‘The Daughter o

'The Daughter of Eve Unfallen'

MARY IN THE THEOLOGY AND SPIRITUALITY OF JOHN HENRY NEWMAN

BY THE REVEREND NICHOLAS L. GREGORIS

NEWMAN HOUSE PRESS

2003

With ecclesiastical approval
Rome: Pontifical Faculty of Theology, Marianum
4 December 2001
Elio M. Peretto, O.S.M
Emanuele Boaga, O.Carm.

Revised Edition

ISBN 0-9704022-7-9

Text composed in Linotype Janson Text fonts
Printed in the United States of America

As a grateful alumnus of my alma mater
the Pontifical North American College,
whose motto is *Firmum est Cor Meum*, which calls to mind the
motto of the Venerable John Henry Cardinal Newman,
Cor ad Cor Loquitur, I dedicate this book:

With heartfelt gratitude to the Most Blessed Virgin Mary
for her spiritual maternity and heavenly intercession
as Patroness of the Pontifical North American College
under her titles of
the Immaculate Conception and Our Lady of Humility;
to St. Philip Neri, Apostle of Rome,
on whose feast I was ordained to the Sacred Priesthood;
and to his spiritual son,
the Venerable John Henry Cardinal Newman
on the occasion of the bicentenary of his birth
on 21 February 1801,
in prayerful hope that he be deemed worthy
of being raised to the honors of the altar
and of being declared a Doctor of the Church.

The Reverend Nicholas L. Gregoris

CONTENTS

ACKNOWLEDGMENTS

With sincere gratitude to His Holiness Pope John Paul II on the occasion of the twenty-fifth anniversary of his accession to the Chair of Saint Peter; to His Excellency, the Most Reverend James Clifford Timlin, D.D., Bishop Emeritus of Scranton, who ordained me to the Sacred Priesthood on 26 May 1997, to the present Bishop of Scranton, the Most Reverend Joseph F. Martino, H.E.D., and to the Most Reverend John M. Dougherty, S.T.L, Auxiliary Bishop of Scranton. To the Very Reverend Peter M. J. Stravinskas, Ph.D, S.T.D., for being my teacher, spiritual mentor, and closest friend in the Priesthood. To the members of the Priestly Society of the Venerable John Henry Newman (Newman House), based in Omaha, Nebraska, for their collaboration on this project and for their fraternal support.

To the seminarians and my brother priests of the Pontifical North American College, especially to the Most Reverend Timothy M. Dolan, Ph.D., former rector of the College and now Archbishop of Milwaukee. To the Reverend Monsignori: Stephen J. Raica, J.C.D., Superior of the Casa Santa Maria; Charles W. Elmer, J.C.D., P.A., former Superior of the Casa Santa Maria and my spiritual director while in Rome; Richard Mahowald, S.T.D., and Roger Roensch, S.T.L., for their continual prayers, spiritual advice and priestly solicitude. I also extend my gratitude to all the other faculty and staff members of the Pontifical North American College for their kindness to me throughout my sojourn in the Eternal City, especially to the Religious Sisters of Mercy of Alma, Michigan, the Sisters Servants of Mary Immaculate, Las Hermanas Josefinas de Mexico, Sisters: Rebecca Abel, O.S.B.; Mary Carol Kinghorn, O.S.B.; Benedicta Clauss, O.S.B.; and Beth Ward, I.H.M., as well as to the late Brother Randal Riede, C.F.X.

I wish to thank in a particular way the Scalabrinian Fathers of my home parish of Saint Joseph in New York City, the Apostles of the Sacred Heart of Jesus who taught me at Our Lady of Pompei and Saint Joseph Grammar Schools, the Reverend Monsignor Eugene Clark for providing me with access to a Catholic high school education, the Marist Brothers of Saint Agnes Boys High School in Manhattan, the De La Salle Christian Brothers of St. Peter's Boys High School on Staten Island, the Reverend Monsignor James Turro, S.S.L., Ph.D., and the Reverend Stanley Jaki, O.S.B., whose love for Our Lady and Newman was inspirational for me when I was a college seminarian at Seton Hall University. A special word of gratitude to the Reverend Fernando Minoggio, Ph.D., whose friendship, spiritual direction and particular love of Cardinal Newman were extremely important for my priestly formation during my years as a seminarian at the Pontifical North American College. To the Reverend Stefano De Fiores, S.M.M., who first taught me Mariology at the Pontificia Università Gregoriana and then at the Marianum. To my classmates and to the faculty members of the Pontificia Facoltà Teologica "Marianum," most especially to the Very Reverend Ignacio Calabuig, O.S.M., former President of the Faculty, and to the Reverend Luigi Gambero, S.M., my thesis moderator, who has been my professor since I first began my studies in Mariology at the International Marian Research Institute at the University of Dayton in Ohio. A word of gratitude is also extended to the Reverend Fathers Elio Peretto, O.S.M., Emmanuele Boaga, O.Carm., and Alberto Valentini, S.M.M., who acted as the official revisori of the examining board for the doctoral defense. A special word of thanks is also extended to the Most Reverend Angelo Amato, S.D.B., whose course on Marian cooperation at the Marianum provided me with invaluable insights into my topic.

I am also most appreciative of the great personal support and scholarly assistance provided during my doctoral studies by the following individuals and communities: His Beatitude, Angelo Cardinal Scola, Patriarch of Venice; their Eminences, James Francis Cardinal Stafford, Augustin Cardinal Mayer, O.S.B., Zenon Cardinal Grocholewski; their Excellencies, Archbishop J. Michael Miller, C.S.B., Archbishop Silvano Tomasi, C.S., Archbishop John Foley, Archbishop Elden F. Curtiss, Archbishop Sean O'Malley, O.F.M. Cap., Bishop Rino Fisichella, Bishop Allen Vigneron, Bishop Philip Boyce, O.C.D., Bishop Vincenzo Paglia; the Reverend Clergy of the Villa Stritch, as well as the Reverend Monsignori Daniel Flores, S.T.D., and Joseph C. Shenrock, P.A., and the Reverend Fathers John Henry Scott

Newman, J.C.L., James Watkins, S.T.L., Ph.D., Gerald O'Collins, S.J., Ian Ker, Louis Bouyer of the Oratory, Jean Stern, M.S., Bertrand de Margerie, S.J., Giovanni Velocci, C.Ss.R., Edmondo Caruana, O.Carm., Ignatius Harrison, C.O., Hermann Geissler, and Paul Chavasse, C.O., the present postulator of Newman's Cause.

Many thanks are due as well to the Comunità di Maria Sedes Sapientiae at the Monastery and Basilica of Saint Benedict in Norcia, most especially to the Prior of the Monastery and Rector of the Basilica, the Reverend Father Cassian Folsom, O.S.B. A special word of thanks to the Sisters of the International Centre of Newman Friends at Rome and at Littlemore, as well as to Sister Mary Christopher Ludden, S.C. I am most grateful for the support of such friends at Priests for Life as the Reverend Father Frank Pavone, Mr. Anthony DeStefano and the Honorable Vito DeStefano, along with Miss Marijane Camilleri and Dr. Pia de Solenni; furthermore, for the dedicated and professional assistance of the late Mr. Gerard Tracey, Archivist of the Birmingham Oratory and of Brother William Fackovec, S.M., of the Marian Library at the University of Dayton, Mrs. Nicole Domenici-Pecheux, and Mr. Peter R. Heyne.

Finally, a most special word of thanks to my parents, family members, and all my other friends and benefactors who throughout the years have encouraged me in faithfulness to my priestly vocation and to the pursuit of academic excellence.

FOREWORD

BY THE VERY REVEREND PAUL CHAVASSE
Postulator for the Cause of the Venerable John Henry Cardinal Newman

The Cloisters of the Oratory in Birmingham contain a series of memorials to the priests who have served that church over the years. Pride of place is given to that of Cardinal Newman. His memorial contains the famous words which act as a summary of his whole life: *Ex umbris et imaginibus in veritatem*—from shadows and images into the truth.

The history of Cardinal Newman's religious life and thought amply reflects the veracity of those words he chose. We see Newman the youth, almost Calvinist in his theology; Newman the Oxford don, striving to avoid the errors of Rome on one hand and the horrors of evangelicalism on the other; finally Newman the Catholic, rejoicing in his membership of the "one fold of the Redeemer" and the peace and certainty to which the "kindly light" had brought him.

His progress in general towards Catholic truth is shown in particular in his beliefs concerning the Blessed Virgin Mary. As an Anglican he was deeply suspicious of what he regarded as Roman accretions in connection with the Blessed Virgin. As his knowledge of Scripture and the Fathers grew and matured, he came to understand more and more fully the pivotal role the humble Virgin occupied in the great scheme of things which God had ordained for our salvation. As a Catholic, of course, his Mariology reached fruition and some of his most inspiring prayers and meditations are concerned with Our Lady. It is interesting to note just how readily Newman, the Oratorian priest, incorporated Roman customs and devotions both into his community and into his private spiritual life. As his biographer, Wilfrid Ward, noted: "Indeed, his own personal taste in devotion was always far more in sympathy with the Continental forms than was that of the old Catholics." [1]

What Newman did not approve of with regard to Our Lady was untheological exaggerations. He maintained that a sound

Mariology must always rest on the Scriptures and the teaching of the Fathers. These guidelines are as valid for us today at the beginning of the twenty-first century as they were in the middle of the nineteenth. Therefore,

I am particularly pleased to have been asked to write these few words to form a Preface for Fr. Nicholas Gregoris's important contribution to the field of Newman studies. If there is one issue in contemporary Mariology which is much discussed, it is that concerning Mary's role in our salvation and the rightness or otherwise of calling her by the titles of Co-Redemptrix, Mediatrix and Advocate. Fr. Gregoris, using Newman's writings and theological principles, helps us to see the best, the truly "traditional" way of both understanding and using these titles.

As Cardinal Newman allowed himself to be led into the fullness of Catholic truth, so may this work help to deepen our theological thinking about the immaculate Mother of God.

The Oratory, Birmingham
September 24, 2003
Feast of Our Lady of Walsingham

PREFACE

BY THE MOST REVEREND PHILIP BOYCE, O.C.D.

Bishop of Raphoe (Northern Ireland)

It might seem strange that Cardinal Newman, steeped as he was in Anglican theology and culture, should be read and studied as a Mariologist of considerable fame. Nevertheless, certain providential circumstances of his life led this great Oxford convert to study in depth various truths about Our Lady which seem so unacceptably difficult to those who have not the faith of the Catholic Church in its fullness. His Mariology is based on Scripture and on the writings of the Fathers of the Church. He displays a marked ecumenical sensitivity in his exposition of Marian doctrine and, as always, his teaching is expressed in elegant and faultless English.

Numerous scholars have examined his teaching on the Blessed Virgin. It has been the subject of various doctrinal theses. The present work is the most recent example to be published. It was presented and successfully defended at the Pontifical Theological Faculty, the *Marianum*, in Rome, two years ago.

The author, Fr. Nicholas L. Gregoris, is to be congratulated on this study in which he focuses on Mary's cooperation in the work of salvation with particular attention to what Newman has to say on her role of mediation in her Son's redemptive sacrifice. This is linked with what contemporary discussion has to say on the meaning and possibility of such titles as Mediatrix and Co-Redemptress.

Noteworthy is Newman's emphasis on Mary's intercession, an aspect of her mediation. She is the greatest exemplification of the power of prayer. Because of her holiness, her union with the divine will, and her nearness to God, she is the most powerful Advocate of the human race before the throne of God. Intercession springs from the doctrinal truth of the Communion of Saints and is theologically explained by the creature's sharing through grace in the mediation of Christ, the universal Mediator.

Guided by Newman, Fr. Gregoris examines how far this mediation can be attributed to Mary and in what sense certain titles could be given to her. "Co-Redemptress" is used very rarely by Newman. He does write at length, however, about the concept of mediation and Mary's active cooperation in the work of Redemption, distinguishing it carefully from that of Christ. Like all of us, Mary too was redeemed by her Son, although in a different manner. While Newman readily understood the exaggerated language used at times by devotees of Our Lady, he would not advocate a dogmatic definition of every popular title given to Saint Mary by her fervent admirers. The distinction between doctrine and devotion is very important in understanding Catholic veneration for the Mother of God. "While dogma is one, devotion is multiform; while faith is fixed, devotion is free." This principle would be very important for Newman in the present discussion.

Fr. Gregoris has provided us with a very richly-documented study on a discussed topic of Mariology. It will be a reference point for all who will in the future write on the subject of Our Lady, especially on her cooperation in the work of Redemption.

ABBREVIATIONS

AP   *Apologia pro Vita Sua: Being a History of His Religious Opinions*

Dev. D.   *An Essay in the Development of Doctrine*

Diff I,

  Diff II *Certain Difficulties Felt by Anglicans in Catholic Teaching* (2 vol.)

DMC   *Discourses to Mixed Congregations*

ES   *Essays and Sketches*

EHC   *Essays Historical and Critical*

FP   *Faith and Prejudice*

GA   *An Essay in Aid of a Grammar of Assent*

HS   *Historical Sketches*

LD   *Letters and Diaries*

MD   *Meditations and Devotions*

OUS   *Oxford University Sermons*

OxCath *Fifteen Sermons Preached before the University of Oxford*

PPS   *Parochial and Plain Sermons*

SN   *Sermon Notes*

VM   *The Via Media of the Anglican Church*

AAS   *Acta Apostolicæ Sedis*

CCC   *The Catechism of the Catholic Church*

CSEL *Corpus Scriptorum Ecclesiasticorum Latinorum*

CSCO *Corpus Scriptorum Christianorum Orientalium*

DS   *Denzinger-Schönmetzer (Enchiridion Symbolorum, Definitionum et Declarationum de Rebus Fidei et Morum)*

FC   *Familiaris Consortio*

GS   *Gaudium et Spes*

LG   *Lumen Gentium*

MC   *Marialis Cultus*

NAB   *The New American Bible*

NDM   *Nuovo Dizionario di Mariologia*

NDT   *Nuovo Dizionario di Teologia*

OssR   *Osservatore Romano*

PG   *Patrologia Greca*

PL   *Patrologia Latina*

RM   *Redemptoris Mater*

SC   *Sources Chrétiennes*

SD   *Salvifici Doloris*

INTRODUCTION

The Venerable John Henry Cardinal Newman has been called a pioneer, precursor, and prophetic voice of the Second Vatican Council.[1] One of the most significant of the Venerable Newman's contributions in this regard is his Marian theology and spirituality, in particular, as this work seeks to demonstrate, his understanding of Mary's cooperation in the *œconomia salutis*.[2] Although Cardinal Newman never set out to treat of this topic in any systematic form,[3] one finds that the whole of his life and thought was imbued with his knowledge and love of the Blessed Virgin Mary, so much so that to understand Newman is to understand his Mariology.[4]

In a certain sense, this work maintains that a fuller comprehension of Newman's Mariology is best achieved when one takes into consideration the particular treatment of Marian doctrine and devotion in the eighth chapter of *Lumen Gentium*.[5] Furthermore, the Mariological insights of the great Newman—when read in the light of the Council and against the background of his own personal development of doctrine and profound experiences of conversion—are likewise reflected in the writings of some notable modern theologians, as well as in the documents of the contemporary Magisterium. Therefore, with these necessary connections made, this volume seeks to ascertain how Newman's understanding of Mary's cooperation in the economy of salvation offers a unique perspective from which the better to comprehend the contemporary theological discussion concerning the titles of Mary as Co-Redemptrix, Mediatrix, and Advocate.

Why is Newman's contribution so important? Perhaps, in part because, as will be explained, Newman's criteria in writing about the Blessed Mother are so much akin to those of the Council. In other words, Newman succeeds in presenting the fundamental truths of Catholic Marian doctrine—in contradistinction but not in contradiction to devotion—as firmly rooted in the Sacred Scriptures and Sacred Tradition such as in the writings of the Fathers and Doctors of the Church, clearly manifesting the timeless appeal of Sacred Truth and thoroughly engaging both mind and heart of Catholic and non-Catholic alike in the concrete circumstances of his reality—past and present. Newman's appeal is a Catholic appeal, that is to say, a universal and genuinely ecumenical one. His Mariology, like the Council teaching itself, is most dogmatically sound yet neither limited to dogmatic formulations nor closed to theological speculation.[6]

Salvatore M. Perrella, O.S.M., in "Maria di Nazareth nel Mistero di Cristo e della Chiesa e la *Tertio millennio adveniente* (1959–1998)," summarizes the unique contributions of the Second Vatican Council's treatment of Marian doctrine and devotion in chapter 7 of *Lumen Gentium*. Father Perrella begins his analysis by re-proposing the insights offered by Salvatore Meo, S.M.M.,[7] in which the Council's methodology is delineated according to biblical, anthropological, ecumenical, and pastoral criteria.[8] Furthermore, Perrella highlights the Council's emphasis on the *Historia Salutis* (history of salvation) as a perspective or *modus interpretandi* (mode of interpretation) of the conciliar treatment of Mariology in relationship to Christology, ecclesiology and the other theological disciplines. The *historia salutis* or *œconomia salutis* (economy of salvation)[9] is, in fact, the main prism through which the Newmanian contribution to Mariology is studied in the present work.[10] Likewise, key to this thesis is the term "cooperation"—a concept which more than adequately expresses both Newman's and the Second Vatican Council's understanding of Mary's role in the work of salvation.[11] Father Perrella explains the reason why that is true of Vatican II; it is the hope of the author that it will be equally the case for Newman. Perrella proceeds to recapitulate the main ideas of these conciliar criteria or instances in application to Mariology, all of which, to one degree or another, can also be considered as foundational in the Marian thought and spirituality of the Venerable John Henry Cardinal Newman.[12]

METHODOLOGY: AN APPLICATION OF
THE CONCILIAR CRITERIA

Chapter One, "The Trajectory of Newman's Mariology," examines Newman's theory of the development of Christian doctrine in relation to the development of the Church's Marian doctrine and devotion and to his own personal theological and spiritual development which resulted, in part, from his ever-deepening knowledge and love of the Blessed Virgin. Therefore, Newman's conversion and subsequent growth in understanding of the Marian mysteries of the Faith cannot be understood apart from his obvious ecumenical concerns—as he sought both to assimilate the truths about Our Lady and to communicate them to others, for example to his fellow scholars at Oxford, most notably the Reverend Edward Pusey and his parishioners at Saint Mary's Church.[13]

Chapter Two is concerned with Newman's use of key Marian passages in the Sacred Scriptures is examined. This book does not pretend to make a comprehensive study of Newman's biblical scholarship regarding the Church's teaching on the Virgin; however, it does attempt to appreciate Newman's insights into Marian dimensions of Holy Writ through a careful analysis of some of his more notable Marian sermons and discourses. Mention of his other Marian writings in the analysis of these sermons and discourses is made to underscore the development of Newman's Mariological reflection, as well as the overall interconnectedness of the topics treated in them. Furthermore, modern biblical scholarship and the contribution of the Magisterium are highlighted where deemed necessary.

Chapter Three demonstrates how Newman drew from the well-spring of the Church's patristic heritage to give evidence of the continuity of the Church's Marian doctrine and devotion throughout the centuries, examining Newman's appropriation of particular Mariological themes in selected Fathers of the Church relating to Mary's cooperation in the economy of salvation.

Chapter Four is a reflection on Newman's understanding of Mary under the titles of *Theotokos* (God-bearer) and New Eve as "instances" of her free, loving, obedient cooperation in the economy of salvation. Newman's considerations stem primarily from his reflections on the scriptural and patristic data, from which he makes highly significant anthropological inferences of tremendous soteriological import.

Chapter Five treats of Newman's theology of *compassio* (compassion or co-suffering) as it concerns the cooperative role in the economy of salvation of Christians in general and of Mary in particular.

Chapter Six explores the vital connections that exist among

Newman's theology of mediation, the communion of saints, and Mary's cooperation in the economy of salvation as expressed in his writings on Mary's spiritual maternity[14] and her intercessory role as Mediatrix and Advocate—a special instance of her spiritual maternity. Therefore, one can say that in this chapter is revealed the special ecclesiological instance or a pastoral criterion according to which Mary's motherhood of the Divine Redeemer and Head of the Church is extended to all the redeemed and, in a particular way, to all her spiritual sons and daughters in the Church—Christ's Mystical Body. Her wholehearted solicitude for the Holy One of God Incarnate allows her to encompass in her immaculate and maternal bosom all the holy ones, that is, the whole *communio sanctorum* (communion of saints) and, indeed, all of mankind, for whom she continually prays as Queen of Heaven and Earth, Queen of Angels and Saints. Her objective cooperation in the salvific work of her Son is characterized by the logic of her ongoing cooperation in that same salvific work, by which the infinite grace and merits of the Redemption, first and most fully applied to her, are subjectively applied to all believers. Thus, Mary is presented as the "the first-fruits of the redemption," primordial believer, the *Mater* and *Typus Ecclesiæ* (Mother and Type of the Church), the eschatological icon of the Church whose cooperation in the *œconomia salutis* is the most perfect expression of the Lord's work of Redemption brought to completion.

Chapter Seven endeavors to offer some Newmanian insights into the contemporary question of Mary's Co-redemption by considering certain passages of his ecumenical work the *Letter to Pusey* and by making a speculative application of the seven notes (tests) of authentic doctrinal development as explained in Newman's *An Essay on the Development of Christian Doctrine*.

UNIQUENESS OF THE STUDY

The question may be asked by some: Why study Newman? All of the Popes from Blessed Pope Pius IX to our present Holy Father have gladly undertaken to offer a personal response to this question.[15] But, perhaps, one observation can be singled out as the most striking of these responses, coming from his Holiness Pope Paul VI at a general audience held on 28 October 1963.[16]

Another simple question may be asked: Why study Newman's

Mariology? While much has been said and written on Mary's cooperation in the mystery of Redemption, a major source of potential enlightenment on the question of the Co-redemption has been largely ignored, namely, the insights of John Henry Cardinal Newman. Michael Schmaus surveys the history of Mariology by noting how the title of "Redemptrix" for Mary from the ninth century evolved into "Co-Redemptrix" in the fifteenth century. He then considers a certain high-point to have been reached with this development: "A Mariology founded on the patristic data was introduced by J. H. Newman and M. J. Scheeben. The main questions centered on Mary's share in the redemption." [17] In addition to the patristic dimension, a special consideration in this study is given to Newman's use of Scripture, especially as exhibited in his Marian sermons, as well as to his treatment of the central Marian doctrines in relationship to his understanding of key Marian titles, namely, *Theotokos*, New Eve, Mediatrix, Advocate, Mother of the Church. Yet again, the Very Reverend Ignatius Harrison, Provost of Brompton Oratory, suggests the feasibility of this prospect when he says:

> [Newman] came to acknowledge Our Lady as Queen and Mother, writing of her and praying to her with the tenderest devotion. At the present time, there is a growing instinct among the People of God, a wholesome *sensus fidelium*, an instinct for the Magisterium to pronounce more fully than hitherto on Our Lady's role in the economy of redemption. Newman's insight into the development of doctrine surely has a great deal to contribute to this debate. . . . [Our Lady] knows how much benefit the wise and prudent teaching of John Henry Newman would bring to the Church in the uncharted centuries ahead. [18]

This study takes seriously the invitation of Father Harrison.

SCOPE AND LIMITATION OF THE STUDY

The scope of the present study is an investigation of the writings of Cardinal Newman as they are related to Mary's cooperation in the economy of salvation. Other aspects of Newman's theology are mentioned in their connection to this precise topic. Excluded from consideration are Mariological and all other theological issues not directly germane to the precise topic of the study.

Although the present study does not intend in any way to take sides in the matter of the proposed Marian dogmatic definition of the titles "Co-Redemptrix," "Mediatrix," and "Advocate" according to the delineations of the contemporary debate, it would be less than forthright not to admit that this debate has surely served as an impetus for this study. The purpose of this work is not to enter into the merit of either position directly but to explore the Marian theology and spirituality of the great nineteenth-century theologian and convert from Anglicanism, the Venerable John Henry Cardinal Newman, in the hope that his understanding of Mary's role of cooperation in the *œconomia salutis* and the related titles under consideration will shed ample light on the contemporary controversy and therefore contribute to a more fruitful discussion.

SOURCES, STYLES AND PERSPECTIVE

The study utilizes, for the most part, primary sources. Examples of relevant material are: Newman's *Letter to Pusey* in *Certain Difficulties Felt by Anglicans*, Part II; his *Parochial and Plain Sermons*; *Discourses to Mixed Congregations*; *Meditations and Devotions*; *An Essay on the Development of Christian Doctrine*; *Apologia pro Vita Sua*; and *Grammar of Assent*. Analysis of these and other works is done and related to the concerns of this study, in an effort to provide intelligent conjecture on how Newman might respond to the contemporary debate. This information is gleaned especially by looking at Newman in a holistic fashion, by surfacing connections and relations which he saw or which can be legitimately be drawn from his opus. Sometimes passages from the Newman corpus are repeated because they apply equally to more than one section of the study, thus facilitating the reading and more importantly the comprehension of the material. Secondary sources are integrated into these considerations as the opinions of acknowledged experts are consulted and evaluated in the light of Newman, and vice versa.

In order to lend a more universal appeal to this study, and to maintain a more scholarly and integral approach to language, I have deemed it useful at times to cite certain texts in their original languages (e.g., Latin, Greek, Italian, Spanish, French, German), both in the body of the text and in the footnotes. The translations of all foreign texts are my own, unless otherwise noted.

Furthermore, it should be noted that this study of Newman's Mariology is done with a sort of Janus-like view: With Newman, it glances backward at the scriptural and the patristic sources; it also gazes forward, that is, beyond the time of Newman, to the contributions of the Second Vatican Council, the contemporary Magisterium and contemporary theologians—many of whose insights into our topic are anticipated in Newman's thought.

It should also be mentioned that, given the time-periods covered in this work, an effort has been made to make consistent styles of spelling, punctuation, and grammatical constructions, lest the stylistic differences become a distraction. For the sake of clarity, bibliographical abbreviations are used only in the footnotes. The study culminates in a summary of the main findings, a discussion of questions of a speculative nature calling for further research, and a reflection on ecumenical implications. The study concludes with recommendations, a detailed bibliography, two appendices, including a glossary, and indexes.

A Trajectory of Newman's Mariology in Relationship to His Personal Development, His Theory of the Development of Christian Doctrine, and Mary's Place within That Development

I. NEWMAN'S DEVELOPMENT IN A CATHOLIC CONTEXT[1]

(a) Newman and Saint Thomas Aquinas

Some commentators on Newman are fond of pointing out that one goes to the great Cardinal in vain to discover precise scholastic definitions and distinctions;[2] this also helps to explain why he is occasionally misunderstood by some scholastics and neo-scholastics.[3] However, in *Newman: Il Coraggio della Verità*,[4] the Reverend Giovanni Velocci, C.Ss.R., briefly explains the significance of Saint Thomas in the development of Newmanian thought.[5] His final analysis is that Thomas and Newman agree substantially, but differ in approach. Newman's study of Thomas was not happenstance or peripheral to his philosophical and theological speculation. Rather, the intellectual and spiritual patrimony of Aquinas was incisive in Newman's own theology and spirituality; Newman arrived at many of the same conclusions, but by different means, as Father Velocci asserts.

Velocci relates that Newman, while a fellow at Oriel College at Oxford, owned 28 volumes of Saint Thomas' works, including his *Summa Contra Gentiles*. Newman, in his *Lectures on Justification*, cites the great Doctor in order to appropriate Thomas' analysis of the relationship between grace and love into his own understanding of the doctrine of justification. In his *Essay on the Development of Christian Doctrine, The Idea of a University, A Grammar of Assent*, and *Apologia pro Vita Sua*, Newman incorporates aspects of Thomistic thought since he recognized it as having firm roots in the teachings of the Fathers of the Church, and thus an integral part of the Church's Tradition. In a personal letter to Pope Leo XIII, Newman expressly adheres to the Holy Father's statements in his encyclical *Æterni Patris*, supporting a revival in Thomism.[6]

Nonetheless, Newman is not easy to categorize in a particular theological school not only because he did not identify himself readily with any given system of thought, for example Thomism, or school of theology but also because his theological development was heavily influenced by his personal experience of life.[7] He was just what Cardinal Dulles says, "personalist to the core."[8] Hence, it would be important to show at the outset how his life and his theology evolved together, indeed how his personal development affected his doctrinal development. Interestingly, when Newman had to select a cardinalatial motto, he exhibited his very personal mode of thinking by apparently borrowing a line from Saint Francis de Sales: *"Cor ad cor loquitur."*[9]

This personal dimension is highlighted by the litany of friends who influenced him and whom he influenced, especially in and through the Oxford Movement. Names like the following dot the landscape: Robert James Wilberforce; Henry Cardinal Manning; John Keble; Edward Pusey; Richard Hurrell Froude; Charles Lloyd; Charles Simeon; W. E. Gladstone. To these, one should add Catholic personages like: Nicholas Cardinal Wiseman; Father Charles Russell; Father Giovanni Perrone, S.J.; Bishop Bernard Ullathorne; Alessandro Manzoni; Blessed Antonio Rosmini, Blessed Dominic Barberi. Numerous works document the relationships among these individuals and how those personal elements had a profound effect on both theirs and Newman's theological investigations and spiritual journeys.[10] However, while the extraordinary impact of Newman's Anglican contemporaries on his theological and spiritual development is discussed at various points throughout the thesis, here the impact of three great Italian thinkers and spiritual writers namely, Alessandro Manzoni, Blessed Antonio Rosmini and Blessed Domenico Barberi, will be summarized precisely because they are three very notable Catholic—but non-Anglo-Saxon—contemporaries formative for Newman. Their genius, individually and collectively and distinguished by a vast array of extraordinary theological, philosophical and literary achievements, combined with a life of intense spirituality and love of the Virgin Mary, helped to shape Newman's personal life and conversion, as well as the history of the nineteenth century and the history of our present age.

(b) *Newman and Alessandro Manzoni* [11]

Father Velocci dedicates a chapter of *Newman: Il Coraggio della Verità* to a discussion of the relationship between Newman and Manzoni, recalling Newman's expressed desire to encounter Manzoni during his stay in Milan—20 September to 30 October 1846—en route to Rome from England. Despite their mutual correspondence, Newman and Manzoni never had a personal encounter. Nevertheless, Newman was able to meet Don Ghilanda[12] on different occasions, from whom he was able to learn much about Manzoni's literary genius. Newman was not reluctant to express his esteem for Manzoni and his work, most especially for his magnum opus, *I Promessi Sposi* (The Promised Spouses).

In his *Apologia pro Vita Sua* (The Apology for His Life), Newman quotes from Manzoni's poem *In Morte di Napoleone* (On the Occasion of Napoleon's Death). Beyond this anecdotal information, Velocci underscores that both Newman and Manzoni underwent transformational conversion experiences. Newman's first conversion was in the autumn of 1816 at the age of fifteen when he begins to adhere to a "definite creed";[13] Manzoni recounts that on 2 April 1810, while praying in the Church of Saint Roch in Paris, he experienced an interior conversion—receiving a special grace to recognize his Creator and Lord after having strayed from the practice of the Catholic Faith in which he had been educated. Furthermore, Velocci writes that in 1833 Newman and Manzoni both had other life-altering conversion experiences resulting from personal trials. For Newman the cross to be borne was his illness in Sicily when Newman thought he was so sick that he was going to die. While, in Manzoni's case, his tribulation lay in having to cope with the death of his beloved wife, Enrichetta Blondel.[14] Furthermore, Velocci regards Newman and Manzoni having an intellectual affinity as regards above all the study of history and divine providence. Velocci explains that these two themes were fundamental to the *weltanschauung* of both men.[15] Finally, it should be mentioned, given the nature of this present work, that Manzoni's affinity to Newman and the process of conversion can also be inferred by way of reference to his devotion to the Virgin, which can be deemed key to the renaissance of his Catholic identity. This fact is indeed evident in some of his Marian writings.[16]

(c) *The Venerable Newman and Blessed Antonio Rosmini* [17]

The former President of Italy, Francesco Cossiga, briefly describes the circumstances of Newman's first failed attempt to meet Rosmini in an article he wrote to celebrate the hundredth anniversary of Newman's death. His insights into this particular relationship are particularly apropos as we pass now the two hundredth anniversary of Newman's birth on 21 February 1801. Cossiga explains that by the time Newman made his second visit to Italy in 1846, he had already "left the Church of England and been received into full communion with the Catholic Church." What was the purpose of this second trip? He was going to the Eternal City to prepare for "his ordination to the priesthood and to search out the kind of priestly vocation to which he was best suited."

President Cossiga goes on to remark that "upon investigation, neither the Dominicans nor the Jesuits appealed to him, nor was he attracted by the newly founded Institute of Charity." However, before he could reach the latter conclusion in a definitive way, Newman made his way north from Rome to Milan "to meet Antonio Rosmini, its founder and the greatest Italian philosopher of the nineteenth century, but for a variety of reasons the meeting never took place." Cossiga adds: "Before leaving England, however, Nicholas Wiseman, the future Cardinal, had encouraged him to consider the Oratorians. It was good advice." Cossiga also explains the spiritual and intellectual affinity between Newman and Rosmini.

Undoubtedly, "Newman and Rosmini were two great masters who fought in defense of truth and Christianity. But, while their teaching coincided on many points, there were also many differences." Cossiga identifies the "depth" and "power" of these two great "Christian thinkers" in their remarkable capacity to maintain a "delicate and complex alliance" between faith and reason in their theology, philosophy of life, and spirituality. Cossiga justly points out that "anything less they saw as a threat to the integrity of Christian believing," and that "while sharing the same basic Christian frame of reference, the character of their genius was distinct." Their distinctive genius lay in that while both men "gave priority to a concrete way of thinking," they did so from two unique philosophical perspectives, namely, "Rosmini's was metaphysical, Newman's existential." In any case, both men "prized reality," according to Cossiga.

More essential, however, is Cossiga's final statement that "Newman and Rosmini emerge today as two exalted spirits, two prophets and pioneers in the Church, who suffered for their love of truth." Finally, Cossiga's words are once again useful in obtaining a deeper appreciation of the Newman-Rosmini connection, especially in terms of their combined impact on ecclesial life in the nineteenth century and, for that matter, on the ecclesial life of "our time": "Antonio Rosmini-Serbati (1797–1855) can in many ways be viewed as the Italian Newman, indeed, Newman as the English Rosmini. For both of their lives were characterized by a concern for the Church to come to terms with the modern world, though this was set within a continued deep loyalty to her teachings." [18]

(d) *The Venerable Newman and Blessed Domenico Barberi della Madre Di Dio*

Blessed Domenico Barberi della Madre di Dio was a Passionist missionary to England whose extraordinary ecumenical work, spiritual writings (of considerable interest is his Mariology) and spiritual direction were essential instruments of the Divine Providence, which led the Venerable John Henry Cardinal Newman to follow the kindly light of truth so as to move from Anglicanism to Catholicism.[19] It was the Blessed Dominic Barberi who heard Newman's first confession and received him into the Church on 9 October 1845. As to the significance of Newman's conversion experience in the lives of both Newman and Blessed Dominic Barberi as well as for the whole Church, Pablo Garcia writes that it was one of the most significant works of Father Barberi's entire priestly apostolate, served as a harbinger of a "new springtime" for the Catholic Church in England and could be considered the greatest conversion in the history of the Catholic Church after that of Saint Augustine of Hippo.[20]

Concerning the arrival of Blessed Dominic Barberi at Littlemore and the subsequent reception of John Henry Newman into full communion with the Catholic Church, Donald A. Withey, in his *John Henry Newman: the Liturgy and the Breviary*, incorporates Frederick Oakeley's vivid description of these historic events in connection with the striking and providential incorporation of

Marian antiphons into the Tractarian recitation of the Roman Breviary—which antiphons, along with other Roman usages, had been hitherto omitted, and comments thus:

> The Breviary offices were recited continuously at Littlemore for some three years including the two years which Newman spent in lay communion after resigning the living of Saint Mary's and when he was working to complete his book *Essay on Development*. We can imagine that they greatly sustained Newman during this difficult period. These offices were still being recited by the residents when Father Dominic Barberi received Newman, Bowles and Stanton into the Roman Catholic Church on 9 October 1845. This was followed by a significant change in the office: the Antiphons of the Blessed Virgin Mary were now included, the various omissions at Prime restored, and the Italianate pronunciation of Latin adopted. There is a graphic, though slightly inaccurate account, of this by Frederick Oakeley. "It was a memorable day that of 9th October 1845. The rain came down in torrents. . . . The wind, like a spent giant, howled forth the expiring notes of its equinoctial fury. . . . The 'monastery' as more than usually somber and still. Egress and ingress there were none that day; for it had been given out, among friends accustomed to visit there, that Mr. Newman 'wished to remain quiet.' One of these friends, who resided in the neighborhood, had been used to attend the evening office in the oratory of the house, but he was forbidden to come 'for two or three days, for reasons which would be explained later.' The ninth of the month passed off without producing any satisfaction to the general curiosity. All that transpired was that a remarkable-looking man, evidently a foreigner, and shabbily dressed in black, had asked his way to Mr. Newman's on the day but one before; and the rumor was that he was a Catholic priest. In the course of a day or two the friend before mentioned was readmitted to the evening office, and found that a change had come over it. The Latin was pronounced for the first time in the Roman way, and the antiphons of Our Lady, which up to that day had always been omitted, came out in their proper place. The friend in question would have asked the reason of these changes, but it was forbidden to speak to any of the community after night-prayers. Very soon the mystery was cleared up by Mr. Newman and his companions appearing at Mass in the public chapel at Oxford. He had been received into the Church on the 9th by Father Dominic,

of the Congregation of the Passion. Thus noiselessly and unob-
trusively did the event come to pass by which . . . must be pronounced to have been, if not the providential end of the
Tractarian Movement, at any rate the symbol and measure of
its true significance." [21]

II. A BIOGRAPHICAL SKETCH OF NEWMAN'S THEOLOGICAL DEVELOPMENT AS AN ANGLICAN

In the *Apologia Pro Vita Sua*, Newman writes that at the age of
fifteen (in 1816), he had his first deep spiritual experience: "I fell
under the influences of a definite creed, and received into my
intellect impressions of dogma which through God's mercy, have
never been effaced or obscured." [22] This was the beginning of a
process of moving, *"Ex umbris et imaginibus in veritatem"* ("From
shadows and images into the truth"),[23] which process would continue for the rest of his life, leading him from Evangelical Protestantism to Anglicanism to Catholicism. This Latin phrase served
as Newman's personal motto because it effectively summarized
his interior or spiritual conversion and his intellectual development, of which his growth in knowledge of Marian doctrine and
personal devotion to Mary were an intrinsic part.[24] In fact, Newman's whole life can be said to be encapsulated in this saying that
he chose to have inscribed as an epitaph on his tombstone (actually found as an inscription in the Oratory at Birmingham) which
"aptly summarizes both his aspiration to the higher world of the
divine and his keen sense of its elusiveness." [25]

Another saying that would have a profound influence on Newman's thought and which is related to his motto is taken from the
evangelical writings of Thomas Scott: "Growth, the only evidence of life." And yet another pithy expression that made an
impact on Newman was the canon or rule of Saint Vincent of
Lérins on the universality and continuity of the faith, *"quod ubi-
que, quod semper, quod ab omnibus"* ("that which is believed always,
everywhere, and by everyone").

In 1827 Dr. Pusey gave Newman copies of the Fathers of the
Church; seven years later, Newman's pupils gave him thirty-six
volumes of the Fathers. In 1828 Newman began a systematic
study of the Fathers; he would never be able to put them down.[26]
Their reading would prove to be the major influence on his

thought and spirituality, and it would be in the study of the writings of the Alexandrian Fathers, in particular, Saint Athanasius of Alexandria, in connection with the history of the Arian controversy that he would discover and apply the principle of the development of Christian doctrine.[27]

The culmination of Newman's study of the Arian controversy led him to write in 1833 his first major scholarly work, *The Arians of the Fourth Century*.[28] Newman believed a proper understanding of the Arian controversy to be key to a proper understanding of how doctrines had developed into dogmas in the Church and became an integral part of the Christian profession of faith without in any way adding to the truth found in Sacred Scripture, but merely as a way of explaining it and handing it down in new historical circumstances.

Briefly stated, what did Newman learn from the Arian crisis? First, that the crisis was responsible for the convocation of two ecumenical councils, Nicea I and Constantinople I, to confront the theological problems posed by Arius and other heretics such as the Macedonians who denied the divinity of the Holy Spirit. Second, that the methodology employed by the Fathers of those two councils was an innovation, in that they used extra-biblical terminology to expound biblical truths, for example the use of the Greek terms *homoousios*, *hypostasis*, meaning "consubstantial" and "subsistent being," respectively. Third, that the result of the theological discussion at those councils led to the doctrinal formulations, subsequently enshrined in creedal statements of dogma, most notably in the Nicean–Constantinopolitan Creed. Fourth, that Newman came to see that what emerged at the councils was not something new, but the explication of what was already held from apostolic times and attested to by the Scriptures implicitly.

His study of the Fathers,[29] and especially the Arian controversy, led him to seek the Early Church's recognizably legitimate heir. Continuing the search, nothing seemed to him more obvious than that Protestantism was not the Church of the Fathers. He then turned to Roman Catholicism, which he considered to be, in principle, on the right track. But only in principle, not in practice.[30] This dilemma caused him to look yet more to find a place in between the doctrinal under-development of Protestantism, and the doctrinal over-development of Catholicism.

He hoped that the Church of England might be the realization of that ideal middle path between two opposite kinds of error, arguing in defense of that hope in a work appropriately entitled, *The Via Media of the Anglican Church*, whose two volumes contain Newman's most elaborate criticism of the doctrinal position of the Roman Catholic Church, as well as his strongest defense of the Anglican position. As he surveyed the reality of it all, he began to see that this was but a pipe-dream. The Reverend James Gaffney notes: "The *Via Media* was, he sadly concluded, only a theory, and a theory whose departure from the facts had become flagrant. This forced Newman to look once more to Rome, as he launched out on a program of reinterpretation of Roman Catholic doctrine, and especially of those doctrinal features that seemed neither scriptural nor, in any acceptable sense, traditional. To accomplish that reinterpretation, the notion of doctrinal development was absolutely crucial." [31]

Newman delivered *Lectures on the Prophetical Office of the Church*,[32] which was formative for him, with special reference to his ideas on the development of doctrine. Geoffrey Rowell writes: "In these lectures he had necessarily to consider the nature of tradition, the character of the bonds of corporate believing, and the way in which the Church was able to maintain a common faith throughout the changes of history. As such it was a necessary stage in a process which led him to consider what was involved in doctrinal development." [33]

Newman investigated this concept with great seriousness, devoting much effort to research and preaching on it. An important record of his thinking on this is the last sermon in a series of fifteen preached before the Oxford University community at Saint Mary's called "The Theory of Developments in Religious Doctrine," poising him to undertake his major study of this topic in his famous *Essay on the Development of Christian Doctrine*.[34] Burke notes: "It is a significant fact that the last writing of Newman as an Anglican was his *Essay*. It was begun just as he was finishing his long journey from Oxford to Rome. In it he glorifies the beauty ever ancient, ever new that he found in the dogma of Catholicism. *The Essay on Development* is almost a *Te Deum* which he composed while standing outside the very threshold of the Church." [35]

With this basic biographical sketch in place, we may now

proceed more profitably to reflect on the specifically theological concerns.

III. NEWMAN'S THEORY OF THE DEVELOPMENT OF CHRISTIAN DOCTRINE

... the highest and most wonderful truths, though communicated to the world once for all by inspired teachers, could not be comprehended all at once by the recipients, but, as being received and transmitted by minds not inspired and through media which were human, have required only the longer time and deeper thought for their full elucidation. This may be called the *Theory of Development of Doctrine*.[36]

If Christianity is a fact, and impresses an idea of itself on our minds and is a subject-matter of exercises of the reason, that idea will in course of time expand into a multitude of ideas, and aspects of ideas, connected and harmonious with one another, and in themselves determinant and immutable, as is the objective fact itself which is thus represented. It is a characteristic of our minds that they cannot take an object in, which is submitted to them simply and integrally. We conceive by means of definition or description; whole objects do not create in the intellect whole ideas, but are, to use a mathematical phrase, thrown into series, into a number of statements, strengthening, interpreting, correcting each other, and with more or less exactness approximating, as they accumulate, to a perfect image. . . .[37]

With the above thoughts, Newman introduces the rationale for his theory of the development of Christian doctrine as a type of grammar of spiritual assent of the mind and heart, of reason and faith, to divinely revealed truths. He likewise identifies these truths as intrinsically linked; thus we discover the significance of the *nexus mysteriorum* (the interconnection of the mysteries) of the Faith in Newman's theology and spirituality.[38] However, before moving directly into Newman's analysis of the development of Christian doctrine, it is essential to recall that for him this development never occurs in a vacuum.

Not only does it take place by engaging the whole of man in an individual act of faith seeking understanding, but it also has another extremely precise context—the ecclesial. It is only by thinking and believing with the Church that man can come to

36

grasp fully the *nexus mysteriorum* of the economy of salvation and of his own insertion into that economy or history of salvation.[39] This study ultimately endeavors to show how Mary is, in a particular way, an essential link in the economy of salvation according to Newman's theology and spirituality. Beyond that, Newman's theology of Mary's singular cooperation in the *œconomia salutis* is also the paradigm of the Church's cooperation for our individual and communal pilgrimage of faith, by which we develop spiritually and so cooperate with God's grace in the working out of our own salvation.[40] Therefore, certain key notions must be posited at the outset, as Newman understood them.[41]

God's self-revelation is preserved in and through the Church.[42] Thus, we read that "the revealed Word of God was committed (to the Church), to be proclaimed by it."[43] Newman maintains that "whereas Revelation is a heavenly gift, He Who gave it virtually has not given it, unless He has also secured it from perversion and corruption, in all such development as comes upon it by the necessity of its nature, or, in other words, that that intellectual action through successive generations, which is the organ of development, must, so far forth as it can claim to have been put in charge of the Revelation, be in its determinations infallible."[44] He also argues that "the word of the Church is the word of the revelation."[45] In that same place, he asserts that "the Church is the infallible oracle of truth."[46] He also observes that Christianity "is a revelation which comes to us as a revelation, as a whole, objectively, and with a profession of infallibility."[47]

The Church he has in mind is the *Ecclesia docens* (the Teaching Church), that is, the Magisterium or body of bishops teaching in union with the Pope, through the gift of apostolic succession. Monsignor Biemer summarizes this point nicely: "The Apostles themselves are present, so to speak, in the bishops and hence the doctrine of the Apostles is also to be heard from them."[48] Newman, however, evaluates the singular importance of the Magisterium in light of the whole economy of salvation, the development of doctrine and the *nexus mysteriorum*:

> . . . so [God] gave the Creed once for all in the beginning, yet blesses its growth still, and provides for its increase. His word shall not return unto Him void, but accomplish His pleasure.

> As creation argues continual governance, so are Apostles harbingers of Popes.
>
> Moreover, it must be borne in mind that, as the essence of all religion is authority and obedience, so the distinction between natural religion and revealed lies in this, that the one has a subjective authority, and the other an objective. Revelation consists in the manifestation of the Invisible Divine Power, or in the substitution of the voice of a Lawgiver for the voice of conscience. The supremacy of conscience is the essence of natural religion; the supremacy of Apostle, or Pope, or Church, or Bishop, is the essence of revealed; and when such external authority is taken away, the mind falls back again of necessity upon that inward guide which it possessed even before Revelation was vouchsafed. Thus, what conscience is in the system of nature, such is the voice of Scripture, or of the Church, or of the Holy See, as we may determine it, in the system of Revelation.[49]

The content of Christian belief is found in the creeds, particularly in the Apostles' Creed, however, it is good to remark that "Newman often treats the Creed in a wide sense as the equivalent of the Deposit [of Faith]."[50] A unique locus of Christian teaching is that of councils, especially ecumenical councils. Their decisions, nonetheless, may be deemed "infallible" only if the Pope so judges; and so, he says that "the seat of infallibility is in him [the Pope], and they [the bishops in council] are adjuncts."[51]

For Newman, an infallible Magisterium was the only guarantee that the transmission of Christian doctrine from age to age could be trusted.[52] He expresses it thus: ". . . and therefore that teaching involves the gift to the Church of not being able to err in those things which are Christian truth or Gospel."[53] Surely we suspect that we are getting a "sneak preview" of the second chapter of Vatican II's *Dei Verbum*[54] when we read: "The Church's infallibility is wholly ministrative to the *depositum* (deposit) . . . and does not exist except as far as she is *custos, testis, judex, magistra depositi*." (guard, witness, judge, and teacher of the deposit).[55] Indeed, in his *Apologia*, Newman insists on the infallibility of the Church "as a provision, adapted by the mercy of the Creator, to preserve religion in the world, and to restrain that freedom of thought. . . . I say that a power, possessed of infallibility in religious teaching, is happily adapted to be a working instrument, in the course of human affairs, for smiting hard and throwing back the immense energy of the aggressive, capricious, untrustworthy intellect."[56]

Finally, the ongoing nature of the need for revelation to be transmitted, particularly in new and different circumstances, called for what he termed "development" , so that the Church could gain deeper insights into the Deposit of Faith as need arose "intermittently, in times and seasons, according as she is guided by her Divine Instructor."[57]

It is this development of doctrine which needs to occupy our attention presently. Newman offers two "master" ideas which help serve as guideposts for our understanding of the development of doctrine. The first "master" idea is that of the living quality of the truth. What does this signify for Newman? Walter Burke summarizes some of the main points of Newman's thought, noting that for Newman the infinite duration of truth requires that "it must be always manifesting the characteristics of a principle of life. It must be active and growing. It must constantly be perfecting and developing itself in the minds of men without suffering any substantial change within itself."[58]

The important phrase "in the minds of men" means that the Church's contemplation or rumination of divine truths allows for development insofar as it means that one arrives at a more profound, subjective growth in their understanding without altering whatsoever their objective signification. Burke further identifies "the dynamic life of truth" as both the cause of the development of doctrine and as a "norm for determining whether or not the doctrinal development of a truth is a genuine development or merely a corruption."[59] In other words, does "the development possess the characteristics proper to a real living thing"?[60] Burke summarizes what he terms the "the master idea of Newman regarding dogmas," in the following way: "The living quality of truth is not only the cause of development but also the criterion for judging a true development of doctrine."[61]

The second "master" idea is the intensity of life in the intellectual order. Once again Burke is worth quoting: "For each human idea is itself a principle of life and activity. It is in this unseen world of ideas and human minds, vibrant beneath the drab world of senses and space and time, that human life and activity reach their highest peak, their whitest heat. It is such a vision that enriches Newman's analysis of the ebb and tide of thought-trends in history, the birth and death of false philosophies, the crooked course of heresies from corruption to decay, and the perennial life and beauty of Christian dogmas."[62] Newman preached thus before the University of Oxford:

> What a remarkable sight it is . . . to see how the great idea takes hold of a thousand minds by its living force . . . and grows in them, and at length is born through them, perhaps in a long course of years, and even successive generations; so that doctrine may rather be said to use the mind of Christians, than to be used by them. . . . Wonderful, to see how heresy has but thrown that idea into fresh forms, and drawn out from it farther developments, with an exuberance which exceeded all questioning, and a harmony which baffled all criticism, like Him, its Divine Author, who, when put on trial by the Evil One, was but fortified by the assault, and is ever justified in His sayings, and overcomes when He is judged.[63]

Burke comments on how Newman's "master idea" of the dynamic (not static) nature of the development of doctrinal truths finds a parallel in Newman's observation of the dynamic development of realities in the physical and intellectual orders. True or authentic development in any order constitutes for Newman a definite sign that something is alive and not a "mere corruption."[64] Ultimately, God's wisdom and providence use the Church as the instrument of making such a discernment and thus is preserved the integrity of the economy of salvation.

IV. NEWMAN'S SEVEN PRINCIPLES OF AUTHENTIC DEVELOPMENT OF DOCTRINE

What are some of these characteristics which can be used to distinguish a true development of doctrine from a corruption? In his *Essay on Development*, Newman establishes seven characteristics of true growth or authentic development of doctrine.[65] Listed and briefly explained, in the order followed by Burke in his commentary, they are:

1) *Chronic Vigor*. Using the image of an oak tree,[66] one can see that it is always alive and, as such, growing and moving toward perfection. In the same way, the truth which is alive must always manifest a continued growth and development; he sees this played in the doctrine of the Incarnation, which has always been

a fruitful source of ongoing contemplation and deeper comprehension in the minds of the great and small alike.[67]

2) *Preservation of Type*. Maintaining the analogy of the oak tree, we can see that a living thing must retain its basic identity and nature, even as it develops. In other words, an oak tree cannot become an apple tree or, even more dramatically, a frog. Similarly, the doctrine of the Incarnation found in the New Testament was substantially maintained, not altered or corrupted, by the Christological definitions of Nicea, Ephesus, Constantinople and Chalcedon.[68]

3) *Power of Assimilation*. As an oak tree takes in water, air, light, etc., it is not corrupted by that process or by those external elements themselves; rather, it is enhanced in its essence. Indeed, without the ability to take in those elements, the tree would die. In like manner, Aristotelian logic and metaphysics enabled the Church to explain the doctrine of the Incarnation in a fashion which was faithful to the scriptural data and, at the very same time, helped her to clarify her understanding of the fundamental revelation, especially in the face of challenges from Arius (e.g., *homoousios*).[69]

4) *Continuity of Principles*. The principles/processes which advance the growth of an oak tree are osmosis and absorption, not chewing or foraging. Likewise, in the growth of doctrine, it is necessary to proceed according to the proper principles which are faith and reason, believing and thinking, with faith always controlling the process. Failure to observe the correct principles results in heresy.[70]

5) *Logical Sequence*. Developments in living things must flow naturally from them, that is, for an oak tree to sprout hemlock leaves or branches would be illogical. Doctrinally speaking, Constantinople II's condemnation of Monothelitism flowed naturally and logically from the fact that Christ has two natures, not one, thus requiring two wills.[71]

6) *Conservative Action*. New branches on an oak tree do not kill the rest of the tree; on the contrary, they take in new life for the entire organism. Genuine doctrinal development ensures not only growth in understanding but also aids in protecting and strengthening what is already known about a given doctrine. Chalcedon improved upon the previous conciliar teachings on the Person of Christ; it did not eviscerate them.[72]

7) *Anticipation of Its Future.* Living things possess, from the outset, certain characteristics of growth, which are maintained throughout. Returning to the oak tree, we find that the process of growth identified in the beginning never changes later on; that is, an acorn and an ancient oak tree exhibit the same basic qualities. The same is true at a doctrinal level: Ephesus' condemnation of Nestorius (acorn) paved the way for Chalcedon's treatment of the two natures in the one Person of Christ (full-grown tree).[73]

These seven principles are re-visited in this paper as they are applied to the question of whether or not the Marian title of Co-Redemptrix participates in legitimate doctrinal development, according to Newman's schema. The other two (Mediatrix and Advocate) are not considered in this paper under the aspect of Newman's seven principles, since both of them are utilized in *Lumen Gentium* VIII. Discussion of the two latter titles centers, rather, upon Newman's explication of their significance. The Reverend Ian Ker spells out the relationship among these seven principles, doctrinal development and ecclesiastical authority thus:

> Newman's fundamental reason, then, for converting to the Roman Catholic Church was the argument from development, and consequently the argument from authority. If an idea like that of Christianity is to be a living idea, it must evidence development. But developments have to be distinguished from corruptions, and although Newman did indeed offer seven "Tests" or "Notes" – which he clearly intended to be tentative rather than exhaustive criteria—this did not remove the need for a living authority to pronounce on the legitimacy of the developments in question.[74]

V. HOW DOCTRINE BECOMES DOGMA

Of fundamental importance for a proper understanding of our topic is a careful consideration of Newman's work *De Catholici Dogmatis Evolutione* (Concerning the Evolution of Catholic Dogma), which he wrote in 1847 as an abridged, Latin version of his earlier *An Essay on the Development of Christian Doctrine*. The purpose for Newman's writing in Latin was to make readily available to Roman theologians a summary in systematic thesis form of his thoughts which were highly debated in those same Roman circles. At first, Newman met with much opposition as his proposal was strongly criticized and ultimately rejected by the Jesuit theologian and personal advisor to Pope Pius IX, Father Carlo Passaglia—who ironically later left the Jesuits, the priesthood and even the Church herself to ally himself with the anti-papal forces of the Italian Risorgimento.[75]

Nevertheless, Newman found a sympathetic ear in another Jesuit theologian, Father Giovanni Perrone, who was a renowned professor of dogmatic theology at what was then known as the Roman College[76] and who eventually became the papal theologian. Father Perrone enthusiastically agreed to read and critique Newman's document, which he did by writing brief, precise and insightful comments in the margins of the work, in spaces which Newman had purposely left. Perrone and Newman were very much "*simpatici*." Perrone read the document with much interest and with an open mind. It is clear from their subsequent correspondence[77] that there existed a profound personal affection between the two. In Perrone's letter to Newman he also assured him of his continued willingness to defend the English convert-scholar against even the most vehement of his Roman critics.

It must be noted that Newman wrote this work as a Catholic and that its style and content are considerably different from other writings of his. Gaffney evaluates it thus:

> As compared with Newman's Anglican writings on development this work is notably more abstract, containing less psychological and historical analysis, and more of an ecclesiological nature. It has overtones of scholasticism, but is not a scholastic exposition. Its references to post-Reformation writers omit favorite Anglican theologians in favor of Roman Catholics, and Perrone himself is cited frequently. Among patristic references, Latin writers, especially Augustine, are more prominent than is usual with Newman, who strongly preferred the Alexandrians. Scholastic references favor sixteenth-century Counter-Reformation Jesuit Thomists, including significantly Francisco Suarez, whose writings against Anglican doctrine had been publicly burnt in the city of London.[78]

Is it far-fetched to suppose that Newman's substitution of the word "dogma" in the title for the earlier "doctrine" indicates that he now wants to show that the development of dogma, although intrinsically related to doctrinal development, is nonetheless distinct from it? While it is beyond the scope of the present paper to make a detailed analysis of Newman's work and Perrone's notes, much of what Newman writes is applicable to the present discussion and therefore worthy of mention. Of particular importance is the careful distinction Newman makes in the first three chapters between the objective and subjective Word of God.[79] Furthermore, the twelve theses that encapsulate Newman's thoughts on the development of dogma are presented in summary form here, which Newman himself provided,* as follows:[80]

"1. In the Deposit of Faith entrusted to the Church by the apostles there did not exist a definite number of articles to be transmitted, to which it was forbidden to make any additions. Rather, a series of dogmas, taught by pastors and learned by the faithful, grew up over the years, and continues to grow. [1]

"2. Those dogmas which in former times the Church did not teach, but afterwards does teach, are not simply minor details. Rather they are serious matters, in virtue of their own inherent force and that of their situation. [2]

"3. That the course of time adds some increment to the deposit is not a matter of chance. It follows an invisible ordinance of God and is regulated by certain laws. That is what the Councils discern when, while exercising human means, they are divinely guided to an irreformable conclusion. [3]

"4. Of these norms what is most important is that whatever additions are made to the deposit are not really new, but evolved out of what is already there. [4] So Christian dogma really grows, rather than accumulates; there is no new beginning of truth, but the continuance of a real tradition. [5]

"5. Even though the dogmas which come into being over the course of time are not so really new in themselves, they may still be new to the Church of those times in which their form is evolving. [6] For one does experience as new what is implicit in what one already holds, as long as one has not yet become aware of the implication.

"6. It is no wonder that, before dogmas are established, even Catholic writers should view them with some uncertainty and confusion, with the result that not only their statements but even their thoughts about them are quite wrong. [7]

* Numbers in brackets indicate places where Father Giovanni Perrone, S.J., commented on the draft text; see note 80.

44

"7. Never have there been writers, or an age, or a span of ages, so disposed that their opinions about matters of faith in dogmas not yet promulgated left nothing to be corrected by succeeding generations. [8]

"8. Until the mind of the Church on a given matter is about to be translated into dogma, the matter is not usually an object of attentive and painstaking contemplation. [9]

"9. Thus it will happen, and fittingly enough, that since truth is one, and given to the Church from the beginning, even those not quite Catholic things that Catholics have brought forth, will generally strike so uncertain and ambiguous a note that, in any serious matter, they prove amenable to pious interpretation. [10]

"10. Once a dogma has finally been formulated in words, there is no more place for dullness of understanding or ambiguity of expression on the part of the faithful. [11]

"11. Even though the Church is enabled, wherever it defines a matter in dogmatic form, to exercise infallibility, it nevertheless proceeds in a timely way to issue its definition, sooner or later, whenever it is willed by the Spirit in whom it is infallible. [12]

"12. Presumptuous persons, who do not wait for the Church to speak, but want by dint of their own struggle to carry off the truth about some matter prematurely, usually achieve not the truth they are seeking, but heresy. [13]." [81]

As with the seven principles of doctrinal development, so too with these twelve theses, specific application is made to the present study in the appropriate place. For the moment, it would be well to highlight some salient insights of Newman in this whole sphere of dogmatic definition; also worthwhile are Perrone's interventions.[82] First, Newman is at great pains to show that dogma, like doctrine, can never be "novel" and so must grow organically out of "a real tradition." Second, what is new about these dogmas is the understanding and/or consciousness of them on the part of the Church as she explicitly formulates that which has been implicitly taught and believed. Third, it should come as no surprise that prior to definition, dogmas are "not usually an object of attentive and painstaking contemplation." Fourth, once a dogma has been defined, it calls for acceptance by all in the Church. Fifth, such dogmatic definitions are acts resultant from divine assistance coming from the charism of infallibility. Finally, Newman cautions against an over-hasty drive toward dogmatic definitions.

Walgrave comments on the ancillary nature of reason (as seen above in Newman's twelve principles); he then goes on to describe the process of definition as one that is useful as a "theological solution," only to the extent that one does not consider such definitions to be exhaustive of the content of the mysterious truths that the definitions are meant to convey and safeguard. Walgrave understands Newman's fundamental principle that reason and faith must cooperate in the process of dogmatic definition but that their functions should never be confused: "The action of reason contributes greatly to the elaboration of the Faith, but the object of faith cannot be comprehended by reason;" he also underscores how the dogmatic definitions of the doctrines of the Immaculate Conception and of the Assumption have successfully demonstrated this ancillary relationship's ability to maintain a sense of the sacred or mystery in religion, concluding:

> Reason, therefore, cannot serve as a principle of a complete and final guarantee in questions of doctrinal development. Its action needs to be completed, from time to time, by the Church's supernatural functioning, and in an intrinsic and positive fashion. This function is exercised by the Magisterium of the Church, where the Holy Ghost, living in the community of the faithful, speaks with authority.[83]

It is precisely the nature of the relationship between the Magisterium and the Lay Faithful in the thought of Cardinal Newman which now occupies our attention.[84] What does Newman mean by "the community of the faithful"? Does he intend to include the hierarchy and the laity together or just the laity by itself? Is the hierarchy, that is, the Magisterium alone responsible for deciding matters of doctrine and dogma or do the laity have a "right" to be "consulted"? What is to be understood by the use of the term "consult" in reference to the laity and doctrinal matters? Furthermore, how is the infallibility of the Church manifested? Does not the body of the Church possess a sort of "instinct" (*phronema*) in matters of doctrine?

These and many other questions are answered by Newman in *"On Consulting the Faithful in Matters of Doctrine,"* found as an appendix with various additions and corrections to the 1871 third edition of his larger opus, *The Arians of the Fourth Century*, which is essential reading for understanding Newman's mind on how doctrine becomes (or rather, as he argues, should become) dogma in the Church. Coulson writes: "This work is fundamental not only to a fuller understanding of Newman's theory of doctrinal development, but to an appreciation of the importance he attaches to the laity in his theology. . . . The importance of *On Consulting the Faithful* is, as Professor Chadwick points out, that it is Newman's first attempt to resolve publicly one of the major difficulties in his theory of doctrinal development: how, before a definition, is the mind of the Church to be discovered?" [85] One cannot truly appreciate this work and its implications without a rudimentary understanding of its historical background, which is briefly summarized here.

Newman originally published his work as an article in the English Catholic periodical *Rambler*, in July of 1859. The article had immediate repercussions, for the most part, due to the highly negative reactions of the Catholic hierarchy both in Rome—even Blessed Pope Pius IX is said to have expressed concern—and in England, including Bishop Ullathorne, Newman's own Ordinary in Birmingham, who were convinced that the work was aimed principally to undermine their authority and to cause rebellion against them by the laity. One can especially comprehend the concern of the English bishops regarding this particular article in the *Rambler* since other articles had previously appeared in which the periodical had seriously questioned and contradicted official stances of the hierarchy in regard to Church–State relations. [86]

Coulson comments that Newman's "publication of this essay was an act of political suicide from which his career within the Church was never fully to recover; at one stroke he, whose reputation as the one honest broker between the extremes of English Catholic opinion had hitherto stood untarnished, gained the Pope's personal displeasure, the reputation at Rome of being the most dangerous man in England, and a formal accusation of heresy proferred against him by the Bishop of Newport." [87]

Although Newman's intent in writing the article was more theological than revolutionary, one cannot deny its polemical nature. Newman is careful to note that the controversy had preceded his treatment of the topic and had indeed been precipitated by another article which appeared in the May issue of the *Rambler*, which on page 122 contained the following statement: "We do unfeigned believe . . . that their Lordships (the Bishops) really desire to know the opinion of the laity on subjects in which the laity are especially concerned. *If even in the preparation of a dogmatic definition, the faithful are consulted*, as lately the instance of the Immaculate Conception, it is at least as natural to antici- pate such an act of kind feeling and sympathy in great practical questions." [88] Although this phrase in itself seems harmless, it was the cause of an uproar, the details of which are beyond the scope of this present paper. Suffice it to say that the hierarchy of England was so enraged that they threatened to close down the *Rambler*. It must also be noted that opposition to the *Rambler's* statement was not limited to the hierarchy but included lay pro- fessors of theology, among whom the most prominent was Doc- tor Gillow who taught at Ushaw.

Newman's work was, for the most part, a noble attempt to shed light on the situation and to "calm the waters," so that the *Rambler* and its opposition could have a common theological ground upon which to find agreement or at least mutual under- standing. Newman, in fact, became the general editor of the *Rambler* for a brief period because both sides were convinced that he was the only person capable of successfully mediating in the precarious situation. Whether or not Newman achieved his pur- pose in writing the work is not an easy question to answer, but its contents are undeniably interesting and constitute an important source for Newman's thought on a subject very dear to him, relevant to his time and quite pertinent to the present work. Having briefly surveyed the historical background to Newman's work, it is suitable to touch on some of the main points he makes, attempting to answer the questions raised at the beginning of this section.

a) What is the community of the faithful? In his *Lecture Notes on the Church* of 1848, Newman observes that the Church is the congregation of the faithful who pass on the revealed Word of God which they themselves have received and believed. It is neither hierarchy alone nor laity alone, but the whole People of God as a body. [89]

b) What does it mean to "consult" the laity in matters of doctrine? The first part of *On Consulting the Faithful* is a painstak- ing attempt to define the term "consult" as used in the vernacu- lar, compared to its more precise and theologically technical Latin usage. Newman is clearly using the term according to its popular English usage, which means to "verify facts" or to "ascertain an opinion" and not to submit to someone's judgment.

Newman uses his definition of consultation by way of analogy to consulting a barometer or a clock. Furthermore, he makes the point: "Thus, a physician consults the pulse of a patient, but not in the same sense in which a patient consults a physician. To consult the pulse of a patient means to get an indication of the patient's state of health." For Newman, the physician could be said to be the hierarchy, while the patient stands for the laity. Even more to the point, "consultation" is by no means a "show of hands" or a plebiscite on the reality or acceptability of a doctrine: "Doubtless their advice, their opinion, their judgment on the question of definition is not asked; but the matter of fact, viz. their belief is sought for, as a testimony to that apostolical tradition, on which alone any doctrine whatsoever can be defined." He goes on to explain that one consults the faithful in the same way that one consults the Church's liturgies and rites—"not that they speak, not that they can take any part in the definition, for they are documents or customs; but they are witnesses to the antiquity or to the universality of the doctrines which they contain, and about which they are consulted." [90] Cardinal Dulles does feel compelled to add, however, that Newman "never suggested that the views of the faithful had infallible normative value apart from, or in opposition to, the teaching of the hierarchy." [91]

How is the Church's infallibility made manifest? At Baptism, each person is endowed with the *sensus fidei* (sense of the faith) as a supernatural gift of the Holy Spirit, made visible in the *sensus fidelium/consensus fidelium* (sense of the faithful/consensus of the faithful)—which is itself a function of the *pastorum et fidelium conspiratio* (the breathing together/joint inspiration of the shepherds and the faithful), that is, a union of the *Ecclesia docens* (the Teaching Church) and *Ecclesia discens* (the Learning Church). As Crowley summarizes it:

> The Church continues to receive and to know the truth of faith to the degree that the faithful, imbued with a sense of faith, assist in transmitting the Faith in its authenticity. This activity of receiving and transmitting is the human foundation of the "mind" of the Church. As this mind becomes explicitly known and universally shared in the *conspiratio pastorum et fidelium*, a real basis emerges for organically relating the authoritative

teaching of the truth of faith by the Magisterium to the confession of faith in the various forms that doctrine assumes. The truth of revelation is the developing subject matter of the entire Church's faith, a faith which the Church receives and transmits in the particular histories which together constitute its collective history.[92]

It must be underscored that this unity within the body is predicated on the absolute necessity of the teaching role of the hierarchy, along with the attendant docility of the faithful. Hence, we read: "It follows that none of these channels of tradition may be treated with disrespect; granting at the same time fully, that the gift of discerning, discriminating, defining, promulgating, and enforcing any portion of that tradition resides solely in the *Ecclesia docens*."[93] All the "theory" or theology on doctrinal development and definition comes into full view as the faithful exhibit what one might call a Catholic "instinct"—Newman's concept of *phronema*[94]—whereby they know intuitively what is or is not "of the faith."[95]

VI. MARIAN DOCTRINE AS THE IMPETUS FOR NEWMAN'S REFLECTION ON DOCTRINAL DEVELOPMENT

"Mary kept all these things, and pondered them in her heart." ... Thus Saint Mary is our pattern of Faith, both in the reception and in the study of Divine Truth. She does not think it enough to accept, she dwells upon it; not enough to possess, she uses it; not enough to assent, she develops it; not enough to submit the Reason, she reasons upon it; not indeed reasoning first, and believing afterwards, with Zacharias, yet first believing without reasoning, next from love and reverence, reasoning after believing. And thus she symbolizes to us, not only the faith of the unlearned, but of the doctors of the Church also, who have to investigate, and weigh, and define, as well as to profess the Gospel; to draw the line between truth and heresy; to anticipate or remedy the various aberrations of wrong reason; to combat pride and recklessness with their own arms; and thus to triumph over the sophist and the innovator.[96]

The above is taken from the last of Newman's sermons delivered before the University of Oxford[97] on the Feast of Our Lady's Purification in 1843[98] and entitled "The Theory of Developments in Religious Doctrine." It was the harbinger of Newman's later *Essay on the Development of Christian Doctrine* and contains important insights into that theory.[99] Surely listeners then and readers now might be surprised that he uses a sermon on a Marian feast to introduce his thoughts on doctrinal development.

The connection between the two may seem *prima facie* to be of little relevance but, in his innovative style, Newman quickly assures all that Mary's life is indeed a paradigm for how the Church relates to the truths of the Faith that she professes and teaches. He is careful to stress the delicate interplay that must occur between faith and reason in the process of the contemplation and the study of "Divine Truth," so that the extremes of rationalism and fideism are both avoided. For Newman, Mary is the exemplar par excellence of the *fides quærens intellectum*[100] of the Church—that process by which one's initial act of faith is nurtured through reflection and contemplation and by which the truth of the Gospel is not simply put forth as intellectual propositions but experienced as internal realties that penetrate heart and mind at one and the same time. Thus, Newman declares:

> A dogma is a proposition; it stands for a notion or for a thing; and to believe it is to give the assent of the mind to it, as it stands for the one or for the other. To give a real assent to it is an act of religion; to give a notional, is a theological act. It is discerned, rested in, and appropriated as a reality, by the religious imagination; it is held as a truth, by the theological intellect.[101]

Moreover, this process is the very foundation for development of doctrine in the Church, that is, the faith which is believed at the outset grows and develops in and through believing, reasoning and living. In this sense, theology is both an intellectual exercise and a pursuit of the soul—a pursuit which holds out an open invitation to the learned and the unlearned alike. However, it is clear that the "doctors of the Church," unlike the lay faithful, have the great responsibility of defending, defining and demarcating the Gospel truth from heresy so that ultimately the true wisdom of God can "triumph" over the world's sophistry. Newman underscores the need to use reason "in investigating the doctrines of Faith" since he views reason as the primary instrument by which "the victory of Faith" is accomplished.

Referring to the writings of the Fathers of the Church, New-man exclaims: "Look along their shelves, and every name you read there is, in one sense or other, a trophy set up in record of the victories of faith. How many long lives, what high aims, what single-minded devotion, what intense contemplation, what fervent prayer, what deep erudition, what untiring diligence, what toilsome conflicts has it taken to establish its supremacy." [102] In other words, he sees the Fathers, and their successors in the Magisterium, as teachers of the Faith who took up from Our Lady the mantle of contemplation, which in turn brings about deeper insights, resulting in doctrinal development.[103]

Mary was not only a model for development; the doctrine about her is likewise a premier example of development. And so, we read:

> As she had increased day by day in grace and merit, while the world knew not of it, so has she raised herself aloft silently, and has grown into her place in the Church by a tranquil influence and a natural process. It was as some fair tree, stretching forth her fruitful branches and her fragrant leaves, and overshadowing the territory of the saints. . . .
>
> Thus was she reared without hands, and gained a modest victory, and exerts a gentle sway, which she has not claimed. When dispute arose about her among her children, she hushed it. When objections were urged against her, she waived her claims and waited. Till now, in this very day, should God so will, she will win at length her most radiant crown, and without opposing voice, and amid the jubilation of the whole Church, she will be hailed as immaculate in her conception.[104]

Some key expressions are worth highlighting. For instance, he speaks of Marian doctrine's development occurring "day by day," "silently" and by a "natural process." [105] Newman also makes a fascinating parallel between Mary's personal growth in holiness and the way doctrine and devotion concerning her has developed in the Church. Likewise connected to this insight is his observation that Mary's holiness has enveloped the whole Church in the aura of that sanctity so much so that the impending definition of the Immaculate Conception (1854) should be serenely assimilated as a logical part of that natural development of Marian doctrine and devotion.[106] One finds a similar train of thought in his meditation on Mary's title of *Virgo Prædicanda*. Newman explains the title not only in terms of its doctrinal content *per se* but precisely in terms of his understanding of the development of Marian doctrine and devotion as we find in the passage below:

> The Virgin who is to be proclaimed, to be heralded; literally, to be preached.
> ... Preaching is a gradual work: First, one lesson, then another. Thus were the heathen brought into the Church and then *gradually* ...
> And in like manner, the preaching of Mary to the children of the Church, and the devotion paid to her by them, has *grown*, grown gradually, with successive ages.
> ... Not so much was preached about her in early times as in later. First, she was preached as the Virgin of Virgins—then as the Mother of God—then as glorious in her Assumption— then as the advocate of sinners—then as Immaculate in her Conception.
> And this last has been the special preaching of the present century; and thus, that which was earliest in her own history is the latest in the Church's recognition of her.[107]

Clearly, Newman regards the gradual nature of Marian preaching and teaching as a pedagogical technique, whereby one is led to and through the doctrine of the Faith in a systematic and orderly fashion and not fed the whole meal at once, if one may use this metaphor, reminiscent of what Saint Paul writes in I Corinthians 3:1–2. Newman says that "creeds and dogmas live in the one idea which they are designed to express, and which alone is substantive; and are necessary only because the human mind cannot reflect upon that idea, except piecemeal, cannot use it in its oneness and entireness, nor without resolving it into a series of aspects and relations."[108] More to the point, in his Sermon XII, "The Reverence Due to the Blessed Virgin Mary," preached on the Feast of the Annunciation while still an Anglican (as a fellow at Oriel College and vicar of Saint Mary the Virgin in Oxford), he stresses that the gradual disclosure of Mary's prerogatives has been for our sake; this development is needed, he maintains, to show that the glories of Mary are "for His [Christ's] sake."[109]

VII. NEWMAN'S THOUGHTS ON THE DOGMATIC DEFINITION OF THE IMMACULATE CONCEPTION AS AN EXEMPLAR OF HIS HERMENEUTIC

The then-impending dogmatic definition of the Immaculate Conception was most formative for Newman, serving as the impetus for refining and explicating his own notions of doctrinal development and dogmatic definition. Chronologically speaking, then, what we have just presented in the section above occurred after the process covered in this section. The rationale for this arrangement, however, is two-fold: First, as a model for contemporary theological discussion, Newman's insights into doctrinal development can be mined without overt reference to the Immaculate Conception because he produced basic principles, independent of any specific doctrine. Second, for our purposes, his analysis of the process of doctrinal development and definition serves as a bridge to our own unique concerns in the sections which follow. With this in mind, let us turn to Newman's detailed and almost magisterial response to Dr. Pusey's objections to Catholic Marian doctrine and devotion, paying particular attention to Newman's references to the Immaculate Conception.

In his *Letter to Pusey*, Newman is careful to ground his apologetic of Mary in the Sacred Scriptures and Tradition, most notably in the writings of the Fathers of the Church. In his discussion of Mary's Immaculate Conception, he goes to great lengths to show that the present doctrine is in fact an authentic development of the primitive teaching of the Church.[110] Before Newman ever speaks directly of Mary's Immaculate Conception, he turns to the Fathers and their treatment of Mary as the Second Eve, believing that this title expresses the fundamental nature of Mary's personal sanctity and role or office as *Theotokos* ("God-bearer"), already developed in the texts of Sacred Scripture. In other words, although the use of the title of "Second Eve" is nowhere to be found in the Bible, the Fathers employed it because they drew inferences from the scriptural data. Thus, they reasoned, if Saint Paul could identify Jesus as the "New Adam," why could they (using the same logic) not identify Mary as the New Eve? This needs to be seen as already a development from the data of Scripture to the incipient stage of early Tradition.

Newman refers to the title and theology of Mary as the New

Eve as "the great rudimental teaching of Antiquity from its earliest date concerning her."[111] He goes on: "She holds, as the Fathers teach us, that office in our restoration which Eve held in our fall."[112] To which Fathers was he referring? He listed and quoted the following: Justin, Tertullian, Irenæus, Cyril of Jerusalem, Ephrem the Syrian, Epiphanius, Jerome, Augustine, Peter Chrysologus, Fulgentius; among these, he singles out for special emphasis the first three whom he dubs "a three-fold cord" which, in his judgment "is not quickly broken."[113] He is quick to point out that "the coincidence of doctrine which they exhibit, and again, the antithetical completeness of it, show that they themselves did not originate it."[114] From where did all this originate? Newman traces it back, in this "three-fold cord," to none other than Saint John the Apostle and Evangelist.[115]

From the patristic identification of Mary as the Second Eve, Newman is led by an almost syllogistic process to the Immaculate Conception. Having explained in great detail the precise meaning of the doctrine, Newman tells Pusey bluntly: "Well, this is simply and literally the doctrine of the Immaculate Conception. I say the doctrine of the Immaculate Conception is in its substance this, and nothing more or less than this (putting aside the question of degrees of grace). And it really does seem to me bound up in the doctrine of the Fathers that Mary is the Second Eve."[116] In short order, he gets even stronger: "I have drawn the doctrine of the Immaculate Conception as an immediate inference, from the primitive doctrine that Mary is the Second Eve. This argument seems to me conclusive. . . ."[117]

In his *Memorandum on the Immaculate Conception* to R. J. Wilberforce, Cardinal Newman writes to aid him in rebutting Protestant arguments against the doctrine recently defined as dogma. In doing so, Newman is careful to ground it solidly in his own theory of doctrinal development, and so he writes: "Next, Was it a primitive doctrine? No one can add to revelation. That was given once for all;—but as time goes on, what was given once for all is understood more and more clearly."[118] He brings to his side once again the Fathers of the Church, even though he admits that such great medieval theologians as Saint Thomas Aquinas and Saint Bernard of Clairvaux denied the doctrine (but only because they did not understand it in the sense that the Church in Newman's time did).[119] He concludes his discussion by challenging Protestants to reflect on their almost hysterical op-position to this doctrine, approaching them in several ways. First, he asks:

> Is it, after all, *certainly* irrational? is it *certainly* against Scrip-ture? is it *certainly* against the primitive Fathers? is it *certainly* idolatrous? I cannot help smiling as I put the questions. Rather, may not *something* be said for it from reason, from piety, from antiquity, from the inspired text? You may see no reason at all to believe the voice of the Church; you may not yet have at-tained to faith in it—but what on earth this doctrine has to do with *shaking* your faith in her, if you have faith, or in sending you to the right-about if you are beginning to think that she *may* be from God, is more than my mind can comprehend. Many, many doctrines are far harder than the Immaculate Conception.

Then he invites them to imagine placing these words on their lips on Judgment Day, in offering the Judge a legitimate defense for remaining outside the visible boundaries of the Catholic Church:

> . . . I say it distinctly—there may be many excuses at the last day, good and bad, for not being Catholics; *one* I cannot con-ceive: "O Lord, the doctrine of the Immaculate Conception was so derogatory to Thy grace, so inconsistent with Thy pas-sion, so at variance with Thy word in Genesis and the Apoca-lypse, so unlike the teaching of Thy first Saints and Martyrs, as to give me a *right* to reject it at all risks, and Thy Church for teaching it. It is a doctrine as to which my private judgment is fully justified in opposing the Church's judgment. And this is my plea for living and dying a Protestant." [120]

One must not forget that the *Memorandum*, unlike the *Letter to Pusey*, was written after the time of the dogmatic definition of the Immaculate Conception. However, it should be noted that while he defends the doctrine˙ in both instances, in the latter case he is even more concerned to defend the rational basis for the Church's definition and her authority to do so in light of the fact that its acceptance was absolutely crucial in his own conversion. Hence, Newman's rhetorical language is aimed at penetrating any preconceived notions on the part of Protestants, tending to dismiss the doctrine as a corruption of the authentic Gospel when, in fact, it is the exact opposite.

At this point, it would be good to recall Newman's seven principles for doctrinal development, as already explained above. Newman believed that one could possibly determine if a development of doctrine was authentic or a corruption by applying these seven tests. Inasmuch as his theory on this was first practiced in his reflection on the process leading up to the definition of the Immaculate Conception, a listing of those qualities would be helpful at this moment. They are as follows: chronic vigor, preservation of type, power of assimilation, continuity of principles, logical sequence, conservative action, anticipation of its future. Finally, for Newman, the doctrinal development of the Immaculate Conception is inseparable from its dogmatic formulation, which process impressed him because of the consultation initiated by the Sovereign Pontiff. Blessed Pope Pius IX, as we have already seen, was careful to include in this consultation not only the world-wide episcopate, but also the whole body of the faithful. Newman lauds the Pope for engaging in this process of consultation but also because the Holy Father is careful to preface the dogmatic definition with a careful enumeration of the various witnesses to the apostolicity of the doctrine: *"divina eloquia, veneranda traditio, perpetuus Ecclesiæ sensus, singularis catholicorum Antistitum ac fidelium conspiratio."* [121]

Newman then entered into the theological mood of the moment (in the pre- and post-definition era of the Immaculate Conception) and used that moment to advance his own thinking on the centrality of doctrinal development in the life of the Church. Taking the process related to the Immaculate Conception as a paradigm, he analyzed the way the Church—from the sub-apostolic age forward—had taken the primary data of Scripture, turned it over in her collective mind and moved forward with ever-deepening insights into the identity of the Virgin Mary and her place in the *œconomia salutis*. He likewise observed how the process grew historically and was subsequently verified by the Pope, in order to ensure that the dogmatic definition was indeed in keeping with authentic modes of doctrinal development.

VIII. NEWMAN'S CRITIQUE OF THE PROTESTANT (ANGLICAN) PROBLEM WITH MARIAN DOCTRINE AND DEVOTION

Newman's Mariology was not developed in a theoretical or theological vacuum. As has already been emphasized, his theology was intensely connected to real-life persons and situations. Therefore, it is not a source of surprise to discover that he engaged in discussions with people—Catholic and Protestant alike—regarding the practical, day-to-day implications of Mariology. In this more "apologetical" mode,[122] Newman seems to identify three problems which surface regularly as Protestants react to Catholic Marian doctrine and devotion. The first is, in fact, their apparent inability to distinguish between doctrine and devotion. Secondly, he indicates that their weak Mariology has led, unwittingly in most cases, to a defective Christology. Third, he accuses Protestantism of a failure to take seriously the historical witness to Mary, especially as seen in its refusal to participate in intercessory prayer. The bulk of this critique can be found, once more, in his *Letter to Pusey*, but also in his *Discourses to Mixed Congregations* and in his *Meditations and Devotions*. The methodology of this section runs along the lines of a catena of citations, with personal commentary.

(a) *Doctrine as Distinct from Devotion*

> I begin by making a distinction . . . the distinction between faith and devotion. I fully grant that *devotion* towards the Blessed Virgin has increased among Catholics with the progress of centuries;[123] I do not allow that the *doctrine* concerning her has undergone a growth,[124] for I believe it has been in substance one and the same from the beginning.[125]

Newman's distinction between doctrine and devotion, especially as regards the Blessed Virgin, is premised on his conviction that the Church's doctrine has not grown, that is to say, changed from one reality into another, but that it "has been in substance one and the same from the beginning" and that the distinction between doctrine and devotion is "like the distinction between objective and subjective truth."[126] Newman is quite careful to avoid any notion that would be like taking a type of Ockham's razor to the realm of doctrinal development. Just as Newman believes that in the economy of nature developments occur that do not necessarily signify substantial change, so too in the economy of salvation developments of doctrine occur which do not change their essence. Furthermore, Newman explains his reasoning by way of an analogy to nature and makes a direct application to the development of Marian doctrine in the Church's Tradition.

> The sun in the spring-time will have shone many days before he is able to melt the frost, open the soil, and bring out the leaves; yet he shines out from the first notwithstanding, though he makes his power felt but gradually. It is one and the same sun, though his influence day by day becomes greater; and so in the Catholic Church it is the one Virgin Mother, one and the same from first to last, and Catholics may have ever acknowledged her; and yet, in spite of that acknowledgment, their devotion to her may be scanty in one time and place, and overflowing in another.[127]

Newman uses this analogy from nature to illustrate the concept of the gradualness of Marian devotion and at the same time points out how it could differ from time to time and from place to place; in other words, it is related to cultural exigencies which may arise from the different spiritual needs of different peoples. In a certain sense, Newman appropriates the meaning of Blaise Pascal's "raisons du coeur"[128] in application to the distinction between doctrine and devotion when he writes: "Religion acts on the affections. . . . They hurry right on to their object. . . . And of all the passions love is the most unmanageable; nay more, I would not give much for that love which is never extravagant. . . ."[129]

Certainly, Newman sees the danger involved when a person's devotion is inordinately expressed so as to distort the very truths which identify the object of a person's affection, especially when those truths govern our worship of God and our reverence for Mary and the other saints. Nevertheless, our human experience teaches us that the heart has reasons of which the mind knows not—such as is one possible rendering of Pascal's adage—and therefore true devotion is always firmly rooted in doctrinal truths. Newman concludes that unnecessarily forcing devotional practices into "formalized" "meditations and exercises," can do a sort a violence to devotional expressions, so much so that they would lose their appeal, and would in fact become ugly. He explains his analogy thus:

> What mother, what husband or wife, what youth or maiden in love, but says a thousand foolish things, in the way of endearment, which the speaker would be sorry for strangers to hear; yet they are not on that account unwelcome to the parties to whom they are addressed. . . . So it is with devotional feelings. Burning thoughts and words are as open to criticism as they are beyond it. What is abstractedly extravagant, may in particular persons be becoming and beautiful, and only fall under blame when it is found in others who imitate them. When it is formalized into meditations or exercises, it is as repulsive as love-letters in a police report.[130]

The metaphor of a love letter is particularly compelling. Newman asks Pusey to reflect about how people are often carried away by emotion pursuing the objects of their heart's desire and applies these insights to the different types of emotions which can characterize people in their Marian devotion. Hence, even though devotion as an expression of love does not admit of cold, clinical language, the language of devotion should never contravene precise doctrinal formulations and should not be unnecessarily forced into doctrinal formulations.

> Now let me apply what I have been saying to the teaching of the Church on the subject of the Blessed Virgin. . . . I say then, when once we have mastered the idea,[131] that Mary bore, suckled, and handled the Eternal in the form of a child, what limit is conceivable to the rush and flood of thoughts which such a doctrine involves? . . . It was the creation of a new idea and of a new sympathy, of a new faith and worship, when the holy Apostles announced that God had become incarnate; then a supreme love and devotion to Him became possible, which seemed hopeless before that revelation. This was the first consequence of their preaching. But, besides this, a second range of thoughts was opened on mankind, unknown before, and unlike any other, as soon as it was understood that the Incarnate God had a mother. The second idea is perfectly distinct from the former and does not interfere with it.[132]

The apostolic preaching, says Newman, had a primary and a secondary consequence. The first was exclusively doctrinal; the second had a devotional component. Thus, the preaching of the mystery of the Incarnation brought an awareness of that doctrine; following closely on that apprehension came a devotion to the Incarnate Word and, rightly in due course, a devotion to the Mother of the Word Incarnate:

> If He had not meant her to exert that wonderful influence in His Church, which she has in the event exerted, I will use a bold word, He it is Who has perverted us. If she is not to attract our homage, why did He make her solitary in her greatness amid His vast creation? If it be idolatry in us to let our affections respond to our faith, He would not have made her what she is, or He would not have told us that He had so made her; but, far from this, He has sent His Prophet to announce to us, "A virgin shall conceive and bear a Son, and they shall call His name Emmanuel," and we have the same warrant for hailing her as God's Mother, as we have for adoring Him as God.[133]

Newman instructs Pusey that Marian devotion is not an aberration but a divinely willed fact of life in the Church. In truth, if Christ promised to preserve His Church in the truth until the end of time, how could He have permitted the introduction of idolatrous thoughts and practices? Newman's strong language ("He it is Who has perverted us") is intended to cause Pusey to reconsider his accusations. "There is a healthy devotion to the Blessed Mary, and there is an artificial; it is possible to love her as a Mother, to honor her as a Virgin, to seek her as a Patron, and to exalt her as a Queen, without any injury to solid piety and Christian good sense:– I cannot help calling this the English style.[134]

Pusey found most of his objectionable Marian material from Italianate devotionals which effused emotionalism and exaggeration which, in combination, seemed to contradict the purity of the Gospel. Newman is quick to point out that Pusey ought not be too quick to confuse differing ethnic styles and manners. What might be offensive to English piety might not be so for the Italians. And so, we should not be surprised to read his personal testimony: "Such devotional manifestations in honor of Our Lady has been my great crux as regards Catholicism . . . they are suitable for Italy, but they are not suitable for England." [135]

Newman shows that he has read carefully what Pusey has surfaced from various devotional sources, as Newman quotes them directly. Much of what Pusey finds objectionable is also objectionable to Newman. In fact, he cannot imagine that these citations are truly to be found in approved prayer books, he says, if they are accurate representations, they are to be spurned. He then summarizes his reaction thus: "I will have nothing to do with statements which can only be explained, by being explained away." [136]

Thus, we arrive at Newman's view of the relationship between Christological doctrine and particular Marian devotions:

> Every church which is dedicated to her, every altar which is raised under her invocation, every image which represents her, every litany in her praise, every Hail Mary for her continual memory, does but remind us that there was One Who, though He was all-blessed from all eternity, yet for the sake of sinners, "did not shrink from the Virgin's womb." [137]

(b) *Christology versus Mariology*

The title of this section could sound provocative, as in fact Newman's own words to Pusey sound provocative, but this title is intended to underscore the polemical situation in which Newman found himself defending the Catholic position on Marian doctrine and devotion, in contrast to liberal Protestant positions—and even those of Anglo-Catholics, to some degree. Newman cannot see any justification for viewing Christology and Mariology to be at odds with each other. On the contrary, the one is inexplicable without reference to the other, and so, we read the following:

> From mere Protestants, indeed, I expect nothing better. They content themselves with saying that our devotions to our Lady *must necessarily* throw our Lord into the shade; and thereby they relieve themselves of a great deal of trouble. Then they catch at any stray fact which countenances or seems to countenance their prejudice. Now I say plainly, I never will defend or screen anyone from your just rebuke, who, through false devotion to Mary, forgets Jesus. But I should like the fact to be proved first; I cannot hastily admit it. There is this broad fact the other way;—that, if we look through Europe, we shall find, on the whole, that just those nations and countries have lost their faith in the divinity of Christ, who have given up devotion to His Mother, and that those on the other hand, who had foremost in her honor, have retained their orthodoxy. [138]

For Newman, Marian devotion should not be seen in competition with Christological doctrine. False and exaggerated devotion, however, is to be rejected as dangerous since it can appear to obscure the Church's true teaching on both Jesus and Mary. Newman's point nevertheless can be summed up in the adage, *Abusus non tollit usum* ("Abuse does not take away use"). He would go on to argue that an orthodox Mariology is crucial to maintain an orthodox Christology, which he demonstrates from the historical record, whereby it is plain to all that the Protestant denominations which abandoned the Marian dimension woke up in Newman's era to discover that they had lost their Christological focus. Newman emphatically states: "We have the same warrant for hailing her as God's Mother, as we have for adoring Him as God." [139]

We have already seen this citation in a fuller context in the previous section, however, it is good to bring this forth in the present discussion since it demonstrates Newman's understanding of the interplay between Christology and Mariology. Likewise, he suggests that the "warrant" for both beliefs is the same, namely, the teaching authority of the Church; accepting a Christological doctrine, for example, Chalcedon's statements on Christ's identity, makes little or no sense if one is not willing to accept another council's statements on Mary, for example, her identification as *Theotokos* at Ephesus, albeit in a Christological vein.

> ...Mere Protestants have seldom any real perception of the doctrine of God and man in one Person. They speak in a dreamy, shadowy way of Christ's divinity; but, when their meaning is shifted, you will find them very slow to commit themselves to any statement sufficient to express the Catholic dogma. ...
>
> And the confession that Mary is *Deipara*, or the Mother of God, is that safeguard wherewith we seal up and secure the doctrine of the Apostle (John) from all evasion. ... It declares that He is God; it implies that He is man; it suggests to us that He is God still, though He has become man, and that He is true man though He is God. ... If Mary is the Mother of God, Christ must be literally Emmanuel, God with us. And hence it was, that, when time went on, and the bad spirits and false prophets grew stronger and bolder, and found a way into the Catholic body itself, then the Church, guided by God, could find no more effectual and sure way of expelling them than that

of using this word *Deipara* against them; and, on the other hand, when they came up again from the realms of darkness, and plotted the utter overthrow of Christian faith in the sixteenth century, then they could find no more certain expedient for their hateful purpose than that of reviling and blaspheming the prerogatives of Mary, for they knew full well that, if they could once get the world to dishonour the Mother, the dishonour of the Son would follow close. The Church and Satan agreed together in this, that Son and Mother went together; and the experience of three centuries has confirmed their testimony, for Catholics who have honoured the Mother, still worship the Son, while Protestants who now have ceased to confess the Son, began then by scoffing at the Mother.[140]

It cannot be overlooked that Newman's language above is rather polemical, yet one must recall that he has been put into that mode by the circumstances of the moment. Putting aside the tone of Newman's language, Newman's adamant defense of the doctrine of the *Theotokos* as an exemplar of a most necessary doctrinal development in light of the early Christological heresies and those attacks on Catholic Marian doctrine and devotion resulting from the Reformation is, nonetheless, quite valid.

Furthermore, one cannot forget that Newman's ongoing battle with Liberal Protestantism would have bolstered his position, as his language itself indicates. Indeed, Protestant Fundamentalism had to be formed in the United States at that very time,[141] precisely to confront the denial of the basics or "fundamentals" of the Christian Faith, including and most especially the divinity of Christ.[142]

His assertion, based on personal observation, was that the Protestantism of his day—in failing to take seriously Ephesus—had ended up denying Chalcedon. Newman identifies the rejection of certain Marian doctrines at the time of the Protestant Reformation as the logical outcome of a failure to understand the full implications of the Christological truths formulated in the early councils. In his *Discourses to Mixed Congregations*, Newman impresses his listeners with an argument in favor of the *nexus mysteriorum* in the divine economy of salvation by which the essential truths concerning the *Theotokos* and her cooperation in this economy are never separated from the truths we hold about her Son:

You see, then, my brethren, in this particular, the harmonious consistency of the revealed system, and the bearing of one doctrine upon another; Mary is exalted for the sake of Jesus. It was fitting that she, as being a creature, though the first of creatures, should have an office of ministration. She, as others, came into the world to do a work, she had a mission to fulfill; her grace and her glory are not for her own sake, but for her Maker's; and to her is committed the custody of the Incarnation; this is her appointed office. . . . As she was once upon earth, and was personally the guardian of her Divine Child, as she carried Him in her womb, folded Him in her embrace, and suckled Him at her breast, so now, and to the latest hour of the Church, do her glories and the devotion paid her proclaim and define the right faith concerning Him as God and Man.[143]

In very human and tender language, Newman presents Mary as the guardian or "minister" of His Sacred Humanity. The guardianship which she exercised during the Lord's earthly life continues, so that her position is not a personal prerogative but one aimed at upholding the dignity and honor of her Son's position as the God-Man. "You will find, that, in this respect, as in Mary's prerogatives themselves, there is the same careful reference to the glory of Him Who gave them to her."[144]

The central insight of this passage can be best summed up in the title of his Discourse XVII, "The Glories of Mary for the Sake of Her Son" and likewise, in Newman's explanation of the Marian title, *Turris Davidica*.[145]

A tower in its simplest idea is a fabric for defense against enemies. David, King of Israel, built for this purpose a notable tower; and as he is a figure or type of our Lord, so is his tower a figure denoting our Lord's Virgin Mother. She is called the Tower of David because she had so signally fulfilled the office of defending her Divine Son from the assaults of His foes. It is customary with those who are not Catholics to fancy that the honours we pay to her interfere with the supreme worship which we pay to Him; that in Catholic teaching she eclipses Him. But this is the very reverse of the truth.[146]

Here, Newman offers an excellent explanation of the title, along with *obiter dicta* regarding the typological questions related to Our Lord and Our Lady. He strenuously defends Church teaching on Mary's proper place in reference to Christ.

Mary, in like manner, is preeminently faithful to her Lord and Son. Let no one for an instant suppose that she is not supremely zealous for His honour, or, as those who are not Catholic fancy, that to exalt her is to be unfaithful to Him. Her true servants are still more truly His. Well as she rewards her friends, she would deem him no friend, but a traitor, who preferred herself to Him. As He is zealous for her honour, so is she for His. He is the Fount of Grace, and all her gifts are from His goodness. O Mary, teach us ever to worship thy Son as the One Creator, and to be devout to thee as the most highly favoured of creatures.[147]

Mary, we learn, is not in competition with her Son; hers is a complementary and subordinate role. In very strong terms, he denounces any kind of devotion which would obscure the centrality of Christ; in truth, he refers to those who engage in such activity as "traitors" to Mary. Implicitly, he deals with the distinctions among *latria*, *hyperdulia*[148] and *dulia*. How are we to understand Newman's mention of Mary rewarding her "friends"? What is this great "reward" that we receive through her mediation but the very gift of God Himself at the moment of the Incarnation and likewise a greater share or participation in the gift of God's life in our souls through this continual mediation? This truth neither makes her "the author of grace," nor the source of any of her privileges in the *œconomia salutis*. Newman's final invocation of Mary reveals that Newman thinks believers ought to relate to her as a creature, even though the most highly favored one. "Lastly, it is Mary's prerogative to be the morning star which heralds in the sun. She does not shine for herself, or from herself, but she is the reflection of her and our Redeemer, and she glorifies *Him*."[149]

In addition to his elucidation of *"Stella Matutina,"*[150] Newman also makes the interesting and critical observation that Jesus is not only "our" Redeemer but also that of His Mother and, therefore, she points to Him and glorifies Him as the morning star does for the Sun. ". . . if lastly all the saints in bliss are called stars, in that they are like stars differing from stars in glory; therefore most assuredly, without any derogation from the honour of Our Lord is Mary His Mother called the Star of the Sea, and the more so because even on her head she wears a crown of twelve stars."[151]

As in the previous selection, Newman indicates Mary's subordinate role to Christ.[152] What is quite interesting, however, is that Newman's apologetic for the Catholic devotion to Mary not only bears in mind this principle of Mary's subordination to Christ but also the principle by which we understand Mary's superiority in regard to the other saints. Newman implicitly indicates a biblical basis for this Marian title of *Stella Matutina* by alluding to the Woman of Revelation 12[153] and to her crown of twelve stars. If the saints can be figuratively referred to as "stars" that differ from each other in the sky, that is, some saints shine more brightly than others according to their degree of sanctity, then she who wears the "crown of twelve stars," in fact "outshines" them all.

This recourse to analogies based on natural phenomena, as we have seen in previous sections, has proven quite useful in enhancing our appreciation of Newman's understanding of the economy of salvation and especially of Mary's particular role in it. Indeed, for Newman, there is in reality only one economy, the economy of salvation which is itself like a star that can indicate the holiness of the saints and the extraordinary holiness of Mary while always having as its ultimate point of reference Jesus the "Light of the World," "the Sun of Righteousness." Therefore, if one properly understands the veneration given to the saints (*dulia*) and the special devotion rendered to Mary (*hyperdulia*) and within this overall Christocentric context of *latria*—worship due to the Triune God alone—then there can be no Christology *versus* Mariology.[154]

(c) *The Historical Witness*

In the citations which follow from Newman's *Letter to Pusey*, certain key words should be noticed: "gradually," "the Fathers," "ancient doctors," "mediæval and modern," "undivided Church," "foundations," "grew up," "gracious persuasion," "gradual manifestation," "natural process." With such words, Newman is attempting to convince Pusey that Marian doctrine and devotion were present in the Church in varying degrees but, like all doctrine, evolved or developed over the centuries yet always in keeping with the oneness of truth and precisely as an example of its fullness.

The historical witness of the Fathers of the Church, in

Newman's mind, should be enough to convince Pusey of the antiquity and authenticity of the Catholic Marian doctrine and devotion. Newman's rather straight forward manner of expression should not be interpreted as lacking in ecumenical sensitivity. Rather, Newman's direct approach is aimed at reminding Pusey of his own lack of consistency in thought and in practice since he too shares, in Newman's estimation, such "high notions of the Blessed Virgin," and makes his own particular appeal to the historical witness of the Fathers and the undivided Church. However, Newman's observations to Pusey that the development of Catholic Marian doctrine and devotion was such a placid process may strike the reader as itself an unhistorical statement, when one considers the upheaval caused by the heresies of Arius and Nestorius that "forced" the Church into defining as a dogma the orthodox doctrine of Mary as the *Theotokos*, a teaching which the Church had always held to be likewise the fundamental doctrine of Christ's divinity.

Newman explains:

> As then these ideas of her sanctity and dignity gradually penetrated the mind of Christendom, so did that of her intercessory power follow close upon them and with them.[155]
>
> . . . Anglicans seem to me simply to overlook the strength of the arguments adducible from the works of those ancient doctors in our favour; and they open the attack upon our mediaeval and modern writers, careless of leaving a host of primitive opponents in their rear. . . . Had you happened in your Volume to introduce your notice of our teaching about the Blessed Virgin, with a notice of the teaching of the Fathers concerning her, which you follow ordinary men would have considered that there was not much to choose between you and us. Though you appealed ever so much, in your defense, to the authority of the "undivided Church" they would have said that you, who had such high notions of the Blessed Mary, were one of the last men who had a right to accuse us of quasi-idolatry.[156]
>
> . . . and thus noiselessly and without strife, as the first Temple was built in the Holy City, she grew up into her inheritance, and was "established in Sion and her power was in Jerusalem." [157] It became her, as a creature, a mother, and a woman, to stand aside and make her way for the Creator, to minister to her Son, and to win her way into the world's homage by sweet and gracious persuasion. . . . No fierce controversy, no persecuted

confessors, no heresiarch, no anathema, were necessary for her gradual manifestation; as she had increased day by day in grace and merit at Nazareth, while the world knew not of her, so has she raised herself aloft silently, and has grown into her place in the Church by a tranquil influence and a natural process.[158]

This development of Marian doctrine and devotion was a true stumbling block for the Anglican Newman. Therefore, Newman can sympathize with Pusey's own difficulties in evaluating whether or the Catholic Church's teaching on the Virgin was in continuity with the historic roots of Christianity. By tenaciously holding on to his Catholic positions as those which the Fathers of the Church—so instrumental in his conversion—espoused and which the Church throughout the centuries has jealously safeguarded as the deposit of apostolic faith, Newman argues that the development of Marian doctrine and devotion—which Pusey himself accepts "does not supercede the Fathers, but explains and completes them." Newman emphatically states this when he writes:

> The Fathers made me a Catholic, and I am not going to kick down the ladder by which I ascended into the Church. It is a ladder quite as serviceable for that purpose now, as it was twenty years ago. . . . And, in particular as regards our teaching concerning the Blessed Virgin, with the Fathers I am content;—and to the subject of that teaching I mean to address myself at once. I do so, because you say, as I myself have said in former years, that "that vast system as to the Blessed Virgin . . . to all of us has been the special *crux* of the Roman system." Here, let me say, as on other points, the Fathers are enough for me. I do not wish to say more than they suggest to me, and will not say less.[159]

The trajectory of Newman's Mariology points to Mary's singular place in the development of doctrine. Therefore, Newman would argue that Catholic Marian doctrine and devotion are not something new or foreign to the Gospel Faith but integral to it. Indeed, his own life's experiences, friendships, pastoral ministry, profound reflection on the written Word of God and study of the Sacred Tradition, most especially the writings of the Fathers, are the *raison d'être* of his conversion to Catholicism and combine to form a most credible historical witness to the authenticity of the Church's Marian teaching and its development.

SUMMARY OF CHAPTER ONE

1) The life of Newman is the epitome of *fides quærens intellectum* (faith seeking understanding)—a process of development and conversion by which faith working together with reason is able to shape and, at times, transform his religious thought, sensibilities, and personal relationships.

2) Newman shares his faith convictions in a pedagogical and apologetical style. He does not engage in petty, polemical *ad hominem* attacks for the sake of proving his point; rather, his aim is to edify and lead men to a more profound understanding and appreciation of the content of the Faith (*fides quae*—the faith which is believed) and the act of faith (*fides qua*—the faith by which one believes).

3) Newman does not interface simply with ideas but with real persons/personalities whose ideas and life events are able to intertwine with his own to form a synthesis of head and heart.

Newman believes that intellectual development must be continually counter-balanced by spiritual development and renewal.

4) Newman does not see theological reflection as divorced from his life of faith and spirituality. He has a genuine *pietas* (piety) without being saccharine.

5) Theology cannot be understood outside an ecclesial context. Newman is a churchman who does not think his ideas in a vacuum, always doing so as a believer who faithfully safeguards the patrimony of the Faith and exercises *sentire cum ecclesia* (to feel/think with the Church).

6) Doctrine and dogma are essential elements of the Church and her theology. They are not static but dynamic expressions of the truth formulated in such a way that while they are suited to a particular time, place and historical period, they also participate in the unchangeability of God Who is Truth Itself. This is best understood and explained through Newman's idea of doctrinal development.

7) Newman understands that the individual believer, whether lay or clerical, is called to holiness, to conversion. He does not think that such conversion can occur without a pursuit of the truth, which begins in the individual conscience (illative sense, *phronesis*) and then seeks to penetrate the whole of man's being. The truth is presented to man in its fullness by the Church,

guided by the Spirit and built up by the incarnational principle (e.g., the sacraments), authentically teaching and interpreting the truth of the Divine Revelation (Sacred Scripture and Tradition) through the exercise of her living teaching office or Magisterium. Nevertheless. the lay faithful, because they possess a *sensus fidei* (*phronema*), combine to form a *sensus/consensus fidelium* so that united with their pastors (*conspiratio*), they share in the charism of infallibility given to the whole Church, which charism is exercised in a unique, supreme way by the Pope and the Bishops. Therefore, Newman concludes that, in matters of faith (doctrine), the laity should be consulted. Newman, however, is always careful to distinguish the *Ecclesia discens* from the *Ecclesia docens*— the latter having the final say in such matters.

8) In relying on Tradition (especially the writings of the Fathers of the Church) and the Church's Magisterium, Newman expresses his keen historical consciousness of the Church and the constant need for vigilance against a spirit of liberalism (i.e., anti-dogmatism) in religion.

9) The truth of doctrines can be discovered not only by relying on the authority of the Magisterium but by the searching of internal evidence. Newman gives seven criteria by which to judge whether or not a certain doctrine is a true development or a corruption. These seven criteria are not absolute but can be helpful to the Magisterium when considering to formulate a dogmatic definition.

10) While the definition of dogmas is not only helpful but necessary at times, it should be used as a last resort, for a sense of mystery needs to be preserved in religion. Newman warns in his twelve theses presented to Perrone that the truth should not be formulated into dogma prematurely since doing so could end up into a perversion of the truth, rather than the preservation intended.

11) Mary is the paradigm for the development of Christian doctrine. He traces and explains the development of Marian doctrine and devotion, seeking to ground them in what he calls the "rudimental" teaching of Sacred Scripture and Tradition, considering the image of Mary as the Second Eve to be the fundamental source for genuine Marian development. He finds the process by which the definition of the Immaculate Conception came about to be an enlightening and enlightened one.

Newman's Use of Sacred Scripture in Support of His Theology of Mary's Cooperation in the Œconomia Salutis

INTRODUCTION

Perhaps it is most appropriate that this chapter begin with an overall evaluation of the importance of the Sacred Scriptures in the life and ministry of the Venerable John Henry Cardinal Newman before the particulars of his biblical hermeneutic and exegetical methods can be discussed, particularly as they relate to the topic of this chapter. Jaak Seynæve, in *Newman's Biblical Hermeneutics*, makes a positive appraisal of Newman's love for the Sacred Scriptures; he highlights, among many things, the fact that already as a child and throughout his evangelical upbringing Newman was fond of reading and memorizing passages from the Bible. He adds:

> He expresses keen approval of the custom of having the Bible read in Church, in the family and in private. Newman read the Bible constantly. Allusions to, and applications of, Holy Scripture are scattered throughout his works. Practically all his sermons draw their main inspiration from Scripture. There is almost no part of the inspired volumes which Newman did not use. Like Saint Augustine and the medieval authors, Newman, in his sermons, employs a mosaic of biblical texts, such that one can hardly tell the difference between the language of the Bible and his own. It is not surprising that scholars speak of Newman as a "biblical theologian," or "an outstanding interpreter of Scripture." While keeping in mind that, in his thought, Scripture and Tradition stand together, one may state that Holy Scripture constitutes the main source of inspiration and reference in Newman's work.[1]

The main focus in this chapter is on the exegetical method which Newman employed, both as an Anglican and then as a Catholic, to explain the Marian theology latent or explicit in some key scriptural texts concerning the Virgin. The main passages most frequently commented on by Newman are: the *Proto-evangelium*[2]; the Infancy Narratives of the Gospels of Saints Matthew and Luke; the enigmatic episodes of the Synoptic Gospels, for example, the praise of Mary by the anonymous woman in the crowd and Jesus' response; the two Marian pericopes in John's Gospel, namely, Mary's presence at the Wedding Feast of Cana and at the Foot of the Cross; and the apocalyptic vision of the twelfth chapter of the Book of Revelation. Within this panoply of sacred texts, other scriptural passages are dealt with based on their relevance to our topic. Of particular interest is Newman's use of Old Testament passages (types and figures) as encountered in his writings about the Virgin and her role in the *historia salutis*.[3] Seynæve makes the following observation:

> We must recollect that few biblical theologians have stressed as much as Newman, the importance of the link between Old and New Testament typology. Time and time again, he underlines that the inspired writers saw in the past "as in miniature and outline," that the past is made the type and pledge of the future. . . . Under the shadows and the figures of the Old Testament are hidden the substance and the reality of the New Testament.[4]

It must be said at the outset that Newman does not pretend to be a Scripture scholar or exegete in the modern sense of the term. Seynæve explains that Newman sought to assimilate into his method of interpretation of the Sacred Text a carefully balanced synthesis of the allegorical, mystical, spiritual school of Alexandria and the literal school of interpretation represented by the Church of Antioch. Nevertheless, Seynæve concludes that Newman's scriptural hermenuetic is not easily categorized since he never fully laid out the principles of his biblical interpretation in a systematic form.[5]

He reads the *Sacra Pagina*[6] in light of the Tradition[7] and relies heavily on patristic sources in order to convey what he is convinced is a faithful rendering of the text's meaning. Newman avoids reading the Scriptures in any sort of vacuum. He is firmly convinced of the *sensus plenior* (the fuller sense) of the sacred texts.[8] He too is aware of the dangers of an approach that does not take into account all the senses of Scripture. Seynæve makes the point that Newman's preference for the "'mystical,' 'allegorical,' 'sacramental,' 'figurative' or 'spiritual' method of biblical interpretation to the critical and literal," as is evident in his work *The Arians of the Fourth Century*, did not stifle his development in "subsequent writings, especially the sermons," of a more "critico-literary interpretation of Scripture." [9]

In his *Essay on the Development of Christian Doctrine*, Newman describes his view of the Scriptures as a sacred text whose richness conceals and reveals at the same time, a multiplicity of meanings, which should be interpreted as shedding light upon the whole of Divine Revelation, not in an isolated fashion. In order to illustrate the interconnectedness of the various literary forms of the Scriptures and the doctrines they teach, Newman uses a topographical analogy: the different terrains or levels of the physical land, express a beauteous harmony of relation that is likewise evident in the relationship among the differing levels of interpretation, structure and style in the one truth of God's Word.

> It is in point to notice also the structure and style of Scripture, a structure so unsystematic and various and a style so figurative and indirect that no one would presume at first sight to say what is in it and what is not. It cannot, as it were, be mapped, or its contents catalogued; but after all our diligence, to the end of our lives and to the end of the Church, it must be an unexplored and unsubdued land, with heights and valleys, forests and streams, on the right and on the left of our path and close about us, full of concealed wonders and choice treasures. Of no doctrine whatever, which does not actually contradict what has been delivered, can it be peremptorily asserted that it is not in Scripture; of no reader, whatever be his study of it, can it be said that he has mastered every doctrine which it contains. [10]

The Reverend Eugene M. Burke discusses Newman's theory of the development of doctrine in relationship to the Church's progressive use and understanding of the Sacred Scriptures as a *locus theologicus* (a theological source) in light of the Tradition. Father Burke is convinced that Newman's theory is an explication of the Church's belief that the Word of God is not a stagnant revelation, but a dynamic revelatory act of the living God, the depths of whose revelation must be plumbed according to the various levels of its interpretation. [11]

Newman wished to avoid at all costs falling into the pitfalls of eisegesis. Seynæve notes that either an exaggerated allegorical and/or an overly literalistic interpretation of Scripture were detrimental to one's understanding of the sacred truths contained therein and to the process of formulating those truths into doctrinal propositions. Ultimately, Newman would argue it is neither the individual Father of the Church nor any particular school of biblical interpretation which must prevail, but the Church's own teaching in accord with the Sacred Tradition. For example, overemphasizing the allegorical sense, with all due deference to the Alexandrian school, could become an abusive tool or "means of evading those more argumentative proofs of the Catholic doctrine, which are built upon the explicit-literal testimonies of Scripture." Cardinal Newman, as Seynæve points out, preferred that the use of allegorism in interpretation be "sober and reverent." Seynæve continues: "In the *Apologia*, he states emphatically that the Fathers of the Church of Alexandria erred 'whenever . . . they proceeded *to obscure* the primary meaning of Scripture and *to weaken the force of historical facts and express declarations.*'"[12]

The Reverend J. Derek Holmes, in "Newman's Attitude towards Biblical Criticism and Biblical Inspiration," reflects on "the evolution of Newman's interpretation of the theological notion of inspiration," according to the influence of several factors. Two of these key factors are the teaching authority of the Church on biblical interpretation[13] and an evaluation of biblical inspiration in light of the discoveries of modern science and historical research. Of all the different notions which Newman held about biblical inspiration, Holmes notes that Newman's "most satisfactory view was that which associated it with the supernatural doctrine or teaching, which could not be given by human means but which was conveyed through the words of the human author." Thus, for Newman, "inspiration was restricted to the divine authoritative voice in Scripture, the sense in which God had spoken. Only the Church, however, could declare what God had actually said through the letter of the Scripture." What then was the common link between the sacred human authors? Their common vocation, to be "inspired for a supernatural object and infallible in their writings or speeches bearing upon it. . . . Historical or scientific accuracy were subordinate to the higher purpose of teaching divine mysteries."[14]

One could say therefore that Newman essentially agreed with

the famous adage of the great Oratorian and Church historian Cardinal Cesare Baronius who remarked, "The Bible does not teach us so much about how the heavens go, as about how to go to heaven." Indeed, the essential hinge of Newman's preaching and teaching is his interpretation of the Sacred Scriptures not as a history or science book but as the divinely inspired and inerrant Word of God written by men for man's eternal salvation.[15] His *Parochial and Plain Sermons* are an obvious example of Newman's constant use of the Bible to exhort his readers to find in the inspired Word of God—preached in the liturgical assembly—the spiritual food for their souls which would fortify them along their pilgrimage of faith in search of Christian perfection and a deeper understanding of the divine mysteries and the truths of faith and morals.[16]

The Reverend Louis Bouyer further convinces us of the theological and spiritual merit of Newman's *Parochial and Plain Sermons*. He explains that for Newman the Word of God is living and dynamic; it penetrates the heart of man piercing the bone and marrow of his earthly existence so as to transform him into the image and likeness of the heavenly Man Christ Jesus. The preaching of the Word of God has as its final aim the urging on of men toward the achievement of holiness in this life as a sure preparation for the holiness of heaven. For the Anglican Newman, the proclamation of the Sacred Scriptures in the liturgical assembly is a quasi-sacrament by which the hearer should receive particular graces for the living out of the Christian ideal.[17]

To understand the preaching of Newman is to appreciate his use of Sacred Scripture, that is, his ability to teach, edify, exhort, correct and to solidify for his audience a foundation for a Christian apologetic. In *The White Stone*, Father Blehl explains how Newman's *Parochial and Plain Sermons* were, in a certain sense, his evangelical attempt at a *mystagogia* (mystagogy). Newman understood his preaching of the Sacred Scriptures as consisting in the role of a *pedagogus* or tutor who leads the People of God— under the inspiration of the Spirit—into the fullness of holiness and truth. His purpose in writing the sermons, as Blehl notes, "was to lead men and women," of Saint Mary's Church at Oxford "to realize vividly for themselves the mysteries of faith and to comprehend authentic Christianity as a concrete way of life, not merely as an abstract program for living."[18] Father Blehl explains that Newman's sermons challenged his congregation to shun any temptations that would cause them to lose their personal sense of sin and the sacred: "By an accumulation of biblical examples, suggestions, and analyses of attitudes of mind, Newman gradually brought his hearers to assimilate the meaning of Christian truths in relation to their lives. Finally, Newman's achievement in these sermons lay in the profoundly difficult task of making the invisible world, so real to him, real for his hearers as well. In this he was, according to the testimonies of the time, entirely successful." [19]

W. D. White, using the colorful and varied brush strokes that make up the wonderful landscape that are the sermons of the Venerable Newman, paints a captivating portrait of Newman's ability to use Sacred Scripture.

> In its fundamental dogmatic basis, Newman's preaching must be seen as doctrinal, though not systematic; in its incarnational and Christological emphasis it is kerygmatic; in its insistence upon holiness of life and obedience to the will of God, it is highly moral and unsentimental; in its peculiar sense of urgency it is apocalyptical; in its awareness of the presence of God and its hope for beatitude it is eschatological; in its unrelenting probings of human motives and facades it is psychologically penetrating; in its critique of the spirit of the age it is prophetic, in its urgent longing for holiness and its exaltation of the heroes and martyrs of the faith it is moving and devotional; in its impregnation with biblical and patristic insights and sensibilities, it is generally Catholic; in its deep sense of the historical Church and its worship it is ecclesiastical and liturgical; in its power to realize lost causes and forgotten truths, it is superbly apologetic. [20]

However, even a cursory reading of some of Newman's more systematic, theological treatises reveals the depth of his knowledge and love of the Scriptures. In this regard, worthy of particular mention is Newman's treatment of miracles. Written from 1825–1826, Newman's *An Essay on the Miracles of Scripture* [21] is a treatise which defends the authenticity of the miracles recorded in the Bible against skeptical rationalists and agnostic empiricists, [22] whose refutation of miracles was primarily intended to undermine the existence of the supernatural order to chisel away at the truth of Divine Revelation, that is, at the divine economy of salvation upon whose foundation are built both the Jewish and Christian Dispensations.

The Reverend Giovanni Velocci, C.Ss.R., emphasizes the importance of Newman's treatment of miracles from the perspective of his biblical exegesis and his philosophical contention with Enlightenment and Post-Enlightenment rationalists and empiricists,[23] who were prone to deny the supernatural, let alone any sort of Divine Economy.[24]

Newman's theology of Divine Providence is an articulation of his understanding of the *œconomia salutis*. Father Velocci explains that Newman's reading of the Sacred Scriptures, that is, his constant meditation on the mysteries of Divine Providence as revealed in the *historia salutis*, mirrored, in a very personal way, the ongoing development of Newman's own spiritual enlightenment—the working out of his own personal history of salvation. Velocci explains this principle of continuity in Newman's sense of Divine Providence. He then draws out the implications of this principle of continuity in Newman's approach to the Bible. It is, in accord with the Divine Providence, that there is maintained in the Sacred Scriptures a fundamental unity between the Old and New Testaments. For Newman, this unity is revealed in a dynamic progression or development of doctrine guided "by the divine, active and omnipotent presence." This unified and dynamic development of the economy of salvation in the Bible is reflected in Newman's own life.[25]

For Newman, there are three living principles or laws which characterize God's governance of the world through Divine Providence: the principle of economy, the principle of the nature of things, and the principle of analogy.[26] The first and most fundamental is the principle of the economy by which, is understood, the pedagogical nature of God's dealings with man throughout the history of salvation. In other words, Newman holds that God reveals Himself and His divine plan of salvation in such a way as to lead men gradually to embrace both. The unfolding of the history of salvation culminates in the Incarnation and in the establishment of the Church as the universal sacrament of salvation. The history of salvation begins, however, with Creation and encompasses each of the successive ratifications of the covenants, until all is fulfilled in the Lord Jesus, the definitive Word of the Father's Revelation and the sole

Universal Redeemer.[27] The progress of the divine economy in the events of the history of salvation is designed, according to Divine Providence, to be accompanied by a gradual illumination of man's conscience, that is, a gradual formation of the conscience by the light of faith and reason so that, "all men might be saved and come to the knowledge of the truth."[28] "The Church, the 'pillar and bulwark of the truth,' has received this solemn command of Christ from the apostles to announce the saving truth."[29]

The Reverend Stanley L. Jaki, O.S.B., noted physicist and professor at Seton Hall University, in a collection of lectures on Newman, gives us some background the better to understand the purpose of his book. He writes in the Foreword: "Newman's chief challenge today, as in his own times, aims at the defense of the supernatural. Of course, the defense of the supernatural for Newman was far more than a mere intellectual enterprise. For him the supernatural was above all an existentially spiritual challenge to be implemented within a plan set by God. Compared with this perspective on Newman, all other facets of his intellectual physiognomy should seem secondary."[30]

In his essay on "Newman and Miracles," Father Jaki also comments on the significance of Newman's apologetic for miracles as a clear instance of his ability to vindicate in the eyes of skeptics the supernatural, in particular, the authority of Divine Revelation and Divine Providence as revealed both in the economy of nature and in the economy of salvation. Jaki relates that Newman's *Essay on the Miracles of Scripture* was a formidable defense of the authenticity of biblical miracles in the criticism of Hume and Gibbon.[31]

Furthermore, Newman's valiant defense of miracles, and thus of the supernatural economy of salvation, is a tribute to him as an apologist, making him a *rara avis* among other Anglican apologists in his day. Jaki holds that Newman believed that the "moral purpose" of biblical miracles could not be grasped, except from "within the framework of a biblical revelation." Likewise, Father Jaki adds that Newman's apologetic on behalf of miracles was designed to impress upon any would-be skeptics that the miracles of the Bible prove that beyond the physical realm "there was a moral universe no less objective than the physical." Jaki explains that this spiritual universe "is a universe of the moral conscience, the universe of a keen awareness of the difference between virtue and sin, a universe pivoted on an infinitely supreme moral Law-giver and final Judge, a universe with an ultimate phase of eternal reward and punishment."[32] Jaki brings our focus back to the centrality of Newman's theology of the economy of salvation explaining that, according to Newman, "biblical miracles were physical because only as such could they effectively draw sinful, fallen man's attention to a plan of salvation which God has set on a plane much higher than the level of mere physical interaction and mere natural life."[33]

One also discovers a particular eloquence and theological prowess in the way that Newman's apologetic of miracles—intended in effect to be an apologetic for Divine Revelation and the economy of salvation—ends up focusing on the central mystery of the economy of salvation namely, the miracle of the Incarnation, and therefore, by necessity, on the figure of the Virgin Mary. Newman writes in his treatise on *Ecclesiastical Miracles*:

> Catholics . . . hold the mystery of the Incarnation; and the Incarnation is the most stupendous event which ever can take place on earth; after it and henceforth, I do not see how we can scruple at any miracle on the mere ground of its being unlikely to happen. No miracle can be so great as that which took place in the Holy House of Nazareth. . . . If, through divine grace, we once are able to accept the solemn truth that the Supreme Being was born of a mortal woman, what is there to be imagined which can offend us on the ground of its marvellousness.[34]

However, before we can examine Newman's use of Sacred Scripture in regard to the Blessed Virgin Mary and her cooperation in the *œconomia salutis*, some further introductory remarks are needed to underscore the fact that Newman's exegetical methods underwent much polishing and refinement before and after his conversion to Catholicism in 1845. His approach to God's Word as an Evangelical is certainly to be distinguished from the approach he takes, for example, as an Anglican preacher at Saint Mary's at Oxford, and, then, as a Catholic priest preaching at the Oratory of Birmingham. Moreover, one cannot overlook the tremendous influence on Newman of the Fathers of the Church and their reading of the Sacred Scriptures.[35] Father Velocci testifies to this vital link between Newman and the biblical interpretations of the Fathers.[36]

Newman's overall scriptural methodology is one that can be rightfully situated within an authentic Catholic approach to the Word of God. Ultimately, Newman does not adhere to the Reformation principle of *sola Scriptura*[37] but, as Jaki asserts, the authority of the living Magisterium of the Church was needed to safeguard the believer from reading the Sacred Scriptures as if they were literal proof-texts for doctrines or simply as containing an inspired message according to the personal interpretation given to it by the believer. In a sense, Newman moves away from the fundamentalist approach to Scripture, in which he was brought up as an Calvinistic Evangelical, in order to adopt an approach to the Bible that takes into consideration not simply the messages of isolated texts but rather situating the particular message of each text and/or book of the Bible in its proper historical, cultural and theological context so that the unified harmony of both testaments, as intended by the Divine Providence in the economy of salvation, is more fully understood. For example, Jaki comments on Newman's *caveat* against a private reading and interpretation of the Scriptures that fails to take into consideration that the Bible, although a book of Divine Revelation, "constitutes no exception to a truth about all books: 'A book, after all, cannot make a stand against the wild living intellect of man.' ... Newman saw only one effective breakwater, the infallible Catholic Church as embodied not in inert texts but in an authority which is forever alive."[38]

For Newman, the Sacred Scriptures, the Tradition and the Magisterium together form a tripod of Divine Revelation.[39] Otherwise, Newman argued that Scripture, without the aid of Tradition and the Magisterium, limps—given that its authentic interpretation and application to the Christian life—utterly depends on all three elements working together in harmonious balance. Father Bouyer explains how his fellow-Oratorian Newman envisioned such a harmonious balance among Sacred Scripture, Sacred Tradition (with special deference to the Fathers of the Church) and the Living Magisterium. Bouyer writes:

> Together with the rediscovery of the Fathers, the needed renewal had to come, Newman thought, through a closer contact with and a firmer grasp of Scripture, the document par excellence of authentic Christianity, as it had been traditionally accepted in the Church. And it goes without saying that

Newman, long before becoming a Catholic, had been per-
suaded that the Bible was never to be divorced, in its use and
its interpretation, from the living understanding of it to be
found in the one, true Church. He went even further, on this
point again, than what was the current teaching and practice
in the Church of the Renaissance and the Counter-Reforma-
tion. As he would make crystal clear, it was not a matter of just
having the Bible *along with* the tradition, but rather of living
the Bible *within* the tradition. This is exactly what Vatican II
was to teach in perhaps the deepest, and certainly the least
read or studied, of its texts.[40] There are not two independent
sources, to be reconciled more or less happily; there is only *one*
source, to be seen always as a living power, using complementary but inseparable means of expression.[41]

For Newman, the danger of isolating the one from the other
or placing the one in opposition to the other (e.g., Scripture vs.
Tradition) is as perilous as pitting Mary and Christ against one
another. Newman's Marian apologetic, to which the use of the
Sacred Scriptures is fundamental, shows the need to keep all
things in proper perspective so that the most orthodox teaching
of the Church is revealed in every instance. The delicate interplay among Scripture, Tradition, Magisterium and the development of Christian doctrine are all essential themes brought
together in the first chapter of this work under the title of "The
Trajectory of Newman's Mariology."

This present section builds on the foundation of that first
chapter to show how in his treatment of the Sacred Scriptures,
Newman's hermeneutical principles are not so much changed,
but refined. However, insofar as Newman does not approach this
topic in any systematic form, it is necessary to offer a method so
as to evaluate more fruitfully Newman's approach to Holy Writ.
The better to appreciate Newman's understanding of Mary and
the Bible, one needs to examine the style and content of various
texts—mostly sermons, discourses or meditations—in which
Newman's constant recourse to the Scriptures reveals his deep
appreciation of the figure of Mary and her cooperation in the
economy of salvation. A general principle of Newman's biblical
hermeneutic, which John Brit identifies and which is directly
pertinent to our discussion, is his having employed, by way of
anticipation, what the Second Vatican Council referred to as "the

hierarchy of truths." Therefore, in discussing Mary's cooperation in the economy of salvation, it is of the upper most importance to begin with a discussion of the centrality of the doctrine of the Incarnation. Brit writes: "Certain doctrines are necessary and higher in significance in relation to God and to the economy of salvation. Newman always kept this mind and indicated that Mary existed only in relation to the Incarnation." [42]

Giovanni Velocci offers his assessment of Newman's treatment of Mary and the Sacred Scriptures. He writes that Newman carefully studied both the Old and New Testaments in order to ground his Mariology, making recourse frequently to the literal sense of the text "applied with scientific vigor." In doing so, Velocci underscores Newman's reliance on such texts as the *Protoevangelium* of Genesis 3:15 and the perennial value of his interpretation of such key texts as regards Mary's role of cooperation in the divine plan of salvation. [43]

1. "Our Lady in the Gospel"

One of the first sermons[44] that Newman preached after his conversion is entitled "Our Lady in the Gospel." He preached this sermon after his return to England from Rome in December 1847—only a few months after his ordination in Rome to the Catholic priesthood on 30 May 1847. He preached this sermon in Saint Chad's Cathedral of Birmingham on the Third Sunday of Lent, 26 March 1848, the previous day being the feast, known in England as "Lady Day," in honor of the Annunciation.

The Gospel upon which Newman preaches is taken from Luke 11:27–28, when an anonymous woman from the crowd praises Mary for her maternal relationship to Jesus, Whom she obviously perceives to be at least a great prophet, if not indeed the Christ. In response to the woman's praise, Jesus swiftly diverts the attention of the crowd to consider the blessedness of His Virgin Mother from a different or, better, higher perspective. Without in any way dismissing the relevance of the woman's praise of Mary's physical maternity, Our Lord is careful to underscore the nature of Mary's spiritual beatitude which, He teaches, is best characterized by the exemplary nature of her faith and discipleship. Newman's sermon is principally concerned with an exegesis of the Lucan pericope in view of this two-fold blessedness of the Virgin. Newman, in support of his own understanding of the passage, relies on the insights of Saint Augustine and Saint John Chrysostom, both of which Fathers of the Church had a profound influence on Newman's approach to the Sacred Text—as becomes clearer in the next chapter of the present work.

Here, one should note the exegetical method that Newman applies to this text of fundamental Marian significance.[45] The text in question, as Newman was well aware, was often misinterpreted as being indicative of a less than positive, or even, a condescending and derogatory attitude on the part of Our Lord with regard to His Mother. However, it was rare to find the latter negative connotation to be so exaggerated as to suggest a complete repudiation of the Virgin.

Although Newman seems to insist that not even the Protestants of his day would have completely dismissed the Virgin based on this text alone, he does offer an excellent apologetical exegesis of this passage which can be used effectively to offset any interpretation that posits an anti-Marian strain in Our Lord's address on that occasion. This sermon of Newman offers an authentic Catholic apologetical interpretation of Our Lord's response to the woman in Luke 11:27–28. In doing so, Newman helps alleviate some serious difficulties which he was aware some Protestants of his day encountered in this text.

Often enough, these difficulties translated into attempts to correct what was viewed as an over-emphasis if not, even worse, an erroneous position of the Catholic Church concerning the nature of Our Lady's blessedness. In other words, even though Newman does not state as much, one possible motivation for writing this sermon could have been to present a Catholic exegesis of a controverted text which would derive its authority from both an integrated use of other scriptural passages as support and a convincing argumentation based on the patristic sources—following the Fathers' own apologetic literary style.

The Fathers of the Church engaged in apologetics, which they often did by means of their sermons/homilies, because they saw that a certain text could fall prey to a variety of misinterpretations. Therefore, they sought to explain a particular text in light of the whole tradition concerning the Virgin and her role in the *œconomia salutis*. Newman makes this point when he writes:

Now a very few words will be sufficient to show that Our Lord's words are no disparagement to the dignity and glory of His Mother, as the first of creatures and the Queen of all Saints. For consider, He says that it is a more blessed thing to keep the commandments than to be His Mother, and do you think that the Most Holy Mother of God did not keep the commandments of God? Of course, no one, no Protestant even—no one will deny she did. Well, if so, what Our Lord says is that the Blessed Virgin was *more* blessed in that she kept His commandments than because she was His Mother. And what Catholic denies this? On the contrary we all confess it. All Catholics confess it. The Holy Fathers of the Church tell us again and again that Our Lady was more blessed in doing God's will than in being His Mother, blessed in two ways. She was blessed in being His Mother; she was blessed in being filled with the Spirit of faith and obedience. And the latter blessedness was the greater. I say the Holy Fathers say so expressly. Saint Augustine says, "More blessed was Mary in receiving the faith of Christ, than in receiving the flesh of Christ." In the like manner Saint Elizabeth says to her at the Visitation, *"Beata es quæ credidisti,* Blessed art thou who didst believe;" and Saint Chrysostom goes so far as to say that she would not have been blessed, even though she had borne Christ in the body, unless she had heard the Word of God and kept it.[46]

The main point which Newman makes, and what needs to be highlighted at the outset, is that Our Lord's response was by no means intended to reprimand or rebuke Our Lady for having violated any precepts of the Law, but to affirm the contrary. Although some Protestants may not conclude from this passage exactly what Catholics do concerning Mary's blessedness, for Newman, any interpretation of our text suggesting Mary's infidelity to the Law, is untenable. He clearly maintains that Mary's blessedness, as many of the Fathers argue, consists precisely in her obedience of faith. This, Newman observes, is a fundamental assertion which needs to be made regarding the text. Newman, after having alluded to Saint Augustine's remark that "more blessed was Mary in receiving the faith in Christ, than in receiving the flesh of Christ," proceeds to comment on Chrysostom's even more striking remark that Mary's maternity would not have been so blest, if it had not been for the faith with which she consented to the mystery of the Incarnation. In other words, the *presupposition* of Mary's entire cooperation with God's plan for our Redemption is her obedience of faith, even before she became the living, physical tabernacle of the God-Man, Christ Jesus.[47] Mary is already blessed by God because she proved herself to be a most worthy disciple by her obedience to the commandments and by means of the integrity and purity of her life. This blessedness, Newman tells us, is clearly acknowledged by the Angel when he greets her at the moment of the Annunciation as κεκαριτομενη or *gratia plena*[48] and is confirmed by Elizabeth's praise of Mary and her acknowledgment of Mary's faith at the Visitation.[49]

Newman stresses here that "the two blessednesses cannot be divided," and that they express in synthesis the truths contained in such Marian doctrines like her Immaculate Conception. He makes this connection by demonstrating how differing passages of Scripture are interconnected and must be viewed as such so the better to appreciate the mystery of Mary's cooperation in the work of salvation. Newman, in a sense, builds a wall around Torah to preserve and reinforce the deepest significance of each individual text by placing them in relationship to one another and to the whole of Scripture. How Newman accomplishes the latter with these texts will become more obvious later on in this section.

What does Mary's two-fold blessedness have to do with her Immaculate Conception? Newman's sermon gives us a scriptural-patristic explanation of this relationship. Simply put, he holds that Mary is "full of grace" from the moment of her conception and that this fullness of grace is already most evident in the life of the Virgin when she consents in faith to be the Mother of the divine Author of that grace. The life of the Triune God, already dwelling in her soul from conception is enhanced in an extraordinary way, as she conceives in her womb that is, as she gives life according to the flesh to the Second Person of the Blessed Trinity.

In his meditation on the title *Virgo Prædicanda*[50] Newman, reflecting on Luke 11:27–28, explains how the response of Jesus to the macarism of the anonymous woman in the crowd is directly related to the blessedness of Mary insofar as she is both immaculately conceived and chosen to be the *Theotokos*. Indeed, for Newman, Mary's sanctity is a prerequisite for her divine maternity. The privileges of the Virgin are always interrelated in the mind of Newman because they are in fact interrelated in the working out of the divine economy of salvation. Mary's blessedness derives in great part from these two singular privileges of her perfect sanctification and bearing of the Word made flesh. Newman writes:

> What is the highest, the rarest, the choicest prerogative of Mary? It is that she was without sin. When a woman in the crowd cried out to Our Lord, "Blessed is the womb that bare thee!" He answered, "More blessed are they who hear the Word of God and keep it." Those words were fulfilled in Mary. She was filled with grace *in order* to be the Mother of God. But it was a higher gift than her maternity to be thus sanctified and thus pure. Our Lord indeed would not have become her Son *unless* He had first sanctified her; but still, the greater blessedness was to have that perfect sanctification.[51]

Newman's last phrase, "but still, the greater blessedness was to have that perfect sanctification," has been a very powerful theological argument in the Tradition in favor of the doctrine of Mary's Immaculate Conception. John Duns Scotus, the fourteenth-century Franciscan theologian, in putting forth his arguments in favor of the doctrine of the Immaculate Conception, said that it was a more fitting and indeed, a greater act of God's redemptive love to have preserved Mary from original sin by means of a prevenient grace, than it would have been for Him to purify her from original sin once she would have contracted it according to the normal course. In this same meditation, Newman explains his reasoning along the lines of the Scotian argument.

> Wherefore, when all seemed lost, in order to show what human nature, His work, was capable of becoming; to show how utterly he could bring to naught the utmost efforts, the most concentrated malice of the foe, and reverse all the consequences of the Fall, Our Lord began, even before His coming, to do His most wonderful act of redemption, in the person of her who was to be His Mother. By the merit of that Blood which was to be shed, He interposed to hinder her incurring the sin of Adam, before He had made on the Cross atonement for it. And therefore we *preach* her who is the subject of this wonderful grace.[52]

Truly, then, she is "full of grace" in both a physical and spiritual way and thus, we can say that she possesses a two-fold blessedness which results from her two-fold inheritance of God's grace. She has a double portion of God's grace, as it were, and likewise a double portion of His blessedness.[53] Newman's sermon proceeds to demonstrate how the doctrine of the Immaculate Conception is, in a sense, the pure fount of her blessedness both as a humble believer who perfectly accomplishes the Father's will and as the Mother of the Sinless One Whose presence consecrates her in all virtue.

> She who was chosen to be the Mother of God was also chosen to be *gratia plena*, full of grace. This you see is an explanation of those high doctrines which are received among Catholics concerning the purity and sinlessness of the Blessed Virgin. Saint Augustine will not listen to any notion that she ever committed any sin, and the Holy Council of Trent declares that by special privilege she through all her life avoided all, even venial sin. And at this time you know it is the received belief of Catholics that she was not conceived in original sin, and that her conception was immaculate. Whence come these doctrines? They come from the great principle contained in Our Lord's words on which I am commenting. He says, "More blessed it is to do God's will than to be God's Mother." Do not say that Catholics do not feel this deeply—so deeply do they [feel] it that they are ever enlarging on her virginity, purity, immaculateness, faith, humility and obedience. Never say then the Catholics forget this passage of Scripture.[54]

Newman defends a Catholic interpretation of Luke 11:27–28 on the grounds that the response of Jesus to the anonymous woman underscores that Mary is "full of grace"[55] and therefore, blessed not merely as the Mother of the Lord but also because she was without sin, indeed, Immaculate in her Conception, as taught by the Fathers and the Council, possessing a pure and integrated faith based on her adherence to the commandments and obedience to the will of God. Therefore, are Our Lord's words in the Lucan pericope laudatory of the Virgin and a decisive confirmation of the veracity of the Angel's and Elizabeth's salutations, rather than what would otherwise be their contradiction?[56]

Newman believes that the key Marian doctrine which acts as a safeguard for the proper interpretation of these scriptural texts is the doctrine of the Immaculate Conception—which, at the time of Newman's sermon, could only be referred to as a "common belief" but not yet an official dogma. The Reverend Ignace de la Potterie, S.J., explains how the greeting of the Angel "Kecharitomene"[57] cannot be fully understood apart from the meaning it acquires in the formulation of the doctrine of the Immaculate Conception.[58]

Newman makes some further points which sustain his apologetical exegesis of Luke 11:27–28, viewing Our Lord's response to the woman in the crowd not as a contradiction of her statement about the blessedness of Mary's maternity but as the explication of the fuller meaning that those words should convey: "The woman in the crowd cried out, 'Blessed is the womb and the breasts of Mary.' She spoke in faith; she did not mean to exclude her high blessedness, but her words only went so far. Therefore our Lord completed them."[59] In this way, Jesus raises the consciousness of His listeners in the crowd from a purely earthly or material level to a more spiritual one.[60] Clearly, Newman tries to get at the intention of the author which may not always be that evident in a strict literal reading of the text. A similar interpretation to that of Newman's is found in Pope John Paul II's *Redemptoris Mater*.[61]

Furthermore, Newman declares the consistency of the Church's interpretation of this passage, insofar as it has been one of the bases found in Sacred Scripture for a distinctively Catholic devotion to Mary. Mary's two-fold blessedness is forever upheld among the children of the Church who invoke her intercession and imitate her faith: "And therefore the Church after Him, dwelling on the great and sacred mystery of His Incarnation, has ever felt that she, who so immediately ministered to it, must be most holy. And therefore for the honour of the Son has ever extolled the glory of the Mother."[62]

The theme of cooperation is key to an understanding of how Newman interprets the nature of Mary's blessedness as revealed in the Sacred Text, exegeting the Lucan pericope along with the Evangelist's account of the Annunciation. Mary's blessedness is not contingent upon her becoming the *Theotokos* because she is already blessed—having never ceased to manifest in her life the fullness of holiness that she received from the first moment of her conception. Thus, Mary's cooperation with God's grace before the Annunciation is an essential aspect of her blessedness. In fact, it can be considered a necessary preparation and condition for meriting that blessedness which would result from the pronunciation of the *fiat*.[63]

The Fathers, as Newman points out, are also convinced that the basis of Mary's divine maternity is related to her vow of virginity,[64] which acts as a powerful sign of Mary's fidelity and obedience to God's will and law which she expresses in the question posed to the Angel Gabriel at the Annunciation: "How can this be since I do not know man?" What Newman says in "Our Lady in the Gospel" is reflected upon in several of his *Meditations and Devotions*. In them, we find confirmation of Newman's interpretation of Mary's response to the Angel Gabriel as not simply a statement of biological fact but as profession of a vow of virginity which, in the light of the *historia salutis*, can be considered to be the most profound expression of the Messianic expectation of the *anawim*.[65]

In his meditation on "May the Month of Promise," Newman explains Mary's *fiat*[66] at the Annunciation fulfills the messianic prophecy of Isaiah 11:1 (see also verses 2 and 3):

> The Prophet says, "There shall come forth a rod out of the root of Jesse, and a flower shall rise out of his root." Who is the flower but Our Blessed Lord? Who is the rod, or beautiful stalk or stem or plant out of which the flower grows, but Mary, Mother of Our Lord, Mary, Mother of God? It was prophesied that God should come upon earth. When the time was now full, how was it announced? It was announced by the Angel coming to Mary. "Hail, full of grace," said Gabriel, "the Lord is with thee; blessed art thou among women." She then was the sure promise of the coming Saviour, and therefore May is by a special title her month.[67]

In other words, Mary is the most faithful daughter of Israel and handmaiden of the Lord who possesses both the physical and spiritual openness and the poverty of the *anawim* who completely rely on the Lord so as to accomplish His will.[68] Therefore, Mary can also be considered the Daughter of Sion *par excellence* predestined by God's grace to be the Mother of the Messiah, and the Mother of the Son of the Most High.[69] Newman, in no uncertain terms, identifies Mary's response to the Angel, as an avowal of virginity which virtue predisposes her to be the *Janua Cæli* (Gate of Heaven) through which, as Newman writes, "Our Lord passed from heaven to earth." Once again, we discover a significant example of Newman's biblical exegesis, especially insofar as he shows the interconnectedness between the Old and New Testaments, but even more so, the fulfillment of the Old in the New. In this instance, Newman focuses on the words of the Prophet Ezekiel found in chapter 44:1–3 which he interprets, according to the Tradition, as a prophecy of the virgin birth. Hence, the use of the title *Janua Cæli* for the Blessed Mary ever-Virgin:

> The prophet Ezechiel, prophesying of Mary, says, "the gate shall be closed, it shall not be opened, and no man shall pass through it, since the Lord God of Israel has entered through it—and it shall be closed for the Prince, the Prince Himself shall sit in it." Now this is fulfilled, not only in Our Lord having taken flesh from her, and being her Son, but, moreover, in that she had a place in the economy of Redemption; it is fulfilled in her spirit and will, as well as in her body.[70]

It should be noted that the very next part of this meditation is tied into a discussion of Mary's cooperation in the *œconomia salutis* as the New Eve whose obedience prepares the way for the coming of the Redeemer, just as Eve's disobedience prepared the way for the sin of Adam. However, it is not the intention to discuss here Newman's theology of the New Eve as this is treated in a separate chapter of the thesis.

Newman concludes this meditation by once again considering Mary's response to the Angel Gabriel in terms of her having made a vow of virginity[71]—a sure expression of her humility:

> Therefore, weighing well the Angel's words before giving answer to them—first she asked whether so great an office would be a forfeiture of that Virginity which she had vowed. When the Angel told her no, then, with the full consent of a full heart, full of God's love to her and her own lowliness, she said, "Behold the handmaid of the Lord; be it done to me according to thy word." It was by this consent that she became the *Gate of Heaven*.[72]

Still further, in Newman's meditation on Mary as the *Virgo Admirabilis* (Wondrous Virgin) we find a sample of his exegetical method as he compares and contrasts various episodes from the Old and New Testaments, so as to highlight the singular importance of Mary's cooperation in the œconomia salutis, making special reference to her extraordinary sanctity, humility and virginal purity. First of all, Newman recalls the episode of the burning bush in Exodus 2:23–25, when Moses hid his face before the Divine Presence for, as God Himself tells Moses, "Thou canst not see My face, for man shall not see Me and live,"[73] and, Saint Paul would later add, "Our God is a consuming fire."[74] Second, Newman speaks of how the Beloved Disciple—whom he identifies as both the Fourth Evangelist and author of the Book of Revelation—"holy as he was, saw only the Human Nature of Our Lord, as He is in Heaven, 'he fell at His feet as dead.'"[75] Third, Newman recounts how the appearances of an Angel to the prophet Daniel[76] and to Zechariah the father of John the Baptist caused both men to tremble in fear.[77] Fourth, Newman compares and contrasts all the previous revelations mentioned with the revelation of the Angel Gabriel to Mary at the Annunciation. He admits that Mary was "overcome indeed, and troubled at his words, but not because she was motivated by dread or doubt." Rather, Newman explains that Mary's response to the Angel was motivated by her profound humility, while the Angel's revelation to Mary was a direct acknowledgment of her unique sanctity and blessedness. He writes, "because, humble as she was in her own opinion of herself, he addressed her as 'full of grace' and 'blessed among women,' but she was able to bear the sight of him."[78] Last, vis-à-vis a comparison with the aforementioned episode of the Angel Gabriel's apparition to the prophet Daniel, Newman offers us two conclusions from his exegesis which determine the significance of his meditation on the title *Mater Admirabilis*. Indeed, Newman's explanations directly relate the wonder, amazement and astonishment that "the children of Holy Church" experience in contemplating the doctrine of Mary's Immaculate Conception to the admiration which we the faithful should have for her exceptional holiness and virginal purity:

> Hence, we learn two things: first, how great a holiness was Mary's, seeing she could endure the presence of an angel, whose brightness smote the holy prophet Daniel even to fainting and almost to death; and secondly, since she is much holier than the angel, and we so much less holy than Daniel, what great reason we have to call her the *Virgo Admirabilis*, the Wonderful, the Awful Virgin, when we think of her ineffable purity.[79]

Moreover, Mary's free-will consent and cooperation, Newman maintains, is so important, that God depends on it in order to accomplish the mystery of the Incarnation. Her cooperation is a ministerial one—for the sake of the economy or "dispensation" of salvation which entails not only her physical motherhood but her whole life of virtue. Newman, like Saint Augustine, speaks of Mary as having conceived Our Lord first by means of her faith and only then in her body. Indeed, her obedience of faith and virtues are considered prerequisites, as it were, of her divine maternity. Once again Newman's sermon underscores the two-fold blessedness of Mary as consisting in her physical and spiritual cooperation in the *œconomia salutis*.

> For when the Angel appeared to her and declared to her the will of God, they say that she displayed especially four graces, humility, faith, obedience and purity. Nay, these graces were, as it were, preparatory conditions to her being made the minister of so high a dispensation. So that if she had not had faith, and humility, and purity, and obedience, she would not have merited to be God's Mother. Thus it is common to say that she conceived Christ in mind before she conceived Him in body, meaning that the blessedness of faith and obedience preceded the blessedness of being a Virgin Mother. Nay, they even say that God waited for her consent before He came into her and took flesh of her. Just as He did no mighty works in one place because they had not faith, so this great miracle, by which He became the Son of a creature, was suspended til she was tried and found meet for it—til she obeyed.[80]

This idea of God anxiously awaiting the consent of the Virgin at the Annunciation is a particularly striking image of which Saint Bernard of Clairvaux was also particularly fond. The second reading of the Office of Readings for December 20 in the late Advent Season is taken from his sermon, *In Praise of the Virgin Mother*. It contains a beautiful description of God's, man's and the universe's breathless anticipation of Mary's loving, free, humble and obedient consent to the message of the Angel, which by faith in her mind brings about the conception of the Word of God in her womb. Upon Mary's consent or cooperation hangs in the balance the whole *œconomia salutis*.[81] Saint Bernard's text is both a theological and spiritual masterpiece of Christian literature and can serve as a marvelous commentary on what we have found briefly mentioned in Newman's sermon "Our Lady in the Gospel." [82]

Newman's sermon masterfully illustrates the interconnectedness of those New Testament passages (Luke 1:26–38; Luke 11:27–28; Matthew 12:48; Mark 3:33; John 2:4) to show the importance of Mary's place in the economy of salvation. His starting point, as we have already seen, is Luke 11:27–28 from which passage he demonstrates that the praise of the anonymous woman in the crowd is inseparable from the blessedness which the Angel Gabriel declares in his greeting of Mary as *gratia plena*. Newman also notes how the apparently enigmatic response of the Lord to the woman in the crowd can be best understood in light of other enigmatic texts in which Jesus relates to Mary. Newman identifies Mark 3:35 and John 2:4 as two of these difficult passages which deserve a careful exegesis in order to arrive at a coherent sense of Our Lord's understanding of Mary's role in the economy. In "Our Lady in the Gospel," Newman offers two explanations of Jesus' words in these passages, introducing his explanations by first summarizing the content of the scriptural texts in question and the dilemma which they present for the exegete:

> It may be asked, why did our blessed Lord even *seem* to extenuate the honor and privilege of His Mother? When the woman said, "Blessed is the womb," etc., He answered indeed, "Yea." But He went on, this, he said when someone told Him that His Mother and brethren were without, "Who is my Mother?" etc. And at an earlier time, when He began his miracles, and had no wine, He said, "Woman, what have I to do with thee? Mine hour is not yet come." These passages seem to be coldly worded towards the Blessed Virgin, even though the sense may be satisfactorily explained. What then do they mean? Why did He so speak?[83]

Newman's exegesis and his theological explanations to the questions raised above take into consideration both the actual texts and the whole scriptural background necessary for a more lucid comprehension of those same texts. He correctly notes that in the Jewish scheme of things it was commonplace to consider marriage to be the highest state in life. The idea that there would be a higher state (i.e., virginity) was culturally and theologically foreign to those who would have heard Jesus' response to the woman in the crowd.[84] Newman explains the lesson Our Lord meant to teach on that occasion, and how it does not diminish Our Lady's role in the economy but rather enhances it—highlighting its uniqueness and even superiority compared to the status which otherwise would have been allotted her as a mere physical instrument. Newman writes: "And therefore when the woman in the crowd cries out the blessedness of the womb that bore Him and the breasts that He had sucked, He taught her and all who heard Him that the soul was greater than the body, and that to be united to Him in spirit was more than to be united to Him in flesh." [85]

The Reverend Aristide Serra exegetes Luke 11:27–28 in terms of the relationship between two biblical symbols—the maternal milk which she offers to her new-born and the milk of the Word of God. Father Serra notes that the anonymous woman's response to Jesus reveals her understanding of Mary's blessedness in terms of Mary's physical motherhood, while Jesus' response is a macarism of Mary, based on the spiritual fecundity that she derives from her spiritual communion with Him.[86]

Newman continues by offering a second, and, what he terms, a "more interesting" argument in support of his exegesis. His use of the Old Testament is illuminating. Quoting from the Book of Deuteronomy, Newman refers to the blessedness of the Levites who, choosing to be free from family ties, are thus made more capable of dedicating themselves wholeheartedly to their duties. At the age of twelve, Jesus is found in the Temple of Jerusalem by Mary and Joseph in the midst of the doctors of the Law. On that occasion, Jesus defends His actions to His parents by claiming His divine origins, that is, His filial relationship to God the Father, and, furthermore, by reminding them of the divine mission which He has received. Thus, Newman sees in this episode of the Finding in the Temple,[87] a foreshadowing of Christ's choice of celibacy in order the more freely to fulfill his priestly, prophetic and kingly mission. Part of that choice of celibacy is his desire to be physically detached from His Mother and putative father Joseph, even from an early age. Admittedly, the same passage concludes by saying that Our Lord then returned with His parents and was obediently subject to them. It seems as though Newman is not far-fetched in his exegesis since what he says about the Levites is not unrelated to the fact that the Lucan passage is itself set in the Temple and thus connected to the office of priesthood and the offering of sacrifice. Newman makes some of these connections clearer thus:

> Therefore it was that from the beginning of His ministry, He gave up His Mother. At the time He did His first miracle, he proclaimed it. He did that miracle at her bidding, but he implied, or rather declared, that He was then beginning to separate from her. He said, "What is between Me and thee?" "Who is My Mother?" etc., meaning, as it would appear, that He had left all for God's service, and that, as for our sake He had been born of the Virgin, so for our sake He gave up His Virgin Mother that He might glorify His heavenly Father and do His work.[88]

Christ does not insist on separation from His Mother to show her up as somehow unworthy of His company because of a lack of faith; on the contrary, Our Lord deliberately takes leave of Mary at Cana ("My hour has not yet come"), so that after He had completed His redemptive mission, she might share in its benefits and so be publically recognized as having cooperated in that mission. The central role which Mary plays at Cana at the outset of Our Lord's public ministry[89] would be taken up again at the foot of the Cross on Calvary. Although certainly not a prominent figure during Our Lord's public ministry, Mary's less-than-conspicuous role does not negate the fact that she enjoyed a particular spiritual union with her Son through obedience to His word and will, which becomes most evident at Calvary. In the end, at Calvary, the words addressed by Jesus to Mary at Cana are less enigmatic because in effect they constitute the heart of a great mystery. Therefore, when Jesus says: "What is this between you and me?" and "My hour has not yet come," Newman offers the following response, put in the form of an intimate, tender dialogue between Jesus and Mary at the feast of Cana or some time thereafter. Our Lord addresses His Mother thus: "The hour cometh when I shall acknowledge thee again, O my Mother. The hour cometh when thou rightly and powerfully wilt intercede with Me. The hour cometh when at thy bidding I will do miracles: it cometh, but it is not yet come."[90]

Thus, it is by a circuitous route that the appropriateness and dignity of Our Lady's virginal state—a definite sign of her complete dedication and cooperation in the economy of salvation—is best appreciated, according to Newman, in relationship to Christ's own choice of celibacy for the sake of being the Author of salvation, the great High Priest, Prophet and King. Therefore, both Our Lord's redeeming work and Our Lady's cooperation in that work—here Newman emphasizes the aspect of Our Lady's mediation such as at Cana—are carried out on a much higher plane than that of the mere physical, so that the merits of both, while distinct, are of eternal value and consequence for the economy of salvation.[91]

Newman rounds out his sermon by directing our attention to the contemplation of Mary at the foot of the Cross. Newman gives to his exegesis of the previous scriptural passages—having to do with some of the perplexing sayings of Our Lord with regard to the Virgin—a finishing touch that provides the reader with a greater clarity of interpretation. From the perspective of Calvary, Newman views the temporary, physical separation of Mother and Son—due to the demands of Our Lord's public ministry—as having been resolved in the indissoluble, spiritual union forged between Jesus and Mary at Calvary. Newman is convinced that such a spiritual bond should unite the Blessed Mother and her children in the Church.[92] Ironically, once again, Our Lord is forced to separate from His Mother in a physical way, by means of the most painful and dramatic of separations known to man—death. However, Jesus does not intend for this separation to be a fruitless departure, for from the tree of the Second Adam's death is born the tree of life laden with the fruit of Redemption under whose shade take refuge the New Eve (Mary) and the company of the redeemed entrusted to her as her spiritual children in the person of the Beloved Disciple. Thus, for Newman, at the foot of the Cross, Mary's motherhood of the Head (*caput*) of the Church becomes also the motherhood of the members (*membra*) of the body of the Church, the Body of Christ.[93]

Therefore, Newman, with great confidence, concludes his sermon by exhorting his listeners to entrust themselves with filial love and devotion to the Virgin, to imitate the blessedness of her faith, to enter into the depth of her sufferings in union with Christ, so as to share in their redemptive merit. And, thus, they too shall be accompanied by her maternal presence into the blessedness of eternal life. Newman's exhortation goes as follows:

> Depend upon it, the way to enter into the sufferings of the Son, is to enter into the sufferings of the Mother. Place yourselves at the foot of the Cross, see Mary standing there, looking up and pierced with the sword. Let her be your great pattern. Feel what she felt and you will worthily mourn over the Death and Passion of your and her Saviour. Have her simple faith, and you will believe well. Pray to be filled with the grace given to her. Alas, you must have many feelings she had not, the feeling of personal sin, of personal sorrow, of contrition, and self-hate, but these will in a sinner naturally accompany the faith, the humility, the simplicity which were her great ornaments. Lament with her, believe with her, and at length you will experience her blessedness of which the text speaks. None indeed can have her special prerogative, and be the Mother of the Highest, but you will have a share in that blessedness of hers which is greater, the blessedness of doing God's will and keeping His commandments.[94]

II. THE ANNUNCIATION: "THE HONOUR DUE TO THE BLESSED VIRGIN"

The theme of Our Lady's blessedness is one which Newman had developed in his first sermon about the Virgin which he delivered on the Feast of the Annunciation on 25 March 1831.[95] Bishop Boyce highlights for us the genius of Newman's exegetical method[96]:

> It may seem strange that a young Anglican curate in Oxford should lament the lack of religious devotion and honour paid to our Lady by members of the Church of England. It shows how grounded in Scripture he was and how deeply he appreciated the full implications of the Incarnation—God the Son taking on our human nature and being born of a woman (cf. Gal. 4:4). The fact that he had a human mother meant that he was truly one of us. As a result of Mary's association with her divine Son she shared in his honour and blessedness. Scripture itself urges us to venerate the Mother of Jesus."[97]

Newman begins his sermon with a quotation from Our Lady's *Magnificat*: "From henceforth all generations will call me blessed," explaining that this sentiment of veneration for the

Virgin is that which has characterized the devotion of the Christian faithful from time immemorial. Mary's own words are then shown to have been fulfilled by way of anticipation in the greetings of the Archangel Gabriel and her cousin Elizabeth. As we have seen, Newman delights in showing the similarity between these two salutations of the Virgin, both of which show a "spirit of reverence and love towards her memory." [98] Furthermore, Rudolf Schnackenburg maintains that Mary's *Magnificat* and Elizabeth's laudatory salutation of the Virgin are both illustrative of the fundamental role of women in the economy of salvation. [99]

Schnackenburg's observations are helpful in introducing the next section of our analysis of Newman's sermon since they clearly underscore what would have been Newman's own most favorable view of the cooperative role that women, especially Mary, exercised *pro mundi salute* (for the salvation of the world). Newman first tackles the thorny issues raised by those who object to Marian veneration based on Saint Paul's teaching that in Christ all are made equal, that is, there is no longer any distinction between Jew and Greek, male and female, and that, therefore, Mary does not enjoy any privileged relationship with her Son beyond that which every believer has. In addition, Newman responds to those who object to a particular devotion to Our Lady as they misinterpret Our Lord's words, claiming that because anyone who does the will of His Heavenly Father becomes in effect a member of His spiritual family and that Mary is no longer worthy of any particular veneration. [100]

However, Newman is adamant in his refusal to accept that there can exist any contradiction among these various texts of Scripture and, therefore, sets out in this sermon to offer an apologetical exegesis which makes clear the basic agreement among the texts as regards the orthodox Christian veneration of the Virgin Mary. [101] Newman considers the meaning of a few of Saint Paul's texts, namely, 2 Corinthians 5:17 and 1 Timothy 5:8, to show that although the baptized believer is indeed to be considered a new creature in Christ, this new spiritual relationship does not, therefore, make illegitimate the believer's natural ties. In other words, Newman does not accept the notion that Our Lord taught disrespect or disregard for His Mother simply because He indicated the need to recognize the importance of the superior nature of the relationship forged by faith and obedience to the will of God. Jesus' response explicates the significance of the first commandment to love of God above all other persons and things.

Newman gives further support to his argument by asking a series of rhetorical questions—a literary technique he often utilizes, especially in his sermons and poetry.[102] He asks: "How then can we consider it pious to forget and irreligious to remember Christ's kindred in our thoughts of Him? How can we suppose that He would separate Himself from His own Mother, when He bids us remember our relations? Certainly He thought of her on the Cross; at the very hour that He was dying for all. And if He remembers her, how can it be right in us to pass by in silence, especially with the implied command, already referred to, to count her blessed to all generations?"[103] Newman develops this idea of sacred memory or remembrance as an integral part of what it means to be part of the human family, arguing that since Our Lord was the perfect Man "with the same heart and affections, soul and body the same,"[104] that He would not forget anything or anyone, most especially, those most intimately associated to His life and ministry.

Our Lord Himself is exemplary in the use of sacred memory as He entrusts Mary to the beloved disciple from the Cross. Newman writes: "Doubtless, having loved His own which were in the world, He loved them unto the end (John 13): Should He not [love] His Mother first of all, whose welfare I say, was on His thoughts even when He was on the cross?"[105] The Evangelist is careful to note that "from that hour," the beloved disciple took Mary into his home.[106] The Greek expression used by the Evangelist (καὶ ἀπ᾽ ἐκείνης τῆς ὥρας ἔλαβεν ὁ μαθητης αὐτην εἰσ τὰ ἴδια) renders both the literal and spiritual sense of this communion and mutual cooperation in the economy of salvation between Mary and John insofar as it is directly related to the reference to Jesus' hour of glorification and indicates that more than a physical custodianship has been willed by Christ whereby John welcomes Mary not only into his home (literally, "among his own things" or "unto his own") but into the depths of his heart as his spiritual Mother.[107] If John the beloved disciple was commanded by Our Lord to be mindful of Mary as his spiritual mother at the foot of the Cross, then how can we not be mindful of her as our own spiritual mother and so call her blessed for all generations?

Indeed, our remembrance of Mary's blessedness stems from Our Lord's own remembrance of His redemptive sufferings in becoming Man and dying on the Cross and of Mary's participation in those salvific sorrows as well.[108] Therefore, Newman writes: "Why is it told to us (Why, what is our very comfort in temptation but) that Christ having suffered under it (Heb 2), is able to succour them that are tempted like as we are? And can He remember His own sorrow, and not the sword which pierced His Mother's soul (Luke 2)?"[109]

It is fascinating that, already in his very first sermon on the Virgin, the Anglican Newman considers Mary's cooperation in the economy of salvation as one most intimately associated in the suffering of Christ. He undoubtedly interprets Simeon's prophecy of the sword that is to pierce Mary's soul as a sword of sorrow and not as some of the Fathers of the Church argued, a sword of doubt or even the temptation to sin.[110] Even if one were to interpret Simeon's sword in terms of a temptation to sin, as some of the Fathers of the Church did, this would not necessarily impute sinfulness to her since, as Newman reminds us in the sermon, Our Lord Himself was tempted in every way that we were, but triumphed over those temptations. Nothing in the Scriptures, however, is ever said about Mary having been exposed to any temptation whatsoever. In any case, one can presume, putting aside the question of the doctrine of Mary's complete sinlessness and her freedom from all concupiscence that, in the above text, even the Anglican Newman would have held that the "succour," in temptation made available to us because of Our Lord's Incarnation and Death, would have been even more readily available to Mary because of His remembrance of her singular cooperation in His salvific activity, and, in a particular way, of her having endured the sword of sorrow in union with Him. Furthermore, Newman asks:

> Can He remember Judas who betrayed Him and Pilate who crucified Him, and not her who bore Him? And when the Holy Spirit has distinctly declared that she is blessed, can it consist with our duty to Him, not to bless her? He is in heaven, but we are to think of Him just as if He were here. . . . Now do we suppose that, if He were here on earth, He would allow anyone to treat His Mother's name with disrespect or rather, would not be pleased with our affectionate and respectful remembrance of

Her? How strange it is to bring the blessing He pronounces on His faithful servants in disparagement of His love towards her? "Whoever shall do the will of God . . ." What does it show but the excess of His attachment to her, that the highest reward He can give them is their being as dear to Him as His Mother and other immediate relatives?[111]

Newman's reflections on the reality of the Incarnation lead him to affirm the reality, the necessity of His human affections and familial ties. It is interesting to note that in his Catholic sermon, "Our Lady in the Gospel," Newman stressed the fact that Our Lord deliberately distanced Himself from His family and from Mary in a particular way in order to accomplish His redemptive mission. In this sermon, on the other hand, the Anglican Newman seeks to establish that Our Lord did not in any way disparage such relations precisely because they were integral to his experience as true Man. In both homilies, Newman emphasizes Mary's blessedness as consisting in her faith and obedience to the will of God, not so much in the fact of her divine maternity as such, especially if only understood as a biological fact. Nevertheless, Newman does not wish to sacrifice the blessedness of Mary's maternity for the sake of developing the theme of her spiritual fecundity, which is characterized by her life of faith and virtue. The two states of Mary's beatitude must remain inexorably linked. Newman defends the blessedness of Mary's divine maternity because he believes its defense is, in effect, a defense of the mystery of the Incarnation. The mysteries of salvation in which she most fully cooperated body and soul are never to be erased from the sacred memory of the Church, her spiritual sons and daughters, for they are forever etched in the mind of her beloved Son and Redeemer. The painful memory of Judas' betrayal and Pilate's condemnation cannot compare with the sweet memory of His most holy Mother.

Therefore, Newman instructs us not to think of Our Lord's words in Matthew 12:46–50, Luke 8:19–21, and Mark 3:31–35 as a "disparagement" of Our Lady but as a cause to recognize her blessedness,[112] in the hope of coming to share in that same blessedness as a reward for our faith and to honor the memory of her name. Here, it should be recalled that in the Sacred Scriptures a certain importance is attributed to a person's name since it is symbolic of a person's identity and mission according to the economy of salvation.[113] To know someone's name in the biblical cultures is to have a sort of power over that person or, better yet, a particular relationship with that person, with a change of name resulting, in most instances, in a change of office, as in the cases of Abraham in the Old Testament and Peter in the New Testament. Although Mary's name is never changed *per se*, we know that the Angel Gabriel refers to her as "full of grace," and Our Lord in the Gospel of John uses the unusual title of "woman," which hearkens back to the title of Eve, "mother of all the living." [114] Is it too far fetched to think that when Newman tells us to remember the memory of her name, he is also bearing in mind these other scriptural texts that declare her blessed for all ages as *Theotokos* and New Eve? Furthermore, if knowing someone's name in biblical terms signifies having a special relationship or friendship with or knowledge of that person, then can we not infer here as well the rudimentary belief of Newman in our relationship to Mary as our spiritual Mother and blessed model in faith? Indeed, just as we are called to keep the Lord's name holy according to the second commandment, so too, we recall the name of Mary, in a particular way, as the most blessed of all creatures, each time we celebrate the memorial of her Son's Passion and Death.[115]

In his meditation "A Short Service for Rosary Sunday," Newman reflects on the theological significance of Mary's name and image as being a memorial of the mysteries of Redemption wrought by God and of her cooperation in these mysteries as the first and most perfectly redeemed and sanctified, the most pure and faithful Virgin, the exemplary model of all "gracious perfections," grace and virtues, especially of virginity and motherhood, Royal Lady and Queen of all saints, "clothed with the sun and crowned with the stars of heaven whom all generations have called and shall call blessed," together with the whole communion of saints for all eternity. Concerning the perpetual memorial of Mary's most blessed name, Newman writes:

> Who can repeat her very name without finding in it a music that goes to the heart, and brings before him thoughts of God and Jesus Christ, and heaven above, and fills him with the desire of those graces by which heaven is to be gained? ... We will take our part in praising thee in our own time and place with all the redeemed of Our Lord, and will exalt thee in the

full assembly of the saints and glorify thee in the Heavenly Jerusalem.[116]

The next part of Newman's sermon is dedicated to a discussion of how God "has made our natural relations the groundwork of our spiritual relations." And so, just as we are bound together in the human family by natural ties, relating to each person in a special way with the hope that we will one day recognize our "earthly friends" in the heavenly kingdom, so too do we know that God has also willed that we be joined togther "by visible bonds of union," in spiritual communion whereby we hope to share in "that benefit which has brought them through God's Providence to heaven."[117] To give biblical support for his theology of the communion of saints, Newman refers to 1 Thessalonians 2. The teaching of Saint Paul, for Newman, contradicts that "cold theory," by which some believe that we will not be able to recognize our "especial intercourse with our earthly friends," in the hereafter and that furthermore "that in heaven all difference between saint and saint is lost, that though the Virgin is dear to Christ, all His saints are equally dear to Him."[118] Undoubtedly, Newman recognizes the biblical roots of the doctrine of the communion of saints as a safeguard against the awful notion that "we should be forced to leave out associations of this world in our anticipation of heaven." Newman asks the following rhetorical question, keeping in mind our common predestination to the life of heaven as members of "one body" who, in Baptism, have received the privilege of sharing in a heavenly rebirth and filial adoption: "And thus having bound together nature and grace in the first days of our existence, shall the two ever be separated?"[119]

One of the keys, therefore, for Newman's understanding of the doctrine of the communion of saints in this sermon, is the notion of sacred memory, which transcends the bounds of time and space without severing the ties that are formed during our earthly sojourn. Perhaps, the notion of sacred memory or "remembrance" in the communion of saints is, for the Anglican Newman, a significant step in coming to understand the notion of God's will that we be saved not simply "through the channel of natural relationship," but through human mediation, that is to say, through human cooperation as it takes place in the sacramental life of the Church and the intercessory prayer of saints—which, although the latter is not formally admitted by Newman in this sermon, is implied and explicated elsewhere in his writings as this work hopes to make manifest. Newman then makes a logical conclusion concerning the special role of cooperation in the economy of salvation which Mary holds and the remembrance that is due to her, not for her own sake only but even more so for "her Glorious Son's sake." Newman returns to the use of the rhetorical question to make this point:

> And if these remembrances of earth remain in heaven, how shall we think that Our Lord does not still with ineffable feelings regard His Mother Mary, and how can we be really said to comprehend His character, to enter into the mind of Christ and to be united to Him in spirit, unless we carefully cherish the remembrance of His doings and feelings while we walk after Him, gathering up the fragments that remain,[120] feeding on those crumbs which He has left us,[121] and though we know not much of the Blessed Virgin, yet making much of what is told to us about her, and knowing her for her Gracious Son's sake?[122]

Newman's words are a profound reflection both on the tender love that characterizes Our Lord's relationship to His Blessed Mother and on our own ability to show our love for Christ and gratitude to Him for the work of our redemption by affectionately calling to mind the cooperation of the Virgin in the same. In a sense, the Anglican Newman has already anticipated in this sermon some of the consequences of a Catholic understanding of Marian devotion whereby we come to Jesus through her. In other words, Newman believes that just as we cannot fully understand and relate to Jesus the Savior without also being mindful of His redemptive activity, including His gift of the memorial of His saving sacrifice in the Eucharist,[123] we cannot fully understand and relate to Mary, the Mother of the Savior, without also being mindful of her role in the work of our Redemption wrought by her Son's saving sacrifice. Although Newman does not deliberately say as much, one can infer from his writing that our remembrance of Mary's cooperation in the economy of salvation is not merely something we accomplish with the head alone but also with the heart, so as to imitate her faith and come to share in our own limited way in Our Lord's own knowledge and ineffable feelings towards the Blessed Virgin, His Mother Mary. Newman proceeds in his sermon to discuss how the Evangelists, Saint Paul and other New Testament writers went to great lengths to impress upon us the reality of Christ's Sacred Humanity as revealed in the mystery of the Incarnation. Christ becomes a Man "to give us an example and a consolation in all we do and suffer."[124] Furthermore, Newman says:

> Christ was not an angel. He was a Man like us, in all points but sin. Have we natural affections? He had them too. Where are we to see them exemplified? He had no brother, sister, wife or father. It is His Mother who concentrates them all. Why should we disjoin Him from human nature, as if He were an angel such as came to Abraham as he sat in the tent door (Gen 18) or to Gideon at the oak of Ophrat (Judge)?[125] John the Baptist in the wilderness.(?) But our Saviour was even characterized by His mixing in the ways of men and feeling with them. Let us use thankfully the instruction given us and in remembering the Mother strive to enter more deeply into the mind of her Son.[126]

Newman argues that the life and ministry of Our Lord reveals that Our Lord in His Sacred Humanity did not intend to scorn or dissociate Himself from human sentiment and relationships. On the contrary, He made every effort to elevate their highest value within the scheme of the economy of salvation. Newman insists on several essential doctrinal points: First and foremost, Christ Jesus is the God-Man and not a mere angel—the latter being the identification often given to Our Lord in Gnostic systems of belief. Secondly, taking his inspiration from Hebrews 4:15, Newman notes that the fullness or perfection of our human nature as revealed in the Sacred Humanity of Christ the High Priest is to be without sin. Third, Newman makes the point that the fullness of Christ's Sacred Humanity is expressed by His having had "natural affections," as we do. Fourth, Newman gives an astonishing testimony of his belief in the perpetual virginity of Mary as he plainly states that Jesus had no brothers and sisters. Newman, then, obviously interprets the mention of Our Lord's brothers and sisters in the Gospels[127] according to the Catholic Tradition, that is, that close relatives, for example, cousins are being referred to or perhaps step-brothers and step-sisters resulting from a previous marriage of Joseph.[128] Fifth, Newman emphasizes Our Lord's celibacy.[129] Sixth, Newman again affirms Mary's virginity and Our Lord's divinity by stating that Jesus had no human father.[130] Seventh, Newman preaches about Mary as having fulfilled in her role as Mother all the other relationships He lacked. Here Newman would appear deficient in his understanding of Our Lord's Sacred Humanity to the extent that he forgets about Joseph's role as the putative father or legal guardian of Jesus. Certainly, Jesus' only Father is God the Father. Nevertheless, the Gospels do not therefore show disregard for Joseph's role as the custodian of the Redeemer.[131] In fact, the infancy narrative of Matthew in particular stresses Joseph's role of cooperation in the work of salvation.[132] The Gospels never say that Mary's divine maternity—as important and intimate as that relationship is—was meant to derogate from Joseph's legitimate role as the foster father of the Christ Child.[133] Eighth, Newman responds indirectly to the ancient heretics who thought of Jesus as an angel (i.e., inferior in substance to the Father) by identifying Him with the angels of the Lord who manifested themselves to men like Abraham and Gideon. Newman's study of the Arian controversy and the writings of the Church Fathers like Saint Athanasius would bring him to understand these Old Testament manifestations in even greater depth, so as to give to them an orthodox interpretation.[134] Ninth, Jesus is distinct from John the Baptist both as a person and for the fact that Jesus, unlike John, did not choose to exercise His ministry in an eremetical way.[135] Last, Newman exhorts us to remember the role of Mary as that which, without doubt, expresses Christ's manifest will that a creature cooperate in the saving mysteries of the Redemption. A brief examination of the life of the Virgin reveals this to be the case. Even though the sacred writers do not describe her involvement in great detail, the historic and salvific significance of those events in which Mary does appear is undeniable. Newman writes:

> She is mentioned at Christ's Incarnation, at His birth, in His childhood and education, during His ministry, at His Death and afterwards His Ascension just before the day of Pentecost as being present with the Apostles in prayer (Acts). Thus she is continually brought before our minds. Yet nothing is told us about her. Or, in other words, that she is to be a subject of our meditation in order to our realizing and fully developing in our hearts the image of her Son.[136]

Newman's readers might ask: "Why all of this mention of Mary in the Sacred Scriptures and yet a lack of details?" And furthermore, given this lack of details about Mary in the Sacred Text, what position does Mary have in the life and ministry of her Son? How should we relate to her, given what we learn about her from the Scriptures? Newman simply states that those details are deliberately removed so that our focus may be placed on the Christ instead of the Virgin. He believes that the scarcity of the material in the Scriptures concerning the Virgin puts the emphasis on her relationship to Jesus since the sacred events in which she is involved are those in which Our Lord takes center stage. This, however, should not detract from the honor and veneration that we show to her. Newman writes: "Hence, we gather first that we are to reverence her memory for His sake. Or, in other words, that she is to be a subject of our meditation in order to our realizing and fully developing in our hearts the image of her Son." [137]

In his Catholic meditation, "A Short Service for Rosary Sunday," Newman writes that "her very image is as a book in which we read at a glance the mystery of the Incarnation, and the mercy of the Redemption." [138] The centrality of Mary's role of cooperation in the *œconomia salutis* is surpassed by no other creature; in fact, Mary deserves our reverence far more than even some of the greatest of saints like the Apostle Paul. Newman explains why:

> Did we pay Saint Paul that honour which we seem called upon to render to the Virgin, we should be in danger of following a human standard and debasing our view of high Christian excellence, because so much is told of him, that, faithful as he was in his obedience, still the history given of him cannot, if we would, too closely imitate, whose name only recalls to us of bright and pleasant thoughts, the emblem of early devotedness to God, guiltless piety, angelic purity (sic), meekness, modesty and patience, shining only in the light of her Son and in the ineffable radiance of that Spirit of power who came upon her and overshadowed her, and hence receiving the prize of that high salutation of Gabriel: "Hail, thou that art highly favoured (filled with divine gifts), the Lord is with thee, blessed art thou among women." Very much might be said in honour of the Virgin or in the apostle's words: "of whom we have many things to say and hard to be uttered seeing you now in debt of hearing" (Hebrews 5). But, since these times are heartless and unbelieving and your hearts profane, I say no more; lest I should say more than we can bear, lest I mean, I should use words instead of

ideas and should outrun the real measure of my own earnestness in my wish to manifest a conformity to Scripture instructions (to what seems a scriptural tone of thought).[139]

In the above passage, Newman expresses his belief that all of the scriptural data about the Virgin, although certainly limited in detail as he has already pointed out, manifests Mary's outstanding holiness; hence, he is unwilling to ascribe to Mary "those infirmities which all the sons of Adam inherit." One can logically conclude that if Newman is so unwilling to ascribe to Mary the consequences of original sin, then he was already perhaps indicating his unwillingness to attribute to Mary any sin whatsoever. Certainly, the virtues of Mary which Newman lists confirm her singular holiness among the saints, for example, Saint Paul "faithful as he was in his obedience." Especially mentioned are her "guiltless piety" and "angelic purity." This is very high praise of the Virgin considering Newman's development of thought and anticipates what Newman says in his Parochial and Plain Sermon, "The Reverence Due to the Blessed Virgin Mary," written almost a year later to the day, when he says: ". . .what must have been the transcendent purity of her, whom the Creator Spirit condescended to overshadow with His miraculous presence . . . for what, think you, was the sanctified state of that human nature, of which God formed His sinless Son; knowing that as we do, 'that which is born of the flesh is flesh,' and that 'none can bring a clean thing out of an unclean'?"[140]

In both sermons Mary's extraordinary holiness, dare we say what Newman believes to be Mary's sinlessness, is understood in terms of her relationship to the Spirit and the Son, that is, we make sense of it only "in the light of her Son and in the ineffable radiance of that Spirit of power Who came upon her and overshadowed her" at the moment of the Annunciation. Her personal sanctity and sinlessness are given her as a singular grace in view of her virginal conception of the Redeemer. For Newman, the "high salutation of Gabriel," is already an indication of Mary's having been "filled with divine gifts," as she has been prepared to receive the greatest "prize," the greatest of all gifts, Who is Christ the Lord. So caught up in awe of the sublime purity of the Virgin and of the profound mystery of her divine maternity is Newman, that he believes that if he were to continue in his encomium of the Virgin, the praise would exceed the capacity of his listeners to assimilate it. However, Newman also realizes the need to limit his praise of the Virgin, lest his words convey ideas about the Virgin which do not "manifest a conformity to Scripture instructions (to what seems a scriptural tone of thought)."[141]

Noteworthy are the two principal conclusions which Newman draws from his reflection on the scriptural evidence as he understands it at this point of his theological development. The first is that Mary's holiness is not exalted for its own sake, but indicates the greater holiness of her Son to Whom she is most configured, both as His Mother and as His most perfect disciple. The Christocentrism of Newman's Mariology is a characteristic which is considerably evident throughout his writings. This kind of Christocentric theology, especially a Christocentric Mariology, is also appreciable from an ecumenical point of view since it is a concern which is as important for Protestants today as it was for those non-Catholic Christians who listened to Newman's first sermon on the Blessed Virgin. Indeed, the title of Mary "Mother of Our Lord, (or, as the Church has since expressed it, the Mother of [Him Who is] God)," as Newman explains, is a safeguard of the orthodox teaching on the distinctness and unity of the two natures in the one divine Person of Christ. Newman's appeal, in essence, is not only an appeal to the truths of Sacred Scripture but also to the truths explicated in the Sacred Tradition such as at the Ecumenical Councils of Ephesus and Chalcedon. Newman reminds us that when we "divide the divine and the human nature in Christ," we do so only "in idea." In reality, as Newman reiterates, there is "only one Christ," in Whom the human and divine natures are united without losing their distinctiveness. To divide the human nature from the divine nature so as to create two Persons—one human and one divine—is what was understood to be the erroneous teaching of Nestorius. In other words, Newman is reminding us that a mother does not conceive and give birth to a nature but to a single human person. The two natures are as inseparable from the one divine Person of Christ as are His body and soul and the body and soul of each one of us. Newman writes, "as truly as soul and body make but one and the same person, so God and man was one Christ."[142] Furthermore, according to the "divine Providence," the Virgin Mary's cooperation in the economy of salvation as *Theotokos* has afforded her "an untold holiness," which "is intimated to us by the favour of the mysterious blessing from her God," so that, we can only conclude that "the Virgin should have been better than the other daughters of Adam," [143] and in fact was. It is to be hoped that this aspect of Newman's theology is made more apparent in Chapter Four (and elsewhere) once we have examined how Newman's study of the Fathers of the Church led him to understand Mary's cooperation in the *œconomia salutis* as the New Eve.

Newman's second conclusion offers us a timeless principle of how to approach the study of Mariology in relationship to Christology and Ecclesiology. These three areas of theology cannot be divorced from one another. Newman exhorts us at the end of his sermon:

> ... how shall we duly conceive of her, who was the only one whom Christ served on earth? His only natural superior?[144] When we estimate the reverence which her Son showed her, then may we know how fitly to honour her memory. Now then let us ascribe to her Son glory for ever and ever more bless Him for His great condescension in becoming, as on this day, incarnate to save a guilty world.[145]

Newman's conclusion reaffirms the Church's veneration for the Virgin Mother of God; it is clearly a Christocentric sermon in that the Marian veneration which Newman advocates is directed to the honor and glory of Christ, that is, to Him Who is the source of Mary's ultimate beatitude and of her eternal salvation and ours. In fact, Mary's divine maternity is that doctrine which best encompasses and expresses the mystery of the Incarnation. Mary is that creature who is most physically and spiritually united and conformed to Christ because of her two-fold blessedness, namely, her physical maternity and her spiritual fecundity, stemming from her singular devotion to the mystery of Our Lord's Person and from her own unique cooperation in the mystery of His redemptive mission.[146] Last, we can see that the ecclesiological implications of the sermon are also disclosed in such a way that our veneration of the Virgin is not only fitting and just for its own sake, but also a definitive source of inspiration for the living out of the Christian vocation to holiness in the obedience of faith.

III. "THE REVERENCE DUE TO THE
BLESSED VIRGIN MARY"

The next sermon to be considered is the first Marian sermon of Newman's to be published, preached on the Feast of the Annunciation, 25 March 1832, "shortly after his move from Evangelicalism to Anglicanism."[147] John Brit explains that Newman's use of Scripture in this sermon is "a confirmation of his teaching concerning how we come to truth and in applied sense."[148] This application is made to the Virgin so that Newman's understanding of Mary's sanctification is clearly contrasted with the sanctification of the other saints and of all other human creatures. Newman also envisions Mary's sinlessness as having "freed her from the experience of the Atonement." Newman's application of this type of biblical hermeneutic, according to Brit, indicates that Newman has undergone a certain theological maturity from his focus on the Atonement in his evangelical period and has shifted to a focus on the mystery of the Incarnation, and consequently, on the mystery of Mary's divine maternity and sinlessness. Brit likewise points to this sermon as having achieved a "rare use of Scripture," whereby Newman was able to combine a *lectio divina* approach to the *Sacra Pagina* "with a scientific analysis of the passage."[149] This approach permitted Newman's listeners to enter into a deeper contemplation of the mystery or mysteries being discussed, so as "to capture the event and its meaning as it was originally intended."[150] Boyce's comment is also helpful in introducing this sermon: "It is a very remarkable piece of religious writing and the most outstanding Marian sermon by the Anglican Newman. It is a fine example of a theological meditation, resting firmly on Sacred Scripture. . . . it contains the best summary we have of Newman's Anglican thoughts on our Lady."[151]

Newman develops a theological triptych by placing side by side, as it were, the greeting of the Angel Gabriel, the salutation of Elizabeth, and Mary's own words in the *Magnificat*: "All generations will call me blessed."[152] He sees in "the great event of the Annunciation," that is, in the greeting of the Archangel Gabriel and in the macarism of Elizabeth, the anticipated fulfillment of Mary's own prophetic utterance in the *Magnificat*. Newman makes an interesting comparison between Mary and her cousin Elizabeth by stating:

... though she was filled with the Holy Ghost she spake, yet, far from thinking herself by such a gift equaled to Mary, she was thereby moved to use the lowlier and more reverent language. "She spake out with a loud voice, and said, *Blessed art thou* among women, and blessed is the fruit of thy womb. And whence is this to me, that the mother of my Lord should come to me?" ... Then she repeated, "Blessed is she that believed; for there shall be a performance of those things which were told her from the Lord." [153]

Newman's exegesis moves quickly to show how the *Magnificat* text cited should be seen not only as an appropriate response of the Virgin to Elizabeth's macarism but likewise as a hymn of praise—an "utterance" filled with the "many and complicated" "feelings" of Mary, a mystery of the economy of salvation, into which we too are called to enter when "we repeat her hymn day after day" "in the Evening Service." [154] Elizabeth's macarism and Mary's canticle of praise are reflected upon by Newman as the fulfillment of the prophecy contained in the *Protoevangelium*. In other words, the justification of Mary's pronouncement in the *Magnificat* is that she is indeed the New Eve, in whom "the destinies of the world were to be reversed, and the serpent's head bruised," and upon whom "was bestowed the greatest honour ever put upon any individual of the fallen race." [155] Mary is to be revered, to be considered blessed by all generations because "God was taking upon Him her flesh, and humbling Himself to be called her offspring;—such is the deep mystery!" [156] At the heart of Newman's exegesis of the *Magnificat* is the sublime mystery of the Incarnation, so sublime that, as Newman says:

> She of course would feel her own inexpressible unworthiness; and again, her humble lot, her ignorance, her weakness in the eyes of the world. And she had moreover, we may well suppose, that purity and innocence of heart, that bright vision of faith, that confiding trust in her God, which raised all these feelings to an intensity which we, ordinary mortals, cannot understand.[157]

The loftiness of the mystery of the Incarnation, as recognized in the life of the humble Virgin of Nazareth, leads us to venerate the mystery of her person, so that even though we cannot fathom the depths of her feelings in being chosen the Mother of the Incarnate Word,[158] we can, nevertheless, admire and imitate to

the best of our ability her virtues. Mary's *tapeinosis*[159] is underscored by Newman in such expressions as her "inexpressible
unworthiness," "humble lot," "her ignorance," "her weakness in
the eyes of the world." Modern biblical scholars seem to have
concurred in attributing to the Greek word ταπείνωσις both a
profound physical and spiritual connotation.[160] Both of these
connotations are included in the theological reflections of the
Magisterium on the *Magnificat* in light of the Church's Tradition,
however, the primary focus is placed on the blessedness of Mary's
spiritual or evangelical poverty as the first of the *anawim* in the
historia salutis.[161] Other aspects of the *Magnificat* emphasized by
Newman are those expressions that point to "purity and innocence of heart," [162] "bright vision of faith," and the "confiding
trust" of Mary—"the most highly favoured, awfully gifted of the
children of men." [163] Newman develops the main body of his
sermon as an explication of the reasons why Mary merits the
veneration the Angel first gave her—that veneration which the
Church has never ceased to give her in every age.[164] He considers
Mary's blessedness from the perspective of her role as the New
Eve, making reference to Galatians 4:4—a key Mariological text
of which a full and proper exegesis is beyond the scope of this
paper. Newman cites the text in passing and relates it to the
Protoevangelium. For the woman of Genesis 3:15, whose seed is
the promised Redeemer, is that same woman from whom that
seed takes on flesh in the fullness of time, according to Galatians.
In both instances, Mary is unnamed and is simply referred to as
the "woman." In both passages, the woman (i.e., Mary) is placed
at the center of the *œconomia salutis*. To Eve is given by the sacred
author a title ("woman"), which Our Lord Himself would later
directly use in addressing Mary at Cana and at Calvary—at the
beginning and end of His public ministry. Furthermore, the title
of "woman" in reference to Mary is also connected to the vision
of Apocalypse 12, in which another unnamed woman is mentioned in association with other figures reminiscent of those
mentioned in Genesis 3:15, namely, a child and a serpent.

Newman's exegesis is capable of reconciling some important
texts of both theological and anthropological significance as he
concludes that Mary's role as the New Eve is a vindication of the
dignity of all women, as well as a confirmation of the special role
that Mary plays in the economy of salvation. This confirmation

of Mary's special role of cooperation as Mother of God and New Eve is likewise a seal on the dignity of our human nature and the dignity of womanhood. He shows not only the anthropological implications of the texts but also highlights their soteriological import.[165] Newman emphasizes the singularity of Our Lord's birth from the virginal womb of Mary with respect to the creation of Adam from the ground and Eve's creation from the side of Adam, finding great significance in this contrast in the new order of the salvific economy inaugurated with the Incarnation of the Second Adam from the Second Eve. Thus, Newman writes:

> But, far from this, God sent forth His son (as Saint Paul says), "made of a woman." For it has been His gracious purpose to save and to change *us*. And in like manner all that belongs to us, our reason, our affections, our relations in life. Therefore, instead of sending His Son from heaven, He sent Him forth as the Son of Mary, to show that all our corruption can be blessed and changed by Him. The very punishment of the fall, the very taint of birth-sin, admits of a cure by the coming of Christ.[166]

Galatians 4:4, from which Newman quotes in the above passage of this sermon, is, as Otto Semmelroth explains, also that precise text with which the Fathers of the Second Vatican Council thought it most fit to introduce the *Proœmium* (no. 52 of chapter 8) of *Lumen Gentium*. Semmelroth attributes various levels of significance to this text which, when viewed in parallel fashion to the comments of Newman's sermon, help to illustrate the multi-layered significance of the pericope.

Semmelroth refers to the uniqueness of this Marian text and to its theological weight in the Pauline corpus. The fact that the Anglican Newman utilizes it to foster reverence for the Virgin and affords it such Mariological weight, which is not commonly given to this text in Protestant circles—the focus being more often than not on the figure of Mary in the Gospels—is an extraordinary testimony to the keenness of Newman's insight into the Scriptures. Secondly, Semmelroth notes that Galatians 4:4 expresses in a formulaic fashion "the ancient Church's confession of faith," about the "salvific Incarnation of God's Son by saying that He 'was born of a woman' . . . to deliver us from bondage to the history of damnation." Newman pin-points the salvific activity of the Incarnation in the reversal of the Fall through Mary's cooperation, alluding to Mary as the New Eve. Third, Semmelroth concludes that this Pauline inclusion is "the marrow which makes Marian formularies so important for orthodox faith in the mystery of Christ." Newman, in the context of commenting on Galatians 4:4, affirms that Mary's divine maternity, that is, Christ being formed of her, is a guarantee of God the Son's entrance into a definitive state of communion with our human nature. Fourth, this entrance of the Son of God into our human history through Mary's ministration marks the culmination of salvation history so that Our Lord is able to redeem us and to root our salvation in the life of the Church. Indeed, the Church herself is, as Semmelroth writes, "engrafted" by Christ's Incarnation "into history." For Newman, the ecclesiological implications based on this text are likewise essential to mention. As a result of the Son of God's birth from "the woman," the Virgin Mary, Newman tells us that: "All that belongs to us, our reason, our affections, our pursuits, our relations in life, needs nothing put aside in His disciples, but all sanctified." And immediately following the latter statement, Newman, once again alluding to the Pauline text, adds that Christ's birth "as the Son of Mary," was intended to transform all "our sorrow and all our corruption." [167] Last, Semmelroth argues that if the mystery of Christ's salvific work "in the fullness of time," and the mystery of His whole Person is Marian, then the Church too be must be essentially Marian in her life and ministry. [168] Newman, in commenting on Galatians 4:4, links together the birth of Christ from Mary and the recapitulation of womanhood and the particular elevation of marriage as "the outward symbol of the heavenly union betwixt Christ and His Church." [169] Newman is therefore neither a Manichean nor a Jansenist.

Newman reads Galatians 4:4–5 and Genesis 3:15 in light of their anthropological implications in relationship to the status of women in general and to the status of Mary in particular. He argues his points by relating the Genesis passage to such New Testament passages as 1 Peter 3:7 and 1 Timothy 2:15:

> But when Christ came as the seed of the woman, He vindicated the rights and honour of His mother. Not that the distinction of ranks is destroyed under the Gospel; the woman is still made inferior to man, as he to Christ; but the slavery is done away with. Saint Peter bids the husband "give honour unto the wife,

because the weaker, in that both are heirs of the grace of life." And Saint Paul, while enjoining subjection upon her, speaks of the especial blessedness vouchsafed her in being the appointed entrance of the Saviour into the world. "Adam was first formed, then Eve; and Adam was not deceived but the woman being deceived was in the transgression." But "notwithstanding, she shall be saved through the child-bearing;" that is, through the birth of Christ from Mary, which was a blessing, as upon all mankind, so peculiarly upon the woman. Accordingly, from that time, marriage has not only been restored to its original dignity, but even gifted with a spiritual privilege, as the outward symbol of the heavenly union subsisting betwixt Christ and His Church. Thus has the Blessed Virgin, in bearing Our Lord, taken off or lightened the peculiar disgrace which the woman inherited for seducing Adam, sanctifying the one part of it, repealing the other.[170]

Newman indicates that Christ's coming as Man "born of a woman" inaugurates a kind of spiritual and anthropological revolution, or better yet, a recapitulation. This is most apparent when one considers the notion of slavery and the low social status of women in Jesus' time. Our Lord's Gospel, as Newman understands it, especially in light of the pastoral applications which it receives in the epistles of Saints Peter and Paul, clearly indicates that, while there is still a definite differentiation between men and women that must be upheld, there cannot be any basis for considering woman to be inherently or essentially inferior to man. The subjection of woman to man, resulting as part of the curse inherited from original sin, ended up, in Newman's view, in women being considered of a lower status than man, ruled over by their husbands as the weaker sex, and in many cases, even disrespected and debased to the point of enslavement and tyranny.[171] The disorder and disharmony between man and woman resulting from original sin is not one-sided according to Newman. He explains that not only women but men too have had to suffer negative consequences.[172] He also explains how this sad situation had been exemplified in the practice of polygamy and divorce "which was suffered under the patriarchal and Jewish dispensation,"[173] but then reversed according to the new dispensation established by the coming of Christ—born of a woman, born under the Law. Newman explains the nature of the recapitulation of the male and female relationship in the new dispensation according to the antithetical parallels Adam/Christ, Eve/Mary.[174]

Newman's exegesis of the Petrine and Pauline texts mentioned merit some explanation. Newman's reading of these texts is that the anthropological complementarity of man and woman in God's plan of salvation does not imply a lack of differentiation, likewise to be reflected in their different roles of cooperation in the economy of salvation.[175] Newman makes this significant theological distinction clear in the context of determining Mary's role, concluding that the subordination of Eve to Adam in the economy of salvation finds a providential parallel in the subordination of Mary to Christ: "Adam was formed first, then Eve; and Adam was not deceived, but woman being deceived was in the transgression.' But 'notwithstanding, she shall be saved through Child-bearing;' that is, through the birth of Christ from Mary, which was a blessing, as upon all mankind, so peculiarly upon the woman." [176]

Are women saved through childbearing? To this question, raised by Saint Paul in 1 Timothy 2:15, Newman responds affirmatively, quickly adding that it is first and foremost the birth of Christ from the Virgin Mary that elevates the dignity of woman and her status not only vis à vis man, but also in terms of her relationship to God. Therefore, Newman admits of a true Christian feminism which, while respecting the order of creation wherein man and woman are equal but different, still he insists upon the subordination of the female to the male insofar as authority is concerned. At the same time, Newman also shows how this subordination based on authority finds its paradigm in the marriage relationship between Christ and the Church. Obedience and love in the male-female relationship do not contradict one another, but are each other's complements since both obedience and love are, in the Christian economy, virtues renewed and elevated by Our Lord's redeeming sacrifice—integral to the bringing about of a new creation.[177] In this wonderful activity of recreation, Christ finds in His Mother Mary a free, loving, obedient partner who does not, in any way, grasp at equality with Him, just as He did not deem equality with His Heavenly Father something to be grasped at but chose to empty Himself in perfect love and obedience.[178] Thus, we find in Mary the epitome of the woman who, according to Paul, perseveres in faith, love and holiness with self-control, and so is saved,[179] insofar as she responds faithfully to her vocation to be the Mother of the Redeemer and the redeemed alike.[180]

Therefore, it is not accidental that Saint Paul, when speaking about the salvation of woman through childbearing, does so precisely in reference to the economy of salvation. He notes that Adam, not Eve, was formed first; and that Eve, not Adam, was deceived by the serpent. A consequence of this subordination in the economy, according to Saint Paul, is that women must therefore be subordinate to men in the exercise of authority in the Church (hierarchical order), just as men are subordinate to Christ.[181] If this is indeed the case, as Church teaching maintains, then there should be no obstacle to our understanding that Mary the New Eve is subordinate to Christ the New Adam in the economy of salvation.[182]

Newman also emphasizes that a consequence of the particular respect and honor shown to the Virgin Mary is also meant to indicate a greater respect and honor paid to women by men in general. Christ's redemptive sacrifice involves the elevation of mankind—males and females alike, who are made children, sons and daughters of God and heirs of the Kingdom.[183] This offer of salvation, divine sonship, benediction, and heavenly inheritance is made by the Second Adam to all mankind directly and, through Mary, extended to women in a particular way.[184] Furthermore, the role of the Virgin is seen as pivotal in the process of recapitulation which, in effect, is realized in the raising up of the institution of marriage to the level of a sacramental union expressive of the sacrificial love which Christ and the Church share in their espousal relationship.[185] Mary, therefore, is the one who best represents the Church and every single human being in relationship to Christ the Second Adam—the Bridegroom of the Church—following the analogy of Saint Paul in his Epistle to the Ephesians.[186]

What follows in Newman's sermon is an eloquent praise of the Virgin's many merits and virtues, most especially as they directly flow from her intimate association with the Incarnation and, therefore, with the *œconomia salutis*:

> But further, she is doubtless to be accounted blessed and favoured in herself, as well as in the benefits she has done for us. Who can estimate the holiness and perfection of her, who was

chosen to be the Mother of Christ? If to him that hath, more is given, and holiness and divine favour go together (and this we are told), what must have been the transcendent purity of her, whom the Creator Spirit condescended to overshadow with His miraculous presence? What must have been her gifts, who was chosen to be the only near-earthly relative of the Son of God, the only one whom He was bound by nature to revere and instruct day by day, as He grew in wisdom and in stature? This contemplation runs to a higher subject, did we dare follow it; for what, think you, was the sanctified state of that human nature, of which God formed His sinless Son; knowing as we do, "that which is born of the flesh is flesh," and "none can bring a clean thing out of an unclean"?[187]

Referring back to the event of the Annunciation in the above passage, Newman asks a series of rhetorical questions that bring us to contemplate the mystery of her sinlessness in direct relation to her privilege of the divine maternity, and vice versa. The visitation of the Angel Gabriel is the prelude to the much greater visitation of the Holy Spirit Who overshadows her with His sanctifying presence so that she might conceive in her womb the sinless Son of the Eternal Father.[188] However, the sinlessness of the Christ Child does not preclude His having simply received from Mary the transmission of life but likewise, according to the development of His human nature, the transmission of wisdom and knowledge.[189] Thus, just as Mary's *fiat* is an integral part of her cooperation in the Father's plan of salvation, so too an integral part of Christ's obedience and submission to the Father's plan of salvation is His obedience and submission to Mary and Joseph.

Newman, then, returns to an overview of the mysteries of Mary's life according to the scriptural evidence which, although limited "after the circumstances of Christ's birth and infancy,"[190] is nonetheless a powerful attestation to her blessedness. He highlights two events in particular as indicative of Mary's cooperation: "She is mentioned as attending Christ to the Cross, and there committed by Him to Saint John's keeping; and she is mentioned as continuing with the Apostles in prayer after His ascension."[191] Newman adds that "in this silence we find instruction as much as in the mention of her."[192]

Newman's exegesis explains why this is the case by setting

down a hermeneutical principle which states: "Scripture was written, not to exalt this or that particular saint, but to give glory to Almighty God."[193] Following this principle, Newman cites as an example the figure of the prophetess Anna, who is introduced by the Evangelist Luke not for her own sake but to glorify the Christ Child, and who is never again mentioned after the Presentation in the Temple.[194] Newman also considers the Apostle John as one of those biblical figures about whom there is little mentioned, precisely because, as Newman speculates, he is so intimately associated with the Person of Christ, "his personal friend," and is indeed "Christ's favoured Apostle."[195] In fact, he remains unnamed in the Fourth Gospel and is simply known as "the disciple whom Jesus loved," or the "beloved disciple."

One could then ask: How much more so will be the reserve with which Our Lady is treated in the Sacred Text since, of all the saints, she was the most intimate with her Son? Newman explains his reasoning thus: "I say, Scripture is written to show us the course of God's great and marvelous Providence, and we hear of those saints only who were instruments of His purposes, as either introducing or preaching His Son."[196] In other words, saints are not introduced for their own sake but *ad maiorem Dei gloriam.*

Newman continues his explanation: "These were not to be exposed, as unfit for the world to know,—as dangerous, because not admitting of being known, without risk lest the honour which those Saints received through grace should *eclipse in our minds the honour of Him who honoured them*" (emphasis added).[197] Newman is not suggesting that the saints do not deserve honor. Rather, the Anglican Newman fears that an overexposure to their sanctity might be a possible distraction for those who seek to honor Christ. We must be careful here not to misinterpret what Newman is saying. A key phrase of the above paragraph is "in our minds," that is, in the popular imagination. Newman's pastoral concern is that the honor due to Christ as the Son of God and the honor offered to the saints as creatures should neither be theologically confused nor that these distinctions be lost in personal devotion—since, as he would later more fully understand, the former pertains to what is commonly referred to as *latria* or worship, while the latter is known as *dulia* or that veneration proper to the saints.

In fact, in the *Letter to Pusey* Newman spends much time

explaining to Pusey these very distinctions from a Catholic perspective.[198] Here, these distinctions are simply reinforced, as we note that the present sermon is one that comes from Newman's Anglican period and therefore, is all the more appreciable since it shows that Newman already understood their importance for the purpose of obviating any misconception on the part of his audience concerning the authentic scriptural roots of the veneration of Mary and the other saints. In this sermon, Newman seeks to prove the opposite, to some extent. He does this by means of a series of admonitions to his congregation favoring a frugal approach to the veneration of Mary and the saints; this is more than comprehensible, given Newman's historical circumstances, but somewhat foreign to the devotion to Mary and the saints in the traditions of both the Eastern and Western Churches.

One such admonition is given in the passage immediately cited below. Newman's intent is to establish the basis for a proper veneration of the saints and in particular for the Virgin, without, however, suggesting any sort of extreme whereby our adoration of the Lord would be overshadowed or eschewed by our love and reverence for her (them). Newman reinforces his general principle which he believes to be derived from the Scriptures by reiterating it in these words:

> When a saint is seen working *towards* an end appointed by God, we *see* him to be a mere instrument, a servant though a favoured one; and though we admire him, yet, after all, we glorify God in him. We pass *from* him to the work to which he ministers. But, when anyone is introduced, full of gifts, yet without visible and immediate subserviency to God's designs, such a one seems revealed for his own sake. We should rest, perchance, in the thought of him, and think of the creature more than the Creator. . . . The higher their gifts, the less fitted they are to be seen.[199]

Though Newman's general principle concerning a balanced Christologically focused and scripturally based devotion to Mary and the other saints is also a Catholic principle,[200] a particular limitation of this principle as applied by the Anglican Newman is due to the fact that it falls short of permitting direct invocation of them. Nevertheless, Newman's own argument that the veneration of the saint "passes through" to become adoration of the Lord is similar to the reasoning of the Second Council of Nicea

(787 A.D.) in its defense of the use of icons when it states: Ἡ γὰρ τῆς εἰκόνος τιμὴ ἐπὶ τὸ πρωτότυπον διαβαίνει καὶ ὁ προσκυνῶν τὴν εἰκόνα προσκυνεῖ ἐν αὐτῇ τοῦ εγγραφομένου τήν ὑπόστασιν.[201] Even though Newman himself does not explicitly state that this is the logic behind his expression, it could be helpful, especially as an apologetical and ecumenical argument, in taking the meaning of Newman's expression to its logical conclusion.

Nor can one ignore, for example, a historical criticism of *The Reverence Due to the Virgin Mary*, most especially of Newman's emphasis in the sermon on the reserve with which one should venerate the Virgin (which reserve Newman attributes to the sacred authors' own insights into the mystery of Mary's place in the economy of salvation) as offered by Michael Perrott in his book, *The Mariology of Newman*. Perrott maintains, without doubting the sincerity of Newman's biblical hermeneutical principles, that the Anglican Newman encouraged such frugality in Marian devotion because he felt himself caught between the Scylla of the Anglican Thirty-nine Articles, especially Article 22, which explicitly prohibited invocation of and undue reverence to the saints, and the Charybdis of Catholicism, which did not hesitate, both in its official Liturgy and in private devotions, to extol the Virgin, her merits and privileges and likewise those of the other saints while invoking their intercession.

Perrott's conclusion is that the Anglican Newman's attempt to forge a *via media* was a clear indication of his unwillingness to challenge the established Church of England, so as to give full expression to the Catholic beliefs and/or sentiments regarding Our Lady which he harbored in his heart during this period and which he would labor to convey until his conversion to Catholicism in 1845. While Perrott certainly acknowledges the remarkableness of many of Newman's statements in "The Reverence Due to the Virgin Mary"—especially given the historical, cultural and theological milieu of the day—he is still not convinced that Newman's Anglican Mariology should be considered of such an affinity to his Catholic Mariology as not to notice the contrasts that exist between the two.

Perrott especially notes that at the heart of the Anglican Newman's inability to reconcile himself with the full implications of Catholic Marian doctrine and devotion lies primarily Newman's attachment to Anglican liturgical forms and in the Protestant belief that the Catholic doctrines, for example, of grace, merit and the invocation of saints, were not in keeping with the authentic Gospel message and practice of the early Church. Perrott explains:

> The prohibition on invocation enshrined in the Anglican Articles of Religion, Newman loyally respected. Such a practice was said to impede the all-sufficient mediation of Christ, a fact Newman clearly concurred with, seemingly unaware of the same problem arising if one allowed the saints to pray for the faithful, without their actually being invoked. The rejection of a theology of lesser mediation, through prayer and penance, by Cranmer led to this suspicious attitude toward the cult of the saints—a clear example of doctrinal and devotional interdependence.[202]

More subtle, however, according to Perrott, is the reason why Newman is wary of Mary's mediation. It is not just a question of invocation but a more fundamental misunderstanding of how Mary's extraordinary holiness is to be properly appreciated in light of the singular sanctity of Christ:

> "Ordinary saints," he asserts, "do not obscure the worship the [sic] God's grace in them, because they can be "seen working *towards* an end appointed by God, we *see* Him to be an instrument." With Our Blessed Lady it is different; first, the nature of her vocation is so sublime, so intimate and so incomprehensible, that "it is a dangerous thing, it is too high a privilege, for sinners like ourselves, . . . we cannot bear to see such men (women) in their own place, in the retirement of private life, and the calmness of hope and joy." This is not a question of invocation impeding the all-sufficiency of Christ's sacrifice, but the sheer overwhelming sanctity of the individual. Such a degree of sanctity, Newman maintains, because of its awesome degree, and private nature, threatens to keep our devotional attention focused on her, a creature, rather than God the originator of such grace and sanctity. It is for this reason, Newman concludes, "that so little is revealed about the Virgin Mary, in mercy to our weakness."[203]

Newman treats the veneration of the saints as a legitimate practice yet one tempered even within the Scriptures themselves for our sake. Likewise, Newman turns his attention to the issue of our veneration of the Blessed Virgin and the question of its appropriateness in light of what is contained and what is not contained in the biblical texts. Newman plainly writes that:

> Had the blessed Mary been more fully disclosed to us in the heavenly beauty and sweetness of the spirit within her, true, *she* would have been honoured, *her* gifts would have been clearly seen; but, at the same time, the Giver would have been somewhat less contemplated, because no design or work of His would have been disclosed in her history. She would have seemingly been introduced for *her* own sake, not for His sake.[204]

Once again, it becomes clear that Newman does not wish to minimize veneration to the Virgin but hopes that a balanced approach will be taken in regard to such veneration following the moderation with which the Scriptures themselves demonstrate veneration for her, so that she might not be seen as an obstacle to our relationship with Jesus but be venerated as the one creature who expresses the greatest possible love for and adoration of her Son. Similarly, Newman notices that the peculiar silence about the Virgin (comparatively and relatively speaking, that is, to what is mentioned about the other apostles and disciples) does not indicate any intention whatsoever on Our Lord's part to diminish our veneration of Mary. Rather, according to Newman's logic, it is a tribute to her since all that could have been said about her virtues and merits was not said.

Consequently, as Newman points out, we are safeguarded from idolatry. Mary's holiness is so great, in Newman's mind, that it is quasi-angelic in nature. He believes that God did not at once fully reveal all that concerns Mary's holiness because we are limited by our sinfulness in the true perception and understanding of such mysterious realities. And so, taking as his point of reference the example of Saint John, who, according to the book of Revelation, "was twice tempted to fall down in worship before an Angel who showed him the things to come,"[205] Newman concludes that "if he who had seen the Son of God was thus overcome by the creature, how is it possible we could bear to gaze upon the creature's holiness in its fulness . . . ?"[206] This latter statement is an outstanding admission of Newman's belief in Mary's sanctity or, to adopt a most venerable term of the East, one could say that Newman considers Mary as the παν-άγια—"all-holy."[207] Newman is so enamored of Mary's singular sanctity that he admits that, naturally speaking, the fullness of her holiness, if more fully contemplated, could lead us to lose sight of "the infinite perfections of the Eternal Godhead." [208] Newman's argument should be appreciated not so much for what he believes as an Anglican to be the just measures of Marian devotion but more so for the exceptional reverence, most especially for Mary's fullness of holiness, to which he does admit in the sermon.

This latter point is confirmed in another of Newman's statements: "Therefore, many truths are, like the 'things which the seven thunders uttered,'[209] 'sealed up' from us. In particular, it is in mercy to us that so little is revealed about the Blessed Virgin, in mercy to our weakness, though of her there are 'many things to say,' yet they are hard to be uttered, seeing we are dull of hearing.' "[210] We can infer from such a text—as from the whole of this sermon—that the Anglican Newman clearly had a high regard for the Most Blessed Virgin, especially for her sinlessness. And even though Mary is mentioned only on a few occasions in the Sacred Scriptures, those instances provided Newman with ample evidence of the importance of her cooperation in the economy of salvation.

Perhaps Newman's appreciation of Our Lady's cooperation in this sermon is best summarized by acknowledging that Newman, starting from an objective appraisal of Mary's cooperation as *Theotokos* and holiest of all creatures, is then able to make a particular assessment of how the individual believer should conform his personal devotion to the Virgin based on what Newman understands as explicitly taught about her person in the Sacred Scriptures, as well as in the liturgical worship of the official Anglican Church. Lest one cultivate an unbalanced devotion to Mary apart from the mystery of her Son, a recognition of Mary's proper place in the economy of salvation as the highest of all creatures next to God and in the Church, Newman writes:

> But, further, the more we consider who Saint Mary was, the more dangerous will such knowledge of her appear to be. Other saints are but influenced or inspired by Christ, and made partakers of Him mystically. But as to Saint Mary, Christ derived His Manhood from her, and so had an especial unity of nature with her; and this wondrous relationship between God and man it is perhaps impossible for us to dwell much upon without some perversion of feeling. For truly, she is raised

above the condition of sinful beings, though by nature a sinner; she is brought near to God, yet is a creature, and seems to lack her fitting place in our understanding, neither too high nor too low. We cannot combine in our thought of her, all we should ascribe with all we should withhold. Hence, following the example of Scripture, we had better only think of her with and for her Son, never separating her from Him, but using her name as a memorial of His great condescension in stooping from heaven, and not "abhorring the Virgin's womb.'[211]

And this is the rule of our own Church, which has set apart only such Festivals in honour of the Blessed Virgin, as may also be Festivals in honour of Our Lord; the Purification[212] commemorating His presentation in the Temple, and the Annunciation commemorating the Incarnation.[213]

Newman dwells upon the relative silence about the Virgin in the Scriptures as indicative of the wise and providential plan designed by God to prevent us from putting Mary on the same level as that of Jesus. Newman believes that the silence of Scripture in regard to Mary is in fact an eloquent testimony to her blessedness, that is, to the truths of her many merits and privileges by reason of which she has the preeminent position in the communion of saints and in the whole of creation.

In this passage, Newman fully admits of Mary's sanctity but does not yet adhere to the Catholic teaching about the Immaculate Conception. It is difficult to determine from the context of this sermon alone as to exactly how Newman envisioned Mary's fullness of sanctification, vis à vis original sin. Undoubtedly, he places her in that realm of holiness nearest to the Triune God— thus, surpassing the holiness of all the saints. Here, Newman does not directly compare Mary's holiness to that of the angels as he does, for example, in his meditation, "On the Annunciation," where Mary is called *"Regina Angelorum."*[214] Yet how is one to interpret Newman's statement about Mary being "by nature a sinner" in light of his praise of Mary's fullness of holiness?

Newman seems to imply that Mary is a sinner not in the sense that she was tainted by sin in any real way but only insofar as she was born into a sinful human race. Even if we cannot determine for sure Newman's thought on the doctrine of Mary's Immaculate Conception based on this text, at least we can safely estimate that Newman did not impute to Mary any stain of actual sin. Later developments in his theology, nevertheless, bring Newman to a full acceptance of the Catholic doctrine of the Immaculate Conception firmly based on the Scotian notion of prevenient grace, which he very much prized.[215] Mary's sanctification, her fullness of grace, will then be understood as having taken place from the moment of her conception, so that her human nature could no longer be considered sinful (in the proper sense of the term) since she had no part in sin, whether original or actual.

This passage, moreover, corroborates the fact that Newman's Mariology is expressed in this sermon in clearly Christocentric terms which, he insists, are based on equally evident biblical principles. In some fashion, the Christological focus of Newman's Anglican Mariology lays the groundwork for his Catholic appropriation of the truth expressed in the adage *Ad Iesum per Mariam* ("to Jesus through Mary"). The veneration (*hyper-dulia*) of the Virgin is subordinate to the adoration (*latria*) of Christ, and this subordination serves as a "memorial" of the great mystery of the Incarnation. Mary, for Newman, is never to be separated from her Son, but thought of "with and for her Son."[216] Beyond that, Newman's reference to a veneration which is "neither too high nor too low" is a way of cautioning his listeners to apply the philosophical principle, *in medio stat virtus*,[217] to their personal Marian devotion. Newman's prudent admonition should be read in combination with the words that conclude this section of the sermon: "And with this caution, the thought of her may be made most profitable to our faith; for nothing is so calculated to impress on our minds that Christ is really a partaker of our nature, and in all respects Man, save sin only, as to associate Him with the thought of her, by whose ministration He became our Brother."[218]

Once again, Mary's role in the economy of salvation is defined in terms of her strict relationship to the mystery of her Son's Person and His redemptive work—with special emphasis placed on her divine maternity. Just as Newman here considered the truth of Mary's cooperation, her "ministration" in the Incarnation, the chosen means by which Christ became our Brother, so too do the Fathers of the Second Vatican Council Fathers speak of Mary's "maternal charity," by which "she cares for the brethren of her Son."[219]

Dr. John R. Griffin, in reference to Newman's views on the sanctity (sinlessness) of the Virgin as expressed in the *Parochial and Plain Sermons*, writes the following:

> ... in the *Plain and Parochial Sermons* [sic] we find abundant evidence of Newman's own devotion to Our Lady. Mary was always identified in Newman's mind as the person who was closest to Christ. In one of his sermons Newman went very close to an avowal of a belief in the doctrine of the Immaculate Conception, for it must be that the one who was chosen to bear the Son of God was unique in the history of mankind. There is a mystery in any direct act of Providence, but the scheme, as Saint Paul said, of God "being made of a woman" absolutely reversing the judgment that has been given against Eve in Newman's words: "instead of sending His Son from heaven, He sent Him forth as the Son of Mary, to show that all our sorrow and all our corruption can be blessed and changed by Him. The very punishment of the Fall, the very taint of birth-sin, admits of a cure by the coming of Christ." [220]

The sermon, to which Griffin refers in his commentary, is precisely "The Reverence Due to the Virgin Mary." In the conclusion to this sermon, Newman enjoins us to consider Mary as a necessary part of the economy of our salvation. Mary's motherhood—to which she consented at the moment of the Annunciation—not only should "impress on our minds that Christ is really a partaker of our nature, and in all respects save sin only, as to associate Him with the thought of her, by whose ministration He became our Brother," [221] but is likewise "profitable to our faith" because we learn from Mary's example of selfless cooperation that God wills to sanctify us in the ordinary circumstances of our lives. Of course, the event of the Incarnation is most extraordinary, but what Newman is reflecting upon is the fact that the Angel visited Mary in the course of her everyday life and that the wonder of this mystery which occurs through her "ministration" teaches us that "the highest graces of the soul may be matured in private." [222] Newman reinforces this point in the following way: "God gives His Holy Spirit to us silently; and the silent duties of every day (it may be humbly hoped) are blest to the sufficient sanctification of thousands, whom the world knows not of. The Blessed Virgin is a memorial of this; and it is consoling as well as instructive to know it." [223] In fact, if one were to consider, for example, that the Annunciation is probably the most depicted of biblical events, in all of sacred art, and that likewise one usually finds Mary depicted as being alone, apart from the presence of the Angel and/or a symbol of the Holy Spirit, in the obscurity of Nazareth, then one may the better reflect on the significance that God gives to the dignity of the individual person and to that person's free-will and the ability to say yes or no to His plan of salvation within the context of ordinary daily life.

The final section of Newman's masterful sermon is revelatory, as is the entire sermon, of his combined love for the Sacred Scriptures and the Blessed Virgin. He extols the Blessed Virgin as the "chief (of the) undefiled followers of the Lamb." [224] Father de la Potterie's insights are helpful in explaining the significance of this image taken from the Book of Revelation, so that we can focus better on the merits of Newman's own exegesis. De la Potterie identifies the "undefiled followers of the Lamb" in Revelation 14:1–4 as the faithful, virgin disciples of Christ Crucified and Risen, who obediently accompany Him before the throne of His heavenly Father in the "celestial Jerusalem." The faithful obedience of these heavenly disciples is understood by de la Potterie as expressing the continuity of the New Testament's disciple of Jesus.[225] Of all those who left everything to follow Our Lord unreservedly, Mary stands out for her singular purity of heart as first among the Lord's *anawim*[226] and as the personification of the "Daughter of Zion." Thus, in her sacred virginity and holiness of life, Mary can be considered not only the model of the perfect disciple of Christ but also the eschatological model of the Church "victorious," of whom she is also the spotless Mother.[227]

Newman also indicates that Mary's ability to consent to the Angel's message in all humility is due to the fact that, unlike those whose faith and obedience are constantly in need of purification and renewal because of the effects of sin, Mary did not suffer these consequences precisely because she was redeemed and sanctified in such a way as to make her the chief of the undefiled followers of the Lamb.[228] Although Newman's application of this text of the Book of Revelation 14:1–14 in this context cannot be taken on face value as proof of Newman's belief in Mary's sinlessness from the moment of her conception, it does indicate that she, according to the divine pleasure,[229] was preserved from sin by "heavenly grace," despite her being born into a sinful human race, requiring her to overcome "the various temptations to evil" which "successively present themselves."[230] A Catholic application of this text of Revelation to the Virgin can only be fully and most properly made if Mary's undefilement or sinlessness is understood as a unique privilege given to her by God and not merely as a privilege that she shared with other followers of Our Lord but enjoyed in the most noble or exemplary of ways. Nevertheless, the Anglican Newman's insights into the Sacred Text, especially as regards the question of Mary's sanctity, do not therefore go unappreciated.

Newman continues in this last part of the sermon to demonstrate his aptitude for biblical exegesis by comparing the faith of Abraham and the faith of Mary and by contrasting the faith of Mary with the doubt of Zechariah the father of John the Baptist:[231]

> Strong in the Lord, and in the power of His might, she "staggered not at the promise of God through unbelief"; she believed when Zacharias doubted,—with a faith like Abraham's she believed and was blessed for her belief, and had the performance of those things which were told her by the Lord. And when sorrow came upon her afterwards, it was but the blessed participation of her Son's sacred sorrows, not the sorrows of those who suffer for their sins.[232]

The first phrase of this passage alludes to Mary's words in the *Magnificat*, praising the Lord for His mercy and might as He has proven this throughout the economy of salvation and, in a particular way, by choosing Mary to be His humble handmaid and Mother of the Redeemer.[233] Newman assures us that Elizabeth's *confessio laudis* (confession of praise) concerning the blessedness of Mary's faith in Luke 1:45 is both a verification of Mary's *fiat* at the Annunciation and looks forward, in a sense, to her unwavering faith at Calvary.

The Reverend Frederick L. Miller comments on the present Holy Father's Mariology with regard to the same contrasting parallelism as found in Newman's sermon. Both Newman and Pope John Paul II understand Mary's faith as the culmination of the Old Testament faith epitomized by the patriarch Abraham who is also the perfect exemplar of faith in the New Testament and for all believers in Christ.[234]

Another striking aspect about the aforementioned passage is

that the Anglican Newman expresses belief in Mary's union with the redemptive suffering of Christ, which he terms a "blessed participation," and that the Virgin's sufferings do not result from her sinfulness. Perrott notes:

> Given the Protestant theology of grace and merit enshrined in the Prayer Book, such a passage is, nevertheless, truly remarkable. The reference to the sorrows of Our Lady, carries with it a veiled reference to her co-mediation resulting from her proximity to that Divine Suffering of her Son. He clearly states that Our Lady's suffering is qualitatively different from that of sinners which is partly punitive; hers by contrast is participatory, and that in an unique way. We see in this sermon the embryonic devotion to Our Lady which is such a notable feature of Newman's Catholic writings; here indeed, is a genuine continuity between the Newman of Oriel College and the Newman of Birmingham Oratory. It is also a splendid illustration of the *lex orandi lex credendi* principle.[235]

Newman's statement, professing belief in Mary's sinlessness, dovetails with another statement found earlier on in the same sermon: "Who can estimate the *holiness and perfection* of her who was chosen to be the Mother of Christ? If to him that hath, more is given, and holiness and divine favour go together (and this we are expressly told), what must have been the *transcendent purity* of her, whom the Creator Spirit condescended to overshadow with His miraculous presence?" (emphasis added).[236] Bishop Boyce writes in reference to this text that:

> This paragraph gave rise to much speculation among Anglicans. They took it to mean that the preacher secretly adhered to the Roman Catholic belief in the Immaculate Conception of the Blessed Virgin Mary. To his accusers when this sermon was published three years later (1835) Newman gave an evasive response. . . . In the *Apologia* (in 1864), he recalls how he *"made much of"* our Lady's *"Immaculate Purity"* in this Anglican sermon (cf. *Apologia*, p. 165). It would seem that he personally saw the constraining fittingness and evidence for this doctrine but did not profess it explicitly in his Anglican period, wishing to remain loyal to the teaching of his own Church."[237]

Therefore, one should recognize the way in which Newman is able to derive from the Scriptures a logical argument in support of Mary's sinlessness or, as he describes it, her "transcendent purity." He makes a clear reference to the presence of the Holy Spirit at the Annunciation and considers the Spirit's descent upon the Virgin to be an affirmation and an intensification of her sanctity. In other words, Newman believes Mary possesses a singular holiness before the event of the Incarnation, that is, her personal holiness is seen as a direct preparation for her divine maternity.[238]

Although Newman does not declare in an explicit way his belief about the beginnings of Mary's extraordinary sanctity, his Catholic intuition in this sermon regarding the doctrine of the Immaculate Conception can be sensed easily nonetheless, as it was probably perceived by Newman's own contemporaries in the Anglican Church. In fact, one could argue that "The Reverence Due to the Virgin Mary" is perhaps the closest the Anglican Newman comes to an articulation of what would later be defined and most wholeheartedly embraced by him as the Catholic dogma of the Immaculate Conception.

The conclusion of Newman's sermon takes the form of an exhortation with an eschatological outlook. Mary is held up by Newman as a model of "God's unspeakable gift" of innocence and holiness, which Newman exhorts his listeners to imitate and enter into with grateful hearts and joyful hope, if they have not already been doing so from the time of their youth. Newman also exhorts them to imitate Mary's sanctity and virtue, so that having overcome their sinfulness, they will be configured to Christ once they, like her, will have completed their earthly course. Because holiness is considered by Newman to be an indelible mark of Mary's person and characteristic of the whole of her history,[239] he encourages us to strive in our own lives to allow God to "cleanse away the marks of sin," so that we may come at last to behold "that Sacred Countenance . . . which no sinner ever yet could see and live."[240] Indeed, Newman urges his listeners to fix their countenances on Mary who, together with all the saints, is a shining example of those who already await the fulfillment of "the promise pledged to the Church on the Mount of the Transfiguration."[241] In other words, Mary already shares in the glory of her Son's Resurrection; she already beholds the countenance which she helped form and to which she was most conformed as the most pure Mother of Christ in the company of "the saints of the Lord." Therefore, those of us who are still in this vale of tears and who "bear but the countenance of common men" can pursue the universal call to holiness by imitating Mary's holiness with the hope that we "will wake up one by one after His likeness," on the day of the General Resurrection.

Newman draws his sermon to a close with a humbling reminder of our sinfulness when compared to the holiness of the saints in light and yet offers us these hopeful and comforting words which conjure up for us the image of the communion of saints which, as the Apostle John describes, culminates in the possession of our filial inheritance, our total conformity to Christ the Pure and Righteous One and our entrance into the beatific vision:[242]

> It will be "good" to be with those whose tabernacles[243] might have been a snare to us on earth, had we been allowed to build them. We shall see Our Lord, and His Blessed Mother, the Apostles and Prophets, and all those righteous men whom we now read of in history, and long to know. Then we shall be taught in those mysteries which are now above us. In the words of the Apostle, "Beloved, now we are the sons of God, and it doth not yet appear, we shall be like Him, for we shall see Him as He is: and every man that hath this hope in Him, purifieth himself, even as He is pure.'"[244]

IV. "THE GLORIES OF MARY FOR THE SAKE OF HER SON"

The next sermon to be studied is one of a series of sermons that Newman preached during the Spring-Summer of 1849 in the Oratory Church—then located at Alcester Street—in Birmingham.[245] They are entitled *Discourses to Mixed Congregations* because his audience was made up of both Catholics and Anglicans.[246] Newman, a convert of only three and a half years and a Catholic priest of two years, undertakes in this work to present a Catholic apologetic for Marian doctrine and devotion. Seven years earlier in 1842, Doctor Charles Russell, an Irish priest and President of Maynooth College, sent Newman some of Saint Alphonsus Liguori's sermons, including some Marian writings. Much to his surprise, Newman found nothing in these works that disedified him.[247] On the contrary, Newman believed them to be doctrinally sound works that engendered true devotion. Indeed, one can suppose that the title of Saint Alphonsus' *Le Glorie di Maria* ("The Glories of Mary") may have served as the basis for the title of the discourse we are presently discussing, even though, in the *Letter to Pusey*, Newman admits of never having read the work.[248] Newman was well aware of the opportunity he had to offer Catholics and Anglicans alike a sermon that could establish the scriptural foundation for a proper and well-balanced approach to the Marian dimension of the Church's teaching in accord with the Tradition.

Newman begins his discourse by situating Mary in the grand scheme of the economy of salvation.[249]

Using texts from Sirach[250] and Genesis,[251] he sets out to show how they attest to order and harmony in creation as planned by God, to Whom he refers as the "Great Architect." The text from Sirach explains that everything in creation has its opposite and that all things in the universe are created according to the Creator's standard of perfection. The Genesis text refers to the heavens and the earth that counterbalance one another and are evidence that there are no longer chaos and emptiness in the universe. Newman spells this out at the very outset of the discourse: "We know, my brethren, that in the natural world nothing is superfluous, nothing incomplete, nothing independent; but part answers to part, and all details combine to form one mighty whole. Order and harmony are among the first perfections that we observe in this creation."[252] One may ask: What does all this have to do with Our Lady? Newman makes the connection for us. He moves from a discussion of the natural order to a discussion of the supernatural order. The unity and harmony of the first creation is restored by the coming of Christ in the Incarnation which is the *nodus* of the *nexus mysteriorum*. Newman introduces this theme in the following way:

> The case is the same as regards the supernatural world. The great truths of Revelation are all connected together and form a whole. Every one can see this in a measure even at a glance, but to understand the full consistency and harmony of Catholic teaching requires study and meditation. Hence, as philosophers of this world bury themselves in museums and laboratories, descend into mines, or wander among woods or on the seashore, so the inquirer into heavenly truths dwells in the cell and the oratory, pouring forth his heart in prayer, collecting his thoughts in meditation, dwelling on the idea of Jesus, or of Mary, or of grace, or of eternity, and pondering the words of

holy men who have gone before him, till before his mental sight arises the hidden wisdom of the perfect, "which God has predestined before the world unto our glory,"[253] which He "reveals unto them by His Spirit."[254]

Newman compares the discovery of the truths of the natural order by scientists and philosophers to the discovery of monks and theologians whose meditation on the *mirabilia Dei* (the marvels of God) reveals to them the *nexus mysteriorum* in the supernatural order. A right contemplation of the economy—which admits of no contradiction between the truths of the natural and supernatural order—should lead one into the heart of the mystery of the Incarnation which encompasses within it the truth about the God-Man, His Mother and His gift of "enlightening grace," leading to salvation. Newman clearly states that his discourse is intended to show that these two persons, these two mysteries of our Faith, are indissolubly united to one another in the perfect order and harmony of the economy, as he writes: "This is simply the point which I shall insist on—disputable indeed by aliens of the Church, but most clear to her children— that the glories of Mary are for the sake of Jesus; and that we praise and bless Mary as the first of creatures, that we may duly confess Him as our sole Creator."[255]

Here, not only does Newman link the mystery of Christ the God-Man to the mystery of Mary His Mother and vice versa but the mystery of the Church is, for him, likewise indissolubly united to these two mysteries, so much so that they cannot be fully comprehended outside of her communion. Although not stated explicitly by Newman in this particular passage, one can see here a logical connection between the motherhood of the Church and the motherhood of Mary not only in terms of her physical maternity of the Church's Lord and Head but also insofar as she is the "first of creatures," and therefore first of believers and Mother of the Church. This conclusion will be made more evident at the end of this discourse.

Newman's subsequent arguments consist in a solid presentation of the Church's teaching on the Incarnation and how Marian doctrine flows directly from it. He begins his reflections by summarizing the Johannine school of thought, most especially the "high" Christology which the Prologue to John's Gospel reflects. Quoting from John 1:1,14, he chooses two verses which contain in essence the mystery of Christ's eternal, divine pre-existence in the bosom of the Father and the mystery of His Incarnation in the fullness of time by which God becomes Man and pitches His tent in our midst.[256]

Newman emphasizes that the Incarnation, as defined by the Scriptures and confirmed by the councils of the Church, is not a doctrine which is fully comprehended by many Protestants[257] because they have not fully grasped the significance of the hypostatic union, so much so that their preaching tends, not necessarily in any deliberate way, toward a reiteration of such ancient heresies as Arianism, Nestorianism and Monophysitism. What Newman knows from his personal experience as a former Evangelical and then as an Anglican is that oftentimes the preachers he heard tended "to comment on the Gospels," speaking of Our Lord "not simply and consistently as God, but as being made up of God and man, partly one and partly the other, or between both, or as a Man inhabited by a special divine presence. Sometimes they even go on to deny that he was in heaven the Son of God, saying that He became the Son when He was conceived of the Holy Ghost."[258]

One of these consequences is that many Protestants lacked a firm belief in the doctrine of Mary as Mother of God, *Theotokos-Deipara*. The contention of the Fathers and of the early councils of the Church is Newman's contention as well: The Incarnation is safeguarded by the doctrine of Mary's divine maternity. The Humanity or Manhood of Christ is inseparable from the Motherhood of Mary. If one admits that Jesus is the Son of God from all eternity and that He becomes Man in the Incarnation, then one must also admit that in becoming Man in the fullness of time, Christ became the Son of Mary according to the flesh without ceasing to be the divine Person He was from all eternity.[259] Newman writes:

> If you would bring distinctly and beyond mistake and evasion, the simple idea of the Catholic Church that God is Man, could you do it better than by laying down in Saint John's words that "God *became* Man"? and again could you express this more emphatically and unequivocally than by declaring that He was *born* a Man, or that He had a *Mother*? The world allows that God is Man; the admission costs it little, for God is everywhere, and (as it may say) is everything; but it shrinks from confessing that God is the Son of Mary.[260]

John Saward explains the essence of Newman's statements thus far by explaining how in the theology of Pope John Paul II this same notion of the "indissoluble bond" between Mary and Christ, is, in a unique way, forged at the moment of the Incarnation. Saward asserts that "the Blessed Virgin is the very air that the Pope breathes." Mary, as Saward explains, is, for the Pope, "a supremely Christocentric person, and the surest way for every person to true Christ-centeredness." Mary's "whole mission is to bring Christ to men and men to Christ." The Virgin's cooperation during Our Lord's earthly life, as the Pope considers it, is one in which "her whole personality," is involved. Mary's Immaculate Heart is totally consecrated to the love and the service of her Son's Sacred Heart. This cooperation, according to Pope John Paul, continues to be exercised in heaven. Mary's "motherly intercession" has a Trinitarian orientation directing our focus "to the Son and so to the Father in the Holy Spirit." Furthermore, "the Son of God is inseparable from the woman in whose flesh and by whose faith He became Man. . . . The Pope's Christocentricity is Marian, and his Mariology is Christocentric. . . . With the Fathers of the Second Vatican Council," he contemplates, "the Blessed Virgin Mary, Mother of God," not in isolation, but "in the mystery of Christ and the Church." In order to illustrate this Christocentricity of the Pope's Mariology, especially in regard to the centrality of Mary in the mystery of the Incarnation, Saward refers to *Redemptoris Mater* (no. 4) wherein the Pope takes "a text from *Gaudium et Spes* concerned with the Christocentricity of Christian anthropology and transforms it into an axiom for Mariology." Saward quotes from *Redemptoris Mater* (no. 4): "If it is true, as the Council itself proclaims, that 'only in the mystery of the Incarnate Word does the mystery of man take on light,' then this principle must be applied in a very particular way to that exceptional 'daughter of the human race,' that extraordinary 'woman' who became the Mother of Christ. Only in the mystery of Christ is her mystery fully clear. . . .'" Finally, Saward, citing von Balthasar, writes "that the Pope demonstrates clearly that 'the whole of Mariology belongs within Christology and can be only justified and made comprehensible by Christology.' No Christology without Mariology, no Mariology without Christology."[261]

In his sermon, Newman continues to hammer away at the

point that the Incarnation is indeed a concrete, historic event by which "the Almighty is introduced into His own world at a certain time and in a definite way." [262] Newman adamantly rejects any heretical notion of the Incarnation that the doctrine is merely a poetic, pious exaggeration or a symbolic, mystical doctrine,[263] rather than one rooted in the economy of salvation. Quoting from Hebrews 10:5, Newman cites a key Christological text which reveals Our Lord's direct conversation with the Father about the nature of the Incarnation in terms of its being a fulfillment of the Old Testament sacrifices and offerings.[264] He adds immediately another inestimable quotation from 1 John 1:1–3, which beautifully expresses the sacred author's direct knowledge of the Incarnation as a mystery that both he and his community have experienced first-hand, that is, felt, seen, contemplated, touched, heard and spoken about. Any teaching to the contrary is to be considered propaganda of the Antichrist, according to 1 John 4:2–3. Newman explains: "And the confession that Mary is *Deipara*, or the Mother of God, is that safeguard wherewith we seal up and secure the doctrine of the Apostle from all evasion, and that test whereby we detect all pretenses of those bad spirits of 'Antichrist which have gone out into the world.'"[265] After this negative or defensive evaluation, Newman then makes a positive statement saying that: "If Mary is the Mother of God, Christ must be literally *Emmanuel, 'God with us.'*"[266] The scriptural references are to Isaiah 7:14 and Matthew 1:23.[267] Father Serra explains how these two texts are have both a Christological sense and a Mariological sense, which are intrinsically linked.[268]

Newman's ecumenical audience does not inhibit him from making very direct affirmations and observations, convinced as he is that the doctrine of Mary as the Mother of God is essential to the formulation and preservation of the Church's orthodox teaching regarding the Person of Christ. Thus, Newman goes so far as to accuse the Protestants of having fallen into Christological heresy because of their refusal to accept Mary as the *Theotokos* (*Deipara*): "The Church and Satan have agreed together in this, that Son and Mother went together; and the experience of three centuries has confirmed their testimony, for Catholics who have honoured the Mother, still worship the Son, while Protestants who now have ceased to confess the Son, began then by scoffing at the Mother."[269] Newman's remarks are not intended as attacks on persons but as a firm prodding of certain persons to accept the full consequences of an orthodox confession of Christ's divinity, one essential consequence being the doctrine of the *Theotokos*. Newman prefaces his remarks to this effect by reminding his "brethren"—a term of affection—about the premise of his entire discourse, namely, "the harmonious consistency of the revealed system, and the bearing of one doctrine upon another." [270]

Returning to the prophecy of Isaiah 7:14, Newman takes up the title of his discourse by saying that "Mary is exalted for the sake of Jesus," and again "her grace and her glory are not for her own sake, but for her Maker's." Newman recaps some of the more significant points of his Mariology. He reiterates the Christological principle by which our devotion to Mary is considered "fitting," insofar as she is the most highly favored of creatures and our devotion to her is subordinated to our worship of Christ. This privileged yet subordinate position of the Blessed Mother is deemed by Newman "an office of ministration," by which she actively cooperates in the work of Redemption. Mary's "appointed office" (work, mission) in the economy of salvation is particular to her since it results from singular graces and privileges, especially because "to her is committed the custody of the Incarnation." However, as Newman notes, Mary's singular cooperation is indicative of God's will that all persons should have a "work to do," and "a mission to fulfill." [271] Both Mary's person and office are clearly recognized and venerated in the Church in her devotional life, but they should not be viewed apart from their reference to the Triune God, to the "Maker": to God the Father, Originator of the plan of salvation; to God the Holy Spirit, by Whose power her virginal womb is made physically and spiritually fecund to give birth to God the Son, "Emmanuel," with Whom she has an unparalleled intimacy as the special guardian and memorial of the mystery of His Incarnation.[272] Newman writes: "As she was on earth, and was personally the guardian of her divine Child, as she carried Him in her womb, folded Him in her embrace, and suckled Him at her breast, so now, and to the latest hours of the Church, do her glories and the devotion paid to her proclaim and defend the right faith concerning Him as God and Man." [273]

Having dwelt upon the fulfillment of the Isaiah prophecy in

Matthew's Gospel, Newman then returns to the context of the Old Testament and considers the Church's devotion to Mary under the title of the *Turris Davidica* explaining the title's Mariological significance as an expression of the doctrine of Mary *Theotokos*. Mary's divine maternity serves to protect, to defend, and to safeguard the Person, work, honor and dignity of Our Lord. Newman's comment reveals the interconnectedness among different aspects of the symbolism of the title as he emphasizes its scriptural and liturgical use. The logic of his explanation is developed. First, Newman explains that the Tower of David is "the high and strong defense of the King of the true Israel." [274] Secondly, incorporating a quotation from the Canticle of Canticles 4:4,[275] Newman makes this further comparison between the doctrine of the *Deipara* and the symbol of the *Turris Davidica*: "For consider; a defense must be strong in order to be a defense; a tower must be, like the Tower of David, 'built with bulwarks,' 'a thousand bucklers hang upon it, all the armour of valiant men.'" [276] Last, he illustrates how this image is also applied to the Virgin in the context of the Sacred Liturgy: "The Church also addresses her in the Antiphon,[277] as having 'alone destroyed all heresies in the whole world.'" [278]

Having established that the doctrine of the divine maternity is necessary as a support and safeguard of the doctrine of the Incarnation, Newman argues that the privileges of Mary, particularly her superior sanctity, are necessary according to the divine economy in order the better to sustain our devotion to the Virgin:

> It would not have sufficed, in order to bring out and impress on us the idea that God is Man, had His Mother been an ordinary person. A mother without a home in the Church, without dignity, without gifts, would have been, as far as the defense of the Incarnation goes, no mother at all. She would not have remained in the memory, or the imagination of men. If she is to witness and remind the world that God became Man, she must be on a high and eminent station for the purpose. She must be made to fill the mind, in order to suggest the lesson. When one attracts our attention, then, and not till then, she begins to preach Jesus. "Why should she have prerogatives," we ask, "unless He be God?" and what must He be by nature, when she is so high by grace? This is why she has other prerogatives besides, namely, the gifts of personal purity and intercessory power, distinct from her maternity; she is personally endowed

that she may perform her office well; she is exalted in herself that she may minister to Christ.[279]

Once again, one notices that Newman speaks of Mary's role in the economy of salvation in terms of her necessary yet subordinate office of ministration to the mystery and ministry of Jesus. Newman plainly says, in language that should have resonated in a particular way with his Evangelical and Anglican listeners, that Mary "preaches Jesus," not only insofar as she gives flesh to the Eternal Word of God but also because her life of outstanding holiness and virtue is a resounding lesson for the whole Church, indeed, for the whole of creation, of the abiding presence of that Word in our midst. Mary's perfect discipleship of the Word-made-flesh teaches us the inestimable lesson of Christian discipleship as no other creature's can. Mary's office of ministration, therefore, is one of service to the Word. However, her cooperation in the redemptive ministry of her Son is not simply exemplary; it extends beyond the earthly bounds of our imitation of her virtue, so that the Word of God, Who is Christ, may continue to be formed in us as members of His Mystical Body, the Church. She does this, in a particular way, through her mediation. As she is personally endowed with an abundance of grace, so too she acts in accord with the divine plan of salvation that we may receive a share in that abundant life of grace through her maternal intercession.

In the next section of his discourse, Newman returns to an exegesis of some significant scriptural texts concerning the privileges of Mary. As we have seen, some of these texts were already touched upon by Newman in his Anglican sermons about the Virgin, and thus can be considered texts to which he ascribes a special value in establishing a foundation for a scriptural apologetic of Mary's place in the economy of salvation. However, Newman does not hesitate to draw from the scriptural commentaries of the Fathers of the Church, such as those of Saint John Chrysostom and Saint Augustine, to lend further support to his biblical exegesis. Newman prefaces his appropriation of Chrysostom and Augustine by offering a summation of his own comments on Luke 11:27–28—to which Newman refers in other sermons, most notably, "Our Lady in the Gospel." This pericope is examined by Newman in conjunction with those of the Annunciation and the Visitation.

Newman makes several important affirmations. First, he states that Mary "has been made more glorious in her person than in her office."[280] Secondly, he writes that "her purity is a higher gift than her relationship to God."[281] What Newman means by Mary's "relationship to God" is not her spiritual relationship but her "physical" or maternal relationship to Christ. Thus, Newman explains that Our Lord's words in Luke 11:27–28 are meant to underscore the "higher blessedness" of Mary's spiritual relationship to Our Lord in regard to her purely physical or biological relationship. Newman identifies, among her many virtues, Mary's "purity" as a particular expression of that spiritual relationship. Newman explains that "this is what is implied in Christ's answer to the woman in the crowd, who cried out, when He was preaching, 'Blessed is the womb that bare thee, and the breasts which Thou hast sucked.' He responded by pointing out to His disciples a higher blessedness; 'Yea, rather, blessed,' He said, 'are they who hear the Word of God and keep it.'"[282] Newman adds an important clarification of the principle of Marian doctrine and devotion that he sees as underlying Our Lord's response in the Gospel:

> You know, brethren, that Protestants take these words in disparagement of Our Lady's greatness, but they really tell the other way. For consider them; He lays down the principle, that it is more blessed to keep God's commandments than to be His Mother; but who, even of Protestants, will say that she did *not* keep His commandments? She kept them surely, and Our Lord does but say that such obedience was in a higher line of privilege than her being His Mother; she was more blessed in her detachment from creatures, in her devotion to God, in her virginal purity, in her fulness of grace, than in her maternity. This is the constant teachings of the Holy Fathers.[283]

Newman is concerned that Our Lord's response to the woman in the crowd not be misinterpreted as a contradictory statement about the nature of Mary's faith and blessedness. On the contrary, Newman interprets Jesus' response as having not only confirmed the blessedness of His Mother in terms of her physical closeness to Him, but also in terms of its having elevated Mary's beatitude to a supernatural level whereby she is most highly blessed because of her exemplary faith and obedience to the will of God in accord with the singular role allotted to her in the work of salvation. To defend his position, Newman relies on the exegesis of Chrysostom and Augustine, as he does in "Our Lady in the Gospel"; those Fathers connect the above passage to the episodes of the Annunciation and Visitation to show that Mary indeed possessed a two-fold blessedness. The first is related to her extraordinary faith and holiness: "Full of Grace," "Blessed are you because you believed." The second is associated with her divine maternity: "Blessed are you among women." In essence, Mary's beatitude consists in her holiness in soul and body.[284] Augustine and Chrysostom confirm both. However, both Fathers are careful to emphasize that Mary's physical union with Christ as His Mother does not overshadow the truth of her spiritual communion with Christ as His most perfect disciple. While this two-fold beatitude cannot be disjoined, the physical union should be seen as a consequence of the spiritual union: "She who was chosen to supply flesh and blood to the Eternal Word, was first filled with grace in soul and body, she had a double blessedness, of office and of qualification for it, and the latter was the greater."[285] For Newman, Mary's cooperation in the economy of salvation is not merely functional, it is ontologically based.

Newman thinks it necessary to lay the foundation for the theology of Mary as New Eve through a synthetic commentary on the Genesis story of the creation of Adam and Eve and their fall from grace. Newman interprets the *Protoevangelium* (Gen 3:15), in light of Saint Paul's Letter to the Romans, in which Christ is said to be the Second (Last) Adam Whose Incarnation signals the beginning of a new creation, by which grace is made to super-abound where sin once abounded (cf. Rom 5:20). At the center of this new creation, that is, of this redemption and recapitulation of man and the universe,[286] the figure of Mary cannot be overlooked. Although she is not explicitly mentioned in the Scriptures as the New Eve, the analogy is sustained in the Tradition of the Church, most notably by the Fathers.[287] Furthermore, the doctrine of the Immaculate Conception develops the theology of the New Eve along the lines traced out in the writing of the Fathers, so that Mary's conception in the fullness of holiness and grace is seen as that first work of the new creation/redemption whereby Christ and Mary cooperate in crushing the head of the ancient Serpent.[288]

Newman explains: "Mary then is a specimen, and more than a specimen, in the purity of her soul and body, of what man was before his fall, and what he would have been, had he risen to his full perfection."[289] Does Newman limit Mary's singular holiness as New Eve to the possession of the preternatural gifts *per se* or to the perfection of those gifts as Adam and Eve would have enjoyed them before the Fall? The speculative nature of this question makes it a difficult one to answer in the present context. However, given Newman's reliance on the Fathers of the Church, for example, in the writings of Peter Chrysologus,[290] and his theology of the New Eve, then perhaps Newman could have also considered Chrysologus' theology of Adam's creation already with a view to the Incarnation of Christ the Second Adam.[291] Following the logic of Chysologus, Newman could have concluded that Mary's holiness was not only to be determined in relationship to Adam and Eve's state before the Fall, but even more importantly in relationship to the perfection of man in Christ the Perfect Man. Nevertheless, putting aside any speculative theology, once the event of the Incarnation is revealed as part of God's divine plan for our salvation, so too is Mary's role of cooperation as the New Eve and therefore her sinlessness from conception:

> The coming of the Emmanuel . . . was a season of grace and of prodigy, and these were to be exhibited in a special manner in the person of His Mother. . . . It was fitting, for His honour and glory, that she, who was the instrument of His bodily presence, should first be a miracle of His grace; it was fitting that she should triumph where Eve had failed, and should "bruise the serpent's head" by the spotlessness of her sanctity.[292]

For Newman, Mary is a miracle of grace prepared by God in view of the conception of the Author of Grace. It is interesting to note that rather than concentrating on the antithetical parallelism Eve–Mary as is more frequently found in his Mariological writings, in this sermon, Newman is concerned with a comparison between Adam's creation by God in original grace and the holiness of Mary's own Immaculate Conception.[293] Newman argues that if Adam was given all the necessary strength or grace needed to preserve him from sin, then why can we not also say that such a privilege had been extended to the Mother of the

Redeemer, the Second Adam? Indeed, all the privileges which Mary receives are fundamentally oriented toward the accomplishment of Christ's redemptive mission, in which she had been chosen to cooperate.[294]

Citing Proverbs 4:18,[295] "The path of the just, which, as shining light, goeth forward and increaseth even to the perfect day,"[296] Newman refers to the singular path of holiness and purity which the Virgin trod and which reaches a particular height at the moment of her Annunciation—the moment of her *fiat*.[297] Besides a contemplation of Mary's privileges in terms of her divine maternity, her Immaculate Conception, and her outstanding faith and personal holiness or purity, Newman also considers the privilege of Mary's intercessory power. In discussing the latter, Newman strings together a *catena aurea* of biblical citations that serve as examples of those in both Testaments who were chosen instruments of intercession (mediation) on behalf of God and His faithful: John 9:31, in which it is said that God will hear the prayer of the man who adores Him and does His will; James 5:16, which assures us that the continual prayer of the just man is heard; Genesis 20:7, wherein Abraham is asked to pray for the prophet Abimelech; Job 42:8, a reference to Job's prayer for his friends; Exodus 17:11–13, which recounts how Moses invoked the Lord with outstretched arms before commencing his battle with Amalech; John 12:20–22, the story of how the Gentiles sought after the apostle Philip so that they might gain access through him to Jesus. Newman concludes from the above texts that if all of these patriarchs, prophets and apostles could exercise an intercessory role, then Mary, who is above all the saints, most definitely possesses, to an even greater degree, a share in the power of intercession.

Newman rounds out this *catena* with a reference to Philippians 2:7, in which Saint Paul speaks of Our Lord's *kenosis* in the Incarnation, asking how, if God, the Creator of the Universe, could become a Man, then why could He not raise up a creature as holy as Mary to become the Queen of Heaven and Earth—a clear reference to the twelfth chapter of the Apocalypse.[298] The line of demarcation, however, is never lost between Creator and creature. Yes, Mary intercedes, but she intercedes as the most perfect of creatures and the Queen of Heaven and Earth; she does not intercede in the same way that Christ or the Holy Spirit intercedes on our behalf before the Father. Newman makes some other important observations when he notes that, even after Our Lord's Ascension into heaven, Mary did not assume a conspicuous role in the life of the Church, as was befitting the apostles. He explicitly says that Mary never assumed a priestly identity and that she in fact would have humbly participated in the Eucharistic Sacrifice celebrated by the apostles of the Lord. In other words, Mary is firmly rooted in ecclesial life and communion without, however, participating in the hierarchical and sacerdotal offices for which the apostles and their successors were designated. Mary's role of intercession is therefore exercised not so much on earth as in heaven where she is rightfully honored as Queen at the right hand of her Son.[299]

The apologetical thrust of Newman's sermon is three-pronged: Christological, Mariological and ecclesiological, and so he begins this next-to-last section of the sermon by showing how the Church as "oracle of divine truth" receives the divine Revelation which she in turn safeguards as the multi-faceted diamond or pearl of great price, whose "beauty" and "harmony" are only fully appreciated when observed from its many sides. The many-faceted truths of the Deposit of Faith are so inexorably linked that to remove a facet would be the equivalent of destroying the integrity of its beauty and true value as it has been entrusted to the Church by Christ and safeguarded by the Apostles and their successors. It is precisely the *nexus mysteriorum* most evident in the divine economy of salvation that fascinates believer and unbeliever alike, so much so that one is willing to sell everything to obtain this pearl of great price. The Church's teachings on the Virgin Mary, as Newman considers them, are of intrinsic value to the whole system of belief. Furthermore, "the Church's dispensation of them," under the guidance of the Holy Spirit is what allows one to appraise fully, not just in part, the singular beauty of Mary's prerogatives in the light of the Christ's splendor. All the Church's doctrines, therefore, but especially those about the Virgin, are put into their proper perspective.

Newman, taking up again the title of his sermon, writes: "There is the same careful reference to the glory of Him Who gave them [glories] to her."[300] But, how can this be illustrated in the *historia salutis*? Newman's point of departure in answering this question is Holy Writ. For Newman, the person and office of Mary in the economy of salvation manifests her willingness to cooperate in a subordinate way in the work of her Son. Newman looks to the beginning of Our Lord's public ministry and to the time before His Ascension into glory—once the saving mysteries of our Redemption had been accomplished—to show how Mary's cooperation was characterized by a holy simplicity or humility that gained its reward not in trying to interfere in Christ's singular work or by vying for the ministerial offices of Christ's apostles but rather in her heavenly exaltation. Newman's explanation takes us a step further—bearing in mind the historical development of Marian doctrine and devotion in the Early Church—by depicting Mary as exercising a sort of celestial humility whereby "she remained waiting for the time, when her own glory should be necessary for His." [301]

That concrete time would come, as Newman observes elsewhere in his writings, when the Church "the living Oracle of Truth," would show forth the beauty and interconnectedness of both Christological and Mariological truths." Newman sets up an interesting contrast between the historical preaching of the kerygma as regards the divinity of Christ and the development of the Church's understanding of Mary's role of cooperation in the economy of salvation. While the Church, for example, from the very beginning never ceased to proclaim that Jesus is God—one in substance with the Father—the truths about Mary were not as readily or explicitly preached, not because they were not always believed but rather because, as Newman explains:

> It became her, as a creature, a mother, and a woman, to stand aside and make way for the Creator, to minister to her Son, and to win her way into the world's homage by sweet and gracious persuasion. So when His name was dishonoured, then it was that she did Him service; when Emmanuel was denied, then the Mother of God (as it were) came forward; when heretics said that God was not incarnate, then was the time for her own honors. And then, when as much as this had been accomplished, she had done with strife; she fought for herself. No fierce controversy, no persecuted confessors, no heresiarch, no anathema, were necessary for her gradual manifestation; as she had increased day by day in grace and merit at Nazareth, while world knew not of her, so has she raised herself aloft silently, and has grown into her place in the Church by a tranquil influence and a natural process. [302]

Thus, the three-fold prolonged thrust of the sermon reveals Newman's keen sense of the *nexus mysteriorum*. The events of the natural order, in this case of the development of doctrine in the history of the Church, is inseparable from the supernatural and supra historical truths that are being revealed in the economy or history of salvation. Mary's role of cooperation is gradually revealed not because it did not already have importance as such; rather, the Divine Providence guided the Church in such a way that the full integrity of Mary's importance would not be made known apart from the disclosure of those truths that regarded her Son. Certainly, there exists the *nexus mysteriorum*. Nevertheless, within this interconnectedness there is also a hierarchy of truths that needs to be considered so that the multi-faceted diamond or pearl of great price is never depleted of its salvific value.

All of this is brought home to us by Newman in the next to the last section of his sermon, wherein he compares Mary's growth in grace and merit within the Church to the image of "some fair tree, stretching forth her fruitful branches and fragrant leaves, and overshadowing the territory of the saints." Newman adds to this image that of Mary as the dwelling place of God in Zion which, like a tree, establishes its roots among the people and the holy ones of Israel. Beyond that, Mary is compared to a cedar of Lebanon and to a cypress which, firmly planted on Mount Sion, extend their branches like a terebinth and whose leaves are symbols of honor and peace. These images are taken from the Book of Sirach 24:8, 10–13, 16 and were applied to the Virgin in the antiphons of the Roman Breviary of Newman's time.[303] Furthermore, Newman's use of these images in reference to the Virgin are incomprehensible apart from an understanding of the biblical theology of the Daughter of Sion[304] and its subsequent Marian application in the Tradition.[305]

Newman concludes this sermon by clearly intimating his love for and devotion to the Virgin as spiritual Mother who, through the power conceded her by God in Christ and through the Holy Spirit, intercedes on behalf of her spiritual children, so that we too might benefit from the grace that she herself received and which she now fully possesses in the glories of heaven. Mary leads us to Him, Who is the Treasure of all grace and eternal beatitude. Her glories are thus not only for the sake of her Son, but for ours as well.[306] Newman directly addresses Mary in these words:

> Such art thou, Holy Mother, in the creed and in the worship of the Church, the defense of many truths, the grace and smiling light of every devotion. In thee, O Mary, is fulfilled, as we can bear it, an original purpose of the Most High. He once had meant to come on earth in heavenly glory, but we sinned; and then He could not safely visit us, except with a shrouded radiance and a bedimmed Majesty, for He was God. So He came Himself in weakness, not in power; and He sent thee, a creature, in His stead, with a creature's comeliness and luster suited to our state. And now thy very face and form, dear Mother, speak to us of the Eternal; not like earthly beauty, dangerous to look upon, but like the morning star, which is thy emblem, bright and musical, breathing purity, telling of heaven, and infusing peace. O harbinger of day! O hope of the pilgrim! lead us still as thou hast led; in the dark night, across the bleak wilderness, guide us on to Our Lord Jesus, guide us home.
>
> > *Maria, Mater gratiæ,*
> > *Dulcis parens clementiæ.*
> > *Tu nos ab hoste protege*
> > *Et mortis hora suscipe.*[307]

This final invocation of the Blessed Virgin which brings to a close Newman's sermon reminds us of the principal points he has endeavored to make. On three occasions in his invocation, Newman affectionately addresses Mary in terms of her spiritual maternity. The first time that Mary is invoked as Mother, Newman, following the principle of *lex orandi, lex credendi* (the law of praying is the law of believing) refers to Marian doctrine and devotion in the creed and worship of the Church as the bulwark of Christological truths, so that the *nexus mysteriorum* is exemplified in the indissoluble bond that unites Christology, Mariology, and Ecclesiology. Mary's motherhood is both spiritual and physical, temporal and eternal. She is the bearer of the fullness of grace, having received the particular privilege of her Immaculate Conception in accord with the divine plan of salvation, and so Newman speaks of "an original purpose of the Most High," having been fulfilled in her. Mary's sinlessness, then, becomes, according to that same plan, the chosen means by which the Creator becomes the Son of a creature.

In the second instance, Mary, in her role as Mother, not only reminds us of the Incarnation and the saving events of her Son's earthly life but she also "speaks to us of the Eternal," that is to say, Mary our "dear Mother," is a sign of eschatological hope for her sons and daughters in the Church. As Mother of the Incarnate Word, Mary points us back to the Crib and to Calvary, while at the same time, indicating that our present pilgrimage of faith is directed to the time of our future union with Christ in heavenly glory. It is, in this sense, that we invoke Mary our Mother as "the morning star."[308] Newman's language about the *chiaro* and *scuro* ("light and dark") of our spiritual journey or pilgrimage of faith is reminiscent of the language he used in his poem commonly known as "Lead, Kindly Light,"[309] in which the Anglican Newman invokes God the Holy Spirit in the midst of the storm-tossed Mediterranean sea on his way back to England—an event which Newman considered a turning point in his conversion. On the other hand, in this *Discourse to Mixed Congregations*, the Catholic Newman quite comfortably invokes Our Mother Mary as her who can best guide us to her Son.

V. "ON THE FITNESS OF THE GLORIES OF MARY"

The next sermon to be examined is again taken from Newman's *Discourses to Mixed Congregations* and was delivered during the month of August, probably on a day close to the feast of the Assumption. Therefore, Newman preaches a sermon that is perfectly in harmony with the liturgical calendar. Furthermore, as we shall discover in this sermon Newman makes ample use of the Scriptures to show that the doctrine of the Assumption, although not explicitly revealed in the Bible, is, nonetheless, a doctrine which is implicitly contained in the Sacred Text as that passage which has been understood in light of the Church's Tradition. The *regula fidei* (the rule of faith) serves to solidify the Church's teaching on the Virgin and to integrate it with other teachings (*nexus mysteriorum*) into the seamless garment of doctrines that has been woven together by the Holy Spirit by means of a happy collaboration among Scripture, Tradition and the Magisterium. Newman recognizes the importance of the *regula fidei* as a sure guide, by which the interpretation and preaching of the Sacred

Scriptures is kept in conformity with what Sacred Tradition has already given as its proper meaning.[310]

Newman introduces his sermon by establishing a scriptural basis for what he terms the "argument of convenience."[311] The "argument of convenience"[312] in regard to Our Lord is verified, according to Newman, in the Lucan narrative of Emmaus in which Jesus tells the disciples on the road that the Messiah had to suffer and die in order to enter into His glory.[313] Newman also cites Hebrews 2:10,[314] in which it is stated that "it *became* Him," he says, "for Whom are all things, and through Whom are all things, Who had brought many sons into glory, to consummate the Author of their salvation by suffering."[315] The argument of convenience is then related by Newman to the principles of the "the *analogy* or rule of faith," and the *nexus mysteriorum*[316] of divinely revealed truths, some of which are latent in the Sacred Text and so in need of explication in preaching and in the teachings of the Magisterium. Newman believes these principles to be established within the canon of Scripture itself according to the writings of Saint Paul.[317] Newman writes:

> Elsewhere, speaking of prophesying, or the exposition of what is latent in Divine truth, he bids his brethren, exercise the gift "according to the *analogy* or rule of faith"; that is, so that the doctrine preached may correspond and fit into what is already received. Thus, you see, it is a great evidence of truth, in the case of revealed teaching, that it is so consistent, that it so hangs together, that one thing springs out of another, that each part requires and is required by the rest. This great principle, which is exemplified so variously in the structure and history of Catholic doctrine, which will receive more and more illustrations the more carefully and minutely we examine the subject, is brought before us especially at this season, when we are celebrating the Assumption of Our Blessed Lady, the Mother of God, into Heaven.[318]

Thus, Newman argues that according to the divine economy it was most convenient that Mary be assumed body and soul into heaven. As Mary shared most fully in the mystery of the Incarnation, so she participated in the fullness of heavenly glory by sharing in the full benefits of the Paschal Mystery of her Son:[319]

> We receive it on the belief of ages; but, viewed in the light of reason, it is the *fitness* of this termination of her earthly course

which so persuasively recommends it to our minds: we feel it "ought" to be; that is, "becomes" her Lord and Son thus to provide for one who was so singular and special, both in herself and her relations to Him. We find that it is simply in harmony with the substance and main outlines of the doctrine of the Incarnation, and that without it Catholic teaching would have a character of incompleteness, and would disappoint our pious expectations.[320]

Newman convinces his hearers that the doctrine of the divine maternity is a bulwark which protects the integrity of the doctrine of the Incarnation. The profundity of this great mystery of our salvation is inexhaustible. Mary not only gives her flesh and blood to the Second Person of the Blessed Trinity, but she also adheres to His Sacred Humanity, showing Christ the most affection and tenderness that a mother could possibly demonstrate to a son. Mary is enveloped by the mystery of Our Lord's Incarnation, and vice versa. It is impossible to contemplate the fullness of the mystery of the Incarnate Word without also meditating on the beautiful mystery of Mary's divine maternity. So great is this communion between Creator and creature in the Incarnation that Mary's participation in the economy of salvation includes a singular and anticipatory share in the benefits of Our Lord's Passion, Death, and Resurrection.

Newman identifies the main purpose of his sermon as showing how Marian doctrine and devotion are linked together in the history of the Church: "I will first state what the Church has taught and defined from the first ages concerning the Blessed Virgin, and then you will see how naturally the devotion which her children show her, and the praises with which they honour her, follow from it." [321]

What follows in the sermon is a review of the mysteries of Our Lord's life in the Scriptures and of the Blessed Virgin's participation in those saving events in her role as "the Mother of the Word Himself, the Word Incarnate." [322] In truth, the foundation of Mary's cooperation in the *œconomia salutis* and in a particular way of her Assumption—as the heavenly event which crowns her earthly cooperation—is Mary's divine maternity, whereby "God, in the Person of the Word, the Second Person of the All-glorious Trinity, humbled Himself to become her Son. *Non horruisti Virginis uterum*, as the Church sings, 'Thou didst not disdain the

Virgin's womb.'"[323] In a practical manner, Newman does not simply synthesize for us the facts of the infancy narratives; he expresses in devotional terms the tender emotions that those sacred mysteries have engendered in the heart of the Church throughout the ages and in his own heart. He hopes that similar emotions and devotional expressions of them will be likewise engendered in the hearts of his listeners. Newman's description of these events helps the listener to enter into the reality of the Incarnation and into the unfathomable depths of the communion between the Mother of God and her only Son.[324] The connection, therefore, between doctrine and devotion is already firmly established at the outset of his sermon. We read:

> He took the substance of His human flesh from her, and clothed in it He lay within her; and He bore it about with Him after birth, as a sort of badge and witness that He, though God, was hers. He was nursed and tended by her; He was suckled by her; He lay in her arms. As time went on, He ministered to her, and obeyed her. He lived with her for thirty years, in one house, with an uninterrupted intercourse, and with only the saintly Joseph to share with Him. She was the witness of His growth, of His joys, of His sorrows, of His prayers; she was blest with His smile, with the touch of His hand, with the whisper of His affection, with the expression of His thoughts and feelings, for that length of time.[325]

Newman then asks: "Now, my brethren, what ought she to be, what is it *becoming* that she should be, who was so favoured?" Newman answers his own question by leading us in an appreciation of the doctrine of the Assumption in light of the ancient practice by which kings manifested their love and respect toward those most intimately associated to their reigns. He illustrates this point by referring to Esther 6:1–14, which recounts that Mordecai's report about the assassination plot of two royal eunuchs saved the life of King Ahasuerus, with the result that Mordecai was duly rewarded by being crowned with a royal diadem and made to have as his attendants the most honored of the King's closest ministers (e.g., princes and presidents).[326] If this was the case with men who saved the lives of ancient, earthly kings, how much more fitting is the honor that the King of Kings shows to his Holy Mother who gave Him the gift of life? Newman explains:

So stands the case with Mary; she gave birth to the Creator, and what recompense shall be made her? What shall be done to her, who had this relationship to the Most High? What shall be the fit accompaniment of one whom the Almighty has deigned to make, not His servant, not His friend, not His intimate, but His superior, the source of His second being, the nurse of His helpless infancy, the teacher of His opening years? I answer, as the king was answered: Nothing is too high for her to whom God owes His human life; no exuberance of grace, no excess of glory, but is becoming, but is to be expected there, where God has lodged Himself, whence God has issued. Let her "be clad in the king's apparel," that is, let the fulness of the Godhead so flow into her that she may be a figure of the incommunicable sanctity, and beauty, and glory, of God Himself: that she may be the Mirror of Justice, the Mystical Rose, the Tower of Ivory, the House of Gold, the Morning Star. Let her "receive the king's diadem upon her head," as the Queen of Heaven, the Mother of All the Living, the Health of the weak, the Refuge of sinners, the Comforter of the afflicted. And "let the first amongst the king's princes walk before her," let the angels and prophets, and apostles and martyrs, and all the saints, kiss the hem of her garment and rejoice under the shadow of her throne.[327]

Newman compares the Virgin to that person who is rightfully honored by the King with a royal status, that of a Queen. He recalls a passage from 1 Kings 2:19, in which King Solomon is described as rising up from his throne to greet his mother and to pay her homage,[328] culminating in her enthronement at his right hand.[329] Newman is confident that such an exaltation is most fitting in those cases and should be deemed such in the case of the Mother of the Messiah and Lord. The Reverend Xavier Léon-Dufour, S.J., extrapolates on this title "queen mother" which, in Hebrew, is rendered *gebîrah*:

> *The queen mother*—A special role seems to be incumbent on the mother of the king, who alone and differently from his wife enjoys a special honor before the reigning princess. She is called the great lady, as was Bathsheba (1 K 15:13; cf. 2:19) or the mother of King Asa (2 Chr 15:16). This practice may clarify the appearance of maternity in the framework of royal Messianism; and it is not without interest to point out the role of the Mother of Jesus who among the devout has become "our Lady" [Notre Dame].[330]

Thus, in keeping with this pattern of the economy of salvation in Sacred Scripture, Mary is dutifully recompensed for her divine maternity in being crowned by Our Lord as Queen of Heaven and Earth, of all the Angels and Saints. The Assumption and subsequent coronation of the Virgin are appropriate ("convenient"), direct consequences of her association with the great mystery of the Incarnation. Thus, Newman addresses the congregation: "We should be prepared then, my brethren, to believe that the Mother of God is full of grace and glory, from the very fitness of such a dispensation. . . . Consider, then, that it has been the ordinary rule of God's dealings with us, that personal sanctity should be the attendant upon high spiritual dignity of place or work." [331] Can we not aptly here apply to the Assumption Eadmer of Canterbury's principle, *"Potuit plane et voluit; si igitur voluit fecit,"* [332] which he first used to defend the *sensus fidelium* regarding the Immaculate Conception? [333]

Newman describes Mary's royal status in connection with some of the titles which form part of the Litany of Loreto, such as Mirror of Justice, Mystical Rose, Tower of Ivory, House of Gold and Morning Star. He adds to these titles others: Queen of Heaven,[334] Mother of the Living,[335] Health of the Sick, Refuge of Sinners, Comfort of the Afflicted. These titles are expressions of Mary's singular "spiritual dignity of place or work," in the economy of salvation just as the prophets received "not only gifts but graces," so that their interior holiness prepared them for the particular preaching mission they received; so too before them the angels, who minister about the throne of God, are revealed by Sacred Scripture to be divided according to particular ranks,[336] corresponding to the particular degrees of holiness and "their contemplation of that Holiness upon whom they wait." [337]

Perhaps, here, it is a worthwhile digression to consider Newman's *Meditations and Devotions* that contain two separate meditations on the Marian title "Mystical Rose" (*Rosa Mystica*) for the month of Mary—one being written as a meditation on the Immaculate Conception, the other as a meditation on the Assumption. In the latter meditation, which is most pertinent to our present discussion, Newman reflects on Mary as "the most beautiful flower that ever was seen in the spiritual world." She is the mystical or hidden rose because she has been assumed body and soul into heaven and, unlike the other saints, her tomb and her relics have never been found or venerated. And so, that is, "it is by the power of God's grace that from this barren and desolate earth there have ever sprung up at all flowers of holiness and glory. And Mary is the Queen of them. She is the Queen of spiritual flowers; and therefore she is called the *Rose*, for the rose is fitly called of all flowers most beautiful." [338]

Newman's meditation on Mary as the *Domus Aurea* (House of Gold) is most scripturally based as it refers to the golden splendor of the Holy City of Jerusalem. He quotes from the Book of Revelation where "the 'City,' says Saint John, 'was pure gold, as it were transparent glass.'" [339] Newman explains that "Mary too is golden; because her graces, her virginity, her innocence, her purity, are of that transcendent brilliancy and dazzling perfection, so costly, so exquisite, that the angels cannot, so to speak, keep their eyes off her any more than *we* could help gazing upon any great work of gold." [340] Newman not only describes Our Lady as golden in terms of her possessing the perfection of beauty, holiness, virtue and grace; he also describes her as golden because she is to be considered the golden house or palace of Christ the Great King. It is from Him that she receives her queenship, splendor and heavenly glory. Newman explains:

> But why call her a *house* or *palace*? And *whose* palace? She is the house and palace of the Great King, of God Himself. Our Lord, the Co-equal Son of God, once dwelt in her. He who was her guest; nay, more than a guest, for a guest comes into a house as well as leaves it. But Our Lord was actually *born in* this holy house. He took His flesh and His blood from this house, from the flesh, from the veins of Mary. Rightly then was she made to be of pure gold, because she was to give of that gold to form the Body of the Son of God. She was *golden* in her conception, *golden* in her birth. She went through the fire of suffering like gold in a furnace, and when she ascended on high, she was, in the word of our hymn, "Above all the Angels in glory untold. Standing next to the King in a vesture of gold. [341]

What makes Mary's exaltation so appropriate is not only the fact that she is the Mother of the King of Kings and Lord of Lords, but also that she reflects in every word and action, the eloquent, luminous essence of His holiness. [342] Newman quotes from Hebrews 12:14, where the author says that "no one will see

God without holiness." Newman also cites Isaiah 6:3, wherein Isaiah has a vision in the Temple of the angels who sing, *"Sanctus, Sanctus, Sanctus Dominus Deus Sabaoth."*[343]

At this point, Newman deliberately digresses to highlight the importance of mediation in the Old and New Testaments. He convinces his audience that the Scriptures abound in examples of holy men who, by means of their holiness, give witness to the holiness of the One Who sent them to preach. Newman derives consolation from this fact since he perceives himself as having been inspired to the vocation of preaching and confessing evangelical truth on behalf of God and His faithful. Newman impresses upon his audience the important idea that the effectiveness of the prophet/preacher lies in the continuity which the Word should find in his personal life of faith.

Holiness is the best expression of the efficacy of God's prophetic word in the life of the believer, and Mary's life epitomizes this efficacy. Her bodily Assumption is the crowning of her life's fidelity to the Word of God both in thought and in deed. Mary is at the head of a long list of holy persons, among whom Newman identifies prophets, apostles, evangelists and doctors of the Church, who have cooperated in the *œconomia salutis*. He argues that one can better ascertain the nature of an individual's cooperation in the work of salvation by bearing in mind that their works are, to different degrees and according to their various personal gifts and historical circumstances, the fruit of the working of the Holy Spirit. In other words, their cooperation in the economy of salvation is not merely instrumental as though detached from their personal merits and individual lives of holiness but a truly genuine cooperation in the very holiness of God that results from their capacity to respond to God's grace in charity and in the freedom of the children of God. In the passage that follows, one should bear in mind that Newman's primary concern is with the particular divine inspiration of the writers of Sacred Scripture and only in a secondary fashion with the inspiration enjoyed by the doctors of the Church. Newman writes:

> The Divine Word is begotten in them, and the offspring has their features and tells of them. They are not like 'the dumb animal, speaking with a man's voice,' on which Balaam rode, a mere instrument of God's word, but they have "received an

unction from the Holy One, and they know all things," and "where the Spirit of the Lord is, there is liberty;" and while they deliver what they have received, they enforce what they feel and know. "We have *known and believed*," says Saint John, "the charity which God hath to us." So has it been through the history of the Church; Moses does not write as David; nor Isaias as Jeremias; nor Saint John as Saint Paul. And so of the great doctors of the Church, Saint Athanasius, Saint Augustine, Saint Ambrose, Saint Leo, Saint Thomas, each has his own manner, each speaks his own words, though he speaks the while the words of God. They speak from themselves, they speak in their own persons, they speak from the heart, from their own experience, with their own arguments, with their own deductions, with their own modes of expression. Now can you fancy, my brethren, such hearts, such feelings to be unholy? How could it be so, without defiling, and thereby nullifying, the word of God?[344]

Newman's analysis is remarkably in line with the teaching of the Second Vatican Council. In numbers 11–13 of *Dei Verbum*, the Council Fathers, while affirming that God is the ultimate author and inspiration of the Sacred Text, clearly instruct us to recognize the authentic nature of the human means by which the canonical texts of Scripture were written. The Council Fathers emphasize, for example, the importance of the sacred writers, their respective languages and their differing modes of thought and communication of the sacred truths according to their various historical and cultural circumstances. However, perhaps Newman's discussion of the personal holiness of the sacred writers in connection with the works they produced is not as fully dwelt upon in the Dogmatic Constitution as we find in this sermon.

Likewise interesting is Newman's idea in this sermon that God has used as His instruments in the work of salvation even those who can be categorized as lacking faith, or maybe even opposed to the truth, or those who preach the truth with the wrong intention and/or without proper delegation.[345] Belonging to the first and more noble list of personages are men like: Enoch,[346] Noah,[347] Moses,[348] Samuel,[349] David,[350] Job, Elijah, Isaiah, Jeremiah, Daniel, John the Baptist, the apostles Peter and Paul and John the Evangelist. Belonging to the second category are the prophet Balaam,[351] Caiaphas the High Priest,[352] and Judas

Iscariot. Furthermore, Newman makes two analogies based on ordinary life experiences and quotations from Our Lord's teaching on "false prophets," in Matthew 7:1–20 and his teaching on "A Tree and Its Fruits," in Matthew 13:33–37, to explain how unlikely it is that saints could produce unholy works. In other words, the cooperation of holy men and women in the economy/history of salvation is made evident, in part, in the writings they produce as their interior cooperation with God's grace bears fruit in an outward cooperation.[353] Newman's exegesis is very keen and insightful. What appears to be an *excursus* on the nature of prophecy is actually an introduction to a discourse on the sanctity of Mary and her divine privileges, such as her glorious and bodily Assumption, which derive from her sanctity.

Consequently, we find a most illuminating passage about Mary's singular role of cooperation: Newman sees the Virgin as directly linked in such an intimate association with the mystery of the Incarnation that her fullness of sanctity is seen both as the most precious of all the fruits of redemption and as an exemplary holiness she was able to communicate to the Redeemer Himself according to his Sacred Humanity. Mary's holiness is also the exemplar of the perfection of holiness among all other creatures redeemed by her Son. Just as she most fully participated in the life of grace by the most direct and intimate contact with the reality of Our Lord's Sacred Humanity, so too are we able, but in a notably distinct way, to cooperate in the work of salvation, in a spiritually fruitful manner, to the extent that our souls participate in the life of grace—which we receive in a unique way through reception of Our Lord's Body and Blood in Holy Communion. This passage reads as follows:

> So then is it the case of the souls; but, as regards the Blessed Mary, a further thought suggests itself. She has no chance place in the Divine Dispensation; the Word of God did not merely come to her and go from her; He did not pass through her, as He visits us in Holy Communion. It was no heavenly Body which the Eternal Son assumed, fashioned by the angels, and brought down to this lower world: no; He imbibed, He absorbed into His Divine Person, her blood and the substance of her flesh; by becoming Man of her, He received her lineaments and features, as the appropriate character in which He was to manifest Himself to mankind. The child is like the parent, and

we may well suppose that by His likeness to her was manifested her relationship to Him. Her sanctity comes not only of her being His Mother, but also of His being her Son. "If the first fruit be holy," says Saint Paul, "the mass also is holy; if the mass be holy, so are the branches." [354]

The last quotation, taken from Romans 11:16, when read in the overall context of chapter 11, is important to consider insofar as it relates to our topic of cooperation in the economy of salvation. Saint Paul—"the apostle to the Gentiles" – addressing the Christians at Rome, reminds the Gentiles in that community that they have inherited from Israel the gift of salvation prepared for in the Old Covenant. Of particular importance are the covenants made with the patriarchs. Paul views his preaching of the Gospel of Christ in the New Covenant as one of the chosen means by which this economy of salvation has continued, so that the Gentiles can consider themselves as "a wild olive shoot . . . grafted in their place . . . to share in the rich root of the olive tree." This continuity of cooperation in the economy of salvation is proof of several truths: The divine election of the Jews, for "the gifts and calls of God are irrevocable"; the triumphant power of God's mercy, especially toward the Gentiles; "the depth of the riches and wisdom and knowledge of God," namely, His "inscrutable judgments" and "unsearchable ways" in the working out of our salvation through the redemptive ministry of Christ and the apostolic ministry of the Church. Paul concludes this chapter with a doxology and so redirects our attention to God as the origin of all holiness and salvation. All cooperation in the economy, in other words, is always subordinate to the Lord's own work and can only have meaning by final reference to Him. Thus, one is able the better to understand the significance of this Pauline citation in the context of this Marian sermon.

In making these significant statements about the Blessed Mother's unique collaboration in the work of Redemption, Newman also makes the important link between her objective role in the Redemption and her subjective role, whereby she is most fittingly considered under the titles: Seat of Wisdom,[355] Gate of Heaven, Mother of Mercy, "the Mother of beautiful love and of reverential fear, of knowledge and of holy hope," [356] ". . . who has left in the Church a fragrance of cinnamon and balsam and sweetness similar to that of chosen myrrh." [357] Newman is careful to distinguish Mary's role from that of Christ, and the titles themselves help to clarify the subordinate role that Mary has in the work of salvation: "He is the Wisdom of God, she therefore is the Seat of Wisdom; His Presence is in Heaven, she therefore is the Gate of heaven; He is infinite mercy, she then is the Mother of Mercy."[358]

A solid biblical foundation for calling Mary "the Seat of Wisdom" is given by Newman in his *Meditations and Devotions*. The intimacy of the Mother-Son relationship between Our Lady and Our Lord is not only posited on the physical level but on the spiritual as well. He writes: "Mary has the title in her Litany, because the Son of God, Who is also called in Scripture the Word and Wisdom of God, once dwelt in her, and then, after His birth of her, was carried in her arms and seated in her lap in His first years. Thus, being, as it were, the human throne of Him Who reigns in heaven, she is called the *Seat of Wisdom*."[359]

Newman recalls this title's affinity to that of "Mirror of Justice" so as to underscore how, because of Mary's intimate communion with Jesus, she is given the privilege of a unique share in the sanctity of her Son the Incarnate Word and Wisdom of the Eternal Father. Furthermore, Mary's closeness to Christ inspires Newman to ask several rhetorical questions, one of which is the following: "Would He not unfold to her the solemn eternal decrees, and the purposes and will of God?"[360] In other words, Mary is no foreigner to the *œconomia salutis*. Newman concludes his meditation on the title *Sedes Sapientiæ*,[361] precisely along the lines of a comparison between Moses' cooperation in the economy of salvation and that of the Blessed Virgin. The prophet Moses had the privilege of receiving God's wisdom and revelation—seeing God face to face "now and then, from time to time." However, far greater was the nearness of the *Theotokos* to the divine Source of all Wisdom: "But Mary for thirty continuous years saw and heard Him, being all through that time face to face with Him, and being able to ask Him any question which she wished explained, and knowing that the answers she received were from the Eternal God Who neither deceives nor can be deceived."[362]

Newman proceeds in this sermon to extol Mary's holiness which, although inferior to that of her Son, her Creator and Lord, is nonetheless superior to that of all saints, indeed of all creation: "No limits, but those proper to a creature, can be assigned to the sanctity of Mary."[363] He compares Our Lady's sanctity to that of several important figures of the Bible:

> Did Abraham believe that a son should be born to him of his aged wife?[364] then Mary's faith must be held greater when she accepted Gabriel's message.[365] Did Judith consecrate her widowhood to God to the surprise of her people? much more did Mary, from her first youth, devote her virginity.[366] Did Samuel, when a child, inhabit the Temple, secluded from the world? Mary too was by her parents lodged in the same holy precincts, even at the age when children first can choose between good and evil.[367] Was not Solomon on his birth called "dear to the Lord"?[368] and shall not the destined Mother of God be dear to Him from the moment she was born? But further still; Saint John Baptist was sanctified by the Spirit before his birth;[369] shall Mary be only equal to him? is it not fitting that her privilege should surpass his? is it wonderful, if grace, which anticipated his birth by three months, should in her case run up to the very first moment of her being, outstrip the imputation of sin, and be beforehand with the usurpation of Satan?[370]

It is logical to conclude from this passage that Newman was familiar with apocryphal literature. Therefore, it is likewise comprehensible to assume that he was able to make the comparison between Samuel and Mary, based on the *Protoevangelium of James*, which has as a central theme the purity of the Virgin Mary and attributes to the Temple a prominence in the life of the Virgin, so much so that she is said to have been entrusted by Joachim and Anne to the Temple priests to be reared in virtue and taught the Law of the Lord. In like fashion, the prophet Samuel—as a young boy—was entrusted by his mother to the priests to be consecrated as a servant of the Lord. Beverly Gaventa, a Protestant professor of New Testament literature at Princeton Seminary, whose work was highly praised by the Reverend Raymond E. Brown, S. S., offers the following insights on the importance of the *Protoevangelium*:

> I intend by it [sacred purity] a shorthand version of Peter Brown's elegant depiction of Mary in the *Protoevangelium* as "a human creature totally enclosed in sacred space." Mary's purity is established by Anna's care, preserved by the Temple priests, guarded by her marriage to Joseph, confirmed during her

pregnancy, and finally maintained even as she gives birth. The unfolding drama of the *Protoevangelium* is the drama of maintaining and defending Mary's sacred purity.[371]

Newman also compares the sanctity of Mary to that of John the Baptist. In entertaining such a comparison, one should bear in mind the theological questions raised, especially by the medievals, concerning the nature of the Virgin's sanctification in comparison to that of the Baptist, questions which found a theological resolution in the formulation of the doctrine of the Immaculate Conception. Saint Thomas Aquinas' treatment of Mary's sanctification, like that of Saint Bernard's, fell short of a fully developed understanding of this teaching, partially because they based their views on the faulty biology of their time and because they did not see a way to reconcile Mary's sinlessness from conception with the Church's teachings on the universality of sin and the concomitant universal need for Redemption. Duns Scotus happily resolved the apparent dilemma by positing the notion of prevenient grace. Thus, the sanctification of the Baptist occurs at the moment of the Visitation, as Newman suggests, while that of the Virgin occurs at "the first very moment of her being," that is from the moment of conception.[372]

Having made all these necessary comparisons, Newman summarizes his argument in these words: "Mary must surpass all the saints; the very fact that certain privileges are known to have been theirs persuades us, almost from the necessity of the case, that she had the same and much higher besides. Her conception was immaculate, in order that she might surpass all the saints in the date as well as in the fulness of her sanctification."[373] Therefore, without hesitancy, Newman exhorts his audience to bear in mind the nature of the "festive season," in which they are celebrating the feast of Mary's Assumption, so that never separating doctrine from devotion, they might "offer specially to the Blessed Virgin the homage of [their] love and loyalty."[374]

Newman goes on to develop his initial theme of the *nexus mysteriorum* in the *œconomia salutis* by describing Mary's Assumption in terms of its being a miracle which God saw fit to accomplish in view of the miracle of the Incarnation and in anticipation of Christ's Second Coming. Therefore, a careful reading of Newman's sermon can lead one to infer that the first coming of the Lord as a body-soul unity and the hope of His return in glory—

body and soul– is thus linked, in Newman's thought, to Mary's conception—body and soul—in the fullness of grace, her sanctity of life and her anticipated experience of the full benefits of the Redemption through her assumption—body and soul—into the glories of heaven as a reward for her having cooperated wholly, that is, as a body-soul unity, in the economy of salvation. Hence: "It was surely fitting then, it was becoming, that she should be taken up into heaven and not lie in the grave till Christ's second coming, who had passed a life of sanctity and of miracle such as hers. All the works of God are in a beautiful harmony; they are carried on to the end as they begin." [375]

This harmony in the economy of salvation is expanded upon by Newman so that his listeners might be able to consider, in a different light, not only the rational nature of miracles in general but the fittingness of the miracle of Mary's Assumption in particular. Given the historical context in which Newman lived,[376] then Newman's philosophical and theological discussion of miracles, in the context of this apologetic discourse on the Assumption, is most illuminating. He says:

> This is the difficulty which men of the world find in believing miracles at all; they think these break the order and consistency of God's visible world, not knowing that they do but subserve a higher order of things, and introduce a supernatural perfection. But, at least, my brethren, when one miracle is wrought, it may be expected to draw others after it for the completion of what is begun. Miracles must be wrought for some great end; and if the course of things fell back again into a natural order before its termination, how could we but feel a disappointment? And if we were told that this is certainly what was to be, how could we but judge the information improbable and difficult to believe? Now this applies to the history of Our Lady. I say, it would be a greater miracle if, her life being what it was, her death was like that of other men, than if it were such as to correspond to her life. Who can conceive, my brethren, that God should so repay the debt, which He condescended to owe to His Mother, for the elements of His human body, as to allow the flesh and blood from which it was taken to molder in the grave? Do the sons of men thus deal with their mothers? Do they not nourish and sustain them in their feebleness, and keep them in life while they are able? Or who can conceive that that virginal frame, which never sinned, was to undergo the death of a sinner? Why

should she share the curse of Adam, who had no share in its fall?[377]

Furthermore, stemming from this connection with the mystery of the Incarnation, is Mary's Assumption body and soul into heaven. Newman returns to the argument of convenience and maintains that it was most fitting that the Virgin's body be preserved from all sin and corruption due to sin since it was from that same body that the Son of God took flesh, was nurtured, and grew into manhood. Referring to Genesis 3:19, Newman explains that Mary, unlike sinful Adam, would not have her body reduced to dust and ashes but glorified in accord with the merits that flow from her singular participation in the *historia salutis* and, more specifically, in Our Lord's Passion, Death and Resurrection.[378]

Newman then occupies himself with the question of the death of Our Lady. Did Mary actually experience a physical death? Newman seems to think that she did indeed experience a physical death—not as consequence of sin—but as a participation in the Lord's Death and as it would be considered the end of the normal course of her human existence. Nevertheless, Newman argues that because Mary enjoyed the privilege of the Immaculate Conception and lived a life free from all sin, her holiness would, according to the divine economy of salvation, have been fittingly rewarded with a physical death without corruption. He explains:

> She died, then, as we hold, because even Our Lord and Saviour died; she died, as she suffered, because she was in this world, because she was in a state of things in which suffering and death are the rule. She lived under their external sway; and, as she obeyed Caesar by coming for enrolment to Bethlehem, so did she, when God willed it, yield to the tyranny of death, and was dissolved into soul and body, as well as others. But though she died as well as others, she died not as others die; for, through the merits of her Son, by Whom she was what she was, by the grace of Christ which in her had anticipated sin, which had filled her with light, which had purified her flesh from all defilement, she was also saved from disease and malady, and all that weakens and decays the bodily frame. Original sin had not been found in her, by the wear of her senses, and the waste of her frame, and the decrepitude of years, propagating death.[379]

There has been much debate throughout the centuries concerning the question of Mary's death, so much so that when Pope Pius XII defined the doctrine of the Assumption in 1950, he did not include in the official bull of promulgation any statement about the exact manner of Mary's earthly passing.[380] Newman is firm in his belief (a theological opinion) that Mary indeed died although, as he remarks, she did so "in a hidden way." The Eastern Churches tend to hold that Mary fell asleep—hence, the word "dormition" , or in Greek Κοιμῄσις—and that this falling asleep constituted her death. In the West, some theologians hold, as did Newman, that Mary experienced a physical death; others maintain that Mary was raptured into heaven while still alive.[381]

In any case, the Church has not solemnly defined nor holds as doctrine any particular theological opinion about the issue of Mary's death.[382] Newman would probably argue that it was most convenient or fitting that she would have experienced physical death so that she might be conformed to Christ in this way, thus sharing in His triumph over death and its corruption. Newman maintains that although Mary suffered during her physical life, her suffering was mostly relegated to the realm of the spiritual rather than the physical. However, Newman's language, if not properly understood, could lead one to believe that a quasi-dualistic principle is presupposed in his thought, by which Mary is considered immune from physical pain but not from spiritual suffering.

Newman, in his *sermon note* for August 15 (Eleventh Pentecost) entitled "Of Our Lady As in the Body," writes: "It was becoming that she who was *inviolata, intemerata*, should have no wound."[383] One should notice how Newman's phrasing, "it was becoming," is indicative of his preference for the "argument of convenience"—most commonly used as one of the theological arguments to substantiate the Marian doctrines of the Immaculate Conception and the Assumption. Also worthy of remark is how Newman ties together Mary's immunity from sin (and so, his use of the adjectives *inviolata, intemerata*) and her immunity from physical harm—("No wound"). Again, we read: "And hence she brings before us the remarkable instance of a soul suffering, yet not the body."[384]

Furthermore, this tension between body and soul is explicated in Newman's pious conjecture concerning Mary's last days: "It was a *contest* between body and soul. The body was so strong, the soul so desirous to see God. No disease could kill that body. What killed it? The soul, that it might get to heaven." [385] Certainly, Newman distinguishes between the physical suffering of the martyrs and the spiritual martyrdom of Mary *iuxta crucem* and that of other saints. Likewise, he admits that the sword of suffering (prophesied by Simeon) indeed pierced Mary's heart, causing her "mental pains like bodily." Nevertheless, Newman's piety leads him to describe Mary as having "died from love" not, of course, as a consequence of sin, but because her death is a sign that, although freed from any and all corruption due to sin, she was able, in accord with her own spiritual disposition and heavenly aspiration, to reap the full benefits of the Redemption by participating in the mystery of Our Lord's dying and rising. Thus, for Newman, belief in Mary's physical death, her participation—body and soul—in the sufferings of Our Lord (i.e., her *compassio*) and in the doctrine of her Assumption are in no way opposed. Newman concludes his *sermon note* thus: "Hence (it was) fitting that, when she did get loose, her Son should not let the body be so overmatched and overcome, but at once that the soul had got the victory, He raised up the body without corruption. Our Advocate in Heaven." [386]

"On the Fitness of the Glories of Mary" is a confirmation of the aforementioned distinctions and succeeds in drawing a clear line of demarcation between Our Lord's Death on the Cross and Mary's painless passing. In the first place, Newman says that Our Lady did not die as a martyr, as did her Son for our expiation. Following this logic, one is led to believe that Newman would not have considered Mary's cooperation in the economy of salvation to be best described in relation to the title our Co-Redemptrix if, by that title, one intends to assert that Mary's cooperation is equally as important as the singular act of Redemption that occurs through the shedding of Jesus' Blood on the Cross. Thus, the major theological distinction is soteriological in nature. Mary's death cannot merit our salvation as the death of Christ merited it. Christ alone is our Redeemer and Savior. Mary's death constitutes, in Newman's view, the natural end of her earthly pilgrimage and is most fitting, insofar as it points to her conformity to her Son. Newman would hold that Mary died a physical death in union with the physical death of her Son. However, even though Mary does not die a martyr's death, she is the Queen of Martyrs by virtue of her unique participation in the sufferings of Christ and in the glory of His Resurrection.[387]

Her physical incorruption is a link between the two doctrines of the Immaculate Conception and the Assumption. Mary's Assumption, like her Immaculate Conception, is an anticipated participation in the infinite, salvific merits of her Son's Paschal Mystery. As she was united to her Son most fully in life and therefore free from sin, so should she be most fully united to Him in her earthly passing and therefore not undergo the corruption due to sin. Secondly, the Assumption is the crowning of Mary's life of holiness and faith and, in this sense, it can be understood as the crowning of her merits:

> She died, but her death was a mere fact, not an effect; and, when it was over, it ceased to be. She died that she might live, she died as a matter of form or (as I may call it) an observance, in order to fulfil, what is called, the debt of nature,—not primarily for herself or because of sin, but to submit herself to her condition, to glorify God, to do what her Son did; not however as her Son and Saviour, with any suffering for a special end; not with a martyr's death, for her martyrdom had been in living; not as an atonement, for man could not make it, and One had made it, and made it for all; but in order to finish her course, and to receive her crown.[388]

This passage is of essential importance for a more precise comprehension of Newman's thought on Mary's cooperation in the economy of salvation. Newman fully adheres to the Church's teaching on the Assumption and even takes it upon himself to address some issues that, while certainly worthy of theological speculation, have never been officially decided upon by the Magisterium. Newman suggests that what he holds as a private theologian finds ample support in the Tradition of the Church and therefore could be an argument put forth with strong conviction. He also entertains the question of where and when Mary died—apparently relying on the Apocryphal Gospels and the *Transitus Mariæ*.[389] Although Newman does not explicitly acknowledge his reliance on these sources, it would be a reasonable opinion that Newman must have been familiar with them, given the non-biblical data about Mary's death that he recounts.

He does not hesitate to present this information in an authoritative manner which bespeaks not only his familiarity with the sources of the Tradition but also his own personal spiritual devotion nourished by a contemplation of the Virgin's death and resurrection.

He begins by noting that Mary died in silence as she had so humbly lived in obscurity. Furthermore, Newman contrasts the *fittingness* of her silent passing to the *fittingness* of the public ignominy of Our Lord's Death on Calvary. This contrast is not presented by Newman as a historical fact but as belying an important theological distinction between Mary's cooperation in the work of Redemption and Christ's singular redemptive act. Newman explains Mary's silent passing by way of allusion to his theology of the New Eve—hence, also to her title of Mystical Rose:

> And therefore she died in private. It became Him Who died for the world, to die in the world's sight; it became the Great Sacrifice to be lifted up on high, as a light that could not be hid.[390] But she, the lily of Eden, who had always dwelt out of the sight of man, fittingly did she die in the garden's shade, and amid the sweet flowers in which she had lived. Her departure made no noise in the world.[391]

Newman then puts together an account of Mary's Assumption after her death "in private" based, it would seem, on the apocryphal literature. He situates Mary's quiet passing in the context of the wide-spread early persecutions of the Church and the consequent death of the martyrs. Once "the rumour spread abroad that the Mother of God was no longer upon earth,"[392] Christian pilgrims from all over came in search of "her relics but they found them not."[393] Newman's theology, as is proper to reiterate especially for ecumenical purposes, includes not only the firm belief in Mary's bodily Assumption but also explains, according to what he is convinced is a proper application of the theological principle or argument of convenience, that the Blessed Virgin first fell asleep in death. Just as Newman's speculation leaves open the question of Mary's death, so too does it leave open the question concerning the location of Mary's earthly passing insofar as he recalls, following the two most ancient traditions, that since the "reports varied," that it most likely occurred either at

Ephesus or at Jerusalem. Similarly, Newman's account makes room for the question of whether or not the pilgrims found Mary's tomb.

However, one must be careful about the details of Newman's story since he immediately bases it on the one tradition that has Mary's Assumption occurring after two events, namely, first the pilgrims are said to have inspected the tomb and instead of finding her body, they found lilies in its place; second, Newman's account, incorporating the apocryphal tradition's reliance on the Jewish notion that at death the soul leaves the body and lingers about the body of the just man,[394] speaks of the time for Mary's soul "to pass in triumph before the judgment-seat of her Son," and the apostles being miraculously reunited from their various places and gathered about her tomb—some, curiously, however, remaining[395] in "the Holy City" of Jerusalem—to witness "the joyful ceremony."[396] After Our Lady had been in the tomb for three days in imitation of Our Lord, says Newman, the apostles return to the tomb, find the tomb empty and hear choirs of angels "singing night and day the praises of their Queen."[397] He concludes his narrative by saying:

> But, however we feel towards the details of this history (nor is there anything in it which will be unwelcome or difficult to piety), so much cannot be doubted, from the consent of the whole Catholic world, and the revelations made to the holy souls, that, as is befitting, she is, soul and body, with her Son and God in heaven, and that we are enabled to celebrate, not only her death, but her Assumption. Whatever would be our reaction to the details of this story . . . that it was convenient (fitting), that Mary now is found body and soul, with her Son and God, in heaven, for whom we can celebrate not only her death but also her Assumption.[398]

Newman ends this sermon by making a heartfelt appeal to his "mixed congregation," whose members he affectionately terms, "my dearest sons and young people," by charging them to lay claim to an affectionate and integrated devotion to their Heavenly Mother and Queen. He exhorts them to find consolation in the doctrines of the Immaculate Conception and the Assumption because together they point the way to hope for salvation. Newman reassures us that our faith in the power of Christ's Death and Resurrection, as is most effective in the life of the Virgin, should allay any fear we have of death—our mortal destiny—and strengthen our resolve in our daily struggle against sin. Our Lord's triumphant victory over sin and death, in which Our Lady participates and actively cooperates, is a victory in which we also hope to share as we follow her example.

Furthermore, Newman says that what was fitting for Mary as the highest of all creatures is also fitting for us, that is, that we should be without sin and come to share in the joy of the Lord's Resurrection. He reminds his congregation that "her glories are not only for her Son: her glories also touch us." [399] He proceeds by urging his "dear brethren" to imitate the virtues of the Virgin, as made evident in the Sacred Scriptures. Newman reflects on the mysteries of Mary's life recounted in Sacred Scripture in a cursory way, so that one is reminded of the style used by Pope Paul VI in *Marialis Cultus*, no. 57. He mentions: Mary's patience in listening to the Angel Gabriel's message;[400] her obedience in giving birth to Our Lord in Bethlehem under very extreme conditions;[401] her spirit of meditation which has her reflecting on the mysteries of her Son's life;[402] her fortitude in experiencing the piercing of a sword of sorrow;[403] her abandonment to God in separating from her Son, so that He might accomplish His saving mission and in standing beneath the cross of her Son;[404] her purity, especially insofar as she preserved her virginity and was willing to do so even to the point of questioning the Angel.[405]

Newman writes:

> And now, my dear brethren, what is befitting in us, if all that I have been telling you is befitting in Mary? If the Mother of Emmanuel ought to be the first of creatures in sanctity and in beauty; if it became her to be free from all sin from the very first, and from the moment she received her first grace to begin to merit more; and if such as was her beginning such was her end, her conception immaculate and her death an assumption; if she died, but revived, and is exalted on high; what is befitting in the children of such a Mother, but an imitation, in their measure, of her devotion, her meekness, her simplicity, her modesty, and her sweetness? Her glories are not only for the sake of her Son, they are for our sakes also. Let us copy her faith, who received God's message by the angel without a doubt; her patience, who endured St. Joseph's surprise without a word; her obedience, who went up to Bethlehem in the winter and bore Our Lord in a stable; her meditative spirit, who pon-

dered in her heart what she saw and heard about Him; her fortitude, whose heart the sword went through; her self-surrender, who gave Him up during His ministry and consented to His death.[406]

Newman's final words to his "dear children, young men and women," is a reinforcement of much of what he has previously said concerning the doctrines of the Immaculate Conception and the Assumption, which are expressive of the privileges and honors paid to her by her Son, but also reflective of those virtues, especially her virginal purity, which Christians should strive to imitate so as to share in her celestial glory. Newman encourages his audience not merely to imitate the Virgin but also to ask her intercession as Mother and Queen, so that she might accompany them as they strive to conform themselves to Christ in imitation of her who most closely resembles His beauty and holiness among all creatures. The exhortation is a fine instance of Newman's uncanny ability to harmonize doctrine and devotional expressions.[407] He concludes this sermon thus:

> Above all, let us imitate her purity, who, rather than relinquish her virginity, was willing to lose Him for a Son. O my dear children, young men and women, what need have you of the intercession of the Virgin-Mother, of her help, of her pattern, in this respect! What shall bring you forward in the narrow way, if you live in the world, but the thought and patronage of Mary? What shall seal your senses, what shall tranquillise your heart, when sights and sounds of danger are around you, but Mary? What shall give you patience and endurance, when you are wearied out with the length of the conflict with evil, with the unceasing necessity of precautions, with the irksomeness of observing them, with the tediousness of their repetition, with the strain upon your mind, with your forlorn and cheerless condition, but a loving communion with her! She will comfort you in your discouragements, solace you in your fatigues, raise you after your falls, reward you for your successes. She will show you her Son, your God and your all. When your spirit within you is excited, or relaxed, or depressed, when it loses its balance, when it is restless and wayward, when it is sick of what it has, and hankers after what it has not, when your eye is solicited with evil and your mortal frame trembles under the shadow of the tempter, what will bring you to yourselves, to peace and to health, but the cool breeze of the Immaculate and

the fragrance of the Rose of Sharon?[408] It is the boast of the Catholic Religion, that it has the gift of making the young heart chaste; and why is this, but that it gives us Jesus Christ for our food, and Mary for our nursing mother? Fulfill this boast in yourselves; prove to the world that you are following no false teaching, vindicate the glory of your Mother Mary, whom the world blasphemes, in the very face of the world, by the simplicity of your own deportment, and the sanctity of your words and deeds. Go to her for the royal heart of innocence. She is the beautiful gift of God, which outshines the fascinations of a bad world, and which no one ever sought in sincerity and was disappointed. She is the personal type and representative image of that spiritual life and renovation in grace, "without which no one will see God."[409] Her spirit is sweeter than honey, and her heritage is sweeter than the honeycomb. They that eat her shall yet be hungry, and they that drink her shall thirst. Whoso hearkeneth to her shall not be confounded, and they that work by her shall not sin.[410]

VI. THE PURIFICATION OF MARY[411]

The next sermon to be examined is the last of fifteen sermons Newman preached before the University of Oxford with this one being delivered on 2 February 1843, the Feast of the Purification of Mary. It deals primarily with the relationship between faith and reason and was considered as the foundational text for his later magnum opus, *An Essay on the Development of Christian Doctrine*. The reader will recall the earlier treatment of this work in relationship to the development of Marian doctrine in Chapter One.[412]

For our Mariological purposes, an analysis of first three paragraphs of the sermon in which Newman compares the faith of Mary to the lack of faith expressed by the doubt of Zachariah will suffice. In analyzing these three brief paragraphs, the aim is to explain Newman's theological insights into the Scriptures in light of some contributions of modern biblical scholarship and the Magisterium. John Brit contextualizes Newman's use of Scripture in this sermon vis-à-vis his rather scarce use of it in *An Essay on the Development of Christian Doctrine*: "Newman used Scripture as an example of a deeper sense through which the implication of Mary's act would be understood and developed."[413]

The primary act of Mary upon which Newman focuses in this sermon is the contemplation of the divine mysteries of salvation as she experienced them and cooperated in them in the various events of her life. However, before Newman directly deals with Mary's contemplation as such, or rather, as Luke highlights this contemplation in 2:19 and 2:51, he begins his sermon by referring to two scriptural events, which precede those recounted in the two aforementioned passages of Luke, wherein Mary is not only described as contemplating the Divine Revelation but also as actively interacting with the divine messenger by posing him questions. Furthermore, Mary's active contemplation of the Angel's message at the Annunciation is complemented by the active contemplation of Mary and her role in the economy of salvation on the part of those to whom those sacred events are recounted by her, such as on the occasion of her visitation to Elizabeth. Newman begins his sermon thus:

> Little is told us in Scripture concerning the Blessed Virgin, but there is one grace of which the Evangelists make her the pattern, in a few simple sentences—of faith. Zacharias questioned the Angel's message, but "Mary said, Behold the handmaid of the Lord; be it done to me according to thy word." Accordingly Elizabeth, speaking with an apparent allusion to the contrast thus exhibited between her own highly, favoured husband, righteous Zacharias, and the still more highly-favoured Mary, said, on receiving her salutation, "Blessed art thou among women, and blessed is the fruit of thy womb; Blessed is she that believed for there shall be a performance of those things which were told her from the Lord." [414]

Newman's opening reflections immediately establish Mary as a model of faith who, filled with grace, pronounces her *fiat* at the Annunciation. The Angel's greeting of the Virgin is seconded by the greeting of Elizabeth. The words of Elizabeth confirm Mary's exemplary faith, praising both her divine maternity and her trust in the fulfilment of the Lord's promises to her.

Newman further illustrates these truths by having recourse to those Scriptures in which Mary is described by the evangelists as having pondered in the depths of her being the meaning of the salvific mysteries in which she was given the grace of a particular cooperation:

But Mary's faith finds not end in a mere acquiescence in divine providences and revelations: as the text informs us, she "pondered" them. When the shepherds came, and told of the vision of Angels which they had seen at the time of the Nativity, and how they had seen at the time of the Nativity, and how one of them announced that the Infant in her arms was "the Saviour, which is Christ the Lord," while others did but wonder, "Mary kept all these things, and pondered them in her heart." Again, when her Son and Saviour had come to the age of twelve years, and had left her for awhile for His Father's service, and had been found, to her surprise, in the Temple, amid the doctors, both hearing them and asking them questions, and had, on her addressing Him, vouchsafed to justify His conduct, we are told, "His mother kept all these sayings in her heart." And accordingly, at the marriage-feast in Cana, her faith anticipated His first miracle, and she said to the servants, "Whatsoever He saith unto you, do it." [415]

In order for Mary to pronounce her *fiat* and to do so again, in a certain sense, at the Wedding Feast of Cana and still further reiterate that "yes" throughout the rest of Our Lord's earthly life and ministry until she would give her silent consent to His self-immolation on Calvary, Mary could not merely passively allow those saving events to happen to her without also actively desiring to contemplate the mysteries of the Lord and their meaning in her own life, in the life of her people Israel, and in the life of her Son and of His Church. Therefore, as the evangelists tell us, Mary cultivated the art of listening—which is an act that is both passive and active in nature. This means that she cultivated the art of obedience to God's Word, Will and Law, not in any superficial sense, but by means of a profound meditation and dialogue with God whereby she was able to assimilate in her sacred memory the evangelical truth and its significance for the economy of salvation. [416]

The Reverend Alonso Luis Schökel, referring to the Second Vatican Council's Dogmatic Constitution on Divine Revelation, explains that Mary's cooperation in the history of salvation, which entailed her most profound contemplation of the mysteries of faith from the beginning to the end of her life, is likewise, indicative of the way in which those same mysteries have been meditated upon in the Church's Tradition. [417]

The Reverend Stefano De Fiores, in light of *Marialis Cultus*

37, explains the interconnection between the active and passive elements of Mary's ongoing spiritual dialogue with God as an integral aspect of her cooperation in the economy of salvation. Indeed, her *fiat* is exemplary of the *fiat* of Israel and of each individual believer in the history of God's covenant with man.[418]

The importance of memory in the history of salvation is illustrated in the ratification of the first covenant with Israel after the events of the Exodus—recounted, for example, in Deuteronomy 4:9, 23—as the Israelites in the Babylonian exile are exhorted not to forget the covenant (*berît*) made on Mount Sinai.[419] This sacred memory, as Serra explains, (*zikkaron* in Hebrew, *anamnesis* in Greek) is that faculty which, pertaining to the whole people of Israel and to the Church throughout salvation history, is personified in Mary.[420] Serra speaks about the dynamic memory of Mary by which she recalls (*symballousa*) the events (mysteries) of Jesus' life in which she cooperates so as to give to them a personal interpretation, explanation and exegesis.[421] Serra, citing Henri de Lubac, confirms the ecclesial meaning of sacred memory and how Mary's is the ecclesial figure which *par excellence* exercises this collective, sacred memory within and on behalf of the Church.[422]

In this Oxford University Sermon, Newman first briefly introduces the reader to the Mary–Zechariah comparison. Secondly, he concentrates on the figure of Mary portrayed in Luke 2:19–51 as she ponders the meaning of all those things, most especially the mysteries of her's Son life and ministry, giving as examples three events: the Visitation of the Shepherds to the Manger, the Finding in the Temple, and the Wedding Feast at Cana. In doing so, Newman's brief mention of the Cana episode in the context of this sermon underscores Mary's command to the servants, "Do whatever He tells you," as a clear sign of the Blessed Virgin's share in divine wisdom which results from her obedience to her Son and her intimate association with His redemptive mission. Newman also contrasts Mary's silent meditation on these occasions[423] to the shepherds whose joyous account of the Lord's birth leads to utter amazement on the part of those who heard their message.[424]

Although Newman does not say as much, he must have also perceived the subtle contrast between Mary's silent meditation on these mysteries[425] and the jubilant praise and preaching of the shepherds upon their departure.[426] He likewise points out the affinity between the pericope of the Finding in the Temple and that of the Wedding Feast at Cana. After Mary finds Jesus in the Temple and is told by Him that He had to be about His Father's business, Mary returns home to contemplate the meaning of those words and the events that transpired in Jerusalem on that occasion.[427] Newman then writes: "And accordingly, at the marriage-feast in Cana, her faith anticipated His first miracle and she said to the servants: 'Whatever He saith unto you, do it.'"[428]

Father Serra's exegesis of the Cana pericope illustrates the similarity between the words spoken by the people of Israel to Moses to ratify the covenant on Mount Sinai: "What the Lord has said, we shall do" (Ex 19:8; 24:3, 7.) and the response of the Virgin at the Wedding Feast at Cana: "Do whatever he tells you," which marks the beginning of Christ's public ministry—the beginning of the new and everlasting covenant. Serra explains that Mary's role at Cana can be understood in terms of a feminine personification of the role of ancient Israel in her messianic expectations. Mary's *fiat* at Cana is pronounced in the name of God's people Israel in accepting the new wine of the Gospel, which fulfills and surpasses the water of the Mosaic law, for example as concerns the Jewish laws of purification.[429]

Last, Newman returns to the parallel between Zechariah and Mary to substantiate his principal point that Mary listens and obeys God but also reflects and meditates on the truths revealed to her as they contain not only the mystery of the Lord's work of Redemption but also the mystery of her cooperation in that work:

> Thus, Saint Mary is our pattern of faith, both in the reception and in the study of Divine Truth. She does not think it enough to accept, she dwells upon it; not enough to submit to the Reason, she reasons upon it; and not indeed reasoning first, and believing afterwards, with Zacharias, yet first believing without reasoning, next from love and reverence, reasoning after believing. And thus she symbolizes to us, not only the faith of the unlearned, but of the doctors of the Church also, who have to investigate, and weigh, and define, as well as to profess the Gospel; to draw the line between truth and heresy; to anticipate or remedy the various aberrations of wrong reason; to combat pride and recklessness with their own arms; and thus to triumph over the sophist and the innovator.[430]

Zechariah is contrasted with Mary because he expressed an initial doubt for which he was made mute, while the Virgin listened and accepted with faith the divine revelation and then later reflected on its meaning in the depths of her heart.[431] There is also a subtle contrast, to which Newman does not make explicit reference, but which is implicitly hinted at, namely, that Zechariah represents the learned priests while Mary represents the common folk, and still, that it would have been expected that a priest would have been wiser and more prudent in his response to the Angel than a young maiden from Nazareth.

Newman posits the fault of Zechariah in the fact that he tried to use reason—before consenting in faith. On the other hand, Mary's question to the Angel does not betray any sort of doubt but reveals her sense of integrity in keeping her vow of virginity and her ability to allow head and heart to work together in consenting to the obedience of faith.[432] Because of her obedience of faith and her contemplation of the divine mysteries, Mary can be called the model of faith for the simple and the learned alike. Mary is the first exegete of those mysteries which are later reflected upon and described by the inspired authors of the New Testament.

What Newman says in this sermon on the verge of his conversion to Catholicism is made even clearer in his meditation on Mary's title *Sedes Sapientiæ*.[433] Newman is quite effusive in his praise of Mary's wisdom in this meditation. He writes about Mary as having been so close to her Son during her earthly life that her conversations with the Divine *Sophia* Incarnate afforded her such a depth of knowledge that it paralleled the depth of her sanctity and could be conceived as having surpassed "in her knowledge of creation, of the universe, and of history . . . the greatest of philosophers, and in her theological knowledge the greatest of theologians, and in her prophetic discernment the most favoured of prophets."[434] He proceeds in this meditation to pose an array of questions, by which he is then able to speculate about the nature of Mary's extraordinary share in divine wisdom and knowledge.

Newman asks: "What was the grand theme of conversation between her and her Son but the nature, the attributes, the Providence, and the works of Almighty God?[435] Indeed, Mary's wisdom penetrates to the very heart of the queen of all sciences (i.e., theology), insofar as she was able to engage not simply in the study of truths about God but to study God with God as He indeed "was carried in her arms and seated in her lap," as "He was under her rule . . . lived with her in her house, til He went forth to preach—that is, for at least a whole thirty years." [436] Newman does not merely situate Mary at the center of the *œconomia salutis* in direct collaboration with her Son, but he speculates about Mary's wisdom and knowledge in such a way as to suggest that Our Lord revealed unto her even "the solemn eternal decrees, and the purposes, and the will of God. . . ." [437] One should not think Newman to have ascribed to Mary a certain type of secret *gnosis*. Newman's speculation follows the logic of the argument of convenience, which is, in effect, the logic of God not the logic of man; Newman believes that Mary's particular *cor ad cor loquitur* with her divine Son involved a type of enlightenment in matters doctrinal and otherwise that came from a kind quasi-prevenient grace,[438] by which she obtained that knowledge and love of divine truths which would only later be fully expounded on and defined by the apostles and their successors.

Newman's speculation in describing Mary's wisdom and knowledge can be perhaps considered excessive when he writes that: "All that is obscure, all that is fragmentary in revelation, would, so far as the knowledge is possible to man, be brought out to her in clearness and simplicity by Him Who is the Light of the World," [439] since it would seem to suggest *prima facie* that Mary understood Divine Revelation in a fuller sense than is actually understood by the Church. However, such a query with Newman should be taken up in light of what he writes in the *Letter to Pusey*.[440]

Reflecting upon Mary's presence at Pentecost and her reception of the gift of the Holy Spirit together with the apostles, Newman never once suggests that Mary shared in the magisterial authority of the apostles and their successors. Furthermore, Newman never posits anything contrary to the Church's teaching concerning the completion of Divine Revelation with the death of the last apostle. Perhaps, then, any insights of Mary into the content of the Deposit of Faith which she received from Our Lord were actually insights that were confirmed only after the Resurrection and her reception of the Pentecostal Spirit together with the apostles. Therefore, Newman's underscoring the particular spiritual communion that Mary and John shared, especially from the foot of the Cross to the day of Mary's earthly departure, might serve as the missing link between what she was taught by Our Lord during his thirty years at Nazareth and the subsequent confirmation and illumination in what she would learn from Saint John and the other apostles.[441]

Finally, perhaps, the words of the Holy Father Pope John Paul II are most instructive and useful in bringing out what Newman is truly hinting at in his sermon, namely, that Mary's sacred memory was not something which she hoarded for herself; rather, her sacred memory is an ecclesial memory which acts as a *chiave di lettura* ("key to the reading of documents") of the history of salvation even until the present time in which she continues to exercise her maternal care for the Church. Mary's memory is the memory of the Church; her contemplation of the sacred mysteries of our Faith as revealed by God in the Sacred Scriptures and in Sacred Tradition is paradigmatic of the Church's own contemplation, occurring from within the depths of the mystery of Christ and the Church,[442] not as parallel to it.

The Holy Father prays to Our Lady: "Tu sei memoria della Chiesa! La Chiesa impara da te, Madre, che essere Madre vuol dire essere una viva memoria, vuol dire 'serbare e meditare nel cuore' le vicende degli uomini e dei popoli, le vicende gioiose e quelle dolorose...."[443]

SUMMARY OF CHAPTER TWO

1) Newman's Evangelical and Anglican background provided him with a profound love of the Sacred Scriptures, as is most clearly evident, for example, in his *Parochial and Plain Sermons*.

2) Newman's hermeneutical/exegetical principles stemmed in part from his deep appreciation of the literal and allegorical interpretation of Scripture in the ancient schools of Antioch and Alexandria, to which the writings of the Fathers (e.g., Saint John Chrysostom; Saint Athanasius of Alexandria) bore for him a most noble witness.

3) His reading of Sacred Writ is closely bound up with his belief in Divine Providence, the fundamental unity of Scripture (Old and New Testaments), the *nexus mysteriorum* in the *œconomia*

salutis, and a theological and pastoral sense of the hierarchy of truths.

4) The Christocentricity of the Word of God necessarily calls into focus for Newman and thus also for his congregation the centrality of Mary's cooperation in the mysteries of her Son's salvific life and mission and in the whole of *historia salutis*.

5) Newman's Catholic sermon, "Our Lady in the Gospel," is primarily a reflection on the Lucan pericope concerning the macarism of the anonymous woman in the crowd (Lk 11: 27f.) that highlights the two-fold nature of Mary's blessedness, namely, her obedience of faith and her divine maternity in accepting the message of the Angel at the Annunciation.

6) "The Annunciation. The Honour Due to the Blessed Virgin," Newman's first Marian sermon as an Anglican, is noteworthy among many things for its particular emphasis on the importance of venerating Mary, both in accord with the veneration shown her in the Sacred Scriptures and as fulfillment of her own prophecy in the *Magnificat* that "all generations will call me blessed."

7) "The Reverence Due to the Virgin Mary" is most striking for its treatment of Mary's extraordinary sanctity in light of the scriptural data and insofar as the Anglican Newman postulates Mary's sinlessness, without however fully espousing the Catholic doctrine of the Immaculate Conception.

8) "The Glories of Mary for the Sake of Her Son" is a Discourse to Mixed Congregations, in which Newman exhorts his listeners to contemplate the mystery of Mary's divine maternity and to invoke her maternal intercession since these two fundamental aspects of her cooperation are clearly expressed in the prophecies of the Old Testament and in the writings of the New Testament.

9) "On the Fitness of the Glories of Mary" is also a Discourse to Mixed Congregations, and its particular genius, both theologically and from a literary perspective, lies in the way Newman is able to show how the argument of convenience—evident in the natural and salvific economies—can be applied to the doctrine of Our Lady's bodily Assumption, so as to show this doctrine's scriptural roots and its full integration in the Sacred Tradition.

10) "On the Purification of Mary" is the harbinger of Newman's *An Essay on the Development of Christian Doctrine* and serves

to underscore Mary's role of cooperation in the *œconomia salutis* in terms of her having faithfully pondered the Word of God as its sacred and saving mysteries unfolded in her life.

Selected Fathers of the Church in Newman's Theology of
Marian Cooperation in the Œconomia Salutis

INTRODUCTION

The influence of the Fathers of the Church on the theology
and spirituality of Newman is undeniable.[1] Indeed, he has been
referred to by some as a modern-day Father of the Church.[2] The
Reverend Giovanni Velocci, C.Ss.R., writes: "The familiarity
with those ancient teachers reveals itself in his Mariology, totally
impregnated with his spirit and with his thought."[3] Newman's
early reading of the Fathers as a young scholar at Oxford led him
to appreciate the full riches of the Church's Tradition, most
especially those fundamental doctrines formulated and eventually defined in the creeds of the early councils. The Reverend
Stanley Jaki, O.S.B., offers some historical background against
which to situate Newman's conversion to Catholicism; he
affirms that Newman's turn to the Fathers of the Church for
theological and spiritual enlightenment was the result, among
other factors, of a powerful nineteenth-century revival in patristic studies.

The three most notable figures of this revival, according to
Father Jaki, were Johann Adam Moehler, John Henry Newman
and Matthias Joseph Scheeben. Moehler, as Jaki reports, re-
gained "his Christian soul through the readings of the Fathers."
Newman claimed that his reading of the Fathers of the Church
was "simply and solely the one intellectual cause" of his conversion to Roman Catholicism. Jaki explains that one of the supreme
motivations behind Newman's conversion was that he found the
ethos of the Catholic Church of his day remarkably similar to
the one animating the Church of the Fathers, many of whom
were great theologians as well as great saints. Newman, as Jaki
relates, had therefore no choice but to exclaim: "Be my soul with
the saints!"[4] In a sense, what Newman so admired in the great
Fathers and Doctors of the Church was not simply their intellec-

tual orthodoxy but above all their sanctity, which was embodied in his own heart and soul.

Furthermore, Joseph Milner's *History of the Church of Christ* gave Newman a great love for the Fathers of the Church, and Milner would eventually be a major influence in his conversion to Catholicism, a point stressed by Jean Cardinal Honoré.[5] Newman writes about Milner's influence in the *Difficulties of Anglicans I:*[6]

> My testimony, then, is as follows. Even when I was a boy, my thoughts were turned to the early Church, and especially to the early Fathers, by the perusal of the Calvinist Joseph Milner's Church history, and I have never lost, I have never suffered a suspension of the impression, deep and pleasurable, which his sketches of Saint Ambrose and Saint Augustine made on my soul. Since then, the vision of the Fathers became for my imagination, I should say like a paradise of delight for all the times my work permits me.[7]

In the writings of the Fathers, Newman recognized the religion of the early Christians, the religion of the primitive Church.[8] Newman gradually became more and more enamored of patristic thought, so that all of his subsequent writing would be refined and enriched by his having come into contact with these giants of Catholicism.[9] W. Ward remarked that once Newman had begun his preaching at Saint Mary's, Oxford, it seemed as though the spirit of an Ambrose or Augustine had been revived.[10]

Honoré begins the fifth chapter of his book entitled "The Patristic Source," by describing the origins of Newman's love affair with the writings of the Fathers of the Church starting with the period of 1826–1830 and the beginning of "his patristic investigations," as a young fellow at Oriel College. Honoré recalls that Newman wrote a letter to his mother in which he spoke of having "heard the call" from those whom he described as "my huge fellows," namely, the Fathers of the Church. Furthermore, Honoré tells us that Newman "devoted himself to studying them with meritorious perseverance. The readings from the Fathers inaugurated a patristic loyalty in Newman which never diminished. The richness of their teachings happily prolonged the great lessons of spiritual detachment and otherworldliness for which prior events in his life had prepared him. In view of the fact that he lost his tutorship, he now had the leisure for such studies." [11]

One must remember, however, that a strongly anti-Catholic sentiment or bias which many had imbibed almost by osmosis in Anglican circles at Oxford, even among the most scholarly of men, was bound to have its impact on Newman. Newman could not help for a time to be affected by this negativity, so much so that he sought to develop a whole line of theological thought— the *Via Media*—in order to preserve an Anglican identity in contradistinction to both Catholicism and Liberal Protestantism. Michael Ffinch observes that Newman's study of the Fathers, while a part of the Oxford Movement, had such an impact on him that it led him to the inexorable conclusion—much against his own personal desire—that the Church of the Fathers was co-extensive with the Church of Rome.

The words of Saint Augustine *"Securus judicat orbis terrarum"* [12] were particularly disturbing to Newman's conscience, for they implied that the judgment of antiquity, that is, of the Church from time immemorial, as concerns matters of faith and morals, without doubt, unanimously favored the teachings of the Church of Rome, thus making his *Via Media* position untenable. Ffinch tells us of the precarious situation in which Newman found himself once he realized "the rising tide of doubt that now threatened to drown him," and that the Oxford Movement "had sprung a leak." Ffinch chronicles how Newman "confided in Henry Wilberforce that, though he prayed that it might never happen, in the end he might find it his duty to join the Roman Catholic Church. Perhaps there was still a way out." [13]

Father Velocci recalls the turmoil that Newman underwent as a result of his eventual break from Anglicanism. Newman's search for certainty is described by Velocci as "patient, severe, punctilious, which prolonged itself for years." He became per-suaded that, as dear as Anglicanism was to his heart, that his search for the truth above all things was leading him away from her bosom to the bosom of Catholicism. The reaction to New-man was disastrous in part causing him to suffer much at the hands of his contemporaries for the sake of safeguarding the integrity of the truth as he viewed and understood it. [14]

As a member of the Oxford Movement, Newman contributed to a series of pamphlets known as *Tracts for the Times*, in which various theological, philosophical and historical questions were addressed, especially those most controverted between Catholics and Anglicans. Newman wrote approximately twenty-seven of these tracts. Bishop Boyce writes:

> In 1836, Newman wrote a whole Tract which was to be a manual for use in Anglican controversy with Roman Catholics. He pointed out what he then considered to be the weak points and some errors in certain Catholic beliefs. The honor paid to our Lady was one point particularly condemned. He quoted from some Catholic authors who ascribe a certain 'omnipotence' to the Blessed Virgin. On account of her office as Mother of God, she is said to be able 'to command' her divine Son with a mother's authority." [15]

For Newman and some of his contemporaries, this was tantamount to idolatry or, as it was termed, "Mariolatry" and was a direct offense against the centrality of Christ in doctrine and devotion. A notable exception was the influence of Richard Hurrell Froude, whom Newman met in 1826. O'Brien makes the point that "Froude, who was not, of course, a Roman Catholic, led Newman to develop an admiration for the Church of Rome, a belief in the Real Presence of Christ in the Eucharist, and the idea of devotion to the Blessed Virgin, whom Froude saw as the great pattern for virginity which he held in the highest esteem." [16]

But, as Providence would have it, the more Newman systematically read the Fathers of the Church, the more he began to see how Mary's role in no way detracted from Christ's, but was a direct consequence of her singular position in relation to Him. Newman became aware that the Anglican Church, which he so desperately tried to salvage by means of the *Via Media*, could not withstand the combined witness of the Fathers of the Church since they bore testimony to the unique authenticity and authority of the Roman Church. Boyce comments that Newman's Via Media theory, which was part of the backbone of the Oxford Movement, began to become rather brittle as a result of Newman's study of the Fathers: "The reading of the Fathers of the Church, and especially of St Augustine, convinced him that the Church of Rome was the legitimate successor of the Church of the Apostles and of early Christianity. He resigned his Anglican offices and withdrew to Littlemore, a hamlet near Oxford, for three years of prayer and study." [17]

Having read a copy of Cardinal Nicholas Wiseman's article "The Anglican Claims of Apostolic Succession," in which the words of Saint Augustine of Hippo, *Securus judicat orbis terrarum*, appeared, Newman's attempt at establishing a *Via Media* was, by his own admission, "absolutely pulverized."[18] It would eventually prompt him to venture across the threshold of conversion so as to enter the fold of the Catholic Church. Newman compared the Fathers of the Church to a type of ladder by which he had made his way into the Church and which he was unwilling to kick down, having climbed too far and overcome too many obstacles.[19]

Initially, Newman did not imagine that his study of the Fathers would lead him away from his beloved Church of England to become a Catholic. In fact, Newman, in a letter addressed to Mrs. Froude on April 5, 1844, writes the following:

> My confidence against the Church of Rome lay in two things, first my feeling that we had the Apostolic Succession—next my conviction that her peculiar doctrines were not held by the Fathers. As to the first of these, I acknowledged great irregularity in the transmission, and vast and various disorders and faults in our Church. But I got over all by the parallel of the Jewish Church which was a Church when Christ came, in spite of anomalies as great as ours. . . . As to the second it was to me as clear as day (as it is now) that the honours paid in the Church of Rome to Saint Mary were not primitive.[20]

The *Via Media* had been designed simply because Newman was convinced that along that middle path lay that virtue which neither Catholicism nor Protestantism had seemed to obtain. Newman held that Catholics misused the Fathers to argue certain points of doctrine and were not faithful to the whole of their message. His evaluation would subsequently change as he began to understand that the Catholic Church did not appeal to individual Fathers for their own sake, but as an assembly of formidable witnesses to a Tradition united in faith and practice.[21]

Nevertheless, Newman admits that the impact of the Fathers on him was perceptible from an early stage. Newman recounts in the *Apologia* that his first contact with the Fathers came at the age of fifteen—a year before entering Trinity College at Oxford—and would leave an indelible mark on his theological and philosophical formation.[22] In his introductory remarks to Pusey,

Newman recalls how even as an Anglican, just the sight of the Fathers' works on his shelves, stirred up within him a holy zeal that would continue to burn as he deepened his study of their works:

> I recollect well what an outcast I seemed to myself, when I took down from the shelves of my library the volumes of Saint Athanasius or Saint Basil, and set myself to study them; how, on the contrary, when at length I was brought into Catholic communion, I kissed them with delight, with a feeling that in them I had more than all that I had lost; and, as though I were directly addressing the glorious saints, who bequeathed them to the Church, how I said to the inanimate pages, "You are mine now and I am yours, beyond any mistake." [23]

Thus, Newman came to the realization that in order to share more fully in the Fathers' life of faith and devotion, he had to leave the Anglican Communion and enter the Catholic Church. However, in his *Apologia pro Vita Sua*, it is clear that Newman's initial romance with the Fathers did not prevent him from making a severe criticism of those Catholic Marian doctrines and devotions which, as he openly declares, constituted a great cross (*crux*) to bear, that is, they formed a stumbling block to his acceptance of Catholicism as the truest form of Christianity.[24]

However, the attraction of the Fathers of the Church would sway Newman and begin to have an impact on his preaching and teaching. The influence of the Fathers would be most detectable throughout. In a particular way, his reading of Church history was broadened by the insights which the testimony of the Fathers offered. O'Brien draws out some of these connections; Newman's discovery of the Church Fathers permitted him to find confirmation for many of his "own long-held ideals."

Of utmost importance was his profound intuition about the economy of salvation and the role of the sacraments in the life of the Church. As regards the sacraments, Newman cherished the fact that the sacraments bespoke a material world permeated by invisible realities. O'Brien explains: "The exterior world, physical and historical, was but the outward manifestation of realities greater than itself." As concerns the economy of salvation he recognized a development of divine pedagogy: "He saw Judaism and Paganism as an outer framework 'which concealed yet suggested the living truth'; the framework had not been intended to last. Changes came slowly but steadily with one disclosure following another until the whole was revealed." [25]

The central doctrine of the Incarnation and its soteriological import formed the foundation of Newman's appropriation of the patristic patrimony. Newman's particular fondness for the thought of Saint Athanasius of Alexandria, as most fully expounded in his controversy with the Arians, sets the stage for Newman's love of Christology and was a sure inspiration for the development of his Mariology. [26] Even though Athanasius himself does not concentrate on the figure of the Virgin *per se*, but vis-à-vis his defense of an orthodox Christology against the heresy of Arius, he implicitly establishes her link to the mystery of the Incarnation.

Boyce's notes are quite helpful in offering some historical background to Newman's reflections on Athanasius' defense of the Incarnation and the use of the title of *Theotokos*: "During the summer of 1841 Newman began a translation of *Selected Treatises of Saint Athanasius* against the Arian heresy. The doctrinal cogency of this great saint and theologian was the occasion of another doubt in Newman's mind about the position of the Anglican Church." Boyce quotes Newman from the *Apologia* [27] as evidence of Newman's attempt to assimilate the thought of Athanasius and his frustration at seeing its incompatibility with his theory of the *Via Media*. However, as Boyce points out, it was not until 1881, when Newman completed his emendations to his complete Anglican works—including the two volumes on *Selected Treatises of Saint Athanasius*—that Newman demonstrates a particular theological prowess by integrating his use of refined theological terminology with his study of "the history of this Marian title [*Theotokos*] and then on the doctrinal truth which the title conveys. He quotes extensively from the Fathers of the Church." [28]

Furthermore, Newman's reliance on Saint Cyril of Alexandria and his writings in controversy with Nestorius and the subsequent formulation of the Christological teaching at Ephesus, is most significant for Newman's development of a profound love for the doctrine of the *Theotokos*, officially ratified by that same Council. [29] In addition, Newman begins to plumb the depths of the mystery of Mary's cooperation in the work of salvation by studying the works of Fathers like Justin Martyr, Irenæus of

Lyons, Tertullian, John Chrysostom and Augustine—to name a few. In fact, Newman will never tire of reiterating that his love for the Person of the God-Man is indissolubly linked to his reverence for the *Theotokos* (*Deipara*), with the opposite true as well. Beyond that, the doctrine of Mary as the New Eve provided Newman with ever greater insights into the figure of Our Lady and her importance for the economy of salvation. For Newman, a separation between Christology and Mariology or Mariology and Ecclesiology or any compartmentalization in theology is unthinkable and perilous, resulting in heterodoxy since, as the Fathers show, an orthodox Marian teaching is a necessary protective shield for an orthodox Christology and an orthodox Ecclesiology.

The central Marian doctrines that occupy Newman are those concerning Mary's divine maternity and her title of "Second Eve," from which Newman sees as derivative all other essential Marian dogmas, such as her Immaculate Conception and bodily Assumption. All of these themes are treated in Newman's Anglican writings *in semine* and reach greater development and refinement in his *Letter to Pusey* and in other writings. F. J. Friedel expands on this: "This doctrine [the New Eve] is the central point of Newman's Mariology as exposed in his *Letter to Pusey*. From it he derives the doctrines of Mary's dignity, her sanctity, her Immaculate Conception, and Assumption." Friedel lauds Newman's *Letter to Pusey* as a Mariological masterpiece precisely because he was able to harmonize his use of Sacred Scripture and the writings of the Fathers: "His treatment of Mary's position as Second Eve really merits the designation of '*magistrale*' as given it by Terrien. His method is not merely historical; the foundation for the belief is indirectly placed in Scripture. He explains it and then strengthens it by the testimony of the Fathers." [30]

The continuity between his thought expressed in his Anglican sermon, "The Reverence Due to the Virgin Mary," and the *Letter to Pusey* can be illustrated by taking into consideration his treatment of Mary as the New Eve and thus, the doctrine of Mary's Immaculate Conception as that doctrine which, first of all, illustrates the beginning of her cooperation in the economy of salvation. For example, in the sermon he writes: "The Seed of the woman, announced to guilty Eve, after the long delay, was at length appearing upon earth, and was to be born from her. In her the destinies of the world were reversed, and the serpent's head bruised. On her was bestowed the greatest honour ever put upon any individual of our fallen race. God was taking upon Him her flesh, and humbling Himself to be called her offspring—such is the deep mystery."[31]

The antithetical parallelism between Mary and Eve is a theme that pervades Newman's Mariological writing and is a direct consequence of his reliance on patristic sources. Michael Schmaus spells this out: "The antithesis 'Eve–Mary,' stemming from the *Protoevangelium* and developed by Justin and still more by Irenæus, proved very fruitful. It was for a long time the keynote of Mariological thinking on the faith. The unbelief and disobedience of Eve brought ruin, the faith and obedience of Mary brought salvation. . . . A Mariology founded on the patristic data was introduced by J. H. Newman and M. J. Scheeben. The main questions centered on Mary's share in the redemption."[32]

Since this parallel is inferred from the Genesis text known as the *Protoevangelium* (Gen 3:15), Newman did not hesitate to propose it to his Anglican brethren, as the Fathers of the Church had first done for the early Christians.[33] Like the Fathers, Newman saw in this parallel the root of many Marian doctrines which, although not part of official Anglican doctrine, did not, in his opinion, openly contradict any particular teaching. Not only did this parallel form the basis of any discussion of Mary's cooperation in the work of salvation, but it also laid the foundation for a discussion of Mary as free from any stain of sin, most especially, original sin.

Of course, as an Anglican, Newman could not simply argue in a direct manner in favor of the doctrine of the Immaculate Conception since he would have been suspected of Romanism. However, by employing the arguments of the Fathers, what is the argument of Tradition, Newman was most capable of putting forth a rather convincing apologetic for Mary as the New Eve, and therefore implicitly succeeded in laying the groundwork for an acceptance of the Church's belief in Mary's immunity from sin.

Boyce writes that Newman's readings of the Fathers guided him in discovering the significance of the antithetical Mary–Eve parallelism, so much so that he was led to consider, at a very early stage of his development, the doctrine of Mary having being preserved from all sin "at the dawn of a new creation" just as Eve had been without sin at the dawn of her creation in the Garden of Eden. Boyce writes: "The balance in the argument then would seem to favor his personal acceptance of this doctrine." Boyce adds: "In fact, his response to his Anglican accusers in 1835 when the sermon was published, was simply that 'there was nothing against the doctrine in the Thirty-Nine Articles' of the Anglican faith." [34]

In order to see how Newman's Anglican thought about the Virgin ties into his Catholic thought, one must turn to his response to the *Eirenicon* of his long-time personal friend and fellow member of the Oxford movement, Dr. Edward B. Pusey. Newman's response comprises the second part of his work, *Certain Difficulties Felt by Anglicans in Catholic Teaching*. Most scholars agree that this is the only so-called "systematic" treatise that Newman ever wrote on the subject of Mariology and that it is an astounding apologetic of Catholic Marian doctrine and devotion—being both quite ecumenical in tone and yet uncompromising in its defense of the truth. Boyce affirms this latter point: "In an age when there was an inflation of popular and devotional writing on our Lady and when many Mariological treatises did not show a thorough knowledge of or respect for Patristic literature, Newman's *Letter to Pusey* appeared as a breath of fresh air. It dissipated many prejudices and was widely acclaimed." [35]

The *Letter to Pusey* gives us direct insight into Newman's use of the Fathers of the Church in support of his position on the Virgin. Boyce elucidates the matter: "Even those Catholics who had a difference outlook from Newman, such as Cardinal Manning and W. G. Ward and F. W. Faber, could not but acknowledge the theological depth and patristic knowledge displayed by the author." [36] It was a harbinger of much development in the field of Mariology, in ecumenism, and in many other areas of theological research. Friedel offers the following: "Newman, too, wished to give a new impulse to Catholic studies so as to enable the Catholic to meet the Protestant on the common footing of Antiquity. His small work, priceless for its profundity, solidity, and conformity to all the canons of historical criticism, was the forerunner of considerable subsequent research on similar lines and in other domains of theology." [37]

The theme of the Immaculate Conception, which Newman traces in his Anglican sermons, is pursued with greater vigor and clarity in the *Letter to Pusey*. Boyce holds that the doctrine of the Immaculate Conception was "the focal point of Newman's teaching on our Lady: it touched on many points of his Mariology. He contemplated it as a logical consequence of Mary being the Second Eve." However, one might ask: How did Newman derive such a faithful adherence to this truth of the Faith? Boyce responds to this question: "The point that seemed to Newman 'to be conclusive' in proving the Immaculate Conception of Mary was that it flows as an immediate inference from that other doctrine (already taught by the Fathers and universally accepted in the Christian tradition) of Mary being the Second Eve. This argument has a strong ecumenical weight as well." [38]

In Chapter One of this book, an analysis of this very point was given to illustrate the hermeneutic of Newman's concept of the development of Christian doctrine. Here, the principal concern is to show the continuity between Newman's Anglican and Catholic thought concerning the Virgin Mary and her cooperation in the economy of salvation, precisely by demonstrating that Newman's deepened sense of the Catholic position regarding Our Lady results from his reading of the Fathers of the Church. The doctrine of the Immaculate Conception is a key doctrine developed by Newman as a result of his heightened awareness and appreciation of the patristic texts. However, Newman's overarching theme is Mary's cooperation in the *œconomia salutis*. Thus, the doctrine of the Immaculate Conception is one piece of a much larger mosaic. Some of the other pieces of this mosaic, which receive particular attention in Newman's thought, are the doctrines of Mary as Mother of God and her spiritual motherhood of the Church, from which also flows a discussion of her mediation and advocacy. Here we specifically refrain from saying that Newman developed a theology of Mary's co-redemption because he does not seem to have favored this term to describe Mary's role. Newman, following the intuition of the Fathers of the Church—which is also the line of thought adopted by the Fathers of the Second Vatican Council– preferred the use of "cooperation" or equivalent expressions.

In this chapter, Newman's use of the Fathers of the Church is examined. The Fathers of the Church, to whom Newman refers in the *Letter to Pusey* and in other works are the surest witnesses for Newman to a combined Tradition in favor of Catholic doctrine concerning Mary and her cooperation in the economy of salvation. This collective witness and its import for Newman is highlighted by Boyce who surveys Newman's *Letter to Pusey* in order to highlight how "Newman's reading of the Fathers and of the history of the early Church led him to begin his theological exposition on our Lady, by recalling what he terms 'the great rudimental teaching of Antiquity from its earliest date' concerning Mary." Boyce also notes Newman's selection of ten Fathers of the Church, who lived between the second and sixth centuries and represented the apostolic tradition in both the Eastern and the Western Church.

The united Church of East and West, as Boyce comments on Newman, "from the beginning, regarded Mary as the Second Eve." Likewise, Boyce indicates that Newman, "gives considerable weight to the fact that these authors, especially the first three he mentions, namely, Saint Justin, Tertullian and Saint Irenæus, witness independently of each other and derive their knowledge from a common source—namely, the universal faith of the early Church, which in turn was derived from an apostolic tradition." [39]

Newman's treatment of Mary as the New Eve is without doubt a focal point of his apologetic, but it does not exhaust it. Nevertheless, we consider, in a particular way, the thought of certain Fathers who seem to have exercised the most influence on Newman's Mariology, not only as revealed in the *Letter to Pusey*, but also as made evident elsewhere in his writings. The selection has to be limited simply because it is the intent to offer a panoramic view of Newman's use of the Fathers and not to engage in any sort of exhaustive study, which could easily be the subject of an entirely separate discussion.

Likewise, it must be noted that being dealt with are Newman's view of the Fathers and his use of their texts as he understood them. Following the general methodology of this paper, Newman's thought is placed in juxtaposition to the thought of patrologists, contemporary theologians and the Church's Magisterium adding further commentary when deemed suitable. Furthermore, it should be noted that Newman made many of his own direct translations of the Fathers into English and that these are the translations most often used here. Hence, there is a certain obligation to rely on Newman's translations, marking, however, any discrepancies from the originals. At the same time, it should be noted that this work quotes from the original Latin or Greek texts, especially when they are given in Newman's own writings.

Bishop Boyce provides us with a commentary that captures the essence of what Newman was able to absorb from the scriptural and patristic sources regarding Mary and her cooperation in the economy of salvation, so much so that he could be considered a precursor of the Second Vatican Council, most especially since he anticipated the Council Fathers' effort to revive the fundamental patristic doctrine of Mary as the New Eve. Boyce propounds a summary appreciation of Newman's Mariology in direct relation to his appropriation of the scriptural and patristic data and so considers him a forerunner of the Second Vatican Council:

> In fact, Newman's Mariology is profound and solid. It is based above all on what Sacred Scripture tells us about our Lady. . . . Moreover, Newman learned much from his Patristic readings. The Fathers had led him into the Church and were his guides in theology. At the beginning of his *Letter to Pusey*, he declares that the Fathers are enough for him: 'I do not wish to say more than they suggest to me, and will not say less'. From them he came to appreciate the depth of meaning in the title of Second Eve which was the rudimentary teaching of the early centuries on our Lady. This intuition was to have immense consequences for his Marian doctrine. It is a truth of Marian doctrine which has been reiterated in many papal documents during the present century. Most significantly of all, it was used in the dogmatic Constitution on the Church, *Lumen Gentium*, of the Second Vatican Council in its chapter on our Lady.[40]

Before we consider each selected Father, a few general observations of a methodological nature need to be mentioned. The Fathers are cited by Newman in the Latin or Greek original as they were accessible to him. These texts are included by Newman in his notes to the *Letter to Pusey* (cf. pp. 119–123). Newman also provides his own English translation for these texts in the main body of the letter (cf. pp. 33–35; 39–44). Nevertheless, on occasion, Newman, for whatever reason, included the whole Latin or Greek text of a given Father yet saw fit to omit a part of the text in translation. These missing portions of the Fathers' texts have been added where deemed necessary. In the case of Saint Ephrem the Syrian, Newman relied on a Latin translation of the Syriac, which he provides. When other texts of Ephrem are quoted in this work, only an English translation of the original Syriac has been used. When other texts of the Fathers are cited in the book in order to provide a context in which the better to situate the actual texts quoted by Newman in the *Letter to Pusey*, these texts are either included as quotations and explained or the reference to their Latin or Greek original is given in the footnote and their content summarized and/or explained in the body of the text. Newman develops an apologetic for the New Eve theology in the immediate context of the *Letter* itself based on a general appropriation of the Fathers' contributions. Nonetheless, Newman did not set out to present Pusey with a step-by-step analysis of the texts cited. Therefore, in this chapter, just such a more detailed analysis of these selected texts (e.g., of Saint Irenæus) is made, so that one might appreciate more fully their theological significance both in general and as they are integral to Newman's theology of Mary's cooperation in the *œconomia salutis*. The reader should bear in mind that a more comprehensive study of Newman's theology of the New Eve is made in Chapter Four and that Newman's other Mariological writings are relied upon to show exactly how Newman's theology and that of an individual Father are interconnected—albeit the literary genre of their respective writings quite different at times, for example a doctrinal treatise as distinct from a devotional meditation.

I. NEWMAN AND SAINT JUSTIN MARTYR

The central theme of Justin's Mariology is the Person and work of Christ the Redeemer.[41] Mario Maritano acknowledges that Justin considers Christ as the one Who, standing at the center of the economy of salvation, reveals the Father thus enabling one to understand the meaning of the Sacred Scriptures, especially their most profound soteriological sense.[42] Furthermore, in Justin's theology, Mary's role as Second Eve is not conceived apart from the mission of Christ, Who restores mankind's relationship to God in the context of a new economy. This is clearly stated by

Mario Maritano when he analyzes the Mariological contribution of Justin in this Christological framework.

Maritano prefaces his discussion of the Christocentric nature of the Marian doctrines in Justin by employing the principle of *Lumen Gentium* (no. 60) concerning the subordination and dependent relationship between Mary's mediation and Christ's, noting that based on this relationship Mary "enters unto her full title, because with her divine maternity she proclaims the reality of the Incarnation of the Son and, cooperating virginally, makes evident the dignity of the Messiah and His divinity." Therefore, Maritano explains that "for Justin the Virgin Mary had an essential role: she helped to comprehend the mystery of Christ, True God and True Man, and at the same time, in her religious dimension, she constituted a true value as a human person transparent to the divine." In the overall context of Justin's writings, Maritano makes this further important observation: "Justin, as do the rest of the Christian authors of the earliest centuries, normally speaks of Mary ... when he explains the Bible or plumbs the depths of the salvific event of the Redeemer or presents the truths of the faith and confutes error or illustrates a model of Christian life."[43]

With this basic background in mind, one can better grasp Newman's use of Justin in *Letter to Pusey*. In the *Letter*, Newman cites Justin as the first Father of the Church to testify in an explicit way to the theology of Mary as the New Eve.[44] Justin does so as a representative of the Palestinian tradition of the second century (120–165 A.D.).[45] He quotes from Justin's *Dialogue with Trypho* (100), in which Justin asserts that the undoing of the serpent's guile and the disobedience which arose out of it were due to God's salvific plan, fulfilled at the moment of the Annunciation when Mary said "yes" to the Archangel Gabriel.[46]

Mary's *fiat* is decisive in the plan of salvation because her cooperation is willed by God as representative of man's own free and active cooperation in the work of his own salvation, just as once he had cooperated freely and actively in the disobedience which signaled the beginning of his fall from grace. For Justin, Mary has a role of representation of the human race which is nonetheless subordinate to the role of Christ the God-Man, in much the same manner as Eve's role was subordinate to that of Adam.[47] Justin writes:

We know that he before all creatures, proceeded from the Father by His power and will, . . . and by means of the Virgin became man, that by what way the disobedience arising from the serpent had its beginning, by that way also it might have an undoing. For Eve, being a Virgin and undefiled, conceiving the word that was from the serpent, brought forth disobedience and death; but the Virgin Mary, taking faith and joy, when the Angel told her the good tidings, that the Spirit of the Lord should come upon her and the power of the Highest overshadow her, and therefore the Holy One that was born of her was the Son of God, answered: "Be it to me according to thy word." [48]

In this passage from Justin's *Dialogue with Trypho* (100), Justin builds up the parallel between Eve and Mary through comparison and contrast. The first area of similarity is that both Mary and Eve are virgins whose participation in the economy of salvation is part of the Father's will. In the *Dialogue* (84), for example, Justin reflects on Eve's creation from the side of Adam and sees it as prefigurement of Mary's virginal conception in the fullness of time.[49] What Justin affirms at the outset of the *Dialogue* (100) leads one to affirm that the participation of both Eve and Mary— whose antithetical parallelism forms the heart of the *Dialogue* (100)—is one that is preceded by the participation of the Son Who, from all eternity, consents to the Father's plan of salvation[50] and Who, in the fullness of time, takes on flesh in the womb of the Virgin Mary, so that the economy of salvation might be restored by means of a perfect act of cooperation in His Person.[51]

To make this point more affirmatively Justin, following the main purpose of this apologetical letter, tries to convince Trypho the Jew that the Incarnation is a historical event whereby the same God of the Patriarchs and Prophets has revealed Himself in the flesh. For Justin, therefore, the node of the economy of salvation is the revelation of the Father by the distinct but co-equal Son in His Incarnation. Justin emphasizes the scriptural evidence[52] that shows the continuity between the salvific economy of the Old and New Testaments, indeed, the fulfillment of the latter in the former in the coming of "the Son of the Patriarchs," "the Son of Man," born of a virgin.[53] Therefore, the Christological emphasis of Justin's *Dialogue with Trypho*, can be considered, in a certain sense, to be encapsulated in chapter 100.

However, it is precisely in this Christological vein that the Virgin Mary is mentioned by Justin in this text. Her pivotal role in the economy of salvation, as the Virgin Mother of the Son of God and the Messiah, leads Justin to consider Mary as having collaborated with the God-Man in reversing the negative effects of Eve's unhappy collaboration with the serpent.[54] The second point of comparison is that both Eve and Mary are virgins[55] and that their virginity is associated with the virtue of purity, both in a physical and a spiritual sense.[56] The third element of commonality is that both Mary and Eve are involved in the reception of a message that is symbolically referred to as the "conception" of a word. Eve symbolically conceives, that is, accepts the word of the serpent, bringing forth the fruits of disobedience and death. Mary, on the other hand, hears the word of the Angel and her obedience brings forth, by the power of the Holy Spirit, the fruits of faith and joy in the Person of the Word-made-flesh.[57]

Father Gambero stresses the importance of Justin's contribution to the theology of Mary's cooperation as the New Eve in the economy of salvation. He explains that the Virgin Mary's role as the New Eve, as Justin was the first to reflect upon it, underwent doctrinal development and formulation as a logical consequence of the Church's reflection on Mary's divine maternity. Gambero accentuates the soteriological importance that the antithetical parallelism Eve–Mary had in determining "the Blessed Virgin's function in the divine plan for our salvation." Gambero, furthermore, reflects that the antithetical parallelism's soteriological import: "demonstrates that the primary concern of the earliest theological reflection about Mary was focused less on her person than on her role in relation to Christ. Mary has a role in relation to Christ, the second Adam, just as the first Eve had a role in relation to the first Adam." Consequently, Gambero writes: *"Cardinal John Henry Newman rightly asserts that the truth about Mary as new Eve constitutes a rudimentary but extremely important Marian doctrine left to us by ancient Christianity.* It is the first meditation on her and on her mission, the fullest profile of her, the view of her that has been handed down to us in the patristic writings" (emphasis added).

The Reverend Jim McManus, C.Ss.R., maintains that "according to Cardinal Newman, Justin's teaching on this parallel between Eve and Mary was a fundamental theological insight, a Mariological insight. We do not know whether Justin was the first to see this parallel between Eve and Mary or whether this was pointed out to him when he was educated in the Faith. It is quite possible that the Church community in which he was baptized was already using this parallel in its catechetical instruction of its members."[58] With all of this said, we are now in a position to see where Justin's trajectory is picked up in the writings of Tertullian and Irenæus.[59]

II. NEWMAN AND TERTULLIAN

In the *Letter to Pusey* Newman cites Tertullian's *De Carne Christi* 17, 5,[60] wherein he treats of the parallelism between Eve and Mary.[61] This quotation deserves to be briefly introduced by recalling some of the many merits of the theology of Tertullian, considered by many to be the first great theologian of the Latin Church.[62] Although Tertullian is not considered a Doctor of the Church since he expressed some extremist, heretical, schismatic views such as Montanism, his theological prowess was demonstrated in a particular way in his ability to defend the Church's teaching against several Trinitarian and Christological heresies stemming from the Gnostic views of Hermogenes,[63] Valentinus,[64] Marcion,[65] and Praxeas,[66] among others. Furthermore, his contribution to Trinitarian theology cannot go unappreciated since he practically coined the terms by which the concept of the Trinity as *"una substantia, tres Personæ"* (one substance, three Persons) is understood in the West.

Indeed, he was also the first Christian writer to use the word *Trinitas*. In considering Tertullian's Mariology, one then begins to appreciate even more his avid defense of an orthodox Christology, especially those truths concerning the reality of the Incarnation against the Gnostic heretics (e.g., Marcion) in his writings.[67] Even though his writings on the Virgin are few and, at times, can evince a rather harsh, literal interpretation of the Sacred Text,[68] his impact in the field of Mariology is remarkable.[69]

In *An Introduction to the History of Exegesis*, the Reverend Bertrand de Margerie, S.J., dedicates a chapter to Tertullian, in which he analyzes his principles of biblical interpretation, referring to Tertullian as "the first great exegete of Latin Christianity." [70] Father De Margerie lists and explains Tertullian's hermeneutical principles, among which are included the *regula fidei* and the principle of totality, by which was excluded any heretical attempt to "interpret the whole Bible in the light of a few isolated sentences." [71] These criteria of biblical interpretation helped Tertullian in his apologetical work against the Gnostics who relied on an exaggerated form of literary and/or allegorical interpretation to oppose orthodox beliefs. [72]

Newman is particularly concerned with Tertullian's understanding of the Scriptures in terms of the parallel between Christ and Adam and, by extension, between Eve and Mary, showing how these comparisons form the basis of the economy of salvation. To understand Tertullian's views about the Virgin, it is helpful to summarize his thought about Mary's relation to the mystery of the Incarnation. Tertullian logically argues that the most convincing proof of Our Lord's Incarnation, that is, the reality of His Sacred Humanity, is that of being born of a woman, the Virgin Mary. [73]

Tertullian argues that Mary is a descendent of the great patriarchs and prophets of Israel, tracing her genealogy back to the messianic line of David, as well as she is a daughter of Eve, a true descendent of Adam. Thus, she guarantees Christ's entrance into humanity, [74] and it is His Sacred Humanity which is the primary instrument of our salvation. Hence, Tertullian's famous adage: *Caro cardo salutis* ("the flesh is the hinge of salvation"). [75] If this is true, then it follows that Mary's giving birth to Our Lord according to the flesh constitutes her as the primary human "cooperatrix" in the work of our salvation. It is along these lines that Tertullian develops a deeper understanding of the Virgin Mary's role in the *œconomia salutis*. [76]

Before we discuss the actual passage that Newman offers from Tertullian, a brief look at some of the content that precedes and follows that quotation might be helpful since it serves as an introduction to Tertullian's treatment of the Eve–Mary parallel by first establishing the Adam–Christ parallel and its ties to the figure of the Virgin. The basic argument of Tertullian is an analogy between the formation of Adam from a virgin earth and the Second Adam's conception in Mary's virginal womb. [77] Thus, Mary provides that all-important link by which the Second Adam is able to make possible a regeneration of humanity by means of his virginal birth, which is due both to the work of the Holy Spirit and to the obedient cooperation of Mary as the New Eve.[78]

At this point, Newman cites Tertullian, who writes: "... ne mihi vacet incursus nominis Adæ, unde Christus Adam ab Apostolo dictus est, si terreni non fuit census homo ejus? Sed et hic ratio defendit, quod Deus imaginem et similitudinem suam a diabolo captam æmula operatione recuperavit."[79] Newman, curiously enough, though he provides an excerpt from Tertullian's *De Carne Christi* (17) in Latin, does not give an English translation of this first question and the next clause that preceeds "quod Deus ... operatione recuperavit." For the sake of clarity, this question and first clause are translated here: "Lest the occurrence of the name Adam have no meaning for me; why is Christ called Adam by the Apostle, if his man (human nature) was not considered of the earth? However and here reason explains that." Newman's translation continues: "God recovered His Image and Likeness, which the devil had seized, by a rival operation."[80] In other words, by becoming Man in the Incarnation, God was able to repair man's disfigured humanity—conforming it to the image and likeness of Christ's perfect Humanity. Tertullian sees in Christ the Word-made-Flesh the form of every man and the hinge of his salvation. All men were created in the image and likeness of the Second Adam and thus have that image and likeness which He recovered (*recuperavit*).

By His Incarnation, Christ transfigures man, so that he might ever more resemble his Creator as he did before the Fall and thus, with body and soul, come to share in the full benefits of the Resurrection, arriving at complete restoration to God's image and likeness on the last day.[81] The rival operation of the devil is one that contributes to the deformation of man, the disfigurement of God's image and likeness. Christ's coming as Man from the Virgin defeats the devil's wily plan, aimed at the death and destruction of mankind's harmony, while the economy of God ultimately succeeds because it is based on the principles of life and unity as Christ's Incarnation effects a recapitulation of the human condition.

In this process of recapitulation, the cooperation of the Virgin Mary is willed in a particular way, so that mankind is made whole and, at the same time, the female sex is restored to its own proper dignity in God's image and likeness. In this way, Mary's cooperation in the work of salvation as the New Eve is not limited to a general representation of humanity but also acquires a particular significance in that she also represents womankind: "In virginem enim adhuc Evam irrepserat verbum ædificatorium mortis. In virginem æquæ introducendum erat Dei verbum exstructorium vitæ; ut quod per eiusmodi sexum abierat in perditionem, per eundem sexum redigeretur in salutem." [82]

This passage of Tertullian continues by furthering the antithetical parallelism between Eve and Mary along the lines of the contrast between their respective responses to the messages made to them. Eve's belief of the serpent's word is "blotted out" by the consent of Mary to the Word announced to her by the Angel Gabriel. Tertullian writes: "Crediderat Eva serpenti; credidit Maria Gabrieli; quod illa credendo deliquit, hæc credendo delevit." [83] Tertullian also points out in that same passage the consequences of both Eve's and Mary's responses. Eve's "yes" to the serpent spawns a series of evil consequences, beginning with the fratricide of Abel by Cain. [84] Mary's *fiat*, on the other hand, is the seed of salvation insofar as her acceptance of the Word of God leads to the birth of the Savior and mankind's Brother Who, by His sacrifice on the Cross, blots out the sin of Cain.

Thus, one concludes that the cooperation between Jesus and Mary in the economy of salvation as understood from this text of Tertullian cited by Newman is best appreciated for the soteriological and anthropological dimensions so as to reverse the evils of the original fall: to restore to man his dignity as a child of God created in the divine image and likeness, indeed his likeness to the Word-of-God-made-flesh.

III. NEWMAN AND SAINT IRENÆUS OF LYONS

Undoubtedly, Saint Irenæus is a major font of inspiration for Newman and a prime source of his knowledge and appreciation of Mary under the title of New Eve. In the *Letter to Pusey*,[85] Newman cites two fundamental texts concerning the Mary–Eve parallelism which are found in Irenæus' *Adversus Hæreses*.[86] However, it bears noting immediately that in the *Letter to Pusey* Newman cites the Latin text of Irenæus at greater length and does not translate it in its entirety.

The first text begins with a quotation of Mary's words to the Angel at the Annunciation prefaced by a statement concerning the Virgin Mary's obedience that leads to her *fiat*: "Consequenter[87] autem et Maria virgo obediens invenitur, dicens, Ecce Ancilla Domini fiat mihi secundum verbum tuum."[88] Mary's *fiat*, for Irenæus, expresses in synthesis the virtue of Mary's obedience in contrast to the disobedience of the virgin Eve. Irenæus contrasts the effects which both Mary's and Eve's actions have in terms of the economy of salvation. The disobedience of Eve becomes the *causa mortis* ("cause of death") for herself and for the whole human race. Similarly, the obedience of the Virgin Mary is said to be the *causa salutis* ("cause of salvation") both for herself and for the whole human race.[89] Irenæus writes: "Eva vero inobediens: non obedivit enim, adhuc quum esset virgo. Quemadmodum illa, virum quiden habens Adam, virgo tamen adhuc existens inobediens facta, et sibi et universo generi humano causa facta est mortis: sic et Maria, habens prædestinatum generi humano causa facta est salutis."[90]

Irenæus' reflection on the antithetical parallelism of Eve and Mary is, at one and the same time, of anthropological and soteriological significance. The salvific causality of Mary's cooperation is explained as a consequence of her personal assent, a virginal obedience of faith, which is glaringly contrasted to the lack of faith or disobedience of the virgin Eve. Nevertheless, this salvific causality is affirmed of Mary insofar as she is dependent upon and subordinate to the action of "prædestinatum virum" ("the predestined man") Christ Jesus, just as the disobedient refusal of cooperation with God's plan of salvation on the part of Eve leading to man's fall is placed in direct relationship to her husband, Adam.

The deliberate emphasis placed on the state of virginity shared by both Mary and Eve is an indication not only of a desire on Irenæus' part to report a biological fact testified to by the Scriptures, but also to underscore its theological significance.[91] The virginity of Mary is symbolic of her personal virtue, of her openness and docility in relationship to the Lord and her willingness to consent with her whole person as handmaiden of the Lord to the Word delivered to her by the angel. Eve's virginal state, unlike that of Mary, is not integrated into the fullness of her personhood and thus does not have the profound significance that

Mary's virginity obtains. Mary's virginal motherhood and her virginal faith are considered by Irenæus to be two essential aspects of Our Lady's cooperation with Christ in the regeneration of humanity. Furthermore, Mary's cooperation as the Virgin-Mother of the Incarnate Word is the beginning of that spiritual regeneration of God's children which culminates in the womb of the Church[92] and which also points to our own cooperation in the economy of salvation.[93] Eve's virginity, on the contrary, lacking the spiritual fecundity which Mary's possessed because of the purity and integrity of her faith/obedience, is degenerative. Tainted by sin and death, Eve becomes a counter-symbol of the economy of salvation.[94]

Irenæus is careful not to dissociate either Eve from Adam or Mary from Christ. In both instances, he explicitly refers to their respective associations in such a way that the antithetical parallelism Eve–Mary is incomprehensible apart from the antithetical parallelism Adam–Christ. Irenæus formulates the antithetical parallelism Eve–Mary by explaining that Mary the Virgin, espoused to Joseph as was Eve to her husband Adam, was involved in the salvific work of Christ as the historic counterpart to Eve in the economy of salvation. The *recirculatio*[95] ("recycling") of Eve in Mary takes place, so that both Eve and her descendants bound by sin are then loosed through the faith expressed in Mary's cooperation and bound back to God.[96] Irenæus then turns to the Scriptures,[97] so that Christ's primary importance in the economy of salvation should be fully recognized.

> Et propter hoc Dominus dicebat, primos quidem novissimos futuros, et novissimos primos. Et propheta autem hoc idem significat, dicens, "Pro patribus nati sunt tibi filii." "Primogenitus" enim "mortuorum" natus Dominus et in sinum suum recipiens pristinos patres, regeneravit eos in vitam Dei, ipse initium viventium factus, quoniam Adam initium morientium factus est. Propter hoc et Lucas initium generationis a Domino inchoans, in Adam retulit, significans, quoniam non illi hunc, sed hic illos in Evangelium vitæ regeneravit.[98]

From this passage one ascertains that Adam and Christ are the main protagonists, the formal causes of man's fall and Redemption, respectively, while Eve and Mary are cooperating agents. It is clear that Irenæus, following the evangelical teaching of Saint Luke and Saint Paul, attributes to Christ, the Second Adam, the work of man's regeneration; while, on the other hand, man's degeneration is rightfully posited of the first Adam.[99] The passage, already cited above, concerning the Eve–Mary antithetical parallelism, that is, the contrast between the obedience of the Virgin Mary and the disobedience of the virgin Eve, is not interpreted by Newman to be equated, in a soteriological sense, with the obedience of Christ and the disobedience of Adam. Newman champions Mary's necessary, active and yet subordinate role to Christ in the work of redemption in the following passage from the *Letter to Pusey* by the means of an inferential argument. Newman, by affirming that Eve's subordinate cooperation with Adam in the Fall was a necessary aspect of the economy of salvation thereby leads one to appreciate the fact that the cooperation of the New Eve was likewise a *sine qua non* of the salvific economy.

> She listened to the Evil Angel; she offered the fruit to her husband and he ate of it. She co-operated, not as an irresponsible instrument, but intimately and personally in the sin: she brought it about. As the history stands, she was a *sine-qua-non*, a positive, active, cause of it. And she had her share in its punishment; in the sentence pronounced on her, she was recognized as a real agent in the temptation and its issue, and she suffered accordingly. . . . We are able, by the position and office of Eve in our fall, to determine the position and office of Mary in our restoration.[100]

Newman's text deserves a brief commentary, since without it a proper understanding of his statement might be lost. Indeed, Newman's theology of the New Eve, along the lines traced out in Irenæus, considers Mary as having had an active and real agency or cause of our salvation through her cooperation such as Eve was considered to have been an active and real agent or cause of the Fall. Nevertheless, Newman carefully notes that it is the from *the position of Eve*, that is, from *her* office in the Fall, that we are then able "to determine the position and office of Mary in our restoration." In other words, Mary's role in the economy of salvation is viewed by Newman in direct relation to that of Eve and not to that of Adam. Following the logic of Newman's argumentation, therefore, Christ must enjoy a singular position or office in "our restoration," that is, in the economy of our salvation, just as Adam's office is clearly to be distinguished from that of Eve's in the fall. Therefore, neither Irenæus nor Newman implies that Mary's virginal obedience is regenerative and salvific in and of itself, but only insofar as Mary is associated to Christ the Author of that regeneration and salvation.

In his *Sermon Notes* for December 9, entitled "On Man as Disobedient by Sin as Contrasted with Mary," Newman writes: "What a contrast Our Lady to this—our Saviour God cannot afford the contrast. Immaculate in her conception—so sweet, so musical, etc. She holds up to us what man is intended to be, as a type, the most perfect submission to God. . . . Christ the source, Mary the work of grace." [101] In Newman's *Sermon Notes* for the beginning of the Month of Mary (May 1), we find a brief meditation entitled "On Mary as the Pattern of the Natural World," which explains that May is the month of Mary because "it is the youth of the year; its beauty, grace and purity. Next is its fertility: all things bud forth. The virgin and mother. . . . Such is the comparison. Nothing so beautiful in the natural world as the season when it opens. Nothing so beautiful in the supernatural world as Mary." [102] Furthermore, Newman goes on to explain that the spiritual beauty and fecundity of Mary Virgin and Mother is even more appreciated when one recalls that the beauty of nature as originally created by God has been disfigured by sin and that the proof of this truth is found in the example of Eve. Thus, Newman makes the following comparison which is, in effect, another application of the Eve–Mary antithetical parallelism so dear to the Fathers of the Church, such as Saint Irenæus of Lyons:

> And thus she [Mary] is a better Eve. Eve, too, in the beginning may be called the May of the year. She was the first-fruits of God's beautiful creation. She was the type of all beauty; but alas! she represented the world also in its fragility. She stayed not in her original creation. Mary comes as a second and holier Eve, having the grace of indefectibility and the gift of perseverance from the first, and teaching us how to use the gifts without abusing them. [103]

Newman's meditation on the Marian title *Janua Cæli* ("Gate of Heaven") in his *Meditations and Devotions* [104] is extremely important because it is a *chiave di lettura* of the soteriological implications of Mary's cooperation in the economy of salvation as implied in the theology of the Fathers of the Church like Irenæus. The first point that Newman makes is that Mary's role in "the economy of Redemption" is not limited to her physical maternity but likewise "fulfilled in her spirit, soul and body." Secondly, Newman makes a crucial distinction between Eve's cooperation in the Fall and the actual sin of Adam which constitutes the core of original sin. "Eve had a part in the fall of man, though it was Adam who was our representative, and whose sin made us sinners." Thus, one finds here a confirmation of that logical inference which had been made based on the text of Diff II, 32 previously cited.

Newman expounds on this point by remarking about the Genesis account and how Eve "tempted Adam," concluding that "it was fitting in God's mercy that, as the woman began the *destruction* of the world, so woman should also begin its *recovery*, and that, as Eve opened the way for the fatal deed of the first Adam, so Mary should open the way for the great achievement of the second Adam, even our Lord Jesus Christ, Who came to save the world by dying on the cross for it." This conclusion is carefully worded by Newman to show that according to the divine economy of salvation the antithetical parallel between Eve and Mary—the Second or New Eve—is subordinate to the antithetical parallel between Adam and Christ—the Second or New Adam. The actual "fatal deed" leading to man's fall can, in a full and proper sense, be attributed only to Adam not to Eve, so too the "great achievement" of our salvation can, in a full and proper sense, be attributed only to Christ, not to Mary. Indeed, it is Christ's physical death on the Cross which is the ultimate and unparalleled cause of our salvation. Third, having made such a vital theological distinction, Newman once again appeals to the Scriptures and the Fathers of the Church to determine Mary's role as the "second and better Eve" who, according to "God's will" (i.e., His economy of salvation), undertook "*willingly* and with *full understanding* to be the Mother of our Lord, and not to be a mere passive instrument whose maternity would have no merits and no reward." Newman considers Mary's tremendous "lot," as that which afforded her the greatest intimacy "near to the Redeemer of men." This intimate association with Christ the Redeemer is exemplified in her *fiat* at the Annunciation, as Newman describes it, her "full consent of a full heart, full of God's love to her and her own lowliness," and in her compassionate union of her sufferings with the redemptive sufferings of her Son on Calvary.

The second passage cited by Newman from the *Adversus Hæreses* 3, 19, serves to reinforce the antithetical parallelism Eve–Mary using the figurative language of loosing and binding, reminiscent of the language used by Our Lord in Matthew 16:13–20 and by introducing the idea of Mary as the Advocate of Eve, reminiscent of the language used by Jesus in his discourse about the promised gift of the Holy Spirit in John 15:26–27. However, this passage should be introduced by referring to the passage which immediately precedes it in the *Letter to Pusey* and to which it is directly linked. Irenæus writes: "Sic autem et Evæ inobedientiæ nodus solutionem accepit per obedientiam Mariæ. Quod enim alligavit virgo Eva per incredulitatem, hoc virgo Maria solvit per fidem." [105] The second passage reads as follows:

> Quemadmodum enim illa per Angeli sermonem seducta est, ut effugeret Deum, prævaricata verbum ejus; ita et hæc per Angelicum sermonem evangelizata est, ut portaret Deum, obediens ejus verbo. Et si ea inobedierat Deo; sed hæc suasa est obedire Deo, uti Virginis Evæ Virgo Maria fieret advocata. Et quemadmodum adstrictum est morti genus humanum per Virginem, salvatur (solvatur) per Virginem, æqua lance disposita, virginalis inobedientia, per virginalem obedientiam. [106]

From the outset, this passage of Irenæus can be properly understood only by making reference to Newman's explanatory note of the Latin verb "salvatur" for which he gives "solvatur" (meaning, "[that] it may be loosed,") as having a synonymous meaning in both Irenæus and Augustine. [107] Newman, in fact, insists that "this variety of reading does not affect the general sense of the passage," and that "moreover, the word 'salvation' occurs in the former of these two passages." However, it is important to relate the above passage and the meaning of the expression "salvatur" to Irenæus' other theological terms, such as *causa salutis* and *advocata*, which he uses to explain his understanding of the Virgin Mary's cooperation in the economy of salvation. Making these connections is also necessary if we are to appreciate the full meaning of Irenæus's theology in light of Newman's appropriation of it. [108]

A first conclusion to be drawn from the above text is that Mary cooperates in a particular way, indeed, in a personal way, as advocate in the salvation of Eve, as she does in that of all other members of the human race.[109] Nevertheless, what Ireænus exactly meant by the use of the expressions "*advocata*" and that of "*causa salutis*" needs to be discussed.

(a) *Mary as "Advocata Evæ"*

Newman's brief apologetic commentary in the *Letter to Pusey* should shed some light upon Irenæus' use of the title Advocate for Our Lady in *Adversus Hæreses* V, 19, 1.[110] He writes:

> Tertullian says that Mary "blotted out" Eve's fault, and "brought back the female sex," or "the human race, to salvation;" and Saint Irenæus says that "by obedience she was the cause or occasion (whatever was the original Greek word) "of salvation to herself and to the whole human race;" that by her the human race was saved; that by her Eve's complication is disentangled; and that she is Eve's Advocate, or friend in need. It is supposed by critics, Protestant as well as Catholic, that the Greek word for Advocate in the original was Paraclete; it should be borne in mind, then, when we are accused of giving Our Lady the titles and offices of her Son, that Saint Irenæus bestows on her the special Name and Office proper to the Holy Ghost.[111]

Gambero comments on Irenæus' use of the title "*Advocata*," by making several points. He notes its historic significance insofar as it is the very first time in all of ancient Christian literature that it is employed in reference to Mary. However, Gambero quickly adds that "unfortunately, the original Greek versions of these texts have been lost, so that we do not know for certain what Greek term was translated by the Latin word *advocata*. The Armenian version seems to indicate that the original Greek word was *parakletos* (defender, advocate, intercessor)." Gambero, furthermore, asks the question: "But in what sense can Mary be Eve's advocate?" and answers this question by pointing out that Irenæus speaks of Mary's obedience as that which properly constituted her the "Advocate" of Eve. Father Gambero is even more precise in answering this question when he writes: "He does not in any way appear to mean that Mary made intercession or offered her merits on Eve's behalf. She simply did the opposite of what Eve had done; that is, she obeyed, and thus removed the deplorable consequences of Eve's disobedience. Therefore, Eve is no longer condemned as being responsible for the ruin of the human race, because this ruin has been removed by Mary's obedience."[112]

The use of the term "advocate" is quite interesting since it is the same word that the Scriptures use in reference to Christ and the Spirit, as Newman observed.[113] The term advocate, as used by Irenæus for Mary, seems, therefore, to imply not so much a reference to Mary's intercessory prayer for Eve as to Mary having actually represented Eve in undoing the work of her disobedience by means of her obedience.[114] However, even if one were to interpret Irenæus as having emphasized Mary's role as Advocate of Eve in terms of her intercessory power, it would be nonetheless necessary to distinguish it from the roles of both the Second and Third Persons of the Trinity. Mary represents or stands before God as a creature representing another creature. On the other hand, the mediation of Christ and the mediation of the Spirit are infinite, ineffable utterances which occur within the immediate sphere of the Godhead, that is, in the depths of the Trinitarian mystery and communion in which the creature participates by grace, not by nature. Only the Spirit searches the depths of the Heart of God; only Christ can fully and most efficaciously represent God to man and man to God since He alone is both the expressed image of the Father[115] and perfect Man. And thus, in this ontological sense, Jesus Christ is the Only Mediator between God and Man which does not exclude but rather gives rise to other forms of subordinate and participatory mediatorial roles among creatures.[116]

The hypostatic union affords Our Lord a power of advocacy, mediation, intercession *pro nobis apud Deum* (for us before God) which no other person, neither the highest of angels nor the most perfect of all creatures, i.e., the Blessed Virgin, possesses.[117] In the Gospel of John, the Holy Spirit is called the Second Advocate by Our Lord[118] ; according to the Letter to the Romans (8:26f.), the Spirit articulates on our behalf those prayers which we ourselves are unable to utter since they are contained in the unfathomable recesses of our hearts.[119] The term "advocate" is also properly attributed to Our Lady by the Tradition of the Church. However, the effectiveness of Mary's mediation results primarily from her singular participation in the superabundant grace, merits and omnipotent power flowing from the Godhead, that is, from the Father through Christ the God-Man and Redeemer in union with the activity of Holy Spirit the Paraclete. Mary's intercessory power is subordinate to and dependent upon this Trinitarian communication and activity and derives its efficacy from it.[120] Newman's discussion of Mary's mediation along with her title of Advocate in the *Letter to Pusey* is likewise taken into further consideration in Chapter Six.

(b) *Mary as "Causa Salutis"*

Irenæus' use of the terms "*causa mortis*" and "*causa salutis*" in reference to Eve and Mary must be properly understood in light of the principal roles which Adam and Christ play in the *œconomia salutis*.[121] Lino Cignelli's study entitled "*Maria Nuova Eva nella Patristica Greca*" makes a major contribution to our understanding of the significance of the theology of the New Eve. Cignelli's insights, furthermore, are reflections not only on the nature of Mary's cooperation in the economy of salvation but also on the nature of human cooperation with God in general as epitomized in her.

Cignelli understands that the work of salvation, which Irenæus terms a *recirculatio*, is a redemptive act that can only be fully and properly attributed to the God-Man. Cignelli writes: "the salvific work is commanded by the principle of 'recapitulation'. . . . The redemption is therefore a divine-human work, a theandric work." Furthermore, Cignelli explains the salvific efficacy of this cooperation of God and Man in Christ Jesus from the perspective of the divine economy and the principle of *opus Dei per hominem* (the work of God through man). In other words, the Incarnate Son of God is the only One Who can fully bridge this gap between God and man in the work of salvation. Cignelli writes: "Christ, inasmuch as He is a man, represents precisely the human dimension or causality of the theandric work of redemption." However, in the theology of Irenæus, as Cignelli points out, this theandric dimension of the work of salvation in the Christ the New Adam is also directly related to the human cooperation exemplified in Mary the New Eve and in the antithesis of this divine-human cooperation epitomized by Eve.

Cignelli makes clearer this connection and underscores how the cooperation of Mary and Eve is nonetheless subordinate to the roles of Christ and Adam, just as Satan must be viewed as a

subordinate protagonist compared to God. He writes: "The antithesis of Eve/Mary bespeaks feminine cooperation, in the sense
that the two women work side by side with the two Adams and
participate in their ministerial and meritorious causality. Eve and
Mary move respectively in the sphere of Adam and Christ's activity, and they also work in full dependancy on the transcendent
antithesis between Satan and God." Cignelli explicates these
points further from what he understands to be the perspective of
Irenæus' theology: "Naturally the feminine cooperation does
not find itself on the same level of equality with respect to that of
the masculine. This point merits attention. Whether in her being
or in her work the *mulier* (woman) is ordered to the *vir* (man).
Eve and Mary work subordinately to the two Adams, who are
respectively the primary ministerial agents in the fall and in the
redemption." Therefore, following Cignelli's study of Irenæus,
one concludes that the same texts of the Bishop of Lyons which
indicate a full and responsible causal relationship between Eve's
disobedience and the fall and between Mary's obedience and the
redemptive work of Christ, do not hesitate to further substantiate
the claim that the salvific efficacy of this feminine cooperation is
nonetheless subordinate to and dependent on the roles of their
respective male partners. Cignelli strengthens his argument thus:
"The biblical doctrine concerning the antithesis between Adam
and Christ clearly orients us in this sense. . . . As concerns the
rest, the notion of head ($\chi\varepsilon\varphi\alpha\lambda\acute{\eta}$) is appropriately applied only to
vir [man], and 'head' bespeaks a principal direction and responsi-
bility (cf. 1 Cor 11:3–9; Eph 5:22–33)." [122]

What kind of causality is intended by Irenæus, direct or indirect? [123] Cignelli treats of this topic by distinguishing the disobedience of Adam as *causa formale* ("formal cause") of the fall and
Eve's disobedience as the *concausa formale* ("subordinate formal
cause"). This distinction is then applied to the obedience of
Christ *causa formale* of our salvation and to the obedience of
Mary *concausa formale* of our salvation. Cignelli explains the causality of Eve's and Mary's subordinate cooperation *vis-à-vis* the
principal agency of Adam/Christ in the economy of salvation.
Firstly, the antithesis between Satan and God is firmly established so that they are described as "respectively the transcendent
and principal artisans of the fall and of the redemption. Irenæus
underscores this truth with much force." Secondly, Cignelli ac-

counts for the human element of cooperation in the economy of salvation in view of God and Satan as the primary, transcendent protagonists: "But Satan like God work in the world making use of man. Their transcendent causality does not annul human causality. Man, created free and remaining free, is constituted therefore co-responsible fro his own destiny. On man's part, both sexes concur actively to determine humanity's sort, but not however in the same measure." Third, Cignelli narrows his focus to consider how Adam and Christ the New Adam correspond, each in an unique way, to the role of the human cooperation with the divine in the work of salvation. Cignelli articulates these notions thus: "Ruin and salvation gravitate around the two Adams. As concerns Christ the New Adam, He can redeem because He is the God-Man. As God, He guarantees victory over the devil and communicates life, incorruptibility, and immortality, which are essentially divine gifts; as Man, He is the primary ministerial cause of salvation and the antithesis of Adam—the cause of universal ruin." Fourth, Cignelli turns his attention to the cooperation of the two virgins Eve and Mary who, according to his interpretation of Irenæus, "besides being dependent respectively on Satan and on God, they are ordered in their activity to the two Adams. with whom their share ministerial causality." Fifth, the cooperative roles of Eve and Mary—although clearly causative in nature with regard to our salvation at a ministerial level with respect to the primary roles of Adam and Christ, means that their roles must be understood as "an intermediate and subordinate work." Cignelli clarifies the term subordination, so to give his interpretation of the terms *causa mortis*, predicated of Eve, and *causa salutis*, predicated of Mary:

> Subordination does not mean however being a mere accessory. Irenæus clearly redirects the ruin and salvation of the human race to feminine causality. Eve is 'the cause of death' and Mary is 'the cause of salvation' for all humanity. This feminine causality, ministerial with respect to Satan and God and subordinate with respect to Adam and Christ, is not understood as a purely material fact. It is a true and proper formal cooperation, that is to say a conscious and free act and therefore co-responsible for human destinies.[124]

What then does Irenæus mean when he writes: "Et quemadmodum adstrictum est morti genus humanum per Virginem, salvatur (solvatur) per Virginem."[125] For example, it seems that Newman correctly interprets Irenæus[126] and the other Fathers when he asserts:

> Now, what is especially noticeable in these three writers, is, that they do not speak of the Blessed Virgin merely as the physical instrument of Our Lord's taking flesh, but as an intelligent, responsible cause of it; her faith and obedience being accessories to the Incarnation, and gaining it as a reward. As Eve failed in these virtues, and thereby brought on the fall of the race in Adam, so Mary by means of the same had a part in its restoration.[127]

Some observations on Newman's explanation are necessary.

The juxtaposition of Mary's physical cooperation—her divine maternity—and the exercise of the virtues of faith and obedience—singled out by Justin, Tertullian and Irenæus—is ascribed to an intelligent, responsible, meritorious causality in the work of our Redemption begun at the Incarnation. However, this causality is described by Newman in subordinate terms. The key phrase being "accessories to the Incarnation," which does not detract from the unicity or primacy of Christ's redemptive role. This point is reinforced by Newman who, without undermining the negative consequences of Eve's disbelief and disobedience, carefully notes that her lack of virtue leads to the fall of the human race not in herself but "in Adam." Likewise, Newman speaks of Mary as having had "a part" in the restoration of the human race; he does not say that Mary's virtues of faith and obedience are the primary, direct cause of that restoration, redemption, since they could not have such an inherent salvific efficacy, properly speaking or: these virtues cannot of themselves cause salvation.

The concept of recapitulation is central to Irenæus' theology. The Reverend René Laurentin explains that the comparison between Eve and Mary "it is not in fact a simple parallel, but the almost necessary consequence of an essential idea: the salvific plan of God is not a simple reparation of the first work of creation. It is a new beginning, a regeneration by the Head, a recapitulation in Christ." The idea of recapitulation in Saint Paul is assimilated into Irenæus' writings as recirculation, signifiying that the Christ event, that is the whole mystery of His Person and work, effected a renewal of human existence and of man's relationship to God, to other men and to the whole of creation, not in any superficial way but at a root level.

Father Laurentin explains that "in this radical renewal every one of the elements, corrupted at the moment of the fall, is radically renewed. The *recapitulatio*, a Pauline theme, becomes *recirculatio* in the writings of Irenæus. It is a new theme that one can reassume thus: the evil contracted from the beginning is resolved with a *circuitio contrario*: Christ recalls Adam; the cross, the tree of the fall. In this ensemble, Mary, who recalls Eve, occupies a prime place." Furthermore, Laurentin also accounts for this idea of *recirculatio* in terms of a *circuitio contrario* ("reverse course") as a necessary consequence ("*consequenter*") according to the economy of salvation. He adds: "It is not a simple *connection* to be expressed, but a *consequence* that appears, in Irenæus' theology of history and anthropology, as a type of necessity: that being one of a reprise or recapitulation of everything in Christ." [128] The term *recapitulatio*[129] is most often employed by Irenæus to indicate the restoration of man and the universe, brought about by the Incarnation.[130] In Christ all things are regenerated and recreated in the image and likeness of God according to the original plan of creation, so that every aspect of creation is made to participate in the redemptive and unifying life of God.[131] In God, all creation lives, moves and has its being.[132] Furthermore, man is destined to reach full realization by means of a perfect communion with the Triune God in the life of heaven.[133] The sin of Adam interrupted this primordial harmony and introduced into the world those elements which conspired to further mankind's alienation. Eve's disobedience cooperates in the sin of Adam's rebellion and brings about man's ruin; the *fiat* of the New Eve at the Annunciation[134] cooperates with the Second Adam and brings about man's restoration and recapitulation.[135] De Margerie assesses Irenæus' contribution, precisely as it is a rendering of the meaning of the New Eve theology latent in the sacred texts.

The obvious starting point for De Margerie is Romans 5:14 since: "For Irenæus, Eve is the type, the prefigurement of Mary, as Adam is of Christ." The second scriptural point of reference to which Irenæus appeals, as we have already seen in the texts cited by Newman, is the pericope of the Annunciation. De Margerie explains: "At the moment of their dialogues with angels, Eve and Mary are both betrothed spouses and virgins. By their free acts, both intervene in the historical drama of salvation. . . . In any case, clearly Irenæus ascribes a privileged role in the economy of salvation to the Virgin Mary herself and to her obedience to the Word of God." Thus, according to De Margerie's study of Irenæus, it is primarily on the basis of Mary's free-willed and obedient cooperation that the Bishop of Lyons then is led to give Mary the appellation of "causa salutis," "sibi, et universo generi humano." De Margerie also makes precise that Mary can be considered the "cause of salvation," for herself and for the whole human race only "in dependence on Christ."

De Margerie champions the interpretation of Irenæus given to the scriptural data , for example, Luke 1:38, since he believes that just such a rendering of this text's meaning was made by the Church in the formulations of the dogmas of Mary's Immaculate Conception and Assumption. De Margerie concludes that these dogmas highlight Mary's role of cooperation in the *œconomia salutis* as characterized in a particular way by "the free consent of Mary to the divine maternity." Thus, "implying an awareness on the part of Irenæus of the existence in the writings of Saints Luke and Paul of a principle of privileged and unique association that represents an implicit New Testament grounding of the doctrines of the Immaculate Conception and the Assumption of Mary, the Second and New Eve. For if Paul could view Christ as the New Adam, was he not implicitly viewing Mary[136] as the New and Second Eve, as Irenæus understood her to be?"[137]

The Reverend John Dillon summarizes well the impact of Irenæus on subsequent patristic thought when he writes: "Toward the end of the second century, Mary's part in salvation is clearly described owing to the work of Saint Irenæus. After him, the Eve–Mary comparison became a commonplace among the Fathers."[138]

IV. NEWMAN AND THE TRIUMVIRATE OF JUSTIN, TERTULLIAN, AND IRENÆUS

Newman's treatment of Irenæus is not limited to the fact that he cites two of the most important texts concerning the Eve–Mary parallel in the *Adversus Hæreses*; the *Letter to Pusey* also strives to develop and comment on Irenæus' thought—presenting it as a most intuitive and reliable testimony to the Church's theology concerning the Virgin's cooperation in the economy of salvation. Newman does not read Irenæus in isolation, but as reflecting the cumulative wisdom of the Church's Tradition. The Fathers, for the most part, are for Newman those spotless mirrors into which one can safely gaze, so as the more clearly to perceive the *sensus plenior* (the fuller sense) of the Church's Marian doctrine and devotion. Newman writes:

> Having then adduced these Three Fathers of the second century, I have at least gone so far as this: viz, that no one, who acknowledges the force of early testimony in determining Christian truth, can wonder, no one can compare that we Catholics should hold a very high doctrine concerning the Blessed Virgin, unless indeed stronger statements can be brought for a contrary conception of her, either of as early or at least of a later date. But, as far as I know, no statements can be brought from the ante-Nicene literature, to invalidate the testimony of the Three Fathers concerning her; and little can be brought against it from the fourth century, while in that fourth century the current of testimony in her belief is as strong as in the second; and, as to the fifth, it is far stronger than in any former time, both in its fulness and its authority. That such is the concordant verdict of "the undivided Church" will to some extent be seen (as I proceed).[139]

Newman regards Justin, Irenæus and Tertullian as a formidable theological trio, which he describes as forming "a three-fold cord [that] is not quickly broken." Newman handles the theology of Mary as the New Eve in each of the three Fathers in such a way that the complementarity and cohesiveness of their thought makes for greater comprehension and clarity concerning the whole of the Church's teaching on the Virgin. Newman explains:

> So much as to the nature of this triple testimony; now as to the worth of it. For a moment put aside Saint Irenæus, and put together Saint Justin in the East with Tertullian in the West. I think I may assume that the doctrine of the two Fathers about the Blessed Virgin, was the received doctrine of their own respective times and places; for writers after all are but witnesses of facts and beliefs, and as such they are treated by all parties in controversial discussion. Moreover, the coincidence of doctrine which they exhibit, and again, the antithetical completeness of it, show that they themselves did not originate it.[140]

The final considerations which Father Laurentin makes in "Nuova Eva" in the *Nuovo Dizionario di Mariologia* serve as an interesting historical footnote to the whole question of the theology of the New Eve, the opposition and/or indifference paid to it within various theological circles, the contribution of Newman to the reappraisal of the theme and the renewed interest found in it by contemporary theologians and the Church's Magisterium:

> Overlooked in these last centuries, the theme of the New Eve has been taken up again honorably by Cardinal A. Billot *and even before him by John Henry Newman*. The Second Vatican Council in its turn picks up the theme of the Eve–Mary parallelism (LG 56). . . . The Eve–Mary theme, forgotten at the time of the Counter Reformation by a Mariology based on the privileges of Mary, has been rightfully restored to a place of honor due to reasons worthy of renewed interest. This theme in fact, pertains to a symbolism that was too much forgotten according to a certain theological rationalism, whether it be on the part of Scholasticism or by a Mariology that was reduced along the lines of demythologization. This theme belongs to a theology of *the history of salvation*, set aside by concepts that were too abstract and reductive. . . . The Fathers of the Church developed a positive parallel for holy women and for every Christian soul. It is important not to patent this theme as a simple comparison more or less subtle in nature. It is a way by which to understand the plan of God in the history of salvation, whereby Mary is a new point of departure: the New Eve, the Mother of the New Adam according to the spirit, so that He might be born according to the flesh[141] [emphasis added].

V. NEWMAN AND SAINT AMBROSE: THE VIRGINITY OF MARY AND HER SPIRITUAL MATERNITY

Introduction

The aim of this section is to examine these important aspects of Saint Ambrose's Mariology[142] and to relate them to the Mariology of Cardinal Newman. Because Newman does not provide us with a detailed commentary the better with which to understand the significance of Saint Ambrose's Marian teachings, it is necessary, as we have been doing with the other Fathers, to situate Newman's use of Ambrose in the wider context of Ambrose's own writings and to show how Newman's own Marian theology mirrors that of Ambrose. It is hoped that this will effectively demonstrate how the Mariological thought of these two great theologians are linked together in the Tradition.

However, before this can be effectively achieved, perhaps a general introduction to Saint Ambrose's Mariological thought is needed.[143] The Reverend Gerardo Di Nola's synthesis is excellent and deserves attention here. The key points that Di Nola makes are the following: The figure and example of Mary are afforded a special place in the Marian thought of Saint Ambrose. Ambrose has a profound veneration for the Virgin Mary that is characterized as deriving, "not from a pietistic sentimentalism, but from a precise consciousness of her singular place with regard to everyone else: for which she becomes a singular model in the mystery of salvation: first for the virgins, afterwards for mothers, for widows and for each faithful one."

Furthermore, Di Nola describes Mary's exemplarity in the life of faith as the fruit of Ambrose's reflection on Mary's pre-eminent holiness in the life of the Church.[144] He makes the interesting point that Ambrose's love of Mary's purity was so great that on occasion he felt the need to make an apology for it when faced with the objections of Eastern writers to whom he himself looked for inspiration. Ambrose's Mariology is also fascinating, according to Father Di Nola, not simply for its delineation of Marian doctrine and devotion but because it also reveals, "the psychological itinerary of Ambrose before Mary since one senses in Ambrose an attempt at introspection into the soul of the Virgin and into the thought of God that willed her to be in His plan, for the purpose of overcoming progressively the 'difficulties' that the Gospels do not cease to put before modern exegesis." He makes several other observations on Ambrose's "Marian thought," which he terms "rich and articulated," even if Ambrose did not present us with a systematic Mariological treatise as such. Some of the dogmas emphasized by Ambrose in his Mariology are the following: the virginal conception of Jesus and its ancillary doctrine of Our Lord's sinlessness; the divine maternity of Mary as a necessary dogmatic corollary of the Christological dogmas of the early councils; he develops and adds to the New Eve theology of earlier Fathers.

Related to these dogmatic considerations of Ambrose's Mariology, Di Nola also notes that there is an ethical and spiritual aspect in which Ambrose adamantly defends the virginity of Mary and upholds Mary as the exemplary model of virginity according to the Lucan portrait of Mary that is drawn in the account of the Annunciation.[145] As Di Nola recalls, Ambrose's exposition on Mary's virginity finds inspiration in the theology of Saint Athanasius.[146] He writes: "following Athanasius, he proposes the Virgin as teacher and model to all virgins according to her true and evangelical portrait of virginal modesty, of attentive listening to the Word of God, of humility of heart, of incessant activity, of solicitous charity toward the poor, of daily asceticism, of interior balance, of ardent, virginal desire for the Spouse Who is continually sought after and always faithfully followed." In Ambrose's theology, there is an interrelationship between the doctrine of Mary's Virginity and his understanding of Mary as the exemplar of all the other Christian virtues. Di Nola explains: "After the Annunciation, Ambrose discovers and highlights in the Virgin-Mother all the fundamental Christian virtues: faith, untouched by any doubt whatsoever; humility, that each day renders her more similar to Christ, by means of an attentive attitude aimed at knowing Him better in order the better to imitate Him."

However, the doctrine of Mary's perpetual virginity[147] is, without doubt, a key doctrine that Ambrose believed necessitated a special defense against the attacks of heretics.[148] Thus, Di Nola comments: "Because of this Ambrose is forced to overcome exegetical doubts and difficulties, favoring arguments in the tradition of both East and West, it seems that new roads open up for him, which reconnected themselves to the same eternal thought of God, Who purposely chose Mary, because He knew her to be worthy and capable of a perfect, indefectible gift of love." One finds in Ambrose's Mariology also a predilection for the evangelical depiction of her beneath the Cross with the beloved virgin disciple John. In fact, Father Di Nola praises Ambrose's unique contribution to Western theology in this regard noting that he expressly demonstrates how Mary is "thus indissolubly united to her Crucified Son, to the point of desiring to die before Him, out of maternal love, or at least to die with Him through her faith as His disciple, in order to rise also together with Him in the end, accomplishing one unique 'paschal mystery' of life, and of redemption, if it had been necessary to unite her own mind to the sacrifice of her Son—the Redeemer."

Finally, Di Nola indicates that Ambrose's Mariology is of particular importance in light of the Second Vatican Council's appropriation of his thought on Mary as *typus Ecclesiæ* ("type of the Church").[149] He explains that this ecclesial typology developed in Ambrose involves different types of parallelisms, namely, "a typological parallelism between Mary and the Church, between the maternity of Mary and the sacraments of the Church, between Mary and every member of the faithful in the Church, regarding precisely the virginity of faith and the fecundity of the Spirit."

Therefore, Father Di Nola concludes that Ambrose's parallel of Mary and the Church leads, practically speaking, to the one image being superimposed on the other. This is also illustrated in Ambrose's theology when one considers that Mary is the Virgin Mother of Christ both for her own sake and for others. He synthesizes these very important aspects of Ambrose's Mariology in the following manner: "Mary, for Ambrose, remains the perennial model of how every member of the Faithful can conceive, bear in his heart and generate Christ in his own life."[150]

(a) *Mary's Virginity*

Therefore, with this background in mind, the first major theme to be discussed is that of Mary's virginity since it is one that is of particular importance in both the theology of Saint Ambrose and Cardinal Newman. Ambrose exalts the Virgin as the model of holiness and virtue for all virgins. Virginity became a type of spiritual or white martyrdom after the official persecution of Christians by the Roman Empire had ceased although it re-emerged from time to time in the fourth and fifth centuries A.D.[151] Ambrose wrote several works on our topic that are important historical and theological documents of this era.[152]

His treatise *De institutione virginis et sanctæ Mariæ virginitate perpetua ad Eusebium liber unus* is particularly critical for Mariology since it holds up the Virgin Mary as the model of virginity both for those consecrated to virginity in the religious life and for all Christians who should strive to imitate the spirituality of the consecrated virgins, that is, to seek the perfection of the virtues, most especially those of patience, chastity and charity. Therefore, in Ambrose, virginity is both a physical and spiritual consecration—a sign of unreserved dedication to the service of the Lord and ideals of His Kingdom which, in the person of the Virgin, is perfectly realized. Ambrose is convinced that the *via perfectionis* ("way of perfection") for all Christians is ideally found in living consecrated virginity since it is the way preferred by Our Lord Himself and by His Blessed Mother Mary Ever-Virgin.[153]

Writing to his sister Marcellina, Ambrose encourages her to be faithful to the vow of consecrated virginity she had made, based, first and foremost, on the example of Christ the Virgin, Who exemplifies virginity and virginal purity in both His essence as the Son of God existing in the bosom of the Father from all eternity and insofar as He was conceived without sin from the Virgin Mary in time. Thus, the Incarnate Son becomes the model *par excellence* of a virginal, celibate, sinless life. Marcellina is therefore exhorted to imitate Christ's integrity and unity of life in the living out of her own vow of virginity.

> Quid autem est castitas virginalis, nisi expers contagionis integritas? Atque ejus auctorem quem possumus æstimare, nisi immaculatum Dei Filium, cujus caro non vidit corruptionem, divinitas non est experta contagionem? Videte igitur quanta virginitatis merita sint. Christus ante virginem, Christus ex virgine: a Patre quidem natus ante sæcula, sed ex virgine natus ab sæcula. Illud naturæ suæ, hoc naturæ utilitatis est. Illud erat semper, hoc voluit.[154]

In the *Letter to Pusey*, Newman refers to Saint Jerome and to Saint Ambrose as having deemed the Virgin Mary "the great pattern of Virgins."[155] Newman does not give an exact reference to Ambrose's writings but perhaps the following quotation is a good example of his teaching on Mary as the model of virginity.

> Hæc est imago virginitatis. Talis enim fuit Maria, ut ejus unius vita omnium sit disciplina. Si igitur auctor non disciplicet, opus probemus; ut quæcumque sibi ejus exoptat præmium, imitetur exemplum. Quantæ in una virgine species virtutum emicant? Secretum verecundiæ, vexillum fidei, devotionis obsequium: virgo intra domum, comes ad ministerium, mater ad templum.[156]

Giordano Frosini writes: "But, as Saint Ambrose confirmed, 'the life of Mary is a mirror for everyone'"[157] Furthermore, in *La*

Vergine Maria nella Formazione Intellettuale e Spirituale, we read: "Among all believers she, Mary, is like a 'mirror' in which 'the great works of God' are reflected in the most profound and limpid way." [158] In fact, we find, in Ambrose, this figurative language that characterizes Mary as the mirror of virginal purity and sanctity when he writes:

> Sit igitur vobis tanquam in imagine descripta virginitas vita Mariæ de qua velut speculo refulgeat species castitatis et forma virtutis. Hinc sumatis licet exempla vivendi, ubi tanquam in exemplari magisteria expressa probabitatis, quid corrigere, quid effigere, quid tenere debeatis ostendunt.[159]

Pope John Paul II, in his Apostolic Letter *Operosam Diem*, written on the occasion of the 1600th anniversary of Saint Ambrose's death, confirms Ambrose's teaching on the exemplary nature of Mary's virginity and motherhood and of Mary's faith and purity, proposing her as the sublime model of virtue for all of Christ's faithful.[160] The Pope's Apostolic Letter also affirms Ambrose's appreciation of Mary's singular role of cooperation in the history of salvation. She is, in other words, that spotless mirror into which each member of Christ's Faithful can gaze, so as to catch a glimpse of the beauty of holiness to which each one of us is called to reflect in our own lives whether as priests, consecrated religious or lay members of the Church.[161]

Newman's own keen appreciation of the exemplarity of Mary's virginity and chastity is revealed in several passages from his *Meditations and Devotions*, where he dwells on the essence of *virginitas mentis, corporis et animæ* so emphasized in the theology of Saint Ambrose.[162] In his *De Virginibus* Ambrose lists a series of the Virgin Mary's virtues, which cultivated in body and soul in cooperation with the Lord's plan of salvation. Thus, Ambrose exhorts all other virgins to do the same by following Mary's example. Some of those virtues that characterized Mary's bodily and mental virginity are described by Ambrose as follows: "corde umilis, verbis gravis, animi prudens, . . . intenta operi, verecunda sermoni, arbitrum mentis solita non hominem, sed Deum quærere, . . . rationem sequi, amare virtutem . . ." [163]

Likewise, Newman reflects on Mary's luminous exemplification of physical and spiritual virtues, such as those mentioned by Ambrose. In what is referred to as his "Meditations for Eight

Days," Newman's meditation for "Saturday" is dedicated to the contemplation of Mary as the model of virgins. He invites the person who meditates to imagine Mary as "robed in white, like the lily," which brings our attention to her purity. Newman then instructs us to address the Virgin in these words:

> Thou, Mary, art the Virgin of Virgins. To have a virgin soul is to love nothing on earth in comparison to God, or except for His sake. That soul is virginal which is ever looking for its Beloved Who is heaven, and which sees Him in whatever is lovely upon the earth, loving earthly friends very dearly, but in their proper place, as His gifts, and His representatives, but loving Jesus alone with sovereign affection, and bearing to lose all, so that she may keep Him . . . O Mary, when will you gain for me some little of this celestial purity, this true whiteness of soul, that may fix my heart on my true love?[164]

In almost mystical language, Newman has us engage Our Lady in a *cor ad cor loquitur* ("heart speaks to heart") by which we express to her not only our admiration of her virginity, purity, chastity and holiness for their own sake but also because we seek to ask her to intercede for us that we might come to share in those same virtues. Ultimately, the purpose of our meditation on Mary's spiritual and physical virginity is aimed at a mystical union or marriage of our souls with Christ the Bridegroom of our souls. As Mary's heart "was with Jesus only"[165] so too we long to have Jesus reign at the center of our hearts. Our freedom from sin is absolutely essential for Christ to make His royal entrance. Perhaps this is why Newman begins this meditation by directing us to read from Isaiah 35:1–10, in which Israel's deliverance from exile in Babylon is prophesied, according to which only the holy ones, "no one unclean," the "redeemed," the "ransomed," will pass over "the holy way" "and enter Zion singing, crowned with everlasting joy." For Christians, this passage of Scripture refers not only to the historic return of the Israelites to their homeland after the exile but also to the hope that one day all those redeemed by Christ will be able to enter the heavenly homeland—the new and everlasting Jerusalem or Zion.

Certainly, Newman's meditations on the Marian titles *Virgo Purissima* (Virgin Most Pure) and *Virgo Prædicanda* (Virgin to Be Preached), which are part of a series of meditations on the doctrine of the Immaculate Conception, are meant to enhance our love of Mary's purity, that extraordinary gift of integrated holiness, body and soul, that forms the essence of her being from the very beginning of its existence. Mary's sinlessness from the moment of her conception is, as Newman reflects in his meditation *Virgo Purissima*, her divine "prerogative," "the foundation of all those salutary truths which are revealed to us concerning her."

Mary is the New Eve for she was, as Newman says, "a child of Adam and Eve as though they had never fallen," one who "inherited the gifts and graces (and more than those) which Adam and Eve possessed in Paradise." Thus, even though we neither share in her privilege of an immaculate conception nor enjoy the gift of pristine holiness, Newman urges us, as sons and daughters of Adam and Eve fallen from grace yet redeemed by Christ, to join our voices with "all holy souls" in entreating the *Virgo Purissima*: "*Virgin Most Pure, conceived without original sin, Mary, pray for us.*" [166]

The title *Virgo Prædicanda* is likewise partially based on a reflection on Mary's sinlessness from conception. Newman upholds Mary as "deserving to be preached abroad because she never committed any sin, even the least; because sin had no part in her; because, through the fullness of God's grace, she never thought a thought, or spoke a word, or did an action, which was displeasing, which was not most pleasing, to Almighty God; because in her was displayed the greatest triumph over the enemy of souls." [167] Thus, according to Newman, "first, she was preached as the Virgin of Virgins," and only last (up until his time in 1854) was she proclaimed as "Immaculate in her Conception," showing how Mary's sacred virginity and her sinlessness are two doctrines which enfold the mystery of Our Lady's life. [168]

Newman, in his *Essay on the Development of Christian Doctrine*, quotes Saint Ambrose as saying: "Mary was alone and wrought the world's salvation," adding that Ambrose's makes this point in connection to Mary's virginal conception of the Redeemer. [169] Furthermore, as Newman points out, Mary is prefigured by the pillar of cloud [170] which guided the Israelites, according to the same Father; and she had 'thus great grace, as not only to have virginity herself, but to impart it to those to whom she came.'" [171]

The above text is repeated practically verbatim in the *Letter to Pusey* (66), save the comparison of Mary to the pillar of cloud referred to in Exodus 40:34–38. One may ask, why does Newman consider these texts of Ambrose important? And, what does Ambrose mean when he says that Mary not only has virginity herself, but also communicates it to others? Given the context in which Ambrose writes this phrase, namely in commenting on Mary's visitation to Elizabeth, one can understand the meaning of Ambrose's words as referring to the graces of purity, chastity, and holiness which Mary exemplified—by word and example—and to the fact that the Church continues to derive spiritual benefits, as through her mediation, from her cooperation in the economy of salvation.[172]

Thus, Mary's visit to Elizabeth is seen by Ambrose in this passage as cited by Newman from *De Institutione Virginis* as a model act of virginal purity and faithful obedience by which she was able to share with others those gifts of grace she had received in a special way for the sake of the economy of salvation. Mary's visitation to Elizabeth corresponds in other words to a selfless act which becomes a means of evangelization, that is of cooperation, which is meant to enhance the salvation of those to whom the message of her virginal conception of the Messiah and Savior is announced.[173]

Ambrose notes that Mary's visitation, which is prolonged for three months, helped John the Baptist become fortified for his mission ("Nec immerito mansit integer corpore, quem tribus mensibus oleo quodam suæ presentiæ et integritatis unguento Domini Mater exercuit"), insofar as he was then brought closer to the infant precursor of her Son Who Himself would serve the Lord in complete chastity. In that same passage, Ambrose comments that Mary's later entrustment to John the Evangelist, with whom she would take up her final earthly dwelling place, was himself a virgin "coniugium nescienti" ("as to one ignorant of conjugal relations"). As Mary joyfully received the Annunciation of the Angel and cooperated by saying "yes," so too Ambrose envisions Mary's visitation to Elizabeth as a joyful annunciation on her part that allows that "yes" then to resound in the life of others. Concerning the wonderful exchange of Mary and John the Evangelist, he writes: "Unde non mirror præ ceteris locutum mysteria divina, cui præsto erat aula cælestium sacramentorum."[174]

In the treatise *De Institutione Virginis*, Saint Ambrose exhorts the consecrated virgins to consider their state of virginity as sacred, indeed, as a celestial gift, likened to the pillar of cloud that hovered over the Israelites in the desert, signifying the abiding presence of God's grace. However, it is Mary's virginity and her virginal conception, that are exalted by the Doctor of Milan as that most sacred and most pure of conduits by which the waters of Christ's salvific grace have come down from the clouds of heaven to bring about our Redemption, the re-creation of mankind. He likewise compares this salvific grace to a type of heavenly, perfumed oil that anoints man with the truth, enabling him to co-operate in the work of salvation. Sacred virginity, therefore, is understood by Ambrose to be a constant sign both of the spiritual fecundity of the Church's life and of that new creation wrought by the coming of the heavenly dew of Christ's redemptive grace into the world through the virgin birth of the New Eve.

> O divitias Marianæ virginitatis! Quasi olla ferbuit et quasi nubes pluit in terras gratiam Christi. Scriptum est enim de ea: *Ecce dominus venit sedens super nubem levem.* Vere levem quæ coniugii onera nescivit; vere levem quæ levavit hunc mundum de gravi fenorum peccatorum. Levis erat, quæ remissionem peccatorum utero gestabat. . . . Excipite igitur, excipite, sacræ virgines, nubis huius pluviam spiritalem temperamentum flagrantiæ corporalis, ut corporis omnes restinguatis ardores atque interna mentis vestræ humescant. Huius imbrem nubis sacratæ patres nostri annuntiaverunt nobis salutem mundi futuram. Hunc imbrem significabant esse venturum *stillicidia stillantia super terram,* Hierobaal poposcit et meruit. Bonam nubem sequimini, quæ fontem intra se genuit, quo rigavit orbem terrarum. Excipite ergo voluntariam pluviam, pluviam benedictionis, quam hereditatis suæ dominus effudit. Excipite aquam, et non effluat vobis. Quia nubes est, diluat vos et sacro humore perfundat. Quia olla est, spiritu vaporet æterno. Excipite itaque ex hac Moabitide olla gratiæ cælestis unguentum, nec veramini ne deficiat; quod exinanitum est et plus redundat, quandoquidem in omnem terram odor eius exivit, sicut scriptum est: *Unguentum exinanitum est nomen tuum; propterea adulescentulæ dilexerunt te.* Descendat istud unguentum in ima præcordia viscerumque secreta, quo non deliciarum odores sancta Maria, sed divinæ gratiæ spiramenta redolebat. Hæc pluvia Evæ restinxit appetentium, Hoc unguentum hereditarii erroris abstersit.[175]

(b) *Mary's Spiritual Maternity*

In *De Institutione Virginis* Ambrose speaks of Mary's virginal conception of Christ in terms of her having received into her womb Christ the *odor suavitatis* and the *odor sanctitatis* ("fragrance of sweetness," "fragrance of sanctity") par excellence. Christ's own sanctity overflowed into Mary's life and continues to do so in the life of the Church, most especially in the life of consecrated virgins who willingly follow her example in receiving Christ into their lives. This reception of their Lord and Master involves their being sanctified and anointed body and soul as His Spiritual Brides.[176]

Newman is remarkably similar to Ambrose in his use of symbolism, for example, the mention of perfumed oil, in reference to the Virgin when he writes, "is it wonderful then that she has left behind her in the Church below 'an odour like cinnamon and balm, and sweetness like to choice myrrh'?"[177] Newman chooses these images inspired by the Book of Sirach to describe Mary's sanctity (*odor sanctitatis*) as exceeding that of every creature and of every member of the Church. Newman is not content to underscore the importance of Mary's example of holiness; his discourse is also particularly aimed at encouraging a more fervent devotion to the Virgin, so that the holiness of the Mother might be extended to her children in the Church.[178]

Invoking the Blessed Virgin under such venerable titles as Seat of Wisdom, Gate of Heaven and Mother of Mercy, Newman desires that these titles be acknowledged as expressive of Christological doctrine. Furthermore, these titles indicate Mary's extraordinary relationship to Christ and His work of Redemption, and an invocation of her under these titles as an expression of our filial devotion to her as our spiritual Mother,[179] who spurs us on toward greater union with her Son and an evermore fervent collaboration in the work of salvation, of which the Church is the universal sacrament.[180]

Newman explicitly refers to "Mary as Our Mother," in his *Sermon Notes*. His point of departure is John 19:25–27 wherein the Crucified Savior entrusts His Blessed Mother to the Beloved Disciple and vice versa, as part of His last will and testament.[181] Ambrose, too, interprets the scene at the foot of the Cross in terms of its significance in the salvific economy. Mary, as Ambrose relates, is entrusted to the Beloved Disciple so that, all things being accomplished, Mary's cooperation in the work of salvation is then carried out, in a particular way, as the spiritual mother of the members of Christ's Body the Church.[182]

Thus, Our Lord, as Newman explains in the *Sermon Notes*, not only provides His Church—according to His last will and testament—with spiritual shepherds, pastors, as in the persons of Peter and the other apostles, but also provides the Church with a spiritual mother, Mary, whose maternal solicitude, that is, "a mother's special gift–fostering care, tenderness, compassion, unfailing love," aims to bring the Church into ever closer union with her Son. Newman explains that more than any other maternal figure in our lives. He uses the analogies of country, schools, colleges, universities. Mary's spiritual maternity fulfills, to the most excellent degree, the maternal role of the Church. Then, Newman makes the following concluding points: Even if "many lose their mothers, or have unkind mothers," "our heavenly Mother cannot fail and cannot err, cannot obscure her Son and Lord, but reminds of Him. Let us try to get this filial feeling, though we can only learn it by degrees and cannot force ourselves into it." [183]

As we have already seen, Ambrose also adopts from Saint Irenæus the theme of the Eve–Mary parallel. As the Bishop of Lyons emphasized this parallel's soteriological importance, so the Bishop of Milan explored its ecclesiological underpinnings, particularly that of Mary's spiritual maternity. Ultimately, the two aspects are intertwined in the writings of both Fathers. Ambrose considers Eve's salvation to be in the Church, best represented by the figure of the Virgin Mary. Both Mary and the Church can be considered the New Eve, in the thought of Ambrose,[184] and have essential roles in the economy of salvation. For example, Ambrose writes:

> Si quæris quæ vita sit, si moveat quod factum sit in ipso, adcipe. Nempe vita Ecclesia est. In ipso facta est, in eius costa, in ipso resuscitata Eva. Eva autem vita, hoc est, quod factum est; quia Eva quæ perierat, salva facta est per Ecclesiam, hoc est, per filiorum suorum generationem, sicut scriptum est quia delictum superioris prævaricationis sobria emendavit hæreditas.[185]

As Eve is created from the side of the sleeping Adam, so the Church is created from the side of Christ Who sleeps the sleep of death on the Cross.[186] In both instances new life is generated. Eve, generated in the first creation, loses the gift of immortality. In the second creation, through the Death and Resurrection of the New Adam, Eve, represented by the Church, is reborn to everlasting life and thus is also recreated and redeemed as part of renewed humanity.[187] Kelly comments on Ambrose's theology of Mary's spiritual maternity as an integral part of Our Lord's last will and testament given from the Cross: "Christ's words from the cross to Mary and John (Jn 19:26f.) were really addressed to the Church, with which she was virtually identified and to its members." [188]

The new life of this renewed or recreated humanity is most fully revealed in the life of the Church—the Body of Christ, the whole company of the redeemed. Christ is the Life, Who communicated this life to the members of His Body the Church so that, by means of her, that life may continue to be transmitted to future generations of believers. Salvation, therefore, is Christ's gift to His Church and through the sacraments, most especially through Baptism, the Church gives birth to new children for God the Father in the power of the Holy Spirit.[189] And these new children reborn by water and the spirit in the bosom of the Church are also placed under the maternal care of the Virgin Mary.[190] The spiritual maternity of the Church and of the Virgin Mary are therefore inexorably linked since, as Saint Ambrose writes, "Deipara est ecclesiæ typus, ut iam docebat in ordine scilicet fidei, caritatis et perfectæ cum Christo unionis." [191]

Ambrose's theology of Mary's spiritual maternity is expounded in several other passages from his works—from his letters, his treatise on the institution of virgins and the perpetual virginity of Mary, and in his commentary on the Visitation in Luke's Gospel.[192] Ambrose, in his *Epistula* 63, extols Mary's virginity and divine maternity because it is the means by which salvation has been generated for the universe. Thus, Ambrose also notes that it is through the cooperation of the Virgin in Christ's redemptive work that men and women are rejoined to God, those same men and women who in the persons of their first parents had been ejected from the Garden of Paradise. Ambrose writes: "Quid autem loquar quanta sit virginitatis gratia, quæ meruit a Christo eligi ut esset etiam corporale Dei templum, in qua corporaliter ut legimus habitavit plenitudo divinitatis? Virgo genuit mundi salutem, virgo peperit vitam universorum . . . Per virum autem et mulierem caro eiecta est de paradiso: per Virginem iuncta est Deo." [193] Along similar lines, in *De Institutione Virginis*, Ambrose praises the virginal womb of Mary which brings forth the fruit of Redemption by the power of the Holy Spirit, so that "per fidem credentium fieret omnis viri caput Christus" and furthermore, "quod erat carnis assumpsit ex Virgine, atque in illa novissimi Adam immaculati hominis membra formavit." [194]

In other words, because it is from Mary's body that the New Adam has been formed, God has willed that in her should likewise be formed the members of the immaculate New Adam Who is both Head of humanity and Head of the Church. In this way, Mary's divine maternity becomes the source of her spiritual motherhood of mankind, redeemed in Christ and incorporated into His Body, the Church. Finally, in his commentaries on the Visitation, Ambrose emphasizes how the presence of Mary pregnant with the Christ-Child invigorates the Baptist in the womb of Elizabeth and acts like a consecration or anointing in preparation for his prophetic mission as precursor of the Messiah. Once again, Mary's divine maternity is interpreted in an ecclesiological sense by the Doctor of Milan since it is a mystery which envelopes the very first members of the Church, for example, John the Baptist, allowing God's grace to make them spiritually fruitful and strong, "in utero situs matris a mensura perfectæ coepit ætatis plenitudinis Christi." [195]

Thus, one finds, in Newman's final exhortation in his sermon "On the Fitness of the Glories of Mary," a masterpiece of Marian spirituality that contains a veritable treasure house of his theology and spirituality concerning the maternal relationship that should be enjoyed between Our Lady and her spiritual children in the Church. This text, though lengthy, merits inclusion at this point:

> And now, my dear brethren, what is befitting in us, if all that I have been telling you is befitting in Mary? If the Mother of Emmanuel ought to be the first of creatures in sanctity and beauty; if it became her to be free from all sin from the very first, and from the moment she received her first grace to begin to merit more; and if such as was her beginning, such was her end, her conception immaculate and her death an

assumption: if she died, but revived, and is exalted on high; what is befitting in the children of such a Mother, but an imitation, in their measure, of her devotion, her meekness, her simplicity, her modesty, and her sweetness? Her glories are not only for the sake of her Son, they are for our sakes also. Let us copy her faith, who received God's message by the angel without doubt; her patience, who endured Saint Joseph's surprise without a word; her obedience, who went up to Bethlehem in the winter and bore Our Lord in a stable; her meditative spirit, who pondered in her heart what she saw and heard about Him: her fortitude, whose heart the sword went through; her self-surrender, who gave Him up during His ministry and consented to His death. Above all, let us imitate her purity, who, rather than relinquish her virginity, was willing to lose Him for a Son. O my dear children, young men and young women, what need have you of the intercession of the Virgin-mother, of her help, of her pattern, in this respect! What shall bring you forward in the narrow way, if you live in the world, but the thought and patronage of Mary? What shall seal your senses, what shall tranquillise your heart, when sights and sounds of danger around you, but Mary? What shall give you patience and endurance, when you are wearied out with the length of the conflict with evil, with the unceasing necessity of precautions, with the irksomeness of observing them, with the tediousness of their repetition, with the strain upon your mind, with your forlorn and cheerless condition, but a loving communion with her! She will comfort you in your discouragements, solace you in your fatigues, raise you after your falls, reward you for your successes. She will show you her Son, Your God and your all. When your spirit is excited, or relaxed, or depressed, when it loses its balance, when it is restless and wayward, when it is sick of what it has, and hankers after what it has not, when your eye is solicited with evil and your mortal frame trembles under the shadow of the tempter, what will bring you to yourselves, to peace and to health, but the cool breath of the Immaculate and the fragrance of the Rose of Sharon? It is the boast of the Catholic Religion, that it has the gift of making the young heart chaste; and why is this, but that it gives us Jesus Christ for our Food, and Mary for our nursing Mother? Fulfil this boast in yourselves; prove to the world that you are following no false teaching, vindicate the glory of your Mother Mary, whom the world blasphemes, in the very face of the world, by the simplicity of your own deportment, and the sanctity of your words and deeds. Go to her for the royal heart of innocence. She is the beautiful gift of God, which outshines the fascinations of a bad world, and which no one ever sought in sincerity and was disappointed. She is the personal type and representative image of that spiritual life and renovation in grace, "without which no one shall see God." "Her spirit is sweeter than honey, and her heritage than the honeycomb. They that eat her shall yet be hungry, and they that drink her shall still thirst. Whoso hearkeneth to her shall not be confounded, and they that work by her shall not sin." [196]

What can we gather from this rich text? Newman presents us with a very solid theology of Mary as *typus Ecclesiæ*. Indeed, for Newman, Mary is the *Mater Ecclesiæ* since he plainly regards Mary's spiritual maternity as deriving from and intrinsically connected to all of her other privileges exercised in the Church and on behalf of the Church's spiritual children. In this final exhortation, he praises Mary's virtues and exhorts the members of the Church to imitate them, insisting that her privileges, above all her sinlessness (e.g., Immaculate Conception), and her purity or holiness in body and soul (e.g., Assumption), have been given to the Virgin Mary not only for herself but are also for our sake, that is, for our sanctification and salvation. [197]

Thus, Newman cleverly takes up again the theme expressed in his earlier discourse, "The Glories of Mary for the Sake of Her Son," and accentuates its ecclesiological significance. He effectively makes this accentuation by reviewing the mysteries of Our Lady's life according to the scriptural data, to highlight as worthy of imitation those particular virtues exemplified by the Virgin Mother. Indeed, as we have already seen in the theology of Saint Ambrose, Newman is quite fond of Mary's sacred virginity and divine maternity. His discourse is addressed primarily to his young audience whom he fervently exhorts to seek Mary's heavenly intercession and patronage, especially in times of trial, tribulation and temptation. Newman reassures us that anyone who has had "sincere" recourse to Mary's maternal intercession has never been "disappointed."

Although Newman himself does not quote Saint Bernard of Clairvaux in this context, his exhorting words call to mind the *Memorare*, attributed to Bernard: "Remember, O Most Blessed

Virgin Mary, that never was it known that anyone who fled to thy protection, implored thy help or sought thy intercession was left unaided. Inspired by this confidence, I fly unto thee, O Virgin of Virgins, My Mother. To thee I come, before thee I stand, sinful and sorrowful. O Mother of the Word Incarnate, despise not my petitions, but, in thy clemency, hear and answer them." [198] In his exhortation, Newman is convinced, and he wants the young people he is addressing to be convinced too, that they have most definite need of Mary's maternal care and intercession precisely because they are young and will most likely find it difficult to persevere in following Mary's "pattern" of purity, holiness and spiritual fecundity.

Also noteworthy in this regard is Newman's brief but poignant statement where he links the Sacrament of the Eucharist and Mary's spiritual motherhood of the Church as sources of spiritual nourishment—founts of abundance of grace needed to mature in the life of virtue, especially in the virtue of chastity. Newman writes: "It is the boast of the Catholic religion that it has the gift of making the young heart chaste; and why is this, but that it gives us Jesus Christ for our Food, and Mary for our nursing Mother?" [199] It is fascinating to note that Newman in one of his *Sermon Notes*, entitled "On Mary As Our Mother," compares Our Lord's love for His children in the Church to that of a mother[200] who, "bearing us in pain," an implicit reference to His Passion, fulfills the words of the Prophet Isaiah: "Shall a mother forget her suckling child?" by "nourishing us with the milk of the Holy Eucharist." [201]

Newman, then, concludes by assuring his "dear young people" that their Holy Mother's mediation is effective also in the crowning of their own merits; and that their communion with her is but a communion with her Son. He writes in this regard: "She is the personal *type* (emphasis added) and *representative image* of that spiritual life and renovation in grace, "without which no one shall see God" (emphasis added).[202]

He also concludes his sermon "The Glories of Mary for the Sake of Her Son" with a supplication that sums up the filial attitude that should be commonplace in every believer. The reader will quickly recognize in this passage that, for Newman, Trinitarian theology, Christology, Mariology, ecclesiology and eschatology are all intimately connected in the economy of salvation as they are likewise interconnected in the doctrine, worship and devotional life of the universal Church, and therefore, are also meant to be integrated into the individual lives of her spiritual sons and daughters. Nothing about Mary is accidental; she is especially chosen by the Heavenly Father to be the sinless Mother of His Only-Begotten Son. Her sinlessness is likened to a radiant beauty and holiness that helps make possible the recapitulation of our fallen human race in Christ, that is, the restoration of the "original purpose of the Most High."

Yet, because she is a creature like ourselves, indeed, our spiritual Mother, we look to Mary and imitate her virtues in a special way, so that, in doing so, we may one day be led by her to gaze upon the countenance of her Son. Everything in Mary, every grace, every privilege, every glory, is, as Newman prays, meant to act as a beacon of light along our pilgrim way to Our Lord and to guide us to the bosom of His and our Heavenly Father and to that heavenly home whence He first descended to earth for our salvation "conceived of the Holy Spirit and born of the Virgin Mary."

> Such thou art, Holy Mother, in the creed and in the worship of the Church, the defense of many truths, the grace and smiling light of every devotion. In thee, O Mary, is fulfilled, as we can bear it, an original purpose of the Most High. He once had meant to come on earth in heavenly glory, but we sinned; and then He could not safely visit us, except with a shrouded radiance and a bedimmed Majesty, for He was our God. So He came Himself in weakness, not in power, and He sent thee, a creature, in His stead, with a creature's comeliness and lustre suited to our state. And now thy very face and form, dear Mother, speak to us of the Eternal; not like earthly beauty, dangerous to look upon, but like the morning star, which is thy emblem, bright and musical, breathing purity, telling of heaven, and infusing peace. O harbinger of day! O hope of the pilgrim! lead us still as thou hast led; in the dark night, across the bleak wilderness, guide us on to Our Lord Jesus, guide us home.
>
> *Maria, Mater gratiæ,*
> *Dulcis parens clementiæ,*
> *Tu nos ab hoste protege*
> *Et mortis hora suscipe.*[203]

(c) *Mary and Zechariah: An Example of Antithetical Parallelism in Newman and Ambrose*

In his *Expositio Evangelii secundum Lucam*,[204] Ambrose develops the parallel between Mary and Zechariah, the father of John the Baptist. He compares and contrasts their responses to the angelic messages and thus highlights the superiority of Mary's faith and obedience to the Word of God in saying "yes" to the divine maternity, while Zechariah is reprimanded for his doubt. Mary's *fiat* is the fruit of a life-long contemplation of the Word of God that never allows to cease in her life the desire for greater illumination in order to achieve a more precise understanding of her role in the *œconomia salutis*.

Thus, Ambrose gives his commentary on the question which the Blessed Virgin Mary poses to the Archangel Gabriel when she says, "How can this be since I do not know man?" Ambrose explains:

> Videtur hic non credidisse Maria, nisi diligenter advertas; neque enim fas est ut electa es generandum unigenitum Dei Filium, fuisse videatur incredula. Quo autem modo fieri matris, cui profecto fuit amplius deferendum, sed ut præ-rogativa major, major etiam fides ei debuit reservari, quo ergo modo fieri posset, ut Zacharias qui non crediderat, silentio condemnaretur: Maria autem si non credidisset, Spiritus Sancti infusione exalteretur? Etenim cum dicit: *Quomodo fiet istud?* Non de effectu dubitavit, sed qualitatem ipsius quæsivit effectus (licet salva prærogativa sit. . . . Quam cito ergo etiam de impari conceptione credidit Maria! Quid enim tam impari quam Spiritus Sanctus, et corpus? Quid tam auditum, quam virgo prægnans contra legem, contra consuetudinem, contra pudorem, cujus charior cura est virgini? Zacharias autem non de impari conditione, sed de senili ætate non credidit nam conditio congruebat. . . . Maria autem cum dicit: *Quomodo fiet istud?* . . . non videtur dubitare de facto, sed de facti qualitate quæsesse. Liquet enim quia faciendum esse crediderat, quæ quomodo fieret, interrogavit. Unde et meruit audire: *Beata quæ credidisti?*. . . . Et vere beata, quæ sacerdote præstantur, cum sacerdos negasset, virgo correxit errorem. Nec mirum si Dominus redempturus mundum, operationem suam inchoavit a Maria . . . ut per quam salus omnibus parabatur, eadem salus omnibus parabatur, eadem prima fructum salutis hauriret ex pignore.[205]

Father Gambero offers an analysis of this text explaining that for Ambrose the narrative of the Annunciation pertains to the core of Mary's life and mission. The meeting of Our Lady with the Angel is a direct encounter with her God and constitutes a central aspect of the mystery of her existence and her cooperation in the economy of salvation, revealing her utter reliance on God and profound faith. Gambero explains that Ambrose, in developing the antithetical parallelism between Zachariah–Mary, seems to have drawn a direct inference from the writings of Irenæus on the antithetical parallelism Eve–Mary. Father Gambero elucidates this point: "Mary, by her conduct, repaired the error of the priest, just as the idea of reparation was present from the beginning in the classic Eve–Mary parallel." In this way, as Gambero acknowledges, Ambrose presents Mary as the first creature to have benefitted fully from the fruits of the redemption so that she might receive a particular role of collaboration in the economy of salvation. Gambero concludes: "For Mary, the mystery of the Incarnation was the fulfillment of her personal salvation; her salvation was Christological, as it is for all other men. The Redeemer began his saving work with his own Mother." [206]

This parallelism between Mary and Zechariah is also treated in the writings of Cardinal Newman. [207] In "The Reverence Due to Her," delivered on the Feast of the Annunciation, Newman reflects on the theological import of the Angel's words to Mary and of Mary's response to the Angel. His sermon begins by showing the continuity between the Angel's salutation of the Virgin and the greeting that Elizabeth extends to Mary on the occasion of her Visitation. Furthermore, Newman points out the significance of Mary's *Magnificat* wherein she prophesies her own blessedness throughout all generations.

The sermon is meant to explain the theological reasons for which the Church, in turn, has taken seriously Mary's praise in Sacred Scripture and so continues to laud her throughout the ages. The legitimacy of the Church's reverence for the Virgin is to be found both in the Scriptures and in the Sacred Tradition. Newman, taking his inspiration from Mary's words in the *Magnificat*, believes that her blessedness and, therefore, our duty to reverence her, begins with the acknowledgment of her role in the economy of salvation. The Annunciation to the Virgin, that is, the mystery of the Incarnation, is the culmination of God's revelation to man and the fulfilment of His promises to Abraham and his descendants.

In fact, Newman, following the patristic interpretations of the Scriptures, identifies the beginning of the promise of salvation in the Genesis account in which "the seed of the woman, announced to guilty Eve, after long delay, was at length appearing upon earth, and was able to be of her. In her the destinies of the world were to be reversed and the serpent's head bruised. On her was bestowed the greatest honour ever put on any individual of our fallen race." [208] Once Newman establishes the Eve–Mary parallelism, as he does so frequently in his Mariological writings, he then turns his attention to the Zechariah-Mary parallel about which he writes in order to give evidence of the extraordinary nature of Mary's faith and obedience in which she persisted, even when faced with much suffering. Newman, like Saint Ambrose, recognizes the meritorious quality of Mary's faith and thus exhorts us to imitate it. Mary's faith is particularly astounding because she preserves its integrity, despite being surrounded by doubt, confusion and uncertainty—the very hindrances to which Zechariah succumbed.[209] Herein lies the major distinction between the Virgin's faith and that of Zechariah.

> Observe the lesson which we gain for ourselves from the history of the Blessed Virgin. When we quench the grace of Baptism, then it is that we need severe trials to restore us. This is the case of the multitude, whose best estate is that of chastisement, repentance, supplication, and absolution, again and again. But there are those who go on in a calm and unswerving course, learning day by day to love Him Who has redeemed them, and overcoming the sin of their nature[210] by His heavenly grace, as the various temptations to evil successively present themselves. And, of these undefiled followers of the Lamb, and God through unbelief; she believed when Zacharias doubted, —with a faith like Abraham's she believed and was blessed for her belief and had the performance of those things which were told her by the Lord. And when sorrow came upon her afterwards, it was but the blessed participation of her Son's sacred sorrows, not the sorrow of those who suffer for their sins.[211]

The Holy Father's understanding of the antithetical parallelism is brought out in his Wednesday audience on 3 July 1996. He warns that a "a superficial reading of the two announcements might consider Zechariah and Mary as having given similar responses to the divine message: How shall I know this? For I am an old man, and my wife is advanced in years, Zechariah said; and Mary: How can this be since I have no husband? (Lk 1:18, 34)." He then explains the main reason why such a superficial reading is unacceptable; this reason is likewise the main argument in the writings of Ambrose and Newman. The Pope writes: "but the profound difference between the two attitudes of the principals in these two episodes can be seen in the words of the angel who rebuked Zechariah for his disbelief, while he immediately replied to Mary's question. Unlike Elizabeth's husband, Mary fully submitted to the divine plan and did not condition her consent on the granting of a visible sign."[212]

In the final analysis, one can conclude that both Saint Ambrose and Cardinal Newman share a deep appreciation for the virginity of Mary and for the pure, unadulterated faith which sustained both her physical and spiritual integrity throughout her life, most especially during such crucial moments as the Annunciation and, as Newman emphasizes, at the foot of the Cross. For both Ambrose and Newman, Mary's virginity and her spiritual maternity are two hinges of her cooperation in the *œconomia salutis*. Mary's consecrated virginity is a paradigm of faith and holiness for all believers and not simply for those who make vows of chastity and celibacy.[213]

VI. NEWMAN AND SAINT AUGUSTINE

(a) *Mary's Sinlessness and Spiritual Maternity*

In discussing the doctrine of the Immaculate Conception, Newman notes that Saint Augustine's teaching in *De Natura et Gratia* 36, 42, to which Pusey makes reference in his *Eirenicon*,[214] is not by any means to be considered a repudiation of the doctrine, even though Augustine's response is admittedly not easy to grasp, *prima facie*. On the contrary, both in the *Letter to Pusey*[215] and in the *Essay on Christian Development*,[216] Newman cites Augustine as a patristic witness to the Church's belief in the sinlessness of the Virgin.[217] Although Augustine does not speak of her exemption from original sin in this text as such, Newman certainly interprets Augustine as not having precluded the possibility.

> I cannot believe that the doctrine (of the Immaculate Conception) would have ever been opposed; for an instinctive sentiment has led Christians jealously to put the Blessed Mary aside when sin comes into discussion. This is expressed in the well-known words of Saint Augustine, All have sinned "except the Holy Virgin Mary, concerning whom, for the honour of the Lord, I wish no question to be raised at all, when we are treating of sins." [218]

In the *Letter to Pusey*, Newman admits that he was unaware of the circumstances which elicited this response from Augustine. [219] Therefore, it is necessary to situate the text in question in relationship to those controversies between Augustine and Pelagius and Julian of Eclanum, which prompted it. [220] Jurgens comments: "*De Natura et Gratia ad Timasium et Iacobum contra Pelagium*, [221] dating from the year 415, is treated in Augustine's *Corrections* 2,68. It was written in refutation of Pelagius' *De Natura* at the request of two young Pelagians who were beginning to see the light, Timasius and James. They continued to correspond with Augustine and may be counted among his converts." [222]

Equally important is Augustine's polemic with Julian, the Bishop of Eclanus, an apostate supporter of Pelagius. In their lively exchange, Augustine is accused by Julian of having invented the concept of original sin and thus of having consigned Mary from her birth to the Devil as a victim of original sin. For Julian, this is unfathomable; his reading of Augustine is mistaken. Augustine is forced to respond to Julian, as he did in his controversy with Pelagius a quarter of a century earlier, by making the following corrections of Julian's accusations. First, Augustine seems to deny that Mary was born with original sin since she received the grace of rebirth, as a type of what would be later referred to as a prevenient grace in view of the redemptive, salvific merits of Christ. Secondly, Augustine seems to exclude Mary from having had any personal sins in that she did not suffer the consequences of original sin. [223] Furthermore, although Newman quotes the best known and core part of the text, Augustine's reasoning is only clear if more of the text is cited. Thus, we read:

Excepta itaque sancta virgine Maria, de qua propter honorem Domini nullam prorsus, cum de peccatis agitur, haberi volo quæstionem—unde enim scimus quid ei plus gratiæ collatum fuerit ad vicendum omni ex parte peccatum, quæ concipere ac parere meruit, quem constat nullum habuisse peccatum?—, hac ergo Virgine excepta, si omnes illos sanctos et sanctas, cum hic viverent, congregare possemus et interrogare, utrum essent sine peccato quid fuisse reponsuros putamus? utrum hoc quod iste dicit, an quod Ioannes apostolus, rogo vos. Quantalibet fuerint in hoc corpore excellentia sanctitatis, si hoc interrogari potuissent, una voce clamassent: *Si dixerimus quia peccatum non habemus, nos ipsos decipimus et veritas in nobis non est.*[224]

In his Catholic sermon "Our Lady in the Gospel," Newman makes reference to this famous passage from Augustine which, as he observes, subsequently was upheld in the Council of Trent's "Decree on Justification," insofar as the Council made a positive statement about the doctrine of Mary's sinlessness very much akin to the positive statement[225] one finds in Augustine's *De Natura et Gratia* (42). Newman, therefore, believes that both Augustine and the Council of Trent pave the way for the formulation of the dogma of Immaculate Conception in conformity to what was always believed by the Church (e.g., *sensus fidelium*). The dogma of the Immaculate Conception was solemnly defined in 1854—six years after Newman's sermon.[226]

It should be noted that Augustine's impetus for dealing with the idea of Mary's relationship to original sin resulted not only from the fact that he felt compelled to answer Julian's attacks on the doctrine but also because Pelagius had propagated misconceptions about the relationship of nature and grace both in reference to the Virgin and to several other holy men and women of the Bible.[227] Pelagius considered the grace of the Immaculate Conception not only as a singular privilege of the Blessed Virgin but also a state of quasi-perfection in which several individuals had also been made to participate.[228] From this belief, Pelagius argues that man is then a liberated, autonomous creature capable of achieving holiness or perfection without the help of God's grace. According to Pelagius' scheme, man's efforts alone seem to suffice for salvation. Augustine is diametrically opposed to Pelagius' notions which eschew the fundamental belief in man's

inheritance of original sin from Adam and Eve through propaga-
tion and its debilitating effects on man's nature. Augustine, while
defending man's use of free will and reason, is adamant in his
insistence that both of these God-given faculties must be understood as working together in cooperation[229] with divine grace and
not independent from it.[230]

Nevertheless, Newman's reading of *De Natura et Gratia* (42)
leads one to conclude that he undoubtedly favored a positive
appraisal of Augustine's statement in defense of the sinlessness of
Mary.[231] Newman concludes his reference to Augustine on this
topic with the following comment: "Certainly, in the spirit which
they (i.e., Augustine's words) breathe, are well adapted to convey
the notion that though her parents had no privilege beyond other
parents, she had not personally any part in sin whatsoever."[232]
Although Augustine did not accept Mary's Immaculate Conception[233] as we know it to be formulated, he does vehemently
uphold Mary's sinfulness and is concerned with the question of
her holiness and the role which she played in the work of redemption.[234] Newman's handling of the same topic strives to
maintain these links so that Mary's privilege of the Immaculate
Conception is never isolated from her other privileges, especially
from her roles as *Theotokos* and New Eve. Furthermore, all of
Our Lady's privileges are Christocentric, that is, Newman, like
Augustine, views Mary in strict relationship to her Son and never
apart from Him.

In order the better to understand Newman's appreciation of
Augustine's *De Natura et Gratia* (42)—in which Augustine refers
to the exemption of Mary from sin as being *propter honorem
Domini* (for the sake of the honor of the Lord)—perhaps it would
be useful to rely on the commentary of one of the foremost
Augustinian scholars, Agostino Trapè. Trapè explains the importance of this phrase, showing its implications for the development of a balanced Mariology in Augustine's thought:

> With the expression for the motivation of "the honor of the
> Lord," Augustine gives us precious key with which to speak of
> Mary. We must speak of Mary in a Christological key. Mary is
> the true Mother because she gave human nature to Jesus, and
> therefore she is the creature most joined to Jesus. This motive
> becomes even more important when one treats of speaking
> of those privileges that God conceded to Mary: the key for

affirming them and for understanding them will always be Christological.[235]

There is no lack of supporting evidence for this Christo-centric approach to Mariology in the writings of Cardinal New-man. The *Letter to Pusey* frequently supplies us with pertinent examples of the need to establish this bond between Christology and Mariology.[236] Both Newman's theological writings and his devotional works contain key illustrations of the Christocentric focus of his Mariology, especially as regards his treatment of Mary's sinlessness and Immaculate Conception. Newman's reflections on Mary's Immaculate Conception in his *Meditations and Devotions* are replete with such illustrations. In his medita-tion on Mary's title, *Rosa Mystica*,[237] Newman begins by reflec-ting on the whole of creation as, in some way, manifesting an attribute of God:

> All that God has made speaks of its Maker; the mountains speak of His eternity; the sun of His immensity, and winds of His Almightiness. In like manner flowers and fruits speak of his sanctity, His love and His Providence . . . by flowers and fruits are meant, in a mystical sense, the gifts and graces of the Holy Ghost, so by a garden is meant mystically a place of spiritual repose, stillness, peace, refreshment and light.[238]

It is in this Mystical Garden, reminiscent of the Garden of Eden, that Newman sees as firmly planted the Mystical Rose, that is, Mary, the New Eve. Mary is the fairest fruit of God's creation, who blossoms because she is filled with the graces of the Holy Spirit and because of her particular nearness to the Tree of Life—the Cross of her Son. She is near that Tree of Redemption from the very moment of her Immaculate Conception, and per-sonal sin would never remove her from her privileged position. In fact, she is the first fruit of the Redemption, having experi-enced redemption in anticipation by means of a prevenient grace. She is the first to drink of the delightful waters flowing from the side of the pierced Savior. Furthermore, as Newman argues, the beauty of Mary's holiness enhances the beauty of the garden of the New Creation because she is not only created without origi-nal sin but, as Newman poetically puts it, "in those blessed gardens, as they may be called, she lived by herself, continually visited by the dew of God's grace and growing up a more and more heavenly flower, till at the end of that period she was meet for the inhabitation in her of the Most Holy." [239]

One should notice that throughout Newman's meditation, the holiness of Mary from the moment of her conception is always described in direct relationship to the beauty and holiness of the sinless Son of Whom she would become both Mother and Companion (*Socia*). Mary is "full of grace," but never is it suggested that she is the author of that grace. Rather, it is the Spirit's gift and the redemptive work of Christ, symbolized by the Tree of Life, that are the principal sources of her singular sanctity, making her "the fairest rose in the paradise of God."

In his meditation *"Virgo Veneranda"* (Virgin to Be Venerated), Newman concludes his reflection by establishing the inexorable connection between Mary's holiness and the supereminent holiness of God. And, at the same time, Newman encourages us to rejoice in her privileges as what points to our own vocation to holiness as children in the Church, the New Israel and People of God:

> And so of the Great Mother of God, as far as a creature can be like the Creator; her ineffable purity and utter freedom from any shadow of sin, her Immaculate Conception, her ever-virginity—these her prerogatives . . . are such to lead us to exclaim in the prophetic words of Scriptures both with awe and with exultation, "Thou art the glory of Jerusalem and the joy of Israel; thou art the honor of our people; therefore hath the hand of the Lord strengthened thee, and therefore art thou blessed forever." [240]

Saint Augustine's admiration of Mary's virtues of chastity, virginity,[241] and pure faith,[242] which the Church's maternal care engenders in the life of the believer, is directly tied to his love of Mary as Virgin and Mother.[243] For Augustine, Mary is both the pre-eminent member of the family of faith as well as the spiritual Mother of the faithful.[244] The theology of Augustine concerning Mary as Virgin and Mother is mostly explicated in his discourses, in his scriptural commentaries, and in his theological treatises.[245] For example, in *De Sancta Virginitate*, Augustine writes:

> . . . Quæ imitatur matrem viri sui et domini sui. Nam Ecclesia quoque et mater et virgo est, cuius enim integritati consulimus, si virgo non est? Aut cuius prolem alloquimur, si mater non est?

Maria corporaliter caput huius corporis peperit: Ecclesia spiritualiter membra illius capitis parit. In utraque virginitas fecunditatem non adimit. . . .[246]

Some of the more significant texts of Augustine that demonstrate his theology and spirituality of Mary's cooperation in the economy as spiritual Mother of the Church are found in his *De Sancta Virginitate* and are discussed in this section. In this first text, Augustine explains that the sacred virginity and maternity of Mary are the model of the Church's own purity and fecundity.[247] Both virtues have a spiritual and a physical connotation. There is no hint of Gnostic dualism in Augustine's thought; he clearly views both Mary and the Church, following Mary's example, as espoused to the Lord, body and soul. Mary's maternal relationship to the Head of the Church is inexorably linked to her spiritual motherhood of the members of His Body, the Church.[248] In the second text, to be quoted below, Augustine asserts, "to one woman alone, to Mary, belongs the right to be both spiritually and corporally, Mother and Virgin."

While fully asserting the rights of Mary's spiritual motherhood of the Church, Augustine likewise notes that Mary is the spiritual mother of Jesus insofar as she is the mother of the "whole Christ" (*totus Christus*), that is to say mother of both head and members.[249] Augustine considers the Church "wholly virgin" and spiritual mother of Christ insofar as she engenders in her members the life of a pure and unadulterated faith in view of the Kingdom.[250] This, according to Augustine, is the life of the saints in light. In other words, the Church gives birth to spiritual children through her celebration of the sacraments, engendering in them the very holiness of Christ their Head, so that they might achieve eternal communion with Him.

In synthesis, Augustine makes clear that the perfect cooperation of Mary—body and soul—in the economy of salvation, is the model by which the Church, Virgin, Spouse and Mother in imitation of Mary, continues to cooperate in the mediation of salvific grace that regenerates men for the life on high. Augustine gives two examples of how the Church exercises her spiritual maternity. First of all, virgins and other women consecrated to the Lord can be said to be the spiritual mothers of Christ, insofar as their works of charity bespeak their spiritual fecundity according to the Father's will. On the other hand, married couples participate in this spiritual maternity by bringing into the world sons and daughters of Adam who are then reborn as children of God and as members of Christ's Body, the Church through the sacraments.[251] The interconnectedness of these mysteries is brought to light by Augustine in the following passage from his *De Sancta Virginitate*:

> Ac per hoc illa una femina non solum spiritu, verum etiam corpore, et mater est ipse Salvator, ex quo magis illa spiritualiter nata est ... sed plane mater membrorum eius, quod nos sumus; quia cooperata est charitate, ut fideles in Ecclesia nascerentur, quæ illius capitis membra sunt. ... Sola ergo Maria et spiritu et corpore mater et virgo; et mater Christi, et virgo Christi: Ecclesia vero in sanctis regnum Dei possessuris, spiritu quidem tota mater Christi est, tota virgo Christi; corpore autem non tota, sed in quibusdam virgo Christi, in quibusdam mater, sed non Christi. Et coniugatæ quippe fideles feminæ et virgines Deo dictæ, fide non ficta, quia voluntatem Patris faciunt, Christi spiritualiter matres sunt. Quæ autem coniugali vita corporaliter pariunt, non Christum, sed Adam pariunt, et ideo currunt ut Sacramentis imbuti Christi membra fiant partus earum, quoniam quid pepererint norunt. [252]

Trapè comments on this text in what he interprets as revelatory of Augustine's firm belief in Mary as type and mother of the Church.[253] Even if, admittedly, Augustine does not strictly use the precise title of *Mater Ecclesiæ* in reference to the Virgin, his theology, like that of Saint Ambrose,[254] seems to encapsulate the fundamental theological understanding that this precise title receives in Pope Paul VI as one reads in his discourse at the third session of the Second Vatican Council and[255] in his apostolic exhortation *Signum Magnum*.[256] Therefore, this makes Trapè's interpretation all the more significant.

> Augustine speaks of Mary as the type and mother of the Church. As Mary is virgin and mother in her body, thus the Church must be virgin and mother in all her members. Virgin because of the integrity of faith: her faith must be integral, total and invulnerable. And it is because of this virginity or integrity of faith that the Church must be a virgin. But the Church is also a mother, because she generates for Christ sons and daughters through the sacraments. She is mother by means of charity, the fervor of charity. Mary is therefore the example of faith; and the

extraordinary miracle; accomplished by God so that she might also be physically mother and virgin, it serves to indicate this fundamental prerogative of the Church that must be virgin and mother.[257]

Newman's theology is not far removed from that of the great fourth-century Doctor of the Church when he treats of Mary's exemplary holiness in the Church—a holiness which outshines that of the other saints, insofar as it most clearly reflects that of her Son's. Newman does not hesitate to praise the saints for their lives of faith and charity—which have led to so many conversions, or to acknowledge their suffering and "superabundance of merits." Nevertheless, it is Mary alone who is "full of grace" from the moment of her Immaculate Conception and thus most deserving of the adjective "holy" as far as it can be applied to a creature. While, as Newman points out, we are regenerated by the gift of grace and holiness in the Sacrament of Baptism—in the womb of the Church, Mary is already created "completely beautiful" and sanctified in the womb of her mother to be "without the stain" of sin.[258]

In this sense, Mary's spiritual motherhood of the Church is implied since Newman obviously views her as the embodiment of that holiness which is to be the distinctive characteristic of the children of God reborn in Baptism. Newman writes in his devotion for "May, the Month of Joy," that "She is the first of creatures, the most acceptable child of God, the dearest and nearest to Him. It is fitting then that this month should be hers, in which, we especially glory and rejoice in His great Providence, in our redemption and sanctification in God the Father, God the Son, and God the Holy Spirit." [259]

In his meditation on Mary as *Speculum Iustitiæ* (Mirror of Justice) Newman uses an analogy to indicate the brilliance of Mary's holiness and its illuminating effect on the holiness of the Church. First, Newman establishes the logic of the analogy by explaining the function of a mirror in relationship to the image it is meant to reflect: "A mirror is a surface which reflects, as still water, polished steel, or as a looking glass. What did Mary reflect? She reflected Our Lord—but *He* is infinite *sanctity*. She then, as far as a creature could, reflected His Divine Sanctity, and therefore she is the *Mirror* of Sanctity, or as the Litany says of *Justice*." [260]

Secondly, and interestingly, Newman explains how Mary came to reflect the sanctity of Christ by way of another analogy—that of the human family and the love which is shared among its members. Thus, Newman, in an implicit manner, sets up the Mother-Son relationship between Christ and Mary as the paradigm of holiness and charity for the rest of the human family and, most especially, for the family of the Church. The conformity of Mary to the image of her Son is described by Newman as "a sanctity of an angelic order, reflecting back the attributes of God with a fulness and exactness of which no saint upon earth, or hermit, or holy virgin can remind us." [261] Newman emphatically concludes: "She is the *Speculum Iustitiæ*, the *mirror* of divine *perfection*." [262] Perhaps, then, Newman would have us conclude from this meditation that it is not sufficient to perceive and admire the holiness of God perfectly mirrored in Mary, but that we must strive to mirror that holiness in our own lives by a greater conformity to the image of her Son and by a greater union with her who, in the words of Newman, "loved her Divine Son with an unutterable love." [263]

In the meditation *Mater Admirabilis*, Newman explains the spiritual dynamic by which Mary is able to demonstrate the depth of her maternal love in relationship to both Christ and the Church. Mary is the quintessential personification of divine love among all creatures and in the communion of saints, manifesting the love of God in her very being because she is the first redeemed, the antithesis of sin and the exemplar of holiness. For all of these reasons, she is most worthy of the title, *Mater Amabilis*. "Why is she *Amabilis* thus specially? It is because she was without sin. Sin is something odious by its very nature, and grace is something bright, beautiful, attractive." [264]

The loveliness and the lovableness of the Virgin are characteristics which Newman terms "angelic" and "heavenly." However, these words should not create in our minds a distorted image of the Virgin. The Virgin is not placed by Newman on so high a pedestal that we must strain our necks to get a glimpse of her amiableness, sweetness and attractiveness. On the contrary, Mary is our Mother and, although she is certainly unlike us by being completely free from sin, it is precisely her sinlessness which causes our admiration and likewise creates within us filial sentiments of love and devotion. Newman is convinced that if we were not children of the Church, we would not be capable of appreciating Mary's full attractiveness in a spiritual sense. It is by living the life of grace in the bosom of the Church that we come to recognize Mary as *Mater Amabilis—in se et pro nobis* (Lovable Mother—in herself and for our sake). Newman writes: "But our Blessed Virgin Mary is called *Amabilis*, or lovable, as being such to the *children of the Church*, not to those outside of it, who know nothing about her."[265] Mary's amiability is then explained by Newman as also consisting in our ability to imitate her virtues and thus to enter into the mystery by which she loved God and neighbor. Newman gives an apt description of Mary's amiableness when he writes, "Her innocence, her humility and modesty, her simplicity, sincerity, and truthfulness, her unselfishness, her unaffected interest in everyone who came to her, her purity—it was those qualities which made her so lovable."[266]

Elsewhere, in his meditation on the title of Mary as *Turris Eburnea* (Tower of Ivory), Newman develops an analogy whereby Mary's virtues are compared to those of the Twelve and Our Lord's other disciples in such a way that they are said to strike a perfect balance between strength and gracefulness—a more feminine quality. Mary is, as it were, a synthesis of those virtues which should characterize the most genuine sort of discipleship in Christian men and women. Newman explains:

> In this magnanimity and generosity she is compared with the Apostles, fitly imaged as a *Tower*. But towers, it may be said, are huge, rough, heavy, obtrusive, graceless structures, for the purposes of war, not of peace; with nothing of the beautifulness, refinement, and finish which are conspicuous in Mary. It is true: therefore she is called the Tower of *Ivory*, to suggest to us, by the brightness, purity, and exquisiteness of that material, how transcendent is the loveliness and gentleness of the Mother of God.[267]

Saint Augustine, as Newman reflects in the *Letter to Pusey*, speaks of her as more exalted because of her sanctity than because of her maternal relationship to the Lord. In other words, Augustine is making the point that Mary's importance exceeds her biological ties to Jesus. First and foremost, Mary's blessedness lies in the obedience of faith which she expresses consistently throughout her life and which, at the moment of the Annunciation, takes on added significance as she consents to become the

Mother of the Lord. Saint Augustine is affirming that Mary is, above all, a perfect disciple of the Lord and that it is because of her fidelity that she is then also most worthy of the divine maternity.[268] Secondly, Mary gives birth not only to the Head but also to the members of the Church—the Body of Christ. She is the preeminent member of the Church; however, she is never to be considered outside the Church.[269]

In both Augustine's and Newman's writings, special emphasis is placed on the theme of the exemplarity of Mary's faith and holiness as integral aspects of her role as Mother of the Church. Trapè provides several insights into Augustine's theology of Mary's spiritual maternity of the Church—a theology which, although less formally developed in Newman's doctrinal treatment of Mary, nevertheless is certainly evident from his devotional writings, as we have already shown. Trapè writes:

> Mary was redeemed by Christ in an eminent way and she is part of the Church of Christ; she must be seen therefore also in relationship to the Church. But when one says that Mary is a member of the Church, it is necessary to add that she is an eminent member, a sublime member, the highest, the most noble, the holiest and worthy of veneration. To this effect we have an important passage of Augustine (*Serm* 72/A,7). For Mary it was more important to have been a disciple of Christ than the Mother of Christ, to have believed than to have generated Christ. This affirmation is difficult but, if one thinks well about it, it is exact. As an eminent member of the Church she is near to us, our sister, although redeemed in a more profound manner, still she is the daughter of the Spouse. They are Augustinian words, namely even if in a higher and more intimate manner: she is our sister, she is in the Church not outside of it, as some Protestants contest to Catholics. She is in the Church and she is Mother of the Church.[270]

(b) *Newman and Augustine on Mary's Two-Fold Blessedness*

The influence of Saint Augustine's thought on Newman's Mariology is quite evident in Newman's Catholic sermon, "Our Lady in the Gospel," which is a compendium of Newman's insights into the scriptural foundations of a Catholic apologetic in defense of the Church's traditional Marian doctrine and devotion.[271] A complete analysis of this sermon is given in the second chapter of this work on Newman, Mary and Scripture. Here, the primary goal is to underscore those elements of Newman's arguments that are directly related to his reliance on Saint Augustine's interpretation of the Sacred Text. Some of the material from this section must be deliberately reiterated for the sake of providing clarity and context so that the reader may more readily see how Newman's and Augustine's exegeses lead to many of the same, fundamental, theological conclusions.

The starting point of Newman's sermon is the passage from Luke 11:27–28, in which the woman in the crowd addresses Our Lord in praise of Mary by saying: "Blessed is the womb that bore Thee and the breasts which Thou hast sucked." [272] To which, Our Lord responds: "Yea, but blessed are those that hear the word of God and keep it." [273] Our Lord's response, so often misinterpreted by Protestants as a rebuke of Our Lady and even a drastic denial of her faith, is understood by Newman, in light of the scriptural and patristic evidence, most especially, that of Saint Augustine, as a confirmation of Mary's blessedness based on her unique relationship to Jesus not only as His Mother but also as His perfect disciple. Newman writes: "Saint Augustine says, 'More blessed was Mary in receiving the faith of Christ, than in receiving the flesh of Christ.'" [274] In addition, Newman gives supporting evidence to Augustine by citing Saint John Chrysostom, whose interpretation of Elizabeth's praise of Mary at the Visitation ("*Beata es quæ credidisti*," "Blessed art thou who didst believe") strengthens Augustine's statement. "Saint Chrysostom goes so far as to say that she would not have been blessed, even though she had borne Christ in the body, unless she heard the Word of God and kept it." [275]

Although Newman accepts Chrysostom's interpretation as a correct one, he is concerned that it can be easily misunderstood. Hence, Newman writes the following to give further precision to his reading of Chrysostom:

> Now I have used the expression "Saint Chrysostom goes *so far* as to say," not that it is not a plain truth. I say, it is a plain truth that the Blessed Virgin would not have been blessed, though she had been the Mother of God, if she had not done His will, but it is an extreme thing to say, for it is supposing a thing impossible, it is supposing that she could be so highly favoured and yet not be inhabited and possessed by God's

grace, whereas the Angel, when he came, expressly hailed her as full of grace.[276]

The reverence which the woman in the crowd manifests towards Mary in regard to her physical cooperation in the economy of salvation is deepened and not diminished by Jesus' response, which does not downplay or deny His filial relationship to Mary but affirms it. Our Lord's response elevates our understanding of that physical relationship, Mother-Son, to a supernatural level by confirming the importance of faith as constituting the heart of discipleship in the spiritual family of the Church. Mary, therefore, is twice a Mother to Jesus. She is His Mother in a physical sense; she is His Mother in a spiritual sense through faith and discipleship. She hears the Word of God and puts it into practice and in this way becomes our model of perfect discipleship.[277]

Perhaps this is why Newman, like Augustine, so emphasizes the blessedness of Mary's faith since, in fact, it is her response of faith (*fiat*) which precedes and therefore makes possible the mystery of the Incarnation. Consequently, Mary's cooperation cannot be limited to being simply a physical instrument but must also take into consideration her life of faith, purity, holiness—all already firmly established in her having become the Mother of Christ. Newman writes: "And therefore when the woman in the crowd cried out upon the blessedness of the womb that bore Him and the breasts that He had sucked, He taught her and all who heard Him that the soul was greater than the body, and that to be united to Him in spirit was more than to be united to Him in the flesh."[278] Trapè offers several insights into Augustine's commentary on Luke 11:27 which are likewise those which we have seen in Newman's interpretation of the same text.

Trapè evaluates Augustine's exegesis of Luke 11:27 as a text upon which Augustine established "a very interesting spiritual doctrine regarding the blessedness of Mary and the blessedness of Christians." He explains that Augustine's consideration that Mary "is more blessed because of her faith in Christ than for having borne Christ in her womb," is most evidently not a desire to underestimate "the value of physical generation of Christ, because, . . . this is the highest honor to which Mary could be elevated; Saint Augustine, however, wishes to establish a hierarchy of values, he intends to speak of Mary and of all Christians, who are blessed because of their faith, because they believe in Christ, and because they adhere to Christ."

Consequently, Trapè captures the essence of Augustine's exegesis of Luke 11:27–28 when he writes: "and in Mary there are these two aspects: she is the Mother of Christ corporally but also and above all she is a faithful disciple of Christ because she believes in Him."

From this hermeneutical principle of Augustine's exegesis, Trapè believes that Augustine draws one extremely important conclusion, namely that, "Mary has conceived through faith; and it is her faith that by means of the action of the Holy Spirit has conceived Christ in the womb. As we can see, here the reflection on Mary extends to ecclesiology, to the spiritual life, and becomes a program of life for each one of us." [279]

In "Our Lady in the Gospel," Newman has recourse to the Fathers of the Church, and in doing so seems to rely heavily upon Augustine's notions of Mary's two-fold blessedness that results first through her faith whereby she conceives the Word of God in her mind and secondly through her virginal conception of Christ the Word made flesh. These passages, of Augustinian inspiration, give further weight to his notions of Mary's sinless cooperation in the economy of salvation:

> The Holy Fathers of the Church tell us again and again that Our Lady was more blessed in doing God's will than in being His Mother. She was blessed in two ways. She was blessed in being His Mother; she was blessed in being filled with spirit of faith and obedience . . . And the Holy Fathers have ever gathered the exact obedience and sinlessness of the Blessed Virgin from the very narrative of the Annunciation, when she became the Mother of God. For when the Angel appeared to her and declared to her the will of God, they say that she displayed especially four graces, humility, faith, obedience and purity. Nay, these graces were as it were, preparatory conditions to her being made the minister of so high a dispensation. So that if she had not had faith, and humility, and purity, and obedience, she would not have merited to be God's Mother. Thus it is common to say that she conceived Christ in mind before she conceived Him in body, meaning that the blessedness of faith and obedience preceded the blessedness of being a Virgin and Mother. Nay, they even say that God waited for her consent before He came into her and took flesh of her. Just as He did no

mighty works in one place because they had not faith, so this great miracle, by which He became the Son of a creature, was suspended till she was tried and found meet for it-till she obeyed . . . The Holy Fathers always teach that in the Annunciation, when the Angel appeared to our Lady, she showed that she preferred what Our Lord called the greater of the two blessednesses to the other.[280]

Conclusion to Newman and Saint Augustine

1) Newman does not hesitate to refer to Saint Augustine as a formidable patristic source in favor of Mary's sinlessness. Although he cannot claim Saint Augustine as a definitive advocate of the doctrine of Mary's Immaculate Conception, Augustine's theology of sin, grace and redemption, properly understood, do not necessarily exclude a fundamental intuition on Augustine's part in support of the veracity of this dogma insofar as he readily admits of her sinlessness.

2) Newman, building upon the foundation of Saint Augustine's theology of grace, envisions Mary's Immaculate Conception as the exordium of a new creation. Christ's redemptive work is inaugurated at the very origins of Mary's existence. Thus, that grace, divine life, original harmony, justice, righteousness, holiness, which enveloped Adam and Eve before the Fall, is restored in Mary, and made even more abundant since she conceives in her womb the Author of grace and eternal life.

3) The extraordinary holiness of the Virgin Mother is, for both Augustine and Newman, the high-water mark of man's cooperation with God in the *œconomia salutis*. She is not simply holy because she is conceived without Original Sin; she is all-holy because she exemplified the holiness of God in her purity of life, chastity, consecrated virginity, maternal care, perfect discipleship of her Son, and also in her solicitude for and spiritual maternity of the redeemed in the Mystical Body of Christ, the Church.

4) Both Augustine and Newman conclude that Mary's faith, even more than her divine maternity, is that virtue, never separated from hope and love, that makes of the Virgin the most sublime paradigm or type of the Church. She is the Church's most excellent member and model. All of Christ's faithful should be drawn, in body, mind, soul and spirit, to imitate Mary's faith so as to share in the eternal blessedness that she now enjoys.

5) Perhaps Jean Guitton's statement, "I think that Newman is a Saint Augustine projected into our time," goes beyond the boundaries of what this present chapter is intended to demonstrate, namely, the interconnectedness of the respective mariologies of these two titans of theology. Nevertheless, it is precisely the boldness of Guitton's affirmation that impresses us with the hope that its truthfulness will become ever more evident in the "age to come." [281]

VII. NEWMAN'S CRITIQUE OF SOME ANOMALOUS STATEMENTS OF SAINTS BASIL, CHRYSOSTOM, AND CYRIL IN THE "LETTER TO PUSEY"

Introduction

Newman understands the Fathers of the Church and their interpretation of the Sacred Scriptures from the perspective of the unity of the faith and the principle of the non-contradictory nature of truth. In his notes, found in the form of an appendix to the *Letter to Pusey*, Newman treats what he refers to as the "anomalous" (*anomala*) statements of Saints Basil, Chrysostom and Cyril about the Blessed Virgin Mary.[282]

The anomalous nature of Chrysostom's exegesis of certain Marian scriptural texts such as those dealt with by Newman is well summarized by the Reverend Ermanno Toniolo in his article, "Il Caso Crisostomo," in *Nuovo Dizionario di Mariologia*. Father Toniolo entitles this article, "Il Caso Crisostomo," perhaps to emphasize the "difficult" nature of some of Chrysostom's Mariological writings. In any case, one can see how Toniolo's analysis is affirmative of Newman's own critique of Chrysostom while, on the other hand, pointing out the stronger areas of his Mariology. Father Toniolo mentions that even though Chrysostom defends "with lively and profound arguments" the doctrine of Mary's virginity and her divine motherhood (*Theotokos*) in his preaching, he nonetheless is not as adamant in Mary's defense "when he speaks of the 'ethical-spiritual' figure of Mary, that is of her sanctity, he expresses himself in way totally different from his contemporaries." Toniolo, however, does not make a blanket statement of criticism. On the contrary, he gives solid references

257

to Chrysostom's exegesis of certain Marian scriptural passages in his works as proof of the veracity of that criticism. He notes that because Chrysostom belonged to the Antiochean school and therefore tended to favor a rather literal exegetical method, that he also was very careful to interpret Marian passages by way of comparison with parallel texts, "especially the facts of the public life of Jesus: the Wedding Feast of Cana, her arrival and that of his 'brothers' a Capernaum, the acclamation of the anonymous woman (Jn 2:1–12; Mt 12:46–50; Lc 11:27–28)."

Thus, Toniolo explains that the case of Chrysostom and his anomalous exegetical statements end up, in part, creating of Mary "an image of a 'mommy,' that was making good on her maternal rights over her Son, and did not have a clear and perfect idea of Him: who therefore, for example at Cana, asked a miracle of the Lord in order that the guests would give glory to her." Toniolo does not rest "the Case of Chrysostom" solely on these grounds. He acknowledges that Chrysostom's interpretations should not be considered as having summarily dismissed a favorable view of Mary: "Therefore Jesus, willing her to be immune from every defect would have adopted toward her a divine pedagogy, correcting her and bringing her slowly to have higher sentiments, to comport herself in a less human way, to become a 'disciple'(cf. for example, *Homilies on John*, 21–22, PG 59, 129–135; *Homilies on Matthew*, 44, PG 57, 463–466)." Father Toniolo also makes an important further distinction in Chrysostom's defense when he explains that "this reading of Mary on the part of Chrysostom as a creature engaged in a slow pilgrimage of faith equal to us was never contested in his time: this goes to show that the Church back then had not yet arrived at the point of having an idea of the person of the Virgin as being immune from imperfections: to this understanding the Council of Ephesus (431) and the Latin Tradition will contribute a great deal."

Toniolo concludes his explanation of the Chrysostom case by making the following appraisal: "But perhaps it is precisely the exegesis of Chrysostom that unwittingly renders us a precious service: it helps us to understand the true interior greatness of Mary as a believer and as a disciple, in her daily struggle to overcome the impulses of the flesh and blood,[283] in order to see and to act only in the light of the Word."[284]

(a) *Newman and Saint John Chrysostom*

For the moment, let us single out what Newman says about Chrysostom, to compare and contrast their exegetical methods with regard to the Sacred Scriptures and its implications for a discussion of Mary's cooperation in the *œconomia salutis*. It must be noted at the outset that Newman is, on the whole, most appreciative of Chrysostom's works, theological insights and exegetical methods; he is not, however, uncritical of some of Chrysostom's interpretations of certain scriptural passages concerning the Virgin, as this section hopes to reveal.

Newman makes the following assessment of Chrysostom's method:

> Saint Chrysostom is *par excellence* the commentator of the Church. As Commentator and Preacher, he, of all the Fathers, carries about him the most intense personality. In this lies his very charm, peculiar to himself. He is overflowing with thought, and he pours it forth with a natural engaging frankness, and an unwearied freshness and vigour. If he really was in the practice of deeply studying and carefully criticizing what he delivered in public, he had in perfection the real art of concealing his art. He ever speaks from himself, not of course without being impregnated with the fulness of a Catholic training, but, still, not speaking, by rule, but as if, "trusting the love of his own loyal heart." On the other hand, if it is not a paradox to say it, no one carries with him so little of the science, precision, consistency, gravity of a Doctor of the Church, as he who is one of the greatest. The difficulties are well known which he has occasioned to school theologians: his *obiter dicta* about Our Lady are among them.[285]

Newman's criticism of Chrysostom in the *Letter to Pusey* is based on Chrysostom's view of the Virgin resulting in part from his interpretation of selected texts. The first text that Newman analyzes is taken from Chrysostom's fourth homily in his commentary on the Gospel of Saint Matthew dealing with the Evangelist's account of the Annunciation, which Chrysostom explains by way of reference to Luke's account of the same event. The second passage chosen by Newman is taken from Chrysostom's 44th homily on the Gospel of Matthew, in which he treats of Mary's attempt to encounter Our Lord during His public ministry and Our Lord's response to the crowd's announcement of the arrival of his mother, brothers and sisters. Chrysostom, in discussing this latter episode, relates it to Mary's presence at the foot of the Cross. Thus, Newman also refers Pusey to a third passage, namely, Chrysostom's 21st homily in his commentary on John's Gospel. Furthermore, in a later section of the *Letter*, Newman also briefly refers to one of Chrysostom's homilies on the Gospel of John in reference to the Cana pericope.[286] The first text (*In Matth. Hom.* iv) is quoted by Newman as follows:

> "Wherefore," a man may say, "did not the Angel do in the case of the Virgin (what he did to Joseph" viz., appear to her after, not before, the Incarnation), "why did he not bring her the good tidings after her conception?" Lest she should be in great disturbance and trouble. For the probability was, that, had she not known the clear fact, she would have resolved something strange (ἄτοπον) about herself, and had recourse to the rope or sword, not bearing the disgrace. For the Virgin was admirable, and Luke shows her virtue when he says that, when she heard the salutation, she did not at once become extravagant, nor appropriated the words, but was troubled, searching what was the nature of the salutation. One then of so refined a mind (διικροβωμένη) would be made beside herself with despondency, considering the disgrace, and not expecting, whatever she may say, to persuade anyone who hears her, that adultery had not been the fact. Lest then these things should occur, the Angel came before the conception; for it beseemed that the womb should be without disorder, which the Creator of all entered, and that the soul should be rid of all perturbation, which was counted worthy to become the minister of such mysteries.[287]

Newman's commentary on this passage of Chrysostom makes several important points. First and foremost, Newman states that, "Saint Chrysostom, in this passage (*In Matth. Hom.* iv), does not impute sin to her at all."[288] Rather, he implies that Mary was predisposed by grace to overcome any temptation to act contrary to the Divine Will. "He (Chrysostom) says God so disposed things for her as to shield her from the chance of sinning."[289]

Therefore, Newman interprets Chrysostom as having considered that Mary's *fiat* was made possible precisely because of her having received a special grace even before the moment in which she received the Angel's message which allowed to have the right spiritual disposition in order to cooperate in the economy of salvation as it was unfolding. Newman interprets Chrysostom's understanding of Mary's spiritual disposition at the Annunciation—characterized by what one may term a "prevenient grace"—prevented Mary from falling into sin since "she was too admirable to be allowed to be betrayed by her best and purest feelings into sin."[290]

Thus, Newman and Chrysostom would essentially agree that in order for Mary or any other human person to say "yes" to God, but most especially given the very difficult circumstances in which the Virgin Mary found herself at the moment of the Annunciation, the assistance of God's grace was absolutely essential. Chrysostom believes that if Mary had not been spiritually disposed by God's grace, if she had not received the message of the Angel that "the probability was, that, had she not known the clear fact, she would have resolved something strange [ἄτοπον] about herself, and had recourse to rope or sword, not bearing the disgrace."[291] Newman explains this text in the following manner:

> All that is implied repugnant to a Catholic's reverence for her, is, that her woman's nature, viewed in itself and apart from the watchful providence of God's grace over her, would not have the strength to resist a hypothetical temptation,—a position which a Catholic will not care to affirm or deny, though he will feel great displeasure at having to discuss it all.[292]

In the passage as Newman cites it, Chrysostom does not seem to refer to the weakness of Mary's sex *per se*, as Newman does in his commentary, but to the idea that, any virgin living in Mary's historical-cultural circumstances found pregnant outside of marriage, could have been easily tempted to avoid this particular "disgrace" by having "recourse" to suicide. It seems as though the main question with which Chrysostom is concerned in this passage is not so much the weakness of Mary insofar as she is a female; rather, he is concerned with underscoring that the human nature—severely debilitated by sin—could not, by itself, without "the watchful providence of God's grace," conform itself to the divine will. Perhaps, therefore, it is important here to state that one should not read this particular text of Chrysostom or Newman's commentary for that matter as evidence of "misogynism" in Chrysostom. Such a conclusion would be simplistic and unfair to Chrysostom as it does not reflect what seems to be the meaning of this text.

Even though Chrysostom's talk about a "hypothetical temptation" of Mary to commit suicide rightly resonates as a bit harsh to the Catholic ear, as Newman himself points out, Chrysostom's point is not that Mary was actually and naturally prone to such despondency and despair but that Mary could have succumbed to such a temptation, if she had not received a particular grace which "duly" prepared her in body, mind and spirit,[293] to be "counted worthy to become the minister of such mysteries."[294] Here, the simple observation that temptation to sin does not equal sin or even concupiscence for that matter, as is clear from Our Lord's own life, can also be made, calling to mind Newman's own pithy saying: "Ten thousand difficulties do not make a single doubt,"[295] and the common theological principle: *"Gratia supponit et perficit naturam"* (grace builds upon and perfects nature).

In fine, a credible case can be made that Chrysostom's exegesis of the Annunciation pericope in this text, if read in light of Newman's explanation does not show that Chryosostom lacked reverence for the Virgin. On the contrary, Newman seems to want to convince Pusey that Chrysostom's exegesis expresses his firm belief that at the moment of the Annunciation the balance between the working of divine grace and Mary's own co-operation in that grace was preserved in accord with the divine economy of salvation—a clear sign of Divine Providence and confirmation of the integrity of Mary's faith and virtue. Therefore, despite any temptation, hypothetical or real—the Evangelists do not give any indication of either possibility in Mary's regard—Chrysostom's exegesis of this text should not be relied upon, as Newman interprets it, to say anything contrary to Mary's full participation in the life of grace and her exemption from any sin both before and after she learned about God's will for her virginal conception.

An analysis of the second text (*In Matth.*, hom. 44) provokes in Newman a negative criticism of Chrysostom because the Father of the Church seems to impute to Mary the sin or imperfection of vainglory.[296] According to Chrysostom, Mary gave evidence of vainglory when she came "to show to the people that she had power and authority over her Son, in nothing ever as yet having given herself airs [φαντάζομένη] about Him. Therefore, she came unseasonably. Observe then her and her rashness [ἀπόνοιαν]." [297]

The texts of Scripture to which Chrysostom is referring are Matthew 12:46–50; Mark 3:31–35; Luke 8:19–21. Newman quotes from Chrysostom's commentary on the Matthean version of the episode. Chrysostom interprets Mary's attempt to visit Our Lord during His public ministry to be not simply inopportune but going beyond untimeliness to reflect a serious lack of virtue. Chrysostom believes that Mary's search for her Son during His public ministry was motivated principally by an inordinate desire to exercise power and control over Him, to impede, to a certain extent, the full accomplishment of His redemptive mission by reinstating the importance of familial ties. Our Lord, therefore, according to Chrysostom, corrects Mary's imprudence, "not, that is, as wishing to cast her into perplexity, but to release her gradually to the fitting thought concerning Him and to persuade her that He is not only her Son, but also her Master." [298] Newman admits that the exact meaning of Chrysostom's thought is not so easy to decipher.

Nevertheless, Newman offers the following remarks: "All that can be said to alleviate the startling character of these passages is, that it does not appear that Saint Chrysostom would account such vainglory in a woman as any great failing." [299] In other words, Chrysostom's understanding of the female character leads him to account for this character flaw (vainglory) in the Virgin without necessarily identifying it as sin. Newman tries to explain how this could, in fact, be the case:

> When then Saint Chrysostom imputes vainglory to her, he is not imputing to her anything worse than an infirmity, the infirmity of a nature, inferior to man's and intrinsically feeble, as though the Almighty could have created a more excellent being than Mary, but could not have made a greater woman. Accordingly, Chrysostom does not say that she sinned. He does not deny that she had all the perfections which women could have; but he seems to have thought the capabilities of her nature were bounded, so that the utmost grace bestowed upon it could not raise it above that standard of perfection in which its elements resulted, and that to attempt more, would have been to injure, not to benefit it. Of course, I am not stating this as

brought out in any of his writings, but it seems to me to be the real sentiment of many of the ancients.[300]

The views of Chrysostom and Newman's interpretation of them, ultimately, must be understood in the light of the accumulated wisdom of the Church,[301] as reflected in her official doctrines. The teaching of the Church on Mary's personal sinlessness also implies, as a logical consequence, her freedom from any imperfection whatsoever, most especially the sin of vainglory, which is a direct consequence of original sin. Indeed, one could ask: Is not vainglory so intimately related to the sin of pride which lies at the heart of the *mysterium iniquitatis* (mystery of iniquity)? Would not the presence of such a serious defect be due not simply to a flaw in character or the weakness of one's sex but to a more severe lacking of that grace and moral virtue which, as Chrysostom seems to admit in the first passage discussed, were necessary for her own salvation and for her cooperation in the mystery of the world's salvation?

Furthermore, the Church's teaching on anthropology does not allow for Chrysostom's presupposition that a woman's weaker physical constitution is likewise proof of a female's greater propensity to suffer the consequences of original sin, concupiscence, disordered passions, while a man's physical strength would indicate somehow a greater moral capacity to overcome imperfection. Likewise, it should be borne in mind, as Newman writes to Pusey, that for certain Greek Fathers especially, an admission of sinfulness or weakness on Mary's part, would not have prohibited them necessarily from engaging in an "exercise of love and devotion to her,"[302] even if, as Newman adds, "though I am not pretending that there is proof of any such exercise on their part in fact."[303]

Newman offers another piece of theological speculation as a possible, logical justification of why these or other Fathers might not have completely understood the full doctrine on Mary's sinlessness and yet still have maintained a deep sense of devotion to her. Newman remarks: "And for this simple reason, that if sinlessness were a condition of inspiring devotion, we should not feel any devotion to any but Our Lady, not Saint Joseph, or to the Apostles, or to our patron saints."[304] In any case, Chrysostom's exegesis of the Gospel passages in question though starkly literal and not completely unsubstantiated from a socio-cultural perspective,[305] nevertheless demand reconsideration in light of the Church's full appreciation of the fundamental complementarity of the sexes vis-à-vis each other, the society and God. Certainly, the question of man's ability, both as males and females, to co-operate in God's grace and the effects of that cooperation are crucial issues in reference to the present discussion.

An exegesis of Chrysostom's twenty-first homily on John's Gospel is not easy and reveals that his interpretation of Jesus' response at Cana is one that is inseparable from his interpretation of other texts (Mk 3:33; Lk 11:27), in which Jesus' responses are likewise as enigmatic as the one given in John 2:4. For example, Chrysostom writes: Τίς ἐστιν ἡ μήτηρ μου, καὶ τίνες ἐσὶν οἱ ἀδελφοι μου; Οὐδε πω γὰρ ἦν ἐχρῆν περι αὐτοῦ δόξαν εἰχον· αλλ' ἐπειδὴ ᾤδινεν αὐτὸν, ἠξίου κατὰ τήν λοιπὴν τῶν μηετέρων συνήθειαν, οὕτως ἅπαντα ἐπιτάττειν αὰτῷ, δέον ὡς Δεσπότην σέβειν καὶ προσκυνεῖν. Likewise interesting is the interpretation that Chrysostom gives the Cana pericope since Jesus' response to Mary, according to Chrysostom, is considered to be a correction of Mary based on what Jesus perceives to have been a request betraying a certain lack of faith and/or lack of proper understanding of the nature of His salvific mission on the part of the Virgin. Chrysostom explains that response to Mary indicated that her untimely request on behalf of the newly wedded spouses and their invited guests was not going to be fulfilled as some sort of cheap magic trick meant to appease their utilitarian sense: Τί ἐμοὶ καὶ σοί, ὦ γύναι; Καὶ δι' ἀναγκαίαν αἰτίαν οὐχ ἧττον. Ποίαν δὲ ταύτην; Ὥστε μὴ ὑποπτευθῆναι τὰ γινόμενα θαύματα. Παρὰ γὰρ τῶν δεομένων παρακληθῆναι ἐχρῆν, οὐ παρὰ ἐχρῆν, οὐ παρὰ τῆσ μητρός. Τί δήποτε; Ὅτι τὰ μὲν ἐκ τῆς τῶ νοικείων παρακλήσεως γινόμενα, κἀνμεγάλαῇ, προσίσταται τοῖς ὁρῶσι πολλάκις· ὅταν δὲ οἱ ξρείαν ἔχοντες, οὗτοιδέωνται, ἀνύποπτον τὸ θαῦμα γίνεται, καὶ κατθαρὸς ὁ ἔπαινος, καὶ πολλὴ ἡ ὠφέλεια.

It seems as though Jesus' response is directed more to those for whom the request is made than to Mary herself. Jesus' intent is to perform this miracle as a sign appropriate to the nature of the new dispensation about to unfold and not as arrogant refusal of the honor of His mother or her proper role of cooperation in the dispensation. Τὶ ἐμοὶ, καὶ σοὶ, γύναι; παιδεὺων αὐτὴν εἰς τὸ μέλλον μηκέτι τὰ τοιαῦτα ποιεῖ. Ἔμελε γὰρ αὐτῷ καὶ τῆς εἰς τὴν μητέρα τιμῆς, πολλῷ δὲ πλέον τῆς σωτηρίας τῆς κατὰ ψυχὴν, καὶ τῆς τῶν πολλῶν εὐεργεσίας, δι᾽ ἥν καὶ τὴν σάρχα Οὐ τοί νυν ἀπαυ θαδιαζομένου πρὸς τὴν μετέρα ταῦτα τὰ ῥήματα ἦν, ἀλλ᾽ οἰκονομίας πολλῆς ῥυθμιζούης αὐτήν τε ἐχείνην, καὶ τα θαύματα μετὰ τῆς προσηκούσης γενέσθαι παρασκευαζ οὔσης ἀξίας.[306]

Chrysostom understands Jesus' reply as seeking to elevate Mary's understanding of the "economy" of salvation, that is to say, of Jesus' mission and identity from a purely natural level whereby she asserted her maternal authority over Him[307]—to a higher and more supernatural level, so that He could assert His divine authority as Redeemer. Chrysostom does not, however, consider the Lord's response to be an outright rebuke of Mary, as some might hold. On the contrary, Jesus performs the miracle and in doing so likewise honors the Virgin.[308]

Newman's interpretation of the Cana pericope has already been discussed in Chapter Two. Mary's request at Cana, although perhaps considered by some as "inopportune,"[309] certainly should not be considered sinful. Otherwise, Our Lord would neither have fulfilled it nor would it have most likely served as the means by which an extraordinary manifestation (σημεῖον) of Christ's glory (δόξα) takes place, inspiring faith in the disciples. Similarly, Mary's request to visit with her Son during His public ministry should not be equated with "vainglory" but should be appreciated as a sincere attempt on Mary's part to draw closer to her Son and to the mystery of His redemptive mission. The overall interpretation given to this text by the Fathers reveals that Our Lord's words in the Gospel are never condemnatory of the Virgin but actually commendatory of her exemplary faith and extraordinary holiness. Nowhere does the angel's salutation of the Virgin as κεχαριτωμένη find opposition or contradiction in any other passage of Scripture. Newman's attempt to reconcile Chrysostom's interpretation of the discussed texts is noble but somewhat inconclusive and must therefore be evaluated in light of what other Fathers have said on the issue.[310]

Newman writes in the *Letter to Pusey*: "Nor do they agree together in their interpretation of those passages; which either one or other of them interprets so harshly; for while, Saint Chrysostom holds that Our Lord spoke in correction of His Mother at the Wedding Feast, Saint Cyril on the contrary says that he wrought a miracle which He was Himself unwilling to work, in order to show 'reverence to His Mother,' and that she, 'having great authority' for the working of the miracle, got the victory, persuading the Lord, as being her Son, as was fitting."[311] Newman seems to think that Saint Augustine's interpretation of the Cana pericope reflects more effectively the Church's own sense of the Scriptures and, therefore, of Mary's role in the work of salvation.[312]

As we have seen, while defending Chrysostom in some areas, indeed seeking to offer an apologetic for some of Chrysostom's more controversial positions concerning the Virgin, Newman is also aware that his tendency toward exaggerated literalism can lead to some faulty interpretations of the Sacred Text. Newman explains to Pusey that Chrysostom's exegetical writings in which he seems to impute sin to Mary are better understood, even if they are certainly wrong, when one considers that Chrysostom came from Antioch in Syria, and that the fourth-century theological schools of Antioch, as in other parts of Asia Minor at the time, tended to be Arian and semi-Arian, at least in influence, if not declaredly so.

Newman rightly concludes that these two heresies, Arianism and Semi–Arianism, propounded a heterodox Christology that "denied the tradition of His divinity," and therefore, "forgot the tradition of her sinlessness."[313] Newman proceeds to offer a disclaimer to his explanation. He fairly points out that even the best of Christians, "however religious themselves, however orthodox their teachers, were necessarily under peculiar disadvantages," given the widespread influence of certain heretical theological schools in Syria and Asia Minor. Newman prefaces his application of this historical argument to the case of Chrysostom, by making a similar application to Saint Basil the Great, who "grew up in the very midst of Semi-Arianism" and dealt on a consistent basis with teachers of theology who had first rejected the teaching of Nicea on the "*homoousios*" ("consubstantial") but who eventually were reconciled. Therefore, Newman is not surprised nor should Pusey be surprised, that a great Father of the Church like Saint Basil, given the historical and theological ambience, did not have "a firm habitual hold upon a doctrine which (though Apostolical) in his day was as yet as much in the background over all Christendom, as our Lady's sinfulness."[314] Newman deduces further that, while a most illustrious theologian and scriptural exegete of the "celebrated Antiochean School," "celebrated, that is, at once for its method of scriptural criticism, and (orthodox as it was itself),"[315] that Chrysostom was, perhaps, at times, "like a sheep in the midst of wolves," given the numerous outbreaks of heresy in the Antiochean theological camp.[316] Newman concludes his critique of the selected passages of Chrysostom with what he terms a "natural explanation," namely, that all of the above, when taken together, helps to demonstrate "why Saint Chrysostom, even more than Saint Basil might be wanting, great doctor as he was, in a clear perception of the place of the Blessed Virgin in the Evangelical Dispensation."[317]

(b) Newman, Saint Basil of Cæsarea, and Saint Cyril of Alexandria

In the notes that are included as an appendix to the *Letter to Pusey*, Newman tackles some thorny issues of biblical interpretation in the writings of three significant Fathers of the Church: Saints Basil,[318] Chrysostom,[319] and Cyril of Alexandria. What concerns Newman most particularly are the Marian implications of their exegesis and how their points of view do not necessarily reflect the overall Tradition of the Church in such matters. Newman explains why some of the Fathers of the Church, given the cultural milieu in which they lived, were prone at times to give negative evaluations of women. He also explains the repercussions such a negative attitude toward women could have on their understanding of Mary.

> However, the strong language of these Fathers (e.g., Basil the Great, Cyril of Alexandria, John Chrysostom) is not directed against Our Lady's person, so much as against her nature. They seem to have participated with Ambrose, Jerome and other Fathers, in that low estimation of woman's nature which was general in their times. In the broad imperial world, the conception entertained of womankind was not high; it seemed only to perpetuate the poetical tradition of the *"Varium et mutabile semper."* Little was there known of that true nobility, which is exemplified in the females of the Gothic and German races, and in those of the old Jewish stock, Miriam, Deborah, Judith, and Susanna, the forerunners of Mary.[320]

Newman's notes are intended to clarify the meaning of their writings, so that Pusey and anyone else can be relieved of any needless preoccupations concerning the Marian doctrine which the Church has consistently taught to be implicitly or explicitly revealed by those sacred texts. The Scripture texts which come under scrutiny have to do with certain events in the life of the Virgin. Saint Basil's 260th Epistle, addressed to Optimus, is cited by Newman in his *Letter to Pusey*. Newman gives the following translation of Basil's text:

> [Symeon] uses the word 'sword' meaning the word which is tentative and critical of the thoughts, and reaches unto the separation of soul and spirit, of the joints and marrow. Since then every soul, at the time of the Passion, was subjected in a way to some unsettlement (διακρίει), according to the Lord's Word, who said, "All ye shall be scandalized in Me," Symeon prophesies even of Mary herself, that, standing by the Cross, and seeing what was doing, and hearing the words, after the testimony of Gabriel, after the secret knowledge of the divine conception, after the great manifestation of miracles, Thou wilt experience, he says, a certain tossing (σάλος) of thy soul. For it beseemed the Lord to taste death for every one, and to become a propitiation of the world, in order to justify all in His blood. And thee thyself who hast been taught from above the things concerning the Lord, some unsettlement (διάκρισις) will reach. This is the sword; "that out of many hearts thoughts may be revealed." He obscurely signifies, that, after the scandalizing which took place upon the Cross of Christ, both to the disciples and to Mary herself, some quick healing should follow upon it from the Lord, confirming their heart unto faith in Him.[321]

Basil's exegesis of Simeon's prophecy that a sword would pierce Mary's heart gives way to various interpretations of this prophecy which, in light of the Tradition, Newman finds objectionable and which became a source of confusion for Pusey and others who seemed to accept such interpretations as officially representing the thought of the Catholic Church or, who perhaps believed that the Church in ignoring such interpretations had erred in her teachings about the Virgin. Basil identifies the sword as a symbol of the doubt ("unsettlement" as the Greek word *diakrisis* suggests), which would have overcome Mary and the other disciples once she (they) stood beneath the Cross of her Son. Basil, however, does imply that this sword which pierces to the marrow of heart and soul would by the mercy of God be removed, so as to permit the Virgin and the other disciples to recommit themselves in faith to the Lord. Nevertheless, the sin of doubt is implied which although not considered by Basil to be a grave sin, is nonetheless a sign that Our Lady would have allowed herself to be scandalized by the Cross.[322] In fact, Basil, in his epistle, makes reference to Our Lord's words in the Gospel, "All ye shall be scandalized in Me."[323]

Newman explains that Basil's notions about Simeon's prophecy of the sword are based on Origen's interpretations of the same passage.[324] Newman says that the hermeneutical principle applied by Origen suggests his preference for "scientific reasoning to authority," that is, to the authority of Tradition.[325] Origen, as Newman points out, was incapable of reconciling the truth of the universal need for salvation and Mary's personal sinlessness. Origen reasons, as did many of the theologians who followed him, especially in the Middle Ages, that if Mary is "one of the redeemed, she must at one time or another have committed an actual sin."[326] Newman quotes Origen as writing: "Are we to think, that the Apostles were scandalized, and not the Lord's Mother? If she suffered not scandal at Our Lord's Passion, then Jesus did not die for her sins. If all have sinned and need the glory of God, being justified by His grace and redeemed, certainly Mary at that time was scandalized."[327]

Saint Cyril arrives at similar conclusions, explaining that Simeon's sword represented the doubt that Mary could have entertained (at least mentally) when faced with Our Lord's sufferings.[328] Cyril reasons that if Peter, the first and greatest of the apostles, could resort to doubt and be scandalized by the prospect of the Lord's Death, then why is it unfathomable that the Mother of the Lord should be equally doubtful and scandalized? Cyril accepts such sentiments as perfectly normal, humanly speaking, especially in a woman,[329] in light of such difficult circumstances:

> And it is very natural that the woman in her (*to gunaion*), not knowing the mystery, should slide into some such trains of thought. For we must conclude, if we judge well, that the gravity of the circumstances was enough to overturn even a self-possessed mind; it is no wonder then if a woman (*to gunaion*) slipped into this reasoning. For if Peter himself, the chosen one of the holy disciples, once was scandalized ... so as to cry out hastily, Be it far from Thee, Lord ... what paradox is it, if the soft mind of womankind was carried off to weak ideas?[330]

Newman's observation in the above text is confirmed in the article, "Padri della Chiesa," by Father Toniolo in *Nuovo Dizionario di Mariologia*. He writes, in commenting on Cyril and indeed on the text cited above, "The sword prophesied by Simeon, which Origin and Basil had interpreted as a doubt of faith at the foot of the Cross, in Cyril is still 'a sword of sorrow,' and 'a sword of doubt,' with one grave addition: he in fact admits that a woman is weaker than a man, and that therefore Mary was not stronger than the apostles, who weakened during the Passion of the Lord." [331]

Newman offers the following estimation of Cyril's thought: "Lastly, as to Saint Cyril, I do not see that he declares that Mary actually doubted at the Crucifixion, but that considering she was a woman, it is likely she was tempted to doubt, and nearly doubted. Moreover, Saint Cyril does not seem to consider such doubt, had it occurred, as any great sin." [332] Newman understands Cyril's remark about the weakness of the female sex, as he considers it from a psychological perspective, not so much as disrespectful of Our Lady *per se* but rather as reflective of a general attitude toward women which was common among some Fathers of the Church, given the limitations of their cultural situation.

Newman is more than willing to accept an interpretation of the sword of Simeon as symbolic of the trials and temptations to which the Blessed Virgin could have been subject during her life, especially during the Passion of her Son, but he does not equate such a temptation/doubt with sin. Newman neither thinks Saint Cyril to have made such an equation nor does he consider it as being reflective of the overall Tradition:

> However, I am not unwilling to grant that, whereas Scripture tells us that all were scandalized at Our Lord's passion, that some sort of traditional interpretation of Simeon's words, to the effect that she was in some sense included in that trial. How near the apostolic era the tradition existed, cannot be determined; but such a belief need not include the idea of sin in the Blessed Virgin, but only the presence of temptation and darkness of spirit. This tradition, whatever its authority, would be easily perverted, so as actually to impute sin to her, by such reasonings as that of Origen. [333]

Newman categorically rejects the idea that the sword of Simeon should be interpreted as a sign of Mary's having succumbed to such trials and/or temptations adding that: "As to the words of Simeon, indeed, as interpreted by Saint Basil and Saint Cyril, there is nothing in the sacred text which obliges us to consider the 'sword' to mean doubt rather than anguish." [334] In other words, Newman holds that the preferred interpretation of the sword of Simeon is that it is symbolic of Mary's sorrows but in no way indicative of her sinfulness. In fact, regarding Saint Cyril, Newman adds the following defense:

> As to Saint Cyril, as I have said, he does not, strictly speaking, say more than that Our Lady was grievously tempted. This does not imply sin, for Our Lord was "tempted in all things like we are, yet without sin." Moreover, it is this Saint Cyril who spoke at Ephesus of the Blessed Virgin in terms of such high panegyric, as to make it more consistent in him to suppose that she was sinless, than that she was not. [335]

Newman is not reticent in disassociating Basil's interpretation of the sword of Simeon as symbolic of Mary's lack of faith from what is the apostolic Tradition, which preserves the integrity of her faith through and through. Newman asserts that "his statement then of the Blessed Virgin's wavering in faith, instead of professing to be the tradition of a doctrine, carries with it an avowal of its being none at all." [336] Newman, having presented the teachings of these Fathers, explains to what extent they can or cannot be held, according to their conformity to or variance from the Apostolic Tradition:[337]

> Such then is the teaching of these three Fathers; now how far is it in antagonism to ours? On the one hand, we will not allow that Our Blessed Lady ever sinned; we cannot bear the notion, entering, as we do, into the full spirit of Saint Augustine's words, "Concerning the Holy Virgin Mary, I wish no question to be raised at all, when we are treating of sins." On the other hand, we admit, rather we maintain, that, except for the grace of God, she might have sinned; and that she may have been exposed to temptation in the sense in which Our Lord was exposed to it, though as His Divine Nature made it impossible for Him to yield to it, so His grace preserved her under its assaults also. While then we do not hold that Saint Simeon prophesied of temptation, when he said a sword pierce her, still, if any one likes to say he did, we do not consider him heretical,

provided he does not impute to her any sinful or inordinate emotion as consequence to it.[338]

Friedel sums up Newman's evaluation of the scriptural exegesis of these three Fathers of Church hitherto examined in terms of their doctrinal and dogmatic validity, vis-à-vis the Apostolic Tradition:

> The remarks of Basil, Chrysostom, and Cyril by no means suppose a tradition in the Church as do the affirmations of other Fathers on Mary's role in the redemption. 1. They do not witness to any belief; they are interpreting passages of Holy Writ, and, further, do not interpret one and the same text; neither do they agree in the interpretation of the same text. It can hardly be inferred that a positive belief existed among the Christians that Our Lady had committed actual sin; even if it be supposed that there was a tradition about her sinfulness, a contrary tradition could not be presumed in consequence. 2. The very form of the statements shows that the Fathers are not witnessing to an apostolical tradition. They do not claim their opinion to be such, nor do they testify to one and the same doctrine. Hence they do not fulfill the requirements for an apostolic tradition. They are merely commentators of Scripture and so may be supposed to be giving a private and personal opinion, rather than to be making a dogmatic statement.[339]

(c) *Newman and Saint Ephrem the Syrian*

In the *Letter to Pusey*, Newman includes two brief citations from the works of this Syriac doctor,[340] serving both to reaffirm what the other Fathers, some already mentioned, have to say about the Eve–Mary parallel and to situate that parallelism within the aura of Mary's entire person and work.[341] Newman sees Ephrem as an important witness of the Syriac tradition concerning the Virgin.[342] These isolated quotations from Ephrem are best understood when placed within the context of the whole of his Mariological writing. Ephrem's literary style is highly poetic and characterized by mystical interpretations of the Sacred Scriptures.[343]

Owen F. Cummings writes:

> If we are to understand some of Ephrem's poetic Mariology, then we must first grasp something of the Syrian Father's conviction that the two Testaments of Holy Scripture derive

from a single Revelation, and that the Old Testament acts as an icon of the New. It is a Christ-centered view of Scripture in which the whole Bible speaks of Christ either directly, as in the New Testament, or indirectly through prophecy, type, and allegory. Ephrem and his peers in the Syriac Church would have only two "doctrines" of Mary, as it were—that she is ever-virgin and that she is the Mother of God incarnate. But, because they were saturated in Scripture, images and types of Our Lady were found by them everywhere, and in these images and types the roots of later doctrinal formulations may be found.[344]

The Genesis account of Creation and the Fall of Adam and Eve supplied Ephrem with much food for spiritual contemplation.[345] The antithetical parallelisms, which other Fathers of the Church like Justin and Irenæus theologized about, do not elude Ephrem and, in fact, receive from him fresh insights, most often born out of his mystical musings over the Sacred Text. Even Ephrem's more prosaic treatments of the Genesis story result in exegesis which bears the mark of mystical inspiration. Cummings offers us examples of both Ephrem's prosaic and poetic use of the Eve–Mary typology in his interpretation of Genesis. As concerns Ephrem's prosaic use, Cummings relies on Ephrem's *Commentary on the Diatesseron* II, 2:

> Saint Paul interprets Christ as the second Adam, so that the first Adam becomes a type of Christ for him. It is then but a short step to think of Mary as a second Eve, with the first Eve as a type of Mary. Ephrem develops this thinking: "Mary gave birth without the participation of a man. Eve was born from Adam without there having been any carnal union, so it is with Joseph and Mary, the Virgin, his spouse. Eve brought the murderer Cain into the world; Mary, the Giver of Life. Eve brought into the world the one who shed his brother's blood; Mary Him Whose blood was shed by His brothers." This passage is a splendid example of how Ephrem uses the Old Testament. Since all of Scripture is a word spoken by God, in the Word of God made flesh, we have the key to Scripture, which unlocks all manner of insights.[346]

As concerns Ephrem's poetic use of typology, Cummings notes: "A slightly different type of Adam–Eve typology emerges in Ephrem's *Hymns on Paradise*." Ephrem writes:

274

Naked, Adam was handsome;
His diligent wife
Toiled to weave for him a garment of defilements:
The garden seeing him
And finding him hideous, thrust him outside.
But a new tunic was made for him by Mary.
Clothed in this robe, and according to the promise,
The Thief was resplendent:
The garden, seeing Adam again in him,
Embraced him.[347]

Owen Cummings comments on this text as follows:

The old Adam with his robe made by Eve is expelled from the garden. The new Adam, with his "robe of flesh" taken in Mary's womb, is the one in whom the old Adam finds himself, his redeemed self, and so the garden embraced him. This is an interesting passage because the embrace of the garden is really the embrace of the risen Christ by Saint Mary Magdalene in the garden of the tomb. It seems as though Ephrem has deliberately combined the Magdalene with the Mother of God. Ultimately, however, this is not problematic for Ephrem, as the poetic effect fosters faith and devotion.[348]

Father De Margerie[349] gives the example of Ephrem's commentary on Genesis 2:21–23, dealing with Eve's creation from the rib of Adam. De Margerie notes Ephrem's use of typology[350]—a literary device which, for example, allows him to identify in the figure of Adam, formed without "carnal link," that is, from virgin earth, a prefigurement or type of the virgin birth of the Second Adam.[351] Ephrem explores the depths of this typology, showing the interconnectedness among the symbolism of Adam's side from which Eve is formed, the miraculous birth of Christ from Mary's virginal womb, and the side of Christ pierced by the soldier's lance from which flow blood and water—symbols of the sacramental life of the Church.[352] Moreover, Eve is seen as the prefigurement or type of Mary and of the Church.[353] This latter relationship between Mary and the Church is an important aspect of Ephrem's Mariology. Father Gambero provides us with a concise overview of some important texts in which Ephrem explains the significance of Mary's relationship to the Church. For example, Gambero offers the following quotation from Ephrem's sermon for Easter night, in which he clearly identifies Mary as a figure of the Church (*Typus*

Ecclesiæ): "The Virgin Mary is a symbol of the Church, when she receives the first announcement of the gospel. And, it is in the name of the Church that Mary sees the risen Jesus. Blessed be God, who filled Mary and the Church with joy. We call the Church by the name of Mary, for she deserves a double name."[354]

As Gambero also points out, the antithetical parallelism between Mary and Eve is a theme which Ephrem utilizes as a *chiave di lettura* to understand Mary's role in the *œconomia salutis*. Mary epitomizes an attitude of openness to God. In fact, Ephrem describes her as having a "luminous eye," enlightened by grace and symbolic of the purity of her faith. In direct contrast to Mary is placed the figure of Eve who is described as having an eye obfuscated and "obscured" by sin.[355] Ephrem portrays Mary as the personification of a new creation redeemed, "re-pristinized" and recapitulated by Christ.[356] Ephrem describes this recapitulation in terms of the reunification of humanity resulting from the free and meritorious cooperation of the Virgin in the luminous work of salvation.[357]

An interesting comparison can be made between Ephrem's use of imagery having to do with light and that of Romanos the Melodist. Both hymnographers use the image of light as a primary symbol of the new creation that is inaugurated with the coming of Christ. Mary is one of the many biblical figures to be enveloped by this light. However, in a certain sense, Mary receives a particular illumination because she is the one who, among all creatures, most brilliantly reflects the radiant beauty,[358] both in a physical and spiritual way, of Him Who enlightens every man who comes into the world.[359]

In the *Letter to Pusey*, Newman gives the following texts from Ephrem concerning the Eve–Mary antithetical parallel:

> Per Evam nempe decora et amabilis hominis gloria extincta est, quæ tamen rursus per Mariam refloruit.[360] Initio protoparentum delicto in omnes homines mors pertransiit; hodie vero per Mariam translati sumus morte ad vitam. Initio serpens, Evæ auribus occupatis, inde virus in totum corpus dilatavit; hodie Maria ex auribus perpetuæ felicitatis assertorem excepit. Quod ergo mortis fuit, simul et vitæ exstitit instrumentum.[361]

Ephrem's use of typology is evident. As he had contrasted Mary's and Eve's eyes, here he contrasts their ears as instruments by which two different messages are heard, resulting in two contrary effects for the economy of salvation. Mary's reception of the word of the Angel results in the birth of the "champion of eternal happiness"; Eve's acceptance of Satan's insidious proposition leads to the unhappy conclusion of death. In his *Homily on the Nativity*, Ephrem continues to develop this antithetical parallelism drawing from it the consequences for our eternal salvation:

> Therefore this day resembles the first day of creation:
> that day created things were established,
> on this, the earth is renewed, and because of Adam it is
>   blessed—
> having been cursed because of him.
> Eve and Adam through sin
> introduced death into the created world;
> creation's Lord gave us, by His-Only begotten
> through Mary, new life again.
> By means of the serpent the Evil one
> poured out his poison in the ear of Eve;
> the Good One brought low His mercy,
> and entered through Mary's ear:
> through the gate by which death entered,
> Life also entered, putting death to death.[362]

What Newman writes in his sermon "The Reverence Due to the Blessed Virgin Mary" about the feast of the Annunciation bears a close resemblance to what Ephrem writes about the mystery of the Incarnation as the inauguration of a completely new creation, a renewed economy of salvation, by which the ancient curse brought about by the sin of Adam and Eve is reversed through the consent of the Virgin into the ineffable blessing of the coming of the Word made flesh:

> The Seed of the woman, announced to guilty Eve, after long delay, was at length appearing upon earth, and was to be born of her. In her the destinies of the world were to be reversed, and the serpent's head bruised. On her was bestowed the greatest honour ever put upon any individual of our fallen race. God was taking upon Him her flesh, and humbling Himself to be called her offspring;—such is the deep mystery! . . . I observe, that in her the curse pronounced on Eve was changed to a blessing. Christ might have descended from heaven, as he went

back, and as He will come again. He might have taken on Himself a body from the ground, as Adam was given; or been formed, like Eve, in some other divinely devised way. But, far from this, God sent forth His Son (as Saint Paul says), "made of a woman." For it has been His gracious purpose to turn *all* that is ours from evil to good. Had He so pleased, He might have found, when we sinned, other beings to do Him service, casting us into hell; but He purposed to save and to change *us*. And in like manner all that belongs to us, our reason, our affections, our pursuits, our relations in life, He needs nothing put aside in His disciples, but all sanctified. Therefore, instead of sending His Son from heaven, He sent Him forth as the Son of Mary, to show that all our sorrow and all our corruption can be blessed and changed by Him. The very punishment of the fall, the very taint of birth-sin, admits of a cure by the coming of Christ.[363]

Newman, although not directly relying on Ephrem's theology of the Incarnation, does nonetheless approximate, in a less poetic fashion, many of the insights found in Ephrem's *Homily on the Nativity*. For example, Ephrem compares Mary's virginal womb to the burning bush from which God spoke to the prophet Moses on Mt. Horeb:

> It is a source of great amazement, my beloved,
> that someone should enquire into the wonder
> of how God came down
> and made His dwelling in a womb,
> not shrinking from such a home;
> and how a womb of flesh was able
> to carry flaming fire,
> and how a flame dwelt
> in a moist womb which did not get burnt up.
> Just as the bush on Horeb bore
> God in the flame,
> so did Mary bear
> Christ in her virginity.[364]

In his Sermon III, "The Incarnation," Newman discusses this infinitely more sublime mystery of Christ's physical dwelling in the Virgin in the context of an overview of the history of salvation in which God revealed Himself in various forms to the patriarchs and prophets. In fact, Newman turns most of his attention in Sermon III to the revelation of God to Moses from out of the burning bush. However, before discussing its mention in Sermon III, it should also be noted that Newman makes important reference to this story in connection to the Incarnation in his sermon on the Incarnation entitled "The Mystery of the Divine Condescension"[365] and in his meditation on the Marian title *Mater Admirabilis*.[366] What, at first, Moses perceived to be only "the Angel of the Lord" was a revelation of the Lord's "supernatural presence" and later accompanied by the revelation of the Lord's identity as "the God of Abraham, Isaac, and Jacob." These revelations, as Newman explains, are confirmed for Moses on Mount Sinai. But even more striking is Newman's exegesis of these texts as representing revelations of the Eternal or preexistent Second Person of the Blessed Trinity, the Son of God, "in angelic form." Newman writes:

> Now, assuming, as we seem to have reason to assume, that the Son of God is herein revealed to us as graciously ministering to the Patriarchs, Moses, and others, in angelic form, the question arises, what was the nature of this appearance? We are not informed, nor may we venture to determine; still, any how, the Angel was but a temporary outward form which the Eternal Word assumed, whether it was of a material nature, or a vision. Whether or no it was really an Angel, or but an appearance existing only for the immediate purpose, still, any how, we could not with propriety say that our Lord "took upon Him the nature of Angels.[367]

These reflections of Newman on the revelations of God to Moses lead him to conclude that if God revealed Himself by means of created realities—or, using the words of Newman, "created substance"—in the Old Testament (e.g., the Angel speaking from the burning bush), why could He not then have chosen to reveal Himself, not "as a vision or phantom" as heretics have insisted, but rather in the flesh being born of a Virgin as confirmed by the creeds and councils of the Church? Furthermore, Newman's arguments, which are clearly in opposition to any heretical teachings tainted by Gnostic dualism (e.g., Docetism) or adoptionism (e.g., Apollonarianism), affirms, by way of reference to the Athanasian Creed, the reality of the hypostatic union in the womb of the Virgin, so that the same Son of God can rightfully be called the Son of Mary. Newman makes his argument thus:

Now these instances of the indwelling of Almighty God in a created substance, which I have given by way of contrast to that infinitely higher and mysterious union which is called the Incarnation, actually supply the senses in which heretics at various times have perverted our holy and comfortable doctrine, and which have obliged us to have recourse to Creeds and Confessions. Rejecting the teaching of the Church, and dealing rudely with the Word of God, they have ventured to delay that "Jesus Christ is come in the flesh," pretending He merely showed Himself as a vision or phantom;—or they have said that the Word of God merely dwelt in the man Christ Jesus, as the Shechinah in the Temple, having no real union with the Son of Mary (as it were two distinct Beings, the Word and Jesus, even as the blessed Spirit is distinct from a man's soul);– or that Christ was called God for His great spiritual perfections, and that He gradually attained them by long practice. All these words not to be uttered, except to show what the true doctrine is, and what is the meaning of the language of the Church concerning it. For instance, the Athanasian Creed confesses that Christ is "God of the substance of the Father, begotten before the worlds, perfect God," lest we should consider his Divine Nature, like ours, as merely a nature resembling God's holiness: that He is "Man of the substance of His Mother, born in the world, perfect man," lest we should think of Him as "not come in the flesh" a mere Angelic vision; and that "although He be God and man, yet He is not two, but one Christ," lest we should fancy that the Word of God entered into Him and then departed, as the Holy Ghost in the prophets.[368]

Thus, can we not conclude that Newman's more didactic, dogmatic, theological discourse contains in essence the truths that Ephrem sought to explain in more symbolic, allegorical, poetical language? Perhaps, finally, it should be recalled how both the theology of Ephrem and of Newman are confirmed in the Sacred Liturgy. Indeed, the third antiphon for First Vespers for the Solemnity of Mary Mother of God (January 1) in the Roman Rite applies the very text of Exodus 2:1–3 recounting the episode of Moses and the burning bush as an image to describe Mary the Ever-Virgin Mother of God: "*Rubrum, quem viderat Moyses incombustum, conservatam agnovimus tuam laudabilem virginatatem. Dei Genetrix, intercede pro nobis.*"[369]

Returning to the event of the Annunciation, Ephrem high-lights the significance of Mary's response to the angel Gabriel:

"Behold His handmaid am I."
Therefore He came down, in a manner He knows,
He stirred and came in a way that pleased Him,
He entered and dwelt in her without her perceiving,
she received Him, suffering nothing.
He was in her womb like a babe,
yet the whole world was full of Him.
Of His love he came down to renew
the image of Adam grown old.
Therefore, when you hear of the birth
of God, remain in silence;
let the word of Gabriel
be depicted in your mind,
for there is nothing that is hard
for that glorious majesty,
which for our sakes leaned down,
and for our sakes was revealed
for it leaned down toward us,
and among us was born, from one of us.
This day Mary has become for us
the heaven that bears God,
for in her the exalted Godhead
has descended and dwelt;
in her It has grown small, to make us great,
– but Its nature does not diminish;
in her It has woven us a garment
that shall be for our salvation.[370]

For Ephrem, the mysteries of the Annunciation and Nativity, that is, the mystery of the Lord's Incarnation, knit together in the virginal womb of Mary, effect at one and the same time, a mar-velous exchange (*admirabile commercium*) between God and man, heaven and earth, eternity and time, greatness and smallness; thus, bringing about the restoration of humanity and the inaugu-ration of mankind's eternal salvation.[371] Mary's divine maternity is essentially the mystery by which Adam is recapitulated, re-stored to and recreated in the image and likeness of Christ the Second Adam and Divine Physician. Ephrem explains:

Happy is Adam at His birth,
for He has recovered the glory that Adam lost.

Who has ever seen
clay serve as the potter's covering?
Who has ever seen fire
wrap itself in swaddling bands?
Such is the extent to which
God has lowered Himself, for Adam's sake.
To such an extent did God humble Himself
for the sake of His servant
who has exalted himself and transgressed the commandment
at the advice of the Evil one, the murderer.
The Giver of that commandment has now
Humbled Himself to raise us up!
Praise to that mercy on high
which has been brought down to men on earth,
so that the sick world might be healed
by the Physician who has shone forth in creation.[372]

The conclusion of Newman's Sermon III, "The Incarnation," is an encomium to the Incarnate Word as to Him Who heals the brokenness of mankind—fallen from original holiness and grace—by means of the redemptive mysteries of His earthly life and ministry which culminate in the mystery of His Passion, Death, Resurrection and Ascension into glory.

Let us then, according to the light given us, praise and bless Him in the Church below, whom Angels in heaven see and adore. Let us bless Him for His surpassing loving-kindness in taking upon Him our infirmities to redeem us, when He dwelt in the innermost love of the Everlasting Father,[373] in the glory which He had with Him before the world was. He came in lowliness and want; born amid the tumults of a mixed and busy multitude, cast aside into the outhouse of a crowded inn, laid to His first rest among the brute cattle. He grew up, as if the native of a despised city, and was bred to a humble craft. He bore to live in a world that slighted Him, for He lived in it. He came as the appointed Priest, to offer sacrifice for those who took no part in the act of worship; He came to offer up for sinners that precious blood which was meritorious by the virtue of His Divine Anointing. He died, to rise again the third day, the Sun of Righteousness, fully displaying that splendour which had hitherto been concealed by the morning clouds. He rose again to ascend to the right hand of God, there to plead His sacred wounds in token of our forgiveness, to rule and guide His ransomed people, and from His pierced side to pour forth

His choicest blessings upon them. He ascended, thence to de-
scend again in due season to judge the world which He has
redeemed—Great is our Lord, and great is His power, Jesus the
Son of God and Son of man. Ten thousand times more daz-
zlingly than the highest Archangel, is Our Lord and Christ. By
birth the Only-begotten and Express image of God; and in
taking our flesh, not sullied thereby, but raising human nature
with Him, as He rose from the lowly manger to the right hand
of power,—raising human nature, for Man has redeemed us,
Man is set above all creatures, as one with the Creator, Man
shall judge man at the last day. So honoured is this earth, that
no stranger shall judge us, but He who is our fellow, who will
sustain our interests, and has full sympathy in all our imperfections. He who loved us, even to die for us, is graciously appointed to assign the final measurement and price upon His
own work. He who best knows by infirmity to take the part of
the infirm, He who would rain reap the full fruit of His passion,
He will separate the wheat from the chaff, so that not a grain
shall fall to the ground. He who has given us to share His own
spiritual nature, He from whom we have drawn the life's blood
of our souls, He our brother will decide about His brethren. In
that His second coming, may He in His grace and loving pity
remember us, who is our only hope, our only salvation.[374]

The healing powers of the Second Adam and our Final Judge
are unsurpassed by all of creation, and therefore Newman can
conclude that Christ is "our only hope, our only salvation." Yet, it
cannot be forgotten that all of the wonderful mysteries of our
salvation referred to by Newman in his encomium were not
accomplished apart from the principal mystery which is the main
subject of Newman's sermon, that is, the Incarnation of the Son
of God whereby, "He rose from the lowly manger to the right
hand of power."

Cummings also reflects on this use of typology in Ephrem and
shows how Mary's virginal womb is the precise link between the
mystery of our salvation in Christ, the Eucharistic Bread of everlasting life, and the working of the Holy Spirit by which we are
spiritually reborn in Baptism:

> Another aspect of the Eve typology links Mary with the Eucha-
> rist: "The Church gave us the living bread for that unleavened
> bread which Egypt gave. Mary gave us the bread of refresh-
> ment for the bread of weariness which Eve gave."[375] In this

passage the Passover bread in Egypt is the type of the Eucharist in the Church. Ephrem adds to this the typology between Mary and Eve in terms of bread. The point of departure is probably Genesis 3:19, "in the sweat of your brow shall you eat bread." But it seems also to suggest Christ's body itself, taken from Mary—"Mary gave us the bread of refreshment." Because the Eucharist is Christ's body under another form, the Eucharist, the Church and Mary are closely interrelated. One then finds this beautiful stanza in his Hymns on Faith[376]: "In the womb that bore you are Fire and Spirit, Fire and Spirit are in the river where you were baptized, Fire and Spirit are in our baptism too, And in the Bread and Cup are Fire and Spirit." The Holy Spirit brings about the Incarnation, descends upon Jesus at the baptism in the Jordan (as well as on us at our baptism), and transforms the bread and wine into the reality of Christ's Presence. This is an excellent example of how the truths of faith interpenetrate one another. Pull at one of the threads of the tapestry of faith, and one finds the other threads being pulled also. For Ephrem there can be no real separation of the Holy Spirit from Christ, from Mary, from the Church, from the sacraments of the Church. All are interwoven in God's saving plan.[377]

Newman concludes his Easter sermon entitled "The Eucharistic Presence" (Sermon 11, *Parochial and Plain Sermons*) by reaffirming that there exists, according to the economy of redemption, a *nexus mysteriorum*, most evident in the doctrines that flow from the "blessed doctrine of the Incarnation of the Son of God." "His birth of a Virgin," is the exordium of this "gracious economy," in which are also linked the mysteries of His "atoning Death and Resurrection." Newman exhorts his readers to pray that their "real and living insight" into the mystery or "doctrine" of the Incarnation and into the Paschal Mystery might lead them to "desire that the Holy Communion may be the effectual type of that gracious economy."[378] Thus, Newman links together the mystery of the Incarnation and the mystery of Christ's Eucharistic Presence; there is also made in an implicit way a link between Mary and the Eucharist: "No one realizes the Mystery of the Incarnation but must feel disposed towards that of Holy Communion." Newman adds: "Let us pray him to give us an earnest longing after Him—a thirst for His presence—an anxiety to find Him—a joy on hearing that He is to be found, even now, under the veil of sensible things,

—and a good hope that *we* shall find Him there. Blessed are they who have not seen, and yet have believed."[379] Perhaps, Newman's words to the young listeners of his Discourse to Mixed Congregations entitled "On the Fitness of the Glories of Mary" make the connection between Mary and the Eucharist even more explicit: "It is the boast of the Catholic Religion, that it has the gift of making the young heart chaste; and why is this, but that it gives us Jesus Christ for our food, and Mary for our nursing Mother."[380]

In his hymns on the Nativity, Ephrem reflects on Mary's divine maternity and how in the eternal wisdom and love of God her maternal womb becomes that dwelling place in which human and natural contradictions (antitheses) are transformed by the divine power into splendid objects of veneration and marvels of grace according to the economy of salvation:

> A wonder is Your mother: The Lord entered her and
> became a servant; He entered able to speak and He
> became silent in her; He entered her thundering and
> His voice grew silent; He entered Shepherd of all;
> a lamb He became in her; He emerged bleating.
> The womb of Your mother overthrew the orders:
> The Establisher of all entered a Rich One; He emerged poor.
> He entered her a Lofty One; He emerged humble. He entered
> her a Radiant One, and He put on a despised hue and emerged.
> He entered a mighty warrior, and put on fear inside her womb.
> He entered, Nourisher of all, and He acquired hunger. He
>   entered,
> the One who gives drink to all, and He acquired thirst.
>   Stripped and
> Laid bare, He emerged from her womb, the One who clothes
>   all.[381]

Newman's sermon "The Mystery of Godliness," intended for the Feast of Christmas (Sermon VII, *Parochial and Plain Sermons*), is a scripturally rich reflection on the mystery of Our Lord's Incarnation and Birth. The *kenosis* ("self-emptying") of Christ, as Newman reflects, is central to the rebirth and exaltation of mankind. The coming of Our Lord in the flesh "is a figure, promise, or pledge of our new birth, and it effects what it promises."[382] The salvific consequences of the Incarnation are a fulfillment of the Old Testament prophecies and yet exceed every hope and imagining of man, so much so that, as Ephrem aptly and poetically describes in his "Hymn on the Nativity," so too, for Newman, the human and divine elements—of apparently contradictory nature—are marvelously harmonized in the person of the Eternal Word–made-flesh conceived in the fullness of time and born of the Most Holy Virgin—True God and True Man—by the power of the Holy Spirit. Newman describes this *admirabile commercium* thus:

> This is the wonderful economy of grace, or mystery of godliness, which should be before our minds at all times, but especially at this season, when the Most Holy took upon Him our flesh of "a pure Virgin," "by the operation of the Holy Ghost, without spot of sin, to make us clean from all sin." God "dwelling in the Light which no man can approach unto" . . . . He is the True Light, which lighteth every man that cometh into the world. . . . He it was who created the worlds;. . . .Yet this great God condescended to come down on earth from his heavenly throne, and to be born into His own world. . . . He took our nature upon Him but not our sin; taking our nature in a way above nature. . . . He was, as other men, "made of woman" as Saint Paul speaks, that He might take on Him, not another nature, but the nature of man. It had been prophesied from the beginning, that the Seed of the woman should bruise the serpent's head. "I will put enmity," said Almighty God to the serpent at the fall, "between thee and the woman, between thy seed and her seed; It shall bruise thy head." In consequence of this promise, pious women, we are told, were in the old time ever looking out in hope that in their own instance per-adventure the promise might find its accomplishment. One after another hoped in turn that she herself might be mother of the promised King; and therefore marriage was in repute, and virginity in disesteem, as if then only they had a prospect of being the Mother of Christ, if they waited for the blessing according to the course of nature, and amid the generations of men. Pious woman they were, but little comprehending the real condition of mankind. It was ordained, indeed, that the Eternal Word should come into the world by the ministration of a woman; but born the way of the flesh he could not be. . . . Priests among men are they who have to offer "first for their own sins, and then for the people's;" but He, coming as the immaculate Lamb of God, and all-prevailing Priest, could not come in the way which those fond persons anticipated. He came by a new and living way, by which He alone has come, and which alone

became Him. The Prophet Isaiah had been the first to announce it: "The Lord Himself will give you a sign," he says, "Behold a Virgin shall conceive and bear a Son, and shall call His Name Immanuel." And accordingly Saint Matthew after quoting this text, declares its fulfillment in the instance of the Blessed Mary. . . . Because He was "incarnate by the Holy Ghost of the Virgin Mary," therefore He was "Jesus" a "Saviour from sin." Again, the Angel Gabriel had already said to Mary, "Hail, thou art highly favoured, the Lord is with thee: blessed art thou among women." And then he proceeds to declare, that her Son should be called Jesus; that He "should be great, and should be called the Son of the Highest;" and that "of his Kingdom there shall be no end." And he concludes by announcing, "The Holy Ghost shall come upon thee, and the power of the Highest shall overshadow thee; therefore that Holy Thing which shall be born of thee shall be called the Son of God." Because God the Holy Ghost wrought miraculously, therefore was her Son a "Holy Thing," "the Son of God," "Jesus" and heir of an everlasting kingdom.[383]

What are some of these apparent contradictions from a natural standpoint, and how are they reconciled in the mystery of the Incarnation in which Mary has a most definite role of cooperation? First of all, through his birth from the Virgin Mary, He who lives in inapproachable light becomes the light of all men. In the Old Testament it was believed that "no man could see God and live," so overwhelmingly powerful was the radiant beauty of God's holiness, so vastly different the heavenly dwelling place of the divine from the ordinary dwelling places of men. The Incarnation accomplishes the unfathomable. God makes His home in our midst. The transcendent holiness and purity of God operative in the Incarnation by the power of the Holy Spirit is most fully revealed on the countenance of the Christ-Child, the Only-Begotten of the Father. However, we get a glimpse of the transcendent holiness and beauty of the Son when we encounter, at the crib of Bethlehem, His most pure and Virgin Mother. Thus are fulfilled the prophecies of the Old Covenant beginning with that of the *Protoevangelium*, so that "those who dwelt in darkness have seen a great light," that is to say, where sin abounded in the persons of Adam and Eve and their descendants, so grace abounds all the more in Christ the New Adam and in Mary the New Eve.

Secondly, contrary to the expectations of the pious women throughout the history of Israel, who looked forward to becoming the mother of the promised Messiah, the ever more sublime mystery of God's condescension at the moment of the Incarnation occurs—not through the natural course as was naturally expected but through birth from a Virgin betrothed to a man named Joseph of the house of David. Last, here, too, God's Providence makes for an outcome which many in Israel would never have imagined possible, namely, that the Kingdom of David, whose physical restoration was expected to occur as a consequence of the Messiah's arrival, would signify, even more importantly, the inauguration of a spiritual Kingdom that would have no end.

Newman's sermon continues to develop along similar lines of contrast and comparison to demonstrate how from the "thesis" of the Father's plan or economy of redemption the "antithesis" of sinful man's fallen human nature is raised up and transformed by the sinless Savior into a "synthesis" of salvation. Thus, Our Lord's entrance into this world makes of Him "a pattern of sanctity in the circumstances of His life, as well as in His birth." Newman prefaces this by saying:

> This is the great Mystery we are now celebrating, of which mercy is the beginning, and sanctity the end: according to the Psalm, "Righteousness and peace have kissed each other." He who is all purity came to an impure race to raise them to His purity. He, the brightness of God's glory, came in a body of flesh, which was pure and holy as Himself, "without spot or wrinkle, or any such thing, but holy and without blemish;" and this He did for our sake, "that we might be partakers of His holiness." He needed not a human nature for Himself,—He was all-perfect in His original Divine nature; but He took upon Himself what was ours for the sake of us. He who "hath made of one blood all nations of men," so that in the sin of one all sinned, and in the death of one all died, he came in that very nature as it is in His person, that "our sinful bodies might be made clean by his Body, and our souls washed through His most precious blood;" to make us partakers of the Divine nature; to sow the seed of eternal life in our hearts; and to raise us from "the corruption that is in the world through lust," to that immaculate purity and that fullness of grace which is in Him. He who is the first principle and pattern of all things, came to

be the beginning and pattern of human kind, the firstborn of the whole creation, He, who is the everlasting Light, became the Light of men; He, who is the Life from eternity, became the Life of a race dead in sin; He, who is the Word of God, came to be a spiritual Word, "dwelling richly in our hearts" an "engrafted word," which is able to save our souls; He, who is the co-equal Son of the Father, came to be the Son of God in our flesh, that He might raise us also to the adoption of sons, and might be first among many brethren. And this is the reason why the Collect for the season, after speaking of our Lord as the Only-begotten Son, and born in our nature of a pure Virgin, proceeds to speak of our new birth and adopted sonship, and renewal by the grace of the Holy Ghost.[384]

Furthermore, Ephrem's *Hymn on Mary* (no. 7) is an invitation to admire the various aspects of the mystery of the divine motherhood. In doing so, Ephrem uses many colorful metaphors which help to conjure up for us images the better to comprehend the central role the Virgin plays in the economy of our salvation. Saint Ephrem's theology, especially his Mariology, is replete with symbolism. In Newman's *Letter to Pusey*, he quotes Ephrem's description of Mary as "the mystical new heavens," "the heavens carrying the Divinity," "the fruitful vine," "by whom we are translated from death to life."[385] The latter typology is also evident, for example, in the typology employed by Ephrem in the *Hymn on Mary*:

> Come, all you who have discernment, let us wonder
> at the virgin mother, David's daughter.
> Herself most fair, to the Wonderful she gave birth;
> she is the spring that provides the Fountain,
> she the ship that bears joy from the Father,
> that carries good news in her pure womb;
> she took on board and escorts
> the great Steersman of creation
> through whom peace reigns
> on earth and in heaven . . .
> A young dove, she carried
> the eagle, the Ancient of days,
> singing praise as she carried Him
> in her lovely songs:
> "O my Son most rich, in a tiny nest
> You have chosen to grow; melodious harp,

with the lyre whose cords stir the cherubim;
pray let me speak to You.
Your home, my Son, is higher than all,
yet it was Your wish to make me Your home.
Heaven is too small to contain Your splendour,
yet I, poorest of creatures, am carrying You." [386]

Finally, Ephrem compares Mary's womb to the chariot upheld by the cherubim envisioned by the prophet Ezekiel. He puts these words on Mary's lips who reflects on this great mystery and even does so by directly addressing Jesus, the fruit of her womb:

The very chariot stops amazed that I carry its Master;
the cherubim cry out with trembling:
"blessed is your splendour in Your place"
– that place is with me, my bosom is Your home!
Your radiance rests on my knees,
the throne of Your majesty is held in my arms.
Instead of the chariot wheels,
my fingers clasp You, I too will cry out
"blessed are You in Your place." [387]

Several of the Marian titles of the Laurentine Litany of Our Lady or "Litany of Loreto," upon which Newman's reflections in his *Meditations and Devotions* are based, follow a typological reading of the Sacred Scriptures, especially in application to the Virgin; however, these titles are always rooted in the literal sense and are decisively Christological in their focus. They have already been discussed in various sections of this work. Therefore, a detailed explanation of their significance as revealed in Newman's writings would be redundant. However, a synopsis of those Marian titles—whose characteristic typological language directly relates to the mystery of the Incarnation and thus, by necessity, to the mystery of the divine maternity—might be useful at this point to demonstrate how both Saint Ephrem and Newman were able to encapsulate the profound theological significance, Mariological in particular, of the typological sense.

The title *Domus Aurea* (House of Gold), alluding to the apocalyptic vision of the Book of Revelation in which the City of the New and Everlasting Jerusalem is described as the golden palace of God, is also applied to Mary to describe the splendor of her manifold gifts, graces and blessings. However, above all, Mary is rightly compared to the golden palace or house of God precisely because she is the *Theotokos*, the *Dei Genetrix*. Consequently, Mary's womb, in which is conceived, formed as flesh of our flesh and, from which the Incarnate Son of the Most High is born is not simply referred to as a "guest house" of sorts for the infant Savior and "Great King," but as His dwelling-place, His "holy house," His "golden palace."[388] To explain this theology, Newman writes:

> He was her Guest; nay, more than a guest, for a guest comes into a house as well as leaves it. But Our Lord was actually *born in* this holy house. He took His flesh and His blood from this house, from the flesh, from the veins of Mary. Rightly then was she made to be of pure gold, because she was to give of that gold to form the body of the Son of God.[389]

Likewise, the title *Sedes Sapientiæ* (Seat of Wisdom), deriving from the Old Testament theology of Yahweh's dwelling in the tabernacle, the portable meeting tent, the ark of the Covenant and in the Temple at Jerusalem,[390] is applied to Mary insofar as she becomes in Newman's words, "the human throne of Him Who reigns in heaven."[391] Newman reinforces this image by quoting an excerpt of poetry of John Keble. Newman simply states: "In the poet's words," and gives the text as follows:

> His throne, thy bosom blest,
> O Mother undefiled,
> That Throne, if aught beneath the skies,
> Beseems the sinless Child.[392]

This use of typology is also inherent in the Marian title of *Vas Honorabile* (Vessel of Honor). Newman's meditation on the title begins by mentioning Saint Paul's use of the term "vessel of honor" in reference to those "elect or chosen souls" which are deemed thus, as Newman explains, "because through the love of God, they are filled with God's heavenly and holy grace."[393] From this Pauline usage of the title, Newman then makes the following logical deduction, "How much more then is Mary a vessel of honour by reason of her having within her, not only the grace of God, but the very Son of God, formed as regards His flesh and blood out of her."[394]

Last, as Ephrem alludes to the fiery chariot of Ezechiel as a typological symbol of Mary's virginal womb, so in his meditation on the title *Janua Cæli* (Gate of Heaven). Newman alludes to the text of the Prophet Ezechiel in which there is a reference to a gate through which the Lord (Yahweh) alone can enter and exit and in which "the Prince Himself shall sit," as prophetically paradigmatic of Mary's perpetual virginity and of her womb as the dwelling place of the promised Messiah.

SUMMARY OF CHAPTER THREE

1) The "three-fold cord" of Justin, Irenæus, and Tertullian forms for Newman a powerful combined witness to the antiquity of the Church's doctrine of the New Eve as gleaned from these ancient Fathers' reflections on the antithetical parallelism of Christ and Adam in the Pauline corpus, the *Protoevangelium*, and the apocalyptic vision of the woman in Revelation 12.

2) The writings of Saint Ambrose on Mary's cooperation in the economy of salvation indicate his predilection for the dogma of her perpetual virginity, her exemplary virginal purity, and her spiritual maternity of the Church. She is the type of the Church (*Typus Ecclesiæ*) and the model of Christian motherhood. New-man's Marian writings, both doctrinal and devotional, can be viewed as very much akin to those of Ambrose since they underscore Mary's physical and spiritual fecundity as the Virgin–Mother of the Redeemer and the redeemed. Hence also, Am-brose's reliance on the New Eve theology. Furthermore, both Ambrose and Newman emphasize the uniqueness of Mary's co-operation, for example, her exemplary obedience of faith, by way of reference to the antithetical parallelism Mary–Zechariah in Luke's Gospel.

3) Newman draws on Saint Augustine's writings to defend the Church's dogma of the Immaculate Conception, insofar as he clearly sees posited in them an implicit notion of the sinlessness of Mary based on what would later be termed by Duns Scotus as prevenient grace. The themes of Mary's spiritual maternity of the Church and her two-fold blessedness (see Chapter Two) are traced in the writings of Augustine and reflected upon in light of what Newman says concerning these same topics.

4) Newman's critique of the anomalous statements of Saints John Chrysostom, Basil of Cæsarea and Cyril of Alexandria con-cerning Mary's cooperation in the *œconomia salutis*, as based on their interpretation of certain Marian pericopes of Sacred Scrip-

ture, is a noble attempt to temper the theological opinions of these Fathers of the Church in light of the overall Tradition of the Church.

5) Saint Ephrem, "the harp of the Spirit," provides us with several extraordinary examples of mystical and poetic interpretations of the Sacred Scriptures concerning the sublime mystery of the Incarnation; several of Newman's sermons reveal his own mystical musings on the Sacred Text and his profound appreciation of Mary's role as virginal Mother of the Incarnate Word.

4

Newman's Concept of Mary's Cooperation in the Œconomia Salutis *as Theotokos and Second Eve*

INTRODUCTION

With the foundations laid in the previous chapters, we are now prepared to deal with Newman's theology and spirituality of Mary as *Theotokos* and Second Eve[1] as two key points of reference for determining his understanding of the place of Mary in the economy of salvation, which dovetails for the most part with that of contemporary theologians[2] as he distinguishes between an eternal and a temporal aspect of the *œconomia*.[3] God's eternal essence (nature) as Triune God is distinct from but intrinsically related to the way in which God reveals Himself in history, most especially as He reveals Himself in Christ. In other words, the *Deus Absconditus* is the *Deus Revelatus*, and vice versa.

I. MARY AS THEOTÓKOS

(a) *The Christological Foundation of Mary's Cooperation in the* Œconomia Salutis

In Sermon III of *Parochial and Plain Sermons*, "The Incarnation," Newman uses terms reminiscent of the noble simplicity by which Saint Paul in Galatians 4:4 introduces Mary into the economy of the Incarnation, when he states: "Thus He came into this world, not in the clouds of heaven, but born into it, born of a woman; He, the Son of Mary, and she (if it may be said), the Mother of God."[4]

Mary's cooperation in the economy of salvation for Newman is, first and foremost, revealed in the doctrine of the *Theotokos* whereby the substance of Mary's humanity is given to her Son and substantially united to His divine Person in the Incarnation, becoming the primary instrument of our eternal salvation. Newman explains that the reality of the Incarnation depends on the reality of Mary's divine maternity and, to a certain extent, their sanctity is mutually dependent. In other words, there is more than just a physical resemblance between the Virgin Mary and Jesus; their ties are not only physical but spiritual. The bond of unity formed between them at the natural level is forever strengthened and brought to perfection on the supernatural level so that, as Newman writes in his sermon to Mixed Congregations entitled "On the Fitness of the Glories of Mary":

> She has no chance place in the divine Dispensation; the Word of God did not merely come to her and go from her; He did not pass through her, as He visits us in Holy Communion. It was no heavenly Body which the Eternal Son assumed, fashioned by angels, and brought down to this lower world: no; He imbibed, He absorbed into His divine Person, her blood and the substance of her flesh; by becoming Man of her, He received her lineaments and features, as the appropriate character in which He was to manifest Himself to mankind. The child is like the parent, and we may well suppose that by His likeness to her was manifested her relationship to Him. Her sanctity comes, not only of her being His Mother, but also of His being her Son. "If the first fruits be holy," says Saint Paul, "the mass is also holy; if the mass be holy, so are the branches." [5]

Furthermore, once Mary and the beloved disciple have been entrusted to one another, it is said by Newman that John the Beloved of Jesus "who had been put in charge with His Virgin Mother . . . heard from her what she alone could tell of the mystery to which she had ministered." [6] The questions, for example, of Mary's exemplary faith, her obedience to God's Word, her sinlessness, which are all intimately associated with the fundamental mystery of the divine maternity and essential expressions of her role in the economy, are only treated in this sermon in passing but receive greater development elsewhere in Newman's corpus, as this work seeks to demonstrate.

Discourse to Mixed Congregations XIV, entitled "The Mystery of Divine Condescension," contains a few but highly significant passages that delve deeper into the relationship between the God-Man Christ Jesus and His Virgin Mother Mary—into the mystery of her cooperation in the central event of the *œconomia salutis*. Newman exhorts his listeners to contemplate the mystery of the Incarnation by envisioning the beautiful union and tender intimacy that existed between the Virgin and the Christ Child, Who was destined to exchange the crib of Bethlehem for the cross of Calvary. Therefore, as the Blessed Virgin Mary recognized and adored her divine Son both at the crib and at Calvary, so should we prepare ourselves "to see in human flesh that glory and that beauty on which Angels gaze" [7] and to behold "at length 'the brightness of God's glory and the Image of His Substance' (which) is fettered, haled to and fro, buffeted, spit upon, mocked, cursed, scourged, and tortured . . . lifted up upon the bitter Cross." [8]

Elsewhere in that same sermon, Newman invites his congregation to approach "the mystery of the divine condescension" with awe and wonder, to "raise high" their "expectations" since they are "to see Emmanuel, since the 'brilliancy of the Eternal Light and the unspotted mirror of God's majesty, and the Image of His goodness,' is to walk the earth since the Son of the Highest is to be born of woman." [9] In fact, Newman envisions the Incarnation as the means by which "the manifold attributes of the Infinite are to be poured out before your eyes through material channels and the operations of a human soul." [10] Therefore, for Newman, the Incarnation and the Paschal Mystery together fulfill the prophecy of Isaiah 64:3, as cited by Saint Paul in 1 Corinthians 2:9 concerning the wisdom of the divine economy of salvation surpassing every human expectation: "Doubtless, you will say, He will take a form such as 'eye hath not seen, nor ear heard of' before. It will be a body framed in the heavens, and only committed to the custody of Mary; a form of light and glory, worthy of Him, who is 'blessed for evermore,' and comes to bless us with His presence." [11] Newman then contrasts Our Lord's humility in the Incarnation with the expectation of the "pomp and pride of men," who, according to their earthly wisdom, expect to find Our Lord revealing Himself "in kings' courts, or in the array of war, or in the philosophical school." On the contrary, Newman explains: "but doubtless He will choose some calm and holy spot, and men will go out thither and find their Incarnate God. He will be tenant of some paradise, like Adam and Elias, or He will dwell in the mystic garden of the Canticles, where nature ministers its best and purest to its Creator." [12]

Newman marvelously underscores the beautiful reality of the enfleshment of God in the womb of the Virgin Mary by anticipating in his sermon what could be the spontaneous and wrongful conclusion of some members of his congregation that Our Lord's Body was "framed in the heavens, and only committed to the custody of Mary," thinking such a *kenosis* to be beneath the divine dignity. Rather, it is precisely the Incarnation which reveals the ineffable splendor of God's love of creation and of man in particular. Our Lord's Body was not framed in the heavens, but framed (knitted together) in the pure womb of the humble Virgin, so as to be consubstantially united to the Godhead. And so, by means of the Virgin's cooperation, Christ is not only consubstantially united to the Father according to His Divinity but also consubstantially united to us according to His Humanity. The paradoxes of the divine condescension are juxtaposed by Newman in such a way that in affirming the simple but profound truths of Mary's divine maternity and her virginal purity, rejected in one fell swoop are many of early Christological heresies, such as Arianism, Adoptionism, Nestorianism, Monophysitism, and Monothelitism.[13]

Newman's reflections on the mystery of the Incarnation, as given in the above text, should also be read in the light of other texts, which help to flesh out the fullness of his thought about the *Theotokos*. The Sacred Humanity of the Savior is not "prefabricated" in the heavens,[14] but, as Newman himself points out (in sermon 3, "The Incarnation," *Parochial and Plain Sermons*), Christ derived "His Manhood from the substance of the Virgin Mary."[15] Beyond that, Mary is not simply passively entrusted with a mere physical guardianship or custody of the Lord Jesus, for as Newman writes: "And so, as regards the Blessed Virgin, it was God's will that she should undertake willingly and with full understanding to be the Mother of Our Lord, and not to be a mere passive instrument whose maternity would have no merit and no reward. It was no light lot to be so intimately near to the Redeemer of men, as she experienced afterwards when she suffered with Him."[16]

The apex of the Divine Revelation is, of course, the mystery and event of the Incarnation, at the heart of which is found together with the Word of God made flesh, a woman named Mary: "Her (Mary's) very image is as a book in which we may read at a glance the mystery of the Incarnation, and the mystery of the Redemption."[17] Mary is no ordinary creature but the bearer of a unique privilege, insofar as her relationship to the mystery and event of the Incarnation is incomparably more intimate than that of any other creature.[18] She is the *Theotokos*, and her divine motherhood is the most fundamental of all her privileges: "As soon as we apprehend by faith the great fundamental truth that Mary is the Mother of God, other wonderful titles follow in its train."[19] Her Immaculate Conception, perpetual virginity,[20] Assumption, intercessory role and motherhood of the Church, together with her other offices, result directly from her dignity as the Mother of the Incarnate Word,[21] as Newman explains:

> It is this awful title which both illustrates and connects together the two prerogatives of Mary, on which I have been lately enlarging, her sanctity and her greatness. It is the issue of her sanctity; it is the origin of her greatness. What dignity can be too great to attribute to her who is as closely bound up, as intimately one, with the Eternal Word, as a mother is with a son? . . . What fullness and redundance of grace, what exuberance of merits must have been hers, when once we admit the supposition, which the Fathers justify, that her Maker really did regard those merits, and take them into account, when He condescended "not to abhor the Virgin's womb"? Is it surprising then that on the one hand she should be immaculate in her conception? Or on the other that she should be honored with an Assumption, and exalted as a queen with a crown of twelve stars, with the rulers of day and night to do her service? Men sometimes wonder that we call her Mother of life, of mercy, of salvation; what are all these titles compared to that one name, Mother of God?[22]

(b) *The Doctrine of the Theotokos: Mary as Mother and Sinless Spouse of Christ*

The passage just examined is an example of the Catholic Newman's acceptance of the full consequences of Mary's divine maternity in accord with the economy of salvation. However, the Anglican Newman struggled to see how the Church's teaching on the *Theotokos* is intimately associated with the doctrine of Mary's personal sinlessness, making his development all the more interesting to trace, especially as it relates to his understanding of the Virgin Mary's espousal to Christ as the New Eve.[23] Because the

Anglican Newman's theology of Mary's sinfulness can only be said to approximate the Catholic dogma of the Immaculate Conception, his writings during his Anglican period on the Virgin's holiness must be read *cum grano salis* and not confused with his later development, such as we can appreciate in his *Meditations and Devotions*.

In Sermon III on "The Incarnation," the Anglican Newman, while without hesitancy placing the Virgin at the heart of the mystery of the Incarnation, nevertheless refers to her as being tainted by sin: "Mary, His mother, was a sinner as others, and born of sinners; but she was set apart, 'as a garden inclosed, a spring shut up, a fountain sealed,' to yield a created nature to Him Who was her Creator."[24] How is this text to be understood? And what does one learn from it about his theology of Mary's cooperation in the economy of salvation? Mary's divine maternity and her espousal relationship to Christ as the New Eve seem to be the focal points of Newman's theology and serve as a key of interpretation.

The scriptural images used by Newman in the text cited above derive from the Old Testament, most notably from the Canticle of Canticles and have been used by various theologians in the Church's history to describe both Mary's perpetual virginity and her preservation from sin in view of her divine maternity.[25] He interprets the Canticle of Canticles in a Mariological sense, insofar as he sees there a typological prefigurement of the mystical union between the Virgin Mary and her divine Son that occurred at the moment of the Incarnation. Some examples from Newman's writings will suffice to demonstrate how this is indeed the case.

First, a text we have already seen: "He will be tenant of some paradise, like Adam or Elias, or He will dwell in the mystic garden of the Canticles, where nature ministers its best and purest to its Creator."[26] Once again, Newman's treatment of the mystery of the Incarnation is a reflection on Christ as the New or Second Adam Whose birth inaugurates a new creation and a mystical marriage by which heaven is wedded to earth. Although Newman himself does not explicitly make the connection, one cannot help but identify, "the mystical garden of the Canticles" as "the bed chamber" of the womb of Mary the New Eve, "the Mother of all the Living," whose whole person, "ministers its best and purest" "to its Creator" for the sake of our Redemption, as Newman puts it.[27]

Giacomo Cardinal Biffi, in *Il Canto Nuziale*, introduces the reader to the mystery of Mary's cooperation in the economy of salvation by means of the *via anagogica*[28] which he defines as "the tension of man to uplift himself knowingly toward that which is beyond the finite and mutable in which we are immersed"[29] Biffi explains: "Mary therefore appears to us as a figure and the first-fruits of the whole Church. As a figure, we rediscover in her the almost personified ambivalence of humanity in relationship to Jesus, Who is at the same time of our trunk: Mary precedes Christ and generates Him, but together she is taken completely from Him. She gives to the Son of God His nature as man completely, but she also derives from him her every value." Cardinal Biffi amplifies his reflection on the *via anagogica*, so that one can better identify Mary as the Daughter of Zion, in whom "the ancient Israel . . . concludes and the new Israel makes its beginning"; the personification of a redeemed humanity "waiting to receive the salvation of the divine life"; the type or eschatological figure of the Church for she is "the first 'Immaculate Church,' that is without contamination of fault, thus alive in soul and in body after death, thus she is as eschatologically will be the people of those who are made alive, resurrected, and enthroned with Christ (cfr. Ef 2, 5–6). She is the first among all of us 'poor ones of Yahweh,' who are destined to be exalted according to the surprising design of the Father."[30]

Therefore, Newman's speaking of Mary's divine maternity—her role in the mystery of the Incarnation—by which the New Adam entered into "the mystic garden of the Canticles" to espouse humanity by means of her *fiat* as the New Eve, is also a theological reflection that makes use of the *via anagogica*. In other words, Mary's collaboration in the redemptive work of her Son served to inaugurate a new creation and a new espousal relationship between God and man on earth and so is designed from all eternity to lead man and in a particular way the Church, as the Bride of Christ, toward the Wedding Feast of the Lamb in heaven.[31] Newman writes:

> He (Christ) came by a new and living way; not, indeed, formed out of the ground, as Adam was at the first, lest He should miss the participation of our nature, but selecting and purifying unto Himself a tabernacle out of what existed. As in the beginning woman was formed out of man by almighty power, so now,

by a like mystery, but a reverse order, the new Adam was fashioned from the woman ... the "beginning of the" new "creation of God." [32]

The creation of Adam out of the virgin ground and of Eve
from the side of Adam constitutes a primordial marriage union.[33]
With the introduction of the various covenants in the history of
salvation, nuptial imagery is used by the sacred authors, for example, the writer of the Song of Songs and the prophet Hosea, to
express the covenant between the Lord God and His Bride Israel.
Such nuptial imagery, as we find in the Song of Songs, is then
later applied to the Virgin in the writings of some of the Fathers.[34]

The influence of Saint Gregory of Nyssa on Newman in this
regard is noteworthy. Perrott writes that "in his *Commentary on
the Song of Songs*, Saint Gregory gives an allegorical interpretation in which in keeping with the tradition, the soul's union with
the bridegroom is portrayed as the lover pursuing the beloved."
He explains that this allegorical interpretation, "later ... came
to be interpreted as Christ's love for His Mother as well as
Christ's love for His Church." Hence, as Perrott illustrates, "the
titles given to the sections" of the Canticle of Canticles "anticipate some of the titles later given to Our Lady." Therefore,
Perrott mentions the following titles that are either directly or
indirectly applied to Mary: "Lily of the Valley," "The Heavenly
Tabernacle," "The Fruit of the Apple Tree," "The Mirror of
the Church," "An Odor of Sweetness," "The Garden Enclosed,"
"One is my Dove," adding that "this dove, who is Mother of
the 'chosen Dove' (Jesus Christ) is, for Saint Gregory, the
Holy Spirit." Perrott thus concludes: "Later writers would interpret this passage in a purely Mariological sense, and seemingly
less convoluted in the genders used. However, the relevant factor for us is not the precise details of how the different Fathers
rendered their interpretation, but the general method—highly
mystical and allegorical.[35] It was this, which enabled them to
support their doctrinal teaching unashamedly from Sacred
Scripture, and it was this which caught Newman's mind and
heart." [36]

In his meditation on the Marian title *Mater Christi* (Mother of
Christ), Newman reflects on the nature of Mary's response to
the Archangel Gabriel at the Annunciation; he affirms that

Mary's consent presupposed a vow of virginity[37] on her part; therefore, he concludes that "she had been inspired to choose the better way of serving God which had not been made known to the Jews—the state of virginity. She preferred to be His Spouse to being His Mother."[38] The latter reference serves to underscore how the mystery of the Incarnation, that is, the mystery of her divine maternity, likewise contains within it the mystery of Mary's espousal to Christ. His sermon, "The Mystery of Divine Condescension," presents us with a very significant example of Newman's interpretation of the Canticle of Canticles not only from the perspective of Mary's union with Christ at the crib of Bethlehem but also in terms of her union with her Beloved Son at the foot of the Cross. Thus, Newman exhorts his listeners:

> Think you not, my brethren, that to Mary, when she held Him in her maternal arms, when she gazed on the pale countenance and the dislocated limbs of her God, when she traced the wandering lines of blood, when she counted the weals, bruises, and the wounds, which dishonoured that virginal flesh, think you not that to her eyes it was more beautiful than when she first worshipped it, pure, radiant, and fragrant, on the night of His nativity? *Dilectus meus candidus et rubricundus*, as the Church sings; "My beloved is white and ruddy; His whole form doth breathe of love, and doth provoke to love in turn; His drooping head, His open palms, and His breast are all bare. My beloved is white and ruddy, choice out of thousands; His head is of the finest gold; His locks are branches of palm-trees, black as a raven. His eyes as doves upon brooks of water, which are washed with milk, and sit beside the plentiful streams. His cheeks are as beds of aromatical spices set by the perfumers; His lips are lilies dropping choice myrrh. His hands are turned and golden, full of jacinths; His throat is most sweet, and He is all lovely. Such is my beloved, and He is my friend, O ye daughters of Jerusalem."[39]

In this text, Newman quotes from the Canticle of Canticles (5:10b–16), which are actually a response to two previous questions posed by the author in verse 9d, namely, "How does your lover differ from any other, O most beautiful among women? How does your lover differ from any other, that you adjure us so?" These are addressed to a most beautiful woman who searches for her lost lover. It would seem, therefore, according to Newman's allegorical reading of these texts in a Mariological key, that Mary is that most beautiful of all women, who contemplates the beauty of her Son and Spouse (*Sponsa Christi*), both in the mystery of His Incarnation and in the mystery of His Passion. Hence, the absence of Our Lord in death becomes the reason why Mary, His beloved Mother and Spouse, makes a spiritual quest for reunion with Him. This allegorical reading of the text in a Mariological mode is further based on the Song of Songs 6:1 (which follows the above text): "Where has your lover gone, O most beautiful among women? Where has your lover gone that we may seek him with you?" In other words, read in its proper context, the Canticle of Canticles necessitates Mariological and ecclesiological interpretations.[40] Mary does not contemplate the mysteries of her Son and Spouse in isolation. In point of fact, all the members of Christ's Spotless Bride and Mystical Body, the Church, are invited by the sacred author, as by Newman, to enter into this same contemplation and spiritual quest for Christ their beloved Bridegroom.

In contemplating the mysteries of the Incarnation and Passion of Christ, one is led to appreciate, at one and the same time, the beauty of both Jesus and Mary, for the beauty of Christ is most perfectly mirrored in that of Mary, His Mother and Spouse. And the beauty of the Church is most perfectly mirrored in her as well. What is the essence of Mary's beauty as Mother and Spouse? According to Newman, it is her sinlessness.

In his sermon "The Reverence Due to the Blessed Virgin Mary," he suggests an implicit acceptance of the doctrine of Mary's sinlessness, without however accepting it along the lines of the doctrine of the New Eve but not yet in explicit acceptance of the Catholic doctrine of the Immaculate Conception: "In her (Mary) the destinies of the world were reversed, and the serpent's head bruised . . . in her the curse pronounced on Eve was changed to a blessing."[41] Another critical passage occurs in that same sermon:

> And or what, think you, was the sanctified state of that human nature, of which God formed His sinless Son; knowing as we do, that "none can bring a clean thing out of an unclean?"
> . . . But there are those who go in a calm and unswerving course, learning day by day to love Him Who has redeemed

them, and overcome the sin of their nature by His heavenly grace.... And, of these undefiled followers of the Lamb, the Blessed Mary is the chief.[42]

Some observations on the above text are necessary: Newman refers to Mary's "sanctified state" in a clear and direct relationship to the mystery of her motherhood of the sinless Son of God. Therefore, Mary's sanctity is not arbitrary; it pertains to the *œconomia salutis* and to the logic of the Sacred Scriptures as they affirm that, following the normal course, flesh begets flesh and impurity gives way to impurity. Newman says that such logic is applicable in the case of the Incarnation. Not only is the Child Jesus without sin but His Mother Mary is also free from sin for His sake; she is "set apart." Nevertheless, Newman makes a fundamental distinction: Because Mary is a human creature redeemed by Christ, her sanctity belongs to her by grace and not by nature—as it belongs to her divine Son. Mary's sanctity is viewed by Newman as the consequence of both her divine vocation and her cooperation in responding to that call whereby she learns "day by day" the ways of holiness, overcoming her sinful nature with the help of sanctifying grace. The Catholic doctrine of the Immaculate Conception which, at the time of that sermon's delivery, the Anglican Newman did not fully accept, does not admit of Mary as having had a "sinful" human nature insofar as she neither incurred original sin nor suffered its consequences.

Taking his inspiration from the Book of Revelation, Newman refers to Mary as the "chief" of the "undefiled followers of the Lamb." However, Mary cannot be simply considered one among many sinless followers of Christ as the Anglican Newman seems to intimate in this passage. Rather, the Catholic teaching on the Immaculate Conception underscores the uniqueness of Mary's sanctity since she alone, among all creatures, received a prevenient, redemptive grace from the very first moment of her existence.[43] Nevertheless, the Catholic Church teaches, as did the Anglican Newman, that Mary's sinlessness did not inhibit her from making a pilgrimage of faith in overcoming trials, tribulations and perhaps even temptations, so that her pilgrimage of faith is an integral part of what made her the most perfect disciple of the Lord and the most prominent member of the communion of saints.[44] Perrott comments on this sermon in light of another sermon which he delivered five years later:

We have observed that in describing Our Lady as the "Second Eve" and "undefiled," Newman is only hinting at the Immaculate Conception. This has to be stressed; indeed, when set alongside a later sermon, it would seem he was never able to realize fully what he had been implying. A sermon delivered in March 1837, "The Mystery of Godliness," explicitly denies the possibility of her being conceived without original sin: "No one is born into the world without sin; or can rid himself of the sin of his birth except by a second birth through the Spirit." [45] It is interesting to note, however, that in this sermon he uses the same text as in the earlier sermon to argue for mankind's sinful nature, which before he used to illustrate Our Lady's Immaculate Conception—"Who can bring a clean thing out of an unclean." [46]

It cannot be determined from this sermon alone as to what Newman actually believed about Mary's sinlessness. In fact, some questions logically arise when reflecting on this sermon: How does Newman reconcile Mary's sinfulness and yet her being set apart? What does this "setting apart" mean? When and how did God allow it to occur? The sermon itself does not offer these answers. Perhaps Newman understood this "setting apart" as being a type of purification from sin which would have occurred at some point before her divine maternity as many Catholic theologians tended to believe—who were not able to reconcile Mary's Immaculate Conception with the universality of sin and the need for a universal Redeemer. Of course, only once Newman is fully under the influence of the Fathers do his reflections on the theology of Mary as the New Eve lead him not only to proclaim her personal sinlessness but also to pinpoint the origin of her sinlessness in the prevenient grace which she received from God at the moment of her Immaculate Conception. [47]

In any case, "The Reverence Due to the Blessed Virgin Mary," together with the other writings of Newman mentioned in this section, maintain that the concrete reality of Mary's motherhood is essential for the definition of the mystery of the Incarnate Word and that Mary's sinlessness as New Eve and Spouse of Christ is inexplicable apart from her privilege of the divine maternity, and vice versa. The Reverend Roderick Strange reflects on Newman's theology of Mary's divine motherhood and explains its development from his Anglican to Catholic periods as indicative of his real rather than merely notional assent to the full implications of the mystery of the Incarnation. Finally, Father Strange, in quoting from various sermons of both the Anglican and Catholic Newman shows how Newman's preference for real assent leads him to emphasize the reality of the Incarnation and, therefore, the reality of Mary's divine privileges, most especially her divine maternity.

> Several times Newman drove home the genuine character of Christ's Humanity with a concrete argument, typical of his preference for the real, rather than notional disputation. He referred to Mary. In an early Anglican sermon he wrote: "Christ derived His Manhood from her." And shortly afterwards he added that "the thought of her may be made profitable to our faith; for nothing is so calculated to impress on our minds that Christ is really a partaker of our nature, and in all respects Man, save sin only, as to associate Him with the thought of Her, by whose ministration He became our brother." He returned to this theme as a Catholic. He spoke of "the simple idea of the Catholic Church that God is man," and asked "could you express this more emphatically that God had a *Mother*?" . . . "if the Church has exalted Mary or Joseph, it has been with a view to the glory of His Sacred Humanity. If Mary is proclaimed as immaculate, it illustrates the doctrine of her maternity. If she is called the Mother of God, it is to remind Him that, though He is out of sight, He, nevertheless, is our possession, for He is of the race of man. . . ." These passages make it clear that Newman saw Christ's birth of Mary as an impressive guarantee of His genuine and full Manhood.[48]

(c) *Newman's Understanding of the Doctrine of the Theotokos in Light of the Fathers of the Church and the Christological Teachings of the First Seven Ecumenical Councils*

Mary's divine maternity is the essential role that she plays in cooperating with God in the *œconomia salutis*. As Newman points out time and again, the Sacred Scriptures, the Fathers of the Church and the early Councils all testify to the divine maternity as the cornerstone of the Church's doctrine regarding Mary.

In the *Letter to Pusey*, Newman summarizes the history of the use of *Theotokos*. According to Newman, it was Origen who first used the term in the third century. Significant is the testimony of

Socrates who, writing in the fifth century A.D., comments on the use of the title in Origen's commentary on the Epistle to the Romans. The title received "its solemn recognition" according to the ancient Apostolic Tradition at the Council of Ephesus, convoked in 431 to combat the errors of Nestorius.[49] At that time, as Newman recounts, even those not so favorable to the solemn declaration of Mary as *Theotokos* and so-called supporters of Nestorius admitted to the title's historical and theological weight in the Apostolic Tradition and its widespread use in the writings of other ancient ecclesiastical writers such as Theodoret, John of Antioch,[50] Alexander.

Between Origen's use of the title and the Council's official approbation of the same, Newman notes, several Fathers of the Church testify to its orthodoxy, for example, Archelaus of Mesopotamia, Eusebius of Palestine and Alexander of Egypt in the third century; Athanasius of Alexandria, Cyril of Palestine, Gregory of Nyssa, Gregory of Nazianzus, Antiochus of Syria, Ammonius of Thrace in the fourth century. Newman likewise appeals to the example of the Emperors Julian and Constantine the Great as having borne witness to the title's legitimacy. Constantine the Great, as Newman remarks, gave an official address to the Fathers of the First Council of Nicæa, during which he explicitly refers to her as "the Virgin Mother of God." Newman concludes his historical apologetic for *Theotokos* by referring to its use in the writings of other Fathers and ecclesiastical writers of both the East and West, from Saint Ignatius of Antioch and Hippolytus, Amphilochus, Chrysostom, Proclus of Constantinople and Theodotus to Cassian,[51] Vincent, Leo the Great, Hilary of Poitiers, Jerome, Ambrose, Capriolus and Augustine in the fifth century.[52]

In his Sermon III on "The Incarnation," preached on the Feast of the Nativity and found in volume two of *Parochial and Plain Sermons*, Newman writes about the topic in the light of the Scriptures and the Apostolic Tradition. He places a special emphasis on the value of the creeds of the Church as having preserved, in formulaic fashion, the orthodox teaching on the mystery of the Incarnation and its related mysteries.[53] At first, Newman points out that "the first generations of the Church needed no explicit lengthy declarations concerning His Sacred Person." And he gives some reasons why this was in fact the case: "Sight and hearing superseded the multitude of words; faith dispensed with the aid of lengthened creeds and confessions. There was silence, 'The Word made flesh;' 'I believe in Jesus Christ His only Son our Lord;' sentences such as these conveyed everything, yet were officious in nothing." Newman concludes: "In the New Testament we find the doctrine of the Incarnation announced clearly indeed, but with a reverent brevity. . . ."[54]

Having given several quotations from Scripture,[55] Newman immediately adds the following: "But we are obliged to speak more at length in the creeds and in our teaching, to meet the perverse ingenuity of those who, when the Apostles were removed, could with impunity insult and misinterpret the letter of their writings."[56] Furthermore, Newman makes this important point concerning the ancillary nature of creeds in relationship to the primary Christological doctrinal formulations in the Sacred Scriptures:

> True is it the Gospels do much by way of realizing for us the Incarnation of the Son of God, if studied in faith and love. But the creeds are an additional help this way. The declarations made in them, the distinctions, cautions, and the like, supported and illuminated by Scripture, draw down, as it were, from heaven, the image of Him Who is on God's right hand, preserve us from an indolent use of words without apprehending them, rouse in us those mingled feelings of fear and confidence, affection and devotion towards Him, which are implied in the belief of a personal advent of God in our nature, and which were originally derived from the very sight of Him.[57]

In some texts of Newman, as will be seen, the Mariological implications are explicitly drawn out. For example, we find the following reference to the Athanasian Creed and the *Te Deum* in Sermon III:

> For instance, the Athanasian Creed confesses that Christ is "God of the substance of the Father, begotten before the worlds, perfect God," lest we should consider His divine nature, like ours, as merely a nature resembling God's holiness: that He is "Man of the substance of His Mother, born in the world, perfect man," lest we should think of Him as "not come in the flesh," a mere Angelic vision; and that "although He be God and man, yet He is not two, but one Christ," lest we should fancy that the Word of God entered into Him and then departed, as the Holy Ghost in the Prophets.[58]

It is clear, then, for Newman, that we cannot have a complete picture of Who Christ is, that is, an orthodox understanding of the oneness of His Divine Person and His two natures (divine-human) in the mystery of the Incarnation without also contemplating the mystery of the divine maternity. In that same sermon Newman links togther the *Te Deum* and Athanasian Creed when he writes: "the *Te Deum* and Athanasian Creed—are especially suitable in divine worship, inasmuch as they kindle and elevate the religious affections. They are hymns of praise and thanksgiving; they give glory to God as revealed in the Gospel, just as David's psalms magnify His attributes as displayed in nature, His wonderful works in the creation of the world, and His mercies towards the house of Israel."[59]

Newman, however, begins his sermon by referring to the Prologue of John's Gospel which masterfully sets that majestic stage upon which is acted out the great economy of salvation culminating in the coming of the Word of God made flesh. Newman's meditation on this "wonderful condescension," in the fullness of time is also one that glances back at the origins of mankind wherein the first order or economy of salvation established by God with Adam and Eve is disrupted by sin and its repair is promised by God in the form of a prophecy of a future Messiah and Redeemer. Thus, Newman writes in his Sermon III, "The Incarnation":

> As in the beginning, woman was formed out of man by Almighty power, so now, by a like mystery, but a reverse order, the new Adam was fashioned from the woman. He was, as had been foretold, the immaculate "seed of the woman," deriving His manhood from the substance of the Virgin Mary; as it is expressed in the articles of the Creed, "conceived by the Holy Ghost, born of the Virgin Mary."[60]

And so, Newman succinctly writes: "The Fathers speak of the Blessed Virgin as the instrument of our salvation, in that she gave birth to the Redeemer."[61]

Giovanni Velocci makes the following assertion: "The doctrine of Newman, as a consequence of the Incarnation, is attested to by antiquity and is a legitimate development of patristic teaching. He attributes to Saint Athanasius, the first great teacher of the Incarnation, the merit of having placed solid foundations for devotion to Mary."[62] Newman, convinced of the utter centrality of the doctrine of the *Theotokos* and the ensuing devotion in the life of the Church, comments in the *Letter to Pusey*: "This being the faith of the Fathers about the Blessed Virgin, we need not wonder that it should in no long time be transmuted into devotion. No wonder if their language should become unmeasured, when so great a term as 'Mother of God' had been formally set down as the safe limit of it. No wonder if it should be stronger and stronger as time went on, since only in a long period could the fullness of its import be exhausted."[63]

Newman, then, offers a chain of quotations from the Fathers of the Church to show the connection between the Fathers' acceptance of the title *Theotokos* and the development of their belief and devotion in regard to other Marian doctrines such as her perpetual virginity, sanctity, mediation and cooperative role. Concerning Mary's perpetual virginity, Newman quotes Saint Jerome: "The closed gate, . . . by which alone the Lord God of Israel enters, is the Virgin Mary."[64] With regard to mediation, he quotes Saint Basil of Seleucia who says that Mary "shines out above all the martyrs as the sun above the stars, and that she mediates between God and men." Concerning Mary's cooperative role, of particular note are the following quotations: Saint Ambrose says: "She was alone and wrought the world's salvation and conceived the redemption of all." Antiochus refers to Mary as "the Mother of life," while Ephrem adds, "by whom we are translated from death to life." Finally, Newman cites Saint Cyril of Alexandria's panegyric from the Council of Ephesus in which he declares: "Hail, Mary, Mother of God, . . . through whom the fallen creature is received up into the heavens,"[65] Thus, one notices that the doctrine of Mary's singular cooperation in the work of our salvation is firmly inculcated in the theology of Newman. All these sayings of the Fathers show the interdependency of the Marian doctrines on the primary Christological title of *Theotokos*, the confession of which—as Newman writes—

> Is that safeguard wherewith we seal up and secure the doctrine of the apostle [John] from all evasion, and that test whereby we detect all the pretenses of those bad spirits of "antichrist which have gone out into the world." It declares that He is God; it implies that He is man; it suggests to us that He is God still, though He has become man, and that He is true man though

He is God. By witnessing to the *process* of the union, it secures the reality of the two *subjects* of the union, of the divinity and of the manhood. If Mary is the Mother of God, Christ must be literally understood to be Emmanuel, God with us.[66]

The first half of the aforementioned quotation reveals Newman's grasp of the significant battle that the early Christians fought against the heresies of Gnosticism and Docetism, which had already begun to be waged in the first century and were the obvious target of 1 John 4:2–4: "This is how you can know the Spirit of God: every spirit that acknowledges Jesus Christ come in the flesh belongs to God, and every spirit that does not acknowledge Jesus does not belong to God. This is the spirit of the antichrist that, as you heard, is to come, but in fact is already in the world." The second half of the above quotation manifestly demonstrates how the doctrine of the *Theotokos* expresses in synthesis the Chalcedonian formula[67] against Monophysitism.[68] The text ends with a reference to the prophecy of Isaiah 7:14, which finds its fulfillment in the doctrine of the Incarnation (i.e., hypostatic union) to which the doctrine of the *Theotokos* is inexorably linked.

The Councils of Nicæa and Ephesus[69] laid the foundation for the development of all further Marian doctrine and dogma by allowing it to spring naturally from its Christological roots and never to be separated from them.[70] In other words, the defeat of the heresies of Arianism and Nestorianism aimed primarily at the definition of an orthodox Christology also resulted in the full acknowledgment of Mary's cooperation in the *œconomia salutis*. Newman explains that there is a development in Mariological doctrines which directly stems from the development of the Church's understanding of the mystery of Christ. Newman explains that "in the first ages no public and ecclesiastical recognition of the place Saint Mary holds in the economy of grace; this was reserved for the fifth century, as the definition of our Lord's proper divinity had been the work of the fourth. . . ." The watermark of this development of Marian doctrine in the early Church is the Council of Ephesus to the extent that, as Newman writes, "in order to do honor to Christ, in order to defend the true doctrine of the Incarnation, in order to ensure a right faith in the manhood of the Eternal Son, the Council of Ephesus determined the Blessed Virgin to be the Mother of God."[71]

In this sense, every Mariological dogma is a Christological one. One could make the analogy that it is as theologically dangerous to separate Christ's divine nature from His human nature in the unity of His divine Person as it is to separate Mary's divine maternity from the mystery of the Incarnation.[72] Newman writes that, "Mary is exalted for the sake of Jesus. It was fitting that she, as being a creature, though the first of creatures, should have an office of ministration. She, as others, came into the world to do a work, she had a mission to fulfil; her grace and her glory are not for her own sake, but for her Maker's; and to her is committed the custody of the Incarnation . . . her glories and the devotion paid her proclaim and define the right faith concerning Him as God and Man."[73]

Newman confirms the above truths in an avid defense of the title *Theotokos* stating that:

> This word carries with it no admixture of rhetoric, no taint of extravagant affection—it has nothing else but a well-weighed, grave, dogmatic sense, which corresponds and is adequate to its sound. It intends to express that God is her son, as truly as any one of us is the son of his own mother. If this be so, what can be said of any creature whatever, which may not be said of her? What can be said too much, so long as it does not compromise the attributes of the Creator? He indeed might have created a being more perfect, more admirable, than she is; he might have endowed that being, so created, with a richer grant of grace, of power, of blessedness, but in one respect she surpasses all possible creations—that she is the Mother of her Creator.[74]

It is obvious, then, that for Newman Mary's motherhood of God is intrinsic to a proper, orthodox understanding of the identity of Christ because it is an office of ministration to the mystery of the Incarnation and is its primary safeguard among Marian doctrines. Furthermore, the doctrine of the *Theotokos* has a direct bearing on the nature of our salvation since it is a guarantee that Jesus Christ is truly Emmanuel, *"qui propter nos homines et propter nostram salutem descendit de cælis."* Newman also underscores the fact that the doctrine of the *Theotokos* does not detract from but rather enhances our knowledge and love of God and His attributes. Indeed, if Christ is not both God and Man and Mary is not the Mother of God according to the flesh, then we are not saved. However, if by saying that Mary is the *Theotokos* we intend to say that Mary is more than the highest of all creatures, then we have failed to understand Mary's subordinate but nevertheless essential role in the history of salvation. Newman declares in his sermon titled "The Reverence Due to the Virgin Mary":

> But, further, the more we consider who Saint Mary was, the more dangerous will such knowledge of her appear to be. Other saints are but influenced or inspired by Christ, and made partakers of Him mystically. But, as to Saint Mary, Christ derived His manhood from her, and so had an especial unity of nature with her; and this wondrous relationship between God and man it is perhaps impossible for us to dwell much upon without some perversion of feeling. For, truly, she is raised above the condition of sinful beings, though by nature a sinner; she is brought near to God, yet is but a creature, and seems to lack her fitting place in our limited understandings, neither too high nor too low. We cannot combine, in our thought of her, all we should ascribe with all we should withhold. Hence, following the example of Scripture, we had better only think of her with and for her son, never separating her from Him, but using her name as a memorial of His great condescension in stooping from heaven, and not "abhorring the Virgin's womb." . . . And, with this caution, the thought of her may be made most profitable to our faith; for nothing is so calculated to impress on our minds that Christ is really partaker of our nature, and in all respects man, save sin only, as to associate Him with the thought of her, by whose ministration He became our Brother.[75]

In this sense, the whole economy of salvation hinges on the doctrine of the *Theotokos*, without which the doctrines of the Incarnation, the Redemption and our eternal salvation cannot be properly understood.[76] Mary's union with Christ is not merely mystical or spiritual as is the union of other saints; her divine motherhood constitutes much more than just a physical union, since when it is considered along with her sinlessness, she is brought into a far more intimate union with the Incarnate Word than any other creature. Newman's theology permits us to contemplate, at one and the same time, the spiritual, mystical, and physical realities expressed in the Marian doctrines. Mary's sinlessness, her perpetual virginity, her divine maternity are not nebulous concepts. Rather, they are doctrinal truths which assure us of the *admirabile commercium* ("wonderful exchange") brought about by the Incarnation. Mary's role of cooperation ("ministration") in the economy is not peripheral to God's plan for our salvation; but, on the contrary, a permanent participation in and perpetuation of it, and in a particular way because she is a "memorial of His great condescension." Mary's "name," her person, all of the privileges of her office, point to Christ.[77]

When the Anglican Newman says that "we had better only think of her with and for her Son, never separating her from Him," he expresses a profound theological intuition confirmed by the ancient tradition. Indeed, one of the most ancient and venerable of icons in the Eastern Church expresses the indissoluble nature of Mary's union with Our Lord and invites us to enter into the mystery of that communion.[78]

Newman elicits the implications of this all-important interconnectedness (*nexus mysteriorum*) in his meditation on Mary's title "Mother of the Creator":

> Christians were accustomed from the first to call the Blessed Virgin "the Mother of God," because they saw that it was impossible to deny her that title without denying Saint John's words, "The Word" (that is, God the Son) "was made flesh." . . . And what can be more consoling and joyful than the wonderful promises which follow from this truth, that Mary is the Mother of God?—the great wonder, namely, that we become the brethren of our God; that, if we live well, and die in the grace of God, we shall all of us hereafter be taken up by our Incarnate God to that place where angels dwell; that our bodies shall be raised from the dust, and be taken to heaven; that we shall be really united to God; that we shall be partakers of the divine nature; that each of us, soul and body, shall be plunged into the abyss of glory which surrounds the Almighty; that we shall see Him, and share His blessedness.[79]

Thus, Newman leads us in concluding that Mary's cooperation in the *œconomia salutis* as *Theotokos* contains within itself an exemplification of our own cooperation with the mystery of grace. Mary's role, then, as Mother of God, includes the mystery of her spiritual maternity of the children of God, indeed, "the brethren of our God,"[80] insofar as she holds out to us "the wonderful promises," of living the life of grace so as to attain to that blessed salvation in which she already shares body and soul in the communion of saints. Mary is considered by Newman as a special link, therefore, between the Incarnation of the Son of God and His Second Coming for as she cooperated in bringing about the first so too is she the eschatological icon to which the Church looks as she waits for the *"beatam spem et adventum Domini nostri Iesu Christi."* [81]

II. MARY AS THE NEW EVE

(a) *Newman's Understanding of the Title "Theotokos" and Its Doctrinal Development in Sacred Scripture, Sacred Tradition, and the Magisterium*

Newman does not deal with the doctrine of Mary as *Theotokos* in a vacuum or in isolation from his treatment of her as the *Second Eve*,[82] which he also sees firmly rooted in Sacred Scripture, Tradition and the Magisterium.[83] According to Newman, "The title of *Theotokos*, as ascribed to the Blessed Mary, begins with ecclesiastical writers of a date hardly later than that at which we read of her as the Second Eve." [84]

The impetus for Newman's treatment of Mary under the title of Second Eve is primarily to be taken from the writings of Fathers of the Church like Justin, Irenæus, and Tertullian. The Reverend Carleton Jones, O.P., comments that "the faith of the Church concerning Mary from first to last—from the earliest period and forever—Newman defines precisely as her being the Second, or New, Eve." Consequently, Father Jones points out: "The proper starting-point of Catholic Mariology is the so-called protoevangelion[85] of Genesis, as it was first interpreted by Justin, Tertullian and Irenæus whose witness, Newman firmly states, must be to the faith of the Apostles, because these three Fathers, coming so soon after the Apostles, represent the whole Christian world at the time." [86]

Newman accepts and develops their interpretation of such fundamental scriptural texts as the *Protoevangelium* (Gen 3:15) and the twelfth chapter of the Apocalypse, in order to establish the title of Second Eve as a legitimate and essential expression of the Church's teaching regarding Mary and her role in the economy of salvation. Sister Agnes Cunningham writes: "John Henry Newman has brought together for us evidences from earliest times attesting to this parallelism held by the Fathers of the Church, as they receive this doctrine from Christians who had preceded them and transmitted it to those who followed them." In this regard, Cunningham explains that: "Newman cites witnesses from Africa and Rome, from Palestine, Asia Minor, and Gaul, from Syria, Egypt, and Cyprus in defending the recognition of Mary as the 'New Eve.' In the case of Saint Irenæus, Newman points to the Johannine Tradition in which this Father stands, through Polycarp by whom he had been instructed in the Faith." Finally, Sister Agnes notes some of the main characteristics of the New Eve theology in the writings of these Fathers whereby they "contrast Mary's faith with Eve's unbelief; Mary's obedience with Eve's disobedience; the fruits of grace in Mary and Eve's forfeiture of privileges by sin." [87]

Newman writes in his *Memorandum on the Immaculate Conception*: "As to primitive notion about our Blessed Lady, really, the frequent contrast of Mary with Eve seems very strong indeed. It is found in Saint Justin, Saint Irenæus, and Tertullian, three of the earliest Fathers, and in three distinct continents—Gaul, Africa, and Syria." [88] This mirrors that which he had already said in the *Essay on Development*:

> Saint Justin, Saint Irenæus, and others had distinctly laid it down, that she not only had an office, but bore a part, and was a voluntary agent, in the actual process of redemption, as Eve had been instrumental and responsible in Adam's fall. . . . And certainly the parallel between the "Mother of all living" and the Mother of the Redeemer may be gathered from a comparison of the first chapter of Scripture with the last. [89]

In other words, he sees their use of the title of Second Eve as consistent with a genuine development of Marian doctrine within the Church's Tradition as well as an authentic and reliable interpretation of the Church's Scriptures. [90] Newman acknowledges that the Fathers of the Church did not invent the Eve–Mary antithetical parallelism themselves since it is a logical inference from the writings of Saint Paul in which an antithetical parallelism is drawn between Adam and the Second Adam or Christ. [91] Nicolas explains that there exists a direct parallel, that is, antithesis between Eve and the Blessed Virgin, which is a logical inference from the antithetical relationship already highlighted by Paul. The interdependence of these two relationships serves to underscore that Mary's role in the work of salvation is incomparable and absolutely necessary since, by her own free will, she gave her assent to the word of the angel and thus became, along with her Son, *causa salutis*. In like manner, Eve cooperated with Adam in bringing about the fall of mankind from his original state of holiness and innocence; hence, the absolute necessity for the work of redemption. Mary's pivotal role as the New Eve is a clear indication of God's will that, in the restoration of man, the complementarity of the sexes be respected. God directly willed that the *fiat* of His Son should find the most appropriate counterpart in the *fiat* of the perfect daughter of "Eve Unfallen." The *fiat* of Christ and the *fiat* of the Virgin are pronounced with full freedom and love, so that man and woman might be redeemed as a couple—a perfect union of mind and heart. Together, our Blessed Lord and our Blessed Mother form a new humanity and make possible a new creation, restoring its original beauty and holiness through the union of their *fiats*. Nevertheless, it must be made clear that the role of Mary as New Eve is always subordinate to that of her Son since she acts as a creature, while He acts as the Son of God Incarnate. These roles, while most complementary, cannot be equated or interchanged.[92]

Father Jones offers further insights into Newman's New Eve theology by showing the link between the Adam–Christ and the Eve–Mary parallelisms. He explains that: "As mankind fell in Adam (not in Eve), so mankind is restored in Christ (and not in Mary). The precise position of Our Lady in relation to her Son is prefigured by Eve's position in relation to her husband." Jones explicates an essential distinction which is found in Newman's theology of the New Eve. He states that: "not only is Our Lady's personal, intelligent and free cooperation in our redemption emphasized by the analogy, but so is her subordination to the Second Adam." Father Jones lends support to Newman's theology and to this distinction in particular by demonstrating how the writings of the Fathers are its very plausible foundation: "Newman notes the similarity between the patristic run of the argument concerning the two Eves and Paul's (in Romans 5) concerning the two Adams: this similarity in the run of the argument is strong circumstantial evidence of apostolic precedent for the patristic doctrine." Finally, Jones expounds on Newman's theology of the New Eve from a historical—apologetical—perspective with special emphasis on

Newman's *Letter to Pusey*. Jones writes: "Newman is removing the ground from the Protestant objection to the Catholic faith concerning Mary, which seeks to preserve the prerogatives of Christ by reducing Mary's portion in His Incarnation to mere physical instrumentality. Newman proves that this reduction is unnecessary if one considers Christ in the light of Adam and Mary in the light of Eve." [93]

Newman highlights the instrumentality of Eve in cooperating in the fall of man from grace when he writes:

> She listened to the Evil Angel; she offered the fruit to her husband, and he ate of it. She co-operated, not as an irresponsible instrument, but intimately and personally in the sin; she brought it about. As history stands, she was a *sine qua non*, a positive, active cause of it. And she had a share in the punishment; in the sentence pronounced on her, she was recognized as a real agent in the temptation and its issue, and she suffered accordingly. [94]

The Venerable Cardinal also stresses some fundamental ideas that need to be highlighted, especially since they are key to our discussion of what cooperation means and whether or not the title of Co-Redemptrix is one that can be properly applied to Mary. Newman speaks about Eve as having cooperated with Adam in bringing about the Fall and then is quick to support that idea of cooperation with other significant statements about Eve's responsibility, her causal instrumentality, her real agency and personal involvement not only in the temptation that led to the original sin but in the sin itself and its deadly consequences.

Newman believes that Mary counterbalances Eve's fatal cooperation in the mystery of iniquity by her own fruitful cooperation in the mystery of the Incarnation. He understands Mary's privilege of the Immaculate Conception to be a particular proof of the greatness of her sanctity and of her superior capacity to cooperate with God's grace as the Second and Better Eve in reversing the effects of original sin. Newman then asks the following rhetorical questions:

> Is it any violent inference that she, who was to cooperate in the redemption of the world, was at least not less endowed with power from on high than she who, given as a helpmate to her husband, did in the event but cooperate with him for its ruin? If Eve was raised above human nature by that indwelling moral

318

gift which we call grace, is it rash to say that Mary had an even greater grace?[95]

Mary is the personified antithesis of sin because she is the Second Eve, full of grace from the moment of her conception and because her *fiat* at the Annunciation, by which she accepts her role as *Theotokos*, reverses the disobedience of Eve.[96]

Newman observes: "As Eve opened the way for the fatal deed of the first Adam, so it was fitting that Mary should open the way for the great achievement of the second Adam, even our Lord Jesus Christ, who came to save the world by dying on the cross for it.[97] In the *Letter to Pusey* we find a very logical development of thought in Newman which leads him to identify the Church's doctrine of the Immaculate Conception as rooted in the patristic theology of Mary the New Eve, which, in turn, is inseparable from the Fathers' interpretations of the Genesis accounts and Saint Paul's analogy (antithetical parallelism) in Romans between Adam and Christ the Second Adam. One finds the following line of thought in Newman:

> Mary may be called, as it were, the daughter of Eve unfallen. . . . I have drawn the doctrine of the Immaculate Conception as an immediate inference, from the primitive doctrine that Mary is the Second Eve. . . . If Eve was raised above human nature by that indwelling moral gift we call grace, is it rash to say that Mary had even a greater grace? . . . . And if Eve had this supernatural inward gift from the very first moment of her personal existence, is it possible to deny that Mary too had this gift from the very first moment of personal existence? I do not know how to resist the inference. Well, this is simply and literally the doctrine of the Immaculate Conception. I say the doctrine of the Immaculate Conception is in its substance this, and nothing more or less than this (putting aside the question of degrees of grace). And it really does seem to me bound up in the doctrine of the Fathers that Mary is the Second Eve.[98]

Monsignor Friedel comments on this, identifying some of the principal distinctions that Newman makes in his theology of the New Eve. Mary's role of cooperation in the economy of salvation is not compromised in Newman's thought because he firmly believes that the combined witness of the Sacred Scripture, Tradition and the Magisterium treat of it as an essential element, while also pointing out its just circumscription vis-à-vis the unique redemptive work of Christ the Second Adam. He explains Newman's reasoning by thus pointing out that "Jesus was not merely to take flesh of the Blessed Mary by becoming her Son." In other words, Newman evaluates Mary's cooperation not in terms of its being a mere physical instrumentality but as having also contributed to the Person and work of her divine Son through a moral and spiritual cooperation. Friedel then sets up an analogy—based on the distinctions developed by Newman in his theology of the New Eve—to express both Mary's unique participation in God's saving plan and yet to underscore her ontological subordination to Christ, the New Adam.

He writes: "As Adam primarily brought about the fall, so the new Adam would be the principal and absolutely essential cause of Redemption. However, Eve had her share in the first sin; in like manner, Mary was to have her place in the economy of Redemption." Friedel continues: "Eve was responsible and in-strumental in Adam's sin; Mary, too, was to bear a part; she was to be a voluntary agent; she was to be united with her divine Son in spirit and in will, as she was associated with Him in body, by furnishing Him the elements of His human nature." The Virgin's cooperation, for Newman, centering around her role as "the second and better Eve," possesses, according to the divine plan of salvation, an instrumental causality whereby she takes "the initial part in the world's restoration." Mary's cooperation in the economy of salvation is considered by Newman, as Friedel explains, to possess an instrumental causality insofar as her *fiat* is a direct, balanced and harmonious response of free will to the overtures of God's love and His plan of salvation.[99] Friedel writes: "God ever demands a reasonable service and the voluntary coop-eration of creatures in His works; He forces no will, but requires acquiescence in His designs. Though the Incarnation was to be of such tremendous significance for the whole human race, nev-ertheless as for man's fall, so for the restoration, He allowed the accomplishment of His will to rest solely on the fiat of a young maiden."[100]

Newman succinctly puts it that "she holds, as the Fathers teach us, that office in our restoration which Eve held in our fall."[101] However, it is always a question of Eve's role, not that of Adam's role. Just as original sin is, in a full and proper sense, attributed to Adam alone, so must the work of our redemption, in its full and proper sense, be attributed to the New Adam alone. Newman is even more precise in spelling out the nature of Mary's cooperation in the work of Redemption and how she freely exercises this role in a way that is antithetically parallel to the role exercised by Eve when he makes it clear that the Fathers of the Church recognized more in Mary than a mere physical instrument in the work of salvation. Newman explains:

> They declare that she was not a mere instrument in the Incarnation, such as David or Judah may be considered; she cooperated in our salvation not merely by the descent of the Holy Ghost upon her body, but by specific holy acts, the effects of the Holy Ghost within her soul; but as Eve forfeited privileges by the fruits of grace; as Eve was disobedient and unbelieving; that as Eve was a cause of ruin to all; that as Eve made room for Adam's fall, so Mary made room for our Lord's reparation of it; and thus, whereas the free gift was not as the offense, but much greater, it follows that, as Eve cooperated in effecting a great evil, Mary cooperated in effecting a much greater good.[102]

(b) *Newman's Understanding of the Theological Concepts of Merit, Grace, Sin, Free Will, and Good Works, and Their Bearing on His Theology of Mary's Cooperation As the New Eve*

In order the better to situate Newman's discussion of Mary's cooperation as the New Eve in the *Letter to Pusey*, some further points need to be addressed concerning the interrelationship among good works, free will, the nature of sin, and meritorious cooperation in Newman's thought and as directly discussed by him in regard to the Virgin, as in the aforementioned passage from *Difficulties of Anglicans* (2:44).

His sermon "Holiness Necessary for Future Blessedness" is a reflection on the nature of good works as integral to the process by which we achieve holiness and so arrive at salvation. Newman is careful to state that, although good works are necessary as outward proof or evidence of one's inner growth in holiness, they do not suffice for our salvation. He likewise stresses that the salvific efficacy and merit of good works do not reside in the actions themselves, but in the fact that these good works tap into, as it were, the well-spring of the Redeemer's own infinite merits:

321

If a certain character of mind, a certain state of the heart and affections, be necessary for entering heaven, our actions will avail for our salvation, chiefly as they tend to produce or evidence this frame of mind. Good works (as they are called) are required, not as if they had any thing of merit in them, not as if they could of themselves turn away God's anger for our sins, or produce heaven for us, but because they are the means under God's grace, of strengthening and showing forth that holy principle which God implants in the heart, and without which ...we cannot see Him.... These holy works, will be the means of making our hearts holy, and of preparing us for the future presence of God ... impressing our hearts with a heavenly character.... Thus we labour to mold our hearts after the pattern of the holiness of our Heavenly Father, it is our comfort to know ... that we are not left to ourselves, but that the Holy Ghost is graciously present with us, and enables us to triumph over, and to change our own minds. It is a comfort and encouragement, while it is an anxious and awful thing, to know that God works in and through us. We are the instruments but we are only the instruments for our own salvation.... Narrow, indeed, is the way of life, but infinite is His love and power who is with the Church, in Christ's place, to guide it along.[103]

It is clear, then, that Newman does not envision good works as extraneous to Christian holiness, but at its very heart, so much so that they become a privileged means by which we are made active, responsible participants (instruments, agents, cooperators) in the work of our own salvation. Nevertheless, the work of our salvation, etiologically speaking, is final conformity to and communion with the Triune God. Newman's understanding of man's cooperation in the work of salvation is anything but Pelagian. Man cannot work out his salvation alone; hence, the necessity of the indwelling presence of the Holy Spirit Who works, as Newman says, both "with the Church" and "in and through us." Newman, harkening back to the Council of Trent, briefly summarizes the Catholic position on the meritorious nature of good works, when he writes:

Catholics hold that our good works, as proceeding from the grace of the Holy Ghost, cannot be worthless, but have a real and proper value; on the other hand, that the great reward of eternal life is due to them only in consequence of the promise of God. Good works have on this ground a claim on God's faithfulness to His promises, and thereby a claim on His justice, for it would be unjust to promise and not fulfil. The Council of Trent says: "Vita æterna et tanquam *gratia misericorditer promissa*, et tanquam merces *ex ipsius Dei promissione fideliter reddenda*. Again: "Quæ justitia nostra dicitur, illa eadem Dei est, quia *a Deo nobis infunditur per Christi meritum*" (Sess. vi., cap.16.).[104]

In the *Letter to Pusey*, Newman cites *Sermon 140* of Saint Peter Chrysologus, in which he praises Mary for her cooperation in the economy of salvation.[105] Newman then comments: "It is difficult to express more explicitly, though in oratorical language, that the Blessed Virgin had a *real meritorious co-operation, a share which had a 'hire' and a 'price' in the reversal of the fall.*"[106] Newman also speaks of Mary's meritorious acts as those good works which were fruits of her holiness, faith and obedience to God's will.[107] In his *Lectures on the Doctrine of Justification*, he explains that the inner workings of the Holy Spirit, which lead to man's spiritual transformation, do not exclude the notion that "we are justified by our obedience" and that God is also "glorified" by the same. Thus, Newman shows how the virtue of obedience expresses both man's meritorious cooperation in the work of his own justification and yet also serves to underscore the sovereignty of God's salvific grace:

> Of course, even though we did all that the Law commanded, we should after all be unprofitable servants, and could claim nothing on the score of merit; but, since the Great Creator deigns to accept the service of His creatures, we should, as giving it, be pleasing Him by our obedience. In the same sense then in which it can be said that God is *glorified* by our obedience, though His perfection is infinitely above the need of it, so can it be said that we are *justified* by our obedience, though His favour is infinitely beyond the value of it. And this great blessing, it is affirmed, really is bestowed on us in the Gospel; which, by the gift of the Holy Ghost, works in us a new and spiritual life, such as at once glorifies God before His creatures, and justifies us before Himself.[108]

Perhaps, in the passage which follows, following Newman's logic, we can see how Mary's obedience of faith can be considered both an instrumental cause of her own sanctification and an instrumental cause of the mystery of the Incarnation. In other words, as the Fathers of the Church consistently point out, Mary's obedient cooperation is an instrumental cause of our salvation just as Eve's disobedience was the instrumental cause of our fall from grace. Therefore, although, as the Council of Trent assures us, the sole meritorious cause of our salvation/justification is that of Christ's Passion, Death and Resurrection[109]—for Christ alone had the innate and infinite power to redeem mankind—this does not negate God's will to attribute salvific merit to the obedient cooperation of Mary since such merit is awarded her without derogation from or offense to His glory. Newman writes:

> Now, what is especially noticeable in these writers (Justin, Tertullian and Irenæus), is, that they do not speak of the Blessed Virgin as the physical instrument of Our Lord's taking flesh, but as an intelligent, responsible cause of it; *her faith and obedience being accessories to the Incarnation, and gaining it as a reward*. As Eve failed in these virtues, and thereby brought on the fall of the race in Adam, so Mary by means of the same had a part in its restoration.[110]

In other words, Mary's *fiat* is a meritorious act since it is an act of free cooperation with God's grace in the realization of His will for her and our salvation.[111] The Angel's greeting to her implies that Mary was already fully immersed in the life of grace from the time of her Immaculate Conception,[112] so much so, that her *fiat* then becomes an act that is likewise fully meritorious in the economy of salvation.[113] In the *Letter to Pusey*, Newman affirms the meritorious nature of the lives of the saints when he writes that "much more then in the great Kingdom and people of God; the saints are ever in our sight, and not as mere ineffectual ghosts or dim memories, but as if present bodily in their past lives." Newman, quoting from Revelation 14:13, adds the following about the meritorious good works of the saints: "It is said of them, 'Their works do follow them;' what they were here, such are they in heaven and in the Church. As we call them by their earthly names, so we contemplate them in their earthly characters and histories. Their acts, callings, and relations below, are types and anticipations of their present mission above."[114]

Two questions may be asked here: If the works (deeds) of the saints were not meritorious, then would not our imitation of the holiness of their lives, our reliance on their heavenly intercession and our hope of entering into their blessed company be in vain? If this is the case with the saints, then must it not also be the case with their Queen, and to an even greater extent? Newman understands Our Lady's meritorious acts as proof of her high dignity, and so he concludes that: "The only question is, whether the Blessed Virgin had a part, a real part, in the economy of grace, whether, when she was on earth, she secured by her deeds any claim on our memories; for if she did, it is impossible we should put her away from us, merely because she is gone hence, and should not look at her still according to the measure of her earthly history, with gratitude and expectation." [115]

Newman not only recognizes Mary's cooperation in the economy of salvation as consisting of meritorious deeds, he also points to those same deeds, as he did for the other saints, as a fundamental reason for venerating her/their memory. In the *Letter to Pusey*, Newman also treats of Mary's blessedness and holiness as resulting from her unique cooperation in the "economy of grace," that is, from her "meritorious share in bringing about the Redemption." [116] Her cooperation consists in such virtues as faith, obedience,[117] purity, and co-suffering which she exemplified in this life, as well as in the meritorious (effectual) intercession which she exercises on our behalf in "her present state of blessedness":

> If, as Saint Irenæus says, she acted the part of an Advocate, a friend in need, even in her mortal life, if as Saint Jerome and Saint Ambrose say, she was on earth the great pattern of Virgins, *if she had a meritorious share in bringing about our Redemption*, if her maternity was *gained by faith and obedience*, if her divine Son was subject to her, and if she stood by the Cross with a mother's heart and drank in to the full those sufferings which it was her portion to gaze upon, it is impossible that we should not associate these characteristics of her life on earth with her present state of blessedness; and this surely she anticipated, when she said in her hymn that "all generations will call me blessed." [118]

Again, in the same work, Newman discusses the merits of the Virgin and their relationship to her divine prerogatives when he writes: "What dignity can be too great to attribute to her who is so closely bound up, as intimately one, with the Eternal Word, as a mother is with a son? What outfit of sanctity, what fulness and redundance of grace, *what exuberance of merits* must have been hers, when once we admit the supposition which the Fathers justify, *that her Maker really did regard those merits and take them into account*, when He condescended 'not to abhor the Virgin's womb.'" [119]

Newman prefaces his defense of the Immaculate Conception in the *Letter to Pusey* by clarifying an essential distinction between the Catholic and Protestant notions of original sin, as he understood the Catholic position in light of the teaching of the Council of Trent: "Original sin, with us, cannot be called sin, in the mere ordinary sense of the word 'sin,' it is a term denoting Adam's sin as transferred to us, or the state to which Adam's sin reduces the children but by Protestants it seems to be understood as sin, in much the same sense as actual sin." [120] Newman's remarks are particularly interesting since he is writing to an Anglican with whom he believes to share a common notion of sin and doctrine of grace. He expresses bewilderment at the fact that Pusey, and other scholarly and devout Anglicans like him, do not seem to agree as to this presumed commonality. Therefore, Newman feels the need to insist on this distinction: "We with the Fathers, think of it as something negative, Protestants as something positive. Protestants hold that it is a disease, a radical change of nature, an active poison internally corrupting the soul, infecting its primary elements, and disorganizing it; and they fancy that we ascribe a different nature from ours to the Blessed Virgin, different from that of her parents, and from that of fallen Adam." [121] The "negative view" of original sin (i.e., the Catholic view) holds that human nature is not corrupted by sin, but rather debilitated by it. Original sin is not part of God's original plan for man. Hence, even though man inherits original sin from Adam and suffers the consequences of sin, for example concupiscence, that does not mean that each of his acts must be, in some way, tainted by sin. Otherwise, man could never truly perform an objectively good and meritorious work. Rather, because God has created man's nature as inherently good and since God has redeemed man in Christ the New Adam—thus, elevating human nature to an even higher level than it had before the Incarnation—man's good works can be considered meritorious insofar as they remain acts of free will and reason, which are preceded, accompanied and followed by the movements of

grace. Therefore, man is capable, despite sin and its consequences, of cooperating with grace in the divine work of his own
salvation, as well as in the salvation of others, most especially of
his brothers and sisters in Christ. Consequently, any good work
that man accomplishes, is inseparable from the sovereignty of
God, His gift of grace and the ultimate goal of conformity to
Christ, eternal communion with the Triune God and with the
saints.

It is the original harmony and holiness, that is to say man's
original communion with God, himself, and others, that Adam
and Eve enjoyed before the Fall, which Newman ascribes to
Mary. Newman clearly states that Mary does not possess a human nature different from the one possessed by Adam and Eve.
In fact, Newman goes so far as to say that, because she was a
daughter of Adam and Eve, that is to say, a daughter of the
human race, that Mary, according to his speculation, would have
experienced physical death—not, of course, as a punishment for
sin—but as the natural means by which her earthly course
ended.[122] Mary, as Newman instructs Pusey, possesses the pristine, sinless human nature that all of us would have inherited if
Adam and Eve had not committed original sin. Sin, therefore,
according to Catholic doctrine, is most definitely not the final
word on human existence. It cannot be considered a "positive":

> . . . we deny that she had original sin; for by original sin we
> mean, as I have already said, something negative, viz; this only,
> the *deprivation* of that supernatural unmerited grace which
> Adam and Eve had on their first formation—deprivation.
> Mary could not merit, any more than they, the restoration of
> that grace; but it was restored to her by God's free bounty,
> from the very first moment of her existence, and thereby, in
> fact, she never came under the original curse, which consisted
> in the loss of it. And she had this special privilege, in order to
> fit her to become the Mother of her and our Redeemer, to fit
> her mentally, spiritually for it, so that by the aid of the first
> grace, she might grow in grace, that, when the Angel of the
> Lord was at hand, she might be "full of grace," prepared as far
> as a creature could be prepared to receive Him into her bo-
> som. I have drawn the doctrine of the Immaculate Concep-
> tion, as an immediate inference, from the primitive doctrine
> that Mary is the Second Eve. The argument seems to me to be
> conclusive.[123]

Because she was redeemed body and soul, in an extraordinary way in anticipation of Christ's saving Death and Resurrection, Newman envisions Mary's redemption as encompassing the entirety of her life from her Immaculate Conception to her Assumption into heaven. Furthermore, Mary's fullness of redemption, although certainly the result of unique privileges of divine grace—is consistently held out to us, by Newman, as an eschatological sign of hope for all believers. To sum up, Newman understands the doctrine of the New Eve in direct correlation to the dogma of the Immaculate Conception, with the two inexorably linked, so much so that to explain the one is to explain the other in the process. Newman is convinced, and tries to convince Pusey, that this is the case from time immemorial, which is to say that it is the constant teaching of the Church, based upon the written Word of God and the Sacred Tradition, especially as found in the writings of the Fathers of the Church.[124]

(c) *Conclusion: Mary's Meritorious Cooperation in the* Œconomia Salutis *As Theotokos and New Eve*

In the notes found as an appendix to the *Letter to Pusey*, Newman further explains that the doctrine of grace and merits in Mary's regard are teachings implicitly found in the teaching of the Fathers of the Church on Mary as the New Eve and thus, in the doctrine of the Immaculate Conception: ". . . that 'Mary is the new Eve,' is a proposition answering to the *idea* of a Tradition. . . . It is an explicit tradition; and the force of it follows two others, which are implicit: first (considering the condition of Eve in paradise), that Mary had no part in sin and indefinitely large measures of grace; secondly (considering the doctrine of merits), that she has been exalted to glory proportionate to that grace."[125]

The logical flow of Newman's arguments in favor of Mary's title of the New Eve and in support of the doctrine of the Immaculate Conception reaches this conclusion:

> And this consideration gives significance to the Angel's salutation of her as "full of grace,"—an interpretation of the original word which is undoubtedly the right one, as soon as we resist the common Protestant assumption that grace is a mere external approbation or acceptance, answering to the word "favour," whereas it is, as the Fathers teach, a real inward condition or supernatural quality of the soul. And if Eve had this super-

natural inward gift given her from the very first moment of her personal existence? I do not know how to resist this inference:—well, this is simply and literally the doctrine of the Immaculate Conception. I say the doctrine of the Immaculate Conception is in its substance this, and nothing more or less than this (putting aside the questions of degrees of grace); and it really does seem to me bound up in the doctrine of the Fathers, that Mary is the New Eve.[126]

Likewise significant is Newman's reference to Mary's "specific holy acts," in the *Letter to Pusey*.[127] How are we to interpret the meaning of Newman's statement in terms of her role of cooperation in the economy of salvation as *Theotokos* and New Eve? Could we not say that Newman envisions Mary performing an active role, in response to the action of the Holy Spirit within her? In other words, unlike the dominant Protestant view, Mary is not a mere "passive" instrument but active. This does not mean, however, that the grace and holiness that characterize her actions derive from her, as though she herself were the source. It is eminently clear that the Triune God remains the source of any and all goodness that is accomplished in and through Mary. To explain the notion of meritorious works in relationship to the Virgin, it is important to recall not only the fact that Mary cooperated in the work of her and our salvation through these good works but also in what these works actually consist, as Newman reflects upon them.

At one point in his *Letter to Pusey*, Newman discusses the dignity of Mary, affirming that her present heavenly intercessory role is an integral aspect and logical consequence of her earthly cooperation in the economy of salvation: "The only question is whether the Blessed Virgin had a part, a real part, in the economy of grace, whether, when she was on earth, she secured by her deeds any claim on our memories." And again in the same place: "She had a meritorious share in bringing about our Redemption."[128] Most significant are the qualifications that Newman employs to make his point, namely, that Mary's cooperation or her participation in the "economy of grace" is not accidental or extrinsic but "real" and even "meritorious." Mary's role is anything but passive; her deeds are all-important because they have a salvific dimension and value.[129] In that same section of the *Letter to Pusey*, he refers to her divine maternity, faith, obedience, and standing at the foot of the Cross as concrete examples of how her deeds freely and most lovingly performed can be considered "meritorious" and salutary.

In his meditation on the title of Mary as "Gate of Heaven," Newman draws out further conclusions concerning Mary's cooperation in the work of Redemption. He begins the meditation by explaining the biblical image of the Gate of Heaven, through which no man passes but the Lord God of Israel and within which only the Prince can sit down. He then comments:

> Now this is fulfilled, not only in Our Lord having taken flesh from her (Mary), and being her Son, but moreover, in that she had a place in the economy of Redemption. It is fulfilled in her spirit and will as well as in her body. Eve had a part in the fall of man, though it was Adam who was our representative and whose sin made us sinners. . . . It was fitting then in God's mercy that, as the woman began the destruction of the world, so a woman should also begin its recovery. . . . Hence, Mary is called by the holy Fathers a second and better Eve, as having taken that first step in the salvation of mankind which Eve took in its ruin.[130]

It is plain that Newman is pointing out that Eve's cooperation in the fall, although clearly subordinate to the role of Adam, has nonetheless a definite causal quality as concerns the Fall.[131] In like manner, Newman underscores that Mary the Second and Better Eve had a real yet subordinate role to that of the Second Adam in the cause of mankind's salvation.[132]

Newman asks the question in his meditation: "How, and when, did Mary take part in the world's restoration?" His answer is that it happened at the moment of her consent to the message of the Angel, by which consent she merits the title of "the Gate of Heaven." The Annunciation is proof that Mary freely consented to be the *Theotokos* and Second Eve, cooperating fully in the *œconomia salutis*. *Lumen Gentium* concurs in this judgment:

> The Virgin Mary, who at the message of the angel received the Word of God in her heart and in her body and gave Life to the world, is acknowledged and honored as being truly the Mother of God and of the Redeemer. . . . The Father of mercies willed that the Incarnation should be preceded by assent on the part of the predestined Mother, so that just as a woman had shared in bringing about death, so also a woman should contribute to

life. This is preeminently true of the Mother of Jesus, who gave to the world the Life that renews all things, and who was enriched by God with gifts appropriate to such a role.[133]

One notices that Newman once again highlights Mary's cooperation as not being passive but as being active. Furthermore, her essential role as the Mother of God is in fact meritorious and rewarding because it associates her in a unique way with the mystery of Redemption. Not only is Mary situated as the most intimately near the Redeemer because of her maternal role, but she is also said to have "suffered with Him" (*compassio*) and thus to have cooperated in the Lord's redemptive sacrifice.[134] Newman views the divine maternity as the prime expression of how Mary has attained her incomparable nearness to and intimacy with the Lord. He writes: "I say then, when once we have mastered the idea that Mary bore, suckled, and handled the Eternal in a form of a Child, what limit is conceivable to the rush and flood of thoughts which such a doctrine involves? What awe and surprise must attend upon that knowledge, that a creature has been brought so close to the Divine Essence?"[135]

SUMMARY OF CHAPTER FOUR

1) The controlling factor in Newman's discussion of Mary's cooperation as *Theotokos* and New Eve is the *œconomia salutis* which, for him, embraces the entire mystery of God's relationship to man—from the dawn of creation, to the original sin, to the work of Redemption, to the distribution of the fruits of that work in and though the Church until its consummation in eternity.

2) Within the overall *œconomia salutis*, the mystery of the Incarnation holds central place for Newman as he follows a patristic line of thought, exemplified by Fathers like Irenæus and Athanasius, Mary is both the "Mother of the Creator" and our Mother since through baptism we became *filii in Filio* ("sons in the Son") and members of His Mystical Body, the Church.

3) Newman sees the title of *Theotokos* ratified at the Council of Ephesus as a succinct encapsulation of the fundamental Christological truths (indeed, it is primarily a Christological title, albeit with Mariological implications). This, in turn, becomes the *fons et culmen* ("source and summit") of all Mary's privileges as she

safeguards the integral identity of her Son, in no way obscuring or compromising it.

4) Newman's theology, already from his Anglican period, reveals a particular appreciation of Mary's cooperation as the New Eve and the sinless spouse of Christ the Beloved. This appreciation stems from his love of the mystical sense of the Scriptures, most especially concerning the Canticle of Canticles and derives its inspiration, for example, from the writings of Origen and Gregory of Nyssa (see *In Assumpt.* 1, 2; PL 185:188).

5) Inasmuch as Newman is always concerned that genuine doctrinal development arise from the Scriptures and the Fathers (most notably, Justin, Irenæus and Tertullian), he resonates favorably to Mary's description as "the Second and Better Eve." It is this title which allows him to explain her cooperation in the work of Redemption. Eve's involvement in the Fall was essential but subordinate to Adam's; in the same way, Mary's participation in the reversal of the Fall was essential but subordinate to Christ's (the new Adam).

6) Newman keeps in the forefront such scriptural texts as the *Protoevangelium* and Revelation 12 as he expounds on the Fathers' development of the antitheses between Eve and Mary (disobedience/obedience; death/life) and their consequences. The title of Mary as "Mother of all the living" indicates for Newman that Mary's role as New Eve embraces her role as Mother of the Church and therefore her exercise of maternal mediation on behalf of our salvation.

7) In relying on the writings of such Fathers of the Church as Jerome, Ambrose and Peter Chrysologus, Newman emphasizes the agency of both Eve and Mary in their respective works, going so far as to speak of Mary's "real, meritorious" share in the redemptive and salvific mission of Christ "in the economy of grace," so much so that she is worthy not only of our remembrance and imitation but also of our filial invocation as part of our veneration of her blessedness.

8) Newman acknowledges that Mary's "real" and "meritorious" cooperation "in bringing about our Redemption" extends from the moment of her Immaculate Conception and her salutary *fiat* at the Annunciation, throughout her extraordinary life of sanctity, virtue and meritorious good deeds, culminating and being consummated on Calvary. At the foot of the Cross, she

exercises her *compassio*, which is more than a mere emotion or sympathetic feeling; rather, it is a profound expression of her intimate union of mind and heart, body, soul, and spirit with her Son as He accomplishes the work of Redemption, of which she is the primary and most perfect beneficiary.

9) Mary's cooperation "in the economy of Redemption" as the New Eve constitutes her "the daughter of Eve un-fallen," who took "that first step in the salvation of mankind which Eve took in its ruin."

Mary's Compassio *As an Instance of Her Cooperation in the* Œconomia Salutis *in Newman*

INTRODUCTION

Before one can address Newman's theology of Mary's *compassio* or co-suffering, one must treat of his theology of *compassio Christianorum* or Christian co-suffering. Just as Newman's theology of Mary's intercessory role is best understood in the context of his theology of the *communio sanctorum* (communion of saints), so Mary's *compassio* is best understood in the light of his theology of *compassio Christianorum*. The better to appreciate the relationship between the former and the latter, this chapter analyzes a sampling of texts from both Newman's Anglican and Catholic periods, for the purposes of integration and comment. Occasionally, it is shown how Newman's thought on our topic is reflected in the writings of selected contemporary theologians and the contemporary Magisterium, most especially that of Pope John Paul II.

I. COMPASSIO CHRISTIANORUM

Newman's Anglican sermon "Use of Saints' Days," delivered on the occasion of the Feast of All Saints, reminds us of the importance that co-suffering has in the living out of the Christian ideal of holiness, which the martyrs attained in an extraordinary way.[1] An integral part of Newman's notion of sainthood is the saint's ability to unite his sufferings to those of the Savior, without however finding in this "privilege" a cause of pride or an excuse to seek out suffering for its own sake—which is contrary to the Divine Will:

> Let us not forget, that, as we are called to be saints, so we are, by that very calling, called to suffer; and, if we suffer, must not

think it strange concerning the fiery trial that is to try us, not to be puffed up by our privilege of suffering, nor bring suffering needlessly upon us, nor be eager to make out we have suffered for Christ, when we have suffered for our faults, or not at all.[2]

In his sermon "Bodily Suffering," Newman makes some very important theological distinctions which provide further clarification of our theme of co-suffering and its relationship to cooperation in the economy of salvation. He is intent on safeguarding the uniqueness of Our Lord's redemptive act: "This only was our Atonement; no one shared in the work. He trod the wine-press alone, and of the people there was none with Him. When lifted up upon the cursed tree, He fought with all hosts of evil, and conquered by suffering.[3] He prefaces this statement by underscoring the uniqueness of Our Lord's sufferings which Newman refers to as "untold." Furthermore, Christ's sufferings are all-sufficient for redemption and all that is salvific in the Christian economy derives its efficacy from those very sufferings: "Thus, in a most mysterious way, all that is needful for the sinful world, the life of our souls, the regeneration of our nature, all that is most joyful and glorious, hope, light, peace, spiritual freedom, holy influences, religious knowledge and strength, all flow from a fount of blood."[4]

Hence, even though the saints have shared in the suffering of Christ in an extraordinary way, Christ's sufferings alone are meritorious, in and of themselves, for our Redemption. The sufferings of the Blessed Mother and of the other saints are meritorious, insofar as they participate in the infinite merits of Our Lord's redemptive Sacrifice: "He [Christ] indeed, alone meritoriously; they [the saints] because they have been near Him."[5] Nevertheless the value of Christian co-suffering is not diminished in the least by this fact. Rather, its very dependence on the Passion of Jesus gives to our co-suffering its most secure and fullest significance as a means of cooperation in the economy of salvation. In uniting our sufferings to those of the Redeemer, we also unite them to the Mother of the Redeemer. Newman puts it bluntly in his sermon note for September 16 (Sixteenth Pentecost): "*Septem Dolorum*—Election: The Cross of Christ puts a different complexion on the *whole* of life. If a man takes up any new course, his old ways are flat in comparison. *Septem dolorum* in connection—we must take part in her."[6]

Newman's sermon "Bodily Suffering" reinforces that all-important lesson of the Gospels and of the Pauline epistles, that uniting our sufferings to Christ is carried out not only for our own sakes, but on behalf of the Body of Christ, the Church. Therefore, out of the sufferings of Christ, is created a communion, a sacred solidarity, which gives us the "privilege" of sharing in God's work of salvation. Suffering in union with Christ is not the masochism that non-believers might sometimes experience. Pain is part of the sinful human experience, but only the Cross truly gives to our suffering its redemptive value (merit) and provides by means of it, an eternal consolation.[7] In fact, Newman, remaining precisely within the ambit of a theology of merit, ponders Christian co-sufferers as "choice instruments," "active servants" of salvation who, by participating in the uniquely meritorious sufferings of the Cross, likewise gain merit "because they are brought near to Him."[8]

Of all those most intimately associated with Our Lord and His Cross and therefore the greatest beneficiary of the infinite merits flowing from His sufferings, Newman speaks of the Blessed Mother who, "had not clasped Him to her breast for many weeks, ere she was warned of the penalty of that fearful privilege: 'Yea, a sword shall pierce through thy own soul also.'"[9] Co-suffering with Christ transforms the Christian so that he is able to view pain, not as an end in itself, but as a definite source of final communion with God and with all our fellow believers in the communion of saints, that is, with all those who are redeemed and with all those who have denied themselves, taken up their cross and followed in Christ's footsteps.[10] Newman explains the eschatological hope which is rooted in our ability to bear suffering in union with the Cross finding inspiration in Colossians 1:24[11]:

> "I rejoice in my sufferings for you, and fill up in my flesh what remains of the afflictions of Christ for His Body's sake, that is, the Church." And though he is speaking especially of persecution and other sufferings borne in the cause of the Gospel, yet is our great privilege, as Scripture tells us, that all pain and trouble, borne in faith and patience, will be accounted as marks of Christ, grace-tokens from the absent Saviour, and

will be accepted and rewarded for His sake at the last day. . . .
Pain, which by nature leads us only to ourselves, carries on the
Christian mind from the thought of self to the contemplation
of Christ, His Passion, His merits, and His pattern; and,
thence, further to that united company of sufferers who follow
Him.[12]

The thought of Newman concerning man's ability to cooperate in the work of salvation through co-suffering with Christ as
part of the communion of saints can be linked to the thought of
Pope John Paul II. For example, the Holy Father, writing in his
apostolic letter, *Salvifici Doloris*, reflects on the unique redemptive value of Jesus' suffering by which man's own suffering is
transformed, purified and elevated by divine love and the infinite
merits of His grace: "Human suffering has reached its culmination in the Passion of Christ. And at the same time has entered
into a completely new dimension and new order: it has been
linked by love. In the Cross of Christ not only is the Redemption
accomplished through suffering, but also human suffering itself
has been redeemed."[13] In his general audience on 26 October
1988, John Paul II reaffirms both the singular redemptive value
of the sacrifice of Christ and the truth that man is called upon by
God to cooperate in the redemptive mission by uniting his sufferings to those of the Savior:

> This truth of our faith (that is, the redemptive value of Christ's
> Sacrifice) does not exclude but demands the participation of
> each and every human being in Christ's sacrifice in collabora-
> tion with the Redeemer. As we said above, no human being
> could carry out the work of redemption by offering a substitu-
> tive sacrifice "for the sins of the whole world" (cf. 1 Jn 2:2). But
> it is also true that each one is called upon to participate in
> Christ's sacrifice and to collaborate with Him in the work of
> Redemption carried out by Him. . . . If Christ has redeemed
> humanity by accepting the cross and death "for all," the solidar-
> ity of Christ with every human being contains in itself the call
> to cooperate in solidarity with Him in the work of Redemption.
> This is the eloquence of the Gospel. This is especially the
> eloquence of the Cross. This is the importance of Baptism,
> which already effects in itself the participation of every person
> in the salvific work, in which he is associated with Christ by the
> same divine vocation.[14]

II. "COMPASSIO MARIÆ"

Co-suffering, that is, man's spiritual participation in the Passion of the Lord and sharing in its infinite merits, is a theme that pervades Newman's theology and spirituality and which receives a particular application to the life of the Virgin in the *Meditations and Devotions*. Mary's nearness to Christ the Redeemer, her suffering "with Him" at the foot of the Cross and intimate participation in the redemptive Sacrifice is a theme that can be traced throughout Newman's *Meditations and Devotions*. The Reverend Vincent Blehl, S.J. (the late postulator for the Cardinal Newman's cause), observes: "The seventy pages of meditations on *the Litany of Loreto for the Month of May*, which Newman composed, are models of theological accuracy and of heartfelt personal love and devotion." [15] In the passages which follow, we find Newman anticipating the Catechism of the Catholic Church when it states: "In fact, Jesus desires to associate with His redeeming sacrifice those who were to be its first beneficiaries. This is achieved supremely in the case of His Mother, who was associated more intimately than any other person in the mystery of His redemptive suffering." [16] For instance, Newman writes: "When then, He was mocked, bruised, scourged, and nailed to the Cross, she felt as keenly as if every indignity and torture inflicted on Him was struck at herself. She would have cried out in agony at every pang of His. This is called her *compassio* or her suffering with her Son, and it arose from this that she was the '*Vas insigne devotionis*' (Vessel of Singular Devotion)." [17]

He goes on: "But He, Who bore the sinner's shame for sinners, spared His Mother, who was sinless, this supreme indignity. Not in the body, but in the soul, she suffered a fellow-passion; she was crucified with Him; the spear that pierced His breast pierced through her spirit." [18] Newman returns to the image of the sword prophesied by Simeon at the Presentation as it strikes its most fatal blow at the Crucifixion. Although Mary's suffering is not of a physical but of a spiritual order, it nonetheless has a redemptive value since it is indissolubly tied to the Passion of Christ.

Along these same lines, his sermon note entitled "On Our Lady as in the Body for August 15 (Eleventh Pentecost)" emphasizes Mary's sword of sorrow as symbolic of both her physical and spiritual sufferings. However, he considers Mary's spiritual suffering as a keener type of suffering than her physical suffering: "And hence she brings before us the remarkable instance of a soul suffering, yet not the body." This suffering, as Newman relates, intensified for Mary with "the absence of Christ," and he refers to her period of suffering, as he does elsewhere, in terms of a purgatory-like state of anticipation for the time when her body would experience the victory that the soul had won because of her loving and obedient perseverance. However, Mary's victory is not her own but a particular share in the victory of Christ crucified and risen. Her suffering is "with merit and not for sin;" her death is one of love crowned by her bodily Assumption and her becoming "Our Advocate in heaven." [19]

By saying that Mary's suffering has a redemptive value, Newman does not mean that her suffering sufficed or that it was absolutely essential in order for the Redemption to be accomplished. Christ purposely willed Mary's cooperation to include a spiritual crucifixion of sorts, a *compassio* by which she was united in an indissoluble way to His Passion so that her suffering derives all of its salvific value from His. This point is further made by Newman in his meditation on Mary as the "Holy Mother of God": "Therefore, we confidently say that Our Lord, having preserved her from sin and the consequences of sin by His Passion, lost no time in pouring out the full merits of that Passion upon her body as well as her soul." [20]

To answer the question "How does the *compassio Mariæ* directly relate to the *compassio Christianorum*?" one might turn to Newman's meditation on Mary's title *Consolatrix Afflictorum* (Consoler of the Afflicted). He begins by recalling the co-suffering of the Apostle Saint Paul and how he was comforted by Our Lord, so that he, in turn, could learn how to comfort others, particularly his fellow Christians in their afflictions. Newman argues, in effect, that if this is the case with Saint Paul, how much greater must be the ability of Our Blessed Mother—who, in a singular way, suffered with Our Lord—to comfort all others who suffer. Newman unequivocally identifies Mary as our spiritual Mother. He explains the rationale for the appellation *Consolatrix Afflictorum* since he determines that its precise *raison d'être* is, in fact, this spiritual, filial rapport between Mary and all believers according to his understanding of John 19:25–27:

> And this too is why the Blessed Virgin is the comforter of the afflicted. We all know how special a mother's consolation is, and we are allowed to call Mary Our Mother from the time that Our Lord from the Cross established the relation of mother and son between her and Saint John. And she especially can console us because she suffered more than mothers in general.[21]

Nor does Newman generalize about Mary's *compassio*. On the contrary, turning back to Sacred Scripture and Tradition, Newman's meditation highlights some instances of Mary's own *via dolorosa* (Sorrowful Way). Indeed, suffering forms a type of *inclusio*[22] of her whole life. The infancy narratives, for example, depict her as the *Mater Dolorosa* (Sorrowful Mother) during the flight into Egypt, together with Joseph her husband and the Child Jesus. After Our Lord's Ascension, having been entrusted to the care of the Beloved Disciple, as Newman points out, Mary "was a stranger and a pilgrim on earth, in proportion to her greater love of Him Who *had* been on earth, and gone away."[23] Finally, Newman envisions Our Blessed Mother's last earthly days together with the Apostle John as a sort of exile at Ephesus. Thus, Newman concludes this meditation by exhorting all who suffer, especially Christians who suffer persecution for their faith, "to invoke the aid of Mary by the memory of her own sufferings among the heathen Greeks and the heathen Egyptians."[24]

In the *Parochial and Plain Sermons*, as we have already found in the previous section, Newman develops the theology of co-suffering in relationship to the ordinary living out of the Christian life by means of a series of reflections on the writings of Saint Paul. For example, in his sermon, "Watching," we read: "He watches with Christ, who ever commemorates and renews in his own person Christ's Cross and Agony, and gladly takes up that mantle of affection which Christ wore here, and left behind Him when He ascended."[25]

He continues with a series of important quotations from Saint Paul's letters about Christian co-suffering,[26] which demonstrate the Apostle's own willingness to suffer with Christ as an exercise of the theological virtues of faith, hope and charity—all of which are essential to the Christian life of holiness lived in the joyful hope of conformity to Christ in the resurrection of the body. To these virtues, Newman also adds the virtue of "watching" (understood as an expression of the virtue of forbearance) that gives fuller expression to the theological virtues, most especially, in the face of hardship.[27]

The virtue of waiting is also related to the virtue of prudence, which Newman ascribes to the Virgin in his meditation, "*Virgo Prudentissima*" (Virgin Most Prudent). Newman immediately makes the connection between Mary's prudence and her ability to persevere in patient forbearance in the trials and sorrows of her life: "It may not appear at first sight how the virtue of prudence is connected with the trials and sorrows of Our Lady's life; yet there is a point of view from which we are reminded of her prudence by those trials."[28] He writes: "It must be recollected that she is not only the great instance of the contemplative life, but also of the practical; and the practical life is at once a life of penance and prudence, if it be well discharged."[29]

Clearly, then, Our Lady is united to the Sacrifice of Christ not only because she was His Mother and happened to be an eyewitness to His suffering, but also because she experiences her own passion in union with His Passion. Mary did not passively endure her suffering, as if she were a victim of unfortunate circumstances; she suffered and, while doing so, was still capable of performing works of charity which, in themselves, were tests of her prudence and ability to forebear suffering for the sake of the immeasurable love she bore her Son.[30] These works flowed from her sinlessness, were perfected by grace, and assisted her in persevering in faith, hope, love and obedience in and through suffering *usque ad finem*. And so, her cooperation can be described as active, integrated, coherent and, as John Saward reflects, a "beautiful" participation in the economy of salvation.[31]

Newman offers us a spiritual-aesthetic appraisal of Mary's co-suffering when he reflects on the title "*Maria Addolorata*" in his sermon note for "April 15 (Tuesday of Holy Week)." His pious meditation is meant to inspire in us a sense of devotion to the Sorrowful Mother whose co-suffering was not only an integral part of the redemptive mysteries that took place during the first Holy Week but is also held up for us as a perfect model of cooperation in the Lord's work of salvation. Newman exhorts us to reflect on Mary, as he envisioned her, before the Passion, so that we "will understand what she was in her grief." Newman affectionately recalls various aspects of her exemplary "character," the sublimity of her virtues. For example, he considers her physical and spiritual beauty, her gentleness, modesty, chastity, charity and capacity for co-suffering flowing from that charity: "So loving toward others; so pained at sorrow and pain." He also ponders the beauty and exuberant nature of her sanctity so much so that he is led to say that "she inspired holiness" and that "the fulness of the sanctity of Saint Joseph: it was inspired by her." [32]

However, Newman's exhortation, while contemplating Mary's exemplary, inspirational holiness never causes the reader to lose sight of Mary's own personal icon of sanctity, Who is Jesus her Son. Newman is careful to maintain this link between Mary and Jesus and to distinguish between her role of cooperation in the economy of salvation and Jesus' "perfect" work as the Redeemer. Thus, Newman explains the nature of this mysterious bond that is solidified both during their earthly sojourn together and also, in a particular way, as she expresses her maternal *compassio* at the foot of the Cross:

> And she lived with a Son Who cannot be described in this way only, because He is God; Who surpassed her infinitely, but in another order. In the one the attributes of the Creator, in the other the most perfect work. What a picture! what a vision! Mother and Son. Next, that Son has left her. And now the news comes to her that He has to die, to be tortured; that He is to die a criminal's death of shame and torment; His limbs to be torn to pieces, etc., and He so innocent. Why, it is worse than killing and torturing the innocent babe. Under those circumstances, remarkable boldness in coming to see Him die. Does a mother commonly so act? Here the perfection of Mary's character, Hagar, "Let me not see the death of my son," Gen. xxi. 15–16. (She saw) Christ bearing the Cross. Then at the Cross. [33]

Returning to Newman's meditation on the Marian title *Virgo Prudentissima*, Newman considers Mary's co-suffering not so much by contrasting it to her life before the Passion such as one finds in the sermon note just cited but by discussing her *compassio* as expressed in her life following the Passion. This period of Mary's life, leading up to her glorious bodily Assumption—hence this sermon note is entitled "Rejoicing for Mary"—is dubbed "a purgatory," since it was during this period that Mary still had to suffer in anticipation of a joyful reunion with her Resurrected Son: "What a Purgatory! This very circumstance that all her life was God's, made the trial longer. But now, as Christ ascended, so has she." [34]

Mary's *fiat* is a cooperative, "meritorious" work since she carried out her life's duties faithfully[35] in union with the redemptive sufferings of Christ and did not cease to do so to an extraordinary degree when she herself was buffeted by suffering.[36] Newman's meditation concludes:

> But before that death [Mary's death] how much must she have suffered in her life amid an idolatrous population! Doubtless the Angels screened their eyes from the worst crimes there committed. Still, she was full of duties there—and in consequence she was full of merit. All her acts were perfect, all were the best that could be done. Now, always to be awake,[37] guarded, fervent, so as to be able to act not only without sin, but in the best possible way, in the various circumstances of each day, denotes a life of untiring mindfulness. But such a life, prudence is the presiding virtue. It is, then, through the pains and sorrows of this earthly pilgrimage that we are able to invoke her as *Virgo prudentissima*.[38]

For Hans Urs von Balthasar, the *fiat* of Mary consenting to the will of the Father is spoken on our behalf in cooperation with the redemptive plan begun in the Incarnation and consummated on Calvary.[39] The "yes" of the Virgin, for von Balthasar, is proof that Christ expressly wills that man cooperate in the work of his own redemption as a member of the Church, the Body of Christ, although Christ alone can be properly called man's Redeemer. Furthermore, von Balthasar reflects on Mary's co-suffering at the foot of the Cross as having reached the apex[40] of faith and spiritual union with Christ in the New Covenant, so that Mary's presence at the foot of the Cross is "a representation of the nuptial character of the new covenant."[41] He writes:

> The absolute sovereignty of God, who in *Jesus Christ alone* set up His new and eternal covenant with humankind; and the obtaining of a *consensual* "Yes" of humanity as represented by the Cross—the "Yes" which Mary had to give, at the moment of the Incarnation (and for all of its implications) *loco totius humanæ naturæ* especially as nucleus of the new Church. Inasmuch as Christ's vicarious suffering *is not exclusive but inclusive*, His gesture of comprehension can only be one of letting others suffer with him.[42]

Newman's sermon note "On the *Maria Addolorata*—The Seven Dolors for September 28 (Sixteenth Pentecost)"[43] returns to the theology of co-suffering in the life of the Virgin as that spiritual martyrdom by which she cooperated in her Son's work of Redemption. Newman highlights the peculiarity of Mary's spiritual or, as we may term it, mystical, silent suffering—making her worthy of the title "Queen of Martyrs." He compares and contrasts Our Lady's suffering and Our Lord's, so that Our Lord's suffering is always understood as constituting the *causa efficiens et formalis* (the efficient and formal cause) of our Redemption, while Mary's co-suffering (Newman emphasizes her mental anguish) is considered a cooperative act, which is a privileged share in her Son's unique redemptive Sacrifice. He makes these comparisons/contrasts clear when he writes:

> Well, as to the sufferings of the Son of God, they are awful mysteries; but they need not surprise us, for He came to suffer. . . . He came in the place and character of a sinner: no wonder he should suffer. But there was one who neither sinned nor took on her the character of a sinner. What had she to do with blood, or wounds, or grief?. . . . She had on the whole been sheltered from the world, yet she suffered. This makes Mary's suffering so peculiar. She is the queen of martyrs. . . . It is true she was not to undergo that bodily pain and violent death which literally makes a martyr. *He alone suffered all who died for all*. He alone suffered bodily and mentally. Her tender flesh was not scourged, but His was; her virginal form was not rudely exposed, but His was. All this would have been unseemly and unnecessary. *He was to save us by that Body and Blood which she furnished; not she*. He was to be made a *sacrament* for us as well as a sacrifice. Yet she was privileged to share the *acutest* part of His sufferings, the mental, once she came into the midst, at His Crucifixion [emphasis added].[44]

In his meditation on the title, "*Janua Cæli*," Newman gives an explanation of the nature of Mary's cooperation in terms of her *fiat* and *compassio*, by which that intimate association to the redemptive mysteries was enhanced as the Mother of the Redeemer persevered in her pilgrimage of faith. Therefore, her cooperation in the economy of salvation is much more than a mere physical one since her divine maternity and her co-suffering united her to Christ and to His work of salvation, causing Newman to understand them in terms of "merit" and "reward":

> And so, as regards the Blessed Virgin, it was God's will that she should undertake *willingly* and with *full understanding* to be the Mother of Our Lord, and not to be a mere passive instrument whose maternity would have no merit and no reward. The higher our gifts, the heavier our duties. It was no light lot to be so intimately near to the Redeemer of men, as she experienced afterwards when she suffered with Him.[45]

In his meditation on Mary as Queen of Martyrs, Newman writes: "What an overwhelming horror to witness the Passion and Crucifixion of her Son! Her anguish was, as holy Simeon had announced to her, at the time of her Son's Presentation in the Temple, a sword piercing her soul."[46] The sword that pierces Mary's soul at the Presentation is a prefiguration of the suffering she was to endure at the foot of the Cross. However, her pain is not simply that of a mother witnessing the suffering of a son but a true *compassio*, by which Mary enters into that suffering, in a profoundly spiritual way, reaping benefits from the merits of that redemptive suffering in body and soul.[47]

Newman also refers to Mary as the "Tower of Ivory" and the "Singular Vessel of Devotion." She is the "Tower of Ivory" because, unlike towers which we usually characterize as "rough," "huge," "heavy," "obtrusive," "graceless structures," the Virgin is made up, as it were, of different materials, that is, of virtues, which render her, in Newman's words, full of "beautifulness," "refinement," "finish," "brightness," "purity," "exquisiteness," "transcendent . . . loveliness and gentleness," all of which "are conspicuous in Mary." Newman writes:

> This quality of greatness is instanced in the Blessed Virgin. Though she suffered more keen and intimate anguish at our Lord's Passion and Crucifixion than any of the apostles by reason of her being His Mother, yet consider how much more noble she was amid her deep distress than they were. When Our Lord underwent His agony, they slept for sorrow. They could not wrestle with their deep disappointment and despondency; they could not master it; it confused, numbed, and overcame their senses. And soon after, when Saint Peter was asked by bystanders whether he was not one of Our Lord's disciples, he denied it. Nor was he alone in this cowardice. The apostles,

one and all, forsook Our Lord, and fled, though Saint John returned. Nay, still further, they even lost faith in Him, and thought all the great expectations which He had raised in them had ended in a failure. How different this even from the brave conduct of Saint Mary Magdalene! and still more from that of the Virgin Mother! It is expressly noted of her that she stood by the Cross. She did not grovel in the dust, but stood upright to receive the blows, the stabs, which the long Passion of her Son inflicted upon her every moment. In this magnanimity and generosity in suffering she is, as compared with the Apostles, fitly imaged as a *Tower*.[48]

In his meditation, entitled *"Vas Insigne Devotionis,"* Newman makes a comparison between the love which Saint Paul had for Our Lord and the love which the Blessed Virgin expressed for Him in her life of faith and devotion. He cites Saint Paul's reflection on the mystery of his spiritual crucifixion with Christ and how, from that crucifixion, was formed an intense, indissoluble bond with Him. Newman's comparison reveals that the love of Mary for her Son is greater than that of Saint Paul's because greater was her share in the merits of Our Lord's Passion: "But great as was Saint Paul's devotion to our Lord, much greater was that of the Blessed Virgin; because she was His Mother, and because she had Him and all His sufferings actually before her eyes, and because she had the long intimacy of thirty years with Him, and because she was from her special sanctity so ineffably near to Him."[49]

One finds a remarkable reflection of Newman's meditations on the Marian titles *"Turris Eburnea"* and *"Vas Insigne Devotionis"* in Pope John Paul II's *Redemptoris Mater*. The Pope, like Newman, praises the greatness of Mary's faith since it "towers over" that of the apostles who, when faced with the prospect of the Cross, run away in fear. The Holy Father reflects on the importance of Simeon's words to the Blessed Mother, with his prophecy concerning the sword of sorrow as a clear indication that Mary's faith and devotion would have to be of greater intensity and profundity than that of any other of the Lord's disciples. John Paul II also contrasts the steadfastness of Mary's faith with the weakened faith of the fearful disciples who do not possess the fortitude and the courage to deny themselves, take up their cross, and follow Our Lord in making their own spiritual ascent to Calvary:

Simeon's words seem like a second Annunciation to Mary, for they tell her of the actual historical situation in which the Son is to accomplish His mission, namely in misunderstanding and sorrow. While the announcement on the one hand confirms her faith in the accomplishment of the divine promises of salvation, on the other hand it also reveals to her that she will have to live her obedience of faith in suffering, at the side of the suffering Savior, and that her motherhood will be mysterious and sorrowful.[50]

The Pope continues:

Through this faith Mary is perfectly united with Christ in His self-emptying. At the foot of the Cross, Mary shares through faith in the shocking mystery of the self-emptying. This is perhaps the deepest "kenosis" of faith in human history. Through faith the Mother shares in the death of her Son, in His redeeming death; but in contrast with the faith of the disciples who fled, hers was far more enlightened. On Golgotha, Jesus through the Cross definitely confirmed that He was the "sign of contradiction" foretold by Simeon. At the same time, there was also fulfilled on Golgotha the words which Simeon had addressed to Mary: "And a sword will pierce through your own heart."[51]

Newman's meditation *"Turris Eburnea"* puts particular emphasis on Mary as having *stetit* (stood) beneath the Cross,[52] rather than having assumed a stance which would have identified her as a weaker woman, devastated and unconsolable in her grief. For Newman, it is not so much Mary's physical posture beneath the Cross that matters but its symbolic and theological significance.[53] Mary "stands" beneath the Cross because she is actively united to the sufferings of her Son, not passively; she is no mere bystander,[54] but an active participant in the redemptive pain experienced by her Son.[55] Likewise, in his meditation, *Vas Honorabile*, Newman takes note of Mary's courage and strength in "standing" beneath the Cross: "Yet there were no visible signs of this intimate martyrdom; she stood up, still, collected, motionless, solitary, under the Cross of her Son, surrounded by Angels, and shrouded in her virginal sanctity from the notice of all who were taking part in His Crucifixion."[56]

The Reverend Aidan Nichols, O.P., considers Mary's upright position at the foot of the Cross as a physical posture indicative of her unwillingness to abandon her role of cooperation in her Son's redemptive work, to which she consented at the moment of the Annunciation. Her *fiat*, which expressed her free, active, responsible, loving, obedient collaboration as the handmaid of the Lord at the moment of the Incarnation, is prolonged so as to be consummated by the love of her Crucified Son and Savior:

> The Virgin would not have fully brought forth the Savior unless He had become fully the Savior. According to the redeeming plan, He became so in completeness only with the Passion, Death and Resurrection. In saying yes to the Incarnation of the Son, Mary says yes to His redemptive work, and repeats that yes throughout His life, supremely at the foot of the Cross where she is God's privileged *collaboratrix* in the new covenant . . . as *Lumen Gentium* puts it, Mary "associated herself with His sacrifice in her Mother's heart and lovingly consented to the immolation of this Victim Who was born of her." Nor is this merely *passive* virtue. On the contrary: such unfailing readiness to surrender herself to the ever greater demands of her Son's saving mission requires supremely active qualities—generous love, eager obedience. Mary's tears do not flow helplessly, simply in reaction to the tragic historical events in which she is involved. The tears of the *Socia Redemptoris*, the Redeemer's woman companion, "symbolize in a particular way the purifying sacrifice of her Son, which washes sinners of all stain, and gives them new life" [emphasis added].[57]

Likewise, John Saward identifies Mary's *compassio* as a special instance of her cooperation in the *œconomia salutis*. Her *statio* (*stetit*) *juxta crucem* is the culmination of her *fiat* at the Annunciation. Indeed, Mary's *fiat* and her standing at the foot of the Cross are the outward, physical expressions of her spiritual virtue of *pietas*.[58] Although Saward himself does not make reference to the title of Mary as the "*Turris Eburnea*," his reference to "the beauty of Our Lady's cooperation in the work of her Son" seems to be a more than adequate expression of the spiritual aesthetic inherent in the title "Tower of Ivory."

Dr. Saward writes about Mary's *compassio* by using the title Co-Redemptrix as a quasi-synonymous term to sum up the aesthetical aspects of Mary's cooperation in the economy of salvation. Although Newman does not use the title "Co-Redemptrix" in this way, the passage of Saward given below reflects Newman's own theology and spirituality of Mary's *compassio*, by identifying a clear link between Mary's consent to the birth of the Savior and her silent *fiat* at the foot of the Cross. Both Newman and Saward would concur that Mary's cooperation was active, not passive, and indeed a uniquely meritorious cooperation in the economy of salvation. Saward writes:

> Mary is not just a Mother who is sorrowful because her Son is suffering. Standing at the foot of the Cross, Our Blessed Lady does not passively or even just patiently assist at the Sacrifice of her Son. In obedience to the Father's saving will, she gives up His and her Son. She gives, she offers; she does not merely let go. With love, she says yes to the immolation of the Victim Who is the flesh of her flesh, the fruit of her womb. Saint Albert says that Our Lady joined herself to the Father of mercies in His greatest work of mercy when she shared in the Passion of her Son and "thus became the helper of our Redemption and the Mother of our spiritual generation." According to Saint Antoninus, she stands by the Cross in devotion (*pietas*) not only towards her natural Son but also towards her adopted sons, for by her consent she is cooperating with their Redemption. To describe the beauty of Our Lady's cooperation with her Son's saving work, some of the Popes of our century have called Our Blessed Lady "Co-Redemptrix." It is a long and daunting Latin word, but its meaning is summed up in one syllable of Anglo-Saxon—the word that is the true heart of Mary: yes. No word is lovelier when uttered to God's glory, no reality more efficacious, saying yes to God is coredemptive.[59]

In his shorter[60] meditations on the Stations of the Cross, reflecting on the Fourth Station, Newman explains that Mary's participation in the mystery of Redemption is coextensive with the whole of the life and mission of her Son: "There is no part of the history of Jesus that Mary did not have her part in it. There are those who profess to be His servants, who think that her work ended when she bore Him, and after that she had nothing to do but disappear and be forgotten. But we, O Lord, Thy children of the Catholic Church, do not so think of Thy Mother."[61]

Newman refers to Mary's active cooperation and presence in the following mysteries of the Redemption: at the Presentation of the "tender Infant" in the Temple;[62] at the Adoration of the Magi, whereby "she lifted Him up in her arms when the wise men came to adore Him;" during the Flight into Egypt, when "she took Him up to Jerusalem when He was twelve years old;"[63] during Our Lord's hidden life at Nazareth,[64] at the Wedding Feast at Cana, during Jesus' public ministry and finally along His "Sacred Way" (i.e., the *Via Dolorosa*). And because Mary's presence is so prominent in the life of Our Lord, Newman concludes the meditation on the Fourth Station, imploring our "Sweet Mother" to let us think forever of her when we think of Jesus and to aid us by her powerful intercession when we pray to her Son.

Newman's longer version of the Fourth Station could be summed up in these powerful words describing Mary's *compassio*: "Mary would rather have had all His sufferings herself, could that have been, than not have known what they were by ceasing to be near Him."[65] But, of course, for Newman, this *compassio* is never unrequited love: "He, too, gained a refreshment, as from soothing and grateful breath of air, to see her sad smile amid the sights and the noises which were about Him."[66] Moreover, Newman contrasts the joy of Mary during the infancy of Christ and her suffering at the sight of her bloodied Son's "countenance" as He hung upon the Cross. Newman explains it thus, alluding to the figure of the Suffering Servant in Isaiah 53:1–12:

> She had known Him beautiful and glorious, with the freshness of divine innocence and peace upon His countenance; *now* she saw Him so changed and deformed that she could scarcely have recognized Him, save for the piercing, thrilling, peace-inspiring look He gave her. Still, He was now carrying the load of the world's sins, and, all-holy though He was, He carried the image of them on His very face. He looked like some outcast or outlaw who had frightful guilt upon Him. He had been made sin for us, who knew no sin; not a feature, not a limb, but spoke of guilt, of a curse, of punishment, of agony. Oh, what a meeting of Son and Mother! Yet there was a mutual comfort, for there was a mutual sympathy. Jesus and Mary—do they forget that Passiontide through all eternity?[67]

In his shorter meditation for the Fifth Station of the Cross, Newman speaks of how Our Lord allowed Simon to help Him carry the Cross, so as "to remind us that we must take part in His sufferings, and have a fellowship in His work."[68] Newman recalls that although Christ's merit is infinite and perfect in the act of Redemption, "He condescends to let His people add their merit to it." [69] He also notes that "the sanctity of the Blessed Virgin, the blood of the martyrs, the prayers and penances of the saints, the good deeds of all the faithful, take part in that work which, nevertheless, is perfect without them." [70] Thus, Christian co-suffering contributes meritoriously to the Lord's salvific action but is ever distinct from the unique act of Redemption accomplished by Christ alone: "He saves us by His Blood, but it is through and with ourselves that He saves us." [71] Perhaps the overall message Newman is trying to get across here is reminiscent of Saint Augustine's expression: "*Qui ergo fecit te sine te, non te justificat sine te*" (He Who made you without you, does not justify you without you). [72] Newman concludes his meditation by returning to the theme of co-suffering and its merit in the form of a prayer directed to Jesus: "Dear Lord, teach us to suffer with Thee, make it pleasant to us to suffer for Thy sake, and sanctify all our sufferings by the merits of Thy own." [73]

In his longer version of the Fifth Station of the Cross, Newman's meditation is centered on the themes of *compassio Christianorum* and *compassio Mariæ*. Newman treats of Simeon's cooperation in helping Jesus carry His Cross as both inspired by Mary's intercession and as inspiring in us the desire to share in the sufferings of Christ, as "the sight of the Sufferer" pierced Simon's heart. This co-suffering is a divine privilege given to Simon of Cyrene, about whom Newman remarks: "O happy soul, elect of God! he takes the part assigned to him with joy." Newman then turns his attention to the even more exemplary figure of the Virgin Mary who accompanies Christ along the *Via Dolorosa* and manifests to Him a special compassion by means of her motherly affection and "by following Him with her prayers, since she could help Him in no other way." Not only does Newman believe Mary's prayers to have availed as a consolation to Our Lord during His Passion, but he also thinks that Mary's intercession/mediation was a divine means by which Simon himself came to the attention of the soldiers, so that they could, in an ironic twist of fate, cooperate in the work of salvation by recognizing their sinfulness and, at the same time, provide consolation for her Son in the person of Simon of Cyrene. Newman concludes his meditation with an invocation of Mary to assist us by her intercession, most especially as we strive to carry our own cross as co-sufferers with Christ, as she cooperated in the work of salvation by assisting Our Lord, Simeon and the soldiers. Newman prays thus:

> Sweet Mother, even *do* the like for us. Pray for us ever, Holy Mother of God, pray for us, whatever be our cross, as we pass along on our way. Pray for us, and we shall rise again, though we have fallen. Pray for us when sorrow, anxiety, or sickness comes upon us. Pray for us when we are prostrate under the power of temptation, and send some faithful servant of thine to succour us. And in the world to come, if found worthy to expiate our sins in the fiery prison, send some good Angel to give us a season of refreshment. Pray for us, Holy Mother of God.[74]

In his "Litany of the Seven Dolours of the Blessed Virgin Mary,"[75] Newman calls on Mary as the "Mother of Sorrows" and "Refuge of Sinners," through whose "piercing anguish," "maternal pity," and "meritorious prayers," the sinner can be saved.[76] In his "Litany of the Immaculate Heart of Mary," Newman speaks of the heart of Mary as "in union with the Heart of Jesus" and describes that heart as a "victim of love," "nailed to the Cross," "refuge of the sinner," "hope of the dying," and "seat of mercy." Newman concludes that Litany with the following prayer which clearly expresses a direct causal relationship between Mary's participation in the sufferings of Christ and the salvation of sinners: "O most merciful God, Who for the salvation of sinners and the refuge of the wretched, hast made the Immaculate Heart of Mary most like in tenderness and pity to the Heart of Jesus, grant that we, who now commemorate her most sweet and loving heart, may by her merits and intercession, ever live in the fellowship of the Hearts of both Mother and Son."[77] In his "Litany of the Holy Name of Mary," Our Lady is invoked as the one who was "pierced with a sword," "bereft of consolation," "suffering with Jesus," "standing by the Cross."[78] Even his short poem entitled "The Heart of Mary," reveals Newman's sensibility to our theme: "Holy the womb that bare Him, Holy the breasts that fed, But holier still the royal heart That in His passion bled."[79]

Newman's sermon note for "September 28 (Twentieth Pentecost)" on Mary's Seven Dolors may be considered a type of summary of the essential points of his theology of Mary's *compassio.* Having ironically referred to the feast of Our Lady of Sorrows as "the most soothing of all feasts," Newman lists the various sorrowful events of her life as mysteries revealed in Sacred Scripture and in Sacred Tradition. Newman contrasts the joyful events of Mary's life, which he lists as the "Presentation, Annunciation, Visitation, the Nativity, (the visitation of) the Shepherds,[80] the Magi, Purification, to the sorrowful mysteries after Simeon's prophecy of the sword (e.g., the flight into Egypt; avoiding Herod; loss of Our Lord in the Temple; death of Saint Joseph; [Our Lord] leaving her to preach; [His] crucifixion and [her] bereavement."[81]

Newman then lists some scriptural passages as parallels to Our Lady's suffering. He refers to Moses in Deuteronomy 28 recounting the covenant the Lord makes with Moses and Israel at Mount Horeb and to the various sufferings that the Lord indicates as consequences of the Israelites' disobedience to the covenant. In this way, Newman may have intended to show a parallel between Moses' sufferings which resulted from his own disobedience and that of the Israelites and the suffering that Mary endured because of the disobedience she encountered in others during her lifetime; perhaps, Newman shows how the sufferings which Moses encountered because of his fidelity to the covenant can be compared to the sufferings that Mary endured for the sake of her fidelity to the covenant brought to fulfillment in Christ.

Newman speaks of the joyful mysteries of Mary's life as "the calmness before the storm," namely, the time when the sword of sorrow pierced her heart at the foot of the Cross. Newman writes thus: "All along there was the vision of One lifted on the Cross, and the sword pierces her heart." He then adds, as a reminder to himself, "Describe the Cross—and her by it! This is the key of her life on earth."[82] In other words, Mary's cooperation in the economy of salvation is incomprehensible apart from the hermeneutic it receives in the Paschal Mystery.

Newman also notes that a peculiar characteristic of "the sword in Mary's heart" is that it is a mental suffering more than a physical suffering such as is endured by the martyrs. Her *compassio* is much more than a mere emotion or sympathetic feeling; it is a profound expression of her intimate union of mind and heart with those of her Son as He accomplishes the work of Redemption. At one and the same time, Newman underscores this peculiarity as a divine privilege by which Mary cooperates in the work of salvation by means of "internal acts," of compassionate suffering of Mother in union with the suffering of her Child—of what he terms "mere suffering," as distinguished from the physical acts suffered by a "champion" and a "martyr." Newman also compares and contrasts Mary's *compassio* to the suffering of Hagar (who says, "I will not see the boy and die," in reference to her son (cf. Genesis 21:16) and "the brave mother of the Maccabees." Newman writes: "[Yet Mary suffered] not like Hagar, but like the brave mother of the Maccabees. This is the *compassio* of Mary." [83]

Newman says that Mary's ability to cope with mental suffering is exemplary since, as he reckoned, mental suffering was more commonplace in the nineteenth century which held out for Newman "those terrors of an intellectual age—madness and heartache." One is led to think of the negative effects of the French Revolution and the Enlightenment and Post-Enlightenment eras. Here, Newman also speaks of the "remorse at sin," perhaps alluding to the type of suffering needed for repentance, and which may not have been as readily noticeable in his time as it should have been. In any case, Newman caps his sermon note by directing his focus to Mary's *compassio*: "In all Mary is our sympathy and comfort. . . ." [84]

In fine, we might say that Newman's theology of Mary's *compassio*—so clearly rooted in his Marian spirituality and devotion—finds an echo in *Lumen Gentium*, no. 58: "Thus the Blessed Virgin advanced in her pilgrimage of faith, and faithfully persevered in her union with her Son unto the Cross, where she stood, in keeping with the divine plan, enduring with her only-begotten Son the intensity of His suffering, associated herself with His sacrifice in her Mother's heart, and lovingly consenting to the immolation of this Victim which was born of her."

SUMMARY OF CHAPTER FIVE

1) The biblical theology of co-suffering, already established in the Old Testament, for example, the typological figures of Hagar and the mother of the Maccabees, is foundational in Newman's theology of Christian co-suffering (or *compassio Christianorum*) as a form of participation in the Paschal Mystery of Our Lord, based primarily on the Pauline theology of the Cross.

2) This co-suffering of the Christian is considered by Newman to be a unique and privileged way of cooperation in *œcono-*

mia salutis, such as is exemplified in the life of the Blessed Virgin Mary and all the saints.

3) Newman underscores the importance of and distinguishes between a physical type of co-suffering, for example, physical martyrdom, and a spiritual type of co-suffering or spiritual martyrdom. Furthermore, Newman clearly distinguishes between the unique salvific sufferings of Christ the God-Man—the sole Redeemer who dies the supreme martyr's death on the Cross—and the unique participation of Mary in those salvific sufferings by means of her co-suffering, which is, more often than not, characterized by Newman as a profound spiritual type of martyrdom.

4) Newman traces Mary's singular cooperation—body and soul—from the moment of her Immaculate Conception, to the Annunciation, to its culmination on Calvary, where she exercises her role as Mother of the Redeemer and of the redeemed (e.g., Jn 19:26f.). A careful analysis of his *Meditations and Devotions* and some of his other writings demonstrates that Newman had a spirituality nourished by the Marian dimension of the Paschal Mystery, thus dealing on numerous occasions with the symbolism of the sword prophesied by Simeon as it reveals the depths of Our Lady's *compassio*.

6

Newman on Mary's Spiritual Maternity and Intercessory Role (Mediatrix and Advocate): Special Instances of Her Cooperation in the Œconomia Salutis

INTRODUCTION

Having explored Newman's theology of Mary's cooperation in the economy of salvation as the *Theotokos* and New Eve in Chapter Four and having considered his theology and spirituality of Christian co-suffering (*compassio Christianorum*) and of Mary's exemplary co-suffering (*compassio Mariæ*) as Mother of the Redeemer and of the redeemed in Chapter Five, we are now poised to reflect on Cardinal Newman's theology and spirituality in regard to his notion of Mary's spiritual maternity and intercessory role.

Special attention should be paid to those instances in which he refers to the Blessed Virgin under the titles of Mediatrix and Advocate since their proper understanding is essential to comprehending Mary's cooperation in the economy of salvation in Newman's thought. Also of considerable importance is Newman's treatment of these titles in relation to his understanding of key biblical texts, such as that of the Wedding Feast at Cana. The doctrine of mediation in the thought of Newman, most especially as it concerns the intercessory role of the saints and Mary's in particular, cannot be dealt with properly without reference to his *Letter to Pusey*, of which several key passages deserve our attention.[1] A careful examination of their content reveals not only Newman's thought on the doctrine of mediation but also some significant insights into his understanding of how the doctrine of mediation is integral to Mary's cooperation in the economy of salvation.

Seeing both of these doctrines as intrinsically related in Newman's thought will also help to formulate answers to the question of co-redemption as directly or indirectly discussed by Newman, which is the topic of Chapter Seven of this book.

Furthermore, a treatment of our topic would be deficient if one did not take into consideration Newman's study of Marian liturgical texts in the Western and Eastern liturgies, his critique of Marian devotions (e.g., *Raccolta*) as found in the *Letter to Pusey* and in his own *Meditations and Devotions*, all of which reveal that the principle of *lex orandi lex credendi* was quite operative in Newman's Marian theology and spirituality.

Bishop Boyce, in discussing Newman as a Mariologist, notes the centrality of the theme of mediation in his treatment of the Virgin:

> Another remarkable element of Newman's Mariology is the importance, not simply theoretical but practical, which he attributes to the power of Our Lady's intercession. It was clear to him from the Apocalypse (8:3) that the angels and saints do intercede for people on earth. Intercession is a vital part of the life of the Church. The power of their heavenly intercession comes from holiness. So too with Mary, she is powerful by her prayer for us because she is so holy and so near to Christ. In truth, she is our Advocate—*Advocata nostra.* Jesus loves her too much to refuse anything she asks on behalf of her spiritual sons and daughters, of whom she became the Mother in the order of grace, as she stood beneath the Cross, sharing in and consenting to her Son's redemptive sacrifice. Hence, her intercession is called powerful, even all-powerful, "because she has, more than anyone else, more than all Angels and Saints, this great, prevailing gift of prayer." [2]

I. THE ANGLICAN NEWMAN ON THE COMMUNION OF SAINTS AND INTERCESSORY PRAYER

Before we enter directly into our topic, it is essential to lay the foundation upon which these titles are built up in the theology of Newman. It must be noted at the outset that Newman treats the Church's belief in mediation in strict relationship to her more fundamental belief in the mystery of the Incarnation upon which we have already amply reflected. Newman writes:

> The Incarnation preludes the doctrine of the mediation and it is the archetype of the sacramental principle and of the doctrine of the merits of the saints. From the doctrine of mediation follows that of expiation, of the Mass, of the merits of the

saints and of the martyrs, of their invocation, of their cult. From the sacramental principle flow the sacraments properly called, the unity of the Church and of the Holy See, the symbol and center of such unity, the authority of the councils, the sanctity of the rites, the veneration of holy places, of sanctuaries, of images.[3]

For Newman, the whole activity of the Church is based upon the activity of mediation. Twice in the above citation Newman makes mention of the "merits of the saints" and refers to their cult and invocation as deriving from the doctrine of mediation. Already as an Anglican, Newman expressed a very sharp and profound understanding of the nature of the Church as a communion of saints, so much so that this apprehension was a major factor in bringing him to enter into full communion with the Catholic Church. Roger Jupp writes: "The history of Newman's conversion to Catholicism has been described as 'an unwearied pilgrimage in search of the communion of saints.'"[4] Father Velocci comments on the importance of the incarnational and sacramental principles of the Anglican Newman's thought, as he had come to understand their significance through his reading of the Church Fathers[5] and the influence of John Keble, and notes that an important consequence—although not immediately perceived—of Newman's developed belief in the mystery of the communion of saints was his fervent belief in the power of Mary's intercession and therefore of Marian invocation.[6]

Newman, preaching from the pulpit of his Anglican parish of Saint Mary's at Oxford, brilliantly and poetically explains to his parishioners the doctrine of the communion of saints:

> The Church, then, properly considered, is that great company of the elect, which has been separated by God's free grace, and His Spirit working in due season, from this sinful world, regenerated, and vouchsafed perseverance unto life eternal. Viewed so far as it merely consists of persons *now* living in this world, it is of course a visible company; but in its nobler and truer character it is a body invisible, or nearly so, as being made up, not merely of the few who happen still to be on their trial, but of the many who sleep in the Lord. . . . Out of the Church there is no salvation;—I mean to say out of that great invisible company, who are one and all incorporate in the one mystical Body of Christ, and quickened by one Spirit: now, by adhering to the

visible ministry which the Apostles left behind them, we approach unto what we see not, to Mount Sion, to the heavenly Jerusalem, to the spirits of the just, to the first-born elected to salvation, to Angels innumerable, to Jesus the One Mediator, and to God. This heavenly Jerusalem is the true Spouse of Christ and virgin Mother of Saints; and the visible ministry on earth, the bishops and pastors, together with Christians depending on them, at this or that day is called the Church, though really but a fragment of it, as being that part of it which is seen and can be pointed out, and as resembling it in type, and witnessing it, and leading towards it.

Newman does not view the Church as some vague reality but as a true communion of saints, a visible and invisible company of persons forming a mystical Body and Bride for Christ. Together, the living and deceased members of the Church share in the call to holiness and salvation, a process in which they mutually cooperate for each others' sakes without in any way derogating from the supreme mediation of Christ but rather participating in it.[8] Newman proceeds to explain how the Church expresses her invisible communion in a visible way through her ministry of preaching, teaching, sanctifying, administering the sacraments, public witness and suffering for the sake of the Gospel. To appreciate the beauty and depth of the Anglican Newman's understanding of the communion of saints, the following text is worth quoting at this point:

When a child is brought for Baptism, the Church invisible claims it, begs it of God, receives it, and extends to it, as God's instrument, her own sanctity. When we praise God in Holy Communion, we praise Him with the Angels and Archangels, who are the guards, and with the saints, who are the citizens of the City of God.[9] When we offer our Sacrifice of praise and thanksgiving, or partake of the sacred elements so offered, we solemnly eat and drink of the powers of the world to come. When we read the psalms, we use before many witnesses the very words on which those witnesses themselves,—I mean, all successive generations of that holy company,—have sustained themselves in their own day, for thousands of years past, during the pilgrimages heavenward. When we profess the Creed, it is no self-willed, arbitrary sense, but in the presence of those innumerable saints who will remember what its words mean, and are witnesses of it before God, in spite of the heresy or indifference of this or that day. When we stand over the graves, we are in the very vestibule of that dwelling which is "all-glorious within," full of light and purity and of voices crying, "Lord, how long?" When we pray in private, we are not solitary; others "are gathered together" with us "in Christ's name," though we see them not, with Christ in the midst of them. When we approach the ministry which He has ordained, we approach the steps of His throne. When we approach the bishops, who are the centers of that ministry, what have we before us but the Twelve Apostles, present but invisible? When we use the sacred Name of Jesus, or the sign given us in Baptism, what do we but bid defiance to devils and evil men, and gain strength to resist them? When we protest, or confess, or suffer in the Name of Christ, what are we but ourselves types and symbols of the Cross of Christ, and of the strength of Him Who died on it? When we are called to battle for the Lord, what are we who are seen, but mere outposts, the advanced guard of a mighty host, ourselves few in number and despicable, but bold beyond our numbers, because supported by chariots and fire and horses of fire round about the mountain of the Lord of Hosts under which we stand? Such is the City of God, the Holy Catholic Church throughout the world, manifested in and acting through what is called in each country the Church visible; which visible Church really depends solely on it, on the invisible,—not on civil power, not on princes or any child of man, not on its endowments, not on its numbers, not on any thing that is seen, unless indeed heaven can depend on earth, eternity on time, Angels on men, the dead on the living. The unseen world through God's secret power and mercy, encroaches upon this world; and the Church that is seen is just that portion of it by which it encroaches; and thus though the visible churches of the saints in this world seem rare, and scattered to and fro, like the islands in the sea, they are in truth but the tops of the everlasting hills, high and vast and deeply-rooted, which a deluge covers.[10]

For the Anglican Newman, intercessory prayer is a necessary component of the communion of saints and the life of the Church. Newman's sermon on intercession, preached as the Anglican rector of Saint Mary's at Oxford, affords us several insights into the general nature of prayer as exercised by the Christian. He describes the intercessory role of the Christian as an exercise in the common priesthood of all the faithful—a regal privilege of the baptized by which prayer on earth is joined to the mediation of the Savior at the Father's throne of grace and mercy in the heavenly Kingdom.[11] Furthermore, the mediation of the Church, as exemplified in her celebration of the mysteries of the Redemption in the Sacred Liturgy and in the administration of the sacraments, is a foretaste and promise of the heavenly life of the Kingdom. The saints in heaven are not dead but alive with God in Christ;[12] they are members of the Church glorious or triumphant, constituting an invisible reality whose unseen presence, example of holiness and intercessory prayer, lend support to the Church militant, so that it might experience the full benefits of the Redemption and likewise effectively carry out the sacred ministry on behalf of the salvation of souls as the Mystical Body of Christ.

Newman's belief in the communion of saints, that is, in the communion of visible and invisible realities, is rooted in his understanding of the mystery of the Church—one, holy, catholic and apostolic—as both a divine and a human institution that mediates the salvific grace of Christ. For example, concerning the intercessory power of the baptized, Newman writes about the believer's participation in the three-fold *munera Christi* ("offices of Christ") as Priest, Prophet and King:

> Intercession is the characteristic of Christian worship, the privilege of the heavenly adoption, the exercise of the perfect and spiritual mind . . . the especial observance of the Christian, because he alone is in a condition to offer it. It is the function of the justified and obedient, of the sons of God. . . . This, I say, is the Christian especial prerogative; and if he does not exercise it, certainly he has not risen to the conception of his real place among created beings. . . . Viewed in his place (the Christian) in "the Church of the first-born enrolled in heaven," with his original debt cancelled in Baptism, and all subsequent penalties put aside by Absolution, standing in God's presence upright and irreprovable, accepted in the Beloved, clad in the garments of righteousness, anointed with oil, and with a crown upon his head, in royal and priestly garb, as an heir of eternity, full of grace and good works, as walking in the commandments of the Lord blameless, such as one, I repeat it, is plainly in his fitting place when he intercedes. He is made after the pattern and in the fulness of Christ—he is what Christ is. Christ intercedes above, and he intercedes below.[13]

The private prayer of the individual is united to the prayer of the countless hosts of angels and saints who are gathered together "in Christ's Name" and who exercise their intercessory role even with the Lord in their midst, deriving their power from His divine presence. Once again, it is clear that the mediation of the angels and saints does not detract from or undermine Christ's own unique mediation.[14] However, it must be noted that although the Anglican Newman speaks with much affection and reverence for "the unseen company of believers," he would still have considered as "idolatrous" and abusive of God's gifts the idea of actively seeking the intercession of the departed saints since, as will be discussed, it was explicitly forbidden according to Article 22 of the Articles of Religion of the Anglican Church.

Jupp outlines the early development of the Anglican Newman's theology of the communion of saints and of Marian devotion. His paper is an excellent historical synthesis whose main points are recalled in the following section of this Chapter. He explains how Newman's official beliefs as a member of the Anglican Church, with its prohibition of invocation of Mary and the saints according to the Articles of Religion, hampered his ability to accept a too explicit devotion to Mary and the saints.

Jupp reflects on the profound influence of Richard Hurrell Froude, one of Newman's closest friends from their meeting in 1829 to Froude's death in 1836. Froude, as Jupp relates, had an ardent "admiration" of the Roman Church, especially of the Latin medieval writers and their Marian devotion, something which initially disturbed Newman because he perceived the Roman doctrine and practice as having fallen short of the teachings of the Primitive Church of the Fathers. Even more to the point, Froude, who openly declared to Newman his "distaste for the Reformation,"[15] prodded Newman to take him seriously, so much so that Newman writes: "His opinions arrested and influenced me, even when they did not gain my assent."[16] Nevertheless, Froude helped in many ways to confirm many of Newman's earliest intuitions in favor of "'real devotion' for the Mother of Jesus," to mitigate many of Newman's prejudices against Roman beliefs and practices, that is, in the words of Meriol Trevor, "to unveil for him a fresher understanding of the Mother of Jesus."[17] And, as Newman admits in the *Apologia*, Froude "fixed deep" in him "the idea of devotion to the Blessed Virgin."[18] Likewise,

Froude helped Newman to "transform" his "obscure feeling" or intuition concerning his desire, from the age of 15, to live a celibate life, "into a conscious resolution." [19] Newman writes in the *Apologia* about Froude: "He had a high severe idea of the intrinsic excellence of virginity; and he considered the Blessed Virgin its great pattern. He delighted in thinking of the saints; he had a keen appreciation of the idea of sanctity, its possibility and its heights severe." [20]

Jupp maintains that Newman's involvement with John Keble and the beginning of the Oxford Movement in 1833 led him to develop his theory of the *Via Media* and therefore to develop an ecclesial sense—a literary fruit of which were his lectures on *The Prophetical Office of the Church*. Newman deemed Anglicanism as the expression of that pure or true Catholicism of antiquity which he believed to have been corrupted by Roman Catholicism and Protestantism.[21] Newman, in his *Apologia*, recalls how he had rejected "that vast system as to the Blessed Virgin," which "has been the special *crux* of the Roman system" [22] and that he thought at the beginning of his involvement with the Oxford Movement that the Church of Rome was "bound up with the cause of the Antichrist by the Council of Trent"—a "view" which, as Jupp states, "remained with him up to 1843, two years before his conversion." [23] Newman testifies to having held such a negative view of Roman Catholicism in the *Apologia*.[24]

Jupp examines several other passages from the *Apologia*, revealing Newman's Mariological development.[25] He appraises Newman's sermon, "The Reverence Due to the Virgin Mary," as particularly reflective of Newman's heightening sense of Mary's singular role of cooperation in the economy of salvation, for example, the emphasis in that sermon on Mary's sinlessness, in his preaching and teaching at Saint Mary's at Oxford during the period 1832–1845.[26] Jupp also duly notes the contribution of Sister Lutgart Govaert who first brought "our attention to a Marian sermon preached exactly one year earlier, again on the Feast of the Annunciation," [27] entitled "The Honour Due to the Blessed Virgin Mary." And, furthermore, relying on Govaert's *Kardinal Newmans Mariologie und sein persönlicher Werdegang*, Jupp explains that Newman's sermons on the Incarnation contain within themselves important traces of his Mariological development, such as his avid defense of the doctrine of the *Theotokos* and the devotion due to Mary because of this unique privilege: "So much of Newman's message, we find, is united in and around the mystery of the Incarnation, which was the hallmark of the message of the Oxford Movement itself: where Evangelicals concentrated on the Atonement, Tractarians spoke of the Incarnation as the well-spring of faith in Christ." [28] Jupp refers to the Mariological content of the last of Newman's Oxford University Sermons as the precursor of Newman's *Essay on the Development of Christian Doctrine*, "where we find Newman reconciling so much of Catholic doctrine and putting an end to his doubts over what he once felt were excesses of Roman devotion to Mary." [29]

Some other significant influences on Newman's development of doctrine concerning the communion of saints and Marian devotion are his use of the devotionals of the seventeenth-century Anglican divines, most notably, the *Greek Devotions* of Lancelot Andrewes, which he translated in his Tract 88. He spoke of "his desire to participate in celebrating the liturgical year with the whole Church, both visible and invisible, after the example of the early Church," which he expressed in his preaching at Saint Mary's and by his use of the Roman Breviary. These devotionals, in particular, the ones of Lancelot "appealed to Newman most strongly because he found in them a patchwork of liturgical forms drawn from the Fathers, the Eastern Church, the Book of Common Prayer and the Bible. Here Newman found Andrewes praying 'as one to whom the communion of saints was a living reality,' for, as Andrewes asserted, 'there are of God's saints that pray for us with all instancy.'" [30]

Jupp likewise attests to Froude's love of the Virgin and its impact on Newman: "Although Andrewes spoke very strongly in his time of exaggerated devotions to the Blessed Virgin, he did not hesitate to speak of her as 'the all-holy, immaculate, more than blessed Mother of God and ever-virgin Mary.' This balance accorded with Newman's own feeling as well as with his knowledge of, and love for, the Fathers." [31] As regards the Roman Breviary, Jupp recalls that Newman was introduced in 1836 upon the passing of Froude; Newman requested Froude's four-volume set of the Divine Office "as a memento of his friendship with Froude." [32] Relying on the introduction Newman wrote for the Roman Breviary, we come upon the vital connection between Newman's use of the Roman Breviary and his ever-increasing love of the communion of saints: "Newman ends this account . . . by saying, 'I took it, studied it, wrote my Tract[33] from it, and have it on my table in constant use till this day,' finding it to be the 'most wonderful and most attractive monument of the devotion of saints.' "[34]

Nevertheless, despite his love of the Roman Breviary, Newman could not yet bring himself to recite the Marian antiphons, "ancient and simple as they were, and devoted as he was to her," as Meriol Trevor comments.[35] Jupp also offers a bit of historical conjecture, perhaps a true anecdote, based on Horace Keast's *Our Lady in England*, that indicates Newman resisted the direct invocation of Mary and the saints until his conversion in 1845.[36]

However, some more historical background still needs to be considered before directly treating of the topic of Newman's Catholic theology of Mary's intercessory role as Mediatrix and Advocate in the communion of saints. The Anglican Newman struggled, as did his co-religionists, with the doctrinal and devotional implications of Marian intercession and invocation. The latter was a true thorn in the side of most Anglicans because of the nature of Article 22 of the Thirty-nine Articles, which strictly forbade "the Romanish doctrine concerning worshiping and adoration, as well as of images and of relics and also invocation of saints," all of which were deemed "a fond thing vainly invented, and grounded upon no warranty of Scripture, but rather repugnant to the Word of God."[37]

A major contributor to the Oxford Tractarian Movement, Newman wrote Tract 90 in January 1841. He believed that by writing this Tract, he could help demonstrate how the Catholic doctrines reiterated at the Council of Trent, for example, the invocation of Mary and the saints, and the stipulations of the Thirty-nine Articles, written before the decrees of Trent, were reconcilable. Furthermore, Newman believed his own devotional practice to be consonant with the teaching of the Anglican Church. Tract 90 turned out to be one of Newman's last attempts to forge a *Via Media* between Anglicanism and Catholicism. In fact, "Tract 90 provoked a storm of protest and condemnation. Newman, who had sworn to the Articles as a member of Oxford University and as Vicar of Saint Mary's, was abused and vilified for disloyalty, dishonesty, dissimulation and guile. It brought him, as he wrote, to his 'death-bed' as regards his membership in the Church of England. The floods which that storm unleashed swept Newman in April 1842 to Littlemore." [38]

Much of the negative reaction to Tract 90 hinged on the irreconcilable differences between Article 22 and what Friedel says were considered by the Anglican Church to be the "'cut and dried propositions' enunciated in the decrees of Trent." [39] Noteworthy is Newman's reliance on Cardinal Robert Bellarmine's theological treatises defending the teachings of Trent, especially on the doctrine of the invocation of saints. However, Newman's intellectual honesty did not prevent him from listing several abuses of the cult of saints as he understood them. [40] An extraordinarily significant instrument in Newman's conversion process was an Irish Catholic priest by the name of Charles Russell, the President of Maynooth College.

In their correspondence, which began as a result of Father Russell's objection to Newman's misrepresentation of the Catholic doctrine of transubstantiation in Tract 90, Russell sought to answer many of Newman's questions calling into doubt the truth of certain Catholic dogmas. A crucial one for Newman that lay at the heart of the Catholic-Anglican divide was the doctrine of the invocation of saints, and of the Roman Catholic devotion to Mary in particular, which Newman dubbed an offense to the "incommunicable glory" of God. As it turned out, Russell's apologetic eventually help convinced Newman otherwise. There is no doubt that Father Russell's gifts to Newman—some of the Mariological writings of Saint Alphonsus Liguori, together with other Catholic works—were an important impetus in reawakening Newman's attention, so that he could reevaluate many aspects of Catholic Marian doctrine and devotion, which were not all easily assimilated by him at first glance. However, by 1842, Newman began to understand more clearly the non-contradictory relationship between Sacred Scripture and the doctrine of the invocation of saints. [41] Nevertheless, Newman was convinced, for a time, that it was not wise either for him or his fellow Anglicans to disobey the ordinances of the Anglican Church, most especially those related to Article 22.

Jupp comments that, since Newman did not perceive the Anglican divines as having offered a definitive answer concerning the relationship between the saints in heaven and the Church militant, the numerous examples of intercessory prayer of holy men and women in Sacred Scripture warranted a moderate acceptance of the doctrine of intercession, even if the Thirty-nine Articles had somewhat incubated a weariness in that regard. Furthermore, Jupp states that a consequence of Newman's development was his having made a distinction between invocation and intercession, the former being "rejected" because of the clearly contrary statements of the Thirty-nine Articles and the latter "accepted" because it is not even mentioned, let alone condemned, by those same Articles. Nevertheless, within this distinction, Newman maintained that the saints interceded on our behalf "as a body and not individually." [42]

Ambrose Saint John, Newman's dearest friend, who by 1843 had already gone to Littlemore, having been drawn closer than Newman to the threshold of conversion, expressed his belief that devotion to Our Lady and the invocation of saints was, in his reckoning, a most salutary practice consistent with the Apostolic and Catholic Faith. Keble and Pusey were not as enthralled with this notion. Likewise, the correspondence between Frederick Faber and Newman[43] throughout 1844 indicates that Faber resisted Newman's injunction to obey the Anglican prohibition of invocation of the Virgin and the saints, so as "to stifle the outbursts of filial devotion to her who for long years seemed to be haunting his spirit." [44] In the end, Our Lady would be victorious in the hearts of both of these two great Oratorians. However, the influence of such Anglican scholars as Keble and Froude on Newman's thought, especially on his Ecclesiology and Mariology, cannot be overlooked.[45] Newman himself acknowledged this influence.

In his *Apologia Pro Vita Sua*, Newman expressed his gratitude to and admiration of Hurrell Froude, making special note of Froude's particular devotion to the Blessed Virgin.[46] The Reverend Charles Stephen Dessain writes about the influence of John Keble on Newman's Mariological development in the following manner:

> Newman was not alone in speaking thus of Our Lady. He had the warrant, to mention no others, of his spiritual counsellor, that traditional Anglican, John Keble. In his poem on the Annunciation, in *The Christian Year*, published in 1827, Keble writes:

"Ave Maria! Mother blest,
To whom caressing and caressed,
Clings the Eternal Child . . .
Ave Maria! Thou whose name
All but adoring love may claim,
Yet may we reach thy shrine. . . ."

In 1846 Keble brought out another volume of sacred poems, *Lyra Innocentium*, which Newman himself has described for us: "The Virgin and Child is the special vision, as it may be called, which this truly evangelical poet has before him. . . ." After illustrating this, Newman continues: 'The feeling which is brought out into formal statement in these passages is intimated by the frequency and tenderness of expression with which the thought of the Blessed Virgin is introduced throughout the Volume. She is the "Blessed Mary" . . . "the Virgin blest . . . "the Mother-maid" . . . "Mother of God"; "the spotless Mother, first of creatures." [47]

Shortly before Newman's conversion to Catholicism, he adds another important personal tribute to Keble and his Marian devotion in his *Essays Historical and Critical,* underscoring Keble's influence in the Anglican Church and even more astonishingly his contribution to what Newman terms "the revival of Catholicism":

> If there be one writer in the Anglican Church who has discovered a deep, tender, loyal devotion to the Blessed Mary, it is the author of the Christian Year. The image of the Virgin and Child seems to be the one vision upon which both his heart and intellect have been formed; and those who knew Oxford twenty or thirty years ago, say that, while other college rooms were ornamented with pictures of Napoleon on horseback, or Apollo and the Graces, or heads of houses lounging in their easy chairs, there was one man, a young and rising one, in whose rooms, instead of these, might be seen the Madonna of Sisto or Domenichino's Saint John—fit augury of him who was in the event to do so much for the revival of Catholicism. [48]

For our purposes, it is worth continuing with the citation because it gives a clue as to Newman's concept of Marian intercession and the communion of saints. In speaking further of Keble, he writes: "We will never give up the hope, the humble belief, that sweet and gracious Lady will not forget her servant, but will recompense him, in royal wise, seven-fold, bringing him and his at length into the Church of the One Saviour, and into the communion of herself and all saints whom He has redeemed."[49] Father Velocci explains the connection between the thought of Newman and that of Froude and Keble:

> Froude exercised an extraordinary fascination over Newman, he helped him to correct many of his theological opinions, he induced him to regard Rome with admiration and he impressed profoundly in him the idea of devotion to the Madonna. But he was, more than anything, an intermediary, the channel that conducted Newman to the source: to John Keble, from whom he himself had learned the concept of the visible Church, of Apostolic Succession, of the sacramental principle, of the communion of saints.[50]

Although Newman as an Anglican wrestled with the idea of developing a full-blown Mariology, his clear notions of the communion of saints and the role of intercessory prayer in the life of the Church helped pave the way, by which a truly "Catholic" Mariology could be formed, a Mariology which, as we have already shown, is firmly rooted in the Scriptures and Tradition, most particularly in the writings of the Fathers of the Church. Velocci comments:

> He based the power of the intercession of the Madonna on the Christian doctrine of prayer and the communion of saints. With arguments and testimonies of the Scriptures and of the Fathers, he demonstrated the value and the importance of prayer in the immemorial Church and its irreversibility: the mysterious bond among Christian on earth, the souls in Purgatory and the blessed in heaven. To prove the existence and efficacy of the intercession of the saints it cost him a notable effort, because it was denied precisely by the Anglican theology; but there it succeeded victoriously.[51]

II. THE CATHOLIC NEWMAN: MARY AS MEDIATRIX AND ADVOCATE IN THE COMMUNION OF SAINTS

(a) *A Letter to Pusey: An Introduction to the Doctrine of Intercessory Prayer*

The *Letter to Pusey*, Newman's response to Pusey's *Eirenicon*,[52] is, in great part, an attempt to correct Pusey's misunderstandings concerning Catholic teaching on the intercession and invocation of the Blessed Virgin Mary. Pusey relied on Catholic sources such as Salazar, Saints Louis de Montfort (e.g., "Treatise on True Devotion to the Blessed Virgin"), Bernardine of Siena and Alphonsus Liguori, as well as on the writings of Suarez and Faber. Newman was particularly aware of the need to defend Faber's reputation since Pusey had cited and critiqued the texts of his fellow Oratorian in his *Eirenicon*. Pusey's inability to distinguish between doctrinal and devotional statements in these writers led him to misinterpret and thus, to reject some essential Marian teachings. Furthermore, Pusey's sources were limited, and he often latched on to more extreme, sentimental expressions of Marian devotions found in the writings of other less formidable Catholic writers as so-called proofs of the falsehood of what was referred to by many Anglicans as "the Roman system of belief."

As a result of Pusey's *Eirenicon*, Newman accuses Pusey of a superficial reading and misinterpretation, even misrepresentation, of the Catholic Church's teaching on Mary. Perhaps, here, Newman was guilty of overacting and misinterpreting Pusey's intent, insofar as Newman was initially convinced that the *Eirenicon* was partially intended as a direct attack on Catholicism, rather than a sincere attempt at ecumenical dialogue. In other words, Newman perceived, at one point, that Pusey's stated purpose of achieving greater understanding of Church teaching was, in effect, designed to create even further division.[53] Pusey, in a letter dated 2 November 1865, responds to Newman's accusations so as to reconfirm his original intention not to attack Catholic teachings but to inquire about them. On November 3, Newman said he would not reply to Pusey. On December 7, Newman's reply is complete. The timing of the *Letter* is not accidental, coinciding as it did with the December 8 celebration of the Feast of Mary's Immaculate Conception.

Newman's *Letter to Pusey* was not meant to be a systematic treatment of Mariology; it was fundamentally a response of a friend and man of faith to a friend and man of faith. Newman's response, however, was not simply addressed to Pusey, for Newman had in mind a much larger audience, namely, all of Pusey's fellow Anglicans with whom Newman could easily identify since he had to overcome many of the same difficulties vis-à-vis Catholicism that they did. Likewise, Newman could easily sympathize with the desire to follow one's conscience in adhering to matters of faith and morals. Newman's *Letter to Pusey* is proof of his ultimate desire to establish further ground for unity between the Catholic and Anglican Churches. It is a masterpiece of true ecumenism because Newman did not pursue this unity apart from truth and charity. Thus, Newman distanced himself from preconceived notions and *ad hominem* attacks to present, in as clear a way as possible, the unadulterated truths of the Catholic teaching on Mary, most especially those called into question by Pusey.

In doing so, Newman made clear to Pusey several important facts about himself, namely, that he had obviously taken stances on doctrinal and devotional matters that cannot be considered of one accord with many of the official teachings of Anglicanism; that he had moved away from his positions in Tract 90, now admitting the full-blown consequences of the pulverization of the *Via Media* Theory and the happy consequences of his redis-covery of the Fathers of the Church and the authentic develop-ments of Christian doctrine represented by their teaching; that he believed that the combined witness of the Fathers of the Church (i.e., "Antiquity") was a confirmation of the truths of Sacred Scripture, Sacred Tradition and the Magisterium of the Roman Catholic Church.

(b) *A Letter to Pusey: An Introductory Analysis of Its Content Concerning Mary As Mediatrix and Advocate*

Once he became a Catholic, Newman's attitude regarding the communion of saints, intercessory prayer and the direct invoca-tion of the saints, most especially of the Blessed Virgin, would be fine-tuned. Newman writes in his *Letter to Pusey*:

> The saints are ever in our sight, and not as mere intellectual ghosts or dim memories, but as if present bodily in their past selves. It is said of them, "their works do follow them;" what they were here, such are they in heaven and in the Church. As we call them by their earthly names, so we contemplate them in their earthly characters and histories. Their acts, callings, and relations below are types and anticipations of their present mis-sion above.[54]

Newman underscores the continuity that exists between the earthly life of the saints and their present heavenly mission of intercession on behalf of the Church. Our invocation of the saints involves our recollection and emulation of their saintly deeds. Just as the saints interceded for the Church in their earthly life, so too they presently intercede in the Kingdom of God on our behalf.[55] Newman goes on to situate Mary's intercessory role within the context of the communion of saints. He believes that Mary exercised this role in her earthly life and, therefore, can even more effectively carry out this function in "her present state of blessedness." He is convinced that her intercession, like that of the other saints, does not in any way interfere with the mediation of Christ the High Priest. Furthermore, Mary's role of mediation, intercession is an integral part of how she cooperates in "the economy of grace." Newman is certain that Mary has secured a "claim on our memories" and that "it is impossible (that) we should put her away from us, merely because she is gone hence, and should not look at her still according to the measure of her earthly history, with gratitude and expectation."[56] Why this mention of expectation? Newman explains:

> If as Saint Irenæus says, she [Mary] acted the part of an advocate, a friend in need, even in her mortal life; if as Saint Jerome and Saint Ambrose say, she was on earth the great pattern of virgins; if she had a meritorious share in bringing about our Redemption; if her maternity was gained by faith and obedience; if her divine Son was subject to her; and if she stood by the Cross with a Mother's heart and drank in to the full those sufferings which it was her portion to gaze upon, it is impossible that we should not associate these characteristics of her life on earth with the present state of blessedness. And this surely she anticipated when she said in her hymn that all "generations should call me blessed."[57]

This distinction is also implied, for example, in Newman's *Letters and Diaries*.[58] Newman speaks of Mary as our Advocate and in so doing posits his belief in Mary's universal mediation of saving grace. He makes clear that Mary's role of cooperation in the economy of salvation in no way detracts from the unique role of Christ as the Redeemer of Man and Our Advocate with the Father nor from the unique role of the Holy Spirit as our Second Advocate or Counsellor. Thus in a letter to John Keble, Newman writes:

Our received doctrine is, after Saints Justin and Irenæus, as we interpret them, that as Eve had a secondary part in the fall, so had the Blessed Mary in the redemption. And interpreting them still, it is our belief, that whereas all the Saints intercede for us, through the merits and in the grace of Christ, she κατ᾽ εξοχὴν the Intercessor or Helper (Advocata, παράκλιτος, Saint Irenæus)—that this is her distinct part in the economy of human salvation—so that, knowing the Will of Our Lord most intimately, she prays *according* to His will, or thus is the ordained means or channel by which that will is carried out. Therefore "every thing goes through the hands of Mary"—and this is a great reason for our asking her prayers.[59]

Newman highlights Mary's intercessory role as clear proof of her greatness and dignity.[60] Indeed, Mary's blessedness, which she herself prophesied in the *Magnificat*, is subsequently attested to in the practice of the Church throughout the ages.[61] Newman calls to his side, as witnesses or advocates, the Fathers of the Church. Although this work examines Newman's appropriation of patristic thought in Chapter Three, the essential aspects of Marian doctrine mentioned in the above passage are necessary to delineate precisely because Newman presents them as interconnected mysteries, which directly relate to our present topic of Mary's mediation and our invocation of her. Mary's mediation as our Advocate is inexorably linked to her role of cooperation as the Virgin Mother whose *fiat* is a direct participation in the objective work of mankind's Redemption.

Furthermore, her *fiat* is prolonged throughout the whole of her life so that she becomes for us the most blessed model of virginity, holiness and all virtue, most especially in the obedience of faith which stands its greatest test at the foot of the Cross. It is at Calvary that Mary's spiritual maternity of the Church is most fully revealed by a direct participation in the salvific sufferings of her Crucified Lord and Savior. For Newman, Mary's mediation and her advocacy on the part of the Mystical Body of Christ derive all their efficacy from the infinite merits of the Cross, so much so that she not only fully benefits from them herself but also becomes an eternal link in the economy of salvation by which those saving graces are mediated to us. Therefore, Newman can envision no other appropriate response on our part than our filial devotion expressed through a constant remembrance of her blessed cooperation, a fervent imitation of her example, and a confident invocation of her heavenly intercession.

(c) *A Letter to Pusey: Newman's Discussion of Saint Irenæus'*
   Use of the Title "Advocate" in Reference to Mary

The title "Advocate," as used by Newman, in application to the Virgin, is one which he adamantly defends in the *Letter to Pusey*: "It is supposed by critics, Protestant as well as Catholic, that the Greek word for Advocate in the original was Paraclete; it should be borne in mind, then, when we are accused of giving Our Lady the titles and offices of her Son, that Saint Irenæus bestows on her the special name and office proper to the Holy Spirit." [62] However, obviously, "Advocate" cannot possess the exact same theological significance in terms of the *œconomia salutis* when it is attributed to the Virgin as when it is attributed to God the Son and God the Holy Spirit.[63] Father Friedel's comment helps to flesh out this essential distinction: "Newman is always careful to remind his audience that, though Mary is the Advocate of the Church, she did not effect the Atonement—she like all others was saved by her Son, through Whom she has been exalted to the office of Advocate of mankind. This position conferred on her is the result of God's merciful Providence, which permits us creatures to supplicate Him for the dispensation of His favors and graces." [64]

   Irenæus refers to Mary as Eve's Advocate or "friend in need" because Mary's obedience loosens the knot of Eve's disobedience, so that Mary represents Eve and the whole fallen human race before God in saying yes to His plan of salvation. Therefore, Mary's role of advocacy does not seem to be understood by Irenæus primarily in terms of her intercessory prayer;[65] rather, it is a title that sums up the singular contribution which Mary had in the economy of salvation, that is, cooperation. In any case, neither Saint Irenæus nor Cardinal Newman understood the title "Advocate" in reference to Mary as an indication that Mary is co-equal to Christ and the Holy Spirit in bringing about the Redemption or that her intercessory prayer can be put on a par with theirs.

   If this type of equality is what Pusey believed that the title Advocate used of Mary was intended to legitimize, at least as it was used in the popular Marian devotions of his day, then Newman's initial response about its use in Irenæus may leave a little something to be desired in terms of a Catholic apologetic, if taken on its own. However, it is hoped that the rest of this chapter, dedicated to a study of the *Letter to Pusey* in relation to some of his other writings on Mary's mediation, will help offer a more unified vision of his thought and thereby assist us in achieving a better appreciation of Mary's title of Advocate. Furthermore, Newman's interpretation of the twelfth chapter of the Apocalypse, as scriptural evidence for Mary's heavenly presence, is immediately referred to by Newman in this context but only subsequently developed in the *Letter*. For Newman's treatment of Revelation 12, the reader is referred to the Chapter of this book dealing with Newman's use of Sacred Scripture. In this Chapter, attention is given to Newman's mention of Mary's mediation vis-à-vis her presence at Cana and in the Cenacle at Pentecost.

Newman's discussion of Saint Irenæus' use of the title "Advocate," in reference to Mary finds ample complementarity in other of Newman's writings, most notably in his *Sermon Notes*. For instance, he writes in one sermon note linking together Mary's role as the New Eve and the corresponding titles of "Advocate with Clients," and "Mother of All Living," to the Protoevangelium of Genesis 3:15 and Apocalypse 12 as well as to Jesus' words addressed to Mary at the Foot of the Cross "Behold, thy Mother" (cf. Jn 19:27).[66] In another sermon note, Newman simply recalls that Mary is "Our Advocate in Heaven."[67] Furthermore, to explain that we should freely have recourse to Mary as our advocate, he uses the phrase, "We have a friend in court. She is the great work of God's love," and so doing impresses upon us the important notion that Mary's maternal mediation on our behalf should not be opposed based on the "foolish objection, as if (we asserted) she were more loving than God."[68] To enhance his argument, Newman makes an analogy. He asserts that Mary's maternal mediation can be compared to a type of ring which God gives us as a special "pledge" of His favors. Indeed, Newman concludes his analogy by stating that "any favours will be granted" by God as a result of this special token of His omnipotent and infinite love that we have in the person of the Blessed Virgin. Finally, one can conclude that Mary is our advocate insofar as she not only exemplifies the power of Christian intercessory prayer in the economy of salvation but also because her maternal mediation, as "the greatest of God's works" and "the glory of our race," aims at increasing in us a greater love of God and neighbor.[69] Newman exhorts us to pray: "Let us pray at this season and beg her to make us full of that love of herself, and of all those who have God's grace, and of all whom God has made."[70]

(d) *A Letter to Pusey: The Belief of Catholics in
    Mary's Intercessory Power*

The *Letter to Pusey* contains Newman's most systematic explanation of the Catholic doctrine concerning Our Lady's intercessory power, in particular on pages 68–76. At this point, it is useful to make an analysis of that section. Newman begins by reminding Pusey that Our Lady's intercessory power "is the immediate result of two truths," which truths, Newman says, Pusey does not dispute. The first of these that Newman identifies concerns the doctrine of the invocation of saints which was confirmed by the Council of Trent when it said (as quoted by Newman) that "it is good and useful . . . suppliantly to invoke the saints and to have recourse to their prayers."[71] The second truth is "that the Blessed Mary is singularly dear to her Son and singularly exalted in sanctity and glory."[72] However, Newman, admittedly, for the sake of not "becoming too didactic," does not explain the Council of Trent's teaching in any detail but proceeds to "state somewhat more fully the grounds on which it rests."[73]

Suffice it to say that the Council of Trent's teaching regarding the unique Mediatorship of Christ the sole Lord and Redeemer in relationship to the dependency and subordination of the mediation of Mary and the other saints (and likewise of our invocation of them),[74] is an extremely important teaching to bear in mind since it not only helps explain Newman's theology but also anticipates, in many ways, the treatment that these doctrines would receive in chapter 8 of *Lumen Gentium*,[75] of which Newman can be seen as a precursor in his own right.

Newman, therefore, sets forth the doctrine of intercessory prayer and the communion of saints by referring to its historical roots in the life of the early Church. He says that "though its members were scattered all over the world, and its rulers and subjects had so little of unified action, yet they, one and all, found the solace of spiritual intercourse and a real bond of union, in the practice of mutual intercession." [76] Newman recalls that the origins of the Church as recounted in the Acts of the Apostles and the Pauline epistles are directly linked to the practice of intercessory prayer.

(e) *A Letter to Pusey: The Belief of Catholics in*
   Mary's Intercessory Power and Her Presence at Pentecost

Therefore, if Mary can be rightfully called our Advocate, as the Church teaches, then one must remember that Mary, like the other apostles and disciples of the Lord, exercised her intercessory role not as ends but as means, so that in accordance with Our Lord's expressed will, their communal perseverance in prayer would lead to the descent of the Holy Spirit on the Feast of Pentecost.[77] Thus, at the very heart of the nascent Church in the Upper Room, both the intercessory power of Mary and the saints is emphasized, while its subordination to the divine power and presence of the Holy Spirit is likewise affirmed.[78] Newman puts it simply: "It was in prayer that the Church was founded." [79] There can be no conflict among the mysteries of faith. However, to distinguish the intercessory prayer of Mary and the saints from that of the Third Person of the Blessed Trinity does not equal the splitting of theological hairs; rather, it is a *sine qua non* of orthodox theology, based on the clear principles which can be gleaned from the Sacred Scriptures.

Consequently, the Pauline injunctions to pray in the Spirit or in the power of the Spirit, to which Newman himself makes reference in the *Letter to Pusey*,[80] give further proof that all intercessory prayer, whether of the Virgin or of the saints, is contingent not only upon the infinite merits of the redemptive Sacrifice of Christ, "the Mediator of the New Testament," [81] but also upon the ineffable mystery of the Spirit's intercession on our behalf.

(f) *A Letter to Pusey: The Beliefs of Catholics in*
   Mary's Intercessory Power and the Doctrines of Purgatory
   and the Intercessory Prayer of the Saints

Having laid the foundation of a biblical apologetic for intercessory prayer in the communion of saints, Newman directs these questions to Pusey: "Now, was this spiritual bond to cease with life? Or had Christians similar duties to their brethren departed?" Newman answers his own questions when he writes:

377

From the witness of the early ages of the Church, it appears that they had. You (Pusey), and those who agree with you, would be the last to deny that they were then in the practice of praying, as for the living, so for those who had passed into the intermediate state between earth and heaven. Did the sacred communion extend further still, on to the inhabitants of heaven itself? Here too you will agree with us, for you have adopted in your volume the words of the Council of Trent which I have quoted above.[82]

Newman then distinguishes three types of intercessory prayer: prayer for the living, prayer for the souls in purgatory and the intercession of saints. Concerning the last of the three, he makes a clarification: "It would be preposterous to pray for those who are already in glory; but at least they can pray for us, and we can ask their prayers."[83] He illustrates this point by referring to Revelation 8:1–5, in which "angels are introduced both sending us their blessing and offering up our prayers before the Divine Presence."[84] Newman also alludes to the Epistle to the Hebrews in which are introduced "not only angels, but 'the spirits of the just' into the sacred communion."[85] Quoting, in part, from Hebrews 12:22–24, Newman explains who these just spirits are and what role they exercise in the communion of saints:

> "Ye have come to Mount Zion, to the heavenly Jerusalem, to myriads of angels, to God the Judge of all, to the spirits of the just made perfect, and to Jesus the Mediator of the New Testament." What can be meant by having "come to the spirits of the just," unless in some way or other, they do us good, whether by blessing or aiding us? That is, in a word, to speak correctly, by praying for us, for it is surely by prayer that the creature above is able to bless and aid the creature below.[86]

It must be noted how the presence and intercessory roles of the angels and saints does not in any way obstruct the singular mediation of Christ but rather are means by which creatures already saved and sanctified can assist those creatures who have still not reached the end of their pilgrimage and completed their heavenly ascent.[87] Furthermore, Newman is once again careful to link together the intercessory prayer of Christians in the communion of saints and the singular mediation or intercessory power of the Holy Spirit: "Intercession thus being a first principle of the Church's life, next it is certain again, that the vital force of that intercession, as an availing power, is, (according to the will of God) sanctity. This seems to be suggested by a passage of Saint Paul, in which the Supreme Intercessor is said to be 'the Spirit': '—the Spirit Himself maketh intercession for us; He maketh intercession for the Saints before God.'"[88] Newman reinforces his point by referring to other instances in Sacred Scripture where the power of intercessory prayer is affirmed as a general principle "in the form of doctrine and of example."[89] Newman writes: "The words of the man born blind speak the common-sense of nature:—'if any man be a worshipper of God, him he heareth.' And the Apostles confirm them:—'the prayer of the just man availeth much,' and 'whatever we ask, we receive, because we keep His commandments."[90]

Newman is then occupied with the question of how the role of the intercessor or mediator was exercised in the Old Testament by such just and holy men. He begins his list of examples with that of Abraham and Moses, telling Pusey that "we read of the Almighty's revealing to Abraham and Moses beforehand, His purposes of wrath, in order that they by their intercessions might avert its execution."[91] Other important Old Testament personages to whom Newman refers, "as being great mediators between God and His people,"[92] are: Job,[93] Elias,[94] Jeremiah,[95] Samuel,[96] Noah,[97] Daniel.[98] Newman also reminds Pusey of the Lucan passage[99] in which Jesus speaks of the beggar Lazarus who dies and makes his abode in Abraham's bosom. Newman understands this passage as testifying that the "high office" of mediation is one that carries over into eternity. He notes that the language and imagery of such a Gospel passage is most definitely Jewish in origin and that it thus expresses a truth "sanctioned by our Lord Himself." Once again it must be highlighted that not only is the mediation of the saints not offensive to the Lord; on the contrary, it is permitted and promoted by His own teaching.

At this point, Newman enters directly into the question of Mary's place in the communion of saints and the nature of her intercessory power. He begins his remarks by asking two questions: "What do Catholics teach about the Blessed Virgin more wonderful than this? If Abraham, not yet ascended on high, had charge of Lazarus, what offense is it to affirm the like of her, who was not merely as Abraham, 'the friend', but was the very 'Mother of God'?"[100] Newman compares Abraham and Mary—

two figures who exemplify the obedience of faith in the Sacred Scriptures—precisely in terms of their intercessory roles. Newman's comparison is not intended to disparage Abraham's role as "our Father in Faith" or his intercessory role as "friend" of the poor man Lazarus who rested in Abraham's bosom in the dwelling place of all the just (i.e., *Sheol, Hades*) awaiting Christ's final victory over sin and death through His Death and Resurrection (this is the scenario that Our Lord's parable sets up). Rather, Newman's comparison is meant to underscore the uniqueness of Mary's exalted position as the one who intercedes not only as "friend" or "advocate" but as "the very Mother of God." What, of course, is implied by Newman is that her divine maternity is the very basis for her maternal relationship to us who implore her intercession.

Newman makes this very point in a sermon note when he writes: "It is like the divine works to turn things to account. Thus, though she subserved the Redeemer she also subserved the redeemed. Hers is a *ministry* to us, and it was to Him originally."[101] Likewise, in Sermon Note 137 Newman links together Mary's divine maternity and her spiritual maternity of the Church. He explains that Mary is "our Mother as well as God's," making the remarkable analogy that just as Mary is rightfully Mother of the God-Man (two natures in the one Person of Christ) so too is she Mother of both the Redeemer and of the redeemed entrusted to her from the Cross. Hence, Newman makes a parallel between the words of Hebrews 2:13, "Behold I and my children," and the words of Our Lord spoken to Mary at the foot of the Cross, "Behold thy Son—[Behold] thy Mother," intimating that the former are fulfilled in the latter and vice versa. Newman adds another comparison between Mary's divine maternity and her spiritual maternity of the Church: "Her first birth without pain" (alluding to her birth of Christ at Bethlehem) and "Her birth of us with pain," alluding to her spiritual maternity of us on Calvary.

(g) *A Letter to Pusey: The Belief of Catholics in Mary's Intercessory Power/Mediation at Cana and Her Spiritual Maternity in the Economy of Salvation*

Newman's comparison, then, in the *Letter to Pusey*, of Mary's intercessory power—our spiritual mother in the faith—and that of Abraham—our spiritual father in the faith—can only make sense in light of what follows, namely, his brief but significant commentary on the episode of the Wedding Feast of Cana by which he hopes to establish a scriptural basis for Mary's intercessory role in the new economy of salvation. Newman emphasizes the singularity of Mary's intercessory power since Our Lord acknowledges it within the framework of His public life and ministry and uses it as privileged means by which the glory of His hour—that is, the hour of that same final victory over sin and death for which Abraham and Lazarus awaited in the parable—would be achieved at the foot of the Cross.

However, the miracle at Cana was not only effective as a sign of Christ's glory but also that, as Newman's clever play on words points out, Mary's intercession becomes the "medium" of her own glory. Newman tells us that her glory is recognized by Our Lord in a two-fold way: first, Christ honors her by honoring her request and thus performing the first of the seven signs of His glory recorded in the Gospel of John; second, Mary's glory is revealed because Our Lord, by changing the water into wine, "breaks through the appointed order of things," that is, the natural order of physical reality, "for her sake," and in so doing, establishes the beginning of a new "dispensation." Thus, the six jars of water representing the Old Testament and the Jewish laws of purification are transformed into the choice wine of Christ's Gospel and grace.[102]

Without a doubt, therefore, Newman's reading of the Cana pericope leads one to understand that Mary's mediation is central to the whole economy of salvation.[103] The following two passages about Cana are also discussed in Chapter Two. The first passage is, as we have already mentioned, directly related to what Newman says about Abraham's and Mary's intercession in the *Letter to Pusey*. The second passage, commenting on the Cana story, is an excerpt from one of Newman's meditations, entitled "Our Lord Refuses Sympathy":

> And if on one occasion, He (Our Lord) seems to repel His Mother, when she told Him that wine was wanting for the guests at the marriage feast, it is obvious to remark on it, that, by saying that she was then separated from Him ("What have I to do with thee?") *because* His hour was not yet come, He implied, that when that hour was come, such separation would

be at an end. Moreover, in fact He did at her intercession work the miracle to which her words pointed.[104]

> ... The *last* day of the earthly intercourse between Jesus and Mary was at the marriage feast of Cana. Yet even then there was something taken from that blissful intimacy, for they no longer lived simply for each other, but showed themselves in public, and began to take their place in the dispensation which was opening. He manifested forth His glory by his first miracle; and hers also, by making her intercession the medium of it. He honoured her still more, by breaking through the appointed order of things for her sake, and though His time of miracles was not come, anticipating it at her instance.[105]

An interesting point of reference for a better understanding of Newman's commentary on this passage of Saint John's Gospel is Saint Thomas Aquinas' commentary, in which he highlights the notion of the mystical intimacy (Newman calls it the "blissful intimacy") between Our Lady and Our Lord that results from the working of the miracle of Cana—a union that symbolizes the marriage between Christ and the Church and the union between a man and a woman in the Sacrament of Matrimony. Furthermore, Mary's intercessory role is treated not as a mere human intervention but as a specific means by which the glory of God is manifested and the onlookers (the Evangelist notes: "and the disciples came to believe in Him") are brought to faith[106] according to the divine economy of salvation. Newman refers to it as: "the dispensation," and "the appointed order of things."

In other words, Mary's intercession (mediation) at the Wedding Feast of Cana leads to a visible sign instituted by Christ to give grace. Indeed, as Saint Paul would later comment in the Epistle to the Ephesians, Our Lord raised up the natural, human institution of marriage to the higher, supernatural level of being a sacrament, that is, a visible sign of His love for His Bride, the Church.[107] Was not Our Lord's miracle at Cana in the context of a wedding feast the first proof that He intended for just such an elevation to occur? Aquinas writes in his first lecture on the second chapter of his commentary on John: "Mystice autem per nuptias intelligitur coniunctio Christi et Ecclesiæ, quia, ut dicit Apostolus Eph. 5,32, sacramentum hoc magnum est, dico autem in Christo et in Ecclesia" (330). Again: "Mystice autem in nuptiis spiritualibus est Mater Iesu, virgo scilicet beata, sicut nuptiarum consiliatrix, quia per eius intercessionem coniungitur Christo per gratiam" (330). He adds: "Gessit ergo, quantum ad primum, Mater Christi, mediatricis personam; et ideo duo facit: primo enim interpellat ad Filium; secundo erudit ministros, ibi et dicit Mater eius ministris etc." (331). Finally, Saint Thomas reflects: "Quamvis autem Mater repulsa sit, tamen de filii misericordia non diffidit" (332).[108]

(h) *A Letter to Pusey: The Belief of Catholics in
    Mary's All-Powerful Intercession As the Exemplification
    of Christian Intercessory Prayer*

Newman makes an excellent synthesis for Pusey of his thoughts on the doctrines of intercessory prayer, Mary's singular intercessory power and her privileged place in the communion of saints when he asserts:

> I consider it impossible then, for those who believe to be one vast body in heaven and on earth, in which every holy creature of God has its place, and of which prayer is the life, when once they recognize the sanctity and the dignity of the Blessed Virgin, not to perceive immediately that her office above is one of perpetual intercession for the faithful militant, and that our very relation to her must be that of clients to a patron, and that, in the eternal enmity which exists between the woman and the serpent, while the serpent's strength lies in being the tempter while the weapon of the Second Eve and the Mother of God is prayer.[109]

The interconnectedness among the themes mentioned is vital to Newman's apologetic. It is clear that Newman believes that Mary exercises her role as the Second Eve through her intercession, which acts as a weapon in the spiritual war waged against Satan. This spiritual combat in which Our Lady engages is integral to her cooperation in the economy of salvation. The above passages bring out the implications of the *inclusio* established in the Sacred Scriptures whereby the salvific role of "the woman" (the Mother of the future Redeemer prophesied in the *Proto-evangelium*) is a prefigurement of the "woman" in the Apocalypse, and likewise identified with Mary as the Second Eve," Mother of all the living," Advocate and Mother of the Church.

The question of Mary's all-powerful maternal mediation also forms a type of *inclusio* in the *Letter to Pusey*. In an early part of the

Letter Newman tells Pusey that a Jesuit confessor, "one of the holiest, and most prudent men he ever knew," once gave him some important advice as regards Marian devotion. The Jesuit Father told Newman "that we could not love the Blessed Virgin too much, if we loved Our Lord a great deal more."[110] Another significant passage is found when Newman writes: "There is a healthy devotion to the Blessed Virgin, and there is an artificial; it is possible to love her as a Mother, to honour her as a Virgin, to seek her as a Patron, and to exalt her as a Queen, without any injury to solid piety and Christian good sense; I cannot help calling this the English style."[111] However, Newman later adds this distinction: "To say, for instance, dogmatically, that no one can be saved without personal devotion to the Blessed Virgin, would be an untenable proposition; yet it may be true of this man or that, or of this country or that country at this date or that date; and, if that very statement has ever been made by any writer of consideration (and this has to be ascertained), then perhaps it was made precisely under these exceptional circumstances. If an Italian preacher made it, I should feel no disposition to doubt him, at least if he spoke of Italian youths and maidens."[112] The veritable Englishman Newman concludes his *Letter to Pusey* with a straightforward invocation of Mary's salvific intercession: ". . . May that bright and gentle Lady, the Blessed Virgin Mary, overcome you with her sweetness, and revenge herself on her foes by interceding effectively for their conversion."[113] In his notes to the *Letter to Pusey* Newman, basing himself on Canisius' work entitled *"De Maria Deipara Virgine,"* strengthens his arguments in favor of Marian intercession and invocation by acknowledging a plethora of prayers in the liturgical rites and devotionals of both the Latin and Greek Churches that bear witness to these doctrines. Finally, Newman remarks about Mary's all-powerful maternal mediation by reporting an important theological distinction that he discovered in a decree of the Holy Inquisition addressed to the Bishop of Presmilia dated 28 February 1875. It reads in part that "although she has the greatest influence (*possa moltissimo*) with her Son, still it cannot be piously affirmed that she exercises command over Him (*eserciti impero*)," to which Newman adds this explanatory comment, "in order apparently to mark the ministrative office of the Blessed Virgin, and her dependence as a creature on her Son."[114]

Dermot Fenelon acknowledges that Newman, two months before his reception into the Church, placed a miraculous medal around his neck as a clear sign of his devotion to the Virgin Mary, accepting her maternal protection as the Immaculate Conception and therefore also the New Eve—in accord with what he had already been convinced was the teaching of the early Church Fathers. Thus, for Newman, as Fenelon writes, "Mary was acclaimed as actively engaged in the reversal of the Fall. By her prayers she continues her maternal role in the Church.[115] The Immaculate Conception was a means, not an obstacle to unity."[116]

Newman concludes this section of the *Letter to Pusey* with a statement that is quite applicable to our own day as we too live in a generation that is often stymied by spiritual inertia (*acedia*) and enslaved to a notion which the ancient Greeks termed *tyche* (fate, chance). Newman considers the refusal to engage in prayer as being ultimately a denial of Divine Providence, which requires that man, as exemplified by the Virgin Mary, cooperate in his own salvation as well as in the salvation of others. "She (Mary) is the great exemplar of prayer in a generation which emphatically denies the power of prayer *in toto*, which determines that fatal laws govern the universe, that there cannot be any direct communication between earth and heaven, that God cannot visit his own earth, and that man cannot influence God's Providence.[117]

In his sermon note "On the Doctrine of Prayer as Reconciling Us to the Catholic Teaching about Our Blessed Lady," Newman's apologetical remarks are aimed at convincing Protestants that the Catholic teaching regarding the intercessory power of Mary is not to be considered an attempt to make Mary a rival of her Son in the work of Redemption.[118] Her power of intercessory prayer is tied to that same power which has been granted to all believers even though we share in this power to a much lesser degree. In another sermon note, "Our Lady the Fulfilling of the Revealed Doctrine of Prayer," Newman considers that omnipotent intercessory prayer "is the marvel, and the comfort which Revelation gives, . . . that God has broken through His own laws—nay does continually," by allowing creatures to participate in His own power to save through prayer. Newman adds that this aspect of the economy, namely omnipotent intercessory prayer, is even granted by some Protestants and then proceeds to make a statement in favor of Mary's all-powerful maternal mediation:

"Now Our Lady has the gift in fulness; not different from us except in degree and perfection. This is her feast. Hence it is that the more we can go to her in simplicity, the more we shall get."[119] However, to claim that prayer is not intrinsic to the mystery of the communion of saints is an altogether unfounded notion as is the notion that such an inscrutable mystery of Divine Providence could not also provide us with Mary as "the greatest exemplification of prayer."[120]

> Much is said by Protestants against Our Lady's power, but Our Lady's power is nothing else than the greatest exemplification of the power of prayer. We don't give her power of atonement, etc., but simply prayer, as we give ourselves; we in a degree, she in fulness. Now I can understand persons scrupling at the power of prayer altogether; but why, that there should be one instance (i.e., great exemplification) of it? We do not introduce a mystery, but realise it. The great mystery is that prayer should have influence. When once we get ourselves to believe the power of prayer, etc."[121]

Newman's sermon note "On the Healing of the Deaf and Dumb Man"[122] is a significant example of Newman's theology of creaturely, ecclesial mediation as a participation in the one, supreme mediation of Christ, from which likewise flows the mediation of Mary "our Advocate," who is the spiritual Mother of the Church. The note is related to Mark 7:31–37, in which Our Lord heals the deaf and dumb man through the ministry of the disciples. The disciples bring the deaf and dumb man to Jesus, according to what Newman refers to as, "the great ordained system;"[123] that is, according to the divine economy of salvation, the disciples' ministerial role is already preordained. Newman explains this interdependency, this *nexus mysteriorum* in the salvific economy: "Christ does not heal without His disciples, and they cannot heal except as bringing to Him."[124] Nevertheless, it is clear from the Sacred Text that the ministerial role of the disciples is to be distinguished from the saving role that Christ plays. Newman insists on this unicity of Jesus' redemptive activity and upholds the particular mediatorial role of the disciples—as exemplified in this instance—by saying that He and not the disciples is the Author of grace, Who has willed the disciples' cooperation in bringing that healing grace to others. As Newman reflects on Mark 7:31–37, he envisions the apostolic band as having been constituted as Jesus' new spiritual family who "obtaining grace through prayer," [125] thus cooperate in the salvific ministry that affords a peculiar identity to the core of that family.

Newman underscores his conviction that Christ is at all times omnipotent in the exercise of his will for salvation and yet He graciously chooses to involve the disciples in His work, so that they can cooperate with His will by exercising freely their own for the same saving purpose. However, in this sermon note Newman states that what Christ accomplished alone as Redeemer of mankind is distinct from the ongoing salvific work in which He has willed the cooperation of man in the communion of saints. Newman explains: "Christ can do all things. He created, He redeemed without any one else; but He saved [saves?] through the co-operation of others by the saints above and by the Church below." [126]

Furthermore, Newman posits that although Christ indeed wills, in accord with the economy of salvation, that grace be mediated through the cooperation of others, most especially through the ministration of the Church, this does not mean that His saving grace cannot therefore be communicated through other means outside of full communion with the Catholic Church, although such full communion is always intended as the ultimate goal, willed by God to be brought about through visible and or invisible means. In this way, Newman's theology is most akin to that expressed by the Fathers of the Second Vatican Council in *Lumen Gentium*, no. 16, and *Unitatis Redintegratio*, no. 3. [127] Newman writes: "Christ can do all things, and He does not confine Himself to [co-operation of] others, so far as this, that all over the earth, external to His Church, He hears those who call on Him. He has many ways. Every one has a guardian Angel. Case of Hagar. *But* He does this to bring them on into His Church, that *they* too may become His friends." [128]

Newman lends further support to his argument by noting how the Church's salvific solicitude is given a concrete expression through her universal exercise of intercessory prayer and celebration of the Eucharistic Sacrifice of the Mass: "And it must be recollected that the Holy Church Universal is praying everywhere (for them). Mass (continually offered)." [129] Newman concludes this sermon note by enhancing it with references to the intercessory power of Abraham and Moses in the Old Testament and showing how there is continuity in the *œconomia salutis*, insofar as Christ's explicit will was that His apostles, His "friends," continue an intercessory role in the New Testament. Thus, Newman cites Jesus' words in John 16:26–27, "In that day you shall ask in My Name: and I say not to you, that I will ask the Father for you: For the Father himself loveth you," whereby He assures them that they will be able to pray to the Heavenly Father in a direct way for all that pertains to salvation. Newman then considers this intercessory prayer (mediation) as exemplified in that of "Our Lady as our advocate and the saints as intercessors," while distinguishing it as a "lower office," assigned to them in the economy of salvation by Our Lord, indeed, an office which "stands in the higher, of the Giver of Grace."[130] By this expression, Newman intends to indicate that there is a definite link between the unique, supreme role of Christ the One Mediator and Redeemer, and the subordinate role of human cooperation in the work of salvation, most effectively exercised through the ministry of the Church and the intercessory prayer of Christians. Newman remarks in closing: "Thus, the salvation of the world is in our hands. . . . England—Birmingham. Therefore, let us *pray*."[131]

III. MARY'S INTERCESSION AS A UNIQUE EXPRESSION OF HER SPIRITUAL MATERNITY; OUR INVOCATION OF MARY AS A UNIQUE EXPRESSION OF OUR FILIAL DEVOTION

(a) *A Letter to Pusey: "Belief of Catholics Concerning the Blessed Virgin As Coloured by Their Devotion to Her"*

In the *Letter to Pusey*, Newman makes some important clarifications regarding Mary's intercessory power. While acknowledging Mary's singular, indeed, most high dignity among all creatures, especially because of her privilege of being the Mother of the Son of God Incarnate, Newman does not hesitate to refer to Christ as "our sole happiness and our sole salvation." He writes:

> May God's mercy keep me from the shadow of a thought, dimming the purity or blunting the keenness of that love of

Him, which is our sole happiness and our sole salvation! But surely when He became Man, He brought home to us His incommunicable attributes with a distinctiveness, which precludes the possibility of our lowering Him merely by our exalting a creature. He alone has entrance into our soul, reads our secret thoughts, speaks to our heart, applies to us spiritual pardon and strength. On Him we solely depend. He alone is our inward life; He not only regenerates us, but (to use the words appropriated to a higher mystery) *semper gignit*; He is ever renewing our new birth and our heavenly sonship. In this sense He may be called, as in nature, so in grace, our real Father. Mary is only our Mother by divine appointment, given us from the cross; her presence is above, not on earth; her office is external, not within us. Her name is not heard in the sacraments. Her work is not one of ministration towards us; her power is indirect. It is her prayers that avail, and her prayers are effectual by the will of Him Who is our all in all. Nor need she hear us by any innate power, or any personal gift; but by His manifestation to her of prayers which we make to her. When Moses was on the mount, the Almighty told him of the idolatry of his people at the foot of it, in order that he might intercede for them; and thus it is the Divine Presence which is the intermediating power by which we reach her and she reaches us.[132]

In this poignant passage Newman clarifies many aspects of Mary's proper role of cooperation in the economy of salvation. He affirms Mary's spiritual maternity of the Church, noting that Mary was given to us from the Cross. Nevertheless, her maternal role does not interfere with the primacy of Christ's presence working in the Church, most especially through the sacraments. Our Lady mediates and intercedes for her children, but her prayers are made effective because they derive their power not from Mary herself but from God in the order of His Providence and Will. Newman clearly distinguishes Mary's indirect, external office and power of intercession from God's direct, internal presence. Mary's mediation is compared to that of Moses in the Old Testament and the point is made that both of their intercessory roles were indirect and utterly dependent on the "intermediating power" of the "Divine Presence."

Newman reaffirms the uniqueness of Christ's role as the One Who intercedes, by His own innate power as Son of God and

Redeemer, on our behalf. Mary's mediation, which flows from the privileges of her divine maternity and spiritual maternity of the Church, is forever dependent upon and subordinate to the mediation of her Son.[133] Newman makes the analogy that just as the efficacy of Moses' prayers at Mt. Sinai derived not from Moses himself but from *Adonai* (Hebrew: "the Lord God"), so Mary's intercession is profitable for our salvation because of the merits of Christ.

In a sense, Newman provides support for both of the following adages: We pray to Mary through Christ (*Ad Mariam per Jesum*, "To Mary through Jesus"), and we pray to Christ through Mary (*Ad Jesum per Mariam*, "To Jesus through Mary"). However, in the former case, Newman would hold that there is a direct cause-and-effect relationship while, in the latter, there is nothing to suggest that we must *perforce* pray to Christ by necessarily asking the intercession of the Virgin. But, when we do pray to Our Lord relying on Mary's intercession, we know that "her prayers are effectual by the *fiat* of Him Who is our all in all." In other words, Christ's power of intercession/mediation is direct and immediately efficacious because it belongs to Him by nature. On the other hand, Mary's office is one that has been given to her in accord with God's grace, that is, in accord with her role as spiritual Mother.[134]

Newman makes further important distinctions as means of strengthening his apologetic to Pusey concerning Catholic Marian doctrine and devotion:

> He Who charges us with making Mary a divinity is thereby denying the divinity of Jesus. Such a man does not know what divinity is. Our Lord cannot pray for us, as a creature prays, as Mary prays; He cannot inspire those feelings which a creature inspires. To her belongs, as being a creature, a natural claim on our sympathy and familiarity, in that she is nothing else than our fellow. She is our pride in the poet's words, "Our tainted nature's solitary boast." We look at her without any fear, any remorse, any consciousness that she is able to read us, judge us, punish us. Our heart yearns towards that pure Virgin, that gentle Mother, and our congratulations follow her, as she rises from Nazareth and Ephesus, through the choir of angels, to her throne on high, so weak, yet so strong; so delicate, yet so glorious; so modest and yet so mighty.[135]

Therefore, one finds that Newman is most concerned to underscore Mary's proper place at the center of the communion of saints. She exercises a definite intercessory role, but this does not mean that Catholics intend to place her—a creature—on the same level as her divine Son. Mary's power of intercession is incomparable with the power exercised by Christ. Mary intercedes for us as the highest of creatures, but Jesus intercedes for us as the Son of God. Newman's perennial distinction between adoration and veneration is upheld lest, as he says to Pusey, "we should only be dragging Him from His throne, and making Him an Arian kind of God; that is, no God at all. He who charges us with making Mary a divinity, is thereby denying the divinity of Jesus. Such a man does not know what divinity is."[136]

One should note Newman's clear distinction between the adoration given to God alone and the veneration that belongs to the saints and in a special way to the Blessed Virgin Mary. Newman observed how the tone of devotion paid to Mary was altogether distinct from that paid to her eternal Son and to the Holy Trinity, as certainly must be allowed on the inspection of the Catholic services. The tone used toward Our Lord is "severe, profound, awful, as well as tender, confiding, and dutiful. Christ is addressed as true God, while He is true Man; as our Creator and Judge, while He is most loving, gentle, and gracious. On the other hand, towards Saint Mary the language employed is affectionate and ardent, as towards a mere child of Adam; though subdued, as coming from her sinful kindred."[137] However, Newman attributes to Mary's intercessory power a uniqueness in relation to that exercised by the angels and saints. In his meditation on Mary as *Refuge of Sinners*, he writes:

> And if Gentiles at Jerusalem sought Philip, because he was an apostle, when they desired access to Jesus, and Philip spoke to Andrew, as still more closely in our Lord's confidence, and then both came to Him, is it strange that the Mother should have power with the Son, distinct in kind from that of the purest angel and the most triumphant saint? If we have faith to admit the Incarnation itself, we must admit it in its fulness; why then should we be surprised by the gracious appointments which arise out of it, or are necessary to it, or are included in it? If the Creator comes on earth in the form of a servant and a creature, why may not His Mother on the other hand rise to be the

Queen of Heaven, and be clothed with the sun, and have the moon under her feet?[138]

Newman's evaluation of Mary's intercessory power reaches a quasi-zenith in his explanation of Mary's title *Virgin Most Powerful*:

> This is why the Blessed Virgin is called powerful—nay, sometimes, all-powerful, because she has, more than anyone else, more than all angels and saints, this great, prevailing gift of prayer. No one has access to the Almighty as His Mother has; none has merit such as hers. Her Son will deny her nothing that she asks; and herein lies her power. While she defends the Church, neither height nor depth, neither men nor evil spirits, neither great monarchs, nor craft of man, nor popular violence can avail to harm us; for human life is short, but Mary reigns above, a queen forever.[139]

He also speaks quite lucidly about the power of Mary's intercession, which he attributes to her special status as the Mother of God whose intimacy with her Son affords her an access to the Father which surpasses that of even the greatest of the saints.[140] Omnipotence, to be sure, is an attribute that can be ascribed to God alone. However, Our Lady participates in the Lord's power partly because of divine privilege and partly because of her merits.[141] Newman's choice of words is illuminating as he clearly wishes to counter-balance the notion of Mary's intercessory "power" with the concept of her having received this mediatorial role as a gift from God.

Likewise Newman underscores the relationship that the Virgin has in regard to the Church, of which she is both Mother and Queen. It seems that the connection between Mary's motherhood of the Church and her intercession is purposely drawn so that the one is said to hinge on the other, a point stressed by Giovanni Velocci regarding the intimate association that Mary's spiritual maternity and the motherhood of the Church have in Newman's theology. Velocci observes that one of the characters of Newman's novel, *Loss and Gain*, gazing upon a sacred image of the Virgin Mary, remarks that, for him, its preferred allegorical interpretation rests in its identification with the Church. More to the point, writing in 1864, Newman speaks of how his love for the Roman Church as the Mother of Christianity in England was accompanied by his ever-increasing devotion to the Virgin Mother to whom his college was dedicated.[142] Therefore, Father Velocci writes: "It is important here to highlight how the Church and Mary were seen by Newman always on the same level and from the same perspective. Thus, as he drew slowly closer to Rome, he drew ever more closer to Mary, and when he fell into the embrace of the Catholic Church, he likewise found himself into the arms of the Virgin Mary." [143]

The quotation from Newman's *Letter to Pusey* can be explained by another passage of the *Letter* in which Newman warns that "thus to say that prayer (and the Blessed Virgin's prayer) is omnipotent,[144] is a harsh expression in everyday prose; but, if it is explained to mean that there is nothing which prayer may not obtain from God, it is nothing else than the very promise made us in Scripture." In the very next sentence Newman resolves that "to say that Mary is the center of all being, sounds inflated and profane; yet after all it is only one way, and a natural way, of saying that the Creator and the creature meet together, and become one in her womb; and as such, I have used the expression above." [145]

In other words, one can conclude that, for Newman, the profound union between Our Lord and His Blessed Mother in the Mystery of the Incarnation—that is between Creator and creature—is the basis for Mary's exaltation and for her subsequent intercessory power as Mother of the Church. Once again Newman is careful to put all of Mary's prerogatives in proper perspective by giving them a Christological and ecclesiological point of reference.

(b) *A Letter to Pusey: "Anglican Misconceptions and*
    Catholic Excesses in Devotion to the Blessed Virgin."
    The Implications of Certain Liturgical and
    Para-liturgical Invocations of Mary

In the section of the *Letter to Pusey* entitled "Anglican Misconceptions and Catholic Excesses in Devotion to the Blessed Virgin," Newman attempts to allay the fears of Pusey with regard to the appropriateness of Mary's intercessory role. He leads Pusey along a path of logical reasoning which shows that Pusey's own acceptance of the doctrinal heritage of the Fathers of the Church, in particular that of the Greek Fathers, should also imply an acceptance of their Marian devotion which, as Newman observes, is even more florid in expressing their love of the Virgin than is that of the Latins. Newman gives as an example the fact that, in many Eastern Liturgies, Mary's intercession is formally invoked, even within the context of the Eucharistic Prayer, so that "petitions are offered," not "in the name of Jesus Christ," but in that "of the *Theotokos*." [146] Making a further application to the Roman Liturgy, Newman quips to Pusey that, "to make a rule of substituting Mary with all saints for Jesus in the public service, has more 'Mariolatry,' in it, than to alter the *Te Deum* to her in private devotion." [147]

Remaining in the sphere of liturgical and para-liturgical Marian devotion, Newman turns Pusey's attention to the *Raccolta*. In doing so, Newman even modestly criticizes the *Raccolta*'s lack of direct language in the prayers addressed to the Virgin. Nonetheless, his criticism leaves some food for thought because it proposes a very human analogy for understanding the sort of spiritual intimacy one should feel when approaching the Blessed Mother in prayer: "Its anxious observance of doctrinal exactness is almost a fault. It seems afraid of using the words 'give me,' 'make me,' in its addresses to the Blessed Virgin, which are as natural to adopt in speaking to her, as in addressing a parent or a friend. Surely we do not disparage Divine Providence when we say that we are indebted to our parents for our life, or when we ask their blessing. . . ." [148] In a sense, we can say that Newman recognizes the Church's reluctance to sacrifice dogmatic precision on the altar of devotion; instead, the Church prefers to adopt more measured language which preserves the integrity of both, "marking thereby with great emphasis that she (Mary) is nothing more than an Advocate, and not a source of mercy." [149]

(c) *A Letter to Pusey: Mary's Role of Cooperation*
   As Mediatrix of All Grace in the Œconomia Salutis

Newman makes other important observations in the *Letter to Pusey* in the section dealing with excesses in devotion to the Blessed Virgin. He reminds Pusey that the *Raccolta* "commonly uses the phrases 'pray to Jesus for me,' 'speak for me, Mary,' 'carry thou our prayers,' 'ask for us grace,' 'intercede for the people of God.'" [150] Yet, Newman observes that there is a necessary distinction between intercession of the saints on our behalf and our devotion to them. He quotes Saint Alphonsus Liguori's "proposition" that "God gives no grace except through Mary"[151] and explains that it is through her intercession that this grace is bestowed. However, he immediately notes that "intercession is one thing, devotion is another."

Newman then cites Suarez, who says: "It is the universal sentiment that the intercession of Mary is not only useful, but also in a certain manner necessary" and explains that "still it is the question of her intercession, not of our invocation of her, not of devotion to her."[152] Newman is careful to highlight that although invocation of Mary is not in any way prohibited, it certainly cannot be considered a prerequisite for salvation since in that case Protestants among others would not be saved.[153] Furthermore, Newman points out that many of the saints such as John Chrysostom, Athanasius and Augustine do not frequently or directly invoke the Blessed Mother. Salvation is the work of Christ and Mary participates in this work by means of her intercession, praying for those souls that Christ wills to save. Mary does not save anyone by her own power but relies on the power of her Son. Newman writes: "Our Lord died for those heathens who did not know Him; and His Mother intercedes for those Christians who do not know her; and she intercedes according to His will, and, when He wills to save a particular soul, she at once prays for it. I say, He will indeed according to her prayer, but then she prays according to His will."[154]

Newman makes a few, essential distinctions with regard to our devotion to Mary and belief in her intercessory power. First and foremost, he writes to Pusey that: "Though then it is natural and prudent for those to have recourse to her, who from the Church's teaching know her power, yet it cannot be said that devotion to her is a *sine-quâ-non* of salvation." Second, in responding to some Catholic authors to whom Pusey refers in his *Eirenicon* as advocating a belief that, "It is morally impossible for those to be saved who *neglect* the devotion to the Blessed Virgin," Newman makes a distinction between a "simple omission of" devotion to the Virgin Mary and "a deliberate rejection or neglect" of Marian devotion, characterized as "some positive disrespect or insult towards her, and that with sufficient knowledge," which Newman deems a "very grave act," inconsistent with official Church teaching and practice, especially for a

Catholic living "in a Catholic country,"[155] where Marian devotion is fervently practiced and even widely evident, for example, in the country's art.[156]

Newman is very careful to distinguish between direct invocation of the saints and their intercession on our behalf. Pusey finds this distinction very difficult to accept. Mary has a special place within the communion of saints; therefore, prayer addressed to her takes a special precedence. Her power of intercession derives from that of Christ, and no one can be said to obscure the uniqueness of the divine mediation. In effect, her intercessory power relies on His strength and is subordinate to His. Mary does not in any way seek to create distance between the one who prays to Christ and the individual who prays to her.

About midway through the last section of his *Letter to Pusey* Newman takes it upon himself to answer the questions raised by Pusey in the *Eirenicon* concerning whether or not it was "morally necessary," that is to say necessary for the salvation of one's soul as a Catholic Christian, "to pray to our Lady and the Saints."[157] Newman's response begins by referring to the "proposition" of Saint Alphonsus Liguori that: "God gives no grace except through Mary." Newman seems to accept the truth of Saint Alphonsus' statement while, at the same time, adhering to the distinction between direct invocation of Mary and her intercession on our behalf. Therefore, it seems that one could be led to offer the following proposition: If, as Newman postulates in the *Letter to Pusey* and elsewhere in his writings (e.g., *Sermon Notes*), Mary is an all-powerful intercessor—although he does not use the title "Mediatrix" in these instances but rather prefers the term "Advocate" or "Intercessor," who, without derogation from the unique mediation of Christ, intercedes on behalf of our salvation—could not the title *Mediatrix of All Grace*, perhaps, be an expression of this belief in Mary's all-powerful intercessory power as Advocate, even though Newman himself does not use the title "Mediatrix of All Grace," as such? The Newmanian perspective, that one need not directly invoke Mary's intercession does not seem to preclude Mary from being the "Mediatrix of all Grace" since, in accord with God's own omnipotent will and providential economy of salvation, she has been given the privilege (grace) of being for us an all-powerful intercessor who has no equal in all of creation.

(d) *Mary's Mediation: The Notes to the* Letter to Pusey

In his notes on the teaching of the Greek Church regarding the Blessed Virgin in the *Letter to Pusey*, in very scholarly fashion, Newman demonstrates that the invocation of Mary and her intercessory role on our behalf is much more developed in the East than in the West. Having offered a few examples from the Roman liturgy of instances in which Mary's intercession is invoked, he highlights numerous examples of the use of the word *presbeias* (intercession) in the Eastern liturgies in regard to the Blessed Virgin. Pusey, in his *Eirenicon*, makes several objections to the traditional Catholic devotional practices, especially as regards the Blessed Virgin Mary. In particular, he objects to the exaggerated sentimentalism that he discovered so widespread in such countries as Italy, Spain and France. Newman wisely distinguishes between doctrine and devotion and notes that the two should never be confused. Pusey, like Newman in his Anglican years, could not accept the concept of the direct invocation of the saints, yet he agrees that their intercession on our behalf is a necessary part of the life of faith in the context of the communion of saints. He confirms the distinction that Newman makes by retaining the essential distinction between our invocation of the saints and their spontaneous intercession on our behalf.[158] Thus, Pusey refers to the "intercession of the saints as a necessary fruit of perfected love," acknowledging that their intercession does not cease with death by making a specific reference to Origen's notion of the communion of saints, which is the expression of the love of neighbor that flows from the love of God and extends into eternity.[159] Pusey accepts a limited number of Marian titles that are expressive of a genuine faith in her role and in her power of intercession, even though such a role and intercessory power are quite limited. Pusey rejects the titles of Mediatrix and Co-Redemptrix[160] because he finds them irreconcilable with authentic, orthodox Christian teaching which, as he insists, must be rooted in the Sacred Scriptures and in the antiquity of the Church's Tradition. The theology of Newman expressed in the *Sermon Notes* concerning Mary's all-powerful maternal mediation is well summed up in the following exhortation in *Discourses to Mixed Congregations*. His words emphasize this unique divine privilege in direct relationship to her divine maternity, *compassio* and her exemplary pilgrimage of faith. In short, because Mary was all-faithful in her singular cooperation in the economy of salvation, so too are we exhorted by Newman to ask Mary's maternal intercession in order that we might be faithful in our cooperation. Newman writes:

> Interest your dear Mother, the Mother of God, in your success; pray to her earnestly for it; she can do more for you than any one else. Pray her by the pain she suffered, when the sharp sword went though her, pray her, by her own perseverance, which was in her the gift of God of whom you ask it for yourselves. God will not refuse you, He will not refuse her, if you have recourse to her succour. It will be a blessed thing in your last hour. . . . That dread day may be sooner or later . . . but if Mary intercedes for you, that day will find you watching and ready.[161]

Newman responds in part to Pusey's objections by quoting to him the Fathers of the Church, most especially the Greek Fathers such as Basil of Seleucia,[162] Proclus of Constantinople and Cyril of Alexandria who, in turn, rely heavily on the Scriptures as the basis of their theology. The Reverend Bertrand de Margerie, S.J., writes:

> . . . more than a century ago, J. H. Newman already took notice of the impressive thought of Basil of Seleucia. . . . For Basil, Mary's mediation is a result of divine Motherhood, a unique privilege that establishes her as Mediatrix between God and men. Basil justifies the viewpoint by a suggestive biblical reasoning: "If Peter was proclaimed 'blessed' for having confessed Christ, if Paul had been qualified by Him as 'chosen instrument' for having preached His name to the nations, what should we not think of Mary's great power, she who gave him a human body?"[163]

Father De Margerie continues his commentary on Basil of Seleucia: "We can therefore see, in the reasoning of Basil of Seleucia, a first outline of the Church's contemplation of three stages of the mystery of Marian co-redemption: the consent of the Incarnation already seen as Paschal, foreseeing Jesus' Death on the Cross, and explaining that Mary's power in the distribution of graces is the basis of our recourse to her intercession."[164] De Margerie believes that also worthy of consideration are the insights offered by the patrologist Roberto Caro: "Thus we find formulated for the first time in the fifth century (says Caro), with Basil of Seleucia, one of the most fecund principles of 'Mariology': the close link between Mary's motherhood and Word determines in her a fulness of grace by which she transcends in merit all other creatures. To be convinced of the power of Mary suggests that we have recourse to her help and her privileged intercession." [165]

(e) *Mary's Maternal Mediation and Our Filial Devotion to Her in Newman's* Sermon Notes

Here some key passages pertaining to our topic are recalled. In the first one to be mentioned Mary's maternal *compassio* is seen as an instance of her all-powerful intercessory prayer on our behalf. Newman writes: "It became her who was to be a mother to us, to be so far like other mothers as to have pain." To which Newman adds: "Here you have the maternity of Mary. You cannot weary her, she never reproaches, etc. Therefore do we pray her to help us in the *hour* of death, for she will not leave us. Especially as men get old and lose their earthly relations and those who knew them when young. Who are now our constant friends but our guardian angel, who has been with us since our youth, and Mary, who will be with us to the end." [166] In another place, Newman directs our attention to Mary's maternal mediation as a special succor we can be privileged to experience in our last agony, if we but have confidence that even though she is not the source of grace she is indeed capable of gaining the salvific grace we need through her all-powerful intercessory prayer. Newman explains: "Here is the special Office of Our Lady, and its bearing on us. She does not predestinate, she does not give grace, she does not merit grace for us, but she gains it by prayer; She gains perseverance by prayer. Thus She overcomes God, as I may say. Suitable on Rosary Sunday, *Nunc et in hora mortis nostræ*. May we die in peace." [167] In his sermon note entitled "During Exposition for Troubles in India," he concludes by saying—in the presence of the Most Blessed Sacrament—"May Our Blessed Lady, whose Maternity this day is, protect them." [168] Newman's sermon note "Falling Away" concludes with a mention of Our Lady and, immediately following that, a brief exhortation: "Prayer—pray *lest* we fall, if we fall, and for others." Finally, Mary's maternal mediation is joined to the intercession of the whole communion of saints on our behalf, in a particular way when seek salvific grace during the celebration of the Eucharistic Sacrifice. Newman writes: "He is the great High Priest Who is offering up His meritorious sacrifice, and the Mass is but the earthly presence of it. While He offers it above, the whole Church intercedes. Mary on high, and the saints with her. Thus a heavenly Mass is now going on above. Below—not a light benefit that we may intercede." [169]

(f) *Mary's Mediation in Newman's* Essay on the Development of Christian Doctrine

In several places in *An Essay on the Development of Christian Doctrine,* Newman aptly illustrates Mary's role of intercession in the doctrinal and devotional life of the Church. In the section, entitled "Dignity of His Mother and All Saints," Newman hearkens back to the early Christological heresies such as Nestorianism and Monophysitism in order to conclude emphatically that, "the votaries of Mary do not exceed the true faith, unless the blasphemers of her Son came up to it. The Church of Rome is not idolatrous, unless Arianism is orthodoxy." [170] For Newman, it is only by clinging to such heresies that one could end up entangled within a theological web that leads men to "mistake the honour paid by the Church to the human Mother for that very honour which, and which alone, is worthy of her Eternal Son." [171]

Ironically enough, as Newman demonstrates, throughout the history of the Church God has written straight with the crooked lines of heresy, so that, by means of his providential hand, the Church has been led "to determine first the conceivable greatness of a creature, and then the incommunicable dignity of the Blessed Virgin." [172] Velocci explains that:

> Newman proves the legitimacy and the development of devotion to Mary with a linear reasoning, with an essentially patristic method. The gradual comprehension of the nature of the Incarnation, of the person and of the natures in Christ lead to a clearer notion of the dignity and of the mission of the Virgin. . . . The natural result of these struggles against the heresies was the *cultus sanctorum* insofar as texts relative to mediation on the part of creatures ceased to be referred to Christ, so that a place was left for created mediators." [173]

Among these "created mediators," as Velocci explains, Newman treats of the veneration of angels in the Old Testament[174] as a "pledge of the divine presence, and manifestation of it." Furthermore, Newman's study of the early Christological controversies enabled the Church to arrive at a deeper appreciation of man's participation in the unique, ontological mediation of Christ the God-Man through a reflection on man's elevation and deification through the life of grace and divine filial adoption begun in Baptism. This theology of man's creaturely participation in the divine life, developed in a particular way by Origen and Saint Athanasius[175] upon whom Newman relies in his writings, also leads to the conclusion that "Jesus shares His titles with us."[176] Newman writes:

> But intimate indeed must be the connexion between Christ and His brethren, and high their glory, if the language which seemed to belong to the Incarnate Word belonged to them. . . . Christ, in rising, raises His saints with Him to the right hand of power. They become instinct with His life, of one body with His flesh, divine sons, immortal kings, gods. He is in them, because He is in human nature; and He communicates to them that nature, deified by becoming His, that them It may deify. He is in them by the Presence of His Spirit, and in them He is seen. They have titles of honour by participation, which are properly His.[177]

In the *Essay on Development*, Newman proceeds to offer a historical synthesis of how the various Marian doctrines of the Church have come to be formulated. One of these key doctrines (having already discussed Mary's titles of *Theotokos* and New Eve) is that of her mediation. The fondness of Newman for the Greek Fathers as ancient witnesses to this doctrine is made abundantly clear in this section. A few examples of Newman's appropriation of their thought concerning Mary's mediation will suffice. Proclus of Constantinople uses lavish phrases, which Newman terms "oratorical expressions," that make use of figurative and allegorical language to describe Mary's mediatorial role. In every case, the "oratorical expressions" of Proclus are tempered by the fact that what is predicated of Mary is, first and foremost, a statement about Christ. Therefore, when Newman quotes Proclus[178] as calling Mary "the golden altar of holocaust," the Holocaust, to which Proclus refers, is the sacrificial offering of Christ's own Body for our Redemption, a Body which He obtains from the most pure Virgin whom Proclus calls "the unsullied shell which contains the pearl of great price," "the sacred shrine of sinlessness."[179]

These expressions are substantiated by another statement of Proclus that compares Mary to a "heifer whose ashes, that is, the Lord's Body taken from her, cleanses those who are defiled by the pollution of sin." However, it is nonetheless certain that Proclus, while offering outstanding praise of Mary's cooperation in the work of our Redemption, does not fail to differentiate Mary's cooperation from the uniquely efficacious sacrifice which Our Lord alone offers by shedding His Blood on the Cross. There is a difference in preparing the victim and actually being the victim who is sacrificed. Thus, even when Proclus, as Newman cites him, says that Mary is "God's only bridge to man," one must bear in mind that Mary's mediation, as great and powerful as it truly is, could never have sufficed in order to bridge the gap between God and man caused by sin. Only the One Mediator Christ Jesus was able to accomplish that singular redemptive act. Nevertheless, together with Newman, one can affirm what Proclus declares: "Run through all of creation in your thoughts, and see if there be equal to, or greater than, the Holy Virgin Mother of God." [180]

However, just as Mary's mediatorial role of cooperation in the economy of salvation is carefully distinguished by Newman from the singular redemptive work of her Son in which she participates, so too Newman insists on the distinction between Mary's mediation and the work of the Holy Spirit. Newman makes this point in the *Essay on Development* when he distinguishes between the liturgical language used in addressing the Holy Spirit by referring to it as "indescribably majestic, solemn, and soothing" whereby we acknowledge Him as the Third Person of the Trinity Who, together with other Divine Persons, is able to "free, save and vivify us" and the language used in addressing the Virgin, which Newman characterizes as "fond," "full of sympathy and affection," "stirring and animating" to underscore her role of spiritual maternity as distinct from the sanctifying role of the Paraclete.

(g) *Mary's Mediation in Newman's Two Meditations on "Our Lord As Our Advocate Above"*

Perhaps Newman's remarks thus far in the *Letter to Pusey* can be better understood in the light of some of his other writings on mediation. In a series of meditations on the mystery of Our

Lord's Ascension, Newman dedicates two separate meditations to Our Lord as "Our Advocate Above."[181] In both of these reflections, Newman underscores the unicity and supremacy of Christ's mediation, while acknowledging the singular mediation of the Blessed Virgin in the communion of saints. He writes in the first of these two meditations: "I adore thee, O my Lord, as is most fitting, for Thou art gone to Heaven to take my part there, and defend my interests. I have one to plead for me with the Lord of all."[182] Newman then prefaces his discussion of the intercessory role of Mary, the angels and the saints by making a common-sense observation that sets up an analogy between the ordinary, daily influence of men in secular matters and the Lord's omnipotent sway in all affairs temporal and eternal. In other words, if we can ask the intercession of our fellow man in matters over which they have limited influence, then how much more should we ask the Savior of all to intercede before the Heavenly Father on our behalf. Newman's logical argumentation continues thus:

> If I am at present in the society of angels and saints, it is hard if I cannot make interest with them that the fellowship began between them and me should endure. Men of the world know how to turn such opportunities to account in their own matters. If Thou hast given me Mary for my Mother, who, O my God! is Thine, cannot I now establish, as it were, a family interest in her, so that she will not cast me off at the last? If I have the right to pray and the gift of impetration, may I not thereby secure that perseverance to the end, which I cannot merit, and which is the sign and assurance of my destination?[183]

Of tremendous significance and pertinence to our topic is Newman's explicit reference to Mary as his Mother, which he makes with all deference to the unique Mother-Son relationship that she has with Christ. In fact, if it were not for the latter, the former would not be possible. Newman, tenderly addressing Christ the Advocate, seeks, as it were, His permission to deepen his relationship to Mary as His spiritual Mother—a relationship which has consequences not only in terms of the present but also the future, indeed, for eternal life. Newman is obviously concerned to exercise the gift and "right" of intercessory prayer appropriately, so that fully availing himself of this particular means he might procure for himself the necessary grace to arrive at eternal salvation—the aim toward which all prayer is ultimately directed.

His second meditation on this topic is equally significant and pertinent. Newman humbly addresses Our Lord, recognizing his lowliness in the sight of Christ's holiness. Moreover, Newman realizes that despite his lowliness the prayers of the Virgin and the saints redound unto the glory of God since their prayers strengthen him in doing the work of the Church—the salvation of the world. Newman's attitude is one of urgency; he is consumed by a holy zeal and fear of the Lord for which he knows he will be accountable. However, Newman, it must be noticed, gets carried away in his zeal almost as to suggest that prayer becomes obsolete in the "grave" [184]—a teaching which does not square well with the Church's official teaching on purgatory insofar as the holy souls there not only can benefit from our prayers but their prayers can also be beneficial to us.

Nevertheless, Newman's other statement that there is no possibility of merit in purgatory is true, if he means by that statement that one's eternal destination (i.e., heaven) is already determined by being in purgatory, based on the faith, good works and merits of the present life. The purpose of purgatory, however, is not a reward given for good done; on the contrary, it is a process by which one is purged of the temporal punishment due to sin. In this sense, perhaps, one can understand why Newman does not consider "merit" to be an appropriate word to be predicated of the souls in purgatory. With these clarifications made, in the hope that the intentions of the Venerable Newman have been properly comprehended and presented, one can still appreciate his ardent address to Our Lord and its relevance for the present discussion:

> O my Lord Jesus, I will use the time. It will be too late to pray, when life is over. There is no prayer in the grave—there is no meriting in purgatory. Low as I am in Thy all holy sight, I am strong in Thee, strong through Thy Immaculate Mother, through Thy saints: and thus I can do much for the Church, for the world, for all I love. O let not the blood of souls be on my head! O let me not walk my own way without thinking of Thee.... I will ever lift up my heart to Thee. I will never forget that Thou art my Advocate at the Throne of the Highest.[185]

(h) *Mary As Mediatrix and Advocate in*
   Newman's Meditations and Devotions

In the *Memorandum of the Immaculate Conception*, Newman speaks of the intercession of saints as the "White Way" and contrasts it with the "Red Way," which is the redemptive sacrifice of Jesus. Interestingly, while maintaining a clear line of demarcation between the two "ways," Newman also stresses a certain commonality between them when he asserts that "the obedience of Mary becomes the cause of salvation to all mankind. Moreover, the distinct way in which Mary does this is pointed out when she is called by the early Fathers an Advocate. The word is used of Our Lord and the Holy Ghost—of Our Lord, as interceding for us in His own Person; of the Holy Ghost, as interceding in the Saints."[186] Consequently, the intercessory role of the Blessed Virgin is an integral part of the "White Way," which derives its strength from the Cross but which is distinct in kind and form from the "Red Way." This distinction is essential since it helps to put into proper perspective that the mediation of Our Lady and the other saints directly flows from the Cross and depends upon it.

Newman's meditation *"Ave Maris Stella"* is a reaffirmation of the above distinctions as he explains that Mary is the brightly shining star whose brilliance points out for us the way to Christ Who alone is the Light of the World enlightening every man coming into it, as Saint John reminds us in his Gospel.[187] She shines, as Newman indicates, "with the light of Christ." She does not shine for herself or with her own light. Rather, she shines so that catching sight of her we might eventually be brought to the safe embrace of her Son even when we are buffeted by the tempests of life's many trials, tribulations and temptations. Mary does not and cannot save us by herself; her prayers are propitious and salutary to the extent that they assist us, so that we might one day safely reach the harbor of our eternal salvation. She does not give us grace as though she were its source. Rather, she mediates grace to us which flows like an ocean of mercy from the throne of grace—the fountain of which is the Triune Godhead.[188]

The Litanies are also a prime example of the finest expression of Newman's understanding of the power of the intercessory role that the Blessed Virgin plays in the life of the Church. The litanies composed by Newman generally encapsulate his profound appreciation of Mary's role in the communion of saints and highlights the ease with which the Church approaches her in prayer. The concluding prayer of the Litany of the Holy Name of Mary is an example: "O Almighty God, Who seest how earnestly we desire to place ourselves under the shadow of the name of Mary, vouchsafe, we beseech Thee, that as often as we invoke her in our need, we may receive grace and pardon from Thy holy heaven, through Christ our Lord." [189] The Litany of the Seven Dolours of the Blessed Virgin Mary concludes with a list of invocations that demonstrates Newman's confidence in Our Lady's power of intercession: "Preserve us from sudden death. . . . Succor us in our last agony. . . . Gain for us the gift of perseverance. . . . Aid us before the judgment seat. . . . We beseech thee, hear us." The concluding prayer for that litany reads as follows: "O Lord Jesus Christ, God and Man, grant, we beseech Thee, that Thy dear Mother Mary, whose soul the sword pierced in the hour of Thy Passion, may intercede for us, now and in the hour of our death, through Thine own merits, O Saviour of the world. . . ." [190]

One also discovers a connection between Newman's theology of Our Lady's mediation and his personal devotion to the recitation of the Holy Rosary. A particular illustration of this connection is Newman's meditation on Mary as "Help of Christians," in which he describes how Mary has exercised her intercessory role on at least five important occasions, including four major battles in the history of the Christians' dealings with the Turks. It is believed that as a result of her intercession, and the prayers of the Associations of the Rosary all over the Christian world, that these battles were won. The most notable of these victories gained was that at the Battle of Lepanto, in which the Turks were overcome, thus sparing Europe from Muslim control. Consequently, Newman explains, Pope Saint Pius V introduced Mary's title of *"Auxilium Christianorum"* into her Litany and Pope Gregory XIII, his successor, dedicated the first Sunday in October, the day of victory, to Our Lady of the Rosary.[191] Father Blehl explains that "long before Pope Leo XIII instituted the regular preaching of the rosary and October as a month of devotion to her, Newman had introduced daily recitation of the rosary in his own church of the Oratory of Birmingham." [192] Father Friedel attests to the fact that Newman was introduced to the rosary in

1836. Furthermore, he notes that the rosary had a special place in the devotional life of the elderly Newman, so much so that when the aging Cardinal was no longer capable of praying the Divine Office,[193] he would finger his beads as a practice in which "he found solace" on a daily basis. Friedel adds the following: "Towards the end, even this consolation was denied him because of the lack of sensitiveness in his fingers."[194]

When Newman makes reference to the devotional practice of the Holy Rosary, he is careful to underscore that what interested him most was not so much the petitions made imploring Mary's intercession but the reflections made on the mysteries of the life of Christ. Blehl comments:

> It was, however, not so much saying the rosary as a form of petition for Mary's intercession that appealed to Newman; rather it was the opportunity it presented of meditating on the full range of the Christian mysteries, with which Mary was so intimately connected—the economy of the incarnation in its entire scope. This is another example of Newman's recognition that Mary is not the rival of her Son but the "the handmaid of the Lord," His servant, and as such her glories were "for the sake of her Son."[195]

Conclusion

In concluding this chapter on Cardinal Newman's understanding of Mary's spiritual maternity, intercessory role and corresponding titles of Mediatrix and Advocate, it should be likewise evident that any discussion of mediation must by its very nature weigh upon the present theological discussion of the title of Co-Redemptrix. Although Newman's own specific contribution to the latter discussion is treated in Chapter Seven, the words of the noted Mariologist René Laurentin will serve well to summarize what Newman anticipated in his own theology and spirituality regarding the relationship between the Church's doctrine of mediation and the theology of the co-redemption, insofar as it keeps clear the line of demarcation between Our Lord's salvific mediation and Our Lady's participation or cooperation in the same. In fact, Father Laurentin cites a text, as we will discover, which bears a close resemblance to what Newman says in his *Letter to Pusey*: "And how, again, is there anything of incommunicable greatness in His Death and Passion, if He Who is alone in the garden, alone upon the Cross, alone in the Resurrection, after all is not alone, but shared His solitary work with His Blessed Mother,– with her to whom, when He entered on His ministry, He said for our instruction, not as grudging her her proper glory, 'Woman, what have I to do with thee?'"[196] Again, along similar lines, Newman writes in a sermon note for Palm Sunday (March 24) "on Our Lord's Agony": "And now look at that one only God, as we contemplate Him at this time of year. He is still one, sole, and alone. He was one in heaven; He is one in the garden, one on the tree. He trod the winepress *alone*."[197] Laurentin writes:

> That Mary was an integral part of the mystery of the Incarnation, founding member of Christ and of the Church, is evident. . . . Is she also an integral part of the mystery of redemption? This is less evident, more controversial. The preconciliar theology sought to promote the co-redemption. It did not have success. The expression was contested by many classical theologians who criticized it for putting on the same level the Redeemer and "Co-Redemptrix." Pope Pius XII, whose ordinary Magisterium approved the co-redemption—according to certain Mariologists—explicitly declared to Father Balič, President of the Mariological Academia, from which this theme was assigned to the Congress of Lourdes, that it was a question open to the free discussion of theologians. The Council deliberately avoided this expression. It feared, and rightly so, to obscure the fact that Christ is the "one Mediator" (1 Tim 2,5), the only Redeemer. *In effect: He alone had suffered condemnation and the bloody passion, He alone was crucified, He alone died on the Cross, He alone rose in a divine and nocturnal solitude.* Mary, who had a mediatorial function at the beginning of the Incarnation, gave to the world from that moment the only Mediator. From that point forward she does not have a mediatorial role if not with Christ and in Christ, even if she maintained a generous and dynamic initiative, as her intervention at the Wedding Feast of Cana and her presence on Calvary demonstrate. In fact the Incarnation makes of Christ essentially the only Mediator. He is not an intermediary, but a bridge that pertains to two sides: God with God and man with men, since he joins God with man in His person. Therefore He is an ontological mediator: there is no longer any mediation if not in Him and together with Him; and this is valid also for Mary. In this picture, therefore, one must

locate the singular participation of Mary in the redeeming sacrifice, since the confines that we have just fixed are not made to exclude but to establish the association of a creature to the Redeemer Who is God in person [emphasis added].[198]

Perhaps, Father's Friedel's words are a most appropriate summation of Newman's contribution to Mariology (as exemplified in the *Letter to Pusey*), which this chapter has sought to analyze:

> Newman has acted as a guide to the many that have made an attempt to delve into the early history of Marian doctrine and devotion. He has given us an impetus to the study of the great Fathers in their teachings on the Blessed Virgin. His greatest merit is, perhaps the re-insistence on the doctrine of the spiritual maternity of Mary, since she is the Second Eve, and the psychological investigation of devotion to Our Lady.[199]

SUMMARY OF CHAPTER SIX

1) The *nexus mysteriorum* has as its central dogma the Incarnation, from which flow the doctrine of mediation, the sacramental principle and the doctrines of the intercession of the saints, their merits, their invocation and cult in the life of the Church.

2) Newman's ecclesiology and theology of the communion of saints underwent significant refinement and development from his Anglican to Catholic periods. It must be noted that such a development of his thought was due in large part to the influence of the theological and spiritual writings of John Keble and Hurrell Froude. According to Newman, Mary exercises her role of mediation as the preeminent member of the Mystical Body of Christ, which Body is made up of both visible and invisible members and of which she is the first believer and the first redeemed. Mary, both in the practice of her faith and in the exercise of her privileges, especially that of mediation, is always treated from within an ecclesial context.

3) One of the principal activities by which the believer cooperates in the salvific work of Christ is prayer. The chief work of the saints in heaven *pro nobis* is that of intercession. Mary is the disciple of Christ *par excellence* and exemplifies the power of intercessory prayer to the highest degree as Mother of the Church, of the Faithful, and Queen of Heaven and Earth, the Angels and the Saints (cf. Diff II, 76).

4) Mary's intercessory power is clearly a divine privilege which she exercises in subordination to the supreme mediation of Christ and by His sovereign will. The efficacy of Mary's prayer, like that of all believers, is dependent upon that of Christ, Who makes continual intercession on our behalf at the right hand of the Father. In this way, Newman's theology of mediation most prophetically anticipates the treatment of creaturely participation in the one, supreme mediation of Christ the God-Man and sole Redeemer, as expounded upon in *Lumen Gentium*.

5) Newman is careful to distinguish between *latria* (adoration belonging by right to the Triune God alone) and *dulia* (the veneration given to the saints). Furthermore, Newman draws a clear line of demarcation between the mediation or intercessory prayer of Our Lord as a Divine Person and that of Mary as a fellow creature with us, albeit the highest of all creatures (cf. Diff II, 85)

6) In addition, Newman highlights the uniqueness of the cult of Our Lady (*hyperdulia*) within the cult of the saints (*dulia*). Mary plays a pivotal role as Mother of both the Head and the members of the Body of Christ. The prayer of Mary is considered more powerful than that of all the angels and saints because she is their Queen. Indeed, Mary's intercessory power is understood by Newman to be all-powerful insofar as it is the great exemplification of Christian intercessory prayer. Furthermore, her intercession on our behalf is a privileged means, by which God communicates to us His saving grace—albeit to be distinguished fundamentally from the intercession of Christ as God-Man, the intercession of the Holy Spirit, and the mediation of the Church's sacraments (cf. Diff II, 84–85).

7) Newman argues that there is an essential difference between the intercession of the saints and our devotion to them, by which we actively invoke their intercession. In other words, whether or not we directly invoke the saints, that is to say manifest explicit devotion to them, they nonetheless can and do intercede on our behalf. This distinction Newman draws in part, from the distinction of Francisco Suarez, who proposed that God communicated all saving grace through Mary's intercession but not necessarily through our direct invocation of her and always in direct subordination to Christ the only Redeemer and Supreme Mediator. In this context, Newman writes: "Our Lord

died for those heathens who did not know Him; and His Mother intercedes for those Christians who do not know her; and she intercedes according to His will, and, when He wills to save a particular soul, she at once prays for it. I say, He wills indeed according to her prayer, but then she prays according to His will" (cf. Diff II, 105).

8) One can safely infer from Newman's writings his belief in Mary as the Mediatrix of All Grace. However, several important factors need to be considered to arrive at such a conclusion. First and foremost, Newman's understanding of Mary's cooperation as *Theotokos* led him to consider Mary as the Mediatrix of all grace, insofar as she is the chosen instrument (not just physical) who cooperates with the Father's plan for the conception of the Author of grace in Whose life she had a full participation from the moment of her own Immaculate Conception. Second, Newman believed that Mary's divine maternity included a spiritual maternity whereby her cooperation in the *œconomia salutis* extended beyond her earthly life to include her active intercession on behalf of all the redeemed, most especially on behalf of the members of Christ's Mystical Body, the Church. Thus, Newman discerns continuity and fulfillment in her intercessory role which, beginning on earth, continues in the life of heaven and is there perfected (cf. Diff II, 72, 84).

9) Newman's clear predilection for Our Lady's title of "Advocate," as this title was applied to her, for example, in the writings of Saint Irenæus of Lyons, stems from the patristic theology of the New Eve, which in turn is firmly based on their interpretation of the *Protoevangelium*, hence also the significance of the Marian title of "the Mother of the Living," and the pericopes that highlight Mary's maternal mediation, such as at Cana, Calvary and in the Cenacle at Pentecost, all culminating in the vision of the woman of Revelation 12. Mary's mediation as "Our Advocate" is a most certain instance of her spiritual maternity, that is of her spiritual motherhood of the Church, and therefore constitutes for Newman an indispensable and integrated part of her cooperation in the economy of salvation. For example, in the *Letter to Pusey*, Newman writes: "Her office above is one of perpetual intercession for the faithful militant, and that our very relation to her must be that of clients to a patron, and that, in the eternal enmity that exists between the woman and the serpent,

while the serpent's strength lies in being the Tempter, the weapon of the Second Eve and the Mother of God is prayer" (Diff II, 73).

10) The early depictions of Mary in the catacombs in the *orans* position—which Newman considers to be developed by the Christians as a profound meditation on the vision of the mother and child in Genesis 3:15 and Revelation 12, is a concrete piece of evidence in the Tradition for Mary's maternal mediation and of the Church's corresponding filial invocation of her.

11) Furthermore, because of Newman's acceptance of Saint Alphonsus Liguori's belief that "God gives no grace except through Mary" (cf. Diff II, 105), one can safely infer from his writings that he accepted belief in the doctrine of Mary "Mediatrix of All Grace," although he does not use the title as such and would modify this belief by saying that it is not so much a matter of our direct invocation of her as it is a matter of her all-powerful intercession on our behalf according to the will of Him Who "wills that all men be saved and come to the knowledge of the truth." For example, Newman plainly writes in the *Letter to Pusey*: "It is her prayers that avail, and her prayers are effectual by the *fiat* of Him Who is our all in all" (Diff II, 84).

12) Newman affirms in his *Letter to Pusey* that devotion to the Blessed Virgin Mary is not a *sine-quâ-non* of salvation. That having been said, Newman demonstrated a great personal devotion to Our Lady and encouraged it among his flock. In the *Sermon Notes*, for example, he writes about the importance and efficacy of Mary's intercession at the moment of death, such as is contained in the last line of the *Ave Maria*. Newman had a special devotion to the Holy Rosary until his dying day.

13) Of enormous influence on Newman's theological concept of Mary's mediation is the thought of the Greek Fathers, most noteworthy being the "panegyrical" language of Saint Cyril of Alexandria at the Council of Ephesus, the "oratorical" language of Saint Peter Chrysologus and the theology of Mary's mediation of all salvific grace put forth in the writings of Saint Basil of Seleucia and Proclus of Constantinople.

14) Newman differentiates between the *Red Way* (the redemptive Sacrifice of Christ) and the *White Way* (the intercession of Our Lady and the other saints), stressing the dependence of the latter on the former—even as he shows their interrelatedness.

Does Newman Treat of Mary as Co-Redemptrix?
An Analysis of the Letter to Pusey

I. INTRODUCTORY REMARKS

To this point, we have considered how Newman's Mariology is centered around a theology of Mary's cooperation in the *œconomia salutis* by studying his use of the Sacred Scriptures in principal Marian sermons, his reliance on the teachings of the Fathers of the Church, his theology of Mary as *Theotokos* and New Eve, her *compassio*, her spiritual maternity or motherhood of the Church, and her role as Mediatrix (of All Grace) and Advocate. It is hoped that this work has successfully demonstrated that the aforementioned doctrines and the titles intimately associated to them are clearly set forth in both the theological and spiritual writings of Newman and that they are treated by him as essential doctrines or titles having to do with a full and proper understanding of Mary's cooperation in the *œconomia salutis*. Nevertheless, one is still left with the very difficult theological question of the Co-Redemption and the related Marian title of "Co-Redemptrix," or, as Newman refers to it, "Co-Redemptress."

It is not the intention of this Chapter to take into consideration the whole history of this theological question and to relate it to Newman's thought, for such an endeavor is clearly beyond the scope of this discussion, as was already clearly indicated in the Introduction to the book. Rather, what is intended here is to offer the reader a perspective from which this precise topic can be viewed in relationship to the thought of the Venerable Newman. In other words, what concrete contribution did the Venerable Newman make to our topic, bearing in mind that it may or may not have been his direct desire or intent to make such a contribution to this precise topic. Nevertheless, this chapter, after a brief introduction, endeavors to deal with the topic of

Co-Redemption in a more direct fashion through a critical analysis of its mention in the *Letter to Pusey*.

One of the more significant findings of this work, as has already been made clear, is that at the very heart of Newman's Mariology lies the theology of Mary's real and meritorious cooperation in the economy of salvation, that is, in the work of our Redemption. Newman clearly understands Mary to have fully and responsibly participated in the Lord's work of Redemption, not simply through a physical or biological union, but through a spiritual communion that progressed together with the unfolding of all the mysteries of Our Lord's life. Father Blehl writes: "By the Incarnation the Word was made flesh; He was conceived and born of a woman, and she was destined to be associated with Him, not just by giving birth to Him, but in the total economy of the Incarnation."[1] In his meditation on the Fourth Station of the Cross, "Jesus Meets His Mother," for example, Newman explains his theology of the *nexus mysteriorum* in relationship to Mary's cooperation:

> There is no part of the history of Jesus but Mary has her part in it. There are those who profess to be His servants, who think that her work was ended when she bore Him, and after that she had nothing to do but disappear and be forgotten. But we, O Lord, Thy children of the Catholic Church, do not so think of Thy Mother. She brought the tender infant into the Temple, she lifted Him up in her arms when the wise men came to adore Him. She fled with Him to Egypt, she took Him up to Jerusalem when He was twelve years old. He lived with her at Nazareth for thirty years. She was with Him at the marriage-feast. Even when He had left her to preach, she hovered about Him. And now she shows herself as He toils along the Sacred Way with His cross on His shoulders.[2]

Again, for example, in his meditation on the Thirteenth Station, "Jesus Is Taken Down from the Cross," Newman considers how Mary's cooperation in the work of the Redeemer would not falter at the Cross. Rather, Mary's cooperation at the Cross is an expression of her maternal *compassio*, by which she is united to the divine, redemptive love and suffering of her Son: "We rejoice in this great mystery. He has been hidden in thy womb, He has lain in thy bosom, He has been suckled at thy breasts, He has been carried in thy arms—and now that He is dead, He is placed upon thy lap."[3] In this work, some instances have been highlighted in which Newman connects Mary in a direct way with such mysteries of Redemption as the Annunciation, the Presentation in the Temple and the Crucifixion, not unlike the citation we find in *Lumen Gentium*:

> The predestination of the Blessed Virgin as Mother of God was associated with the Incarnation of the Divine Word: in the designs of the Divine Providence she was the gracious Mother of the Divine Redeemer here on earth, and above all others and in a singular way the generous associate and humble handmaid of the Lord. She conceived, brought forth, and nourished Christ, she presented Him to the Father in the Temple, shared her Son's sufferings as He died on the Cross.[4]

However, for the purpose of this present chapter, the *Letter to Pusey* is of invaluable importance. Indeed, the apologetical remarks of Newman in the *Letter to Pusey* concerning our topic need to be introduced by way of a brief analysis of another statement of Newman taken from his *Apologia pro Vita Sua*: "The Catholic Church allows no image of any sort, material or immaterial, no dogmatic symbol, no rite, no sacrament, no saint, not even the Blessed Virgin herself, to come between the soul and its Creator. It is face to face, 'solus cum solo,' in all matters between man and God. He alone creates; He alone has redeemed; before His aweful eyes we go in death; in the vision of Him is our eternal beatitude."[5]

What does Newman mean by this statement and how does it apply to our present discussion? The distinctions that Newman makes are essential. The work of our creation, redemption, sanctification and judgment can be attributed to the Triune God alone in their full and proper sense. The mediation of the Church, her sacraments and sacramentals, her belief in the communion of saints and their veneration together with Marian devotion/invocation are all means by which the creature has access to God and eternal salvation (beatitude), but they cannot replace the necessity for the believing creature to have a direct, personal relationship with the Triune God Himself, either here or in the world to come.

Some might be tempted to dismiss the significance of Newman's adage *"solus cum solo"* by interpreting it along the same lines that accompany a strict interpretation of the Reformation principles of *Solus Christus, Sola Scriptura, Sola Fides, Sola Gratia*—given Newman's Evangelical and Anglican background—but this would lead to a gross misrepresentation of Newman's Catholic understanding of the enunciated principle. Newman, unlike the Reformers, does not intend his adage or theological principle to eschew certain Church doctrines or to underestimate their importance. On the contrary, Newman utilizes "solus cum solo," as a measuring stick by which all other doctrines—which are rightfully taught and believed by the Catholic Church (*fides quæ*)—can be assimilated into a personal relationship of faith in God (*fides qua*) and thus also adhered to according to the Church's hierarchy of truths. Thus, the primacy of God in the economy of salvation is never jeopardized and the subordinate, correlated doctrines are understood as enhancing, not inhibiting one's personal relationship to Him.[6] A proper interpretation of Newman's principle of *solus cum solo* should be kept in mind in our present discussion of Newman's theology and the title of Mary as "Co-Redemptrix."

II. THE MENTION OF MARY AS "CO-REDEMPTRESS" IN THE "LETTER TO PUSEY"

Only on one occasion in his *Letter to Pusey* does Newman directly refer to Mary as Co-Redemptrix:[7]

> ...when they [ordinary men] found you with the Fathers calling her Mother of God, Second Eve, and Mother of all the Living, the Mother of Life, the Morning Star, the Mystical New Heaven, the Scepter of Orthodoxy, the All-undefiled Mother of Holiness, and the like, they would have deemed it a poor compensation for such language that you protested against her being called a co-redemptress and a priestess.[8]

Newman's response is a criticism of Pusey's inconsistency. In other words, if Pusey finds acceptable the whole panoply of Marian titles utilized by the Fathers of the Church, Newman asks why he should bristle at Mary's being called "co-redemptress," or even "priestess" for that matter. Interestingly enough, Newman never goes on to explain in the *Letter to Pusey* what he

understands either title to mean, which, perhaps, is why a deter-
mination concerning his understanding of the title "co-redemptress" cannot be made solely based on this isolated remark to
Pusey; rather, it should be derived from the whole of his Mariological thought as is the aim of this discussion. Hence also the
necessity of reading this chapter with a view to what is said in
the previous chapters of this book, even if they do not pretend to
offer a comprehensive treatment of Newman's Mariological
thought.

Certainly, however, for our immediate purposes, it is most
appropriate to arrive at an understanding of Newman's response
to Pusey cited above in relation to certain other significant statements of Newman which precede and follow it. The overall
context in which it is used is Newman's discussion of the relationship between faith and devotion in regard to Mary. This is a
highly significant point of Newman's *Letter to Pusey* since one of
the most crucial issues that Newman had to clarify for Pusey
was that there exists an essential distinction between what the
Church official teaches as immutable doctrine and what are her
devotions varying from time to time and place to place and
likewise subject to change depending on whether or not the
Church considers them appropriate expressions of her orthodox
teaching. In other words, Newman strives in his apologetical and
ecumenical letter to imbue Pusey with a most certain notion of
this distinction between doctrine and devotion along similar lines
to the distinction that is now commonly made between Tradition
with a capital "T" and tradition(s) with a lower case "t," viz.,
"Tradition" meaning the irreformable deposit of Faith as taught
and lived in the Church down through the centuries, and "tradi-
tion(s)" signifying, among other things, the cultural and historical tokens of that deposit.

III. "BELIEF OF CATHOLICS, CONCERNING
THE BLESSED VIRGIN, AS COLOURED BY THEIR
DEVOTION TO HER"[9]

It is precisely in this section having to do with devotion—as
distinct from the first half of the *Letter*, which focuses on the
Church's official Marian doctrine—that Newman mentions the

title "co-redemptress." Newman's remark clearly reveals that he does not detect in its use anything contrary to the Marian doctrine of the faith hitherto expounded on. Furthermore, he encourages Pusey's acceptance of it, at least as a valid devotional expression, precisely based on the fact that Pusey, like Newman, has given every indication of accepting the doctrinal and devotional authenticity of other Marian titles used by the Fathers of the Church. He has in mind those titles directly connected to the theology of the New Eve and the titles referred to in the panegyric of Our Lady by Saint Cyril of Alexandria at the Council of Ephesus. From Newman's tone in the *Letter*, the reader could get the impression that Newman considered the latter Marian titles to be even more compelling expressions of the Church's belief in Mary's divine privileges than the title "co-redemptress." Furthermore, Newman duly notes that although some of the modern Catholic writers whom Pusey criticized in the *Eirenicon* perhaps exceeded the Fathers in their devotional use of the title of "co-redemptress," "still the line cannot be logically drawn between the teachings of the Fathers concerning the Blessed Virgin and our own. . . . It is impossible, I say, in a doctrine like this, to draw a line clearly between truth and error, right and wrong." [10]

Newman proceeds to argue in favor of a legitimate use of the title "co-redemptress," by basing its devotional use on the notion of doctrinal development, which he deems a concrete and living process. As the Church's understanding of a doctrine develops, so too do the Church's devotional expressions of that doctrine. Nevertheless, Newman is well aware of Pusey's concern that such devotional expressions can tend to be exaggerated in the writings of some and therefore also end up distorting the truths which they were originally intended to express. Newman sums up his general attitude concerning this topic thus: ". . . for myself, I prefer such whenever it is possible, to be first generous and then just, to grant full liberty of thought and to call it to account when abused." [11] It seems clear, therefore, from the immediate context in which Newman responds to Pusey's rejection of the title "co-redemptress," that he believes it to be a legitimate devotional expression of orthodox Catholic belief in Mary's cooperation in the economy of salvation, apart from the question of any abuses that the use of such a title could possibly undergo in the writings of individual Catholics. Newman, however, believes that such an abuse of devotional expressions should neither automatically take away from their legitimate use nor certainly lead us to the extreme of denying the doctrinal truths that they are meant to convey.

In any case, Newman's response encouraging Pusey to accept the title "co-redemptress," along with the other Marian titles mentioned, is particularly enlightening when one takes into consideration, for example, the commentary he makes earlier in the *Letter* concerning Saint Peter Chrysologus' use of "oratorical language," to explicate his understanding of the essential doctrine "that the Blessed Virgin had a real, meritorious co-operation, a share which had a 'hire' and a 'price' in the reversal of the Fall." [12] It seems that in both cases, given the fact that the primary issues at stake were both the orthodox teaching of the Fathers of the Church on Mary's cooperation in the *œconomia salutis* and an ecumenical understanding and acceptance of the same, Newman's promotion of the title "co-redemptress" is most acceptable, insofar as he saw it as constituting a doctrinally sound and devotional title authenticated by the Sacred Tradition. Indeed he viewed it on a kind of par with the panegyrical titles used by Saint Cyril in the third ecumenical council, which form an integral part of his eloquent and most orthodox defense of the title *Theotokos*, as an expression that succinctly expresses and safeguards, at one and the same time, the essential doctrines of the two-natures in the one Person of Christ and that of Mary's divine motherhood of the same Christ.

Another of Newman's more significant statements that can be said to pertain to the question of the Co-Redemption is the following:

> May God's mercy keep me from the shadow of a thought, dimming the purity or blunting the keenness of that love of Him, which is our sole happiness and our sole salvation! But surely He became man, He brought home to us His incommunicable attributes with a distinctiveness, which precludes the possibility of our lowering Him merely by our exalting a creature. He alone has an entrance into our soul, reads our secret thoughts, speaks to our hearts, applies to us spiritual pardon and strength. On Him solely we depend. He alone is our inward life; He not only regenerates us, but (to use the words

appropriated to a higher mystery) *semper gignit*; He is ever renewing our new birth and our heavenly sonship. In this sense He may be called, as in nature, so in grace, our real Father. Mary is our Mother by divine appointment, given us from the Cross; her presence is above on earth; her office is external, not within us. Her name is not heard in the administration of the sacraments. Her work is not one of ministration towards us; her power is indirect. It is her prayers that avail, and her prayers are effectual by the *fiat* of Him Who is our all in all. Nor need she hear us by any innate gift, or any personal gift; but by His manifestation to her of the prayers which we make to her. When Moses was on the Mount, the Almighty told him of the idolatry of his people at the foot of it, in order that he might intercede for them; and thus it is the Divine Presence which is the intermediating Power by which we reach her and she reaches us.[13]

Several observations are needed on this text. Newman is a champion of the love of Christ which must reign sovereignly in our hearts. A debt of gratitude is owed to Him which is owed to no other. The gift of salvation and the goal of eternal beatitude are gifts which God alone can give, even if He has willed that we cooperate, as Mary most fully did, in the work of our own salvation. Nonetheless, one's cooperation and therefore Mary's cooperation can never be put on a par with the singular redemptive work of Our Lord. One should not interpret Newman as having tried to convince Pusey that eternal life can be attained apart from one's communion with Mary and the saints or solely in relationship to Christ. Newman's point is that the definitive anchor of our salvation is Christ and that our communion with Mary and the saints in heaven is only possible if we develop, first and foremost, our relationship to Christ the God-Man and Redeemer, and furthermore that our communion with Mary and the saints should foster our striving for eternal communion (*koinonia*) with the Triune Godhead.

Certainly, as Newman reflects, Mary is our spiritual Mother to whom we were entrusted by Our Lord at the foot of the Cross in the person of the beloved disciple. Furthermore, Mary's obedient and loving cooperation in the work of our Redemption according to the divine plan is brought about in a unique way through her spiritual maternity, that is to say, through her powerful maternal mediation/intercession. Nevertheless, Newman clarifies for Pusey that Mary's spiritual motherhood and maternal mediation do not have the same salvific efficacy as the actual presence of Christ within us. For Newman, as can be gleaned clearly from the study of his writings in Chapters One through Six, Mary is most definitely a conduit, a minister, a means, an instrument of grace, and an instrument of our salvation; but neither can she or does she or any other creature make the claim on our souls that Our Lord has, since grace is the free gift of the supernatural life of God within our souls and not the life of Mary within our souls—though she herself fully shares in this supernatural life as far as a creature can.

This latter point serves to underscore an essential distinction between conformity to Christ as adoptive sons (*filii in Filio*) through the grace of Baptism and the other sacraments, and the reception of grace through devotion to Mary as a direct consequence of the primary relationship to Christ. Once again, Newman is careful to highlight the interconnectedness among the mysteries of Mary's divine maternity of Christ the Redeemer and Head of the Church, her motherhood of the redeemed and spiritual maternity of the members of Christ's Mystical Body, the Church.

The theological principle of *communicatio idiomatum* ("communication of idioms") is employed by Newman when he refers to Christ as our "real Father" by nature and by grace, in contradistinction to Mary who is only "our Mother by divine appointment," that is, by grace alone. There is no tinge of modalism in Newman's thought. What Newman intends to say is that Our Lord's relationship to us has a primacy over Mary's relationship to us since this relationship is inherent to our existence—resulting from the fact that He is the Son of God and therefore from all eternity our Creator and Sanctifier together with the Father and the Spirit, notwithstanding the fact that only the Second Person of the Blessed Trinity and not the Father and the Holy Spirit became Incarnate and died on the Cross as our Redeemer. Therefore, one can speculate that even if the Father and the Holy Spirit fully take part in the work of the Redemption, and the singular redemptive acts of the Incarnation, Death and Resurrection are acts most properly attributed to the Second Person of the Trinity and not to the Father and the Holy Spirit,

Mary's full cooperation as a creature in these singular redemptive mysteries need not detract from the use of the title of "Co-Redemptrix" for Mary according to Newman's understanding of the *communicatio idiomatum*: this is so precisely because he would have clearly understood that the title of "Co-Redemptrix"—whether considered from a doctrinal or devotional standpoint—could never entail attributing to the Virgin Mother of God a share in the work of Redemption that either would put her on a par with Christ the God-Man and sole Redeemer or suggest that her human cooperation was in some way to be equated with the work of the God the Father and God the Holy Spirit.[14]

Perhaps, one can speculate that this use of *communicatio idiomatum* in Newman's thought concerning Mary's cooperation in the *œconomia salutis* can best be understood in light of the theological distinction between *de congruo* and *de condigno*, as Father Friedel explains in his commentary on this passage (Diff II, 84f.):

> Because of her position in the Incarnation, she stands alone between God and the rest of creation; she may thus be called the center of all things.[15] Consequently, a special office is assigned to her distinct from that assigned to Our Lord. In the words of Segneri, she has been made "the arbitress of every effect coming from God's mercy."[16] Because she is Mother of God, the salvation of mankind is said to be given to her prayers *"de congruo,* but *de condigno* it is due only to the blood of the Redeemer."[17] Her prayer is especially powerful because no one has access to God as she has, for she is the Mother of God; could Jesus deny her anything in heaven, who has been so near to Him on earth?[18]

"Her work is not a ministration towards us; her power is indirect," is best explained as a reinforcement of the above distinction, namely, that God's direct presence within the soul through grace is not to be confused with Mary's external cooperation that assists us in coming into contact with that grace through her intercession and/or our invocation of her. Nevertheless, Newman's expression "ministration" could be misunderstood if taken out of its proper context. Newman is not attempting to relegate Mary's office or our devotion to Mary to a distant or foreign realm. He is simply trying to demonstrate to Pusey that Mary's office of intercession and our devotional invocation of Mary are neither contrary to our adoration of God nor operative apart from our adoration of Him. In fact, Mary's own prayers on our behalf are efficacious precisely because of the omnipotent power of God's infinite love and mercy, and desire for our salvation.

In a clever play on words, Newman alludes to this truth by making reference to the *fiat* of Christ on behalf of our salvation. Indeed, Newman's mention of Christ's *fiat* reminds us that it precedes the *fiat* of the Virgin from all eternity according to the divine economy of salvation, directly flowing from Christ's oneness with the divine essence and eternal communion with the two distinct and divine Persons of the Father and the Holy Spirit. Thus, one can observe that Newman's reference to Christ's eternal *fiat* in the bosom of the Father is the very basis for Mary's *fiat* in the fullness of time, according to which He became Incarnate in her virginal womb. Furthermore, based on Newman's text, one could offer the following analogy—not made by Newman but implied nonetheless—in order to explicate the meaning of Newman's own words, namely, that just as Mary's *fiat* at the Annunciation was only possible because of the *fiat* of the Son in the bosom of the Father from all eternity in view of our Redemption. So too, Mary's *fiat*—which is expressed through her maternal mediation and intercession—is forever subordinate to the *fiat* of her Son reigning glorious at the right hand of the Father in view of our eternal salvation.

Thus, Mary's maternal mediation, indeed, the whole of her office in the economy of salvation, can only be fully appreciated when viewed in direct relation and subordination to the unique and supreme mediation of the One Mediator Christ Jesus. Newman's reply to Pusey in this instance and throughout his Mariological writings should be read in the light of *Lumen Gentium*, no. 49 (the participation of the Mystical Body, the Church vis-à-vis the mediation of Christ her Lord and Head) and *Lumen Gentium*, nos. 60–65 (the participation of Mary through her "*maternum munus*" (maternal duty) "*in gratiæ œconomia*" (in the economy or order of grace) by virtue of the superabundant merits of Christ the One Redeemer and Mediator).

IV. "ANGLICAN MISCONCEPTIONS AND CATHOLIC
EXCESSES IN DEVOTION TO THE BLESSED VIRGIN"

(a) *The Main Points of Newman's Apologetic of*
Catholic Marian Devotion and Their Bearing on
One's Understanding of Mary's Proper Role of Cooperation
in the Economy of Salvation

Newman's response is basically twofold. First, he responds by way of a critical analysis of Pusey's objection to the devotional statements which he has singled out as doctrinally problematic. Second, as Newman tells Pusey, he is led "from the consideration of the sentiments themselves," of which Pusey complains, "to the persons who wrote, and the places where they wrote." [19]

The first part of Newman's response is a vindication of Marian devotion in the Catholic tradition. Newman reminds Pusey that the Mariology of the Roman Church like that of the Anglican Church is fundamentally based on the teaching of the Fathers of the Church, so much so that "ordinary men" as Newman terms them would find little difference between the two Mariologies. Second, Newman considers the Anglicans, themselves having such "high notions of the Blessed Virgin," unjustified in their accusation of the Roman Church as quasi-idolatrous. Newman then logically guides Pusey into a consideration of the fact that the law of believing (*lex credendi*) cannot be separated from the law of worship (*lex orandi*). Thus, Newman argues in effect that the acceptance of the theology of the Greek Fathers must be taken together with an acceptance of the Liturgy which they celebrated and the Marian devotion which that Liturgy engenders. Newman illustrates to Pusey that the Liturgy of the Greek Church is even more exuberant in its expressions than the Roman Liturgy, such as when Mary is invoked within the very context of the anaphora. In essence, Newman explains that the diversity of liturgical expression between East and West as regards the Blessed Virgin should not be an obstacle to Pusey's union. Pusey's *Eirenicon*, by way of omission, as Newman indicates, does not do justice to the necessary distinction between doctrine and devotion, so that one might come to the faulty conclusion that Catholics are guilty of Mariolatry in their devotion to the Virgin.

On the contrary, Newman plainly agrees with Pusey not to make excuses for any Catholic "who, through false devotion to Mary, forgets Jesus";[20] he also argues that Catholic Marian doctrine and devotion do not "stop short in her" (the expression used in Pusey's *Eirenicon*), but that "in the Catholic Church Mary has shown herself, not the rival, but the minister of her Son; she has protected Him, as in His infancy, so in the whole of the religion."[21] This statement touches directly upon the question of the Co-Redemption inasmuch as it allays any fears that a non-Catholic may have that Catholic Marian doctrine and devotion are meant to obscure Our Lord's salvific primacy.

Both Marian doctrine and devotion are designed by God to safeguard not only the integrity but also the uniqueness and supremacy of divine worship. Mary's role is one of ministration or cooperation in the *œconomia salutis*. These are the preferred theological terms that Newman consistently uses throughout his writings, both of a doctrinal and devotional nature, when discussing this precise topic.

(b) *Saint Alphonsus Liguori and Saint Paul of the Cross: The Centrality of Christ the Redeemer*

The title "coredemptress," which Newman uses in his *Letter to Pusey*, must be understood against the background of the centrality of Christ the Redeemer. To enhance his arguments, Newman calls Pusey's attention to two important, saintly figures, Alphonsus Liguori and Paul of the Cross, who, renowned for their Marian devotion, nonetheless "have shown their love of her Divine Son, in the names which they have given to their respective Congregations, viz. that 'of the Redeemer,' and that 'of the Cross and Passion.'"[22] These two examples are far from insignificant. Why? Pusey was at least aware of some of the Mariological writings of Saint Alphonsus Liguori and therefore, whatever his queries, Newman sought to assure Pusey that Saint Alphonsus' Mariology did not set up a rival to the throne of Christ the only Redeemer. Furthermore, Pusey was certainly aware that Newman had been received into full communion with the Catholic Church by the Passionist Father, Blessed Dominic Barberi. Both titles express the centrality of the Paschal Mystery—to which Mary is certainly most intimately associated—without, however, substituting for Our Lord in those saving events which He alone could accomplish according to the Father's plan.

(c) *The Text of Father Nepveu: The Uniqueness of Christ in the Economy of Salvation*

Newman is hound-like in his relentless pursuit of truth. He recommends to Pusey an enlightening passage from the work of a French Jesuit by the name of Father Nepveu. Father Nepveu's devotional work is entitled *Christian Thoughts for Every Day of the Year,*[23] and Newman calls it "a fair specimen of the teaching of our spiritual books,"[24] from which he offers the following quotation:

> The love of Jesus Christ is the most sure pledge of our future happiness, and the most infallible token of our predestination. Mercy towards the poor, devotion to the Holy Virgin, are very sensible tokens of predestination; nevertheless they are not absolutely infallible; but one cannot have a sincere devotion and constant love of Jesus without being predestinated. . . . The destroying angel, which bereaved the houses of the Egyptians of their first-born, had respect to all the houses which were marked with the blood of the Lamb.[25]

The choice of this quotation is not accidental; it underscores the truth that our salvation ultimately rests in our possession of the beatific vision and of our final union with Christ, which does not preclude but includes our "love of the poor" or "sincere devotion," to and desire of union with the Virgin, or, for that matter, any other participation in the divine goodness through creaturely communion. Newman impresses upon Pusey that the focus of Catholicism is not obfuscated by its contemplation of the Virgin and that the Church's vision of the Crucified Redeemer is a constant reminder that it is the Blood of Christ the Lamb that washed away our sins, that is, the Blood of His Sacred Humanity derived from the Virgin.

Newman's argument leads to what he proposes—based on the writings of Father Nepveu—is an essential distinction between the "absolutely infallible" nature of Our Lord's place in the economy of salvation by His very nature as the Son of God and Redeemer of mankind and the "not absolutely infallible," subordinate role of cooperation that Our Lady exercises by grace in the economy as the highest and most blessed of all creatures redeemed by her Son.

A brief explanation is necessary, lest one think that Newman's adoption of the contradistinction between "absolutely infallible" and "not absolutely infallible" is intended to call into question the infallible nature of God's design to involve Mary in the work of salvation. On the contrary, this contradistinction is intended to clarify that what Our Lord accomplished is infallibly efficacious in terms of our salvation because of the Hypostatic Union which although brought about through the full cooperation of the Virgin, nonetheless involves singular redemptive actions of the God-Man and sole Redeemer Christ Jesus, that is the shedding of His Blood on the Cross absolutely necessary for the forgiveness of sins and atoning death, which cannot be attributed to the Virgin, let alone to any other creature.

(d) *The Holy Sacrifice of the Mass and Marian Devotion*

What other examples do we have in the *Letter to Pusey* to support what has been said thus far? A powerful argument is posed by Newman in that which immediately follows the quotation from Father Nepveu. Newman returns to the Sacred Liturgy, and more precisely, to the *fons et culmen* (source and summit) of the Church's life, that is, to the mystery of the Eucharistic Sacrifice. For Newman, it is inconceivable that authentic Marian devotion as intended by the Church could ever derogate and certainly not to the point of idolatry from the worship of Our Lord's Real Presence in the Blessed Sacrament, in the Holy Sacrifice of the Mass, and in the reception of Holy Communion. Not even the devotion offered to the image of the Crucified Savior can compare. To this effect, Newman writes:

> When strangers are so unfavourably impressed with us, because they see images of Our Lady in our churches, and crowds flocking about her, they forget that there is a Presence within the sacred walls, infinitely more aweful, which claims and obtains from us a worship transcendentally different from any devotion we pay to her. That devotion to her might indeed tend to idolatry, if it were encouraged in Protestant churches, where there is nothing higher than it to attract the worshipper: but all the images that a Catholic church ever contained, all the

crucifixes at its altars brought together, do not so affect its frequenters, as the lamp which betokens the presence or absence there of the Blessed Sacrament. . . . The Mass again conveys to us the same lesson of the sovereignty of the Incarnate Son; it is a return to Calvary, and Mary is scarcely named in it. . . . Communion, again, . . . is a solemn unequivocal act of faith in the Incarnate God; if any can be such; and the most gracious of admonitions, did we need one, of His sovereign and sole right to possess us.[26]

(e) *Mary's Cooperation in the Economy of Salvation and the Implications of the Statements of Catholic Theologians about Marian Devotion*

Pusey rejects certain aspects of Catholic Marian doctrine and devotion partially because he has not been able to square the writings of Father Frederick Faber, Saint Alphonsus Liguori, Francisco Suarez, and Francisco de Salazar with what he believed to be the orthodox teaching of the Scriptures and Tradition concerning the Virgin. Newman's reply in the *Letter to Pusey* is intended to show how the Catholic teaching on Marian doctrine and devotion is the fullest expression of that orthodox teaching. Furthermore, Newman is unwilling to allow Pusey's objections to rest on the opinions of a few theologians—even the most formidable—since individual Christian thinkers, even the individual Fathers themselves and the most spiritual and holy of Christian writers, cannot be taken singly as the definitive authorities on matters of doctrine and devotion.[27]

Thus, Newman, for instance, defends Suarez's notion that "no one is saved without the Blessed Virgin," by adding this rejoinder, "he is speaking not of devotion to her, but of her intercession." However, Newman does readily criticize Salazar's use of theological terminology since, in his opinion, it is too "ruthlessly logical to be a safe or pleasant guide in the matter of devotion,"[28] yet he does not offer any example of how this is actually the case. Newman admits that he was not fully aware of the sources to which Pusey made reference, or, at least, that he did not have an in-depth knowledge of their content, so as to be capable of responding to Pusey by way of direct commentary on them. Newman humbly tells Pusey: "I hope it is not disrespectful to so great a servant of God to say, that I never have read his *Glories of*

Mary; . . . As to De Montford [sic] and Oswald, I never even met with their names, till I saw them in your book . . ."[29]

This is perhaps a serious limitation of Newman's apology insofar as it could have been even more convincing if he had taken the opportunity to familiarize himself with the actual sources that prompted some of Pusey's misunderstandings. Instead, he dismisses their importance on the basis of his own ignorance or on the presumption that his congregation and fellow clergymen shared his same ignorance in these matters[30] or on the claim that the differing provenance (e.g., Italy, Spain) of these devotions should not be of concern to an Englishman, and that the writings of "saints" are so extraordinarily elevated so as to be almost incomprehensible for ordinary men or even for scholarly men like Pusey and Newman himself.[31]

One should not doubt the sincerity of the Venerable Newman's humility. Certainly, he is correct in pointing out that the popular Marian devotions of a given place need not be the litmus test of the whole of Catholic Marian devotion. Newman justly remarks: "As to his practical directions, Saint Alfonso wrote them for Neapolitans, whom he knew, and we do not know." Yet, perhaps, in this case, Newman tended to underestimate how the devotional writings of one Catholic theologian and spiritual writer of a particular place could have a far-reaching effect on the mind and heart of a non-Catholic such as Pusey or on others of similar background. He writes: "Whatever these writers may have said or not said, whatever they may have said harshly, and whatever capable of fair explanations, still they are foreigners; we are not answerable for their particular devotions. . . ."[32] While Newman's statement regarding devotion is technically true, without desiring to blame Newman, one could consider his response in this latter instance as leaving something to be desired from an ecumenical standpoint.

(f) *Mary's Cooperation in the Economy of Salvation and the Implications of Catholic Marian Devotionals*

Newman continues in the *Letter to Pusey* to discuss the nature of Marian devotion, especially by way of reference to the prayers of the *Raccolta*, drawing a line between Mary's role of mediation as Advocate and the Triune God, Who alone is the source of mercy. Newman responds directly to Pusey's objections to certain prayers of the *Raccolta* which, for example, speak of her being as "reborn spiritually in our souls," by explaining their meaning according to the sense with which Saint Paul writes to his converts speaking to them of his spiritual fatherhood by which his communication of the Gospel message has begotten them in Christ. Newman explains that when we say that we place all our hope in Mary we understand that this entrustment of ourselves to her is based on that much more profound hope which we have in Jesus, Who alone "deserves of us an immeasurable love." [33]

Newman responds to Pusey's criticism that certain unofficial Catholic Marian devotional works at the time tended to foster a type of spiritual rivalry between Christ and Mary, by expressing his dismay, or, as Newman writes, his "grief and almost anger" that these devotionals could be interpreted as having exalted the Church's veneration of the Virgin to the point of obstructing a proper vision of the person and ministry of Christ, so as "to ascribe to the Blessed Virgin a power of 'searching the reins and hearts,' which is the attribute of God alone." [34] Newman ventures on to answer Pusey by means of a series of rhetorical questions:

> And I said to myself, how can we any longer prove our Lord's divinity from Scripture, if those cardinal passages which invest Him with divine prerogatives, after all invest Him with nothing beyond what His Mother shares with Him? And how, again, is there anything of incommunicable greatness in His death and passion, if He who was alone in the garden, alone upon the Cross, alone in the Resurrection, after all is not alone, but shares His solitary work with His Blessed Mother, —with her to whom, when He entered His ministry, He said for our instruction, not as grudging her proper glory, "Woman, what have I to do with thee?" [35]

Newman's response in the above passage salvages both the uniqueness of the Lord's redemptive work and Mary's secondary but nonetheless critical role of cooperation in Christ's salvific mission which she played, not as a rival to His divine attributes or prerogatives, but as one who performed those functions in accord with the "proper glory" attributed to her by Christ Himself in the economy of salvation. [36] Newman's response is an adamant affirmation that it is incorrect to attribute to Mary that "incommunicable greatness," which Our Lord Jesus alone possesses in the mystery of his Passion, Death and Resurrection. In this context, Newman interprets Our Lord's words to His Blessed Mother at Cana as a clear indication of his divine sovereignty in view of His redemptive mission. It is implied by Newman that even at the foot of the Cross Mary's presence did not infringe on that divine sovereignty in any way. This essential distinction is never lost in Newman's writings, so much so that the distinction is maintained even within his most heartfelt meditations on her *compassio* and in his praise of her role as *Theotokos*, New Eve, Mediatrix, Advocate and in her spiritual motherhood of the Church. Newman concludes by saying that to blur such an essential distinction would be a great offense to Mary since it would be equivalent to expressing love for her as a creature which one owes by right to God alone and therefore in a particular way to Jesus her Son, the sole Redeemer. Just as she is unwilling to compromise "in proportion to her love for Him," by accepting reverence which is due to the Redeemer alone, so should we be unwilling to compromise "our love for her, by wounding her in the very apple of her eye," by giving her such reverence.[37]

Pusey's criticism of excesses in devotion to the Blessed Virgin leads Newman to distance himself even further from any statement that would confuse Mary's cooperation in the *œconomia salutis* with the singular operations of the Persons of the Trinity. Newman agrees with Pusey that one ought to reject, "without hesitation," if understood in a strictly literal sense, the following phrases:

> that mercy of Mary is infinite; that God has resigned into her hands His omnipotence; that it is safer to seek her than her Son; that the Blessed Virgin is superior to God; that our Lord is subject to her command; that His present disposition towards sinners, as well as His Father's, is to reject them, while the Blessed Mary takes His place as an Advocate with Father and Son; that the Saints are more ready to intercede with Jesus than Jesus with the Father; that Mary is the only refuge of those with whom God is angry; that Mary alone can obtain a Protestant's conversion; that it would have sufficed for the salvation of men if our Lord had died, not in order to obey the Father, but to defer to the decree of the Mother; that she rivals our Lord in being God's daughter, not by adoption, but by a kind of nature; that Christ fulfilled the office of Saviour by imitating her virtues; that, as the Incarnate God bore the image of His Father, so He bore the image of His Mother;[38] that redemption derived

from Christ indeed its sufficiency, but from Mary its beauty and loveliness; that, as we are clothed with the merits of Christ, so we are clothed with the merits of Mary; that, as He is priest, in a like sense is she Priestess; that His Body and Blood in the Eucharist are truly hers and appertain to hers; that as He is present and received therein, so is she present and received therein; that Priests are ministers as of Christ, so of Mary; that elect souls are born of God and Mary; that the Holy Ghost brings into fruitfulness His action by her, producing in her and by her Jesus Christ in His members; that the kingdom of God in our souls, as our Lord speaks, is really the kingdom of Mary in the soul; that she and the Holy Ghost produce in the soul extraordinary things; and that when the Holy Ghost finds Mary in a soul He flies there.[39]

This series of theologically problematic expressions ends up, according to Newman's estimation, attributing to Mary titles and prerogatives in the economy of salvation that far exceed the boundaries of the Church's official Marian doctrine and the orthodox forms of devotion, only if they are misunderstood according to a strictly literal sense. Newman does not believe that such a strict literal sense was necessarily intended by the authors themselves and that this sense is only held by those, especially Protestants, who misinterpret the texts. However, even though these pious sentiments of devotion to Our Lady are not to be understood in the literal sense of their expression, they are nonetheless strongly objected to by Newman on several bases.

First and foremost, Newman objects to them because they are not altogether consonant with the teachings of Sacred Scripture and Sacred Tradition. He writes: ". . . they seem to me like a bad dream. I could not have conceived them to have been said. I know not to what authority to go for them, to Scripture, to the Fathers, or to the decrees of the Councils, or to the consent of the schools, or to the tradition of the faithful, or to the Holy See, or to Reason."[40] Second, as Newman relates to Pusey, "they defy all the *loci theologici*. There is nothing of them in the Roman Missal, in the Roman Catechism, in the Roman *Raccolta*, in *The Imitation of Christ*. . . ."[41] Third, Newman refutes them because they are, as far as he can judge, foreign to the writings of such notable theologians as "Gother, Challoner, Milner or Wiseman."[42] Fourth, Newman believes them to be offensive and a potential source of confusion both theologically and devotionally insofar as they could conjure up the false idea of Mary as possessing those attributes which can only be attributed to God in their full and proper sense.

Newman illustrates this point by making an analogy. He says that making such attributions to Mary as those given in the expressions cited by Pusey are like "painting up a young and beautiful princess with a brow of a Plato and the muscle of an Achilles," that is to say, Mary's true image is distorted by these sayings, whether well-intentioned or not. Newman writes: "I should but be guilty of fulsome, frigid flattery towards the most upright and noble of God's creatures, if I professed them,—and of stupid flattery too."[43] Fifth, these distortions which "scare" Newman are likewise, in his opinion, the cause of scandal to the learned and unlearned alike.[44] He goes so far as to say "that I had rather believe that there is no God at all, than that Mary is greater than God. I will have nothing to do with statements, which can only be explained, by being explained away."[45] Sixth, Newman, while strongly objecting to the statements as they are found in Pusey's writings, is intellectually honest enough to state that he has never read the original texts and humble enough to admit that he cannot presume that the intentions of the authors were entirely ill-conceived. Perhaps, they even could possibly have a "good meaning," if they were the musings of "saints in ecstasy." Nevertheless, Newman is unwilling to appropriate these expressions himself if they are understood according to the "literal sense which they bear in the mouths of English men and English women,"[46] in the historical context of nineteenth-century England.

Friedel, relying on Newman's own final words of judgment, comments on this passage in the following way: "Of course Newman admits that these sayings may not have so crude a meaning as they seem to have when taken on their face value independently of the context. Their authors probably never understood them in the literal sense. Nevertheless they are 'calculated to prejudice inquirers, to frighten the unlearned, to unsettle consciences, to provoke blasphemy, and to work the loss of souls.'"[47] Therefore, for Newman, the dogmatic inappropriateness of these sayings,[48] predetermines not only their inappropriateness for his own personal devotional life but likewise their inappropri-

433

ateness for the devotional lives of other English Christians. The basic principles of Newman's objection to these expressions are solid. For indeed, from both a doctrinal and devotional point of view, most, if not all of them, would be contrary to the Church's teaching, if they were to be understood at face value. Newman's response, although colored by personal emotion and conditioned by historical circumstance, is, on the whole, a rational and coherent defense of Mary's proper role of cooperation in the economy of salvation vis-à-vis the passage hitherto examined.

Hence, one is brought to appreciate the outstanding merits of Newman's Catholic apologetic of Marian devotion in the *Letter to Pusey* in terms not only of his defense of Marian intercession and invocation (both of which are topics that receive a more in-depth and direct treatment in Chapter Six) but more specifically of those statements in the *Letter to Pusey* which more directly bear upon the topic of Co-Redemption in Newman's Mariology insofar as these statements have not been studied in isolation but situated within their proper theological, historical and literary context. Finally, it is hoped that the contribution of Newman's theology of Mary's cooperation in the economy of salvation, as explored throughout this work and in this chapter in particular, will be able to shed even further light on the contemporary theological discussion of Mary "Co-Redemptrix."

(g) *An Application of the Seven Principles of Doctrinal Development in Newman's* Essay on the Development of Christian Doctrine *to the Question of Mary Co-Redemptrix*

As we round out our reflections in this chapter, perhaps this is the appropriate place to make an application of the seven principles of authentic development set forth in Newman's *Essay on Development* and treated in Chapter One of the present study to the title or better still to the doctrinal question of Mary "Co-Redemptrix"[49] since, in a particular way, this title, of the three proposed Marian titles—"Mediatrix" and "Advocate," being plainly mentioned by the Council Fathers in *Lumen Gentium* (no. 62)—is the most highly debated among theologians and therefore the one that requires the most elucidation. The principles are given, it will be recalled, so that the Church can distinguish authentic development of doctrines from corruptions that are not in consonance with the Sacred Tradition. However, as Newman himself makes clear, these principles are not absolute proofs but "tests" which can be applied; nor did he ever intend that their application be an absolute measure of the authentic development of a given doctrine. Furthermore, Newman is also careful to point out that even an authentic doctrinal development in the Church need not, in every case, warrant a dogmatic definition. This distinction is absolutely essential for a proper understanding of this discussion since nowhere does Newman suggest and certainly not in explicit terms that Mary's cooperation in the *œconomia salutis* cannot be fully and properly understood apart from a dogmatic definition of the precise titles of "Co-Redemptrix," "Mediatrix" (of All Grace) and "Advocate." Yet it is equally difficult to find any objection to Newman's acceptance of these titles based on his understanding of the Church's Marian doctrine and devotion and more precisely that of Mary's cooperation in the *œconomia salutis* as it has been examined in this book. The principles are applied in the following way:

1) The principle of *Chronic Vigor* can be applied to the title of "Co-Redemptrix" because in one form or another it has undergone much development throughout the centuries and yet it remains a definite source of theological speculation although its precise and proper understanding is a question of ongoing discussion in the Church. As Perrella notes: "The theological debate about the Co-Redemption although ignited, has never degenerated into a sterile, harsh, and damaging polemic; it is has been in fact an important and fecund moment for theology in general and for Mariology in particular." [50]

2) Similarly, the principle of *Conservative Action* assures us that legitimate growth is occurring, in that the question of the title of Mary as Co-Redemptrix in no way eviscerates, for example, the doctrine of the New Eve—so essential to Newman's understanding of Mary's cooperation in the economy of salvation. On the contrary, the former, if properly understood against the background of Newman's whole Mariological output, could strengthen the latter. However, Newman's Mariology does not explicitly make this connection for us. While Newman, for example, identified a very close link between the development of the theology of the New Eve and the subsequent dogmatic

definition of the doctrine of Mary's Immaculate Conception, which he so thoroughly promoted, he does not imply that a further definition of Mary as "Co-Redemptrix" would be necessary to give full expression to the Church's teaching on Mary's cooperation in the economy of salvation. Nor does not state that the proclamation or dogmatic definition of the doctrine of Mary "Co-Redemptrix" might not be, at some future time, in fact necessary in order to conserve or more fully express an essential aspect of Mary's cooperation.

3) The principle of *Preservation of Type* would also seem to be applicable in this case. Just as an oak tree cannot become an apple tree, so too, for example, Newman did not consider the patristic theology of Mary as the New Eve as having been enlisted by them to produce an alien image of her contrary to the Scriptural data. In fact, Newman was wholeheartedly convinced that the theology of the New Eve was not only a fitting contribution of patristic thought but that it was even more so a sure proof of authentic development of doctrine and therefore an integral part of the Church's Marian doctrine, even though the doctrine of Mary's cooperation was never dogmatically defined under the title of New Eve. Therefore, according to Newman, the possibility of considering Mary under the title of "Co-Redemptrix,"— even if this title is regarded as simply a devotional title subject to modification (e.g., from a terminological point of view), does not necessarily corrupt or alter the fundamental truth of the biblical and patristic doctrine of the New Eve nor necessarily suggest that the doctrinal underpinnings of this title are not essential to the *preservation of type*. On the whole, it must be said that Newman's Mariology, as far as this work has been able to examine its content, while in no way detracting from a legitimate use of the title "Co-Redemptrix" at least as a devotional expression, nonetheless reveals a clear preference on Newman's part for the theological concept or term of "cooperation" to explain Mary's role in the *œconomia salutis*. Newman consistently uses the term "co-operation" or related theological and devotional expressions throughout his Mariological writings, while the title of Co-Redemptrix is barely mentioned, although in a highly significant fashion, in the *Letter to Pusey*.

4) Also connected here is the principle of *logical sequence*, whereby a particular thought flows consistently and not illogi-

cally from another. This writer holds that, as far as Newman's Mariology is concerned, the title of Mary "Co-Redemptrix" (at least as a devotional expression) is not *per force* a violation of logical thinking from the starting point of the fundamental doctrines of Mary as the New Eve—not to mention all of the other Marian doctrines expounded upon and interrelated (*nexus mysteriorum*) in Newman's Mariological writings. Antonio Maria Calero, citing Carol with approval, summarizes the situation, from his perspective, thus:

> It is clear, however, to those who consider the ascendent line of sparse testimonies across the whole spectrum of the Tradition, and it will appear with equal evidence to them that the doctrine of the co-redemption of Mary, as we know it today, represents the result of many centuries of gradual and progressive development. The idea, a seed which is already incorporated in the concrete composition of "New Eve," and which we find in the first centuries of the Patristic era, has suffered a long evolutionary process, at times imperceptible, before reaching maturity. [51]

A careful study of Newman's Mariological writings reveals that, considering his extraordinarily deep appreciation of the doctrines of Mary *Theotokos*, New Eve and likewise of her singular association to the mystery of Christ's saving passion through her *compassio*, her spiritual maternity of the Church and her maternal mediation of saving grace through intercessory prayer as "Our Advocate," that his belief in these fundamental teachings can be considered strong arguments to back up his acceptance of the title "Co-Redemptrix," as one possible way of expressing the Church's teaching on Mary's cooperation in the *œconomia salutis*.

5) The *power of assimilation* is concerned with the ability of a doctrine to take in additional sources of life without corruption. For Newman, just as the use of Aristotelian metaphysics did not destroy the biblical understanding of the Incarnation, so too, in a similar fashion, the fundamental revelation about Mary as the New Eve—not to mention all the other aspects of her cooperation examined in this book—may not suffer damage by the further theological reflection which leads one to consider her under the title of Co-Redemptrix. Carlos Ignacio González briefly summarizes the history of how the title of "Co-Redemptrix" developed from the Eve–Mary parallelism as a title which may or

may not be the most suitable mode of expressing the theology of Mary as the New Eve:

> From the second century the patristic tradition has perma-nently recognized this mission of Mary at the side of her Son, even if it has developed a way of expressing it. The most com-mon means . . . has been the parallel between Eve and Mary, in connection to the Pauline theology that sees Jesus as the new and second Adam. At the end of the patristic era (around the tenth century) in order to express this doctrine the term *redemptrix* began to be used. . . . Given the theological impreci-sion of the term, between the fifteenth and seventeenth centu-ries the more precise title of Co-Redemptrix began to be used. Slowly this habit was extended, even if it never was completely commonplace nor well received by theologians, and not even by all those who accept the doctrine expressed by such a title.[52]

While González clearly identifies the origin of Co-Redemptrix within the New Eve terminology, he seems to doubt that a genu-ine assimilation is possible; some other authors agree and others disagree with this perspective.[53] The several passages which have been discussed in this section in connection to the *Letter to Pusey*, are rather strong arguments in favor of just such a genuine assimi-lation by Newman, only if this title's doctrinal content is properly understood in light of how other Marian titles have been under-stood and accepted by the Church in her Sacred Tradition.

6) The *continuity of principles* demands that appropriate meth-odologies be employed. Faith and reason are always basic to the process of doctrinal development; both are surely engaged here as one finds an attempt to live the goal of *fides quærens intellectum* (faith seeking understanding). In fact, as Chapter One indicates with regard to Newman's Fifteenth Sermon before the Univer-sity at Oxford for the feast of Mary's Purification, Mary is consid-ered by him to be the exemplar *par excellence* of the theologian and non-theologian alike who ponder in their minds and assimi-late into their hearts the great mysteries of faith, so as to under-stand their interconnectedness and continuity in both a real and a notional sense.

7) *Anticipation of Its Future* is that principle which deals with the analysis of the process of development, so that a past reality ever true provides the gateway for further growth. Once more, following our model of the New Eve theology, the controlling

scriptural and patristic datum of this doctrine held within itself the capacity to become yet even more fully understood upon theological reflection, such as was most appreciated by Newman in the process of the dogmatic definition of the Immaculate Conception. One example of how a theologian employs faith and reason while looking toward future development comes from Mark Miravalle, the personal and driving force behind the movement, *Vox Populi Mariæ Mediatrici*. Regardless of one's personal disposition toward this movement and its goal, one would have to agree that he utilizes well these last two principles of Newman's—using passages of *Tertio Millennio Adveniente* to support his position:

> "The religion (says the Pope) which originates in the mystery of the Redemptive Incarnation, is the religion of 'dwelling in the heart of God,' of sharing in God's very life," a life regained for the human family through the triumphant reconquest of Christ, the New Adam, and Mary, the New Eve. Thus Galatians 4:4–5, this great Pauline-Marian passage as John Paul tells us, "allows the fullness of the mystery of the Redemptive Incarnation to shine forth." . . . The whole truth about Mary, the Woman of Galatians, the Woman of the Redemptive Incarnation, comprises the distinguishing thesis of this theological volume, with a particular accentuation on the providential timing of this thesis within the context of the upcoming "Great Jubilee." [54]

Miravalle rounds out his argument in this way: "The Mother precedes the Son in the historic order of suffering, and as the Father willed that the Mother historically precede the Incarnation, so too is the appropriateness of the proclamation of the whole truth about Mary in precedence for the celebration of the Incarnation in the Year 2000." [55]

Bertrand de Margerie, S.J., makes the following observation concerning Newman and his attitude in regard to the possibility of a dogmatic definition of Mary, Co-Redemptrix:

> At first sight it would seem that Newman, avoiding the signature of any petition, would even have rejected any affirmation contending that Mary was Co-Redemptrix if this word was understood as meaning purely and simply Redemptrix: this is what he rejects in his *Sermon Notes*. In a more general way he would have desired, as in the case of the Immaculate Conception in

1854, a consultation of the Catholic world; he would think today as in 1854 that such a definition by the pope would be valid and licit, but extraordinary; he would add that it would be later received by a Council, the normal mode of deciding points of faith, and in that sense Newman was a prophet: the Vatican II Council received and proclaimed the doctrine of the Immaculate Conception of Mary (LG 56), but Newman today, as in a letter of his to Pusey, would not promise us that there would be no further dogmatic definitions about Mary because the Spirit blows as He wills and one cannot bind over the Holy Ghost to keep ecumenical peace.[56]

SUMMARY OF CHAPTER SEVEN

1) Newman uses *Co-Redemptrix* only once in his *Letter to Pusey* and does so in a positive fashion. The context in which this mention is made reveals that Newman, although he does not explicitly say as much, offers us an explanation of Marian cooperation in the economy of salvation that can safely incorporate the use of this title, even if only as a devotional expression, without in any way derogating from the Church's grounding of Marian doctrine and devotion in Christ's unique and supreme role as the One Mediator and One Redeemer as well as in that of an clearly orthodox ecclesiology. In this sense, Newman's treatment of the title "coredemptress" in the *Letter to Pusey* should be considered as one that makes a special contribution to present and future discussion concerning its proper theological significance and use.

2) The chapter concludes with an application of Newman's seven principles, already explained in Chapter One, by which he distinguishes an authentic development of doctrine from a corruption. Employing those principles in the present situation, one discovers that most if not all of those principles would result in a positive judgment concerning the notion of Mary's cooperation in the work of Redemption encompassing the use of the title Mary "Co-Redemptrix," but not without proper theological explanation. Certainly, Newman cannot be considered as having discouraged use of this title in the *Letter to Pusey* or having forgotten the significance of its theological and devotional underpinnings.

3) The acceptability of the title in Newman's *Letter to Pusey* does not, in and of itself, argue for a further step of dogmatic definition, especially given Newman's general hesitancy regarding resorting to such definitions unnecessarily. This is to say that, before petitioning for any such dogmatic definition, Newman would expect both a clear affirmation of the doctrine's significance among theologians as well as a clear affirmation of these doctrines vis-à-vis Scripture, Tradition and the Magisterium. Also key to a hypothetical push for such a dogmatic definition on Newman's part would be an appeal to the theological principles of *sensus fidelium* and *conspiratio pastorum et fidelium*.

4) I believe that Newman's ecumenical concerns as regards Marian doctrine and devotion can best be summarized in the words of His Holiness, Pope John Paul II, who writes: "Just as Mary's presence in the early community fostered oneness of heart, which prayer strengthened and made visible (cf. Acts 1:14), so the most intense communion with her whom St. Augustine called the 'Mother of Unity,' (*Sermo 192*, 2; PL 38, 1013) will be able to bring Christians to the point of enjoying the long awaited gift of ecumenical unity" (*Mary, Mother of God*, 260).

General Conclusion

I. SUMMARY OF FINDINGS ON THE TITLES OF MARY AS CO-REDEMPTRIX, MEDIATRIX, AND ADVOCATE

(a) *Mary As Advocate*

1) In his *Letter to Pusey*, Newman takes as his point of departure Saint Irenæus of Lyons who considers Mary under the title of *Advocata Evæ* since by means of her obedience (*fiat*) she represented the disobedient Eve before God in view of the reparation and *recirculatio* that would be effected by the coming of the Second Adam. Newman acknowledges the significance of this title in contradistinction to but not in contradiction of the scriptural references to Christ the Advocate and the Holy Spirit the Paraclete. Newman refers to Mary's maternal mediation under the title of *Advocata* in his *Letters and Diaries* so as to designate her singular role of cooperation in the economy of salvation.

2) Newman's two meditations on "Christ Our Advocate Above" in *Meditations and Devotions* can be considered exemplary of the Christocentric focus of Newman's theology of the title Advocate that in no way excludes mention of Mary's maternal intercessory role but rather highlights it. In this way, Newman's theology of Mary's mediation, which neither derogates from, obstructs or obscures the one, supreme mediation of Christ, can be best understood in light of *Lumen Gentium*, nos. 60–62.

3) In the *Letter to Pusey*, Newman speaks of our relationship to Mary as that of "clients to a patron," and does so in the context of a discussion of her maternal mediation. He concludes the main body of his letter with an explicit invocation of Mary: ". . . May that bright and gentle Lady, the Blessed Virgin Mary, overcome you with her sweetness, and revenge herself on her foes by interceding effectively for their conversion." Furthermore, he duly notes a plethora of references to Mary's maternal mediation and intercession in the liturgies of both the East and West (cf. Diff II,

153–164), concluding his *Letter* nevertheless by way of an additional note concerning a decree of the Inquisition (now Congregation for the Doctrine of the Faith) addressed to the Bishop of Presimilia in which it is expressly noted that "although she (Mary) has the greatest influence (*possa moltissimo*) with her Son, still it cannot be piously affirmed that she exercises command over Him (*eserciti impero*). Newman adds that certain images depicting Mary as exercising such command over Our Lord were apparently prohibited at the time by the Holy Inquisition "in order apparently to mark the ministrative office of the Blessed Virgin, and her dependence as a creature on her Son."

4) Other references to Mary under the title Advocate abound in the writings of Newman, such as in his *Meditations and Devotions* and in his *Sermon Notes*. Newman often qualifies the title Advocate by the possessive adjective "our" or by adding the qualifying phrase "of the Church," to indicate that special ecclesial dimension of Mary's role.

(b) *Mary As Mediatrix (of All Grace)*

1) The centrality of Christ Jesus, the God-Man, the New or Second Adam, the One Mediator, Pontifex Maximus, that is, Great High Priest, Prophet, and King, etc. constitutes the ontological basis of Newman's soteriology. This is brought out, for example, in his reflections on the Cana and Calvary pericopes in the *Meditations and Devotions* and in *A Letter to Pusey*.

2) What Our Lord Jesus Christ divinely and sovereignly accomplished as the Son of God Incarnate through the Paschal Mystery does not preclude creaturely participation in His redemptive and salvific mediation but rather promotes it in accord with the economy of salvation.

3) In fact, such a creaturely participation in the mediation of Christ is anticipated, according to Newman, in the ministerial function of angels, patriarchs, prophets and holy men and women of the Old Testament (cf. Dev. D., 135–148) and finds its personification in Mary in the fullness of time (Gal 4:4).

4) First and foremost, Mary's mediation is considered by Newman a prerogative and a divine privilege that derives from her unique cooperation in the *œconomia salutis* as *Theotokos* and New Eve (e.g., Gen 3:15).

5) For Newman, Mary enjoys a singular participation in the life of grace since she has been perfectly redeemed by a prevenient grace in view of the infinite merits of Christ, the sole Savior and Redeemer of Mankind according to the doctrine of the Immaculate Conception.

6) Furthermore, she is the type or exemplar of full human cooperation (body and soul) with God's grace in the communion of saints and in the Mystical Body of Christ, the Church, as the perfect disciple of Christ (exemplified in her *fiat*) and eschatological icon or sign of hope for all believers according to the doctrine of the Assumption. See, for example, Newman's sermon, "On the Fitness of the Glories of Mary," in *Discourses to Mixed Congregations* and his reflections on the Marian title *Stella Matutina* in *Meditations and Devotions*.

7) Mary is likewise, for Newman, the exemplification of Christian intercessory prayer for the salvation of the world; her intercessory role surpasses that of all the angels and saints. Indeed, she is their Queen and "the help of all Christians." See, for example, Newman's litanies in honor of the Virgin and his love of the Holy Rosary.

8) Mary is the spiritual Mother of the Church in the order or economy of grace because she is conceived in the fullness of grace and consents to be the Mother of the Author of Grace at the moment of the Incarnation. The *Meditations and Devotions* contain several examples of Newman's theology of Mary's sanctity which she derives from her singular union with Christ. Furthermore, Mary is, as Newman quotes from William Wordsworth in the *Letter to Pusey*, "Our tainted nature's solitary boast," and therefore, of all creatures, the model of holiness *par excellence*.

9) At Cana and Calvary, in particular, she is presented as the preeminent member of the Church (*typus Ecclesiæ*) and indeed as the Church's Virgin Mother whose office of mediation continues by means of heavenly intercession. See, for example, Chapter Three for Newman's exegesis of John 2:1–11 and John 19:25–27.

10) Her spiritual maternity of the Church (see treatment of this theme in Chapter Three, Newman and Saints Ambrose and Augustine) and of all the redeemed after the Pentecost event in the heart of the nascent Church (cf. *A Letter to Pusey*) is prolonged into eternity on behalf of the pilgrim Church. See, for example, Newman's exegesis of Revelation 12.

11) Mary, in accord with the Father's plan of salvation, is an all-powerful means or instrument by which the supernatural gift of God's life is communicated to our souls, even though Newman is always careful to distinguish Mary's mediation of grace from the indwelling presence of the Holy Spirit and to underscore the truth that she does not supplant the unique mediatorial role of Christ, the Church, the sacraments or the Church's hierarchy. Mary does not share in the ministerial priesthood or in apostolic succession. In fact, Newman gives some significant points of meditation about Mary's participation in the Eucharistic life of the Church after the Ascension. And, furthermore, Newman exhorts us to have recourse to Mary's intercession so as to enter more fully into the life of grace that flows from the celebration of the Eucharistic Sacrifice and the reception of Holy Communion.

12) For Newman, Mary cannot be the source of the grace that redeems and saves us but since she is the highest of all creatures and the most intimately associated with Christ and His redemptive/saving mysteries; she is a privileged medium or conduit of redemptive and salvific grace. Newman accepts the truth of Saint Alphonsus Liguori's saying that: "God gives all grace through Mary," as well as the possibility that God wills to save all through Mary's intercession, even if this does not necessarily involve our direct invocation of her (e.g., the distinction of Francisco Suarez to which Newman makes reference in *A Letter to Pusey*).

13) Finally, Newman's exegesis of the Sacred Scriptures and his reading of the Fathers of the Church permit him to view Mary's mediation as a maternal function or role that is exercised always within the framework of the Church's own maternal mediation as universal sacrament of salvation on behalf of all the redeemed children of God.

(c) *Mary As Co-Redemptrix*

1) Newman relies on Saint Irenæus of Lyons who, drawing from the antithetical parallelism of Adam–Christ in Saint Paul, develops the theology of the Eve–Mary antithetical parallelism already found in the writings of Saint Justin Martyr and Tertullian. Mary is the New Eve and is called the *"causa salutis"* because her *fiat* (obedience of faith) in contrast to Eve's disobedience reverses the Fall. However, Mary's *fiat* is subordinate to the

redemptive work of Christ (all things are recapitulated in Him), just as Eve's disobedience is subordinated to the sin (properly called) of Adam.

2) Just as Newman considers Eve's disobedience to be a *sine qua non* of Adam's sin, that is, of the human fall from grace, so too he considers Mary's obedience (*fiat*) to be a *sine quâ non* of the Redemption.

3) Just as Newman considers Eve's disobedience to have constituted a full engagement of her being (e.g., free will and reason), bringing us death by cooperating in the sin of Adam, so too Mary's obedience constitutes a full engagement of her being (e.g., "My soul proclaims the greatness of the Lord, my spirit rejoices in God my Savior"), bringing us life in the Person of the Savior Jesus Christ and by cooperating with Him in His redemptive and salvific activity.

4) Newman is careful to note that one can determine the position and office of Mary in our Redemption from the position and office of Eve (not of Adam) in the Fall. Indeed, Newman refers to Mary as "the Daughter of Eve Un-fallen." Newman considers that just as the "great achievement" of our redemption/salvation/atonement can only be considered the work of Christ the New Adam in a full and proper sense, so too can original sin be considered in its full and proper sense as the sin of Adam.

5) Mary's cooperation, for Newman, is not limited to her *fiat* but extends to encompass the full range of the redemptive mysteries of Christ and in a special way to the heart of the Paschal Mystery (e.g., *compassio Mariæ* at the foot of the Cross). Mary's *compassio* is exemplary of *compassio Christianorum*.

6) Here, Newman makes an important distinction between the work of the Atonement attributed only to Christ and His physical martyrdom on the Cross (i.e., "the Red Way,") and the spiritual martyrdom (e.g., the prophecy of Simeon's sword) which Mary experiences as an expression of her most intimate union with the mystery of the Cross. (i.e., "the White Way").

7) Newman maintains, according to an argument of convenience such as that governing the doctrine of her Immaculate Conception and Assumption, that Mary would have experienced a physical death not of course as a consequence of sin but as the natural outcome of her earthly sojourn and as an expression of her full participation in the saving Death and Resurrection of

Christ, to Whom she is most perfectly conformed and con-figured as Virgin Mother "full of grace" (cf. Newman's sermon "The Glories of Mary for the Sake of Her Son," in *Discourses to Mixed Congregations*).

8) Of considerable significance is Newman's insistence that Mary's *compassio* is a real, not simply a notional, participation in the work of salvation, that is to say, "the full benefits" of the Paschal Mystery are experienced by her "in body and in spirit." Newman emphasizes the spiritual aspect to underscore the mystical nature of Mary's sufferings and to distinguish them, as has already been said, from the physical sufferings of martyrs, for whom she is nonetheless Queen.

9) Therefore, Newman regards Mary's cooperation as merito-rious insofar as it is indicative of her having shared, by divine grace, in the full benefits of the Redemption, in accord with the divine economy of salvation, not only in her own name but on behalf of the whole Mystical Body of Christ, and indeed of all mankind.

10) Consequently, Newman says that the meritorious coop-eration of Mary has a most definite "claim on our memories," so much so that both her intercession and our invocation of her are a fully integral and salutary part of orthodox Catholic doctrine and devotion.

11) Newman's personal development in this regard is remark-able and must be carefully traced throughout his writings and even in the particular events of his life in order to comprehend more fully how all three of these titles, although to differing degrees, are integrated into his own Marian devotion and under-standing of Marian doctrine.

12) In the *Letter to Pusey* Newman accepts the legitimacy of the title of Mary "coredemptress," against which Pusey protests. Newman's basic argument to Pusey is that if he agrees to accept the many titles of Mary found in the writings of the Fathers of the Church (e.g., panegyrical language of Saint Cyril of Alexan-dria at the Council of Ephesus), then why should he be so op-posed to the title of "coredemptress?" Nevertheless, one should bear in mind that the title of "priestess" is also mentioned by Pusey as objectionable and is treated by Newman in the same vein as that of "coredemptress." Furthermore, it seems as though the title of "coredemptress," as it is being used by Newman in

response to Pusey's objections, possesses a more devotional than doctrinal connotation.

13) In the *Letter to Pusey*, Newman does not directly attribute any particular value, doctrinal or devotional, to the title "co-redemptress" beyond that just mentioned. Furthermore, there is no indication in his Mariological writings that he believed the title "Co-Redemptrix" to contain within itself a Marian doctrine beyond that which he already understood as being fully expressed in the Marian doctrines/dogmas officially taught by the Church and as confirmed in the Sacred Scriptures and in Sacred Tradition.

14) Since Newman never presents us with a systematic, precise definition of the title "Co-Redemptrix" in his Mariological writings and certainly does not deem it necessary that such a title/doctrine be defined by the extraordinary Magisterium—as he had so joyfully welcomed the dogmatic definition of the Immaculate Conception; he clearly prefers the theological concept "cooperation" to describe Mary's role in the *œconomia salutis* to that of the title "Co-Redemptrix." It is the opinion of this writer that although the theological concept, "cooperation," is preferred by Newman, there is nothing inherent in the title of "Co-Redemptrix" itself as Newman understood it, to consider it contrary to right doctrine and devotion. Furthermore, given the particular application of the seven principles of authentic doctrinal development in this book, nothing explicit can be found in either Newman's Marian doctrine or devotion to suggest that the title of "Co-Redemptrix" is not an adequate and theologically sound expression of his understanding of the doctrine of Mary's cooperation in the *œconomia salutis*.

II. FINAL CONSIDERATIONS AND QUESTIONS OF A SPECULATIVE NATURE

Newman, anticipating in a prophetic sense the theology of the Second Vatican Council, affirms the full richness of the Church's Marian doctrine and devotion, avoiding any extremism or exaggerated sentimentalism without precluding, as the Council itself does not, the possibility of doctrinal development and if need be doctrinal definition in theological, especially Mariological matters, not yet fully defined by the Church's official and living

Magisterium. Newman would insist on the scriptural and patristic roots of a Mariology that is consistent with the Tradition yet capable of devotional expressions varying from culture to culture, from time to time, and from place to place.[1] However, he would not perceive the necessity of formulating the entirety of the Church's teaching regarding Mary in terms of magisterial dogmatic definitions. Nevertheless, as Chapter One recalls, Newman expressed a most positive enthusiasm when faced with the prospect of a papal definition of the Immaculate Conception since he believed that such a doctrine had theologically matured enough as part of the Church's constant belief and practice, thus deserving a definitive dogmatic formulation. Newman would probably insist that a proper consultation of the whole episcopate and through them of the lay faithful—as was carried out by Pope Pius IX in the process of the dogmatic definition of the Immaculate Conception and later after his own day by Pope Pius XII in defining the dogma of the Assumption—to be a most fruitful and perhaps a most necessary step in determining whether or not a particular doctrine were an authentic development of doctrine in the Church's Tradition corresponding to the *sensus fidelium*, indeed the *conspiratio pastorum et fidelium*.

However, there is no doubt whatsoever that although Newman fully accepted the Church's belief in the Assumption just as he fully accepted the Church's teaching on papal infallibility, he did not seem to envision or suggest the need for a magisterial pronouncement that would enshrine either doctrine in a dogmatic definition. Indeed, in the latter case Newman expressed his opinion that the Church's dogmatic definition of papal infallibility at the First Vatican Council was untimely. All this having been considered, Newman himself, despite his reluctance to make recourse to dogmatic definitions, clearly left open the possibility for the latter to occur. It is obvious that such future dogmatic definitions would follow very precise criteria, some of which he even suggested, as already pointed out in his seven notes or tests of doctrinal development and in his twelve theses "De Evolutione Dogmatica" (see Chapter One). The ecumenical factor, however, does not appear to be enumerated among the first of his discriminating principles—although it would be in fact a significant issue for the Popes and the Fathers of the Second Vatican Council (which was deemed in an overall sense a "pasto-

449

ral" and not a dogmatic council), leading them not to undertake any further definitions of dogma whether of a Mariological nature or of any other kind.[2]

A careful search reveals that the *Letter to Pusey* contains the only direct reference that Newman makes to the title of "coredemptress" in his writings. He offers no explanation of the doctrinal content of the title "coredemptress," yet Chapter Seven has sought to provide an explanation of Newman's theology, given the overall context in which this title is favorably acknowledged by Newman in reaction to Pusey's vehement rejection of it. Newman defends the use of the title, "coredemptress," in the *Letter to Pusey* simply by way of acknowledging its validity in light of other titles—which he considers not only legitimate, orthodox, doctrinal and devotional expressions used by the Fathers of the Church, but also titles that bear equal respect, and therefore equal acceptance or rejection by Pusey.

The purpose of this book in general and of this Chapter in particular has been to examine, in as comprehensive a way as possible, Newman's Marian theology and spirituality, so as to offer a contribution to the modern and contemporary theological question about the titles of Mary "Co-Redemptrix," "Advocate" and "Mediatrix" (of All Grace) from the perspective of his understanding of Mary's role of cooperation in the *œconomia salutis*. Mary's cooperation in the *œconomia salutis* associates her with the mystery of Redemption in such a surpassing way that after the role of her Son, her role is said to be the most pivotal. One can safely say that Mary's role in the economy of salvation is essential once God has willed to make it so. In any case, Mary's cooperation must always be understood as hinging on the primary redemptive work of her Son. The salvific value, or, shall we say, "merit" of her cooperation relies solely on that of her Son.

The use of the term "Co-Redemptrix" (or "coredemptress") remains quite equivocal; at best, a cautious, reserved employment of the term is recommended. Although the term "Co-Redemptrix" has been used at different times by various theologians and spiritual writers throughout the centuries,[3] the Magisterium of the Church has never officially determined its precise theological meaning nor sanctioned its official use.[4] The Church avoided use of the term in the Dogmatic Constitution on the Church, *Lumen Gentium*, because debate among the

Council Fathers was inconclusive.[5] This author is convinced that although Newman defends its use in the *Letter to Pusey*, he could possibly be hesitant in promoting a dogmatic definition of the doctrine of Mary "Co-Redemptrix" since at this particular point in the Church's life this precise doctrine and its related title still lack proper theological apprehension. This does not exclude the possibility that with deeper reflection the Church might reach a point when the title, "Co-Redemptrix," might be deemed suitable for proclamation, such as has already occurred in the case of Pope Paul VI's proclamation of the title "Mater Ecclesiæ" at the third session of the Second Vatican Council or the explication of the Church's theology of Mary's maternal mediation, as has been most eloquently reflected on by Pope John Paul II in such magisterial documents as his monumental encyclical, *Redemptoris Mater*.

However, the process by which a title is proclaimed is certainly not to be confused with the process by which a doctrine is dogmatically defined. It must also be considered whether or not there exists the precise motivation (criteria) for the solemn definition of Mary as "Co-Redemptrix," whether considered alone or together with the other proposed doctrines/titles of "Mediatrix" (of all grace) and "Advocate," as were taken into serious consideration in the process of defining the two more recent Marian dogmas. Certainly, there is nothing explicitly stated in Newman's writings to suggest that such a dogmatic definition need occur or that, if indeed another definition of Marian dogma were to take place, that any or all of these precise titles need be the focus of such a definition.

One could safely speculate that if Newman were alive today and asked the hypothetical question: "What, if any, of the Marian doctrines do you think merits a dogmatic definition?" he could possibly respond in many different ways. Perhaps he would enthusiastically embrace a dogmatic definition of the proposed doctrines. Or, perhaps, given the solemn proclamation of the title, *"Mater Ecclesiæ"* by Pope Paul VI, Pope John Paul II's elucidation of *Lumen Gentium*'s teaching on Mary's maternal mediation and a hoped-for consensus of the bishops and the faithful as to their precise theological significance, the doctrines of Mary's motherhood of the Church (i.e., spiritual maternity) and maternal mediation might merit dogmatic definition before the Magisterium would consider whether or not the other proposed doctrines centered on the titles "Co-Redemprix," "Mediatrix" (of all Grace), and "Advocate" were as worthy of consideration in terms of dogmatic definition. Or, perhaps, in answering the same hypothetical question, Newman might express his desire for no dogmatic definition whatsoever. Therefore, these theological considerations and speculations about dogmatic definition are quite obviously open to future research and discussion.

In fine, it is necessary to draw some inferences/conclusions from Newman's theology and spirituality to determine his position concerning Mary's cooperation in the economy of salvation. Having answered our initial question, "Does Newman treat of Mary as Co-Redemptrix?" in Chapter Seven, the hypothetical question remains which we have just raised: "Does Newman believe that the Marian titles of 'Co-Redemptrix,' 'Mediatrix' (of all Grace), and 'Advocate' are theologically mature expressions of essential doctrines about Mary which may or may not merit a solemn dogmatic definition?" It must be said that this question finds no simple answer from a Newmanian perspective, especially given his general reluctance to have recourse to such extraordinary exercise of the Church's official teaching office.

This work, however, does conclude that the doctrines encapsulated in the titles of Mary "Co-Redemptrix," "Mediatrix" (of all Grace) and "Advocate," all find ample support in the theology of Newman but always in strict relationship to the other areas of theology, most especially to the Church's Christological and ecclesiological doctrine/dogma. Thus, for example, Mary's divine maternity and spiritual maternity/motherhood of the Church are two fulcrums of his Mariology. Likewise, this work concludes by noting that Newman makes explicit use of the title "Advocate" and in effect explains from his perspective the doctrine concerning Mary's maternal mediation of all grace although he does not use the title "Mary, Mediatrix of all Grace," but nonetheless explains its significance. Therefore, from a careful study of Newman's Marian theology and spirituality, this work also argues that the doctrine concerning Mary's role as "Advocate" and her maternal mediation of all grace—not limited to the precise use of the title "Mediatrix of All Grace"—are integral to Newman's understanding of the Church's Marian doctrine and devotion and more specifically to this book's precise topic of Mary's cooperation in the *œconomia salutis*. One could also speculate that since Newman understood the Church's use of the *communicatio idiomatum* in addressing Mary as "Advocate," that he would also be comfortable—as he seems to be in the *Letter to Pusey*—in addressing Mary as "Co-Redemptrix" following the same theological principle.

Furthermore, this work holds that Newman, who never directly dismisses the theological appropriateness of the title of Mary "Co-Redemptrix," but on the contrary sanctions its use, at least as a devotional expression in the *Letter to Pusey*, indicates throughout most of his Marian theology and spirituality his preference for the use of the theological term of "cooperation" to describe Mary's singular role in the economy of our redemption and salvation. In this way, Newman most certainly anticipates in his thought the conciliar teaching on the Blessed Virgin Mary in chapter 8 of *Lumen Gentium*. Finally, Newman does not seem to ascribe to the title of "Co-Redemptrix" any real significance beyond that which this paper has demonstrated to be the focal points of his Mariology, which was forged by his being steeped in the Scriptures and in the Fathers of the Church.

We have examined the Venerable Cardinal's Mariological thought from numerous angles. How may it all be summed up? How does he want us to view Our Lady?

Newman the theologian has spoken to us in these pages, but there are other sides to the man, which can assist us in the final analysis, especially the poetic side of him. As Blaise Pascal reminds us, "The heart has reasons the mind knows not of." Newman would agree, and the poetic dimension is never far from his theological musings; indeed, it is intimately connected to them and underpins them. And so, if we were to try to find a pithy yet lovely title for the Blessed Virgin, we discover that he has suggested one himself. In that famous *Letter* to E. B. Pusey, he declares: "Mary may be called, as it were, the daughter of Eve unfallen." This sentence, of course, was the inspiration for the title of this book. The reader will note that it brings us right back to the founts of Newman's reflections on the Blessed Mother—Scripture and the Fathers—all the while, providing us with images of the Paradise of our origins and the Paradise we hope to inherit.

The great Cardinal's insights find echoes in the poetic reflections of other authors, some of whom are cited by him. William Wordsworth referred to Our Lady as "our tainted nature's solitary boast," even as Gerard Manley Hopkins compared her to "the air we breathe." And may we conjecture that Paul Claudel obtained inspiration from Newman, so that he would speak of the Virgin Mary as "younger than sin"?

Considering Mary as "Eve unfallen" allows us to glimpse God's original design for us, especially evident in her roles as the compassionate Mother and faithful Mediatrix, who always cooperated with the Lord's plan and continues to be concerned about the salvation of her children. This is Mariology at its best, taking in the Holy Scriptures and their first expositors, the Fathers of the Church—subsumed into language that transcends and encompasses them all, poetry, the language of love and, on that score, the language of God Himself.

May the "daughter of Eve unfallen" enable all of us to know the high calling that is ours, which her holy example inspires us to imitate, and for which her powerful intercession prays.

Glossary of Terms

The following terms are found with some regularity in the Newman corpus, particularly in reference to his notion of the development of dogma; definitions are offered to aid the reader in understanding how a particular expression is understood by Newman. However, it must also be noted that Newman does not operate within a scholastic framework, as already noted in Chapter One of this work; therefore, "definitions" are not as hard and fast as one might expect in some other theological systems.

The present work relies on definitions of these terms from Newman and from commentators on Newman either when Newman himself does not provide his own definitions or when his definitions are more succinctly expressed in commentaries. These definitions are given to facilitate the reader's comprehension of Newman's thought, especially as it is examined in Chapter One.

Assent: see certitude.

Certitude: From Father Velocci, we learn: "In the current language it is commonplace to confuse assent with certitude; but between them there are notable differences. This will be made evident to us in a description of that which Newman defines as *inquiry* and *investigation*. Inquiry designates the research of one who has found the truth and who does not know where the truth is to be found. This research, for the most part implicit, is subjected to a variety of circumstances; implicates doubts, hesitations, hypothesis, errors; it terminates when, on account of various indications and experiences, man gives his assent to that which appears to him to be the truth. At this point one would want to make an account of his judgment, of his assent; he would want to be 'certain' about it. Then he enters into a second phase, that of 'investigation', which can be defined as the return of his consensus concerning antecedent rationales, a reflection on the motives that have brought to a proposition unconditional adherence. With this reflection Newman intends to give order and clarity to 'inquiry', to explicate the logical concatenation and the convergence of indications that served as immediate antecedents to assent. It is important to highlight that this return does not imply the necessity of doubting the assent that has already been given and to suspend it; in some cases however at the end of the 'investigation' the assent can be revealed as not justified and therefore one must reject it. But ordinarily the 'investigation' confirms the assent and makes possible certitude in a strict sense, permitting the intellect to give a new assent to the initial one. Therefore certitude is a reflected assent, fully conscious of its motives and of its antecedents. While simple assent rises up after 'inquiry', certitude derives from a basic assent upon which the spirit returns in order to justify it. In brief certitude is an assent not only to a given proposition, but also to the demand of this proposition to be accepted as true. It is assent to an assent, to that which commonly is called conviction." [1]

Communis fidelium sensus: "Common or universal sentiment of the faithful." [2]

Communitas fidelium: "Community of the faithful." [3]

Conscience: This description comes also from Velocci: "According to the thought of Newman, good dispositions are found above all in the conscience, 'the true light that enlightens every man who comes into the world.' Always, in whatever circumstance, in every situation, man has within him a law, an imperious dictation, an authoritative voice that commands him to do some things and to avoid others. This mysterious law is the conscience. . . . Conscience always means having a relationship to a person; it does not stop at actions, but considers them united to those who accomplish them. The conscience does not repose in itself, but pushes itself further, and discerns a higher sanction for its decisions, as is evident from the acute sense of responsibility that informs it. . . . conscience is truly 'the primitive vicar of Christ; a prophet with its information; a king with its peremptory orders, a priest with its benedictions.' Therefore, according to the thought of Newman, the first preparation for faith comes about in the conscience; to educate the conscience means to educate in the faith." [4]

Consensus fidelium: An intensification and collectivization of *sensus fidelium*.

Consultation: Newman uses the verb *consult* in two primary senses in regard to the involvement of the laity in matters of doctrine. The first sense is a passive one, in which, Newman says, the hierarchy consults the laity as one consults a barometer to see how it behaves. The second sense is an active one, by which Newman means to take notice of the opinion of the laity. Owen Chadwick, summarizing Newman's thought, adds that "this is not the absurd idea that we must conduct polls into people's preferences. It is the conviction that within the body of Christian men and women is the experience of truth, and that this experience has something to say about new creeds or new ways of prayer. He [Newman] defined this consensus of the Christian people as a 'sort of instinct.'"[5]

Depositum fidei: "Newman uses the term 'deposit of faith,' then, to mean the Word of God as fully understood and defined. Since that Word dwells in the Spirit and in the Apostles, fully understood, and in the Church, but partially defined, he was able to speak of the Word in the Church as capable of growth and of the Word as possessed by the Spirit as surpassing the understanding of any single human intellect."[6]

Dogma, Principle of: This principle is found in the "supernatural truths irrevocably committed to human language, imperfect because it is human, but definitive and necessary because given from above."[7] Walter P. Burke makes the following clarification: Newman "is well aware that a dogma is composed of two elements: a formula and a divine truth. The formula, of course, is the organized group of terms which contain and express the divine truth. Even in his appreciation of the formulas, we see the master idea of Newman in action beholding the formula as itself a living thing and participating in the vitality of the truth that it expresses. . . . The formula, then, is readily comprehended as very intimately sharing in the life of the truth it contains and manifests."[8] Next, Chadwick reflects on Newman's concept of dogma, as inseparable from the lived experience of faith: "Religious truth is not to be accepted with the top of the head, like a calculation of the width of the English Channel. The community has to live this truth. Its members meditate on it, dwell on it, draw out its meaning, apply it in moral predicaments, come to an affection for it, learn to give it reverence. In this way a 'dogma' is not a bald, hard, literal sentence. It is a mode of expression which can only be understood rightly in relation to a surrounding of religious life and experience; and it is by leading that religious life that we come to understand the 'dogma' more fully."[9] Finally, Francesco Turvasi demonstrates how all this comes together within the individual believer: To understand the meaning which Newman gives to dogma, we must appeal to the well-known distinction he makes between "real apprehension" and "notional apprehension." To "real apprehension" corresponds "real assent," which is given to concrete reality; to "notional apprehension" corresponds "notional assent," which is given to an abstract concept. Of these two modes of apprehending propositions, real assent is stronger, more vivid, than notional assent, because the experience of concrete

459

facts is more effective than an abstract idea. Applied to religion, Newman calls "real assent" the act of faith to the reality which is proposed by Sacred Scripture (Newman gives the example of the Holy Trinity, Father, Son, and Holy Spirit). He calls "notional assent" the act of faith to the dogmatic propositions.[10]

Ecclesia docens: The teaching Church is the Magisterium, comprised of the Pope and the bishops in communion with him.

Ecclesia discens: The Church that is taught, that is, the whole body of Christian faithful.

Faith and Devotion, the distinction between: "By 'faith' I mean the Creed and assent to the Creed; by 'devotion' I mean such religious honors as belong to the object of our faith, and the payment of those honors. Faith and devotion are distinct in fact, as they are in idea. We cannot, indeed, be devout without faith, but we may believe without feeling devotion."[11]

Fides implicita: "Implicit faith, a technical theological term indicating that aspect of the virtue of faith whereby one accepts the implications of a dogma before they have been formally defined."[12]

Illative sense: "He [Newman] coined the expression to describe the act of assent in the mind based upon a body of grounds in their totality, even though the mind is not aware of all the grounds treated as separate arguments, and may be resting on half-inarticulate experience as well as argument. This was the assent which turned the accumulation of probabilities into certitude."[13] Newman uses *phronesis* as a synonym for the illative sense. Coulson adds: "It is clear that, for Newman, the individual conscience (*phronesis*) finds its fulfillment only in the *phronema*, the common conscience of the Church in her entirety: The one is the mirror of the other—a mirror into which at times we can see ourselves with greater clarity and in which our moral concepts find fulfillment and support."[14]

Judices fidei: The judges of the Church; the teaching Church.

Nexus mysteriorum: Newman, without using the term, explains its meaning: "We know, my brethren, that in the natural world nothing is superfluous, nothing incomplete, nothing independent; but part answers to part, and all details combine to form one mighty whole. . . . The case is the same as regards the supernatural world. The great truths of Revelation are all connected together and form a whole. Everyone can see this in a measure even at a glance, but to understand the full consistency and harmony of Catholic teaching requires study and meditation. . . . I am going to apply this remark to the subject of the prerogatives with which the Church invests the Blessed Mother of God. They are startling and difficult to those whose imagination is not accustomed to them, and whose reason has not reflected on them; but the more carefully and religiously they are dwelt on, the more, I am sure, will they be found essential to the Catholic Faith, and integral to the worship of Christ. This simply is the point which I shall insist on—disputable indeed by aliens from the Church, but most clear to her children;—that the glories of Mary are for the sake of Jesus; and that we praise and bless her as the first of creatures, that we may duly confess Him as our sole Creator." [15]

Objective Word of God: "Newman takes on his general topic 'the Word of God,' that is, divine revelation or 'Gospel truth,' which he distinguishes as 'objective' and 'subjective'. As objective it is given once and for all, simple and integral, existing as such in the mind of God, but also communicated to the Apostles and to the Church where it is the foundation of dogma. This is the Word of God 'in itself' or absolutely, hence unchangeable." [16]

Œconomia (salutis): The dispensation of God's self-revelation (*ad extra; pro nobis*) in the history of salvation. Newman writes: "The word 'Economy' occurs in St. Paul's Epistle to the Ephesians, where it is used for that series of divine appointments viewed as a whole, by which the Gospel is introduced and realized among mankind, being translated in our version 'dispensation'. It will evidently bear a wider sense, embracing the Jewish and patriarchal dispensations, or any divine procedure, greater or less, which consists of means and an end. Thus it is applied by the Fathers to the history of Christ's humiliation, as exhibited in the doctrines of His incarnation, ministry, atonement, exaltation, and mediatorial sovereignty." [17] This should be seen in contradistinction to "*Theologia*," which, for him, is God *in se/ad intra*. In his words, *theologia* is "the collection of truths relative to His [Christ's] personal indwelling in the bosom of God." Yves Congar identifies the affinity between Saint Thomas Aquinas' and Newman's "sense of the salvific economy" ("*le sens de l'Écono-maire salutaire*"): "The work of Revelation and of the salutary teaching (Sacred Doctrine) is coextensive with human history. Leaving aside here the question of progress or that of an explication of dogmatic knowledge in the womb of the Church: it requires a particular development. It is preceded by a progress of Revelation properly called, that to which Saint Thomas gives a particular attention in the concise articles which he dedicated to them, ST, II-II,

I, 7 et 174,6, it would necessary to join a view expressed in passing, ST, III, 61, 3, ad 2, that one should want to join closer the one with that of *Newman*, with much greater depth. . . ." [18]

Pastorum et fidelium conspiratio: The unity of thought and action which should exist between the hierarchy (pastors) and the laity (faithful). Femiano comments: "When Newman speaks of them (hierarchy) joining with the faithful to form a *conspiratio*, he is not speaking of them as 'judges' (*judices*) of the faith but as witnesses to the faith." And again: "Even though there is a *conspiratio* of the laity and hierarchy in the giving of witness, their relations do not cease to be those of the Church teaching (*Ecclesia docens*) and the Church that has been taught (*Ecclesia discens*)." [19]

Securus judicat orbis terrarum: "The whole world judges securely." In his *Apologia*, Newman explains: "For a mere sentence, the words of St. Augustine, struck me with a power which I never had felt from any words before . . . they were like the *'Tolle, lege'* of the child, which converted Saint Augustine himself. . . . By those great words of the ancient Father, interpreting, and summing up the long and varied course of ecclesiastical history, the theory of the *Via Media* was absolutely pulverized." [20] Ker comments: "The words that made such a deep impression on Newman are not altogether easy to translate. Newman's own (free) rendering was: 'The universal Church is in its judgments secure of truth.' The translation makes the point: It was the idea of *the Church*, not a part or branch of the Church, but the Church universal that struck Newman so powerfully." [21] Or, as Chadwick puts it, "if everyone agrees, the verdict must be right." [22] Christopher Hollis puts an even finer point on it thus: "Though himself the most home-loving and insular of men, he yet tried to teach his fellow countrymen, at a time when they were by no means generally ready to learn the lesson, that the last word on all ultimate questions was not necessarily said by an Englishman—that the appeal was to the world's court. . . ." [23]

Sensus fidelium: "Newman described [this]: 1) As a testimony of the apostolical dogma; 2) as a sort of instinct, or *phronema* deep in the bosom of the Mystical Body of Christ; 3) as a direction of the Holy Ghost; 4) as an answer to prayer; 5) as an abhorrence to error, which it at once feels as a scandal." [24] Patterson translates the expression and explains further: ". . . literally, 'sense of the faithful,' but better described as an instinct or power of discernment whereby one who has the faith is able to distinguish between what is true and what is false, what is compatible with his faith and what is not." [25]

Subjective Word of God: "Divine revelation as grasped, partially and distinctively, by each individual believer in her or his peculiar situation of time, place, and innumerable circumstances." [26]

Tradition: Newman offers this: "It [Tradition] is latent, but it lives. It is silent, like the rapids of a river, before the rocks intercept it. It is the Church's unconscious habit of opinion and sentiment; which she reflects upon, masters, and expresses, according to the emergency. We see then the mistake of asking for a complete collection of the Roman Traditions; as well might we ask for a full catalogue of man's tastes and thoughts on a given subject. Tradition in its fullness is necessarily unwritten; it is the mode in which a society has felt or acted during a certain period, and it cannot be circumscribed any more than a man's countenance and manner can be conveyed to strangers in any set of propositions." [27] According to Newman, Tradition is "the living force, the breathing form, the expressive countenance, which preaches, which catechizes." [28]

Via media: Newman's forging of a *tertium quid* between a perceived exaggerated dogmatism within the Church of Rome and the nearly total abandonment of any doctrinal commitment within what Newman dubbed "liberalism in religion," found especially in the Protestantism of his era. Rowell summarizes it thus: "The Church as a school for saints, built up by apostolic creeds, and ministry, and sacraments, was a vision Newman had derived from his study of the Fathers, and it was the appeal to the undivided Church of the first four centuries which seemed to him characteristic of Anglicanism. As the Church of England strove to remain faithful to that tradition, in distinction from the over-systematization of Roman theology and the idiosyncratic individualism of Protestantism, she witnessed to a *via media*." [29]

A Chronological Schema of Significant Events in Newman's Life *

1801–1845
LIFE IN THE CHURCH OF ENGLAND

1801
21 Feb	N. is born in London.
9 April	N. baptized in the Church of St. Benet, Funk.

1808
1 May	Attends school at Ealing; Dr. Nicholas of Wadham College, Oxford (8 years there): skill in writing prose, verse at age eleven; desire to be virtuous but not religious at age fourteen; always possessing a sense of God's presence; meets Rev. Walter Mayer (deep Calvinistic impressions, just before Oxford).

1816
1 Aug–21 Dec	N.'s first religious conversion.
14 Dec	N. enters Trinity College, Oxford.

1817
8 June	N. comes to residence at Oxford.

1818
18 May	N. is elected scholar of Trinity; friendship with John Williams Bowden at Trinity. Reads Gibbon, Locke during long vacation.

1820
	Failure in schools; decides to pursue Holy Orders instead of law.

1822
12 April	N. gains Oriel Fellowship. N.'s association with Keble, Hawkins, Tyler. (1) Liberal influence: Whately; Noetics. (2) Friendship with Hurrell, Froude, and end of Liberal thought.

1824
16 May	N. meets Edward B. Pusey.

* Use of the Chronology as given in the *Positio* for Newman's canonization is gratefully acknowledged.

13 June–4 July	N. takes Holy Orders; accepts curacy of St. Clement's.
1824–1826	Influence of Copleston, Darwin, Whately, Hawkins, Arnold, Blanco White.
1825–1826	N. is vice-principal of Alban Hall under Whately.
1826	N. meets Hurrell, Froude; is appointed public tutor of Oriel; resigns curacy of St. Clement's.
1827	N. has serious illness.
1828	
5 Jan	Death of N.'s sister Mary.
2 Feb	N. vicar of St. Mary's.
	N. begins reading the Fathers.
1829	Catholic Emancipation.
1832	
July	N. finishes writing *Arians.*
Dec 1832–	
April 1833	N. takes Mediterranean trip with Froude (Malta, Naples, Palermo, Egesta, Rome, Sicily; a fever and a crisis in his life).
1833	
16 June	N. writes *Lead, Kindly Light.*
July	N. arrives back in England.
14 July	Keble's sermon "The National Apostasy."
9 Sept	*Tracts for the Times* begins
5 Nov	N. publishes *Arians of the Fourth Century.*
1834	
11 March	N. publishes *Parochial Sermons*, vol. 1.
1835	
27 March	N. publishes *Parochial Sermons*, vol. 2.
1836	N. begins editing the Library of the Fathers; editor of *British Critic*; Hurrell Froude dies
29 Jan	N. publishes *Parochial Sermons*, vol. 3.
10 Feb	N. publishes *Elucidations of Dr. Hampden's Theological Statements.*
1837	
11 March	N. publishes *Prophetical Office of the Church.*
1838	Height of N.'s influence at Oxford.
30 March	N. publishes *Lectures on Justification.*
30 Nov	N. publishes *Parochial Sermons*, vol. 4.
1839	
April; July–Sept	N. begins reading about Monophysite controversy; has first doubts about Anglicanism.
October	N. first hints at becoming Roman Catholic.

1840	"A new position": Church of England is a "branch" of the Church, as Roman Catholicism is; letters mention prospect of N.'s going over to Rome; N.'s plans for possible future monastic community at Littlemore.
	N. publishes *Parochial Sermons*, vol. 5.
1841	Presupposition for Rome's side.
27 Feb	N. publishes Tract 90.
1842	
February	N. publishes *Parochial Sermons*, vol. 6.
19 April	N. moves to Littlemore to live a semi-monastic life.
	N. publishes part one of *Select Treatises of Saint Athanasius in Controversy with the Arians* in the Library of the Fathers.
1843	N. writes to a friend that the Roman Catholic Church is the Church of the Apostles.
18 Sept	N. resigns vicarage of St. Mary's.
25 Sept	N. publishes *Sermons, Chiefly on the History of Religious Belief, Preached before the University of Oxford*.
	N. publishes *Sermons Bearing on Subjects of the Day*.
	N. publishes *Plain Sermons*, vol. 5.
1844	N. publishes part two of *Select Treatises of Saint Athanasius in Controversy with the Arians*.

1845–1846
NEWMAN'S LAST DAYS AT LITTLEMORE

1845	
February	End of Oxford Movement.
Summer	First group of converts from the Movement to Roman Catholicism living at Littlemore: Ambrose St. John, J. B. Dalgairns, Richard Stanton, E. S. Bowles
27 Sept	Dalgairns enters Catholic Church through Blessed Dominic Barberi.
3 Oct	N. resigns Oriel Fellowship.
8 Oct	N. makes general confession to Fr. Barberi in Littlemore Oratory.
9 Oct	N.'s Mass and First Communion at Littlemore.
1 Nov	N.'s Confirmation from Dr. Wiseman at Oscott (Confirmation name: Mary).
1846	N. at Maryvale.
23 Feb	Group from Littlemore moves to Oscott.

	N. preparing for Catholic ministry.
May	N. receives minor orders.
June–July	Pope Gregory XVI dies; Pope Pius IX sends N. a special blessing.
c. Sept/Oct	N.'s trip to Milan.
28 Oct	N. arrives in Rome.
1847	
Jan–Feb	N.'s plans to become an Oratorian.
Spring	Oratorian novitiate set up in Rome at Santa Croce: Newman, St. John, Penny, Dalgairns, Coffin, Stanton, Bowles; led by Fr. Rossi of Rome Oratory.
22 May	Examination for Orders.
26 May	Sub-diaconate ordination by Cardinal Franzoni.
29 May	N. receives Diaconate ordination.
30 May	N. receives Priesthood ordination.
6 Dec	N. departs Rome.
24 Dec	N. arrives in London.

1848–1850
THE ENGLISH ORATORY

1848	N. publishes *Loss and Gain*.
1 Feb	N.'s first Mass at Maryvale; members of new English Oratory assemble at Maryvale: Frs. St. John, Dalgairns, Penny, Stanton, Coffin; Fr. Knox (a novice), three lay brothers.
14 Feb	Frederick Faber and the Wilfridians are admitted.
31 Oct	N. leaves Maryvale for St. Wilfrid's, Cotton.
1849	
2 Feb	Arrangement of new Oratory in Alcester Street, Birmingham; first plan for Fr. Faber and others not in sympathy with N. to form London Oratory.
15 April	Fr. Faber moves to London.
31 May	Formal opening of London Oratory.
November	N.'s *Discourses to Mixed Congregations* published.

1850–1851
"THE PAPAL AGGRESSION" CAMPAIGN (NO PAPACY)

| 1850 | |
| *9 May* | N. begins weekly lectures at King William Street: *The Difficulties of Anglicans*; a high point of optimism in N.s life. |

1851–1854
THE CATHOLIC UNIVERSITY OF IRELAND

1851

6 April	Manning received into the Church.
15 April	Oratorians move to new house in Hagley Road.
May	*Oratorium Parvum* started for lay Catholics.
30 June	N. begins weekly lectures on *Catholicism in England* at the Corn Exchange.
July	Dr. Cullen, Archbishop of Armagh, asks N. to be founding rector of a Catholic university in Ireland.
July	N.s Corn Exchange lecture on Dr. Achilli, apostate priest.
Aug	Achilli's libel suit against N. begins.

1852

10 May	N.'s lectures on the "Scope and Nature of University Education" written; first lecture delivered in Dublin.
7 June	Dublin lectures concluded.
21 June	Achilli trial begins.
25 June	Achilli trial ends; N. found guilty of libel.
13 July	N. preaches sermon "The Second Spring," on the establishment of the restored hierarchy.
22 Nov	Sentencing from trial scheduled; new trial suggested.

1853

26 Jan	New trial refused.
31 Jan	N. fined 100 pounds; avoids prison time.
February	Fr. Joseph Gordon dies (first death among the Oratorians).
Spring	N.'s trial expenses of 12,000 British pounds paid by donations from Catholics from many countries.
August	N. publishes *Verses on Religious Subjects.*

1854–1858
UNIVERSITY LECTURES

1854

	N. publishes *Letters on the Crimean War.*
Jan–Feb	Rumors of plans to make N. a bishop.
February	N. thinks the Irish university is doomed to fail.
7 Feb	N. arrives in Dublin.
20 March	N. returns to England.

22 March	N. opens Brompton Oratory.
4 June	N. installed as rector.
5 Sept	N. returns to Ireland.
3 Nov	School of Philosophy and Letters opened. N.'s inaugural address: *Christianity and Letters.*
1855	N.'s university lectures on freedom of scientific investigation.
November	N. publishes *Christianity and Scientific Investigation.*
1856	N. finishes *Callista* (begun 1849, then laid aside).
April	N. tells Dr. Cullen he will resign the next year.
1 May	N. publishes *Callista, A Sketch of the Third Century.*

1857–1859
NEW UNDERTAKINGS

1857	
March	N. offers resignation (to take effect 14 November 1857)
5 May	The Oratory recalls N. from his leave of absence from Birmingham.
26 Aug	N. invited by Cardinal Wiseman to edit a new English version of the Bible.
27 Aug	N. publishes *Sermons Preached on Various Occasions.*
14 Sept	N. accepts Wiseman's invitation.
	N. works on *Prolegomena* for the Bible translation.
1858	N. abandons work on the Bible project; works with the *Rambler* and *Atlantis*; after November 1858, final resignation of the Irish rectorship, one year of nonresident rectorship.

1859–1862
"THE RAMBLER" AND ROME

1859	
21 March	N. takes over as editor of *The Rambler*.
May	Opening of Oratory School at Edgbaston.
July	Ne resigns as editor of *The Rambler*; publishes article in the July issue "On Consulting the Faithful in Matters of Doctrine."
July	N. continues to make contributions to the *The Rambler* (till July 1860).

1859–1864
SAD DAYS

1859	War between Italy and Austria.
1860	Loss of territory from the Papal States.
1862	*The Rambler* is changed to a quarterly called *The Home and Foreign Review.*
1864	N., thinking he is at the end of his life and career, prepares to die.
21 April	N. begins publication of *Apologia* in weekly installments.
	Success of the *Apologia* wins N. respect in the Catholic world; possibility of establishing a Catholic mission at Oxford blocked.
December	Pope Pius IX publishes *Syllabus Errorum.*
1865	A new archbishop for Westminister; Pusey publishes his *Eirenicon.*
February	Cardinal Wiseman dies.
May–June	N. publishes *Dream of Gerontius.*
June	Manning consecrated archbishop of Westminster.
December	N. publishes *Letter to Pusey.*

1866–1867
NEWMAN'S RETURN TO OXFORD

1866	
31 March	R. W. Church publishes *Times* review of N.'s *Letter to Pusey.*
April	N. is again offered a mission at Oxford.
Summer	N. begins notes on a work on faith and reason (later titled *Essay in Aid of a Grammar of Assent*). Propaganda Fide approves of the Oxford mission by end of year.
1867	
6 April	Permission for Oxford mission revoked (so that N. could not reside at Oxford); key issue of suspicion of N.'s orthodoxy was his refusal to explain or retract his *Rambler* article "Consulting the Faithful on Matters of Doctrine."
	Appeal to Rome; deadlock in higher education.
April–May	Fr. Bittleston and Fr. St. John in Rome to represent N.'s case.
26 June	Vatican Council I announced.

1867–1868
Debates on Papal Infallibility

1867
   13 Oct   Bishop of Birmingham issues pastoral letter discouraging Catholics from attending Oxford.

1868   N. is asked by Pope to help prepare material for Vatican Council I.

   January   N. publishes *Verses on Various Occasions*.

1869–1870
Vatican Council I

1870
   March   N. publishes *Essay in Aid of a Grammar of Assent*.
   18 July   Papal infallibility defined.
   September Loss of the Papal States.
   October   N. publishes *Essays on Miracles*.

1871–1874
After the Council

1871–1874   N. works on revisions of his writings (including Anglican writings): *Essays Critical and Historical*, 2 vols.

1872 (mid)   A period of N.'s friends dying.
1873
   December   N. expresses support for lay and clerical cooperation in running universities.

1874
   November   Gladstone attacks on papal infallibility.
1875
   January   N. publishes *Letter to the Duke of Norfolk*.
   May   Death of Ambrose St. John, N.'s closest friend.
1877   N. made honorary Fellow of Trinity College; the Pope confers the D.D. degree on him.

1878
   April   Election of Pope Leo XIII.
             N. revises *Athanasius*.
1879   Public controversy over the cardinalate; rumor that N. had refused the cardinalate.
             N. receives the biglietto; the *Biglietto Speech*.
   25 Dec   N.'s sister, Mrs. John Mozely, dies.

1880–1890
FINAL TASKS AND LAST YEARS

1883	N. writes on the *Inspiration of Scripture* in nineteenth century.
1885	
October	N. publishes essay "The Development of Religious Error" in *Contemporary Review* (reply to Dr. Fairbairn's attack).
1888	
1 Jan	N. gives his last sermon.
1889	
25 Dec	N. offers his last Mass.
1890	
10 August	N. receives the last sacraments.
11 August	N.'s death.
19 August	N.'s funeral at Rednal.

NOTES

FOREWORD

1. *The Life of Cardinal Newman*, vol. 1 (New York: Longmans, Green, 1912), 204.

INTRODUCTION

1. Cf. Jean Guitton, *Il Secolo che Verrà: Conversazioni con Phillipe Guyard*, trans. Antonietta Francavilla (Milan: Bompiani, 1999), 141. Guitton asserts: "Credo che i grandi Concili siano stati ispirati da grandi pensatori: Il Concilio di Trento da San Tommaso, il Concilio di Nicea da Sant'Atanasio. Penso che il Concilio attuale, nei tempi futuri, considerà con ragione che il personaggio che lo ha più ispirato e meglio spiegato a quelli che non comprendono sia il cardinale Newman." Along these same lines, Jean Guitton writes: "I grandi geni e i grandi avvenimenti storici hanno tra loro un rapporto segreto e reciproco. I grandi geni sono profeti sempre pronti a rischiarare i grandi avvenimenti, i quali a loro volta gettano sui grandi geni una luce retrospettiva che dona loro un carattere profetico. È come il rapporto che intercorre tra Isaia e la Passione, reciprocamente illuminati. Così Newman rischiara della sua presenza il Concilio, e il Concilio giustifica Newman" (OssR, 28 October 1963).

2. God's economy or plan of salvation.

3. Some might argue that Newman's *A Letter Addressed to the Rev. E. B. Pusey* (hereafter *Letter to Pusey*) is just such a treatment. However, it does not seem to have been the intent of Newman to make of it a systematic treatment of Mariology. Although the *Letter to Pusey* is rightly hailed as Newman's most formidable and comprehensive treatment of Marian topics—indeed, it is a veritable treasure-house of the Church's teaching on the Virgin—it does not exhaust Newman's Mariological contribution; besides that, it is most fruitfully studied in relation to his other Mariological writings, most especially his *Meditations and Devotions*, and when viewed as an intrinsic part of his entire output.

4. Jean Guitton has remarked that Cardinal Newman should be considered the *Doctor Marianus* of the nineteenth century.

5. Cf. Michael O'Carroll, "Our Lady in Newman and Vatican II," *Downside Review* 89 (1971), 38–63.

6. It is important to remember that Vatican II, as a pastoral council (rather than a dogmatic council), did not desire to define any Marian dogmas or limit the freedom of theologians to develop currently acceptable lines of theological thought regarding the Blessed Virgin; indeed, theologians were actually encouraged to pursue such work. Second, the Fathers acknowledged various titles in use among the Christian faithful and indicated their propriety, all the while setting parameters for their use; notably absent from the list is that of "Co-Redemptrix" (cf. LG 54, 62).

7. Cf. Salvatore De Meo, "Concilio Vaticano II," in NDM, 384–387.

8. Here, Father Perrella notes the following criteria: "*il criterio biblico, antropologico, ecumenico, pastorale.*" The reader will notice that other criteria (*istanze*, instances) have been added (not mentioned directly by either Father Perrella or Father De Meo), which are likewise operative in the conciliar documents and are equally evident as criteria of Newman's own Mariology.

9. Cf. the article entitled "Mariologia" by the Reverend Stefano De Fiores, S.M.M., in NDT, 904–914.

10. The Reverend Giovanni Velocci, C.Ss.R., writes: "Quello della storia della salvezza è un capitolo della teologia al quale Newman ha portato un notevole contributo": *Newman: Il Coraggio della Verità* (Vatican City: Libreria Editrice Vaticana, 2000), 161.

11. Cf. LG 56.

12. Salvatore M. Perrella, "Maria di Nazereth nel Mistero di Cristo e della Chiesa tra il Vaticano II e la *Tertio Millenio Adveniente* (1959–1998)," *Marianum Ephemerides Mariologiæ*, 60, nos. 153–154 (1998), 432–439, passim. Cf. also Velocci, *Il Coraggio della Verità*, 157–162. Perrella writes: "In questo ambito di stretta unione e *cooperazione*—verbo ricorrente nella dottrina mariana del Concilio—alla persona e all'opera del Verbo incarnato e salvatore e con il ministero della Chiesa suo sacramento di salvezza dovranno essere lette e interpretate la vicenda, la funzione e il carisma della santa Vergine. Ed è sempre in questo contesto di cooperazione della Madre nell'opera della salvezza di Cristo che emergono alcune istanze o criteri operativi nel capitolo VIII della *Lumen Gentium* . . . . *Istanza biblica*, che propone l'itinerario di fede e di associazione di Maria a Cristo in tutta la vicenda evangelica, fin dalle adombrazioni veterotestamentarie . . . . *Istanza patristica* che convalida la figura evangelica della Madre di Gesù mostrandone la sua intima ed esemplare unione con la Chiesa, di cui è membro eccellente e icona amatissima. *Istanza ecumenica* che coinvolge la comunità cattolica a considerare e valutare con verità, carità e lungimiranza i 'beni comuni' non depauperati dalla divisione e insiti nelle altre Chiese, ritenendo le differenze succedutesi nel tempo come fattori di dialogo e di reciproco arrichimento: senza l'unione di tutti i cristiani—afferma il Concilio—non si manifesta in pienezza la cattolicità . . . il nuovo canovaccio dottrinale mariano . . . fondandolo e imbastendolo sul riconscimento del primato assiologico della Rivelazione divina e biblica, sulla lettura dell'evento mariano in ottica prevalentemente cristologica ed ecclesiologica . . . . *Istanza antropologica*, che percorre il passato e l'oggi di Maria di Nazareth nel suo rapportarsi alla Chiesa, all'uomo/donna e al mondo. . . . Volle intenzionalmente mostrare che la sua partecipazione al mistero salvifico non si ridusse ad una mera funzione biologica, ma impegnò ancor più la sua totale disponibilità e cooperazione libera ed eroica con Dio. In tal modo la figura evangelica di Maria si colora di sfumature umane, ma più ancora si mostra in tutta la sua grandezza nella sinergia con la grazia divina, da cui nasce e si sviluppa il suo cammino progressivo di ubbidienza e di fede, di conoscenza, di speranza, di ardente carità."

13. Cf. AP, 24f. Newman writes: "I had a true devotion to the Blessed Virgin, in whose College I lived, whose altar I served, and whose Immaculate Purity I had in one of my earliest printed sermons made much of." The Reverend Stephen Dessain, C.O., in discussing Mary's place in Newman's preaching,

cites the above text and explains that "this was the sermon, The Reverence Due to the Virgin Mary, first preached on 25 March 1832, more than a year before what is usually considered to be the beginning of the Oxford Movement": *Cardinal Newman's Teaching about the Blessed Virgin Mary* (Birmingham, Eng.: The Friends of Cardinal Newman, n.d.), 3.

14. Mary bears the title *Mater Ecclesiæ* (Mother of the Church).

15. Blessed Pope Pius IX, as Velocci explains, "lo [Newman] ricevette più volte in udienza, lo accolse con paterna benevolenza, lo incoraggiò a stabilire in Inghilterra l'oratorio filippino; ma forse non capì il suo genio" (235). Pope Leo XIII created John Henry Newman a Cardinal (12–15 May 1879). Velocci writes: "Lo capì invece Leone XIII e dimostrò la sua stima creandolo cardinale . . . . Quando nel febbraio del 1878 Leone XIII fu eletto papa, l'archeologo Giovanni Battista de Rossi, suo amico da vecchia data, gli chiese quale sarebbe stata la linea del suo pontificato; ed egli rispose: 'Aspettate fino a che non avrete visto il mio primo cardinale. Comprenderete allora quale sarà la nota caratteristica del mio pontificato.' L'uomo a cui si riferiva la risposta, era John Henry Newman, il famoso dotto e predicatore di Oxford, il grande convertito dall'anglicanesimo, che era diventato prete cattolico e viveva da tempo nella solititudine dell'Oratorio di Birmingham. Il Papa aveva una stima immensa per lui e la manifestò in varie circostanze: ne ammirava il genio, la dottrina, la pietà, l'attaccamento filiale alla Santa Sede e i grandi servizi resi alla causa della religione" (235). Pope St. Pius X, in his letter to the bishops of Ireland entitled *Tum illud opusculum*, exonerated Newman of any false accusations of having followed a modernist method in his philosophical-theological speculation. The letter became an occasion for the Pope to vindicate Newman's exemplarity as a philosopher-theologian in contradistinction to those modernists who rejected the Magisterium and resisted obedience to the Vicar of Christ. Velocci clarifies: "Anche se, Newman ha usato un linguaggio nuovo, non è possibile, come vorrebbero i modernisti, forzarlo per sostenere le loro opinioni. Concludendo la lettera, il Papa fa voti che i modernisti studino Newman, non applicando ai suoi libri i loro preconcetti, ma sapendo cogliere con piena oggettività i suoi principi e il suo spirito. E imparino da un simile Maestro una grande lezione: il rispetto per il magistero della Chiesa, la fedeltà assoluta alla dottrina dei Padri, l'ubbidienza al papa che è la salvaguardia della fede" (242). Pope Pius XII did not hesitate, on many an occasion, to add his own accolades to the praises of Newman offered by his predecessors on the Chair of Peter. The *Pastor Angelicus* was an avid admirer of Newman and such an assiduous reader of his works that he had his *opera omnia* in his private library. Velocci concludes his section on Pope Pius XII and Newman by relating Pope Pius' prophetic words (*Deo volente*) to Jean Guitton: "Pio XII manifestò la sua stima e il suo amore per Newman in un incontro con l'accademico di Francia, J. Guitton; dopo aver parlato della grandezza di Newman, della sua santità di vita, dell'altezza e profondità della sua dottrina egli soggiunse: 'Non dubiti, signor Guitton, Newman sarà un giorno Dottore della Chiesa'"(248). Pope John XXIII inherited Pope Pius XII's private collection of Newman's works. On the desk in his study, *il Papa Buono* kept other biographical works having to do with Newman and/or *Pippo Buono*—the nickname for St. Philip Neri, founder of the Oratory at Rome. Pope Paul VI,

during a Cardinal Newman Symposium held in April of the Holy Year 1975, illustrated some of the reasons why he considered Newman to be a prophetic voice of the Second Vatican Council. Velocci recounts: "Nell'udienza concessa ai partecipanti al convegno egli accennò ancora alle mirabili intuizioni di Newman, ma volle mettere in risalto specialmente la sua attualità, il suo 'potente esempio e il suo insegnamento per trarne delle conclusioni pratiche e delle risposte valide per i problemi del tempo presente.' Il Papa mise in rilievo anche la presenza invisibile di Newman al Concilio Vaticano II: 'Molti problemi che egli trattò con sapienza . . . furono i temi delle discussioni e dello studio dei padri di questo Concilio, per esempio, la questione dell'ecumenismo, le relazioni tra il cristianesimo e il mondo contemporaneo, il compito dei laici nella Chiesa, i rapporti tra la Chiesa e le religioni non cristiane'" (252). Pope John Paul I, even during his brief thirty-day reign, made recourse to the writings of the Venerable Newman, citing during a discourse on the Faith, Newman's famous line: "Ten thousand difficulties do not make a single doubt" (254). Finally, we arrive at the present pontificate during which Pope John Paul II has ushered the cause of Newman into the third millennium. Velocci points out that the Holy Father, already within a short period after his election, saw fit to make several mentions of Newman (254–257). Of particular importance is Pope John Paul's Letter to the Church in England on the occasion of the hundredth anniversary of Newman's elevation to the Sacred College of Cardinals. Cf. OssR, English Edition (21 May 1979), 5, as well as his allusion to Newman during the consistory of 2001, coincidentally on the two hundredth anniversary of Newman's birth. See also Pope John Paul II, "Message of His Holiness to the Most Reverend G. P. Dwyer" (OssR, 14 May 1980). Also, the letter of Pope John Paul II to Archbishop Vincent Nichols of Birmingham, England, marking the 200th Anniversary of the Venerable John Henry Cardinal Newman's birth, as found in *Origins* (15 March 2001), 631–632.

16. Pope Paul VI (OssR, 28 October 1963): "Newman, il promotore e la figura più rappresentativa del movimento di Oxford, nella piena coscienza della sua missione—'io ho un lavoro da compiere'—, e guidato solamente dall'amore della verità e della fedeltà a Cristo, tracciò un itinerario, il più faticoso, ma anche il più grande, il più significativo, il più conclusivo che pensiero umano abbia segnato nel secolo scorso, anzi si potrebbe dire durante l'età moderna, per giungere alla pienezza della sapienza e della pace." Cf. also Pope Paul VI, "De l'Actualité de Newman," *Monitor Ecclesiasticus* 95 (1970), 494–496.

17. Michael Schmaus, "Mariology," in *Encyclopedia of Theology: The Concise Sacramentum Mundi*, ed. Karl Rahner (New York: Seabury Press, 1975), 897.

18. "Timeless Truth in an Ever-Changing World," *Friends of Cardinal Newman Newsletter* (Christmas 1998), 11.

CHAPTER ONE

1. Inasmuch as concern with Marian dogma and the development of doctrine is perceived as characteristically Catholic, it is worth considering specifically Catholic influences on Newman at the outset, especially since these are rarely alluded to in standard reflections on his own theological development.

2. Cf. Marvin R. O'Connell, "Newman: The Victorian Intellectual As Pas-

tor," *Theological Studies* (June 1985), 337. The Reverend Edmond Darvil Benard acknowledges Newman's particular place among Catholic theologians. Benard's nuanced opinion can be appreciated, maintaining that it is neither fair to identify Newman as a Thomist (scholastic) nor to cast Newman and his theology into the dark shadows of anti-Thomism, simply because Newman's theological method differed from that of the Angelic Doctor: "As a theologian, John Henry Newman is hard to catalogue. He was certainly not of the Thomistic school; his works betray little or no dependence on the study of the Angelic Doctor. Nor was he a Scholastic in the sense of following either of the other two schools, Molinist or Scotist. . . . But although Newman had . . . almost no training in the theology of the Schools, we must not for that reason automatically picture him as an opponent of the principles which underlie scholastic theology": *A Preface to Newman's Theology* (London: B. Herder), 16. Furthermore, even though Benard is of the opinion that Newman does not manifest any dependence on St. Thomas or the Thomistic schools of thought, he carefully notes the following significant references to St. Thomas in the works of Newman: *Historical Sketches* II, 226f.; *Idea of the University*, 469f.; *Letter to the Duke of Norfolk* (Diff II, 256); *Grammar of Assent*, 503; "Newman refers to his [Aquinas'] sanctity and influence in the *Discourses to Mixed Congregations*, 99 and in the *Present Position of Catholics in England*, 396" (16).

3. Cf. Avery Cardinal Dulles, S.J., "From Images to Truth: Newman on Revelation and Faith," *Theological Studies* (June 1990), 265f.; A. Linera, "La Vida y la Mentalidad del Cardinal Newman," *Las Ciencias* 13 (1948), 385–405.

4. Author's translation of the Italian, unless otherwise indicated: "Newman: The Courage of the Truth."

5. Cf. Giovanni Velocci, "San Tommaso d'Aquino 'Visto' dal Cardinale John Henry Newman," OssR (1 February 1996), 7; H. Francis Davis, "Newman and Thomism," *Newman Studien*, vol. 3, ed. Heinrich Fries and Werner Becker (Nürenburg: Glock und Lutz, 1957), 157–169.

6. Father Velocci makes this conclusive evaluation: "Risulta . . . che Newman ebbe nel corso degli anni una visione sempre più ampia e chiara di San Tommaso. . . . Le due vie però non si elidono, ma si completano a vicenda e ci danno una visione più vera della realtà. È quindi sbagliato il tentativo di mettere in contrasto San Tommaso e Newman, come fu fatto dai modernisti al principio del secolo, i quali inventarono a proposito il dilemma: o San Tommaso o Newman. Corrisponde invece alla verità l'interpretazione dei migliori newmanisti i quali vedono nei due grandi pensatori una varietà di aspetti, ma un accordo sostanziale. Si deve perciò ritenere non l'antitesi ma la sintesi: San Tommaso e Newman."—OssR (1 February 1996), 7.

7. Cf. L. Govaert, *Kardinal Newmans Mariologie und Sein Persönlicher Werdegang* (Salzburg und München: Universitätsverlag Anton Pustet, 1975).

8. Dulles, "From Images," 267. Cf. Sr. Mary Christopher Ludden, "John Henry Newman," *Process: Journal of the Catholic Campus Ministry Association* 5.1 (1979), 16: " . . . his ability to understand himself by penetrating the recesses of his own heart and as a result of this self-knowledge to better comprehend human nature . . . his extraordinary ability to probe the minds and hearts of those to whom he addresses himself and to elicit from them an empathetic

response, be they Oxford scholars, town shopkeepers or simple servants. The power to lay the most gentle yet the most penetrating finger on the very core of things, reading to men their own most secret thoughts better than they knew themselves" (16). Cf. also F. Frost, "Le Personalisme dans l'Itinéraire Théologique et Spirituelle de John Henry Newman," *Mélange de Science Religieuse* 35 (1976), 57–70. See also Avery Cardinal Dulles, S.J., *Newman* (New York: Continuum, 2002), 1–15.

9. Günter Biemer, *Newman on Tradition* (New York: Herder & Herder, 1967), 116f. O'Connell makes the same point in "Newman: The Victorian Intellectual as Pastor," *Theological Studies* (June 1985), 341.

10. See, for example, the following: ON NEWMAN AND DOMINIC BARBERI: Pablo Garcia *Domingo Barberi, Precursor y Profeta* (Salamanca: Ediciones Sigueme, 1997); Denis Gwynn, *Father Dominic Barberi* (Buffalo, N.Y.: Desmond & Stapleton, 1948); Urban Young, *Dominic Barberi in England: A New Series of Letters* (London: Burns Oates & Washbourne, 1935). ON NEWMAN HIMSELF: Meriol Trevor, *Newman: The Pillar of the Cloud* (Garden City, N.Y.: Doubleday, 1962), and *Newman: Light in Winter* (Garden City, N.Y.: Doubleday., 1963); Wilfrid Ward, *The Life of John Henry Cardinal Newman*, 2 vol. (New York: Longmans, Green, 1912); Harold L. Weatherby, *Cardinal Newman in His Age: His Place in English Theology and Literature* (Nashville: Vanderbilt University Press, 1973). ON THE OXFORD MOVEMENT: Henry R. T. Brandreth, *The Ecumenical Ideals of the Oxford Movement* (London: Society for Promoting Christian Knowledge, 1947); Owen Chadwick, *The Spirit of the Oxford Movement: Tractarian Essays* (New York: Cambridge University Press, 1990); Wilfrid L. Knox, *The Catholic Movement in the Church of England* (London: Philip Allan, 1923); Marvin R. O'Connell, *The Oxford Conspirators: A History of the Oxford Movement, 1833–1845* (London: Macmillan, 1969); Minima Parspartis, *Some Side-Lights on the Oxford Movement* (London: Art & Book Co., 1895); Geoffrey Rowell, *The Vision Glorious: Themes and Personalities of the Catholic Revival in Anglicanism* (New York: Oxford University Press, 1983). ON INDIVIDUALS OF THE OXFORD MOVEMENT: Perry Butler, ed., *Pusey Rediscovered* (London: Society for Promoting Christian Knowledge, 1983); Gertrude Donald, *Men Who Left the Movement: John Henry Newman, Thomas W. Allies, Henry Edward Manning, Basil William Maturin* (London: Burns, Oates & Washbourne, 1933); Robert Gray, *Cardinal Manning: A Biography* (New York: St. Martin's Press, 1985); E. E. Reynolds, *Three Cardinals: Newman, Wiseman, Manning* (New York: P. J. Kenedy & Sons, 1958); Henry Tristam, C.O., *Newman and His Friends* (London: John Lane, 1993); Wilfrid Ward, *William George Ward and the Catholic Revival* (New York: Macmillan, 1969 (reprint). ON INDIVIDUALS OF THE OXFORD MOVEMENT AND NEWMAN'S MARIOLOGICAL DEVELOPMENT: Jacques Coupet, O.P., "Le Rôle de Marie dans le Cheminement de Newman," *Nouveaux Cahiers Marials* 17 (1990/1991), 6–12; H. Francis Davis, "La Sainte Vierge dans la Jeunesse de Newman," *Doctrine Mariale*, 535–552; Stephen Dessain, C.O., "Cardinal Newman and Our Lady," *Our Lady's Digest* 27 (January–February 1973), 1972. Jean Stern, M.S., "La Vierge Marie dans le Chemin de Foi Parcouru par John Henry Newman," *Marianum* 52.141 (1991), 42–68; Giovanni Velocci, C.Ss.R., "Maria nella Vita di John Henry Newman," *Theotokos* 6 (1998), 277–300.

11. One of Italy's renowned literary figures, who lived from 1785 to 1873.

12. Manzoni's house chaplain.

13. Ap 4: "When I was fifteen, in the autumn of 1816, a great change of thought took place in me. I fell under the influence of a definitive dogma, which, through God's mercy, has never been effaced or obscured."

14. Velocci, *Il Coraggio*, 219. "Newman e Manzoni ebbero alcuni anni dopo, e precisamente nel 1833, un'altra esperienza religiosa, che segnò in profondità il loro spirito e orientò la loro vita. Per Newman fu la malattia in Sicilia, per Manzoni la morte della moglie Enrichetta Blondel."

15. Velocci, *Il Coraggio*, 222. "In Newman e in Manzoni c'è un'affinità intellettuale che si riscontra sopratutto nello studio della storia e della Provvidenza, due temi fondamentali nella loro visione del mondo." Cf. pp. 215–223 of the chapter entitled "Alessandro Manzoni" from the same work for more detailed information. Velocci recalls, among many things, Newman's fascination with Milan both from an artistic and historical point of view. As concerns the latter, what Newman most admired (according to his *Letters and Diaries*) were the numerous sacred sites of the city related to the pastoral ministry of Ambrose as Bishop of Milan in the fourth century; the garden of St. Augustine's conversion; the ancient baptistry of St. Augustine; the tombs of Sts. Ambrose and Charles Borromeo; the site where Ambrose turned back the Arians; the place of St. Monica's all-night vigil with the "pious people" of Milan held before Augustine's baptism. Cf. also Velocci, "Senso e Teologia della Provvidenza in Newman" (manuscript), a lecture given for a Cardinal Newman Academic Symposium, 3–8 April 1975, at Rome.

16. Cf. *Maria: Testi Teologici e Spirituali dal I al XX Secolo* (Milan: Arnaldo Mondadori Editore, 2000), 1331–34.

17. Antonio Rosmini was born in 1797. He was ordained a priest in 1821, and founded the Institute of Charity in 1828. In 1832–1833 he wrote a controversial work entitled *Delle Cinque Piaghe della Chiesa* (On the Five Wounds of the Church). In 1848 he tried unsuccessfully to convince Pope Pius IX to enter into war against Austria, while failure resulted in some of his books being placed on the Index of Forbidden Books. He died in 1855.

18. Francesco Cossiga, "Newman the Man: Newman in Italy," *Newman: A Man for Our Time*, ed. David Brown (Harrisburg, Pennsylvania: Morehouse Publishing, 1990), 21–23, passim. Cf. G. Pusinieri, "Spiriti Rosminiani nella Conversione di Enrico Newman," *Rivista Rosminiana di Filosofia e di Cultura* 39 (1945), 69f. As concerns Antonio Rosmini's Mariological writings, cf. *Maria: Testi Teologici e Spirituali*, 1005–1009.

19. Cf. Jacques Coupet, O.P. "Le Rôle de Marie dans le Cheminement de Newman," in *Nouveaux Cahiers Marials* (1990), 6–12.

20. Pablo Garcia, *Domingo Barberi Precursor y Profeta: ¿Que Está Sucediendo en el Anglicanismo?* (Salamanca: Ediciones Sigueme, 1997), 170. "La admisión de Newman en la Iglesia católica es el mayor consuelo del beato Domingo e el hecho más destacado de todo su apostolado. Ha sembrado con lágrimas a lo largo de muchos años, esperando contra toda experiencia, y ahora, por la bondad de Dios en quien siempre ha puesto su confianza, recoge con gozo la meyor cosecha del siglo, primicia de una cosecha todavía más rica y preludio de otra

primavera para la Iglesia católica en Inglaterra. Desde la conversión de San Agustín, probabilmente ninguna otra conversión ha tenido repercusiones tan mundiales difundidas como ésta, tanto dentro como fuera la Iglesia católica."

21. Donald A. Withey, *John Henry Newman: The Liturgy and the Breviary, Their Influence on His Life As an Anglican* (London: Sheed & Ward, 1992), 80f.

22. AP, 4.

23. Cf. Madeline Kisner, A.S.C., "From Shadows and Images into Truth: Development As a Personal Journey" (manuscript), a lecture given at the National Newman Conference, 3–5 August 1995, in Rensselaer, Indiana.

24. Cf. Velocci, "Maria nella Vita di John Henry Newman," *Theotokos* 6 (1998), 277–300.

25. Dulles, "From Images," 252.

26. Cf. Govaert. *Kardinal Newmans Mariologie*, 20.

27. Cf. *Select Treatises of St. Athanasius in Controversy with the Arians*, 2 vol. (New York: Longmans, Green, 1903). Cf. also Diff II, 87f.: "We have no proof that Athanasius himself had any special devotion to the Blessed Virgin; but he laid the foundations on which that devotion was to rest. . . ." Also, *The Arians of the Fourth Century*, by John Henry Cardinal Newman, with an Introduction and Notes by Rowan Williams (University of Notre Dame Press, 2001), xix-xlvii, especially pages xxxiiif., wherein we read the following: "Certainly Newman is walking a tightrope, and we can see the germs of the *Essay on Development* pretty plainly. What is different in the *Arians*, though, is the pervasive sense that it is, in the abstract, better not to define mysteries, that the Church is most itself when it feels no need to prescribe formulæ, because Christians can trust one another's spiritual discernment. Nor do we find in this earlier work any real hint of the search for general *principles* of development; There is no *a priori* element in the discussion of doctrinal history. The effect is a strikingly intense rhetoric of initiation, revealed-but-concealed mystery, the holy community guarding its integrity against a hostile world." Furthermore, Rowan Williams offers the following summary of the Arians of the Fourth Century: "In a word, Newman's *Arians* helped to create 'Anglicanism'—that troubled and complex family of attempts to define a reformed Catholicism without the benefit of state endorsement, developing among the ruins of the High Church project for the maintenance of a confessional society. Loss and gain, no doubt (in an appropriately Newmanesque phrase)."

28. Cf. Aidan Nichols, O.P., *From Newman to Congar: The Idea of Doctrinal Development from the Victorians to the Second Vatican Council* (Edinburgh: Clark, 1990), 17–70.

29. From 1833 to 1836, Newman wrote a series of articles on the Fathers of the Church which appeared in *British Magazine*, eventually published as *The Church of the Fathers* (repr. N.Y.: John Lane, 1928). Cf. also Govaert, *Kardinal Newmans Mariologie*, 184, and *The Church of the Fathers*, ed. with an introduction and notes by Francis McGrath, F.M.S. (University of Notre Dame Press, 2002), xi–lxxix, especially xxxviif., wherein we read: "Naturally, Newman's focus in *The Church of the Fathers* had altered since becoming a Roman Catholic in 1845. Gone was the emphasis on the anti-Erastian High Church principles triggered off by the Irish Church Temporalities Bill of 1833. By this stage, he was more

interested in showing how the current Church of England and Bible Christians differed from the early Church. For example, Anthony of Egypt, the father of monasticism, now comes across as a latter-day example of an 'enthusiast.' Had he been living in England as a 'Protestant in the Protestant day' and age, he would have been labeled a fanatic. If he wanted to live the life of a monk, he would most probably have been ostracised for unsocial and un-gentlemanlike behaviour. . . . Contrary to current popular opinion, Anthony's lifestyle was not of the 'vulgar, bustling, imbecile, unstable, undutiful' type as most people imagine it was. If the truth be known, it was 'calm and composed, manly, intrepid, magnanimous, full of affectionate loyalty to the Church and to the Truth.'"

30. *John Henry Newman: Roman Catholic Writings on Doctrinal Development* (Kansas City: Sheed & Ward, 1997), xiv-xv.

31. Gaffney, *John Henry Newman: Roman Catholic Writings*, xv-xvi.

32. These lectures were eventually published in 1837 and then re-published in two volumes as part of *The Via Media* in 1877 and 1883.

33. *The Vision Glorious: Themes and Personalities of the Catholic Revival in Anglicanism* (New York: Oxford University Press, 1983), 61.

34. This essay was left incomplete at his conversion in 1845 and revised in 1878. Cf. R. D. Middleton, *Newman at Oxford: His Religious Development* (New York: Oxford University Press, 1950), 228.

35. Walter P. Burke, "The Beauty Ever Ancient, Ever New," in *American Essays for the Newman Centennial*, ed. John K. Ryan and Edmond Darvil Benard (Washington, D.C.: The Catholic University of America Press, 1947), 207. See also Avery Cardinal Dulles, S.J., *Newman*, 79. Dulles appraises the value of Newman's contribution in writing his *Essay on the Development of Christian Doctrine*: "Newman's *Essay on the Development of Christian Doctrine* is one of the most seminal works of nineteenth-century theology. . . . This single work, far more than any other, established the idea of doctrinal development as a principle of Catholic Theology. Although much has been written on the subject since Newman's time, it would be difficult to name any rival treatise that measures up to his depth and thoroughness."

36. Dev. D., 29f. Cf. Owen Chadwick, *From Bossuet to Newman: The Idea of Doctrinal Development* (Cambridge: University Press, 1957), 48: "The idea of development was the most important single idea which Newman contributed to the thought of the Christian Church."

37. Dev. D., 55. Cf. Dulles, *Newman*, 64–82. On page 74, Cardinal Dulles writes: "The *Essay* is not a brief for a kind of dogmatic Darwinism. From the very outset Newman opposes the 'transformist' view that Christianity is ever in flux and accommodates itself to the times. For him it is axiomatic that the faith of the apostles must perdure. But in order to retain its vitality and ward off new errors, the living Church will sometimes have to articulate its faith in new ways. Granted that development must occur, it must still be asked whether the new formulations are in accord with the ancient faith. To respond to this difficult question her proposed seven texts for authentic development." These seven tests will be discussed later on in this chapter.

38. Cf. Charles C. Hefling, Jr., *Why Doctrines?* (Boston: Cowley Publications, 1984), 125: "In one sense Newman asked the same question that

prompted the medieval compendiums of Christian teaching: how can all the many and various doctrines comprised in Christian teaching be reconciled?" Cf. also pages 5, 9, 127–130.

39. Cf. Dulles, *Newman*, 83–89. On page 76, the Cardinal writes: "Newman's Mariology may be studied as an illustration of all the principles set forth in this chapter. His own theology about Mary developed gradually from his early Anglican sermons, in which he shows a deep veneration toward her but refrains from clear dogmatic statements about her Immaculate Conception and Assumption. In his *Essay on Development* he frequently uses the Church's teaching on Mary as an example to be tested by his seven criteria of authentic development. In his *Discourses to Mixed Congregations*, representing his early enthusiasm with Roman Catholic teaching, he devotes the two final chapters to Mary. And finally, in his *Letter to Pusey*, he responds in a firm but friendly manner to the objections of his former associate in the Oxford Movement."

40. Cf. Jean Stern, M.S., *La Vierge Marie dans le Chemin de Foi Parcouru par John Henry Newman* (Rome: Marianum, 1991), 42–68. Father Stern writes: "À vrai dire, Marie est présentée dans le pélerinage de foi accompli par Newman sinon dès le début, du moins de longues années déjà avant qu'il songe à rejoindre la communion de Rôme, pélerinage qui, une fois découvert le Christ vivant, l'amène à la découverte de l'Église et à l'engagement personnel pour l'Église, même au prix de lourds sacrifices" (44).

41. For the summary that follows, I acknowledge reliance on the synthesis created by the Reverend Monsignor Günter Biemer in *Newman on Tradition*, 92–112.

42. Cf. Dulles, *Newman*, 83–98. A very poignant summary of Newman's thought is offered on page 90: "In the *Essay on Development* Newman has a powerful section on the 'antecedent probability' of infallibility. Revelation itself, he argues, comes to us with a profession of infallibility. If God speaks, His word cannot be false. The common sense of mankind 'feels that the very idea of revelation implies a present informant and guide, and that an infallible one.' The revelation could not long survive in its purity and fullness without an authority that was protected against error. Protestants tend to regard the Bible as such an infallible authority, but Newman has shown that the inspired Scriptures were not intended and are not intended and are not suited to fulfill that purpose alone. Thus we are left with the question of Peter in the Gospel: 'Lord, to whom shall we go?' (Jn 6:68). Scripture, as we have seen, refers to the Church as 'the pillar and ground of the truth' and promises that the Spirit will be with her to the end of time (cf. Is 59:21). Everything therefore conspires to persuade us that Christ will supply an organ of truth, to whose judgments we must securely submit. 'If Christianity is both social and dogmatic; and intended for all ages, it must humanly speaking have an infallible expounder.'"

43. MS A 18, 20 (unpublished manuscript in the Birmingham Archives, cited by Biemer, 92)—*cætus cui traditur verbum revelatum, ut ab eo prædicetur.*

44. Dev. D., 92.

45. GA, 153.

46. GA, 153.

47. Dev. D., 79.

48. Biemer, *Newman on Tradition*, 102.

49. Dev. D., 86.

50. Biemer, *Newman on Tradition*, 95.

51. Diff II, 371.

52. Dev. D., 88f.

53. MS A 29, 4 (from a private transcription by a "Mr. Willson," undated, cited in Biemer, 106).

54. Cf. Jean Stern, M.S., "Le Développement du Dogme selon Newman et la Constitution Dogmatique sur la Révélation Divine du Vatican II," in *Euntes Docentes* 33 (1980/1981), 47–61.

55. MS B 7, 4, also found in J. Derek Holmes, ed., *The Theological Papers of John Henry Newman on Biblical Inspiration and on Infallibility* (Oxford: Oxford University Press, 1979), 140f.

56. AP, 245f.

57. *Gregorianum* 39 (1950), 595.

58. Burke, "The Beauty," 190.

59. Ibid.

60. Ibid.

61. Burke, "The Beauty," 190f.

62. Burke, "The Beauty," 191. This true sense of development Newman contrasts with heresy or false development: "Here, too, is the badge of heresy; its dogmas are unfruitful; it has no theology; so far forth as it is heresy, it has none. . . . Its *formulæ* end in themselves, without development, because they are words; they are barren, because they are dead. If they had life, they would increase and multiply; or, if they do not live and bear fruit, it is but as 'sin when it is finished, bringeth forth death.' It develops into dissolution; but it creates nothing, it tends to no system, its resultant dogma is but the denial of all dogmas, any theology under the Gospel. No wonder it denies what it cannot contain" (OUS, 318).

63. OUS, 316f.

64. Burke, "The Beauty," 201.

65. Cf. Dulles, *Newman*, 77. Cardinal Dulles writes: "In the *Essay on Development* Mary appears principally in the discussion of two of the seven criteria—anticipation of the future (no. 5) and conservative action on the past (no. 6). In the Fathers, Newman concedes, we do not find a developed Marian doctrine, but Mary's virginity is extolled and imitated as a means of union with God; she is seen as actively involved in the process of redemption, and her medieval role as a patroness with clients is anticipated. In considering the sixth note Newman takes cognizance of the Protestant objection that the *cultus* of Mary draws the minds and hearts of Christians away from the more fundamental truth of their relationship to Christ. He replies that the contrary is true."

66. Burke uses the image of the oak tree, which is very helpful to understanding these principles. Newman uses a variety of images from nature.

67. Dev. D., 203.

68. Dev. D., 171f.

69. Dev. D., 185f.

70. Dev. D., 178f.

71. Dev. D., 189f.

72. Dev. D., 199f.

73. Dev. D., 195f.

74. Ian Ker, *Newman and the Fullness of Christianity* (Edinburgh: Clark, 1993), 115.

75. The Italian Risorgimento—literally "resurgence"—in this context, does not refer to the fifteenth-century revival of classical Roman and Greek culture that began in the Italian city of Florence; rather it refers to a nineteenth-century Italian political movement that aimed at unifying the various regions of Italy by overthrowing the monarchy and the rule of the Papal states. The sad enigma of Father Carlo Passaglia is also enhanced when one considers his contribution to Mariology and Ecclesiology. Hugo Rahner makes mention of Passaglia's contribution in the context of a discussion of the virginity of Mary, the nature of the Church, heresy, and the doctrine of the Church's infallibility. See Hugo Rahner, *Our Lady and the Church* (Chicago: Darton, Longman & Todd, repr. Regnery Logos Edition, 1966), 25. See also Carlo Passaglia, *De Ecclesia Christi* 1 (Rome, 1853), 78ff.

76. Today, the Pontifical Gregorian University.

77. In 1867, Father Perrone wrote a letter to Newman in Italian, to which Newman responded in Latin.

78. Gaffney, *John Henry Newman: Roman Catholic Writings*, 5.

79. See Appendix I: Glossary of Terms.

80. Perrone's notes on chapter 4 (p. 25) were as follows:

"(1) If you mean *formulated* dogmas, there were certainly few of them, if any. But if you mean truths considered in themselves, contained severally in the Deposit, then there have been no additions.

"(2) I do not understand what is meant by these *minor details*.

"(3) We should rather express it as divine *assistance*.

"(4) The Deposit is not *expanded*, for it always remained unchangeable.

"(5) Dogma does not grow *in itself*. But it does grow quantitatively in relation to us, evolving into greater explicitness and more distinct awareness of articles that have been defined.

"(6) Only a sanction or formal definition is new.

"(7) That may happen in the case of private individuals, but not of the Church.

"(8) In the sense indicated above.

"(9) That is to say, individuals may have no very profound mental grasp of it.

"(10) In the sense already explained.

"(11) Once they know, all must believe explicitly.

"(12) Namely, as circumstances require.

"(13) It is not for that reason, but because they rashly introduce novelties contrary to what is held in the Church or to what the Church teaches."

81. Gaffney, *John Henry Newman: Roman Catholic Writings*, 23–25.

82. Cf. A. Brent, "Newman and Perrone: Irreconcilable Theses on Development," *Downside Review* 102, 349 (1984), 276.

83. J. H. Walgrave, *Newman the Theologian: The Nature of Belief and Doctrine As Exemplified in His Life and Works* (New York: Sheed & Ward, n.d.), 303. Cf. M. Panido, "Newman e Evoluçao do Dogma Catolico," *Revista Ecclesia Brasilera* 5 (1946), 233–263.

84. Cf. Ian Ker, "Newman's View of the Relationship between Magisterium and Theologians," *Scripta* (manuscript form; Rome: Pontificia Università Urbaniana, 1979).

85. Note: The summary offered here is based on John Coulson's Introduction to Newman's *On Consulting the Faithful in Matters of Doctrine* (New York: Sheed & Ward, 1961); cf. also Aidan Nichols, O.P., *Newman to Congar*, 59–62.

86. Vincent Blehl, S.J., "Newman: The Bishops and *The Rambler*," *Downside Review* 90 (1972), 20–40.

87. Coulson, *JHN: On Consulting*, 2.

88. Cf. Coulson, *JHN: On Consulting*, 8.

89. This is consonant with the 1983 Code of Canon Law, which informs us in cc. 204 and 207 that Christ's faithful are both the lay and ordained and that within the fundamental unity of the Church there is nonetheless a distinction of functions.

90. Coulson, *JHN: On Consulting*, 54f.

91. Avery Dulles, S.J., "Newman on Infallibility," *Theological Studies* (September 1990), 448. Cf. Jean Stern, M.S., "L'Infallibilité dans la Pensée de John Henry Newman," *Recherches de Science Religieuse* 61 (1973), 161–185; Roderick Strange, "Newman on Infallibility," *American Journal* 80 (1975), 61–70.

92. Paul G. Crowley, "The *Sensus Fidelium* and Catholicity," in *John Henry Newman: Theology and Reform*, ed. Michael E. Alsopp and Ronald R. Burke (New York: Garland Publishing, Inc., 1992), 115f. Cf. John Ford, "Newman on *Sensus Fidelium* and Mariology," *Marian Studies* 28 (1977), 120–145; reply, A. McGuire, *Marian Studies* 28 (1977), 146f.

93. Coulson, *JHN: On Consulting*, 63.

94. See Appendix I: Glossary of Terms.

95. Cf. LG 12.

96. OxCath, 313f.

97. Newman's fifteen Oxford University Sermons: 1826–1843.

98. Cf. Giovanni Velocci, C.Ss.R., "Maria nella Vita di John Henry Newman," *Theotokos* 6 (1998), 292. Velocci also explains that Newman upon his return to England from Italy stopped at Loreto to invoke Mary's intercession on behalf of the Oratory he was intending to found at Birmingham. Newman chose as the date of the Oratory's foundation the feast of Mary's Purification, which also happened to be the date of the founding of Oriel College at Oxford where Newman had been a student and fellow (cf. 297).

99. Gaffney remarks: "This (sermon) is an excellent summary of how Newman perceived doctrinal development, and the sermon is an admirable description of how it takes place. Essentially it is a process of gradual unfolding implications, progressively realizing the potentialities of understanding that deliberation and argument bring to consciousness. Newman's subtle and persuasive account of how fundamental ideas seem to expand, deepen, and ramify

under intellectual scrutiny is an impressive contribution to the intellectual side of the psychology of religion. In the light of this analysis of the normal way in which profound ideas gradually disclose their fuller significance, Newman proposed that for Christian doctrine not to develop would be the incredible thing, whereas the evidence of its having developed merely attests its vitality" (*John Henry Newman: Roman Catholic Writings on Development*, xvii).

100. St. Anselm's expression meaning "faith seeking understanding."

101. GA, 98. Cf. also Jean Stern, M.S., "Le Dogme chez John Henry Newman," *Axes* 7.3–4 (1976), 53–62. See also Dulles, *Newman*, 34–47. Cardinal Dulles explains: "Faith, he holds, is an acceptance of mystery, which reason cannot reach by its own powers and can accept only on the basis of testimony. The truths of the faith, being obscure and mysterious, must be treated with great reverence. The rationalist errs by taking himself, rather than the Creator, as his own center. For the rationalist faith is never more than an opinion." On page 36, Cardinal Dulles quotes from a famous passage of one of Newman's seven letters to the *London Times* composed in 1841 as a response to rationalism. Newman writes: "The heart is commonly reached, not through reason but through the imagination, by means of direct impressions, by the testimony of facts and events, by history, by description. Persons influence us, voices melt us, looks subdue us, deeds inflame us. Many a man will live and die upon a dogma: no man will be a martyr for a conclusion. A conclusion is but an opinion. . . ." This text of Newman's is found in GA, 94.

102. OxCath, 315.

103. Stern, *La Vierge Marie*, 53.

104. DMC, 357–60.

105. Cf. also Diff II, 87f; DMC, 357, wherein Newman uses similar language to describe the development of Marian doctrine and devotion in the life of the Church

106. Since Newman presumed that the doctrine of the Assumption was already a doctrine of the Faith by being taught through the ordinary Magisterium and obviously here considers the Immaculate Conception to be the last Marian doctrine to be defined, one can logically ask how he would indeed view the present controversy over the Marian titles here under study.

107. MD, 10f., passim.

108. OUS, 331f.

109. Cf. PPS, II, 134. This expression, or, better yet, the doctrine, is one of the main themes of Newman's sermon "The Glories of Mary for the Sake of Her Son" (cf. DMC, 342–359).

110. Velocci observes: "Anche da Anglicano Newman non dubitò mai della concezione immacolata di Maria; ma si radicò sempre più in questa certezza da quando, abbandonato il liberalismo, cominciò a sentire più tenera e intensa la devozione verso di lei. Egli fu sempre molto esplicito nell'affermare il privilegio dell'Immacolata, anche se non usava il termine proprio per timore di offendere la sensibilità anglicana. Lasciato il protestantesimo inglese, tale dottrina gli divenne ancor più evidente tanto da non poter concepire come alcuni cattolici avessero potuto opporvisi" (*Il Coraggio*, 148).

111. Diff II, 31.

112. Diff II, 44.

113. Diff II, 38.

114. Diff II, 37.

115. Newman's methodology of development is revealed in these lines as he explains the origins for the Marian thought of the Three Fathers. He asks, "Who did (originate the teaching on the New Eve)?" He answers: " . . . for from one definite organ or source, place or person, it must have come. Then we must inquire, what length of time would it take for such a doctrine to have extended, and to be received, in the second century over so wide an area; that is, to be received before the year 200 in Palestine, Africa, and Rome. Can we refer the common source of these local traditions to a date much later than that of the Apostles, since St. John died within twenty years of St. Justin's conversion and sixty of Tertullian's birth? Make what allowance you will for whatever possible exceptions can be taken to this representation; and then, after doing so, add to the concordant testimony of these two Fathers the evidence of St. Irenæus, which is so close upon that of the School of St. John himself in Asia Minor" (Diff II, 37f.). Cf. *The Letters and Diaries of John Henry Newman*, vol. 19 (London, 1969), 346f. See also Philip Boyce, *The Virgin Mary in the Life and Writings of John Henry Newman* (Grand Rapids, Michigan: Eerdmans, 2002), 314f. This last work will hereafter be abbreviated *Mary in the Writings of JHN*.

116. Diff II, 46.

117. Diff II, 49.

118. MD, 81.

119. Cf. LD, 19:346f. See also Boyce, *Mary in the Writings of JHN*, 345.

120. MD, 86.

121. Coulson, *John Henry Newman: Roman Catholic Writings on Development*, 71. "Divine speech, venerable tradition, the perpetual sense of the Church, the single breath of Catholic bishops and faithful."

122. The Reverend Carleton Jones, O.P., in a talk delivered to the annual conference of the New England region of the Mariological Society of America at Providence College on 19 October 1996, makes the following point: "Newman's side of the dialogue concerning Mary should not be thought of as an ecumenical strategy . . . to find the lowest common denominator, but as a genuinely Catholic theological method that is capable of yielding ecumenical results —not in the sense of creating a *tertium quid* between Catholic and Protestant positions, but in the sense of expounding Catholic doctrine in a way that places the burden of proof on the Protestant side by removing their objections to it" (4).

123. One should not pass over his desire to underscore the historical witness here too.

124. Here Newman obviously means the *substance* of the doctrine has not changed, but that should not be interpreted as excluding *development* properly understood.

125. Diff II, 26. The reader should also refer to Appendix I: "Glossary of Terms," under the heading of *Devotion and Faith, Distinction between.*

126. Diff II, 27.

127. Diff II, 27f. Attention should be directed to the historical dimension

here as well as to the distinction drawn. Cf. LD, 19:361–370. This is Newman's second letter to Arthur Osborne Alleyne. The letter is dated 15–17 June 1860.

128. Cf. Lina Callegari, *Newman: La Fede e le Sue Ragioni* (Milan: Edizioni Paoline, 2001), 81–83.

129. Diff II, 79f.

130. Ibid.

131. Clearly, Newman here (as in his *Essay on Development*) uses "idea" as an equivalent of doctrinal belief.

132. Diff II, 82f. The last line, it cannot be overlooked, stresses also the compatibility of Christ and Mary.

133. Diff II, 86. The second half of the citation is also worthy of notice in connection with the inseparability of Christology and Mariology.

134. Diff II, 100.

135. AP, 195.

136. Diff II, 115.

137. DMC, 349.

138. Diff II, 92. In his meditation on *Turris Davidica*, we find again his charge that Protestant countries (Germany, Switzerland, England) which have rejected Marian doctrine and devotion have, in effect, ended up losing an orthodox Christology (cf. MD, 68f.). Cf. Placid Murray, O.S.B., "Tower of David: Cardinal Newman's Mariology," *Furrow* 27 (1976), 26–34.

139. Diff II, 86.

140. DMC, 345–348, passim. Of course, this passage applies equally well to our section demonstrating the historical dimension of Marian doctrine and devotion.

141. Cf. Ernest R. Sandeen, *The Roots of Fundamentalism: British and American Millenarianism, 1800–1930* (University of Chicago Press, 1970), 273–277.

142. Cf. Peter M. J. Stravinskas, *Mary and the Fundamentalist Challenge* (Huntington, Ind.: Our Sunday Visitor, 1998), 25, 40f.

143. DMC, 349.

144. DMC, 356.

145. A Marian title in the Litany of Loreto meaning "Tower of David."

146. MD, 68.

147. MD, 74f.

148. Cf. LG 66: "Placed by the grace of God, as God's Mother, next to her Son and exalted above all the angels and men, Mary intervened in the mysteries of Christ and is justly honored by a special cult in the Church." Also, the Fathers of the Second Vatican Council maintain the above distinction when they state at paragraph 66 of *Lumen Gentium*: "as it always existed, although it is altogether singular, [it] differs from the cult of adoration which is offered to the Incarnate Word, as well as to the Father and the Holy Spirit, and it is most favorable to it."

149. MD, 77.

150. This is a Marian title in the Litany of Loreto, meaning "Morning Star." This title has first and foremost a grounding in Sacred Scripture in relationship to Christ. Cf. Rev 22:16.

151. MD, 265.

152. Cf. Rev 2:28; 22:16. Therefore, the Marian title has its biblical roots in

the use of the Christological title, to which it is subordinate and from which it derives all its efficacy and theological significance in the economy of salvation.

153. Cf. Hugo Rahner, *Our Lady and the Church*, 103–115.

154. Cf. H. Francis Davis, "La Sainte Vierge dans la Jeunesse de Newman," 535–552. As regards the question of the relationship between Christology and Mariology in Newman's understanding of the development of doctrine, see pp. 538–540.

155. Diff II, 73. A personal observation: Newman's claim that history has proven that Marian doctrine and devotion have silently progressed in the life of the Church, that is to say, developed without much turmoil or controversy, seems to be contradicted by the very historical facts that prompted the Church to define, for example, the doctrine of Mary as *Theotokos*. The ongoing theological and personal debates of St. Cyril of Alexandria and Nestorius (e.g., correspondence) were far from being dispassionate expressions of disagreement. It was precisely the bitter (heated) controversy between St. Cyril of Alexandria and Nestorius that served as the basis (among others) of the convocation of the Council of Ephesus (431 A.D.). Indeed, many historians note that Cyril and his entourage deliberately arrived at Ephesus in advance of Nestorius and his supporters, so that the matters at hand could be settled by the orthodox believers without having to engage in any more polemics with Nestorius, which could have obfuscated and, even worse, obstructed the aims of the Council.

156. Diff II, 77f.

157. Diff II, 87f.

158. DMC, 357.

159. Diff II, 24f.

CHAPTER TWO

1. Jaak Seynaeve, "Newman's Biblical Hermeneutics," in *John Henry Cardinal Newman, 1801–1890*, ed. Terrence Merrigan (Louvain: Katholieke Universiteit Leuven, 1990), 282f. Seynaeve, drawing from Newman's own accounts, gives us a feel for Newman's love of the Bible. "On the first page of the *Apologia pro Vita Sua* (1864), Newman states: 'I was brought up as a child to take great delight in reading the Bible.' In a letter (October 13, 1823) written to his sister, Harriet, he declares that he had the practice of learning large sections of the Bible by heart, and that he had committed Paul's Epistle to the Ephesians to memory. He recommended the same practice to her: 'If you have leisure time on Sunday, learn portions of Scripture by heart.' In 1872, at an advanced age, Newman, in a classical passage in the *Grammar of Assent*, describes 'Bible Religion,' as 'both the recognized title and the best description of English religion" (282). Cf. also Vincent Blehl, S.J., *The White Stone: The Spiritual Theology of John Henry Newman* (Petersham, Mass.: St. Bede Publications, 1993), 160.

2. Literally, "the First Gospel," a Latin word used by theologians to refer to the promise of a Redeemer in Genesis 3:15.

3. Cf. LG 55: "The books of the Old Testament describe the history of salvation, by which the coming of Christ into the world was slowly prepared. The earliest documents, as they are read in the light of a further and full

revelation, bring the figure of a woman, Mother of the Redeemer, into a gradually clearer light."

4. The Catechism, relying on St. Augustine, reads: " As an old saying put it, the New Testament lies hidden in the Old and the Old Testament is unveiled in the New" (CCC 129).

5. Seynaeve, "Newman's Biblical Hermeneutics," 284.

6. From the Latin meaning "Sacred Page," that is, the Sacred Scriptures or the Bible.

7. Cf. A. Boekraad, "Newman en die Heilige Schrift," *Schrift und Tradition* 7 (1954), 385–388; Yves Congar, O.P., "Écriture et Tradition comme Forme de Communication," *Istina* 8 (1962), 411–436; J. Stern, M.S., *Bible et Tradition chez Newman* (Paris, 1948); N. Schriffers, "Schrift und Tradition bei John Henry Newman," *Schrift und Tradition* (Essen, 1962), 250–266.

8. Seynaeve asserts: "A careful examination of his writings shows that Newman held the literal sense of the Bible in high esteem, that, indeed, he was very much aware of the role and importance, and the richness, of that sense. He states that God, the main author of Scripture, in revealing His mysteries, used 'the plainest and most exact form of speech which human language admits of.' Furthermore, as a biblical theologian writing or preaching primarily for the edification of the faithful, Newman aimed chiefly at discovering the main trends, the broad outlines or the general principles that underlie the structure of the Bible. This does not imply, however, that he neglected or ignored the details of the sacred narrative. In one passage in particular, the Cardinal observes that even small details, interpreted according to their literal meaning, can be very important. 'A very great deal of doctrine and a very great deal of precept goes with such [details]' " ("Newman's Biblical Hermeneutics," 295).

9. Seynaeve, "Newman's Biblical Hermeneutics," 291f. Cf. CCC 115–119.

10. Dev D, 71. Henri de Lubac, S.J., remarks about this passage from the *Development* that it is "worthy of St. Gregory [the Great]": *Medieval Exegesis: The Four Senses of Scripture*, vol. 1 (Grand Rapids, Mich.: Eerdmans, 1998), 80.

11. Eugene M. Burke, "The Use of Sacred Scripture as *Locus Theologicus*", in Proceedings of the Fourteenth Annual Convention held in Buffalo, New York, June 22–25, 1959 (St. Joseph's Seminary, N.Y.: The Catholic Theological Society of America, 1959), 76. Cf. also John Brit, "Newman's Use of Sacred Scripture in Texts on the Incarnation and Mary," *Marian Library Studies* 24:19.

12. Seynaeve, "Newman's Biblical Hermeneutics," 295f.

13. Cf. Pontifical Biblical Commission, *The Interpretation of the Bible in the Church* (Vatican City: Libreria Editrice Vaticana, 1993).

14. J. Derek Holmes, "Newman's Attitude towards Historical Criticism and Biblical Inspiration," *Downside Review* (January 1971), 27–29; see also the whole article, pages 20–37.

15. Cf. J. Healy, "Cardinal Newman on the Inspiration of Scripture," *Irish Ecclesiastical Review* (1884); H. Johnson, "Leo XIII, Cardinal Newman and the Inerrancy of Scripture," *Downside Review* 69 (1951), 411–427; J. Seynaeve, "La Doctrine Scriptuaire du Cardinal Newman sur l'Inspiration d'après les Articles de 1884," *Ephemerides Theologicæ Louvanienses* 18 (1950), 356–382.

16. The Most Reverend Philip Boyce is quick to point out: "The eight

volumes of *Parochial and Plain Sermons* contain the kernel of Newman's preaching in its most simple and exquisite form. Taken as a whole they constitute a sincere call to a committed Christian life. They seem, even to us who read them today, to make faith more binding, the invisible world more real and the effort to attain the scriptural goal of holiness and conformity with Christ more rewarding. They persuade us that membership of the Church is a precious and comforting privilege, that Christ is really present in the sacraments with His sanctifying power, that Divine Providence pervades our lives, that Scripture is the key we are given to interpret the world, that life is short and eternity is long."—John Henry Newman: The Birth and the Pursuit of an Ideal of Holiness," *John Henry Newman: 1879-May 1979*, ed. M. K. Strolz (Rome: The International Centre of Newman Friends, 1979), 46.

17. Louis Bouyer, *Newman's Vision of Faith* (San Francisco: Ignatius Press, 1986), 17–19.

18. Blehl, *The White Stone*, 21.

19. Blehl, *The White Stone*, 22.

20. W. D. White, *The Preaching of John Henry Newman* (Philadelphia, 1969), 60–61.

21. Equally important is Newman's later work *An Essay on the Miracles of Early Ecclesiastical History*, written in 1842–1843.

22. Cf. Basil Mitchell, "Newman As a Philosopher," *Newman after a Hundred Years*, ed. Ian Ker and Alan G. Hill (Oxford: Random Press, 1990), 223–246. "Locke's careful and sympathetic attempt to delimit the spheres of reason and revelation, while leaving the final judgment with reason, was felt by Newman to be profoundly unsatisfactory, albeit never to be dismissed out of hand" (224). "Newman's response to Locke was not to reject the claims of reason as such but to demand a much more subtle appreciation of the way that reason works, not only in relation to religious truth but also in respect of all matters of serious importance" (226).

23. Velocci underscores the particular threat that the empiricism of Hume held out for an orthodox understanding of the significance of miracles as supernatural realities to which the inerrant Word of God attests and which have been confirmed, time and again, by the concrete experience on the part of man of the benevolence of Divine Providence throughout history: "Per dimostrare la possibilità dei miracoli, Newman deve ribattere le obiezioni di Hume che la negava; egli ritiene di accettare solo i fatti straordinari che coincidono con quello che conosciamo della Provvidenza di Dio e dei suoi attributi. Oltre che sulla ragione, Newman si fonda sulla Scrittura la quale è esplicita nell'ammettere i miracoli come segni di un'azione divina e non di forze segrete e occulte. Le interruzioni nel corso ordinario della natura si attribuiscono all'autore della natura. In realtà sia la Scrittura che la storia della Chiesa presentano dei fatti straordinari, forniti dei caratteri dell'autenticità e dell'oggettività, e provano che Dio è presente al mondo e lo guida con la sua sapienza e con il suo amore" (*Il Coraggio*, 88).

24. Velocci, *Il Coraggio*, 87f. "I miracoli hanno un compito preciso nell'economia della Provvidenza: sono il segno della rivelazione, il criterio del messaggio divino. . . . Nel piano divino i miracoli hanno una dignità e un compito reale,

ma presi isolatamente potrebbero sembrare una deformazione di un sistema armonioso. Essi si giustifichino in una visione unitaria dell'economia della Provvidenza in cui tutte le parti sono interpendenti. La funzione dei miracoli è altamente significativa: essi completano il sistema morale, hanno di mira uno scopo di salvezza, uniscono l'uomo al suo Creatore. Nella visione newmaniana tutte le rivelazioni di Dio sono dei miracoli; Cristo che è la rivelazione suprema è anche il miracolo più grande. Newman giunge così al cuore della teologia della Provvidenza, a Cristo, il punto omega della storia: 'Tutte le Provvidenze di Dio hanno per centro Cristo.'"

25. Velocci, *Il Coraggio*, 76. "Una testimonianza ininterrotta ... una trasmissione, quasi un passaggio, dalla lettura della Bibbia alla sua esperienza personale. L'ascolto della storia sacra fin da quando era bambino, imprese in lui 'l'idea di tutto quello che la Divina Providenza ha fatto per l'uomo dalla creazione fino all'ultimo giorno.' La sua esistenza fu volta in avanti," come direbbe Kierkegaard. Significativo il fatto che da giovane scelse come ideale due principi scomodi. 'La santità piuttosto che la pace'; 'Lo sviluppo è l'unica prova della vita.'"

26. Cf. Velocci, *Il Coraggio*, 79–99.

27. Cf. Congregation of the Doctrine of the Faith, *Dominus Jesus—On the Unicity and Salvific Universality of Jesus Christ and the Church* (Vatican: Libreria Editrice Vaticana, 2000).

28. 1 Tim 2:4.

29. CCC 2032, citing 1 Tim 3:15; LG 17. Cf. also CCC 50–66, 302–314, 758–759, 774–776.

30. Stanley Jaki, *Newman's Challenge* (Grand Rapids, Mich.: Eerdmans, 2000), vii.

31. Cf. Dulles, *Newman*, 53–55, passim. The Cardinal writes: "In the standard manuals of the day, physical miracles strongly emphasized as the signs by which an alleged revelation could be verified, Newman had a lifelong interest in miracles. One of his earliest publications, written in 1825, was an encyclopedia article on biblical miracles. In 1843, when publishing a partial translation of Fleury's *Ecclesiastical History*, he composed a lengthy 'Essay on the Miracles Recorded in the Ecclesiastical History of the Early Ages.' He republished the two essays in 1870 as a 400-page volume, *Two Essays on Biblical and Ecclesiastical Miracles*. The first essay is the more philosophical of the two. It begins with a consideration of the nature of miracles. They do not have to be violations of the laws of nature, Newman contends. An event is a miracle if it is exceptional in the order of nature but intelligible as part of a redemptive economy. From this perspective, Newman meets the objection of David Hume that it is always more likely that the testimony be false than that the account of the miracle be true. Newman would concede this if a miracle were a mere anomaly. But he contends that the biblical miracles constituted a coherent system that shows them to be parts of a higher dispensation. In view of our experience of God's beneficial providence, which Newman regards as an ingredient of natural religion, miracles may be regarded as antecedently probable. The evidence for miracles is cumulative with the probability of each being supported by that of the others. . . . In his second essay, Newman takes up ecclesiastical miracles of post-

biblical times, which in the first essay he had found tainted by superstition and corruption. Correcting this unduly negative assessment, he now contends that since biblical miracles had occurred, it was antecedently likely that miracles should also take place in Church history."

32. Jaki, *Newman's Challenge*, 47.

33. Ibid.

34. *Ecclesiastical Miracles*, 307.

35. Brit makes the point: "The authority switched from *sola Scriptura* in Newman's earlier writings, to the authority of Scripture and Tradition. Those familiar with the Fathers of the Church will easily realize that almost every position taken by Newman could be traced to them" ("Newman's Use of Scripture in Texts on the Incarnation and Mary," 18). He also says: "Once Newman became a Catholic, he noticed how differently Anglicans and Catholics lived the faith. This, together with his life-long struggle against Liberalism, which, he held, had permeated the practice of religion in Anglicanism, caused him to look upon his audience in changing ways—from his earliest days as an Evangelical, through and into his Catholic days. Therefore, his use of Scripture varied as he himself developed" (22).

36. Velocci, *Il Coraggio*, 88: "In opposizione a un cristianesimo così decadente, Newman presentava una visione fresca e autentica della verità della Scrittura. La sua visione era nello stesso tempo patristica e personale. Il carattere patristico, così diffuso nei sermoni, sorge non dalla interpretazione di questo o di quel passo, ma scaturisce dal contatto vitale e dalla riflessione prolungata sulla verità. Per Newman e per i Padri la Bibbia presenta un dramma vivente delle relazioni salvifiche di Dio con gli uomini. Il movimento della storia sacra è diretto verso l'avvento di Cristo, nell'incarnazione prima, alla fine del mondo dopo. Fondamentalmente i sermoni proclamano una chiamata alla santità la quale, per Newman come per i Padri, significa confronto e conformità con Cristo, essenza, modello e motivo della santità." Chapter Three of the present work shows the Fathers of the Church left an indelible mark on Newman's writings, most especially on his Mariological writings.

37. See Geoffrey Rowell, "Newman, John Henry," *The Blackwell Encyclopedia of Modern Christian Thought*, ed. Alister E. McGrath (Cambridge, Mass.: Blackwell Publishers, 1993), 405–408: "The question of creeds and development of doctrine appears in a more ecclesiological context in the *Lectures on the Prophetical Office of the Church* in 1837. In these lectures, developing out of a correspondence with the French Catholic Abbé J.-N. Jager, Newman defends the Church of England as a *via media* between Roman Catholicism and popular Protestantism. Against Roman concepts of authority, which Newman believed discounted the authority of Christian antiquity, Newman sets Scripture and the Fathers, interpreted by the Vincentian canon of what has been believed 'always, everywhere, and by all.' Against the Protestant *sola scriptura*, he points to the importance of tradition—both 'prophetic,' that is, implicit in liturgies, prayers and the life of the Church, and 'episcopal' in the formal pronouncements of bishops and councils. Christianity, he maintains, is corporate and ecclesial, and therefore necessarily involves authority. The individualism of private judgment in Protestantism is fissiparous and leads to rationalism and liberalism. When Newman

republished these lectures as a Roman Catholic (*The Via Media of the Anglican Church*, 1877) . . ., he added an important preface, portraying the Church as reflecting the offices of Christ as prophet, priest and king in its theologically reflective, devotional and political/institutional role, all of which, which needed to be kept in balance for the Church to be true to its own identity" (407).

38. Jaki, *Newman's Challenge*, 33f., passim.

39. A century later, *Dei Verbum* would declare: "Patet igitur Sacram Traditionem, Sacram Scripturam et Ecclesiæ magisterium, iuxta sapientissimum Dei consilium, ita inter se connecti, omniaque simul, singula suo modo sub actione unius Spiritus Sancti, ad animarum salutem efficaciter conferant" (10).

40. Bouyer's reference is to *Dei Verbum*.

41. Bouyer, *Newman's Vision of Faith*, 11f.

42. Brit, "Newman's Use of Sacred Scripture," 17.

43. Velocci, *Il Coraggio*, 159. "Newman fonda la sua mariologia sulla Sacra Scrittura: non c'è testo dell'Antico e del Nuovo Testamento, concernente in qualche misura la Madre del Signore, che egli non prenda in esame e non sviluppi con analisi accurata. E qui è la novità del suo metodo in un tempo in cui, nella teologia cattolica—in particolare in mariologia—dominava una marcata refrattarietà nei confronti della Scrittura. Ma quello è più degno di rilievo è il criterio da lui seguito: l'uso del senso letterale, applicato con vero rigore scientifico. Come esempio possiamo prendere il testo del Protovangelo (Gn 3:15), al quale Newman annette un'importanza fondamentale e a cui si appella ripetutamente; la sua interpretazione è ancora degna di considerazione."

44. This sermon was not written out *in toto* (as was Newman's custom) but simply put into outline form. Cf. Boyce, *Mary*, 167: "As an Anglican Newman wrote out his sermons with exact references to Scripture. He read them as was customary in the Anglican Church. After his conversion, he endeavoured to conform to the Catholic custom of preaching more freely without reading from a prepared text. Consequently, for most of his Catholic sermons, he only jotted down a general outline or schematic notes, and when he did write out his text he gave no scriptural references, or at most incomplete ones."

45. Brit writes: "This is a pivotal sermon since . . . it provided a different approach than those, due to the different expectations Newman could have of his Catholic audience. He did not have to announce a text, and he could preach on Mary without defensiveness. Newman used Scripture to show the harmony of the elements of the Gospel, by depending on the insights of the Fathers and the analogy of faith" ("Newman's Use of Sacred Scripture," 26).

46. *Faith and Prejudice and Other Unpublished Sermons of Cardinal Newman*, ed. the Birmingham Oratory (New York: Sheed & Ward, 1956), 86.

47. Cf. LG 56: "embracing God's salvific will with a full heart and impeded by no sin . . . devoted herself totally as a handmaid of the Lord to the person and work of her Son, under Him and with Him, by the grace of Almighty God, serving the mystery of Redemption."

48. Most commonly translated "full of grace," from the Greek and Latin, respectively.

49. John Saward makes the connection between Mary's blessedness which results from her being chosen as be the ark of the new and everlasting covenant,

for which her cousin Elizabeth praises Mary, and the transfer of the holy ark in the time of the great King David. "There is good reason for thinking that St. Luke's description of Jesus-in-Mary's journey to Elizabeth was intended by the evangelist to recall the transfer of the Ark of the Covenant to Jerusalem (cf. 2 Sam 6). The wonder in Elizabeth's words of welcome match the awe of David when he receives the Ark: And why is this granted me, that the Mother of my Lord should come to me? (Lk 1:43). How can the Ark of the Lord come to me? (2 Sam 6:9). The Ark, like Mary, travels up into the Judaean hills (cf. 2 Sam 6:22; Lk 1:39). The transfer, like the Visitation, is an occasion of delight (cf. 2 Sam 6:12; Lk 1:44). David the King 'leaps and dances before the Lord' (2 Sam 6:16); so does John the Baptist (cf. Lk 1:44). The Ark remains in the house of Obededom for three months (2 Sam 6:11); Mary stays with Elizabeth 'for about three months' (Lk 1:56). . . . The Babe in the womb is God, so the expectant Mother is the definitive Ark, the archetypical shrine and sanctuary of the divine presence. Indeed, Mary's whole life to that point was characterized by those virtues which enabled her to accept the blessedness of Divine Maternity—the sublime vocation for which God had prepared her from the moment of her Immaculate Conception": *Redeemer in the Womb* (San Francisco: Ignatius Press, 1993), 27f.

50. A Marian title found in the Litany of Loreto, meaning "Virgin worthy of being preached."

51. MD, 10.

52. MD, 11.

53. The Reverend Hans Urs von Balthasar recognizes, as did the Fathers and Newman, the twofold nature of Mary's blessedness consisting in, first and foremost, her faith, which allows Mary to spiritually conceive and obey God's Word even before she pronounces her *fiat* at the Annunciation, and, secondly, in the physical conception of that Word in the Incarnation, when he writes: "Mary is the original and generative image of the Church because she is two things in an original and generative way; first, she is the place of the Word's indwelling of mother and child sharing one flesh; and second, she is the place due to the spiritual servant hood of her entire person, body and soul, that knows no law of its own, but only conformity to God's Word" (*Karlstellungen*, 69). Antonio Sicari comments on the above-mentioned text of Balthasar: "At the beginning the Fathers of the Church saw Mary only as an image of the Church, but they soon began to insist on her being 'the Church's deepest origin and unbroken kernel.' The Church is the original contemplative who sits at the Lord's feet and whose attention is entirely directed toward hearing Him; even more, as Virgin-Mother she offers her womb to receive and bear the seed of the Word. Primary attention is, without any doubt, given to Mary's faith, but with an awareness that the Word of God can only become man when the 'helper' does not offer only a vague faith, but a faith that is fully incarnate, that embraces body and soul and spirit, so that, they can become the vessel of God's Word": "Mary, Peter and John: Figures of the Church," *Communio* (Summer 1992), 198f.

54. FP, 87f.

55. Cf. Pope John Paul II, *A Catechesis on Mary, Mother of God*, 87–89.

56. The Reverend Raymond E. Brown's *Mary in the New Testament* assists us

in responding to these rhetorical questions in such a way that one can judge the exegesis of Father Brown as confirmatory of Newman's commentary on the twofold blessedness of Mary in light of the macarism of the anonymous woman and Elizabeth's greeting of Mary, "*Beata es quæ credidisti*, Blessed art thou who didst believe." We read: " 'Blessed are you among women and blessed is the fruit of your womb.' This implies that Mary is blessed because she has conceived a son like Jesus; yet she herself is truly the object of praise. In 1:45 Elizabeth makes it clear that Mary's share in the praise is not purely physical: 'Happy is she who believed that there would be a fulfillment of the things spoken to her by the Lord.' The same contrast may be at work here: the woman praises the mother because she has given birth to a son like Jesus; but Jesus stresses that real beatitude comes from hearing the word of God and keeping it. . . . In the overall Lucan picture of Mary, 11:28 stresses that Jesus' Mother is worthy of a beatitude, yet not simply because she has given birth to a child. Her beatitude must be based on the fact that she has heard, believed, obeyed, kept, and pondered the Word, and continued to do so (Acts 1:14). Implicitly, 11:28 is a more positive way of expressing that, like all others, Mary too must meet a criterion of discipleship (see 2:35a: 'A sword will pierce through your soul'). She herself predicted: 'Behold, henceforth all generations will call me happy' (1:48—*makariousin*), but now we have come to understand why": *Mary in the New Testament* (New York: Paulist Press, 1978), 172.

57. Father de la Potterie explains: "The verb utilized here by Luke (charitoun) is extremely rare in Greek. It is present only two times in the New Testament: in the text of Luke on the Annunciation (Lk 1:28) 'kécharitôméné,' and in the Epistle to the Ephesians (Ep 1:6), 'écharitôsén.' In both cases a form of the verb 'charitôô' is used. The verbs in 'óô' are causative; they indicate an action which effects something in the object. . . . Thus, the radical of the verb 'charitôô' being 'charis' (grace). In addition, the verb used by Luke is in the past perfect participial form."—*Mary in the Mystery of the Covenant* (New York: Alba House, 1992), 17f

58. Cf. Father de la Potterie goes on: " 'Kécharitôménê' signifies then, in the person to whom the verb relates, that is, Mary, that the action of the grace of God has already brought a change. . . . In the bull of 1854, *Ineffabilis Deus*, in which Pius IX proclaimed the dogma of the Immaculate Conception, it is said that in Luke 1:28, 'full of grace,' read in the Tradition, is the biblical text which furnishes the most sure foundation (not the proof) in favor of the Immaculate Conception of Mary" (*Mary in the Mystery of the Covenant*, 17f.).

59. FP, 88.

60. This technique, which is commonly termed irony, is employed frequently throughout the Gospel of John. For example, Nicodemus' misunderstanding about the need to be reborn in a physical sense prompts Jesus to teach him about the necessity of spiritual rebirth by water and the Holy Spirit.

61. RM 20: "The Gospel of Luke recounts the moment when 'a woman in the crowd raised her voice' and said to Jesus: '*Blessed is the womb that bore you, and the breasts that you sucked!*' (Lk 11:27). These words were an expression of praise for Mary as Jesus' Mother according to the flesh. Probably the Mother of Jesus was not personally known to this woman; in fact, when Jesus began His messi-

anic activity Mary did not accompany Him but continued to remain at Nazareth. One could say that the words of that unknown woman in a way brought Mary out of her hiddenness. Through these words, there flashed out in the midst of the crowd, at least for an instant, the Gospel of Jesus' infancy. This is the Gospel in which Mary is present as the Mother who conceives Jesus in her womb, gives Him birth and nurses Him: the nursing Mother referred to by the woman in the crowd. *Thanks to this motherhood, Jesus,* the Son of the Most High (cf. Lk 1:32) is a true son of man. He is 'flesh' like every other man: He is 'the Word [Who] became flesh' (cf. Jn 1:14). He is of the flesh and blood of Mary! But to the blessing uttered by that woman upon her who was His Mother according to the flesh, Jesus replies in a significant way: *'Blessed rather are those who hear the word of God and keep it'* (Lk 11:28). He wishes to divert attention from motherhood understood only as a fleshly bond, in order to direct it toward those mysterious bonds of the spirit which develop from hearing and keeping God's word."

62. FP, 88.

63. Father de la Potterie elucidates these matters: "The resonance of Mary's *fiat* at the moment of the Annunciation is not that of the *'fiat voluntas tua'* of Jesus in Gethsemane, nor that of the formula corresponding to the Our Father. Here there is a remarkable detail, which has only been noticed in recent years, and which even today is frequently lost from sight. The "fiat" of Mary is not just a simple acceptance and even less, a resignation. It is rather a joyous desire to collaborate with what God foresees in her. It is the joy of total abandonment to the good will of God. Thus the joy of this ending responds to the invitation of joy at the beginning" (*Mary in the Mystery of the Covenant*, 34f.). The "joy at the beginning" to which de la Potterie refers is the Angel's greeting of "Rejoice," a translation of the Greek word "chaïré." Father de la Potterie explains: "The Greek word 'chaïre,' in effect can have two meanings. It can be a simple salutation: 'Hello,' but it can also have a stronger meaning, a more pregnant invitation to joy, 'Rejoice.' ... It seems practically certain that Luke had to be thinking here of an invitation to joy" (*Mary in the Mystery of the Covenant*, 14).

64. See Pope John Paul II, *A Catechesis on Mary, Mother of God*, 116–119.

65. The Hebrew word *anawim* is the plural form of the feminine word *anawah*, which is often rendered as "the poor ones" or "the lowly ones," and which refers to all the holy women, forming part of a small remnant of Israel, who awaited the coming of the Messiah. Also, this term implies the open desire on the part of such holy women to become the mother of the Messiah if so especially chosen by God.

66. It is interesting to note that this word used in the Latin Vulgate or Common version of Sacred Scripture is the same word used in reference to the work of God the Creator in Genesis 1–2. For example, the author of Genesis has God saying, "Let there be light." With the Incarnation of the God-Man, He Who is the Light of the World, co-equal with the Father and the Spirit from all eternity, inaugurates with the Virgin's consent a new creation of all mankind through His redemptive life and ministry.

67. MD, 4.

68. Sarah's motherhood of Isaac: Gen 17:15–16; Rebecca: Gen 27; Rachel's

motherhood of Jacob: Gen 30:1–2; the birth of Samson: 1 Sam 1:11, 19–20, 27–28; 1 Sam 2:1; Abigail: 1 Sam 25; Miriam: Ex 15:20–21; Deborah's praise of Jael: Judg 5:24; Huldah: 2 Kings 22:14–20; Judith: Jud 13:7; Jud 15:9–10; the Book of Esther; the mother of the Maccabees: 2 Mac 7:20–23.

69. The Reverend Jean Galot, S.J., explains how Mary's vow of virginity, expressed in her response to the Angel Gabriel "I do not know man," is linked to her identity as the Daughter of Sion and as the most preeminent of the *anawim* in the history of Israel, indeed, in the history of man's salvation. "Sotto due punti di vista essenziali il proposito di verginità di Maria trova appoggio nella tradizione dell'AT. La verginità è una forma di povertà davanti a Dio: rinuncia alla più nobile ricchezza che desideravano le donne ebraiche una posterità. Maria si pone nel prolungamento delle donne la cui sterilità umana ha attirato l'intervento divino in vista d'un figlio predestinato. Ma al posto di subire la sterilità come una costrizione, l'assume volontariamente, attendendo da Dio solo la sua fecondità. Questa scelta volontaria s'ispira ad una forma d'amore esaltata nell'AT: i profeti avevano definito le relazioni di Jahve e d'Israele sotto i tratti dell'unione matrimoniale. Non è dunque strano che Maria sia entrata in questa prospettiva. In particolare, le parole annunciate all'annunciazione: 'Non conosco uomo' sembrano echeggiare la profezia di Osea: 'Ti fidanzerò con me nella fedeltà e *tu conoscerai il Signore*' (Os 2, 22). Maria non vuol 'conoscere' che Dio, e la domanda posta all'angelo risuona come proposta di fedeltà della sposa del Signore. In ciò si comprende meglio come nell'atteggiamento di sposa Maria rappresenta il popolo e si esprime in suo nome. In tutto questo vi è un primo indizio della dimensione ecclesiale della verginità cristiana" ("Maria," in NDT, 840f.).

70. MD, 36.

71. De la Potterie provides some valuable exegetical background that confirms the validity of Newman's own exegesis of the Annunciation pericope, which is consonant with that of St. Bernard of Clairvaux and St. Thomas Aquinas: "In the Greek text we find 'andra ou ginôskô,' and in the Vulgate 'quoniam virum non cognosco,' two expressions that must be translated literally as, 'I do not know man at all,' or, 'since I have not had relations with a man.' . . . the formula of Mary in verse 34 is unique in the whole Bible. . . . But that is in effect not so surprising, since we are dealing with a unique situation in the history of salvation, the Incarnation of the Son of God. . . . But what is the meaning of this in the mouth of Mary? How must we interpret her words? . . . St. Thomas Aquinas . . . employed the expression 'desiderium virginitatis' (a desire for virginity). He added immediately that, after the Annunciation, Mary together with Joseph made a vow of virginity. In such an assertion, there is . . . a type of anachronism which pertains to the medieval frame of devotion. But the expression, 'desiderium virginitatis,' the desire for virginity, describes exactly the sentiment of Mary at the moment of the Annunciation. . . . From her youth—under the impulse of the grace of God which accompanied her from the first years of her life—Mary lived in the perspective of virginity. Even before her Son later proposed it as an ideal, Mary already existentially lived virginity. This is what my explanation of Lk 1:34 had in mind. By the grace of God, by the 'grace of virginity' (St. Bernard), Mary was prepared in an extraordinary way for the fact

that she was going to be the Mother of the Messiah, the Son of God, virginally. This is then the 'grace' which gives us the key to everything; it permits us to explain the entire content of the angelic annunciation to Mary: her desire for virginity, her preservation from sin and concupiscence, but also the grace of her divine maternity and finally of her consent full of joyful enthusiasm for the design of God" (*Mary in the Mystery of the Covenant*, 22–29, passim).

72. MD, 37f.

73. Ex 33:20.

74. Heb 12:29.

75. Rev 1:17.

76. Dan 10:4–12. The Angel who appears to Daniel is probably Gabriel, even if the context which follows (e.g., verse 13) makes a direct reference to Michael "one of the chief princes," who appears and succors Daniel in his need.

77. Lk 1:12–13.

78. MD, 14.

79. Ibid.

80. FP, 89.

81. The Reverend William Most notes: "Paul VI, in *Marialis Cultus*, gives further clarification, in a very remarkable statement of her *awareness of her role* at the Annunciation: "She admitted to dialogue with God, in the *strongly active awareness* of her special role, very actively and freely consented, not to some ordinary thing but on a matter of the ages (n. 37)": "The Knowledge of Our Lady," *Faith and Reason*, 11 (1985), 67f. St. Thomas Aquinas writes: "Per annuntiationem expectabatur consensus loco totius humanæ naturæ" (*Summa Theologiæ*, III, q. 30, a. 1 in c.).

82. Cf. *Ex Homiliis sancti Bernardi abbatis, in Laudibus Virginis Matris*, hom. 4, 8–9 (*Liturgia Horarum*, volume 1). Cf. also hom. 4, 4 (PL 183:83–84). The title of this particular homily is *Super Missus est*. Cf. also Jean Galot, "Maria, l'Immagine della Donna," *La Civiltà Cattolica* (1974), 219f.

83. FP, 91. Father Most comments on Lk 11:27–28 in light of the Tradition and the contemporary Magisterium, especially their treatment in the writings of the Second Vatican Council (*Lumen Gentium*). "As to His words, 'Who is my Mother?' we cannot do better than to quote Vatican II: 'In the course of His preaching, she received the words in which her Son, extolling the Kingdom above the reasons and bonds of flesh and blood, proclaimed blessed those who heard the Word of God and kept it' (as she *was* faithfully doing) (cf. Mk 3:35). In other words, there are two categories: (1) That of dignity: in which she had the supreme dignity of the Mother of God, which Pius XI called 'second only to God.' In fact, Aquinas writes: 'The Blessed Virgin, from the fact that she is Mother of God, has a sort of infinite dignity from the infinite good that God is.' (2) That of hearing and keeping the words of God, 'as she was faithfully doing.' She was the greatest mere human in both categories. Her Son was pointing out that the second was even greater than the first" ("The Knowledge of Our Lady," 61f.).

84. The reader should not take this in an absolutist sense. One notable exception would the Essene community of Qumran at the Dead Sea. Scripture

scholars and archeologists alike confirm that at least some members of this community practiced celibacy, so much so that some speculation has been offered linking the desert-dwelling John the Baptist to this community as well as Jesus through the latter's mediation. Also, of noteworthy interest is the connection between Qumran lustral rites of initiation and the Christian roots of the Sacrament of Baptism already found in the Baptist's own ministry.

85. FP, 92.

86. Aristide Serra, *Maria di Nazareth, Una Fede in Cammino* (Milan: Edizioni Paoline, 1993), 58. "Gesù sposta l'accento della beatitudine, alludendo a un altro latte, ossia al latte spirituale che è la Parola di Dio. In sostanza Gesù ribadisce che la vera grandezza nei confronti della sua Persona non deriva dalla parentela comune ma dall'accoglienza fruttuosa della sua Parola."

87. Lk 2:41–51.

88. FP, 93f.

89. Cf. LG 58 and MC 18.

90. FP, 94.

91. See Pope John Paul II, *A Catechesis on Mary, Mother of God*, 173–178. Also, LG 58: "At the marriage feast of Cana, moved with pity, she brought about by her intercession the beginning of miracles of Jesus the Messiah" (cf. Jn 2:1–11)

92. Cf. Pope John Paul II, *A Catechesis on Mary, Mother of God*, 188–193. Some pertinent highlights of the Holy Father's writings are worthy of note. On p. 189, "After Jesus' statements to his Mother, the evangelist adds a significant clause: 'Jesus, knowing that all was now finished' (Jn 19:28), as if he wished to stress that he had brought his sacrifice to completion by entrusting his Mother to John, and in him to all men, whose Mother she became in the work of salvation." Again, on page 193: "May every Christian, after the beloved disciple's example, 'take Mary into his house' and make room for her in his own daily life, recognizing her providential role in the journey of salvation."

93. De la Potterie draws out some of the same implications which Newman believed to be inherent in the Johannine texts of Cana and Calvary. "Mary, undoubtedly, has a very close relationship to Christ. She has become the Mother of Jesus; this is her historical and unique role in the mystery of the Incarnation and her place in the work of salvation. But because—in Christ—we have become children of God, the maternity of Mary must be continued also in us. That is what the words of Jesus on the Cross mean: 'Woman, behold your son . . . ; behold, your mother' (Jn 19:25–27). . . . Theologically explained, the significance of Mary for us is, then, of exceptional importance. She brought forth Christ totally and as a result likewise the disciples and brethren of Jesus. Certainly, this is not explicitly found in the New Testament; but we believe we can say, conformable to our reading of Jn 1:13, that it is found there implicitly. Since the Mother of Jesus is thus in relationship with the different aspects— both negative and positive (Jn 1:13)—of the Incarnation of the Son of God and since this Incarnation is in turn envisaged as the model of our growth in the filial life of the children of God, it is clear that Mary must likewise fulfill a maternal role in our regard. Extending then to all persons, the virginal maternity of Mary implies an invitation for us to receive her into our life and to consider her as our

Mother, just as she is at the same time the Mother of Christ, our model, since we are called to become like to Him. Since each one of us must be formed to the image of Christ, it is necessary that we too, like Mary—but spiritually speaking—must *conceive* in ourselves and *bring forth* in ourselves Christ" (*Mary in the Mystery of the Covenant*, 119f.). Cf. also CCC 964.

94. FP, 95f.

95. In Newman's time, the feast of the Annunciation was commonly referred to as "Lady's Day" and was both a civil and a religious holiday in England.

96. Boyce explains some of the background: "This is Newman's first sermon on our Lady. It lay unpublished in the Archives of the Birmingham Oratory, until Fr. Stephen Dessain put it at the disposal of Lutgart Govaert. It was published for the first time in her doctoral thesis *Kardinal Newmans Mariologie und sein persönlicher Werdegang* in 1975 (pp. 136–9). Since Newman himself never prepared it for publication, it lacks precise biblical references and has stylistically incomplete sentences. The manuscript has various words and phrases pencilled in by the author" (*Mary in the Writings of JHN*, 105, note 1).

97. Boyce, *Mary in the Writings of JHN*, 106, note 3.

98. Govaert, *Kardinal Newmans Mariologie*, 136.

99. Rudolf Schnackenburg, *La Persona di Gesù Cristo nei Quattro Vangeli* (Brescia: Paideia Editrice, 1995), 298. "L'importanza delle donne nella storia della salvezza emerge nella maniera più decisa nella storia dell'infanzia di Gesù. Nel *Magnificat* che Maria intona è descritto il grande rivolgimento che ha luogo con l'elezione di Maria a madre del Messia. In quanto Dio ha rivolto lo squardo all'umiltà della sua serva, si dovrà riconoscere per il futuro che egli distrugge coloro che nel loro cuore sono pieni di orgoglio. Egli abbatte i potenti dal trono e innalza gli umili (1,48–52). Si compie una svolta escatologica, come quella che Gesù annuncia nelle beatitudini e negli anatemi (6,20–26). Maria è il simbolo reale di questo mutamento radicale contenuto nel piano salvifico di Dio. Anche Elisabetta, che loda Maria come benedetta fra tutte le donne (1,42), è compresa in questa visione."

100. Cf. Govaert, *Kardinal Newmans Mariologie*, 136.

101. Boyce writes: "Notice Newman's power of argumentation. He never fears to present his adversary's case with clarity and force. In the next paragraphs he proceeds to give his own viewpoint, using the same source of demonstration, namely, Sacred Scripture. He confirms it with arguments from his own keen discernment of the laws of human nature" (*Mary in the Writings of JHN*, 107, note 5).

102. Cf. John Brit, "The Use of My Rhetorical Approach to Poetry on Newman and Mary," lecture delivered to the National Danforth Conference at Ohio University, 1994.

103. Govaert, *Kardinal Newmans Mariologie*, 137.

104. Ibid.

105. Ibid.

106. Jn 19:27.

107. Cf. Aristide Serra, *Dimensioni Mariane nel Mistero Pasquale* (Milan: Edizioni Paoline, 1995), 13–37. For example, Serra explains that: " . . . Oltre a questo senso ovvio di base, l'evangelista ci fa capire che il discepolo accolse

Maria in una sorta di casa 'mistico spirituale,' che sarebbe 'la sua fede e la sua unione con Cristo.' Era questo spazio interiore e spirituale, l'ambiente vitale che caratterizzava la sua esistenza come discepolo del Cristo. Ai suoi occhi, ormai, la Madre di Gesù costitutiva uno dei tanti beni morali-spirituali, che egli riceveva in eredità da Gesù, suo Maestro e Signore (cf. Gv 13:13). Se fino a quel momento Maria era soltanto 'la Madre di Gesù,' ella diviene anche 'Madre del discepolo,' il quale rappresenta tutti i discepoli. In quanto tale, cioè come 'sua madre,' il discepolo l'accoglie e la riconosce, in ossequio alla volontà di Gesù" (19). Cf. also RM 25; *Nuovissima Versione della Bibbia: Il Nuovo Testamento*, vol. 1, *I Quattro Vangeli* (Il Vangelo secondo Giovanni a cura di Giuseppe Segala) (Milan: Edizioni Paoline, 1988), 1062f.

108. Cf. Boyce, *Mary in the Writings of JHN*, 109, note 8. "Newman distinguishes between the blessing which God gives and through which Mary is blessed (*eulogémené*: cf. Lk 1:28 and 42) and that which comes to her from all generations who call her 'blessed' (*makarizo*: cf. Lk 1:48). After 'the Holy Ghost . . . declared that she is blessed,' Newman adds '*eulogémené*' in his masnuscript; and after 'our duty . . . to bless her,' he writes '*makarios*' " (cf. Govaert, *Kardinal Newmans Mariologie*, 141).

109. Govaert, *Kardinal Newmans Mariologie*, 137.

110. Cf. Diff II, 140–145, which, in part, contain Newman's explanation of the interpretations of Simeon's prophecy in the writings of Sts. Cyril of Alexandria, Basil the Great, and John Chrysostom. Chapter Three discusses Newman's analysis of these texts.

111. Govaert, *Kardinal Newmans Mariologie*, 137.

112. Father Brown explains the fundamental agreement of these texts as an affirmation of Mary's twofold blessedness. "When Luke comes to the one scene in common tradition where Mary appears in the ministry (Luke 8:19–21 = Mark 3:31–35), like Matthew he leaves out the Marcan introduction (Mark 3:21). It is inconceivable to Luke that Jesus's 'own' (family) would not comprehend Him. More significantly and unlike Matthew, Luke radically transforms the Marcan form of the scene where the Mother of Jesus comes with the brothers asking for Him. In Mark we saw an unfavorable distinction between the natural family and a family of believers. In Luke also the mother and the brothers come and stand outside, asking for Jesus. But when Jesus is told, 'Your mother and brothers are standing outside, desiring to see you,' He does not ask, 'Who are my mother and brothers?' He does *not* point to those inside as His mother and brothers. Rather He affirms in response, 'My mother and brothers are those who hear the Word of God and do it.' That is a highly significant change. There is no longer a contrast between a family of believers and a natural family—to the contrary, the natural family now becomes exemplary believers. Jesus' mother and brothers who stand outside are those who hear the Word of God and do it, and thus are examples of what discipleship should be. In the Annunciation Mary was the first one to hear the Word and do it; she continued to be present in the ministry as the example of those who hear and do" (Brown, *Biblical Exegesis and Church Doctrine*, 93f.).

113. Cf. Xavier Léon-Dufour, *Dictionary of Biblical Theology* (Boston: St. Paul Book & Media, 1995), 377–380.

114. Pope John Paul II, *A Catechesis on Mary, Mother of God*, 111: "Mary's act of faith recalls the faith of Abraham, who at the dawn of the Old Covenant, believed in God and thus became the father of a great posterity (cf. Gen 15:6; RM 14). At the start of the New Covenant, Mary also exerted with her faith a decisive influence on the fulfillment of the mystery of the Incarnation, the beginning and the synthesis of Jesus' entire redeeming mission."

115. In the article of the Reverend Ignacio Calabuig, O.S.M., "Liturgia," in NDM, we read: "La matrice di tale culto è anzitutto la Sacra Scrittura; in essa alcuni testi costituiscono espressione di venerazione e di lode verso Maria di Nazareth: il saluto riverente di Gabriele (cf. Lc 1:28–29); le due benedizioni, piene di ammirazione e di ossequio, che Elizabeth rivolge a Maria di Nazareth per la maternità (cf. Lc 1:42) e la sua fede (cf. Lc 1:45); l'esclamazione della donna anonima del vangelo (cf. Lc 11:27); e, non ultima, la stessa parola profetica della Vergine: 'Tutte le generazioni mi chiameranno beata' (Lc 1:48). . . . Tale è l'indirizzo più genuino della liturgia cristiana: essa è celebrazione anamnetica dei 'mirabilia Dei,' tra cui il grande evento del Verbo compiuto in Maria" (784, 786).

116. MD, 261f.

117. Govaert, *Kardinal Newmans Mariologie*, 137f.

118. Govaert, *Kardinal Newmans Mariologie*, 137.

119. Govaert, *Kardinal Newmans Mariologie*, 138.

120. Cf. Mt 15:37; Mk 6: 43; Lk 9:17; Jn 6:13—referring to the fragments left over in the twelve wicker baskets after the multiplication of the loaves and fishes.

121. Cf. Lk 16:2—Lazarus eating the crumbs that fall from the rich man's table.

122. Govaert, *Kardinal Newmans Mariologie*, 138.

123. Reading this passage, one could interpret Newman's allusions to the fragments and the crumbs left over as having Eucharistic overtones, even if Newman does not explicitly state as much. In the Book of Common Prayer, the following prayer may be said by the clergy and people together before the reception of Holy Communion: "We do not presume to come to this thy Table, O merciful Lord, trusting in our own righteousness, but in thy manifold and great mercies. We are not worthy so much as to gather up the crumbs under thy Table. But thou art the same Lord Whose property is always to have mercy. Grant us therefore, gracious Lord, so to eat the flesh of thy dear Son Jesus Christ, and to drink His Blood, that we may evermore dwell in Him and He in us." Another possible interpretation is that the fragments and crumbs left over stand for all those sacred realities (including the Eucharist and Marian devotion) that the Church receives as part of her spiritual patrimony in accord with the economy of salvation and the Sacred Tradition. Perhaps, then, the cooperation of the ordained ministers of the Church, as stewards and administrators of the divine mysteries, is implied in the sacred texts themselves since, for example, the twelve disciples are employed by Jesus in the gathering up of the fragments into the twelve wicker baskets, with the number twelve, perhaps, being symbolic of the Apostolic College.

124. Govaert, *Kardinal Newmans Mariologie*, 138.

125. The exact reference, about which Newman raises a question, is Judges 6:11.

126. Govaert, *Kardinal Newmans Mariologie*, 138.

127. Cf. Mk 3:31–34.

128. Newman tends to maintain that Joseph was a virgin like Mary and therefore never married and was without children. Cf. "A Triduo to St. Joseph," in Newman's *Meditations and Devotions*, 269–271. For example, Newman writes: "He was a virgin and his virginity was the faithful mirror of the virginity of Mary" (MD, 269).

129. The following scriptural texts are foundational for the Church's teaching on celibacy: Mt 19:1–12; concerning the eschatological dimension of Our Lord's teaching, see Mt 22:23–33, Mk 12:18–27, Lk 20:27–39. Furthermore, a significant Pauline injunction concerning the theological and practical values of celibacy in the Lord's service is found in 1 Cor 7:25–40.

130. Cf. Heb 7:3 on Melchizedech as a type of Christ, "without father."

131. Cf. Pope John Paul II, *A Catechesis on Mary, Mother of God*, 127–129. Also, Pope John Paul II, apostolic exhortation *Redemptoris Custos*, 7.

132. Cf. NDM, 639: "Costituito 'padre' di Gesù da questo sovrana volontà, Giuseppe si inserisce come un elemento necessario nell'esecuzione del piano divino della salvezza ed entra a giusto titolo nella schiera dei patriarchi come il loro massimo esponente."

133. Cf. Newman's "Meditations for Eight Days" (Tuesday), dedicated to St. Joseph, in MD, 213–214. Cf. also the article "Giuseppe," by the Reverend Stefano De Fiores, NDM, 633–655.

134. Cf. Dev. D., 135–148.

135. Although not given as references in Newman's sermon, one can call to mind the following texts that have both John the Baptist and Jesus clearly distinguishing themselves from each other, despite the identification that some had made between the two: Cf. Jn 1:19–28; Mt 16:13–20; Mt 11:2–19.

136. Govaert, *Kardinal Newmans Mariologie*, 139.

137. Ibid.

138. MD, 269.

139. Govaert, *Kardinal Newmans Mariologie*, 139.

140. PPS, II, 132.

141. Govaert, *Kardinal Newmans Mariologie*, 139.

142. Ibid.

143. Ibid.

144. Technically, what Newman says is not true insofar as it does not take into consideration the role proper of Joseph as Our Lord's putative father.

145. Govaert, *Kardinal Newmans Mariologie*, 139.

146. John Saward reflects on the mystery of Mary's womb as the privileged dwelling place of the Word Incarnate. Her womb is no ordinary place of physical repose but, like her whole person, it has been purposely furnished by God Himself in advance with the finest of spiritual gifts, graces and blessings so as to be made the most worthy living tabernacle of the Son of the Most High. Moreover, Mary freely cooperates in this plan of salvation before, during and after the Incarnation. "The first place in which we find Jesus in the Gospels is

the womb of Mary—in her 'innermost parts,' say Matthew and Luke with energetic realism (*en gastri, en tê kolia*, Mt 1:18; Lk 1:31; 2:21). He is not only the inhabitant of the womb; He is also its 'fruit' (cf. Lk 1:42). His Body does not come down from heaven; it is fashioned out of His Virgin Mother's flesh and blood. Indeed, since she is made fruitful by the Holy Spirit, not by male seed (cf. Mt 1:20), He is physically more indebted to her than any other child could be to his mother. Moreover, since in the Bible the body is the sacrament of the spiritual, Mary's enfolding of Christ in her womb is preceded by her soul's assent (cf. 1:38), accompanied by her spirit's rejoicing (cf. 1:46–55), and followed by her heart's contemplation (cf. 1:46–55). She gives Him His humanity in faith and love" (*Redeemer in the Womb*, 23).

147. Cf. LD, 19:346f. The sermon was published in 1835. Newman remarks about its reception: "I was accused of holding the doctrine of the Immaculate Conception for it was clear that I connected 'grace' with the Blessed Virgin's humanity—as if grace and nature in her case never had been separated. All I could say in answer was, that there was nothing against the thirty-nine articles."

148. Brit, *Newman's Use of Sacred Scripture*, 227.

149. Ibid.

150. Brit, *Newman's Use of Sacred Scripture*, 223.

151. Boyce, *Mary in the Writings of JHN*, 115, note 1.

152. Lk 1:48. Cf. Diff II, 125: "All generations have called her blessed." In his footnote (Diff II, 125), Newman recalls the Greek word μακαριοῦσι, which is translated as "blessed." Cf. also Diff II, 85—a further reference to the *Magnificat* in Newman's sermon "The Annunciation of the Blessed Virgin, On the Honor Due to Her" (25 March 1831), published for the first time in Govært, *Kardinal Newmans Mariologie*, 136. Cf. "*Magnificat*," by Elio Peretto in NDM, 853–865. Father Peretto concludes his reflections thus: "Il *Magnificat* non azzarda una definizione di Dio, ma ne descrive le opere salvifiche inziando con la concezione verginale. Sommo mistero della storia, ha un solo testimone e un solo poeta capace di celebrarlo: Maria" (864). Cf. also Alberto Valentini, *Il Magnificat: Genere Letterario, Struttura, Esegesi* (Bologna: Edizioni Dehoniane, 1987); *Mary in the New Testament*, ed. Raymond E. Brown et al. (New York: Paulist Press, 1978), 134–143.

153. PPS, II, 128.

154. Ibid. Cf. LG 66; MC 56–58; CCC 723; RM 35, 1–37, 4. Cf. also Stefano De Fiores, *Corso di Teologia Sistematica: Maria Madre di Gesù Sintesi Storico-Salvifica* (Bologna: Edizioni Dehoniane, 1992), 80–82. De Fiores, relying on the insights of Brown, Valentini, and Schnackenburg, introduces his treatment of the *Magnificat* thus: "Il Magnificat, cantico/inno/salmo di lode posto sulle labbra di Maria, presenta 'il valore rivelativo e kerigmatico della scena,' in quanto 'evidenzia in forma poetica quello che aveva già espresso con brevi parole prosaiche Elizabeth.' Il cantico costituisce 'la più antica teologia mariana,' poiché 'testimonia come il giovane cristianesimo considerava la Madre di Dio'" (80).

155. PPS, II, 128.

156. Ibid.

157. Ibid.

158. Cf. PPS, II, 128f.

159. A Greek word found in Mary's *Magnificat* that is often times rendered as "lowliness" or "humble estate."

160. Cf. Stefano De Fiores, *Maria Madre di Gesù*, 80f.: "Dio, Signore e Salvatore, 'ha guardato alla *tapeinosis* della sua serva (1,48a). La *tapeinosis* è stata recentemente interpretata come 'condizione di umiliazione' (Lyonnet), 'insignificanza e anonimato' (Mussner), 'bassezza/umiltà/miseria' (Valentini). . . . L'espressione indica probabilmente tutto questo, ma in primo luogo l'atteggiamento spirituale proprio dei 'poveri di JHWH,' che include 'piccolezza, povertà, essere indifesa, insignificanza, nullità, assolutta mancanza di influenza e di potere.'"

161. Cf. LG 55, 56, 57; MC 56–58; RM 35, 1–37, 4; CCC 722.

162. Our Holy Father Pope John Paul II writes: "The Council used the expression 'temple' (*sacrarium*) of the Holy Spirit, intending to emphasize the link of presence, love and colaboration that exists between the Blessed Virgin and the Holy Spirit" (*Mary, Mother of God*, 215). Cf. LG 53: "beloved daughter of the Father and the temple of the Holy Spirit."

163. Cf. PPS, 128f. In *Redemptoris Mater*, Pope John Paul II reflects on these virtues of Mary in light of the *Magnificat* when he writes: "The words used by Mary on the threshold of Elizabeth's house are *an inspired profession of her faith*, in which *her response to the revealed Word* is expressed with the religious and poetical exultation of her whole being toward God. In these sublime words, which are simultaneously very simple and wholly inspired by the sacred texts of the people of Israel, Mary's personal experience, the ecstasy of her heart, shines forth. In them shines a ray of the mystery of God, the glory of His ineffable holiness, the eternal *love which, as an irrevocable gift, enters into human history*. . . . In her exultation Mary confesses that she finds herself in *the very heart of this fullness of Christ*. She is conscious that the promise made to the fathers, first of all 'to Abraham and to his posterity for ever,' is being fulfilled in herself. She is thus aware that concentrated within herself as Mother of Christ is *the whole salvific economy*, in which 'from age to age' is manifested He Who, as the God of the Covenant, 'remembers his mercy'" (RM 36, 1).

164. Boyce observes: "The sermon which has just been referred to above . . . is most noteworthy, and gives us one of the best summaries we have of Newman's thought as an Anglican on our Lady. It was preached for the Feast of the Annunciation, 1832. He makes much of the words of the Archangel Gabriel to Mary. These same words form the scriptural foundation of the Church's teaching on the Divine Motherhood, the perpetual Virginity and Immaculate Conception of Mary. While summing up the reasons why the Virgin Mary is called blessed in Scripture, Newman touches on most of his Anglican thought about her. The first reason for this blessedness arises from Mary's parallel role to Eve in the history of salvation, a point which would become a distinctive feature of Newman's Mariology. First of all, in Mary, 'the curse pronounced on Eve was changed to a blessing'. God did not decide to destroy his sinful children who transgressed his original purpose, but he proposed to forgive and save them. Hence he sent his only Son, born of a woman (cf. Gal. 4:4), to redeem them and

initiate a new creation from what had become old and corrupt" (*Mary in the Writings of JHN*, 18f.).

165. The Holy Father's reflection on the *Magnificat* in *Redemptoris Mater* reveals a similar appreciation of Mary's role of cooperation in the *œconomia salutis* as the New Eve: "In the *Magnificat* the Church sees uprooted that sin which is found at the outset of the earthly history of man and woman, the sin of disbelief and of 'little faith' in God. In contrast with the 'suspicion' which the 'father of lies' sowed in the heart of Eve' and the true 'Mother of the Living,' bodily proclaims the *undimmed* truth about God: the holy and almighty God, Who from the beginning is *the source of all gifts*, He Who 'has done great things' in her, as well as in the whole universe. In the act of creation God gives existence to all that is. In creating man, God gives him the dignity of the image and likeness of Himself in a special way as compared with all earthly creatures. Moreover, in His desire to give, *God gives Himself in the Son*, notwithstanding man's sin: 'He so loved the world that He gave his only Son' (Jn 3:16). Mary is the first witness of this marvelous truth, which will be fully accomplished through 'the works and words' (cf. Acts 1:1) of her Son and definitively through His Cross and Resurrection" (RM 37).

166. PPS, II, 129f.

167. Ibid.

168. Otto Semmelroth, "Chapter VIII, The Role of the Blessed Virgin Mary, Mother of God, in the Mystery of Christ and the Church," in Herbert Vorgrimler's *Commentary on the Documents of Vatican II*, vol. 1 (New York: Herder & Herder, 1967), 287. Cf. also NDM, 233; Maria Ka Ho Fung. "Le Nozze di Cana, *Lectio Divina* su Giovanni 2, 1–2," in *Theotokos* 1 (1999), 154.

169. PPS, II, 131. Pope John Paul II comments on the significance of Gal 4:4 as a keystone of LG 8 and its teaching on Mary's spiritual maternity as a relationship that directly flows from our being adopted sons of the Father through union with Christ her Son. The Holy Father writes in his catechesis for 10 January 1996: "Chapter VIII of *Lumen Gentium* shows in the mystery of Christ the absolutely necessary reference to Marian doctrine. . . . She who brought the eternal Son of God to humanity can never be separated from Him Who is found at the center of the divine plan carried out in history. . . . The primacy of Christ is shown forth in the Church, His Mystical Body. In it the faithful are 'joined to Christ the Head . . . in the unity of fellowship with all His saints' (LG 52). Christ draws all men to Himself. Since in her maternal role she is closely united with her Son, Mary helps direct the gaze and heart of believers toward Him. She is the way that leads to Christ. Indeed, she who 'at the message of the angel received the Word of God in her heart and in her body' (LG 53) shows us how to receive into our lives the Son come down from heaven, teaching us to make Jesus the center and the supreme 'law' of our existence. Mary also helps us discover, at the origin of the whole work of salvation, the sovereign action of the Father Who calls men to become sons in the one Son."—*Theotokos: Woman, Mother, Disciple—A Catechesis on Mary, Mother of God* (Boston: Pauline Books and Media, 2000), 57f.; cf. also, for example, RM 1.

170. PPS, II, 130f.

171. PPS, II, 130.

172. Ibid. Newman writes: "Thus, the serpent has triumphed,—making the man still degrade himself by her who originally tempted him, and her, who then tempted, now suffer from him who was seduced."

173. PPS, II, 130.

174. Cf. Boyce, *Mary in the Writings of JHN*, 71. "On this point, Newman was speaking with a prophetic voice for the contemporary world. In these considerations by him, Catholic feminist movements would find enlightened insights into the mystery of woman, in harmony with the divine plan for creation and supernatural salvation. It would help them to safeguard the rights of women in a manner that would not jeopardize their dignity."

175. Cf. FC 23.

176. PPS, II, 131.

177. Cf. FC 20.

178. Cf. RM 46: "This Marian dimension of Christian life takes on special importance in relation to women and their status. In fact, femininity has a *unique relationship* with the Mother of the Redeemer . . . the figure of Mary of Nazareth shed light on *womanhood as such* by the very fact that God, in the sublime event of the Incarnation of His Son, entrusted Himself to the ministry, the free and active ministry, of a woman. It can thus be said that women, by looking to Mary, find in her the secret of living their femininity with dignity and of achieving their own true advancement. In the light of Mary, the Church sees in the face of women the reflection of a beauty which mirrors the loftiest sentiments of which the human heart is capable: the self-offering totality of love; the strength that is capable of bearing the greatest sorrows; limitless fidelity and tireless devotion to work; the ability to combine penetrating intuition with words of support and encouragement."

179. Cf. 1 Tim 2: 11–15.

180. Pope John Paul II reiterates the Gospel teaching on the dignity of women as exemplified in the dignity of the Blessed Virgin when he writes: "In creating the human race 'male and female' God gives man and woman an equal personal dignity, endowing them with the inalienable rights and responsibilities proper to the human person. God then manifests the dignity of women in the highest form possible, by assuming human flesh from the Virgin Mary, whom the Church honors as the Mother of God, calling her the new Eve and presenting her as the model of the redeemed woman" (FC 22).

181. Cf. Diff II, 131. Also, Eph 5:22–33.

182. Cf. Boyce, *Mary in the Writings of JHN*, 118, note 5: "Newman touches here on a topic of extreme relevance at the present time, the dignity and the role of women. The Church, in its official teaching, also looks to Mary in the mystery of the Incarnation as the person in whom every woman finds a model of her true greatness and feminine genius. Pope John Paul II, in one of his Apostolic Letters, makes explicit use of the mystery of the Annunciation and of Mary's role as the Second Eve: 'If Mary is described also as the "new Eve," what are the meanings of this analogy? Certainly there are many. Particularly noteworthy is the meaning which sees Mary as the full revelation of all that is included in the biblical word "woman": a revelation commensurate with the mystery of the Redemption. *Mary* means, in a sense, a going beyond the limit

spoken of in the Book of Genesis (3:6) and a return to that "beginning" in which one finds the "Woman" as she was intended to be in *creation*, and therefore in the eternal mind of God: in the bosom of the Most Holy Trinity. Mary *is* "the new beginning" of the *dignity and vocation of women*, of each and every woman. A particular key for understanding this text can be found in the words which the Evangelist puts on Mary's lips after the Annunciation, during her visit to Elizabeth: "He who is mighty has done great things for me" (Lk 1:49). These words certainly refer to the conception of her Son, who is the "Son of the Most High" (Lk 1:32), the "holy one" of God; but they can also signify *the discovery of her own feminine humanity*. He "*has done great things for me*": this is *the discovery of all richness and personal resources of femininity*, all the eternal originality of the "woman," just as God wanted her to be, a person for her own sake, who discovers herself "by means of a sincere gift of self" (Apostolic Letter, On the Dignity and Vocation of Women on the Occasion of the Marian Year, *Mulieris Dignitatem* [Vatican City, Libreria Editrice Vaticana, 1988], No. 11).' "

183. Cf. Gal 3:26, 28.

184. The Reverend Jean Galot, S.J., in his article *Maria Immagine della Donna*, highlights the uniqueness of Mary's contribution to the economy of salvation. Her cooperation at the moment of the Incarnation is particularly remarkable, given the socio-cultural milieu in which she lived. God's choice of Mary reveals a radical divine initiative and logic that surpasses all human expectation. Mary's *fiat* is pronounced not simply on her own behalf but on behalf of all mankind: "L'episodio dell'Annunciazione manifesta la volontà di Dio di richiedere la cooperazione di una donna a tutta l'opera di salvezza. Si poteva pensare che Dio solo decidesse il compimento del mistero dell'Incarnazione: l'impegno personale del Verbo in una vita umana avrebbe potuto essere soltanto un atto di sovranità divina. Invece, Maria è stata invitata a dare il suo contributo a questa decisione: la realizzazzione del mistero è sottomessa al suo consenso. Maria appare pienamente libera nella sua risposta al messaggio dell'angelo; chiede un chiarimento prima di dare la sua risposta, e solo dopo aver ricevuto dall'angelo la spiegazione sul piano di Dio dice il suo 'si' al progetto divino. Mai una donna ha esercitato una influenza così decisiva sulla storia dell'umanità. Dalla sua cooperazione è dipesa la venuta del Salvatore tra gli uomini. E tutto il destino umano che è stato trasformato, grazie alla risposta al messaggio dell'Annunciazione. Non si è mancato di notare che in questo momento Maria ha espresso il suo 'si' alla venuta di tutta l'umanità: 'Con l'Annunciazione—dice San Tommaso—si attendeva il consenso della Vergine in nome di tutta la natura umana' "—*Civiltà Cattolica* 1 (1974), 220. The citation of St. Thomas Aquinas is from his *Summa Theologiæ* III, q. 30, a. 1 in c.: "Per annuntiationem expectabatur consensus Virginis in loco totius humanæ naturæ," as given by Father Galot in his text.

185. Cf. FC 13.

186. Cf. Eph 5:21–33. In his post-synodal apostolic exhortation *Familaris Consortio*, Pope John Paul II writes: "The communion between God and His people finds its definitive fulfillment in Jesus Christ, the Bridegroom Who loves and gives Himself as the Savior of humanity, uniting it to Himself as His Body. He reveals the original truth of marriage, the truth of the 'beginning,' and,

freeing man from his hardness of heart, he makes man capable of realizing this truth in its entirety. This revelation reaches its definitive fullness in the gift of love which the Word of God makes to humanity in assuming a human nature, and in the sacrifice which Jesus Christ makes of Himself on the Cross for His Bride, the Church. In this sacrifice there is entirely revealed that plan which God has imprinted on the humanity of man and woman since their creation; the marriage of baptized persons thus becomes a real symbol of that New and Eternal Covenant sanctioned in the Blood of Christ. The Spirit which the Lord pours forth gives a new heart, and renders man and woman capable of loving one another as Christ has loved us" (FC 13, 1; 13, 2; 13, 3). Cf. Jer 31:31–34; Ezra 37:25–28. Cardinal Giacomo Biffi acknowledges that Mary as the New Eve enters into a mystical spousal relationship with Christ the New Adam in order to consummate the marriage between God and man in the Incarnation and therefore make possible the birth of a new humanity redeemed from sin and born again unto the supernatural life of grace and the everlasting life of a new heavens and a new earth. Cardinal Biffi explains: "Come Eva è stata tratta interamente da Adamo, così Maria è tutta derivata dal Figlio di Dio suo Salvatore: non c'è in lei alcuna bellezza, alcun valore, alcuna positività che non venga da Cristo; e non c'è in nessun palpito di vita consapevole che non sia donazione piena ed esistenziale a Cristo. In lei la verginità . . . è il suo modo proprio di essere sposa; e al tempo stesso è la misura assolutamente perfetta della sponsalità nella sua verità più sostanziale e profonda. Come Eva si è poi congiunta ad Adamo al servizio della vita da propagare, così Maria misticamente si unisce al Nuovo Adamo e—in lui, con lui, subordinatamente a lui—diventa la 'madre dei nuovi viventi,' cioè dell'umanità riscattata. È, come Eva, un caso unico e inimitabile: lei sola deriva totalmente da Cristo senza che altri sia associato a questa derivazione, cioè senza partecipazione ecclesiale; e lei sola entra come comprincipio della vita soprannaturale di tutte le creature che, dopo di lei e a somiglianza di lei, sono vivificate dal sacrificio del Signore."—*Canto Nuziale* (Milan: Jaca Books, 2000), 86.

187. PPS, II, 131f.

188. Newman alludes to Lk 2:40, 52.

189. Ibid.

190. PPS, II, 132.

191. Ibid. Even though here Newman does not delve into the theological significance of Mary's presence at Calvary and in the Cenacle in this sermon, he does so elsewhere in his writings, most notably in his *Meditations and Devotions*. Noteworthy also is Newman's failure to mention Mary's presence at Cana at this point, although this mystery plays a prominent part in Newman's later Marian reflection.

192. PPS, II, 132.

193. Ibid.

194. Newman writes that the Prophetess Anna "spoke of the Infant Saviour 'to all them that looked for redemption in Jerusalem.' Nay, for what we know, faith like Abraham's, and zeal like David's, have burned in the breasts of thousands whose names have no memorial" (PPS, II, 133).

195. PPS, II, 133.

196. Ibid.

197. Ibid.

198. Chapters One and Six of this work analyze Newman's discussions of the distinction between faith (doctrine) and devotion in the *Letter to Pusey* in relationship to Newman's theory of the development of doctrine and his theology of Mary's mediation, respectively.

199. PPS, II, 134f; cf. Heb 5:11.

200. Cf. Pope Paul VI's apostolic exhortation *Marialis Cultus*, especially nos. 25–39; 40–58.

201. DS, 601. The Latin text: "Imaginis enim honor ad primitivum transit: et qui adorat imaginem, adorat in ea depicti subsistentiam" ("'the honor given to an image goes to the original model,' and the one who venerates an image, venerates in it the person represented by it" (Neuner-Dupuis, *The Christian Faith*, § 1252).

202. Perrott, *Newman's Mariology*, 51.

203. Perrott, *Newman's Mariology*, 52.

204. PPS, II, 133f.

205. Diff II, 134. Cf. Rev 19:10; 22:8–9.

206. PPS, II, 134.

207. Cf. CCC 493.

208. PPS, II, 135.

209. Rev 10:4.

210. PPS, II, 135. Cf. Heb 5:11.

211. Newman seems to be quoting from the *Te Deum*, although he does not explicitly say as much.

212. Cf. PPS, II, 101–116. In a sermon for the Feast of the Purification of the Blessed Virgin Mary entitled: "Secrecy and Suddenness of Divine Visitations," Newman writes: "I say, we are to-day reminded of the noiseless course of God's Providence,— tranquil accomplishment, in the course of nature, of great events long designed; and again, of the suddenness and stillness of His visitations," hence the title of the sermon. Furthermore, Newman duly notes that this feast is primarily a Christological feast, namely, the Feast of the Presentation of Our Lord in the Temple. He offers particular exegetical insights when he explains, according to a twofold reasoning, that Mary need not have presented Jesus in the Temple or undergone the ritual purification of the Law because: 1) "Our Saviour was without sin" ; 2) "It was that the very birth of the Son of God which sanctified the whole race of woman, and turned her curse into a blessing." However, Newman explains the rationale of the feast and therefore of Mary's cooperation in the economy of salvation on this occasion in the following way: "Nevertheless, as Christ Himself was minded to 'fulfil all righteousness,' to obey all ordinances of the covenant under which He was born, so in like manner His Mother Mary submitted to the Law, in order to do it reverence" (PPS, II, 108). Cf. also OUS, 313f; the article of Father Gaetano Meaolo, "Presentazione del Signore," in NDM, 1148–55, and of Father George Gharib "Presentazione di Maria," in NDM, 1155–61. It is also worth noting that in the post-conciliar liturgical reform, the names and foci of the solemnities celebrated on February 2 and March 25, respectively, have

been given a dominical rather than a specifically Marian thrust—something Newman would have undoubtedly appreciated. See also Boyce, *Mary in the Writings of JHN*, 125, note 10: "In the Roman Catholic Liturgy too, feasts in honour of Our Lady are closely associated with the person and redemptive work of Christ. 'In celebrating this annual cycle of the mysteries of Christ, holy Church honours the Blessed Mary, Mother of God, with a special love. She is inseparably linked with her Son's saving work. In her the Church admires and exalts the most excellent fruit of redemption, and joyfully contemplates, as in a faultless image, that which she herself desires and hopes wholly to be.' (Vatican II, Constitution on the Sacred Liturgy, *Sacrosanctum Concilium*, 103). 'The feasts of the saints proclaim the wonderful works of Christ in His servants and offers to the faithful fitting examples of their imitation' (*Ibid.* 11)."

213. PPS, II, 135f. Saward develops the idea of Newman's sermon regarding Mary's name as a "memorial" of the great *kenosis* of Christ in becoming her Child when he comments: " 'A woman,' said Chesterton, 'was His walking home.' The first stage of the divine Word's human life was literally 'in Mary,' in her womb. *O Jesu vivens in Maria.* . . . Before He was among us, He was inside her. Most contemporary Christology, with some notable exceptions, has little to say about what John Donne called this 'well-beloved imprisonment' " (1f.). Cf. also pp. 151, 156–157, 161.

214. "Queen of the Angels." Cf. MD, 29–31.

215. The doctrine of the Immaculate Conception, so essential to Newman's Mariological writings, is dealt with throughout this thesis, most especially in connection with his *Letter to Pusey* and his *Meditations and Devotions.*

216. PPS, II, 135.

217. A version of this expression is found in the writings of Plato and Aristotle on ethics. One recalls, for example, Aristole's famous notion of the "golden mean." Translated from the Latin, it means: "In the middle stands virtue."

218. PPS, II, 136.

219. LG 62. Cf. RM 403. For a more detailed study of Newman's understanding of Mary's cooperative, "ministrative," role in the *opera salutis* as spiritual Mother of the Church, see, especially, Chapter Six and the section of Chapter Three on Newman and Ambrose.

220. John R. Griffin, "Newman and the Mother of God," *Faith and Reason: Essays in Honor of the Centenary of John Henry Cardinal Newman, 1801–1890* (Winter 1989), 93. Cf. PPS, II, 145.

221. PPS, II, 136.

222. Ibid.

223. Ibid.

224. PPS, II, 137.

225. Cf. Mt 4:20–22; Mk 1:18; 2:15; Lk 5:11; Jn 1:38, 40, 43.

226. Cf. 1 Cor 7:35.

227. Cf. De la Potterie, *Mary in the Mystery of the Covenant*, 150f.

228. PPS, II, 136f.

229. Cf. Eph 1:3–10.

230. PPS, II, 137.

231. For a more in-depth study of Newman's understanding of this con-

trasting parallelism between the faith of Mary and that of Zechariah, see this work's treatment of Newman's Oxford University sermon, "The Purification of Mary," in the present chapter and in Chapter Three on Newman and Ambrose.

232. PPS, II, 137.

233. Cf. Lk 1:46–55.

234. Cf. RM 14, 1. Cf. also Frederick L. Miller, "The Marian Orientation of Spirituality in the Thought of John Paul II," *Communio* (Winter 1990), 571.

235. Perrott, *Newman's Mariology*, 51.

236. PPS, II, 131f.

237. Boyce, *Mary in the Writings of JHN*, 120, note 6.

238. Cardinal Ratzinger writes: "'The Holy Spirit will come upon you, and the power of the Most High will overshadow you; therefore, the child to be born will be called holy, the Son of God' (Lk 1:35). Our gaze is led beyond the covenant with Israel to the creation: in the Old Testament the Spirit of God is the power of creation; He it was Who hovered over the waters at the beginning and shaped chaos into cosmos (Gen 1:2); when he is sent, living beings are created (Ps 104[103]:30). So what happens here to Mary is new creation: the God Who called forth being out of nothing makes a new beginning amid humanity: His Word became flesh. The other image in this text—the 'overshadowing by the power of the Most High'—points to the temple of Israel and to the holy tent in the wilderness where God's presence was indicated in the cloud, which hides His glory as well as revealing it (Ex 40:34; 1 Kings 8:11). Just as Mary was depicted earlier as the new Israel, the true 'daughter of Sion', so now she appears as the temple onto which descends the cloud in which God walks into the midst of history."—Joseph Ratzinger, *Introduction to Christianity* (San Francisco: Ignatius Press, 1990), 206.

239. Cf. PPS, II, 136.

240. PPS, II, 137.

241. PPS, II, 138.

242. We can notice how, for Newman, the vision of the Blessed Virgin and the other saints does not obscure our vision of the Lord but is actually an essential consequence of entrance into heavenly glory. It is worth citing here the Catechism of the Catholic Church in this regard: "Mary, the all-holy ever-virgin Mother of God, is the masterwork of the mission of the Son and the Spirit in the fullness of time. For the first time in the plan of salvation and because His Spirit had prepared her, the Father found the *dwelling place* where His Son and His Spirit could dwell among men. . . . The Holy Spirit *prepared* Mary by His grace. It was fitting that the Mother of Him in Whom 'the whole fullness of deity dwells bodily' should herself be 'full of grace.' She was, by sheer grace, conceived without sin as the most humble of creatures, the most capable of welcoming the inexpressible gift of the Almighty" (CCC 721f.).

243. Cf. Mt 17:1–8; Mk 9:2–8; Lk 9:28–36.

244. PPS, II, 138.

245. Cf. Boyce, *Mary in the Writings of JHN*, 129, note 1. As regards these sermons Bishop Boyce notes: "They did not form part of a Eucharistic or liturgical celebration." Also, Boyce, *Mary*, 136, note 7: "All of these eighteen

Discourses to Mixed Congregations display a zeal that is typical of a new convert. Richard H. Hutton describes the peculiar genius of these sermons as follows 'They have more in them of the enthusiasm of a convert than any other of Newman's publications, and altogether contain the most eloquent and elaborate specimens of eloquence as a preacher, and of his sense, if I may so call it, of the religious advantages of his position as a spokesman of the great Church of Rome. They represent more adequately Dr Newman as he was when he first felt himself 'unmuzzled' . . . , than any other of his writings; and though they have not to me quite the delicate charm of the reserve, and I almost say, the shy passion, of his Oxford sermons, they represent the full-blown blossom of his genius, while the former show it only in bud'": *Cardinal Newman* (London: Methuen, 1891), 197.

246. Cf. John Henry Newman, *Discourses Addressed to Mixed Congregations*, with an Introduction and Notes by James Tolhurst—vol. 6 of the Works of John Henry Cardinal Newman, Birmingham Oratory, Millennium Edition, series ed. James Tolhurst (Paris: University of Notre Dame, 2002), ix–lix. See especially page x, wherein Tolhurst writes: "It is perhaps necessary to explain the term *Mixed Congregations* which Newman uses on page 254: 'I trust I need at present to have none in insisting before a congregation however mixed, on the mysteries or difficulties of God's existence.' These discourses were aimed at an audience which comprised many Roman Catholics and also those who may have had a Christian affiliation to another Church or may have had no particular faith. According to Faber, the poor came to the early Masses, and 'shopkeepers' (among a congregation of 600) to late Benediction. Birmingham . . . was a growing industrial city with its share of Unitarians, Plymouth Brethren and Agnostics."

247. Franciscus M. William, O.S.B., "Cardinal Newman Theses De Doctrina et Devotione Mariana et Motus Œcumenicus," *De Mariologia et Œcumenismo* (Rome: Pontificia Academia Mariana Internationalis, 1962), 271: "Lectione absoluta, obstipuit quodammodo Newman, eo quod ibi nihil excessus vel elationis invenire potuit, quæ huic operi vitio verti consueverant." Cf. also Newman's *Discourse for Mixed Congregations*, "On the Fitness of the Glories of Mary."

248. Cf. Giovanni Velocci, "Maria nella Vita di John Henry Newman," *Theotokos* 6 (1998), 289f.; Velocci, "Sant'Alfonso Visto da Newman," *Rivista di Vita Spirituale* 40 (1986), 167–180; Jean Stern, "La Vierge Marie dans le Chemin de Foi parcouru par John Henry Newman," *Marianum* 53 (1991), 51.

249. John Brit examines various sermons of Newman's in order to illustrate the concept of divine Providence as a biblical hermeneutic. One such is entitled, "The Glory of the Christian Church," found in *Parochial and Plain Sermons*. Brit writes: "The first specimen, from just before the heart of the sermon . . . contains as explicit a statement on Providence as we are able to find in Newman: 'Now the system of the world depends, in a way unknown to us, both on God's Providence and on human agency. Every event . . . has two faces; it is divine and perfect, and it belongs to man and is marked with his sin. I observe next, that it is a peculiarity of Holy Scripture to represent the world on its providential side; ascribing all that happens in it to Him who rules and directs it, as it moves along. . . . In other words, Scripture more commonly speaks of the divine *design*

and *substantial work*, than of the *measure* of fulfilment which it receives at this time or that": "Providence and Scripture: Maturity, Subtlety, and Consciousness in Newman," *Marian Library Studies: Mater Fidei et Fidelium*, Collected Essays to Honor Théodore Koehler on His 80th Birthday, volumes 17–23 (1985–1991), 330–344. Cf. also PPS, II, 82f. Brit further acknowledges that Newman's sermon "The Glory of the Christian Church" permits us to comprehend in a more "mature way" Newman's concept of the divine Providence as revealed in order of the divine economy of salvation because Newman followed the hermeneutical principles of the Alexandrian School more than those of the Antiochean School. Thus, Newman is more capable of seeing the divine Providence at work in both an individual and collective sense throughout salvation history because it is from the Alexandrian principles of hermeneutics that "we have the *sensus plenior* as a constant link between the literal sense, which he uses as a starting point, and the typical and allegorical senses, upon which a further insight into the material, so that his applications may be achieved" (Brit, *Providence and Scripture*, 338).

250. Sir 42:24. It is interesting that Newman's very first quotation from Scripture is taken from one of the Deuterocanonical books.

251. Gen 2:1.

252. DMC, 342.

253. 1 Cor 2:7.

254. DMC, 343; cf. 1 Cor 2:10.

255. DMC, 344.

256. The literal meaning of καὶ ὁ λόγος σὰρξ ἐγένετο καὶ ἐσήνωσεν ἐν ἡμῖν (found in Jn 1:14); but this text is usually rendered "And the Word became flesh and *dwelt* among us."

257. Newman sometimes speaks of Protestantism in generalizations, without reference to a specific denomination. His observations about the Protestants of his day are not necessarily reflective of the present situation. Newman does not suggest that "Protestant" preaching consciously aims to promote heretical doctrines but that, in some cases, this was in fact the effect produced. His sermon aims to correct those errors where found and to show how the Catholic Marian teaching is nothing less than the fullest expression of the orthodox, apostolic Tradition. Newman's remarks are not meant to be an attack *ad hominem*, but a constructive criticism and fraternal correction of those who, for example, whether part of the established Anglican Church, members of a dissenting group such as those called the "Freedmen," or members of other ecclesial communions, did not accept all the consequences of an orthodox belief in the reality of the Incarnation.

258. DMC, 346.

259. Pope St. Leo the Great, in his sermons for the Christmas season, is intent upon showing that the early Christological heresies (e.g, Nestorianism and Monophysitism) are also fundamental denials of an orthodox Mariology, with the doctrine of Mary as the *Theotokos* as the pivotal point of dispute. Some excerpts from Pope Leo's sermons might help put into perspective the concerns Newman frequently expresses in his own writings, namely, that the glories of Mary are for the sake of her Son. In other words, the emphasis that Catholics

place on the divine maternity, for example, is essentially a reinforcement or bulwark of the ancient Christological formulations. Pope Leo says: "Multa sunt prodigia falsitatum, quibus enumerandis caritatis vestræ non est fatigandus auditus. Sed post diversas impietates, quæ sibi invicem sunt multiformium blasphemiarum cognatione conexæ, de his potissimum erroribus declinandis observantiam vestræ devotionis admoneo, quorum unus dudum Nestorio auctore consurgere non impune temptavit, alius super pari exsecratione damnandus, Eutyche assertore, prorupit.... Nam ille beatam Mariam virginem hominis tantummodo ausus est predicare genetricem, ut in conceptu eius et partu nulla Verbi et carnis facta unitio crederetur, quia Dei Filius non ipse factus sit hominis filius, sed creato homini sola se dignatione sociaverit. Quod catholicæ aures nequaquam tolerare potuerunt, quæ sic evangelio veritatis inbutæ sunt, ut firmissime noverint nullam esse humano generi spem salutis, nisi ipse esset filius Virginis, qui Creator est matris" (*Sermo* 8, 5.2).

260. DMC, 346f.

261. John Saward, "The Christocentricity of Pope John Paul II," *Communio* (Fall 1991), 345–347, passim.

262. DMC, 347.

263. Newman uses the phrase "mystic economy."

264. CCC 462 quotes from the Letter to the Hebrews 10:5–7, citing Ps 40:6–8 (7–9, LXX): "God sent forth his Son" (Gal 4:4), but to prepare a body for Him (Heb 10:5), He wanted the free cooperation of a creature. For this, from all eternity God chose for the Mother of His Son a daughter of Israel, a young Jewish woman of Nazareth in Galilee, 'a virgin betrothed to a man whose name was Joseph of the house of David; and the virgin's name was Mary.'" (Lk 1:26–27). CCC 488, quoting from LG 56, reads: "The Father of mercies willed that the Incarnation should be preceded by assent on the part of the predestined Mother, so that just as a woman had a share in the coming of death, so also should a woman contribute to the coming of life." The Catechism reveals an obvious aim to reinforce the historicity of the event of the Incarnation and therefore cites different scriptural passages which give specific data concerning the identity of the Virgin and St. Joseph as persons whose predestined role of cooperation in the history of salvation is freely undertaken so that the Father's will might be accomplished. The Virgin's consent ("free co-operation") is what makes possible the realization of the Father's predestined plan that His Son become flesh of a "predestined Mother."

265. DMC, 347.

266. DMC, 348.

267. Pope John Paul II, *Mary, Mother of God*, 64f. "In the Hebrew text this prophecy does not explicitly foretell the Virgin birth of Emmanuel: the word used (*almah*) simply means 'a young woman,' not necessarily a virgin. Moreover, we know that Jewish tradition did not hold up the idea of perpetual virginity, nor did it ever express the idea of virginal motherhood. In the Greek tradition, however, the Hebrew word was translated *parthenos*—virgin. In this fact, which could seem merely a peculiarity of translation, we must recognize a mysterious orientation given by the Holy Spirit to Isaiah's words in order to prepare for the understanding of the Messiah's extraordinary birth."

268. Serra, "Bibbia," in NDM, 242f.: "Mt 1,22–23 rilegge Is 7:14 in senso messianico e mariologico. . . . Potremo dire che la rilettura mateana di Is 7:14 ha due aspetti: l'uno attiene al messia, l'altro alla madre del messia . . . Is 7,14 è il primo degli oracoli veterotestmentari ad essere compreso anche in senso mariologico da un autore del NT. La vergine vi è profeticamente adombrata (cf. LG 55). Se diversi padri, come Giustino, riferivano questa profezia direttamente a Cristo e a Maria, ciò avvenne molto probabilmente sotto l'influsso della polemica con gli ambienti giudaici, che negavano ogni contenuto cristologico all'AT. Rispettando, invece, l'economia progressiva e storicistica della rivelazione, vediamo che solo a partire dalla testimonianza di Matteo è possibile scorgere la figura del Salvatore e della Madre sua dietro i veli del personaggio-tipo del re Ezechia e della regina madre Abia. Ciò che avvenne ai tempi del re Achaz, consegue ora l'adempimento perfetto e definitivo nel mistero della concezione verginale di Cristo, 'figlio di Davide' (cf. Mt 1,20) e 'Dio con noi' (Mt 1:23). Il NT porta a compimento l'AT, superandolo."

269. DMC, 348.

270. Ibid.

271. Cf. also MD, 399–402, passim: "I am created to do something or to be something for which no one else is created; I have a place in God's counsels, in God's world, which no one else has; whether I be rich or poor, despised or esteemed by men, God knows me and calls me by my name. God has created me to do Him some definite service; He has committed some work to me which He has not committed to another. I have my mission—I may never know it in this life, but I shall be told it in the next. Somehow I am necessary for His purposes, as necessary in my place as an Archangel in his. . . . I have a part in this great work; I am a link in a chain, a bond of connection between persons. He has not created me for naught. I shall be an angel of peace, a preacher of truth in my own place, while not intending it, if I do but keep His commandments and serve Him in my calling. Therefore I will trust Him. Whatever, wherever I am, I can never be thrown away. If I am in sickness, my sickness may serve Him; in perplexity, my perplexity may serve Him; if I am in sorrow, my sorrow may serve Him; my sickness or perplexity or sorrow may be necessary causes of some great end, which is quite beyond us. He does nothing in vain; He may prolong my life; He may shorten it; He knows what He is about. He may take away my friends, He may throw me among strangers, He may make me feel desolate, make my spirits sink, hide the future from me—still He knows what He is about. I ask not to see—I ask not to know—I ask simply to be used."

272. Cf. LG 53: "She is endowed with the high office and dignity of being the Mother of the Son of God, by which account she is also the beloved daughter of the Father and the temple of the Holy Spirit."

273. DMC, 349.

274. Ibid.

275. Gianfranco Ravasi briefly evaluates the tradition of a Mariological interpretation of the Canticle of Canticles: "La lettura mariologica del Cantico è, quindi, un atto di libera interpretazione che assume particelle del testo e soprattutto la sua folgorante simbologia, attribuendovi iridescenze, tonalità, ammicamenti, valori inediti e non compatibili col tenore originale, compren-

sibili solo nell'arco globale della Rivelazione e della Tradizione. In questo senso si parla di 'allegoria' (letteralmente 'parlare l'altro'), anche se con una sua legittimità teologica, quella dell'unità del discorso di Dio nell'orizzonte integrale della storia della salvezza, anche se legittime sono le singole, concrete connessioni. Se qualche applicazione mariana è facilmente già reperibile nei Padri della Chiesa, la sposa del Cantico diventa in modo continuo Maria nell'opera *In Cantica de Incarnatione Domini libri VII di Ruperto di Deutz* (1075–1130), abate benedettino di Sant' Erberto. Fino a lui i cenni mariologici sul Cantico erano subordinati a quelli ecclesiali o mistici o morali; con lui e Maria a comandare le applicazioni derivate della Chiesa e all'anima. E lo è sulla base del legame nuziale mistico di Maria con Dio attraverso lo Spirito Santo il cui frutto è la nascita del Cristo. Da allora questa interpretazione avrà un grande successo, anche nell'arte cristiana": *L'Albero di Maria Trentun: "Icone" Bibliche Mariane* (Milan: Edizioni San Paolo, 1994), 121.

276. DMC, 349f.

277. Cf. Boyce, *Mary in the Writings of JHN*, 138, note 11: "The antiphon was used at the time in the *Breviarum Romanum*, cf. the Common of the Feasts of the Blessed Virgin Mary, Matins, 3rd Nocturn, Antiphon 7, and also in the *Missale Romanum*: cf. the Common of Our Lady, *Tract* of the Mass '*Salve Sancta Parens*' (between Septuagesima and Easter) and the second Mass for Our Lady on Saturdays, '*Vultum tuum.*' Newman considered the mystery of Mary to be a safeguard of the Catholic orthodox teaching."

278. DMC, 349.

279. DMC, 350.

280. Ibid.

281. Ibid.

282. Ibid.

283. DMC, 351.

284. Father Serra, in his article "Assunta," in NDM, explains how the readings of the present-day Roman liturgy for the Vigil Mass of the Assumption relate the dogma of the Assumption to the Old Testament theology of the Ark of the Covenant (cf. First Reading: 1 Chron 15:3–4, 15–16; 16:1–2) and the teaching of Our Lord concerning Mary's physical and spiritual beatitude (cf. Gospel Reading: Luke 11, 27–28). Serra makes further allusions to the image of the seat of wisdom (feminine personification) in the sapiential literature of the Old Testament and makes an application to the Virgin thus: "Divenuta sede della sapienza incarnata, nel corpo e nello spirito, ella fu resa partecipe dell'immortalità, dell'incorruzione; un dono, dicono i libri dell'AT, di cui è dispensatrice la Sapienza, cioè l'accoglienza amorosa fatta al disegno di Dio espresso nelle Scritture (Cf. Sap 6, 17–20; 8, 17; Prv 8, 35, ecc.)" (166). See also Ps 131 (132): "Surge, Domine, in requiem tuam, tu et arca fortitudinis tuæ." An English translation: "Rise up, O Lord, into your rest, you and the ark of your strength."

285. DMC, 351.

286. Cf. Louis Bouyer, *The Meaning of Sacred Scripture* (London: Darton, Longman & Todd, 1958), 182–190, passim, on St. Paul and his theology of Christ as the Heavenly Man or Second Adam, in Whom, according to the divine economy of salvation, all men and all of creation are recapitulated.

287. See Chapters One and Four of the present work for a more detailed treatment of Newman's understanding of the New Eve theology. Hans Urs von Balthasar, in his work *The Office of Peter and the Structure of the Church*, links together the scriptural and patristic evidence for the theology of the New Eve. The scriptural evidence, as Balthasar comprehends it, first and foremost, establishes the doctrine of the New or Second Eve in relationship to the Church. For example, he writes: "The infancy narratives, particularly those of Luke, are clearly full to the brim with the theological symbolism—leading from the Old to the New testament—that has a real foundation in the simply told events. As could be expected, the Marian episodes of the Fourth Gospel are essential to its understanding. The Letter to the Ephesians forcefully presents the relationship of Christ and the Church as that of man and wife, and since Paul shows Christ to be the second and final Adam, the Church automatically assumes the role of the second Eve, without reference to Mary."—(San Francisco: Ignatius Press, 1986), 197. Cardinal Newman, as far as has been able to be ascertained in this work, would agree with Balthasar that the Church automatically assumes the role of the New or Second Eve based on the inference from this particular text of Ephesians, as well as in light of the many other Marian Scriptural texts to which Balthasar himself alludes. However, Newman probably would have been reticent in adding Balthasar's second statement that such an inference was initially made "without reference to her [i.e., the Church's] relationship to Mary." Newman would probably assert that the sacred authors, apart from the later theological developments of the New Eve theology in the writings of the Fathers, would have already intuited a link (even if not yet fully explicated) between the Marian and ecclesial aspects of this title. In any case, Balthasar's statement that: "Later reflection follows the path opened up by Paul," would find Newman in fundamental agreement. Balthasar makes special mention of the contributions of Justin Martyr and Irenæus of Lyon. Thus, analogously speaking, both Newman and Balthasar would concur that the New Eve theology hidden in the Scriptures is revealed in the writings of the Fathers. (Cf. von Balthasar, *The Office of Peter*, 196–203).

288. It is fascinating to discover that the official English translation of *The Holy Scriptures according to the Masoretic Text* (Philadelphia: The Jewish Publication Society of America, 1965) translates this text thus: "*They* [that is, the woman and her seed] shall bruise thy head" (6, emphasis added). Cf. Boyce, *Mary in the Writings of JHN*, 55f. Bishop Boyce notes: "Newman, however, not only bases his conviction on theological argumentation but, as always, goes to the sure foundation of Sacred Scripture. He reads the pertinent texts in light of the interpretation given to them by the Fathers of the Church. Thus he recalls the words of Genesis 3:15 and defends the Vulgate reading: 'She bruise thy head'—the same procedure was used by Pope Pius IX in the bull *Ineffabilis Deus*. He adds that the parallel Eve-Mary shows up the full content of the Archangel's words to Mary: 'full of grace.' Newman's exposition is completely in harmony with the mind of the Church and is a fine specimen of theological writing." Cf. CCC 410–412, 490–495.

289. DMC, 352.

290. Cf. Diff II, 42f.

291. Cf. CCC 359. Chrysologus in his *Sermo* 117 speaks of God the Father having formed Adam from the ground and in so doing creating him in the image and likeness of Christ, His Only-Begotten Son with a view to Our Lord's Incarnation as the Last Adam. The much-debated question of whether or not the Incarnation would have occurred if Adam and Eve had not sinned, seems to receive an answer in Chrysologus that it does not receive in the teaching, for example, of St. Augustine and St. Thomas Aquinas, or, for that matter, in the majority of medieval theologians who entertained the question in a particular way (cf. PL 52:520–521).

292. DMC, 353f.

293. Newman's sermon note "On The Peculiarities and Consequent Sufferings of Our Lady's Sanctity," dated 8 December 1853, is precisely concerned with the Eve-Mary parallel in terms of their respective creation in a state of original grace and holiness. Newman believes that the doctrine of Our Lady's Immaculate Conception (to be solemnly defined as dogma the following year—1854) can be logically inferred from the following truths: "Eve, as Adam, had been not only created, but constituted holy, grace given, etc. Eve was without sin from the first, filled with grace from the first. When Adam and Eve fell, this grace was removed; and this constitutes the state of original sin. . . . This is the state into which the soul of man comes on its creation. Nothing can hinder it but a *return* of the great gift. *She* [Mary] was to restore, and more, the age of Paradise. She was promised at the fall. Eve has been deceived. *She* was to conquer. How would this be the case, unless Mary had at least the gifts which Eve had? We believe, then, that Mary had this sanctifying grace from the moment she began to be" (SN, 106f.).

294. Along these lines, Newman writes the following in his meditation on the title of *Virgo Purissima*: "Therefore, she was a child of Adam and Eve as if they had never fallen; she did not share with them their sin; she inherited the gifts and graces (and more than those) which Adam and Eve possessed in Paradise. This is her prerogative, and the foundation of all those salutary truths which are revealed to us concerning her. Let us say then with all holy souls, *Virgin most pure, conceived without original sin*, Mary, pray for us" (MD, 9).

295. The *Catechism* states the following: ". . . the Church's Tradition has often read the most beautiful texts on wisdom in relation to Mary. Mary is acclaimed and represented in the liturgy as the 'Seat of Wisdom.' . . . It was quite correct for the angel Gabriel to greet her as the 'Daughter of Zion': 'Rejoice'" (CCC 721f.). Cf. also "Figlia di Sion," NDM, 580–589.

296. DMC, 354.

297. De la Potterie explains the significance of Mary's *fiat* thus: "The word used here by Luke (*genoito*)—a word that occurs only once in the New Testament—does not express a passive and resigned acceptance, but a joyous consent to enter completely into the design of God. Mary said to the angel: 'I am the servant of the Lord; *let it be done to me* according to your word' (v. 38). The use, in Greek, of the verb "to happen; to be done" (*ginesthai*) in the optative (*optare* = to desire) shows that Luke, here once more, wishes to describe a desire of Mary. The desire manifested in v. 34 is prolonged in that which is expressed in v. 38, viz., the desire to cooperate completely in the realization of God's design. This

was the exact same attitude that the People of God had toward the covenant, as so well expressed by Israel at the moment of the ratification of the Covenant on Sinai: 'All that Yahweh has said, we will do' (Ex 19:8; cf. 24:7). In so expressing her complete consent, Mary became the personification of the Daughter of the Messianic Zion, of the *'Virgo Zion,'* in the context of the Covenant. Rightly then, Tradition has more and more clearly underlined the fact that the *'fiat'* of Mary expresses here the fundamental image of the People of God, the Church, in its relationship with God" (*Mary in the Mystery of the Covenant*, 145).

298. Newman asks: "If we have faith to admit the Incarnation itself, we must admit it in its fulness; why then should we not start at the gracious appointments which arise out of it? If the Creator comes on earth in the form of a servant and a creature, why may not His Mother, on the other hand, rise to be the Queen of heaven, clothed with the sun and have the moon under her feet" (DMC, 355).

299. The fundamental distinction which Newman makes in this sermon between the hierarchical, priestly ministry of the twelve apostles and their successors and Mary's role (e.g., of mediation) within and on behalf of the Church has been the cause of much theological discussion among modern theologians. The following works are most noteworthy: Hans Urs von Balthasar, *The Office of Peter and the Structure of the Church* (San Francisco: Ignatius Press, 1986), 194, 204–225; Yves Congar, *Vraie et Fausse Réforme dans l'Église* (Paris: Cerf, 1950), 95; Congar, *Jalons pour une Théologie du Laïcat* (Paris: Cerf, 1953), 46f.; René Laurentin, *Court Traité de Théologie Mariale* (Paris: Lethielleux, 1953), 109; Laurentin, *Marie, l'Église et le Sacerdoce*, 2 vol. (Paris: Lethielleux, 1952–1953); Charles Journet, *L'Église du Verbe Incarné*, 3 vol. (Paris: Desclée de Brouwer, 1951), 2:438–446.

300. DMC, 356.

301. DMC, 357.

302. Ibid.

303. Cf. Donald A. Withey, *John Henry Newman: The Liturgy and the Roman Breviary, Their Influence on His Life As an Anglican* (London: Sheed & Ward, 1992), 23, 35f., 39, 42, 58, 61, 63, 66, 79, 81. See also Boyce, *Mary in the Writings of JHN*, 147, note 15: "These words taken from Wisdom texts in the Old Testament (cf. Sir 24:11–13, 15–20 in the Vulgate) have been applied to Our Lady by the Church's Liturgy. In the Tridentine Liturgy of Newman's day: cf. for example, *Officium Parvum Beatæ Mariæ Virginis, Ad Matutinum, In Nocturno*, and in the Roman Missal, Mass for the Common of the Feast of Our Lady."

304. Cf. ES, 62:11–12. Also, LG 55; Pope John Paul II, *Mary, Mother of God*, 83–86.

305. It is perhaps useful to summarize the theology to which Newman only alludes in his Mariological writings. Gianfranco Ravasi's reflection on the theology of the Daughter of Sion in his *L'Albero di Maria: Trentun'Icone Bibliche Mariane* will serve well in making this summary: " . . . La locuzione 'figlia di Sion' o 'vergine figlia di Sion' (Lam 2:13) è in ebraico sinonimo di 'Sion è figlia' perché essa è amata da Jhwh che le è sposo e padre e madre (Os 11; Is 49:15). Ma l'elemento più suggestivo che specifica questa 'figlia' è il suo grembo, espresso

con la formula *be-qereb*, che spesso è neutralmente tradotta con la locuzione 'in mezzo.' In realtà, essa significa letteralmente 'nelle viscere, nel grembo' e permette una connessione dell'immagaine di Sion-figlia con quella di Sion-madre. Ma la novità è forte, sopratutto per l'applicazione successiva mariana. Il grembo della figlia di Sion è sede della presenza sapienziale (1 Re 8) e storica (2 Sam 7) di Dio nel tempio e nella casa dinastica davidica: 'Esulta grandemente, figlia di Sion, giubila, figlia di Gerusalemme! Ecco, a te viene il tuo re . . .' (Zc 9:9–10); 'voi riconoscerete che io sono in mezzo a Israele' (Gl 2:23, 27). Esemplare in questo senso è la splendida apostrofe a Sion, presente nel libro di Sofonia e aperta da un appello solenne:

> 'Gioisci, figlia di Sion, esulta, Israele, rallegrati con tutto il cuore, figlia
>   di Gerusalemme!
> Re d'Israele è Jhwh in mezzo a te (*be-quereb*), Jhwh tuo Dio in mezzo a
>   te (*be-quereb*)
> è un salvatore potente. Esulterà di gioia per te, ti rinnoverà col suo
>   amore,
> si rallegrerà per te con grida di gioia come nei giorni di festa' (3:14–18).

. . . In fine Maria è per eccellenza 'la figlia di Sion' nel cui grembo (be-quereb) Dio è presente in modo supremo. In Maria la Parola divina si fa carne, umanità e storia in modo pieno e perfetto: 'Lo Spirito Santo scenderà su di te . . . Colui che nascerà sarà santo e chiamato Figlio di Dio' (Lc 1:35). La nascita è segno di un inizio, è indizio di limite, di tempo, di umanità; la 'santità' e la filiazione divina ci riportono all'infinito e a Dio. Maria è, dunque, la Sion ideale. . . " (79f., passim).

306. DMC, 358f.

307. "Mary, Mother of grace, gentle parent of clemency; from the enemy defend us, and welcome us at the hour of death."

308. See Newman's meditation on the title *Stella Matutina* in MD, 76–77. Cf. also RM 3, 2–3, 3: "Just as this star, together with the 'dawn,' precedes the rising of the sun, so Mary from the time of her Immaculate Conception preceded the coming of the Savior, the rising of the 'Sun of Justice' in the history of the human race. Her presence in the midst of Israel—a presence so discreet as to pass almost unnoticed by the eyes of her contemporaries—shone very clearly before the Eternal One, who had associated this hidden 'daughter of Sion' (cf. Zeph 3:14; Zeph 2:10) with the plan of salvation embracing the whole history of humanity." The Holy Father's reflection on Mary *Stella Matutina* is primarily concerned with Christ's first Advent and its 2,000th year commemoration at the dawn of the third millennium. However, one notices that the Pope also makes reference to "the whole history of humanity," and therefore, without explicating it as such, he considers Mary the shining star who will prepare us to welcome Christ at His Second Coming.

309. The title given to this poem by Newman is "The Pillar of Cloud," repr. in John Henry Newman, *Prayers, Verses, and Devotions* (San Francisco: Ignatius Press, 1989), 572.

310. Cf. Boyce, *Mary in the Writings of JHN*, 149, note 1: "The *analogia fidei*, the analogy or rule of faith, is one of the methods used by theologians to determine whether a doctrine is truly part of divine revelation. It means that the

doctrine in question fits harmoniously and is seen to be consistent with other known truths of Revelation."

311. Convenience is to be understood as "appropriateness" or "fittingness." Newman's use of the argument of convenience is related to his appropriation of the philosophical notion of antecedent probabilities. Cf. Dom. Franciscus M. William, "Doctrina Mariana Cardinal Newman et Motus Œcumenicus," *De Mariologia et Œcumenismo* (Rome: Pontificia Academia Mariana Internationalis, 1962), 258–264. Cf. also Lino Callegari, *Newman: La Fede e le Sue Ragioni* (Milan: Edizioni Paoline, 2001), 68–89.

312. Boyce extrapolates on the terminology: "Another theological method of argumentation, from which divine revelation is investigated and new intuitions are judged, is the so-called argument from 'convenience', viz. Its suitableness or fitness. It is used above all in the judging the truth of propositions that contain the mystery of the divine life which go far beyond all human comprehension, or for truths that are but very implicitly revealed in sacred Scripture. A very obvious example of its use is in the demonstration of the doctrine of our Lady's bodily Assumption into heaven. It is easy for the eye of faith to see how *fitting* this truth is. Naturally, such theological argumentation needs in a particular manner and in all cases the final authoritative acceptance and approval of the Church" (*Mary in the Writings of JHN*, 150, note 2).

313. Cf. Lk 24:25f.

314. Following the tradition of the time, Newman accepts the Pauline authorship of the Letter to the Hebrews.

315. DMC, 360.

316. Cf. Boyce, *Mary in the Writings of JHN*, 318, note 1. "With the phrase 'a family of doctrines which are intimately (connected) united together,' Newman refers to the interdependence of revealed supernatural truths in the corpus of divine revelation. By comparing one revealed mystery with another one, it is possible to get a deeper understanding of them. This method of investigating and obtaining a more penetrating knowledge of revealed mysteries (technically called the 'analogy of faith'): 'the connection of mysteries themselves with each other' was officially stated by the First Vatican Council in its Dogmatic Constitution *Dei Filius* (cf. Denzinger-Schönmetzer, 3016)." See also LD, 19:361–370. Second Letter to Arthur Osborne Alleyne. Letter dated 15–17 June 1860.

317. Cf. Rom 12: 6.

318. DMC, 360f.

319. See Pope John Paul II, *Mary, Mother of God*, 194–95. The Holy Father writes: "Present at Calvary on Good Friday (cf. Jn 19:25) and in the upper room on Pentecost (cf. Acts 1:14), the Blessed Virgin too was probably a privileged witness of Christ's resurrection, completing in this way her participation in all the essential moments of the Paschal Mystery. Welcoming the risen Jesus, Mary is also a sign and an anticipation of humanity, which hopes to achieve its fulfillment through the resurrection of the dead. In the Easter season, the Christian community addresses the Mother of the Lord and invites her to rejoice: *Regina cæli, lætare, alleluia! 'Queen of heaven, rejoice, alleluia!'* Thus it recalls Mary's joy at Jesus' resurrection, prolonging in time the 'rejoice' that the angel

addressed to her at the annunciation, so that she might become a cause of 'great joy' for all people."

320. DMC, 361.

321. Ibid.

322. DMC, 362. Cf. GS 22, CCC 561. See Pope John Paul II, apostolic exhortation *Catechesi Tradendæ*, 9.

323. DMC, 362. The liturgical reference, of which both the Anglican and Catholic Newman is quite fond, is to the *Te Deum*. This hymn is sung at the conclusion of the Office of Readings on Sundays and other solemnities. It is also customary to sing the *Te Deum* at the conclusion of an episcopal ordination/consecration before the newly ordained bishop takes his place at the bishop's chair (*cathedra*). In Rome there is a tradition, revived by Pope John Paul II, of singing the *Te Deum* in order to mark the beginning of a new calendar year by asking God's blessing upon the year's endeavors. On January 1st, according to the liturgical calendar, the Church celebrates one of Our Lady's most ancient feasts, namely, the Solemnity of the Mother of God. The New Year's singing of the *Te Deum* is customarily held at the Jesuit Church of the *Gesù*, where the great counter-reformer and founder of the Society of Jesus, St. Ignatius of Loyola, is buried.

324. Pope John Paul II, *Mary, Mother of God*, 152–154. On page 154, we read in summary fashion: "The importance of the virgin Mother's task remained; from his infancy to adulthood, she helped her Son Jesus to grow 'in wisdom and in stature, and in favor with God and man' (Lk 2:52) and to prepare for His mission."

325. DMC, 362.

326. DMC, 362f. In the discourse, Newman does not give the exact reference himself but presumes, as he does throughout much of his writing, a familiarity with certain Scripture texts on the part of his audience and so omits citations of the passages even when quoting directly from them.

327. DMC, 363.

328. See the article "Adorare," by Bernard Gilliéron, in *Lessico dei Termini Biblici* (Torino: Elle Di Ci Editrice, 1992), 15f.

329. DMC, 363f.

330. Xavier Léon-Dufour, S.J., *Dictionary of Biblical Theology*, 370.

331. DMC, 364.

332. One possible translation of Eadmer's famous saying is: "He could plainly do it, and He willed it; if therefore He willed it, He did it."

333. Eadmer of Canterbury, *Tractatus de Conceptione Beatæ Virginis Mariæ*, 12 (PL 159:305).

334. Rev 12:1–8.

335. Gen 3:20.

336. Of the nine traditional choirs of Angels, Newman here mentions the ranks of Angels and Seraphim.

337. DMC, 364.

338. MD, 66f; Cf. also MD, 20–22. The great medieval poet Dante Alighieri lauds the Blessed Virgin Mary by alluding to the title *Rosa Mystica* in Canto XXIII, verses 88–90, of *Il Paradiso* in his *La Divina Commedia*:

Il nome del bel fior ch'io sempre invoco
e mane e sera, tutto mi ristrinse
l'animo ad avvisar lo maggior foco.
—(Milan: Edizioni San Paolo, 1987), 350.

339. Rev 21:11–18.

340. MD, 15f.

341. MD, 16. The biblical citation is Ps 45:10.

342. DMC, 364.

343. The Latin Vulgate, upon which Newman would have relied in his writings, translates the Hebrew expression *Sabaoth* as *Exercituum*. The text as given here is based on the Church's use of the Latin Vulgate in the *Sanctus* of the Mass.

344. DMC, 367. The pericopes to which Newman is referring in this text are: Num 22:22–40; 2 Cor 3:17; 1 Jn 4:16.

345. DMC, 365; Mt 7:22f.

346. DMC, 366; Gen 5:22; Heb 11:5.

347. DMC, 366; Heb 11:7.

348. DMC, 366; Num 12:3.

349. DMC, 366; 1 Sam 2:18.

350 DMC, 366; Acts 13:22.

351. DMC, 365; Num 22:28–20, 24:1–9; 2 Pet 2:16.

352. DMC, 365; Jn 18:14.

353. Cf. DMC, 368: "If one drop of corruption makes the purest water worthless, as the slightest savour of bitterness spoils the most delicate viands, how can it be that the word of truth and holiness can proceed profitably from impure lips and an earthly heart? No; as is the tree, so is the fruit; 'beware of the false prophets,' says Our Lord; and He then adds, 'from their fruits ye shall know them. Do men gather grapes of thorns, or figs of thistles?' Is it not so, my brethren? Which of you would not go to ask counsel of another, however learned, however gifted, however aged, if you thought him unholy? Nay, though you feel and are sure, as far as absolution goes, that a bad priest could give it as a holy priest, yet for advice, for comfort, for instruction, you would not go to one whom you did not respect. 'Out of the abundance of the heart, the mouth speaketh;' 'a good man out of the good treasure of his heart bringeth forth good, and an evil man out of the evil treasure bringeth forth evil.'"

354. DMC, 368f.

355. Giacomo Cardinal Biffi reflects on the relationship between Mary and the Divine "Sofia" or Wisdom as this has been reflected on by the Church in her reading of the Sapiential Literature of the Sacred Scriptures. He writes: "Noi abbiamo chiarito che la divina Sofia, nella sua significazione prima e originaria, è il disegno del Padre, eletto e destinato all'attuazione tra gli infiniti possibili, come esiste da sempre nel segreto di Dio. Ma non abbiamo avuto difficoltà— allorché la nostra attenzione è passata dal mondo della realtà effettuale—ad affermare che la contemplazione della divina Sofia è al tempo stesso contemplazione di Cristo, perché di fatto il progetto del Padre si è esaurientemente inverato in lui, dal momento che Egli è lo stesso 'mistero nascosto dei secoli' ora reso conoscibile ai credenti attraverso la sua realtà adorabile di Uomo-Dio (cfr.

Col 1:26). Con la stessa logica non esitiamo adesso a vedere in Maria non solo 'la Sede della Sapienza,' come la denomina la preghiera cristiana, ma la Sapienza stessa che si è perfettamente manifestata nella creatura più adeguatamente esemplata su Cristo. Si tratta sempre di analogie successive, ma sono analogie ben fondate. La Sofia—che è, tra le idee divine, quella determinata e scelta dalla volontà divina di salvezza—si realizza con pienezza inarrivabile in Cristo, nel quale 'abita corporalmente tutta la pienezza della divinità' (cfr. Col 2:9). Ma avanza con progressiva attuazione anche nell'universo creato, ricapitolato in Cristo (cfr. Ef 1:10), dove incontra per prima—nell'ordine delle perfezioni— proprio Maria di Nazaret. In lei la Divinità ha preso dimora con una intensità eccezzionale e unica, in virtù di una unione ipostatica (come avviene nel suo Figlio) ma in virtù della sua divina maternità": *Canto Nuziale* (Milan: Jaca Book, 2000), 87.

356. DMC, 369; Sir 24:18.

357. DMC, 369; Sir 24:15.

358. DMC, 369.

359. MD, 33.

360. MD, 34.

361. Friedel writes: "Newman supposes in her an immense knowledge proportional to her sanctity, which had to be inconceivably great." He explains that Newman's understanding of Mary's wisdom is primarily Christologically focused, as the title "Seat of Wisdom" itself suggests. Indeed, she is the creature who is closest to the Source of all wisdom. Newman understands Mary's wisdom according to the same traditional theological terminology of the beatific vision—infused knowledge and acquired knowledge. Although Newman does not speculate as to whether or not Mary enjoyed the beatific vision during her earthly sojourn, he does speculate that Mary received infused knowledge from the very first moment of her conception in the fullness of grace. Nevertheless, as a human creature she had to acquire knowledge through her life's experience, most especially through the practice of the virtues in union with her Son Who, according to His human nature, we are told by the Evangelist Luke, "advanced [in] wisdom, age and favor before God and man" (Lk 2: 40, 52). Interestingly enough, in the immediately preceding verse 52, the Evangelist tells us that Mary contemplated in her heart the meaning on two different occasions (2:19, 51). See also Boyce, *Mary*, 36: "When Rector of the Catholic University in Dublin, he chose *Sedes Sapientiæ* as its title and patroness."

362. MD, 35.

363. DMC, 369.

364. Cf. Gen 18:1–15.

365. DMC, 369.

366. Judith 8:1–8. Cf. Michael O'Carroll, C.S.Sp., "Vow of Virginity, Mary's," *Theotokos: A Theological Encyclopedia of the Blessed Virgin Mary* (Collegeville, Minn.: Liturgical Press, 1982), 363f.

367. Cf. 1 Sam 1:24–28; 2:18–19.

368. 2 Sam 12:24.

369. Lk 1:41.

370. DMC, 370.

371. Beverly Gaventa, *Mary: Glimpses of the Mother of Jesus* (Columbia, S.C.: University of South Carolina Press, 1995), 110. Cf. Luigi Gambero, *Mary and the Fathers of the Church* (San Francisco: Ignatius Press, 1999), 33–42. Gambero comments about the New Testament Apocrypha: "Some of these writings come from the earliest Christian times. They cannot be considered a witness to the official teaching of the Church, but they can at least serve to give a certain idea of the religious interests and Marian piety of their time and of the questions that the faithful asked about the Lord's Mother. These writings note her mysterious presence and important role in the divine work of salvation, which is perpetuated in the time of the Church" (33) As concerns the second century A.D. *Protoevangelium of James*, which is attributed to St. James the Less, and which was most likely written by a non-Jew or by a Jew living in the Diaspora, Father Gambero offers us this fine apraissal. He writes: "In order to understand and evaluate such a 'storybook' text as the *Protoevangelium of James*, it is necessary to keep in mind that its principal objective is to demonstrate the virginal conception of Jesus and Mary's virginity before and during Jesus' birth. It is in this perspective that certain curious facts introduced into the account have to be understood. The bitter water test confirms Mary's virginity before giving birth. The absence of labor pains and the sometimes crudely realistic examinations carried out by the midwife and a woman named Salome, who was then punished for her unbelief, confirm Mary's virginity in the act of giving birth. At the same time, the realism with which the Lord's birth is described leads one to think that the apocryphal gospel means to oppose the error of gnostic Docetism, which considered Christ's body to be a mere appearance or phantasm" (40)

372. DMC, 370.

373. Ibid.

374. Ibid.

375. DMC, 371.

376. Newman's critique of Hume's approach to the interpretation of biblical miracles is mentioned in Chapter Two of this work. One should recall, for example the dubut in Newman's time of Charles Darwin's *On the Origin of Species*, and the post-Enlightenment empiricism and the skepticism oftentimes ensuing from it, especially concerning the content of Divine Revelation and Divine Providence.

377. DMC, 371.

378. Cf. Jacob of Sarug (d. 521), *Discourse on the Burial of the Holy Mother of God*, 87–99, in C. Vona, *Lateranum* 19 (1953), 188; St. Modestus of Jerusalem (d. 634), *Enc. in dormitationem Deiparae semperque Virginis Mariæ*, nos. 7 and 14 (PG 86:3293, 3311); St. John Damascene (d. 704), *Panegyric on the Dormition of the Mother of God*, no. 10 (SC 80:107); Severus of Antioch, *Antijulianistica* (Beirut, 1931), 194f.; St. Germanus I of Contantinople (d. 730), Hom. 1 *in Dormitationem* (PG 98:347), Hom. 3 *in Dormitationem* (PG 98:360); St. John Damascene, *Hom.* 2 (PG 96:741).

379. DMC, 372.

380. DS, 3903: "Quapropter . . . ad Omnipotentis Dei gloriam qui peculiarem benevolentiam suum Mariæ Virgini dilargitus est, ad sui Filii honorem, immortalis sæculorum Regis ac peccati mortisque victoris, ad eiusdem agustæ

Matris augendum gloriam et ad totius Ecclesiæ gaudium exsultationemque, auctoritate Domini nostri Iesu Christi, Beatorum Apostolorum Petri et Pauli ac nostra pronuntiamus, declarmus et definimus divinitus revelatum dogma esse: Immaculatam Deiparam semper Virginem Mariam, expleto terrestris vitæ cursu, fuisse corpore et anima ad cælestem gloriam assumptam" (Pope Pius XII, *"Munificentissimus Deus,"* 1 November 1950). Cf. also LG 59 and CCC 966.

381. See the article "Assunta," in NDM, 163–185; also, Antonio Maria Calero, *La Vergine Maria nel Mistero di Cristo e della Chiesa: Saggio di Mariologia* (Turin: Elle Di Ci, 1995), 225–280; Michael O'Carroll, "Assumption," 55–61.

382. Cf. *Munificentissimus Deus*: AAS 42 (1950), 757, 768.

383. SN, 104.

384. SN, 105.

385. SN, 5.

386. SN, 105.

387. Cf. MD, 48f. Michael J. Miller writes: "Mary is the Queen of Martyrs, but no company of martyrs ever restored the divine life to a child of Adam. Mary offered her Son to His Eternal Father during that bloody Sacrifice on Calvary, but it was (pre-eminently) in the way that lay people offer the Eucharist to God the Father when they reverently attend Mass" ("Mediatrix, Si! Coredemptrix, No!," *Homiletic and Pastoral Review*, February 2001, 28).

388. DMC, 372f.

389. See "Apocrifi," by Elio Peretto, in NDM, 106–125. Also, Stefano De Fiores, *Corso di Teologia Sistematica: Maria Madre di Gesù* (Bologna: Edizioni Dehoniane Bologna, 1992), 110–112.

390. Cf. Mt 5:14–16. See also Jn 1:4–8; 3:1–21; 5:35–36; 6:10–15; 8:12; 9:5; 9:34–41; 12:35–36, 44–46; 13:27–30; 18:2–3, 15–18, 25–27; 20:1; 21:3–4, 15–19.

391. DMC, 373.

392. Cf. DMC, 373. Here, Newman uses a clever literary device, since it can refer either to the fact that Mary was no longer to be found because she was assumed into heaven or simply to the fact that she had died and in this sense was no longer seen on earth.

393. DMC, 373.

394. Cf. CCC 627. The Resurrection of Jesus on the third day served as proof of His veracity since it was believed that bodily corruption revealed itself starting with the fourth day after death.

395. Here, Newman does not allude to the apocryphal tradition that St. Thomas arrived at the tomb of Our Lady before the other apostles, to highlight Thomas' renewed faith in the bodily Resurrection, and intended as a contrasting parallel to his conspicuous absence in the Upper Room on Easter night when Our Lord appeared to the apostles there, according to Jn 20:19–29. Cf. M. von Esbroeck, "Apocryphes Géorgiens de la Dormition," *Analecta Bollandiana* 91 (1973), 55–75; and his "L'Assomption de la Vierge dans un Transitus Pseudo-Basilien," AB 92 (1974), 125–163.

396. DMC, 373.

397. DMC, 374.

398. Ibid. Fortunately, Newman admits of the possibility that the details of the various traditions are historically questionable at best, while clearly

affirming the Church's teaching on the bodily Assumption. Unfortunately, however, Newman seems to have embraced the Apocryphal accounts concerning Mary in such a way that they are presented in the sermon as accepted traditions without, however, pointing out the serious theological problems that these accounts create. However, Newman gives no indication in this sermon that he was even aware of these difficulties, since he claims that, on the whole, they do not impinge on a person's piety. Nonetheless, this study would be remiss not to recall the Gnostic underpinnings of several of the apocryphal accounts (e.g., *Transitus Mariæ*) concerning Mary's earthly passing/death/judgment/assumption, of which Newman was seemingly unaware. Cf., for example, "Apocrifi" in NDM, 120–122.

399. DMC, 374.

400. Lk 1:29.

401. Lk 2:7.

402. Lk 2:19, 51.

403. Lk 2:35.

404. Jn 19:25–27.

405. Lk 1:34. Han Urs von Balthasar, like Newman, envisions Mary's *fiat* at the Annunciation as encompassing each and every aspect of her cooperation in the economy of salvation, not simply expressive of her having personally entered into the mysteries of her Son's redemptive activity but also pointing to the ideal of the Church's own participation in their saving effects. Balthasar writes: "The Marian *fiat*, in its truly *unlimited* availability, is, by grace, the bridal womb, *matrix* and *mater*, through which the Son of God becomes Man, and thus it is by this *fiat* that He also forms the truly universal Church. By the power of the boundless, triune God, this *fiat* that opens up the boundaries of earthly time 'in advance' (in 'anticipatory redemption' in the case of the 'Immaculate Conception') so that what is earthly and temporal—whether Mary, her Son or the Church—should not place any fundamental obstacle to God's indwelling but should be *infiniti capax*. What is basic to the infinite elasticity of the Marian Yes is that it again and again stretches beyond understanding and must consent to what is not within the domain of the humanly possible, foreseeable, bearable or fitting. It must embrace virginal conception by an already married woman, her 'not understanding' the reply of her twelve-year-old, to her being painfully rebuffed by her Son and finally her being abandoned at the foot of the Cross and committed to 'another Son,' John. . . . These events repeatedly challenge her understanding and demand an endlessly growing readiness (without any resistance). In all this, Mary shows herself to be 'truly blessed'" because she has believed (Lk 1:45; 11:28, cf. Jn 20:29), and thus she becomes the 'seat of wisdom.' This is the mold in which the Church is formed. It is to this end that Mary's availability is formed and to this Son is channeled through the disciple to whom Jesus entrusted her as Mother (Jn 19:26–27). From the beginning the Marian principle is thus the exact opposite of any 'partial identification' where discipleship depends on the measure of one's personal comprehension or 'responsible evaluation.' But it is equally the opposite of the passive indifference of a mere instrument that can be manipulated at will. In fact, Mary keeps alert to find at any moment the correct response to a new demand (Lk 1:29, 34; 2:19,

51). At Cana she shows a sensitive solicitude for the poor. Her suggestion, 'Do whatever He tells you'(Jn 2:5), reveals once more her *fiat*, her detachment, in the midst of this care. It is not simply a matter of 'submission to the will of God,' ... rather it is the will to retreat into the background and make possible the encounter between human need and divine grace.... The Marian *fiat*, unequalled in its perfection, is the all-inclusive, protective and directive form of all ecclesial life" (*The Office of Peter*, 206–208, passim).

406. DMC, 374f.

407. Boyce has this to say about the nature of the exhortation: "Newman ends with a paragraph of lyrical beauty and intense devotion" (*Mary in the Writings of JHN*, 165, note 14).

408. The rose of Sharon is described as a kind of crocus, said to grow like a "lily among brambles" (cf. Canticle of Canticles 2:1–2) . Thus, the rose of Sharon becomes a symbol of Mary's virginal purity (sinlessness), despite the fact that she is born into a world of sin. Eadmer of Canterbury, writing in the eleventh century, compares Our Lady's conception in the midst of a sinful world to a chestnut that is able to come out of its thorny shell without being harmed. (Cf. "Immacolata," by Stefano De Fiores, NDM, 685.)

409. Heb 12:4.

410. DMC, 375f.

411. This sermon is entitled by Newman "The Theory of Developments in Religious Doctrine."

412. As a justification for any repetition of texts in this treatment of Newman's sermon, it should be borne in mind that such texts were discussed in the first chapter where the focus was not so much on Newman's use of Scripture as on the theological implications of the analogy which he develops between a theologian's work and that of a non-theologian who, without any formal background, nevertheless contemplates the divine mysteries and enters into the depth of their meaning. Thus, for Newman, Mary is paradigmatic of the *sensus fidei* that should characterize both theologians and non-theologians with respect to the development of particular doctrines and of that sacred reverence which the whole of God's Word demands.

413. Brit, "Newman's Use of Sacred Scripture," 26.

414. OUS, 312.

415. OUS, 312f.

416. *Obædire* (*ob-audire*), "to listen attentively." Mary perfected the art of listening and, therefore, is the creature who perfectly obeying God's Word, Will and Law, most fully cooperated in the economy of salvation. Mary, being a good Jew, would have prayed the *Shema, Israel* ("Hear, O Israel") every day. The Apocryphal Gospels and *Transitus* refer to Mary as praying night and day in the Temple even as a young child. Newman alludes to this apocryphal belief in his *Sermon Notes*: "At length she is taken to the Temple, and there she lives ten years—what a blessed change!—in the presence of her God. But even then, though she looks at the priests as ministers, yet, alas, how she is able to bear the world, even in its best shape!" Although according to Jewish Law women could not be scribes, the Virgin is often depicted as reading the Sacred Scriptures in her home. Newman writes: "Let us suppose her passing out of her first infancy.

She is taught external things. She is taught to read. She learns Scripture." Artists throughout the ages have depicted Mary as reading/studying the Scriptures at the moment of the Annunciation and some have depicted Mary as receiving the Holy Spirit in the form of a dove or a ray of light which enters into her ear, to allow the Word to take flesh according to her consent given to the Angel's message. Thus, Mary had to have the most finely tuned of the spiritual senses so that her listening to the Word of God would result in her free, loving obedience to that Word.

417. Cf. Alonso Luis Schökel, *Il Dinamismo della Tradizione* (Brescia: Paideia, 1970), 216: "La costituzione [*Dei Verbum*] allude a Maria, come tipo di questa tradizione della Chiesa (cfr. Lc 2,19.51). Maria partecipa alla realizzazione del mistero della salvezza ed era testimone immediato e privilegiato dei fatti: non contenta della prima intelligenza, ripensava gli avvenimenti e li meditava dentro di se, aumentando in tal modo la sua intelligenza del mistero, fino alla consummazione escatologica della sua assunzione che la incorpora definitivamente alla piena glorificazione del Figlio."

418. Cf. De Fiores. *Corso di Teologia Sistematica: Maria Madre di Gesù*, 110–112: "Maria, la donna che 'assunta al dialogo con Dio, da il suo consenso attivo e responsabile' (*Marialis Cultus*, 37), diviene immagine viva e prototipa del ruolo umano nella storia della salvezza. Ella mostra l'antropologia teologica che scaturisce da tutta la Bibbia: l'uomo sotto l'impulso della chiamata e della grazia di Dio, risponde liberamente con l'obbedienza della fede. Alla 'luce' del *fiat* di Maria appare la struttura fondamentale dell'antica alleanza. Essa non è solo parola pronunciata da Dio, ma anche risposta dell'uomo, in quanto 'ogni azione o parola di Dio mira a suscitare una reazione dell'uomo.' In altri termini, la storia della salvezza è un 'avvenimento dialogico' in cui la risposta umana 'fa parte del nucleo centrale della teologia.'"

419. Serra, *Maria di Nazaret: Una Fede in Cammino* (Milan: Edizioni Paoline, 1993), 33. Thus, the Reverend Aristide Serra states: "Quella di Israele è una memoria totalizzante perché niente deve tralasciare di tutto ciò che il Signore ha fatto per lui."

420. Serra, *Maria di Nazaret*, 34f. Thus Fr. Serra explains: "Per la Bibbia 'ricordare' equivale ad 'attualizare' il passato nel presente."

421. Serra, *Maria di Nazaret*, 34f.: "E anche il ricordo di Maria è dinamico. Ella, infatti, non solo conserva nel cuore tutti gli eventi che riguardano il Figlio, ma al tempo stesso il pone a confronto, li '*symballousa*.' Il verbo *symballo*, usato qui dall'evangelista, vuol dire mettere insieme diversi elementi o aspetti di una situazione alquanto enigmatica, in vista appunto di interpretarla, di darne la retta spiegazione, insomma di farne esegesi. Ecco allora il momento dinamico e attivo della fede di Maria. Davanti al suo squardo si dispiega tutta la vicenda del Figlio, dalla concezione verginale fino alla Risurrezione. Ella niente lascia cadere di tanto memoriale: tutto conserva. Al tempo stesso, Maria è in grado di rimettere ogni tessera al suo posto, per individuare l'armonia complessiva di tutto il mosaico. Lei attinge questo risultato ermeneutico simbolizzando, ossia confrontando eventi e parole di Gesù con le rispettive prefigurazioni dell'Antico Testamento (come ben documenta il *Magnificat*), e poi situa in rapporto dialettico i vari segmenti dell'itinerario di Gesù: dalla sua discesa nel grembo

materno come Verbo divino Incarnato, fino al ritorno nel grembo del Padre. Dalla Risurrezione, infatti, emanava la luce piena sulla persona e sull'opera di Cristo Salvatore. Dalla sommità del mistero pasquale, la Vergine poteva contemplare la coerenza sottesa al disegno dell'intera storia salvifica. Per così dire, ella fu la prima esegeta di Cristo, suo Figlio." Once again, the words of Serra are helpful: "La sua meditazione (di Maria) si concentra su tutta la storia del Figlio, che va dal grembo materno fino all'altro grembo, cioè alla tomba dalla quale Cristo rinasce con la risurrezione dai morti. Così la Madre ripeteva l'iternario sapienziale che già aveva caratterizzato la fisionomia spirituale di Israele."

422. Serra, *Maria di Nazaret*, 34: "La fortuna di Lc 2, 19.51b è stata immensa nella vita della Chiesa. Quando la comunità cristiana di ogni tempo ripensa all'insegnamento di Cristo, suo Signore, leva lo squardo a Maria come a propria immagine conduttrice. Un decennio avanti l'apertura dei lavori conciliari, padre Henri de Lubac (poi cardinale) avveva asserito nella sua celebre opera *Meditations on the Church*, pubblicata in francese nel 1952: 'Quando (Maria) "Madre muta del Verbo silente," *Verbi silentis muta mater*, aderiva senza comprenderli ai misteri del Dio fatto uomo, osservando tutte queste cose, conservandole e meditandole nel suo cuore, essa prefigura quel lungo lavorio di memoria e di intensa ruminazione che costituisce l'anima della tradizione della Chiesa."

423. Lk 2:19:51.

424. Lk 2:17f.—"And when they saw it, they made known the saying which had been told them concerning this child; and all who heard it wondered at what the shepherds told them."

425. Lk 2:19—"But Mary kept all these things, pondering them in her heart."

426. Lk 2:20—"And the shepherds returned, glorifying and praising God for all they had heard and seen, as it had been told them."

427. Lk 2:51.

428. OUS, 313; cf. Jn 2:5.

429. NDM, 280f.

430. OUS, 313f.

431. St. Augustine remarks in his *Sermo 291*: "She sought the manner; she did not doubt God's omnipotence." See also: Pope John Paul II, *Mary, Mother of God*, 108–111.

432. In this regard, Newman places himself in that long line of Catholic thinkers who would express it thus: *Credo ut intellegam, intellego ut credam* (a popular patristic aphorism often attributed to St. Augustine or St. Anselm); *Fides quærens intellectum* (St. Anselm); *Les raisons du cœur* (Blaise Pascal).

433. MD, 33–35.

434. MD, 34.

435. Ibid.

436. MD, 33.

437. MD, 34.

438. Newman does not use the theological term in this instance. It is used here only analogously, to render more clearly the paths along which Newman treads in his theological speculation in this meditation.

439. MD, 34.

440. Diff II, 69.

441. Cf. for example, Diff II, 57: "If there is an Apostle on whom, *à priori*, our eyes would be fixed, as likely to teach us about the Blessed Virgin, it is St. John, to whom she was committed by Our Lord on the Cross;—with whom, as tradition goes, she lived at Ephesus till she was taken away. This anticipation is confirmed *à posteriori*; for, as I have said above, one of the earliest and fullest of our informants concerning her dignity, as being the second Eve, is Irenæus, who came to Lyons from Asia Minor, and had been taught by the immediate disciples of St. John." One notices that Newman's argumentation flows from his understanding of the completeness of Divine Revelation, from his acceptance of Apostolic Tradition and authority, as well as from his keen understanding of the development of doctrine. For Newman, Marian doctrine and devotion, it can be said, always fall within the parameters of the *œconomia salutis*, never outside it, and likewise, never outside its relationship to the Church and her teaching office. The Catechism teaches that the Marian dimension precedes the Petrine dimension in terms of her cooperation in the economy of salvation. However, this does not mean that Mary's office, is, in any way, equated to that of Peter (cf. CCC 773). Cf. also von Balthasar, *The Office of Peter*, 204–206.

442. The final and much-debated decision of the Council Fathers to treat of Mary within the Dogmatic Constitution on the Church and not in a separate document, as well as the title chosen for Chapter VIII of *Lumen Gentium*, makes this abundantly clear. Cf. G. Philips, *La Chiesa e Il suo Mistero* (Milan: Jaca Books, 1969).

443. Cf. *Insegnamenti di Giovanni Paolo II*, vol. 10.1 (Rome: Libreria Editrice Vaticana, 1987), 7.

CHAPTER THREE

1. Cf. J. Chapman, "Newman and the Fathers," *Blackfriars* 14 (1993), 578–590; E. Hammerschmidt, "John Henry Newmans Patristichen Studien," *Internationale Kirchliche Zeitschrift* 53 (1963), 105–115; F. William, "Kardinal John Henry Newman und die Kirchlichen Lehrtradition," *Orientierung* 22 (1958), 61–66; D. Gorce, *Newman et les Pères* (Bruges: Bayaert, 1947).

2. Jean Guitton, "Newman As a Modern Father of the Church," *Tablet* 218 (1964), 814ff.; Giovanni Velocci, "John Henry Newman, l'Ultimo dei Padri" (OssR, 17 July 1974); W. Strolz, "Newman, Kirchvater der Neuzeit," *Word und Wahrheit* 10 (1955), 396–399.

3. Giovanni Velocci, *Newman: Il Coraggio della Verità* (Vatican City: Libreria del Vaticano, 2000), 160. "La familiarità con quegli antichi maestri si rivela chiaramente nella sua mariologia, tutta impregnata del loro spirito e del loro pensiero."

4. Stanley L. Jaki, *Newman's Challenge* (Grand Rapids, Mich.: Eerdmans, 2000), 295. Cf. Diff I, 259.

5. Cf. Jean Honoré, *The Spiritual Journey of Newman*, trans. Sr. Mary Christopher Ludden, S.C. (New York: Alba House, 1992), 50f.: "At the time of his conversion in 1816, an introductory work on the early Church stimulated his appetite. The book, entitled *The History of the Church* by Milner, was dedicated to Christian antiquity. Milner, an eighteenth-century historian with an Evangelical background, was more anxious to recover an account of the spiritual life

of souls than a summary of doctrines from past patristic history. He reveals to his avid reader some particular images and portraits of the great Fathers, which were always to fascinate the young convert." Cf. also AP, 18, 31.

6. Cf. John Henry Newman, *Anglican Difficulties*, with an introduction and notes by Stanley L. Jaki (Fraser, Mich.: Real-View-Books, n.d.), xxxvi. Jaki writes: "So much of support of the perennial value and sudden timeliness of these Lectures. In their times they could not have sustained an appeal to Catholics as did the *Development*, the *Apologia*, and the *Grammar of Ascent*. These they could take as written above all for them and were found by them invaluable. They could not see so much direct profit in Newman's analysis of the predicament of Anglo-Catholics as set forth in these Lectures. But the Lectures remain an indispensable document to anyone interested in the development of Newman's philosophical and theological thinking. They witness, in gemlike phrases, his thoroughly objectivist epistemology and his insights into the strange dynamics of the human intellect. They contain some of his best pages on what formal faith, submission to apostolic authority, is truly about as distinguished from a merely material faith, or unreflecting acceptance of the creed as a social consensus."

7. Diff I, 370f. Cf. Ap 7. Newman recalls: "I read Joseph Milner's Church History, and was nothing short of enamoured of the long extracts from St. Augustine, St. Ambrose, and the other Fathers which I found there. I read them as being the religion of primitive Christians. . . ."

8. Felicity O'Brien, *Not Peace but a Sword* (England: St. Paul's Publication, 1990), 16.

9. O'Brien offers some biographical insight: "In 1828 Newman was appointed Vicar of St. Mary's University Church, replacing Dr. Hawkins who had become Provost of Oriel College. In the same year, Newman began to read through the Church Fathers in chronological order. This study was to raise considerable alarm in Newman's mind because he could see similarities between the beginnings of Arianism and the growing 'liberal' spirit in the Church of England: the questioning of revealed truths which led into heresy" (*Not Peace but a Sword*, 32).

10. Cf. W. Ward, *Life of John Henry Cardinal Newman*, vol. 1 (London, 1913), 42.

11. Honoré, *The Spiritual Journey of Newman*, 49.

12. "The whole world judges securely." See Appendix I: Glossary of Terms.

13. Michael Ffinch, *Newman towards the Second Spring* (San Francisco: Ignatius Press, 1992), 77.

14. Velocci, *Il Coraggio*, 6. Velocci writes: "Suscitò allora una reazione dei teologi, dei pastori, dei vescovi che lo contrattaccarono, lo contestarono, lo condannarono. Newman ne soffrì moltissimo, ma seguì con coraggio la sua via: *prima di tutto la verità*. Diceva: 'Perisca la Chiesa, sebbene (sia benedetta la promessa) ciò non sia possibile; ma perisca la Chiesa, piuttosto che fallisca la verità.' "

15. Philip Boyce, *Mary: The Virgin Mary in the Life and Writings of John Henry Newman* (Grand Rapids, Mich.: Eerdmans, 2001), 13f.

16. O'Brien, *Not Peace but a Sword*, 30.

17. Boyce, *Mary in the Writings of JHN*, 7.

18. O'Brien spells it out in greater detail: "The theory of the *Via Media* was 'absolutely pulverized' in his view by the thought that 'the deliberate judgment, in which the whole Church at length rests and acquiesces, is an infallible prescription and a final sentence against such portions of it as protest and secede'" (*Not Peace but a Sword*, 45). Cf. AP, 121.

19. Cf. Diff II, 24.

20. *Letters and Diaries*, ed. Stamford and Spark, 99–100.

21. Cf. Boyce, *Mary in the Writings of JHN*, 16f.

22. AP, 4.

23. Diff II, 3.

24. AP, 195.

25. O'Brien, *Not Peace but a Sword*, 33, 4.

26. Cf. O'Brien, *Not Peace but a Sword*, 33, 49, where she demonstrates some historical coincidences regarding Newman's introduction to and study of the works of St. Athanasius of Alexandria. Of course, one cannot fail to mention the importance of Newman's *The Arians of the Fourth Century*.

27. AP, 169f.

28. Boyce, *Mary in the Writings of JHN*, 254, note 1. Cf. also *Contra Paganos* III, 14, 29, 33; *Incarnatio Verbi* 8, 22. These are key texts in which Athanasius refers to the doctrine of the *Theotokos* (*Mater Dei*) in association with the great mystery of the Incarnation. Also, Newman's *Select Treatises of St. Athanasius in Controversy with the Arians*, 2:210–215, 367–369, in which he expounds on the use of the term *Theotokos* in the writings of Athanasius and its history as a theological term. Father Luigi Gambero offers us a synthesis of St. Athanasius' contribution to Mariology: "One of the Fathers who made the greatest contributions to new interest in the person and mission of the Virgin Mary in the plan of salvation was Athanasius, bishop of Alexandria in Egypt. He strongly defended the true Christian doctrine of the divinity of Jesus Christ against Arius and his followers, who denied it. St. Gregory Nazianzen called him 'pillar of the Church'. . . . The bishop of Alexandria became a vigorous defender and assertor of the teaching of revelation on the Mother of the Lord. Against the followers of Arius, he unequivocally holds that Jesus is the Son of God, generated by the Father from eternity, and thus possessing the Father's identical divine nature. On the basis of this premise, he does not hesitate to give the name 'Mother of God' to her who generated Him in His mortal nature. Athanasius uses the term *Theotokos*, which in 431 would be introduced into the official documents of the Council of Ephesus. . . . He is fond of emphasizing the salvific purpose of the Incarnation, which allows him to argue for an (at least) indirect link between Mary's motherhood and human redemption. . . . The salvation of men demanded the destruction of the power of sin, and Jesus took our human flesh from Mary precisely in order to redeem from slavery those who were being held prisoner. . . . Athanasius points out that the virginal birth of the Son of God is an absolutely unique fact. No saint, no prophet, or patriarch of the Old Testament was born virginally. The birth of Jesus is a mystery that goes beyond our power to understand. . . .Athanasius who was a great promoter of the monastic life, insists strongly on Mary's perpetual virgin-

ity, which he presents as a paradigm of the highest holiness to virgins who have consecrated their lives to the Lord": *Mary and the Fathers of the Church: The Blessed Virgin Mary in Patristic Thought* (San Francisco: Ignatius Press, 1999), 99–103, passim.

29. In his *Select Treatises of Saint Athanasius in Controversy with the Arians* (vol. 2), Newman cites the following texts of St. Cyril of Alexandria to show the Father's grasp of the significance of the term *Theotokos* in the controversy with Nestorius and the proceedings of the Council of Ephesus: *Contra Iulianum* 8, 262; *De Recta Fidei*, 49f.; *Letters*, 106f.; *Contra Nestorium* 1:18. St. Cyril of Alexandria was declared a Doctor of the Church by Pope Leo the Great in 1882. Father Gambero highlights some of Cyril's contributions to Mariology: "One can safely state that Cyril of Alexandria inaugurated the much beloved Byzantine homiletic technique in which the preacher would teach Marian truths by means of praises addressed to the Blessed Virgin. . . . The famous homily that he preached during the Council of Ephesus is inspired by these feelings. . . . Cyril's preaching and attitude, redolent withe affection and admiration, greatly contributed to the growth of Marian devotion. In addition, thanks to the intransigence with which he defended the title 'Mother of God', both before and during the Council of Ephesus, Cyril helped awaken an explicit interest in Marian dogma in the Church as well as concern to safeguard a precious tradition of the Alexandria Church, which was already accustomed to invoking Mary under the title *Theotokos*. It appears that this title had been customary in Alexandria for centuries. . . . Cyril considers that it was through the *Theotokos* that God accomplished everything concerning human salvation. His point of departure is the essential relationship between Mary and the Church, which was perfectly known to him; he builds his arguments upon the lapidary statements of the earliest Fathers. In his famous *Homily* 11 . . . he pays tribute to the Virgin, greeting her as the instrument of a long list of God's saving action" (*Mary and the Fathers*, 242–247, passim).

30. F. J. Friedel, *The Mariology of Cardinal Newman* (New York: Benziger Brothers, 1928), 189.

31. PPS, II, 128.

32. Michael J. Schmaus, "Mariology," ed. Karl Rahner, *Encyclopedia of Theology: A Concise Sacramentum Mundi* (New York: Seabury Press, 1975), 896f.

33. Boyce explains: "Scholars discuss and disagree about what Newman really held as an Anglican concerning the doctrine of the Immaculate Conception. Some maintain that until he became a Catholic he did not fully understand or believe this doctrine. Others claim that he did arrive personally at this belief but refrained from saying it explicitly in order not to give offence to his co-religionists" (*Mary in the Writings of JHN*, 23).

34. Boyce, *Mary in the Writings of JHN*, 24.

35. Boyce, *Mary in the Writings of JHN*, 45.

36. Boyce, *Mary in the Writings of JHN*, 45f.

37. Friedel, *The Mariology of Cardinal Newman*, 140.

38. Boyce, *Mary in the Writings of JHN*, 51f.

39. Boyce, *Mary in the Writings of JHN*, 64f.

40. Boyce, *Mary in the Writings of JHN*, 91.

41. Cf. John J. Dillon, "Mary as Second Eve: A Patristic Viewpoint," *Hopes and Visions: Papers of the Ecumenical Society of the Blessed Virgin Mary in the United States of America* (Washington, D.C.: Ecumenical Society of the Blessed Virgin Mary, 1998), 8f.

42. Cf. NDM, 1047: "Ai giudei Giustino prova che Cristo è il compimento dell'AT e delle profezie, le quali nel loro insieme prefigurano e preannunciano tutto il mistero di lui, capo e corpo: prefigurano e preannunciano anche il verginale concepimento."

43. Mario Maritano, "La Vergine Maria negli Scritti di Giustino Martire," *La Mariologia nella Catechesis dei Padri*, ed. Sergio Felici (Rome: Libreria Ateneo Salesiano, 1989), 80.

44. Father Gambero notes: "Justin was probably the first author to use the Eve-Mary parallel. The theological value of this doctrine emerges clearly from its subsequent development in the history of Christian thought" (*Mary and the Fathers*, 46). See also J. N. D. Kelly. *Early Christian Doctrines* (London: Black, 1977), 493: "Justin was the pioneer, although the way he introduced the theme suggests that he was not innovating."

45. Hilda Graef observes: "By the end of the patristic period properly so called the main doctrinal and devotional lines had been traced: the fruitful opposition of Mary to Eve had appeared as early as the first half of the second century and was never lost sight of again": *A History of Doctrine and Devotion* (Westminister, Md.: Christian Classics, 1985), 1:160.

46. NDM, 1047: "Un misterioso legame congiunge la scena dell'annunciazione narrata da Lc 1,26–38 e la scena della seduzione raccontata da Gn 3, 1–20: sono i due momenti generatori della storia, in quanto essa appartiene e all'uomo e a Dio. L'uomo distrugge, Dio riedifica; l'uomo pecca, Dio salva; l'uomo introduce la morte, Dio riporta la vita; ma unico è il binario che guida inversamente il percorso, unico l'antitesi lo strumento: la 'donna-vergine.'"

47. Gambero puts a finer point on this: "Here it is interesting to note how Justin already presents Mary's role in salvation as the consequence of a free and conscious choice in response to the angel's message. However, just as the harmful action of Eve was subordinate to that of Adam, on whom fell the primary responsibility for sin, in the same way the action of Mary, in the order of human salvation, remains absolutely subordinate to the necessary and essential action of Christ, the only Redeemer" (*Mary and the Fathers*, 48). Cf. also NDM, 1047–48.

48. Newman's translation at Diff II, 33. The Greek text of St. Justin Martyr's *Dialogue with Trypho the Jew* (chapter 100) is given by Newman in Diff II, 118 (PG 6:709).

49. Cf. PG 6:673.

50. The Reverend Francesco Spedalieri, S.J. explains the central place that Mary holds in the *œconomia salutis* according to the theology of St. Justin Martyr by means of a critical textual analysis of the *Dialogue with Trypho* (nos. 120, 127): "Oggetto di predestinazione, Maria occupa un posto speciale nei disegni divini: ' . . . ὃν καὶ ἄνθρωπον διά γεγνηθῆναι διά τῆς παρθένου βεβούλεται—[il Padre] volle ch'egli [Cristo] come uomo nascesse dalla Vergine. . . . In Maria dunque, prendono consistenza le promesse fatte ad Abramo e ripetute ai suoi discendenti; anzi Giustino proprio da lei denomina l'economia, i disegni cioè di

Dio nel Vecchio Testamento—κατὰ τὴν οἰκονομίαν τῆς παρθένου Μαρίας":
Maria nella Scrittura e nella Tradizione della Chiesa Primitiva, vol. 1, Studio
diretto sulle fonti (Rome: Herder Editrice e Libreria, 1968), 138f.

51. Cf. PG 6:710–711: ἀπλλαγὴν δε τοῦ θανάου τοῖ   ς μετα γινώσκουσιν
ἀπὸ τῶν φαύλων καὶ πιστευσιν εἰς αὐτὸ νεάζεται. Cf. also Heb 10:5–7, citing
Ps 40:6–8 (7–9 of LXX) quoted in CCC 462 concerning the *fiat* of Christ.

52. Cf. Mt 11:27; 16:15–18, 21; Mk 8:31–39; Lk 9:22–27.

53. Cf. PG 6:709–710. *Dialogus cum Trypho* 100: Οὐδεὶς γινωσκει τὸν
πατέρα εἰ μὴ ὁ Υἱὸς· οὐδὲ τὸν Υἱὸν εἰ μὴ ὁ Πατὴρ καὶ οἷς ἂν ὁ Υἱὸς
ἀποκαλύψη· Ἀπεκάλυψεν οὖν ἡμῖν πάντα ὅσα καὶ ἀπὸ τῶν Γραφῶν διὰ τῆς
αὐτοῦ νενοήκαμεν, γνόντες αὐτὸν πρωτότκον μὲν, τοῦ Θεοῦ, καὶ πρὸ πάντων
τῶν κτισμάτων· καὶ τῶν πατριαρχῶν υἱόν, ἐπει δὴ διὰ τῆσ ἀπὸ γένους αὐτὸν
Παρθενου σαρκοποιηθείς. . . .

54. Spedalieri comments on the *Dialogue with Trypho* (100), highlighting the
antithetical parallelism of Eve and Mary and its consequence for the economy of
salvation: "Essa perciò, eccelle sui patriarchi, e fu prescelta ad essere la Madre
del Salvatore, affinché la via seguita da Dio nell'opera di restaurazione fosse
parallela a quella onde ebbe origine la colpa: 'Ut qua via initium orta a serpente
inobedientia accepit, eadem et dissolutionem acciperet'": *Maria nella Scrittura*,
139.

55. Cf. Kelly, *Early Christian Doctrines*, 493f.

56. Cf. NDM, 1048: "Eva responsabile della morte, Maria della vita, ma
attraverso una sola strada: la verginal ubbidienza. . . . Maria è la madre vera, la
madre-vergine—per risposta di fede e di ubbedienza—della Parola di Dio, che
in lei si incarna per darci la vita."

57. Laurentin comments thus on Justin's use of the parallel Mary–Eve in the
Dialogue with Trypho: "Vi è un parallelismo fra Eva e Maria solo in quanto esse
sono vergini non deflorate, che accolgono una parola, ma il resto è opposizione.
Da un lato Eva crea disobbedienza e morte; dall'altro Maria concepisce fede e
gioia: il Cristo fatto uomo per mezzo dello Spirito Santo. Questa prima esplicitazione, dunque, si fa partendo dall'annunciazione. Più che le analogie e i con-
trasti, i cui ritagli costituiscono l'interesse del tema, è importante il *disegno*
nascosto di Dio, che fa passare la 'soluzione' attraverso la stessa via laddove 'la
disobbedienza' aveva 'avuto la sua origine'; poiché l'opposizione Eva-Maria è
completata da quella del serpente e dell'angelo Gabriele, tutt'e due esplicitamente menzionati" (cf. the article "Nuova Eva," in NDM, 1019). "Il disegno
nascosto di Dio" refers to the *œconomia* or *mysterium salutis*. Cf. Eph 1:1–14; Col
1:26–27; Rom 16:25. CCC 492 cites Eph 1:3–4 in reference to the doctrine of
the Immaculate Conception. Mary has a predestined role in the economy of
salvation. CCC 410–412 is appropriately introduced by a presentation of Mary
the New Eve who, together with Christ the Second Adam, inaugurates the
fullness of time and the Redemption foreshadowed in the prophecy of Gen 3:15.
Thus, the economy of salvation reaches its zenith in the event of the Incarnation, whereby the mystery of salvation is made known to the world in the Person
of the God-Man and by means of Mary's cooperation.

58. Jim McManus, C.Ss.R., *All Generations Will Call Me Blessed* (New York:
Crossroad, 1999), 41.

59. Cf. Kelly, *Early Christian Doctrines*, 494: "Tertullian and Irenæus were quick to develop these ideas."

60. Cf. PG 2:781–782.

61. Gambero notes: "This is an extremely valuable witness. It confirms that the Eve–Mary parallel was known in the West during the first Christian centuries, and that the mystery of the Mother of God was beginning to become an object of theological reflection in the entire Church" (*Mary and the Fathers*, 66).

62. Patrick Hamell weighs the evidence for this claim: "He is the most prolific of all the Latin writers, most original and personal. In no one else is Buffon's phrase, 'the style is the man,' more justified (Ebert)—he always spoke from the heart. His writings are (1) apologetic; (2) dogmatico-polemic; (3) practico-ascetical. The personal note is always present, whether he writes carried away with holy zeal that is harshly rigorous, or as a Montanist raging against the alleged laxity of the Catholic Church. A born controversialist, powerful adversary, eloquent and fiery, a man of biting satire and compact logic, he often overshoots the mark, writes without moderation, sweeps away opposition rather than convinces. His expression is bold, concise, rugged, involved; he does not bother with beauty of form—he is 'daringly creative and suddenly enriches the Latin tongue.' With St. Augustine he is the greatest Western theologian. Western theology is in his debt for many technical terms. Indeed, in a certain sense, he created the clear language of Western theology": *Handbook of Patrology* (New York: Alba House, 1968), 70f.

63. He was a Gnostic who held a dualist theory contrary to the biblical doctrine of creation.

64. Tertullian maintained, as Kelly explains, that "He [Christ] entered into the Virgin, as the angel of the Annunciation foretold, and received His flesh from her (cf. *Adv. Prax.* 26). The birth was a real one; He was born *from* her and not, as the Gnostic Valentinus alleged, simply *through* her, as if she were a mere channel through which He passed (cf. *De carn. Chr.* 20: PL 2:830–831)" (*Early Christian Doctrines*, 150).

65. Hubert Cunliffe Jones gives Tertullian credit as a champion of orthodoxy: "Against Marcion and Valentinus he asserts the reality of Christ's birth. He did not simply appear as man without deriving actual humanity from Mary" (*A History of Christian Doctrine*, 60).

66. Cf. Kelly, *Early Christian Doctrines*, 121, for some historical background concerning the identity of Praxeas and his theology.

67. Cf. Cunliffe Jones, *A History of Christian Doctrine*, 52. Jones highlights Tertullian's efforts defending the goodness of creation, the reality of the Incarnation and the efficacy of the sacramental system against gnostic dualism. Furthermore, Jones illustrates how Tertullian's controversies with Praxeas and Marcion led him to formulate precise soteriological conclusions: "Against Praxeas, it is the Son, distinct from the Father, Who became Man; against Marcion, the Son became fully Man, and did not merely assume a human disguise. Tertullian therefore asserts the scandalous paradox of the Incarnation with the utmost possible vigour. The subject of the human experience of Christ, the subject, indeed, of the Incarnation, is none other than the Son. 'The Son of

God was born; one is not ashamed to confess it, just because it is shameful. And the Son of God died; one can believe it, just because it is absurd. And He was buried and rose; it is certain, just because it is impossible.' (cf. *De Carne Christi* 17, 5). That it is God the Son Who lived and died is the essential truth on which Tertullian's soteriology depends; for, like Irenæus, he interprets the work of Christ for salvation as an interchange of places with mankind [*admirabile commercium*]: 'God lived with man, so that man might be able to live with God; God became small so that man might become great.' (cf. Mk 2:27)" (58f.). It is interesting to note that two very significant theological expressions, based on Tertullian's work *De Carne Christi* 17, 5, which, summarize truths about the essential relationship between the Christian act of faith and the use of God's gift of reason, have been transmitted to us as part of our common theological lexicon. These two phrases are: *"Credo quia absurdum est,"* and *"Credo quia impossibile est."* As regards the former expression, one should also be familiar with this rendition: "Credibile est quia ineptum est."

68. Gambero comments on the severity of Tertullian with regard to the Virgin as revealed in his exegesis of key Marian scriptural texts: "It does not seem that our author is directly concerned about, or sympathetic toward, the Virgin as a person. To the contrary, one must acknowledge that it was characteristic of him to render one of the most severe and rash judgments of the holy Virgin known to patristic literature. He poorly interpreted the Gospel passages that mention the brothers of Jesus (cf. Mt 12:46–50; Mk 3:31–35; Lk 8:19–21). According to him, the Lord was reproving his Mother together with his brothers . . . he understands it to mean sons of the same parents" (*Mary and the Fathers*, 62). Furthermore, Tertullian did not accept the teaching on the perpetual virginity of Mary, believing that she ceased to be a virgin *in partu* because he was convinced that the reality of the Humanity of Christ could not otherwise be fully affirmed against the teachings of the Docetists.

69. Cf. NDM, 1051f.: "La figura di Maria che Tertulliano presenta è indice del punto cui era giunta allora la Chiesa nella formulazione della verità rivelata. Anch'egli afferma con vigore il nucleo primitivo di fede cristologico-mariana, su cui poggia l'intera opera della salvezza: il verginale concepimento e la reale maternità di Maria."

70. De Margerie, *An Introduction to the History of Exegesis*, 2:11.

71. De Margerie, *An Introduction to the History of Exegesis*, 2:14.

72. De Margerie offers this summary appraisal of Tertullian as an exegete: "We can therefore fully endorse Adhémar d'Alès' concluding assessment: 'in spite of its limitations, Tertullian's exegetical contribution remains impressive. . . . He has given the Apostle's words a powerful and generally favorable echo. Less daring than his great contemporaries in Alexandria, he heralded the future school of Antioch through his tendencies. His strong dialectics brought forth from Scripture verities whose splendor easily prevail over the shadows cast here and there by materialistic instincts, and later by sectarian bias. This evaluation of Tertullian's exegesis seems to summarize the main facets of the appraisal made by the Church.' The main ones only: Fr. d'Alès does not say here to what extent moral rigorism, from the time of Tertullian's conversion, warped his exegetical judgment, long before his Montanist period; neither does he

report the overwhelming, deliberate and consistent silence of the Fathers (with the exception of St. Augustine and Vincent of Lerins, both highly critical) in relation to a master whom they read and referred to, particularly in exegetical matters" (2:43f.).

73. Cf. *De carne Christi* 20, 1 (PL 2:830–831).

74. Cf. *De carne Christi* 21, 5 (PL 2:833–834).

75. De Margerie comments: "The pith of Scripture is the Word of God become flesh for the salvation of all flesh, for which He offers Himself in the Eucharist. The entire meaning and direction of Scripture thus derives from the Eucharistic and Paschal Incarnation: *Caro Christi, medulla Scripturarum*. This concise formulation is in harmony with Tertullian's thinking, which it encapsulates admirably. The African theologian's views are just as faithfully expressed in the phrase: *Sanguis Christi et Christianorum, medulla Scripturarum*" (2:46). Likewise, one recalls Tertullian's pithy expression: "*Sanguis martyrum, semen Christianorum.*"

76. Cf. Tertullian, *Adversus Marcionem* 2, 4 (PL 2:289, or CSEL 47:338). Tertullian writes: "God knew that it is not good for man to be alone, and He knew how good it would be for him to have a woman with him, first Mary and then the Church."

77. Cf. PL 2:781: "Qui ideo non putant carnem nostrum in Christo fuisse, quia non fuit ex viri semine, recordentur Adam ipsum in hanc carnem non ex semine viri factum. Sicut terra conversa est in hanc carnem sine viri semine, ita et Dei verbum potuit sine coagulo in eiusdem carnis transire materiam." Cf. also PL 2:782: "Virgo erat adhuc terra nondum opere commessa, nondum sementi subacta: ex ea hominem factum accepimus a Deo in animam vivam. Igitur si primus Adam de terra traditur, merito sequens, vel novissimus Adam, ut Apostolus dixit, proinde de terra, id est, carne nondum generationi resignata, in spiritum vivificantem a Deo est prolatus."

78. *De carne Christi* 17, 1–5 (PL 2:781–782).

79. Diff II, 119.

80. Diff II, 34.

81. Tertullian, *De resurrectione carnis* 6 (PL 11:848–849): "Quodcumque enim limus exprimebatur, Christus cogitabatur homo futurus, quod et limus, et caro sermo, quod et terra tunc" (cf. GS 20).

82. Diff II, 119f. Newman's translation: "For into Eve, as yet a virgin, had crept the word which was the framer of death. Equally into a virgin was to be introduced the Word of God which was the builder-up of life; that, what by that sex had gone into perdition by the same sex might be brought back to salvation" (cf. Diff II, 34).

83. Diff II, 120. Newman's translation: "Eve had believed the serpent; Mary believed Gabriel; the fault which the one committed by believing, the other by believing has blotted out" (cf. Diff II, 34).

84. Cf. PL 2:782: "Nam enixe ut abiecta pareret, et in doloribus pareret, verbum diaboli semen illi fuit. Enixa est denique diabolum fratricidam. Contra, Maria eum edidit, qui carnalem fratrem Israel, interemptorem suum detulit, bonum fratrem, ut memoriam mali fratris eraderet. Inde prodeundum fuit Christo ad salutem hominis, quo homo iam damnatus intraverat."

85. Diff II, 34f. *Adv. Hæreses* 3, 22, 4 (PG 7:958–960); *Adv. Hæreses* 5, 19, 1 (PG 7:1175–1176).

86. The Group of Dombes observes: "Ireneo è il primo padre della Chiesa che suggerisce esplicitamente, verso 180, la presenza di Maria nella predicazione degli apostoli.... L'autorità e l'onestà di Ireneo, il suo fondamento sulla tradizione delle Chiese dell'Asia Minore e particolarmente di Policarpo, la presenza dello stesso tema Maria-Eva a due riprese nella sua grande opera *Contro le eresie*; tutto ciò incita a fidarsi di lui allorché egli situa Maria nell'economia della salvezza grazie a una presentazione della predicazione degli apostoli": *Maria: nel Disegno di Dio e nella Communione dei Santi* (Magnano: Edizioni Qi Quajon/Comunità di Bose, 1998), 28.

87. René Laurentin explains the theological significance of the Latin term "consequenter" in relationship to Mary's singular role in the economy of salvation as willed by God. He writes: "Secondo Ireneo il suo ruolo è *necessario* alla logica del piano divino, e per questo il raffronto Eva-Maria cominicia con un 'consequenter' così audace, così sconcertante che è evitato dai traduttori: 'In stretta connessione' traduce Sagnard. No, non è una semplice *connessione* ad essere espressa, ma è una *consequenza* che riveste, nella teologia della storia e nell'antropologia di Ireneo, una specie di necessità: quella della ripresa o ricapitolazione di ogna cosa in Cristo" (NDM, 1019).

88. Diff II, 120.

89. Bishop Boyce notes: "Consequently Newman is led, from his reading of the early Fathers on this point, to speak of the Blessed Virgin as meriting her place in the plan of salvation, since she actively and personally corresponded with God's grace. At the moment of her own conception she was passive in God's creative hands, but at the moment of the Annunciation, when she became the Mother of God and of divine mercy, she was not simply a passive and physical instrument, but a living, responsible and intelligent cause of God taking flesh within her" (*Mary in the Writings of JHN*, 66).

90. Diff II, 120. Newman's translation: "But Eve was disobedient; for she obeyed not, while she was yet a virgin.... As she, having indeed Adam for a husband, but as yet being a virgin ... becoming disobedient, became the cause of death, both to herself and to the whole human race, so also Mary, having the predestined Man, and being yet a Virgin, being obedient, became both to herself and to the whole human race the cause of salvation" (cf. Diff II, 34).

91. Cf. Spedalieri, *Maria nella Scrittura*, 1:158–161.

92. This connection is highlighted in the following text: "Une contribution plus importante encore d'Irénée à la mariologie fut la découverte de l'analogie ou de l'unité de Marie et de l'Église. Le chemin qu'il suit le conduit de l'idée que 'la naissance nouvelle et inespérée du Christ, du sein de la Vierge' est le fondement et le noyau de notre propre renaissance, à la découverte que la foi et le baptême, l'Église, qui opèrent notre renaissance, correspondent exactement et très profondéement à la Vierge Marie": "Place et Cooperation de Marie dans l'Événement Jésus-Christ," in *Mysterium Salutis*, vol. 13 (Paris: Cerf, 1972), 24.

93. Thus Karl Delahaye: "Pour la Patristique primitive, dès Irénée, la naissance de la Parole du sein de la Vierge se continue donc dans la naissance des chrétiens du sein de l'Église. L'acte rédempteur du Christ devient ici le

fondement de l'humanité rachetée. Par l'extension ou le rénouvellement de la naissance de la *Parole* dans le sein de l'Église l'individu participe à l'action salvatrice de Dieu. . . . Pour Irénée, ce qu'opère l'action divine du salut est une 'nouvelle naissance' (*anagenesis*) qui, de façon merveilleuse et incomprehensible, nous a été donnée par Dieu, comme expression du salut, de la Vierge par la foi. Et que produit cette naissance du Logos dans le sein de l'Église, venant de la Vierge par la foi, qui est l'expression du salut? Par elle nous devenons 'porteurs du Christ' (*christophoroi*) comme le dit déjà Ignace le martyr, et Irénée pense aussi que, par cette naissance, nous portons Dieu. Par cette naissance la marque du Christ s'imprime en nous, de sorte que nous sommes configurés à l'image de Dieu": *Ecclesia Mater chez les Pères des Trois Premiers Siècles* (Paris: Cerf, 1964), 142. Cf. Irenæus, *Adversus Hæreses* 3, 9, 1.

94. Father De Margerie explains: "Recently, within the context of the theology of the Fathers of the second century as a whole, A. Orbe has shown how the Eve-Mary antithesis is, for Irenæus, deeper and more 'existential' than has hitherto been thought. Satan was proposing to the first Eve, under the image of the forbidden fruit, a sexual activity that would anticipate the hour preordained by God and, consequently, a death-bearing motherhood. This explains Irenæus' insistence . . . on the fact that Eve was still a virgin and that she had (as yet) no knowledge of procreation. In contrast, the archangel Gabriel proposes in God's name, to the Virgin Mary, without harm to her virginity, a life-bearing motherhood. The interpretation of Orbe seems quite acceptable and certainly makes this text of Irenæus both more intelligible and more meaningful" (*An Introduction to the History of Exegesis*, 1:63).

95. Father René Laurentin illuminates us as to the theological import of this term in the New Eve theology of St. Irenæus. He writes: "In Ireneo (+202) il tema troverà non solo più rilievo e esplicitazione man uno statuto teologico. Il raffronto tra Eva e Maria qui non è affatto un semplice parallelo, ma la consequenza quasi necessaria di un'idea essenziale: il piano salvifico di Dio non è una semplice riparazione della prima parte. È un ricominiciare dall'origine, una rigenerazione attraverso il capo, una ricapitolazione in Cristo. In questo rinnovamento radicale ognuno al momento della caduta, è rimesso a nuovo radicalmente. La 'recapitulatio' (tema paolino) diventa "recirculatio." È un tema nuovo che si può riassumere così: il male contratto fin dalle origini viene risolto con un *circuito contrario*: il Cristo richiama Adamo; la croce, l'albero della caduta. In questo insieme, Maria che richiama Eva occupa un posto di primo piano" (NDM, 1019)

96. Cf. Diff II, 120. Newman quotes from Irenæus' *Adversus Hæreses* 3, 22, 4. "Et propter hoc Lex eam, quæ desponsata erat viro, licet virgo sit adhuc, uxorem ejus, qui desponsaverat, vocat; eam quæ est a Maria in Evam recirculationem significans: quia non aliter quod colligatum est solveretur, nisi ipsæ compagines alligationis reflectantur retrorsus; ut primæ solutionis habere locum." Newman does not give an English translation of this text in the *Letter to Pusey*.

97. Cf. Ps 44:17; Col 1:18; Lk 3:23–38.

98. Diff II, 120f. Cf. *Adversus Hæreses* 3, 22, 4 (PG 7:959). Newman's translation: "And on account of this the Lord said, that the first should be last and the last first. And the Prophet signifies the same saying, 'Instead of fathers you

have children.' For, whereas the Lord, when born, was the first-begotten of the dead, and received into His bosom the primitive fathers, He regenerated them into the life of God, He Himself becoming the beginning of the living, since Adam became the beginning of the dying. Therefore also Luke, commencing the line of generations from the Lord, referred back to Adam, signifying that He regenerated the old fathers, not they Him, into the Gospel of life" (cf. Diff II, 34f.).

99. Antonio Orbe exegetes this passage of Irenæus in his article, "La 'Recirculacion' de la Virgen María en San Ireneo." His emphasis is on Irenæus' use of the Lucan genealogy (Lk 3:23–38) as a central axis of his Christologically focused soteriology. He writes: "Vástago de los patriarcas, Jesús los hizo 'hijos Suyos,' regenerandolos a la Vida de Dios. El misterioso fenómeno tuvo lugar, al hacerse *initium viventium*. Ireneo simplifica, haciendo al Señor *initium generationis* (resp. *regenerationis*), a raíz del bautismo en Espíritu del Jordán; y *initium viventium*, cuando *Primogentius mortuorum*. El Señor *nació* primogénito de los muertos, cuando 'renacido' ya a la Vida divina en el Jordán, en favor de su iglesia, resucitó en carne de entre los muertos. Reformado según la forma de Dios, o remodelado con la 'segunda plasis,' inaugurò como cabeza vital el linaje humano, en contraste con el inaugurado por Adán. El Obispo de Lión indica la trayectoria que seguirá el nuevo Adàn para regenerar a los hombres; la serie lucana de genealogías, de Jesús por José hasta Adán y Dios. Regenerado en carne por el Esprítu, en el Jordán y hecho 'hijo de Dios' por la unción bautismal, aguardó a resucitar en sentido inverso al de las humanas generaciones. Juntas ambas 'génnesis' (en Espíritu y en carne), y idóneo para influir, en cuanto hombre, sobre Sus hermanos los hombres, desciende el Señor a región de los muertos. Predica allí la Salud a los patriarcas (y justos) que descansaban dormidos con el sueño de la muerte. Los 'dormidos Suyos' (los creyentes) la acogen con fe, y creen en El. Cristo los recibe entre los Suyos para el bautismo de Espíritu. 'Los regenera a la Vida de Dios.' El drama tiene lugar en el Hades, donde el Señor encuentra por vez primera a los justos, 'sus dormidos.' Allá los regenera al Evangelio de la Vida, y les ortorga el denario de la Salud, en orden inverso a su venida de ellos al Hades" (*La Mariologia nella Catechesi dei Padri*, 108).

100. Diff II, 32.

101. SN, 29.

102. SN, 78.

103. SN, 79.

104. Cf. MD, 36–38.

105. Diff II, 121. Newman's translation: "And so the knot of Eve's disobedience received its unloosing through the obedience of Mary; for what Eve, a virgin, bound by incredulity, that Mary, a virgin, unloosed by faith" (cf. Diff II, 35).

106. Diff II, 121. Newman's translation: "As Eve by the speech of an Angel was seduced, so as to flee God, transgressing His word, so also Mary received the good tidings by means of the Angel's speech, so as to hear God within her, being obedient to His word. And, though the one had disobeyed God, yet the other was drawn to obey God; that of the virgin Eve the Virgin Mary might

become the advocate. And, as by a virgin it is saved, the balance being preserved, a virgin's disobedience by a Virgin's obedience" (cf. Diff II, 35).

107. Cited by Newman as "contr. Jul. i. no. 5."

108. Cf. Gambero, *Mary and the Fathers*, 55f.: "The principle of recapitulation is integrated with the principle of 'recirculation,' which introduces a note of salvation history into the theology of Irenæus. While the principle of recapitulation affirms that humanity (fallen because of its first head, Adam) had to be brought back to God by another man—Christ—who would be its second head, the principle of recirculation affirms that this process of restoration accomplished by the Savior had to correspond step by step, but in an opposite way, to the story of the fall. Mary enters this process as the antitype of Eve. Within this vision, the bishop of Lyons shows a desire to consider human history as a unified phenomenon, in which the New Testament is nothing other than the continuation of the Old Testament. The single divine economy, interrupted by Adam, with whom Eve was associated, is resumed and brought to its complete perfection by Christ, with whom Mary is associated. In this perspective we can understand why Irenæus calls Mary *causa salutis*, precisely because she is the antitype of Eve, who was *causa mortis*. Her role is not limited to her purely biological and negative status as Virgin Mother; no, her cooperation includes moral and spiritual motives. For example, her obedience to the word of God was conscious and voluntary; her consent to the plan of salvation had a soteriological character, since she knew that the Incarnation of God's Son was happening for the sake of human redemption."

109. Luigi Melotti offers the following insight: "L'azione salvifica di Maria a favore del proprio sesso è duplice: come 'intercedetrice' e 'avvocata' Maria Vergine obbediente ottiene la salvezza personale di Eva, vergine disobbediente e punita da Dio; come docile 'serva' del Signore, ripara e scioglie la disobbedienza, con le consequenze, di Eva-sesso femminile, nella propria persona ricaptiolatrice": *Maria la Madre dei Viventi: Compendio di Mariologia* (Turin: Editrice Elle Di Leumann, 1989), 53.

110. Cf. PG 7:1175–76.

111. Diff II, 37.

112. Gambero, *Mary and the Fathers*, 56.

113. Cf. Diff II, 37.

114. Cf. Bertrand de Margerie, "Mary Coredemptrix in the Light of Patristics," *Mary Coredemptrix, Mediatrix, Advocate*, ed. Mark I. Miravalle (Santa Barbara, Calif.: Queenship Publishing, 1995), 9f.

115. Cf. Heb 1:3.

116. Cf. LG 62. St. Paul in 1 Tim 2:5–6 writes that "there is one God, and that there is one mediator between God and man, the man Christ Jesus, Who gave Himself as a ransom for all." St. Paul uses the Greek word *heis*, meaning "one," "first" or "primary," and not *monos*, which means "sole" or "only" and could have been employed by St. Paul to designate Christ's mediation as excluding any and all other forms of subordinate and participatory forms of mediation. The Reverend Michael O'Carroll, C.S.Sp., explains that "the practice of addressing Mary as Mediatrix was not and need not be impeded by the Pauline text. The use of 'one' [*heis* not *monos*] emphasizes Christ's transcendence as a

mediator, through the unique value of His redemptive death" (*Theotokos: A Theological Encyclopedia of the Blessed Virgin Mary* (Collegeville, Minn.: The Liturgical Press, 1982), 238).

117. See, for example, Mt 11:25–30 and Heb 5:7–10.

118. Cf. Jn 14:16; 16:7.

119. Cf. Diff II, 71.

120. Cf. LG 62: "This motherhood of Mary in the order of grace continues uninterruptedly from the consent which she loyally gave at the Annunciation and which sustained without wavering beneath the Cross, until the eternal fulfillment of all the elect. Taken up into heaven she did not lay aside this saving office but by her manifold intercession continues to bring us the gifts of eternal salvation. By her maternal charity, she cares for the brethren of her Son, who still journey on earth surrounded by dangers and difficulties, until they are led into their blessed home. Therefore the Blessed Virgin is invoked in the Church under the titles of Advocate, Helper, Benefactress, and Mediatrix. This, however, is so understood that it neither takes away anything nor adds anything to the dignity and efficacy of Christ the one Mediator. No creature could ever be counted along with the Incarnate Word and Redeemer; but just as the priesthood of Christ is shared in various ways both by His ministers and the faithful, and as the one goodness of God is radiated in different ways among His creatures, so also the unique mediation of the Redeemer does not exclude but rather gives rise to a manifold cooperation which is but a sharing in this one source. The Church does not hesitate to profess this subordinate role of Mary, which it constantly experiences and recommends to the heartfelt attention of the faithful, so that encouraged by this maternal help they may the more closely adhere to the Mediator and Redeemer." See also NDM, 920–935.

121. Cf. Lino Cignelli, *Maria Nuova Eva nella Patristica Greca* (Assisi: Studio Teologico "Porziuncola"), 202–254.

122. Cignelli, *Maria Nuova Eva nella Patristica Greca*, 6–26, passim.

123. De Margerie assists us thus: "We do not share the opinion of J. A. de Aldama (*Eph. Mariologicæ* 16, 1966, 319–321: *sibi causa facta est causa salutis*); he believes that the *sibi* does not refer to Mary but to Eve; he supports his interpretation by the argument that it would be impossible to attribute to Irenæus the idea that Mary was the cause of her own redemption (p. 320); but it is by no means necessary to attribute such an idea to Irenæus in order to justify his expression [Mary cause of her own salvation] if we recall that Paul wrote to Timothy, 'Pay close attention to yourself and to your teaching; continue in these things; for in doing this *you will save* both *yourself* and your hearers' (1 Tm 4:16: the verb *sozein* is employed by the author, just as Irenæus, in the text in question, employs the term *soteria*). . . . In the context of the AH III, 22.4., where Irenæus writes of Mary: '*sibi causa facta est salutis*,' it is quite possible that he explicitly intended to allude to another passage of the same letter of Paul to Timothy, namely to 1 Tm 2:14–15: 'Adam was not deceived, but the woman was deceived and became a transgressor. Yet *she will be saved through childbearing*, provided they continue in faith and love and holiness, with modesty.' Is it not possible that, in the statement discussed by Fr. de Aldama, Irenæus meant that Mary was saved, having become herself a cause of salvation, by accepting to

become the Mother of not just any human being, but of the New Adam, the divine Savior? Indeed, the statement of Irenæus suggests that the general and universal law of salvation for woman, namely, maternity, was fulfilled in a unique and transcendent way in Mary, to the extent that in saving herself as well as others, He would be both her and their Savior. This comparison had been suggested by Fr. Spicq. Its particular merit lies in the fact that it shows how much more deeply rooted in Pauline thinking than had previously been suspected is the theology of Irenæus regarding Mary as the new Eve. The interpretation of Fr. de Aldama seems to overlook the whole parallel drawn by Irenæus: Mary saves herself, just as Eve had lost herself. The point is not that Mary redeemed herself: the suggestion is merely made, as later theology will put it, that she cooperated (like each of us, but in a more sublime way) in her own *subjective* redemption, by applying to herself the merits of the one Redeemer who was the sole author of her *objective* redemption" (*An Introduction to the History of Exegesis*, 1:61f.).

124. Cignelli, *Maria Nuova Eva nella Patristica Greca*, 36f.

125. Newman gives an explanatory footnote: "*Salvatur*; some MSS. read *Solvatur*, '(that) it might be loosed;' and so Augustine contr. Jul. i. no. 5. This variety of reading does not affect the general sense of the passage. Moreover, the word 'salvation' occurs in the former of the two passages" (Diff II, 35).

126. Newman's interpretation of Irenæus is equally applicable to Justin and Tertullian by Newman's own admission—he treats them as having put forth a unified theological vision concerning Mary's cooperation in the work of salvation. (cf. Diff II, 35: *Adv. Hæreses* 5, 19, 1).

127. Cignelli refers to Irenæus as having put a particular emphasis on the contrast between Eve's disobedience and Mary's obedience because this antithetical parallel yields consequences of both soteriological and anthropological significance. Cignelli concludes that the antithetical responses and their antithetical consequences also involve a question of personal merit (or, in Eve's case, what the author calls "demerit") and therefore, of personal responsibility and cooperation. Hence, the actions of Eve and Mary are to be evaluated as significant not merely because of their effect on us but also insofar as they have merit/demerit according to both a soteriological and an anthropological point of view (cf. *Maria Nuova Eva nella Patristica Greca*, 32–39).

128. Laurentin, "Nuova Eva," in NDM, 1019

129. The Greek term *anakephalaisosis* is the term that Irenæus uses to refer to the salvific action of Christ as the Second Adam. It best translates the Latin *recapitulatio* or recapitulation. However, there is also a second Greek term, *anakyklesis* (*recirculatio*), which is translated "recycling" and signifies Mary's specific role of cooperation in the salvation of Eve wrought by Our Lord. We find this term used by Irenæus in *Adversus Hæreses* III, 22, when he speaks of Mary's faith as that which unties the knot of Eve's disobedience. This distinction is not merely semantic but theologically significant. De Margerie offers the following explanation: "It is easy to see why Irenæus chose a different term to signify the action of Mary, because he underscores (in the same section) the faith of Mary who repaired Eve's lack of faith. He does not claim that Christ recapitulated Adam through faith. The transcendence implicit in the notion of

recapitulation with respect to that of 'recycling' manifests the transcendence of Jesus with respect to Mary the believer" (*An Introduction to the History of Exegesis*, 2:62).

130. Cf. Kelly, *Early Christian Doctrines* (London: Black, 1977), 172f.

131. Kelly, *Early Christian Doctrines*, 173.

132. Cf. Acts 17:28—Aratus, *Phænomena* 5.

133. Cf. Jones, *A History of Christian Doctrine*, 68.

134. Cf. Luigi Padovese, *Introduzione alla Teologia Patristica* (Casale Monferrato: Edizioni Piemme, 1992), 126.

135. Antonio Orbe explains: "La eficacia salvifica asignada aquí a Maria puede en absoluto concebirse de dos modos: a) causa de salud para todo el linaje humano, a partir de Ella; b) causa de salud para los hombres todos, sin limitación, lo mismo antes que después de Ella. Lo primero limitaria mucho el influyo salvifico de Maria. El contexto irenecano acentuia, al parecer, expresamente su eficacia, de Maria a Eva. E invoca ahi la *recirculatio*. Lo que anuda Eva, desata Maria. Eva anuda la humana *sarx* con la muerte, e inicia la trayectoria *in mortem* de padres a hijos, fundada en la genesis *secundum carnem*. Maria desata el nudo de muerte, e inicia la trayectoria *in vitam* de hijos a padres, fundada asimismo en la génesis *secundum carnem*." He adds: "La 'recirculación' de la Virgen Maria, al igual que los grandes misterios de la vida de Jesús, afecta esencialmente a la *sarx*. Su eficacia es, en absoluto, doble: a) por la obediencia virginal al mensaje de Dios y b) por el fruto de la obediencia. Agradable a Dios por su obediencia, la 'carne' virginal pasará al Hijo, en Quien—regenerada en Espíritu—se vuelve fuente de bendición para la humana familia, hasta Adán."— "La 'Recirculación' de la Virgen Maria en San Ireneo," *La Mariologia nella Catechesi dei Padri: Età Prenicena* (Rome: Libreria Ateneo Salesiano, 1989), 105, 120.

136. Cf. Gal 4:4–6.

137. De Margerie, *An Introduction to the History of Exegesis*, 1:63.

138. John J. Dillon, "Mary As Second Eve: A Patristic Viewpoint," *Hopes and Visions* (Washington, D.C.: Ecumenical Society of the Blessed Virgin Mary, 1998), 12.

139. Diff II, 38f.

140. Diff II, 37.

141. NDM, 1021.

142. Cf. Kelly, *Early Christian Doctrines*, 496: ". . . it was Jerome, Ambrose and Augustine who contributed most to Mariology in the West."

143. For the convenience of the reader here is reproduced the excellent bibliographical information concerning Ambrose's Mariology provided in Father Luigi Gambero's book *Mary and the Fathers of the Church: The Blessed Virgin Mary in Patristic Thought* on page 190, notes 1 and 2. Cf. J. M. Bover, "La mediación universal de María según san Ambrosio," *Gregorianum* 5 (1924), 24–45; A. Pagnamenta, *la mariologia di Sant'Ambrogio* (Milan, 1932); E. Vismara, "Il testamento del Signore nel pensiero di S. Ambrogio e la maternità di Maria SS. verso gli uomini," *Salesianum* 7 (1945), 7–38, 97–143; J. Huhn, "Das Mariengeheimnis beim Kirchenvater Ambrosius," *Münchener Theologische Zeitschrift* 2 (1951), 130–146, and his *Das Geheimnis der Jungfrau-Mutter Maria nach dem*

Kirchenvater Ambrosius (Würtzburg, 1954); G. Joussard, "Deux chefs de file en théologie mariale dans la second moitié du IV siècle: St. Epiphane et St. Ambroise," *Gregorianum* 42 (1961), 5–36, and his "Un Portrait de la Ste. Vierge par St. Ambroise," *Vie spirituelle* 90 (1954), 477–489; G. Rigamonti, *Maria ideale di vita cristiana nella dottrina di S. Ambrogio* (Milan, 1960); Charles William Neumann, *The Virgin Mary in the Works of St. Ambrose* (Fribourg: University Press, 1962); M. Bretagna, "Elementi cultus mariani apud sanctum Ambrosium mediolanensem," *De primordiis cultus Mariani*, vol. 3 (Rome, 1970), 1–15; M. S. Ducci, "Senso della tipologia mariana in S. Ambrogio," *Ephemerides Mariologicæ* 23 (1973), 363–404; S. Folgado Flores, "María modelo de la Iglesia en San Ambrosio," *Estudios Marianos* 39 (1974), 57–77, and his "Contento teológico de la virginidad de María en S. Ambrosio," *Marianum* 44 (1982), 288–315; S-L. Bastero de Aleizalde, "Paralelismo Eva-Maria en S.Ambrosio de Milan," *Estudios Marianos* 50 (1985), 71–88.

144. Cf. St. Ambrose, *Sermo* 195, 2 (PL 38:1013). "'*Speciosus forma præ filiis hominum*': 'beautiful above the sons of men' (Ps 44:3), Mary's Son, Spouse of the Church! He has made His Church like to His Mother, He has given her to us as a mother, He has kept her for Himself as a virgin. The Church, like her, is a virgin ever spotless and a mother ever fruitful. What He bestowed on Mary in the flesh, He has bestowed on the Church in the spirit: Mary gave birth to the One, and the Church gives birth to the many, who through the One becomes one."

145. Cf. Charles William Neumann, S.M., *The Virgin Mary in the Works of St. Ambrose*, vol. 17 of *Paradosis: Contributions to the History of Early Christian Literature and Theology* (Fribourg, Switzerland: University Press, 1962), 47–50.

146. Cf. Neumann, *The Virgin Mary in the Works of St. Ambrose*, 9: "With Athanasius (295–293) the idea of Mary as model of virgins finds unambiguous expression. The most abundant text is the long description of Mary's virginal life in a work called the *Letter to Virgins* and preserved only in Coptic fragments discovered in 1929 by Louis-Théodore Lefort. This writing indubitably inspired Ambrose to make a similar development in his *De Virginibus*...." See also 46f.

147. Cf. Kelly, *Early Christian Doctrines*, 496: "As for Ambrose, despite early hesitations about her virginity *in partu*, he became a powerful advocate of Mary's perpetual virginity."

148. Cf. Neumann, *The Virgin Mary in the Works of St. Ambrose*, 205–272: "Ambrose clearly testifies to Bonosus' denial of Mary's perpetual virginity *post partum*..." (216). "Jovinian seems to have been led to deny Mary's virginity *in partu*... by his desire to prove that virginity was no more meritorious than the married state" (221).

149. Cf. LG 60–69. See also Isaac of Stella, *Sermo* 51 (on the Assumption) (PL 194:1862–63, 1865) and the Second Reading of the Office of Readings for Saturday of the Second Week of Advent.

150. Gerardo Di Nola, ed., *Ambrogio—Cristo Eucaristia La Vergine Madre del Signore: In Occasione del XVI Centenario della Morte di Sant'Ambrogio Vescovo e Dottore della Chiesa e in Preparazione al Giubileo 2000* (Latin-Italian ed., Vatican City: Libreria Editrice Vaticana, 1997), 20–22.

151. Cf. *Storia della Chiesa Cattolica*, ed. Luigi Giovannini (Milan: Edizioni San Paolo, 1989), 179.

152. Cf. *De virginibus ad Marcellinam sororem suam libri tres* (PL 16:187–232); *De viduis liber unus* (PL 16:233–262); *De virginitate liber unus* (PL 16:265–302); *De institutione virginis et sanctæ Mariæ virginitate perpetua ad Eusebium liber unus* (PL 16:305–334); *Exhortatio virginitatis liber unus* (PL 16:35–364).

153. Cf. Kelly, *Early Christian Doctrines*, 496: "His [Ambrose's] intense veneration for her [Mary] sprang from the twin facts that she was the ideal virgin, showing no trace of imperfections but exhibiting all the virtues appropriate to the virginal state." See also the Second Vatican Council's decree on the renewal of religious life, *Perfectæ Caritatis*, 25: "Religious Institutes, for which these norms of up-to-date renewal have been established, should respond generously to the divine call and should be prompt in performing the task allotted to them in the Church today. The holy synod holds in high esteem their way of life in chastity, poverty and obedience, a way of life of which Christ the Lord Himself is the exemplar. It places great hope in their work, which is so fruitful, whether it be hidden or in public. All religious, therefore, with undiminished faith, with charity towards God and their neighbor, with love for the cross and with the hope of future glory, should spread the good news of Christ throughout the entire world, so that their witness will be seen by all men and our Father, who is in heaven will be glorified (Mt 5:16). Thus, through the prayers of the gentle Virgin Mary, Mother of God, 'whose life is a model for all' (St. Ambrose, *De Virginitate*, 2, 2, no. 15) may they increase daily and may they bring more abundant fruits of salvation."

154. *De Virginibus ad Marcellinam sororem suam libri tres* 5, 21 (PL 16:205).

155. Diff II, 52.

156. *De Virginibus* 2, 2, 15 (PL 16:210).

157. *Teologia Oggi* (Bologna: Edizioni Dehoniane, 1996), 247.

158. Lettera della Congregazione per L'Educazione Cattolica: *La Vergine Maria nella Formazione Intellettuale e Spirituale* (Bologna: EDB, 1988), 13.

159. *De Virginibus* II, 2, 6 (PL 16:219).

160. Cf. Pope John Paul II, *Mulieris Dignitatem* 21.

161. The Holy Father writes: "Imaginem eius accuratam ille præstat et amantem et minutatim descriptam, cuius pariter morales virtutes is delineat vitamque interiorem nec non in opere et oratione sedulitatem. Quamvis scribendi genus sit plane sobrium, inde tamen fervida eius erga Virginem pietas elucet, Christi matrem Ecclesiæ speciem vitæque christianorum specimen. In gaudio carminis eius '*Magnificat*' ipsam contemplatus, clamat Mediolanensis Episcopus: 'Sit in singulis Mariæ anima, ut magnificet Dominum, sit in singulis spiritus Mariæ, ut exsultet in Deo.' Quæmadmodum tradit Ambrosius, salutis historiæ Maria tota adminiscetur velut Mater ac Virgo. Quia nimirum aternum Patris unguentum Christus est, 'hoc unguento uncta est Maria et virgo concepit, virgo peperit bonum odorem, Dei Filium.' Cum Christo coniuncta, quando Filius se ex amore offerens 'affixus ad lignum . . . bonum odorem mundanæ fundebat redemptionis' . . . Hoc Mariæ simulacrum est mulieris animosæ ac magnanimosæ, sibi partium consciæ in salutis historia concrediatrum et prompta ad suum exsequendum munus usque ad ipsius vitæ oblationem.

Verumtamen Mediolanensis Episcopus qui eam tantopere celebrat tantumque amat numquam obliviscitur eam totam Christo unico Redemptori subdi et ad illum referri."—as found in *Ambrogio—Cristo, Eucaristia*, 71–72, passim.

162. Cf. *De Virginibus* 2, 7 (PL 16:209). "Virgo erat non solum corpore, sed etiam mente. . . ."

163. Ibid.

164. MD, 221f.

165. MD, 222.

166. MD, 9.

167. MD, 11.

168. MD, 12. It is interesting to note that Newman in enumerating a few of Mary's privileges—gradually taught by the Church in greater or lesser dogmatic form—lists the Assumption as a belief explicitly held by the Church in advance of the Immaculate Conception, even though the former was not yet dogmatically defined and would only come to be so defined in 1950—only sixty years after his death in 1890.

169. Cf. Kelly, *Early Christian Doctrines*, 476: ". . . as the Mother of God she was endued with a special grace, and was associated with man's salvation."

170. Cf. *Exhortatio Virginitatis* 5, 31 (PL 16:345). Ambrose compares the Virgin Mary to a "light cloud" upon which, according to his interpretation of the Prophet Isaiah 19,1, the promised Messiah comes so as to make His entrance into the world amidst the sufferings of a new Egypt. Ambrose writes: "*Nubem* itaque Mariam dixit, quia carnem gerebat; *levem*, quia virgo erat, nullis oneribus gravata coniugii. Ipsa est virga germinans florem, quia pura et ad dominum libero corde directa virginitatis, quæ nullis in hoc sæculo curarum anfractibus reflectitur."

171. Dev. D., 146. The reference for the quotation of Ambrose is: *De Institutione Virginis* 7, 50 (PL 16:319). The Latin text reads: "Cuius tanta gratia, ut non solum in se virginitatis gratiam reservaret, sed etiam his quos viseret, integritatis conferret."

172. De Lubac, relying on St. Ambrose, explains how the Church like Mary, Virgin and Mother, is spiritually fecund and thus communicates that spiritual fecundity to her children: "In St. Ambrose the equation becomes explicit; like Christ's Mother, the Church is wed but virgin; she conceives us virginally by the Holy Spirit, and she bears us virginally without travail." The original quotation from St. Ambrose, to which de Lubac refers comes from *In Lucam*: "Bene disponsata, sed virgo, quia est Ecclesiæ typus, quæ est immaculata, sed nupta. Concepit nos virgo de Spiritu, parit nos virgo sine gemitu" (cf. PL 15:1555B). Dr. Mark Miravalle reflects on the episode of Mary's Visitation to Elizabeth in Lk 1:39–45 as an expression of Mary's cooperation as "Mediatrix of Graces." Mary bears "the Source of all grace in her womb," and her visitation with the unborn Messiah causes the unborn Baptist to leap for joy in Elizabeth's womb, Elizabeth to be "filled with the Holy Spirit," and Elizabeth to praise and bless the Virgin Mother for her exemplary faith and divine maternity. Mary's mediation, the sanctifying presence of the Holy Spirit and the unborn Savior are interconnected mysteries. Mary's presence does not obstruct the salvific and sanctifying activity of the Divine Persons but it is precisely the chosen instru-

ment by which it is mediated to both Elizabeth and John the Baptist.—*Mary: CoRedemptrix, Mediatrix, Advocate* (Santa Barbara, Calif.: Queenship Publishing, 1993), 30f.

173. Our Holy Father Pope John Paul II writes: "In the Visitation episode, St. Luke shows how the grace of the Incarnation, after filling Mary brings salvation and joy to Elizabeth's house. Carried in his Mother's womb, the Savior of men pours out the Holy Spirit, revealing Himself from the start of His coming into the world. In describing Mary's departure for Judea, the evangelist uses the verb *anístemi*, which means, 'to arise,' 'to start moving.' Considering that this verb is used in the Gospels to indicate Jesus' Resurrection (Mk 8:31; 9:9, 31; Lk 24: 7, 46) or physical actions that imply a spiritual effort (Lk 5: 27–28; 15: 18–20), we can suppose that Luke wished to stress with this expression the vigorous zeal which led Mary, under the inspiration of the Holy Spirit, to give the world its Savior. The Gospel text also reports that Mary made the journey, 'with haste.' (Lk 1:39) In the Lucan context, even the note, 'into the hill country,' (Lk1:39) appears to be much more than a topographical indication, since it calls to mind the messenger of good news described inthe Book of Isaiah (52:7)" (*A Catechesis on Mary, Mother of God*, 139.) See also pp. 140–42. Relying on St. Bede the Venerable, a ninth-century Father and Doctor of the Church, Hugo Rahner highlights Mary's visitation to Elizabeth by way of reference to her other evangelical journeys, and furthermore relates their mystical, allegorical typology to our spiritual lives as Christians. He writes: "In one of his most beautiful passages the Anglo-Saxon Bede describes Mary's journey from Nazareth (meaning the "flower") to Bethlehem (the "House of Bread"), as the journey of the Church, God's Mother: 'Today and every day to the end of time is unceasingly conceived at 'Nazareth' and born at 'Bethlehem,' wherever one of the faithful takes to himself the "Flower" of the Word, he is transformed into an everlasting "House of Bread." Every day the Lord is conceived in a virginal womb, that is, in the spirit of the faithful, and brought to birth in Baptism. Every day the Church as God's Mother follows her Master from Galilee (which means the "turning wheel" of life on earth) to that city in Judea (which means the city of "exultation and praise," in order to be inscribed in the register of her dedication to the eternal King. Thus does the Church follow the blessed and ever-Virgin Mary, who is the symbol of her, at once espoused and undefiled. She conceives us by the Holy Ghost, and as a virgin brings us to birth without travail.'"

174. *De Institutione Virginis* 7, 50 (PL 16:319).

175. Cf. *De Institutione Virginis* 13, 81–84 (PL 16:339–340).

176. Cf. *De Virginitate* 63–67 (PL 16:281–283).

177. DMC, 369.

178. Cf. St. Ambrose, *In Evangelium Secundum Lucam*, 2, 7 (CCL 14, 33, 102–106).

179. We read in CCC 501: "Jesus is Mary's only son, but her spiritual motherhood extends to all men whom indeed He came to save: 'The Son whom she brought forth is he whom God placed as the first-born among many brethren, that is, the faithful in whose generation and formulation she cooperates with a mother's love.'"

180. On the question of the Church as universal sacrament of salvation, Newman's teaching can be considered prophetic since it anticipates in its accuracy and theological nuance the teachings of the Second Vatican Council, most especially as found in LG 14, 16, and AG 7. For example, Newman writes the following in a letter to John Douglas Sandford: "Saving Grace is given outside the Catholic Church—but not to those who are *not* in invincible ignorance and in good faith.—Many a soul is saved who does not belong to the visible body" (LD, 28:129; 21, 10, 1876). Furthermore, in his *Discourses to Mixed Congregations*, Newman explains: "God gives grace to all men, and to those who profit by it He gives more grace, and even those who quench it still have the offer. ... Many, we may trust, are enjoying that permanent light, and are coming steadily into the Church; some, alas! may have received it, and, as not advancing towards the Holy House in which it is stored, are losing it, and, though they know it not, are living only by the recollections of what was once present within them. These are the secret things with God; but the great and general truths remain, that nature cannot see God, and that grace is the sole means of seeing Him; and that which grace enables us to do so, it also brings us into His Church, and is never given us for our illumination, without being also given to make us Catholics" (DMC, 188f.).

181. Cf. SN, 80f.

182. Cf. *Expositio Evangelii secundum Lucam* 10, 129–133 (PL 15:1836–38). Also, *Exhortatio Virginitatis*, 31–33 (PL 16:345).

183. SN, 81–82, passim.

184. *De Institutione Virginis*, 33 (PL 16:328): "Si typum Christi illa pariendo a viro meretur audiri, quantum proficiat sexus qui Christum, salva tamen virginitate, generavit! Veni ergo Eva, jam Maria, quæ nobis non solvum virginitatis incentivum attulit, sed etiam Deum intulit." Cf. also Kelly, *Early Christian Doctrines*, 476: "He [Ambrose] elaborated the contrast between her (Mary) and Eve, and found a kinship between her and the Church, both being virgins and both mothers by the operation of the Holy Spirit." Cf. Sir 24:1–31, especially verse 15. The note given in the *New American Bible* is worth citing: "In this chapter, Wisdom speaks in the first person, describing her origin, her dwelling place in Israel, and the reward she gives her followers. As in Proverbs 8, Wisdom is described as a being who comes from God and is distinct from Him. While we do not say with certainty that this description applies to a personal being, it does foreshadow the beautiful doctrine of the Word of God later developed in St. John's Gospel (Jn 1:1–14). In the liturgy this chapter is applied to the Blessed Virgin because of her constant and intimate association with Christ, the Incarnate Word" (845).

185. *In Ps XXXVI Enarratio* 37 (PL 14:1032).

186. Cf. CCC 766, citing *Sacrosanctum Concilium*, 5, "Nam de latere Christi in cruce dormientis ortum est totius Ecclesiæ mirabile sacramentum." More to our point, the Catechism (776) citing Ambrose's commentary on Luke, says: "Sicut Eva de latere Adami formata est, sic ecclesia est nata de corde transfixo Christi in cruce mortui" (St. Ambrose, *In Luc.* 2, 85–89: PL 15:1666–68).

187. De Margerie discusses Ambrose's exegesis of Eph 5:32, which is an interpretation of Gen 2:24 concerning the spousal relationship between Christ

and the Church in *De Paradiso*, 14, 72 (PL 14:33). De Margerie writes: "Paul (and Ambrose along with him) saw Christ in Adam and the Church in Eve. The Church had therefore, in a way, sinned. However, Eve (who represents the Church) was saved by generating Christ through Mary, 'in faith, love and modesty'" (*An Introduction to the History of Exegesis*, 2:81f.). De Margerie explains in his footnote that this sinfulness is not imputed to the Church as a whole but to her individual members—a point which needs to be emphasized in order to preserve the doctrine of the Church's sinlessness as the Spouse of Christ. Spotless holiness is an indelible mark of the Church as are the marks of oneness, catholicity and apostolicity. Therefore, as the Fathers of the Second Vatican Council teach in LG 8, even though the principal rebirth of the children of the Church takes place in Baptism, she continues to embrace in her maternal bosom all sinners, all those who are in continual need of spiritual renewal and conversion. Mary's cooperation in the Incarnation, that is, her divine maternity, characterized, as Ambrose notes, by the virtues of "faith, love and modesty," is a mystery by which God restores to Eve and to her children in the human race the dignity of regeneration and divine sonship in Christ the Second Adam. In this sense, but not only in this sense, can we derive from Ambrose a theology of Mary the New Eve, who is both Mother of Christ the Head and spiritual Mother of the members of Christ's Body the Church (cf. LG 65).

188. Cf. Kelly, *Early Christian Doctrines*, 476f. Here, Kelly refers to Ambrose's *Expositio Evangelii secundum Lucam* 7, 5. See also *De Institutione Virginis* 494 (PL 16:333; *Expositio in Lucam* 10, 132 (SC 52:200).

189. Cf. Ignace de la Potterie, S.J., *Mary in the Mystery of the Covenant* (New York: Alba House, 1992), 153. Cf. also *Lumen Gentium*, 64; Ambrose, *In Ev. Lc.* 2, 7 (PL 15:1635–36): "Didicimus seriem veritatis, didicimus consilium, discamus et mysterium. Bene desponsata, sed virgo; quia est Ecclesiæ typus, quæ est immaculata sed nupta. Concepit nos virgo de Spiritu, parit nos virgo sine gemitu. Et ideo fortasse sancta Maria alli nupta, ab alio repleta: quia et singulæ Ecclesiæ Spiritu, quidem replentur et gratia; junguntur tamen ad temporalis speciem sacerdotis."

190. Cf. St. Irenæus, *Adv. Haereses*, 3, 16, 4; CCC 501; Pope John Paul II, *Mary, Mother of God*, 122.

191. Ambrose, *Expositio in Lucam* 2, 17 (PG 15:1555), cited in LG 63 and CCC 507. Cf. also *De Paradiso* 14, 72 (PL 14:311): "Hæc [Ecclesia] enim vere in prævaricatione ante fuit, sed salva erit per filiorum generationem in fide et charitate, et sanctificatione, cum chastitate." Cf. Gambero, *Mary and the Fathers*, 198: "Ambrose is the first Christian author to call Mary the type and image of the Church."

192. Cf. Gambero, *Mary and the Fathers*, 198–199, passim: "The Mary–Church parallel is based on the virginal motherhood of both, a motherhood that has the same supernatural fructifying principle: the Holy Spirit. However, there is not only a relationship of resemblance between the Virgin and the Church; there is also an operative relationship, made possible by the unity between Christ and His Mystical Body. For, in conceiving Christ, Mary also conceived us in the Church: 'From Mary's womb there came into the world that heap of

grain surrounded by lilies (cf. Song of Songs 7:1), when Christ was born of her.' From the context, it is understood that Ambrose interprets this verse from the Song of Songs in such a way that the lily stands for Christ, while the heap of grain stands for the faithful. The holy Virgin, in giving birth to Christ for the salvation of the world, contracted to building up of the Church into the body of Christ. The context allows us to interpret in this sense another text, which describes the profound communion between Jesus and the faithful: 'The inheritance of the Lord are the sons (cf. Ps 127:3), the reward of the fruit has come forth from Mary's womb. He is the fruit of the womb. . . . Mary is the branch; the flower of Mary is Christ, who, like the fruit of a good tree, according to our progress in virtue, now flowers, bears fruit in us, and is reborn through the Resurrection that returns life to His body.'" Cf. *De Institutione Virginis* 94 (PL 16:342); *Expositio in Lucam* 2, 24 (PL 15:1641–42).

193. *Epistula* 63, 33 (PL 16:1198).

194. *De Institutione Virginis* 16, 1198 (PL 16:328, 329).

195. *Expositio Evangelii secundum Lucam*, 2.29, 30 (PL 15:1562–63). Cf. *De Institutione Virginis* 7, 50 (PL 16:319). Also, Jean-Marie Salgado, O.M.I., *La Maternité Spirituelle de la Très Ste. Vierge Marie: Studi Tomistici* (Rome: Libreria Editrice Vaticana, 1990), 74–77. Cf. Ef 4:13.

196. DMC, 374–376. Cf. John Henry Newman, *Discourses to Mixed Congregations*, ed. Tolhurst, xxiif. Tolhurst explains: "It is this failure, however, to accept the real nature of sin which lay behind much of the venom directed against the structure of the Catholic Church. It was because Catholicism deliberately confronted sin, in its priests, its penances, its confessionals, that it makes the English uncomfortable, who had previously either liked not to discuss such matters or to be free to commit sin in private. This, Newman argued, explained the attack on celibacy, the mockery of holy persons and holy things 'as far as they come across him.' One should not be surprised that Newman would end his *Discourses* by putting before his audience the image of the Virgin Mother of God, and affirming that 'it is the boast of the Catholic Religion that it has the gift of making the young heart chaste.'"

197. Cf. Methodius of Philippi, *Symposion* 8, 5 (PG 18:145). Methodius writes: "Look well at the woman in the sky, clothed with the sun, crowned with twelve stars, and with the moon beneath her feet; yes its is indeed our Church!" See also Pseudo-Ambrose (= Berengaud), *Commentary on the Apocalypse* 4, 3, 4 (PL 17:876). In this ninth-century text we read: "We can indeed say that the woman of the Apocalypse is Mary because she is the Mother of the Church, having given birth to the Head of the Church. Yet she is also the daughter of the Church, and the holiest of her members."

198. The Latin text reads: "Memorare, o piissima Virgo Maria, non esse auditum a sæculo, quemquam ad tua currentem præsidia, tua implorantem auxilia, tua petentem suffragia esse derelictum. Ego tali animatus confidentia ad te, Virgo Virginum, Mater, curro; ad te venio; coram te gemens peccator assisto. Noli, Mater Verbi, verba mea despicere, sed audi propitia et exaudi. Amen."

199. DMC, 376.

200. In applying this analogy of the maternal love of God in the Old Testament for the children of Israel, Newman first makes clear that our Lord fulfills

this analogous role as "our mother" along with several other analogous roles, namely, by being "our physician, our teacher, our ruler or pastor, our father."

201. SN, 81. The reference of Newman is to Isaiah 49:14f. The NAB reads: "But Zion said: 'The Lord has forsaken me.' Can a mother forsake her infant, be without tenderness for the child of her womb? Even should she forget, I will never forget you." *Rahamîm*, the Hebrew word for tenderness used in this text and elsewhere in the Old Testament, has a profound theological significance since it is derived from the Hebrew root word *rehem* which literally refers to the visceral love and compassion that a mother should have for the child of her womb. This type of love, therefore, is referred to by the Old Testament prophets like Isaiah and Hosea (cf. 14:5) to characterize the love of God for the children of Israel. In the New Testament, the Greek noun "splanchon" and related verb "splanchnízomai" meaning respectively "compassion" and "to have compassion" are used to describe Our Lord's deep-seated, visceral emotions expressed in relationship to the children of Israel (cf. Mk 1:42; 6:34; 8:2; 9:22; Mt 14:14; 20:34; Lk 7:13). See also Pope John Paul II, encyclical letter *Dives in Misericordia* (especially pages 118–120) for an explanation of the biblical significance of the term *rahamîm* in relationship to other biblical words (e.g., *hesed, emet, hanan, hamal, hus*) whose definitions express various aspects of the infinite and, ultimately, indescribable love of God. Finally, it may be recalled that one of the traditional symbols of Our Lord is a pelican who picks from her own flesh in order to feed her children. In the Eucharistic Sacrifice, Our Lord feeds His children in the Church with His own Body and Blood as a memorial of His immolation on Calvary. In the Eucharistic Hymn of St. Thomas Aquinas *Adoro Te Devote*, one finds this very metaphor (i.e., "O Pie Pellicane, Iesu Domine").

202. Diff II, 376.

203. DMC, 358f. Cf. also SN, 46f.

204. *Expositio Evangelii secundum Lucam* 2, 14–17 (PL 15:1158–59).

205. PL 15:1640.

206. Gambero, *Mary and the Fathers*, 197.

207. The reader will note that in the first chapter of this book, "Mary and the Development of Christian Doctrine," Newman's last sermon (15) delivered before the University of Oxford is cited wherein he begins by making an interesting parallel between Mary and Zechariah. Newman proposes that Mary's faith is of a superior nature to the faith of Zechariah precisely because, unlike Zechariah, who immediately doubted the angelic message, Mary engages in a process of reasoning: discernment of the Angel's message, followed by her full consent.

208. PPS, II, 128.

209. Zechariah's doubt and Eve's disobedience are analogous to a certain degree, but certainly not of equally grave consequence.

210. Newman is writing this sermon as an Anglican. He does not yet possess a fully Catholic belief in Mary's sinlessness enshrined in the dogma of the Immaculate Conception.

211. PPS, II, 136.

212. "Mary Freely Cooperated in God's Plan," *Mary, Mother of God*, 108. Cf.

also Cardinal Fagiolo's commentary on the Holy Father's treatment of the Mary-Zechariah parallel in *Catechesi Mariane* (Casale Monferrato: Piemme, 1998), 163–169.

213. René Laurentin writes: "Maria è il paradigma della fede? Se ne discute. Secondo Hans Urs Von Balthasar e altri teologi, sulla scorta dei padri greci, il Cristo stesso ha spinto la 'chenosi' e la serietà dell'Incarnazione fino a vivere la sua vita *umana* nella notte della fede. . . . Anche se Cristo è vissuto nella fede (controversia che non pretendo risolvere), la fede di Maria l'ha preceduto. In lei, la lunga elaborazione della fede durante i due millenni dell'Antico Testamento raggiunge la sua perfezione. In lei, la qualità *intensiva* della fede di Abramo è portata al massimo grado. Ed ella beneficia—in tutta la sua ampiezza della rivelazione di Mosè e dei profeti, in cui culmina l'ascensione eroica dei 'poveri di JHWH'. . . . Maria è il paradigma, il prototipo della fede: per la Chiesa e per ogni anima cristiana che fa nascere personalmente Dio nel suo cuore e nel mondo (sempre secondo la dottrina dei padri, studiata da A. Muller). Cf. A. Muller, *Maria-Ecclesia* (Freiburg, 1951). Il *fiat* all'annunciazione—questo supremo atto di fede—non è dunque un evento irrepetibile estraneo alla nostra vita. È l'inaugurazione condivisibile di ciò che ogni cristiano deve vivere cooperando alla nascita continuata di Cristo quaggiù. . . . La sua fede in Cristo è il punto di partenza e il vertice della fede della Chiesa nella sua adesione a Cristo e l'esemplare della fede assoluta in Dio" (*Maria Chiave del Mistero Cristiano*, 68–71, passim).

214. Diff II, 50.

215. Ibid.

216. Dev. D., 146.

217. In both instances the same text of Augustine is quoted: *De Natura et Gratia* 36, 42.

218. Diff II, 49f.

219. Diff II, 50: "words which, whatever St. Augustine's actual occasion for using them. . . ."

220. Cf. Gambero, *Mary and the Fathers*, 218–219, passim: "Augustine considers himself bound to develop a deeper understanding of the question (i.e. doctrine of predestination), in order to defend the dogma of the absolute gratuity of divine grace, in opposition to the Pelagian heresy. He concludes that this gratuity is such an essential reality that the Incarnate Word Himself, as man, is subject to divine predestination. . . . Immediately after the example of Christ comes the example of His Mother. For the Lord, in His absolute and inscrutable will, chose a Mother from whom to be born as man. She is the second in a series of events that He arranged for the realization of His plan of salvation. . . . The Virgin's future destiny depends on this supreme divine act, in which God knows and chooses her. . . . The choice of Mary was not determined by any factor on a human level. The Lord created and chose her according to His unsearchable designs. . . . Augustine thinks that God's initial choice of the Virgin was not determined by any unforseen merits of hers. Mary, then, is a pure grace of the Lord, given to the Incarnate Word and to all humanity."

221. "To Timasius against Pelagius Concerning Nature and Grace."

222. Jurgens, *The Faith of the Early Fathers* 3:110.

223. Cf. Agostino Trapè, *Sant'Agostino—Maria "Dignitas Terrae,"* ed. with introduction, notes, and commentary by Agostino Trapè (Rome: Città Nuova Editrice, 1988), 36–41, 59–67.

224. *De Natura et Gratia* 36, 42 (PL 44:267). An English translation of Augustine's text: "Having excepted the Holy Virgin Mary, concerning whom, on account of the honor of the Lord, I wish to have absolutely no question when treating of sins, for how do we know what abundance of grace for the total overcoming of sin was conferred upon her, who merited to conceive and bear Him in whom there was no sin? So, I say, with the exception of the Virgin, when they were living here, and have gathered together all those holy men and women, (when they were living here) and had asked them whether they were without sin, what do we suppose would have been their answer? Would it be what Pelagius says, or would it be what the Apostle John says? I ask you, however excellent might their holiness have been in the body, if they had been so questioned would they not have declared in a single voice: "If we say we have no sin, we deceive ourselves, and the truth is not in us" (Jurgens, *The Faith of the Early Fathers* 3:11). The commentary on this text by Agostino Trapè is worth citing here: "Celebre testo mariano sul quale si è molto discusso; forse perchè si è voluto leggervi più di quanto esso contega. Che cosa contiene? Questo: Agostino—è la cosa non può non meravigliare—fa un eccezione per Maria alla legge generale del peccato, e ne da un motivo cristologico non solo validissimo ma anche profondo e altamente significativo: *propter honorem Domini*. Ma fin dove si estende questa eccezione? Certamente fino ai peccati personali. Di questi infatti si tratta nel contesto del discorso del Pelagio, per sostenere la tesi dell'*impeccantia*, adduce l'esempio dei santi lodati nella Scrittura. Tra essi l'esempio della Madre del Signore, *della quale*, dice,— quest'aggiunta rivela l'animo suo è il senso cristiano dei fedeli—*la pietà deve confessare che non abbia avuto peccato*. Agostino, risponde a questa tesi dichiarando improbanti gli esempi addotti; con una sola eccezione: Maria. Eccezione che viene indebolita dal fatto che venga proposta sotto la forma di una interrogazione retorica. Ma si puo estenderla al peccato originale? Direttamente no, certo, ma indirettamente credo di sì. Indirettamente, dico, osservando: a) che il motivo cristologico addotto è universale e vale anche per il peccato originale; b) che per Agostino, non commettere peccati personali significa non aver avuto peccato originale (cf. *Contra Iul.* 5, 15, 57). C'è poi un testo direttamente favorevole, letto in se e nel suo contesto, all'immunità di Maria dal peccato originale in *Contra Iul.* op. imp. 4,122, anche se, esso pure, molto discusso. Sembra dunque certo che Agostino, a due leggi generali, sulle quali molto insiste, quella delle inevitabili colpe o imperfezioni personali e quella del peccato originale, abbia fatto per Maria, dietro la provocazione pelagiana, due eccezioni. Le difficoltà in contrario non sono insolubili. Quella, per esempio, proveniente dall'espressione sintomatica di *caro peccati* che Cristo o ha mondato prima di assumerla o l'ha mondata assumendola" (*De Pecc. Mer. et Rem.* 2, 24, 38).

225. Cf. DS, 1516

226. FP, 87.

227. Having listed several important biblical figures (males and females)

from both the Old and New Testaments, Augustine, while certainly in agreement with Pelagius as regarding their sanctity, will not go so far as Pelagius in declaring their sinlessness (*impeccantia*). The only exception for Augustine is Mary. "Ipsam etiam Domini ac Salvatoris nostri matrem, quam, dicit, 'sine peccato confiteri necesse esse pietati'" (*De Natura et Gratia* 36, 42).

228. Jurgens notes: "Pelagius in his *De Natura* had enumerated a considerable list of persons, mostly of the Old Testament, who were according to him, without sin. The final entry on this list is the Mother of the Lord. His basis for considering that all these people were without sin in this life was that in one connexion or another each one of them is mentioned in Scripture as being holy or righteous" (*The Faith of the Early Fathers*, 3:112).

229. See Pope John Paul II, *Mary, Mother of God*, 185. He writes: "St. Augustine already gave the Blessed Virgin the title, 'cooperator' in the redemption (cf. *De Sancta Virginitate*, 6; PL 40:399), a title which emphasizes Mary's joint but subordinate action with Christ the Redeemer." See also pages 186–87.

230. Father Gambero comments: "There seems no doubt that Augustine considered Mary's exemption from sin to be a great grace. But what sins does he mean? Undoubtedly he excludes any personal sin from Mary. Is it possible to hypothesize that Augustine also intended to exclude original sin? Some scholars think so and make him a forerunner of the doctrine of the Immaculate Conception. A full treatment of the question would call for a lengthy discussion. To us it seems safer to adopt the contrary position, which is held by many experts and appears more in accord with numerous Augustinian texts" (*Mary and the Fathers*, 226). In his note 25 on page 226, Gambero gives examples of several studies that support this latter position.

231. Diff II, 50. One need not expect Augustine to have upheld the doctrine of the Immaculate Conception in exactly the same way as it is understood in the official teaching of the Church. The doctrine would be the source of much theological debate in the years following Augustine. The scholastic debate is what finally led the Church to adopt as a satisfactory resolution of the question by adopting the Scotian teaching on prevenient grace. Even great theologians like St. Thomas Aquinas and St. Bernard of Clairvaux were unable to reconcile in their theological speculations the doctrine of the Immaculate Conception with the universality of Original Sin. Furthermore, it should be remembered that the mediævals had some faulty notions of biology, one of which was a temporal distinction between conception and animation (the direct creation of the soul by God in the individual). Until animation occurred, which was believed to happen at different stages in males and females, the individual was not considered a fully human person body and soul.

232. Diff II, 50. Original sin in Augustinian theology is explained, in part, through an understanding of the inheritance of Adam's sin which focuses on original sin as being propagated through sexual intercourse. Our Lord's virginal birth would therefore be the only exemption according to this principle when universally applied. Augustine, however, appears in this passage to have made an exception for the Virgin, at least, as regards personal sin in light of his belief that Mary was predestined unto holiness for the purpose of becoming the Mother of the Word Incarnate.

233. Cf. Kelly, *Early Christian Doctrines*, 497: "The question of her sin-lessness arose in the course of his debate with Pelagius, who had cited the Blessed Virgin as an example of a human being who had remained wholly untouched by sin by her own free will. Augustine denied the possibility for all other men (the saints themselves would have been the first to avow their sinful-ness), but agreed that Mary was the unique exception; she had been kept sinless, however, not by the effort of her own will, but as a result of a grace given her in view of the Incarnation. On the other hand, he did not hold (as has some times been alleged) that she was born exempt from all taint of original sin (the later doctrine of the Immaculate Conception). Julian of Eclanum maintained this as a clinching argument in his onslaught on the whole idea of original sin, but Augustine's rejoinder was that Mary had indeed been born subject to original sin like other human beings, but had been delivered from its effects 'by the grace of rebirth.' "

234. As concerns the question of the antithetical parallelism Eve-Mary in the writings of Augustine and its implications for the *œconomia salutis*, Agostino Trapè has this to say: "Maria è la nuova Eva. Questo confronto ci porta a considerare l'azione di Maria nel piano redentivo di Dio, Maria partecipe con Cristo della redenzione del mondo. È una tesi tradizionale, quindi non c'è nulla di nuovo in Agostino. La troviamo già nei primi scrittori, in S. Giustino (II sec), poi più tardi in maniera esplicita in Ireneo. Il Concilio, nel capitolo della Costituzione *Lumen Gentium*, dedicato a Maria, riprende questo tema e lo espone. (cf. LG 56). Questo tema c'è in Agostino, ma stando alle opere sicuramente non è molto sviluppato; mentre è sviluppato, approfondito, difeso il confronto tra Adamo e Cristo, che fa da fondamento e da la spiegazione a quello tra Eva e Maria . . . Questo raffronto tra Eva e Maria nasce dal confronto tra Adamo e Cristo, e d'altra parte da quello tra Eva e la Chiesa. Se la salvezza è incentrata su questi due uomini, e anche incentrata su Eva e la Chiesa, Eva e Maria. Da questo paragone ha origine poi la dottrina di Maria corredentrice del genere umano" (*Sant'Agostino—Maria "Dignitas Terræ,"* 42–45, passim).

235. Trapè, *Sant'Agostino Maria "Dignitas Terræ,"* 39.

236. Diff II, 92–93.

237. In the *Meditations and Devotions*, there are two separate meditations with this same title.

238. MD, 21.

239. MD, 22.

240. MD, 24f. One hears an echo of this in LG 68f., where Our Lady is considered under the heading: "certæ spei et solatii peregrinanti Populo Dei."

241. Cf. St. Augustine, *De Sancta Virg.*, 4 (PL 40:398; MC 37; RM 43).

242. Cf. Pope John Paul II, *Mary, Mother of God*, 223–25. The notion of *virginitas mentis* is mentioned by the Holy Father in reference to St. Augustine's theology relied upon by the Second Vatican Council.

243. Cf. LG 64.

244. Pope Paul VI's encyclical letter *Christi Matri* is an exhortation to take seriously his proclamation of Mary as *Mater Ecclesiæ* at the end of the third session of the Second Vatican Council by invoking her powerful, maternal intercession. In doing so, he makes reference to St. Augustine's and St. Anselm's

theology of Mary's spiritual maternity of the Church. He writes: "Vogliamo che Le siano rivolte assiduamente intense preghiere, a Lei, diciamo, che durante la celebrazione del Concilio Ecumenico Vaticano II, tra il plauso dei Padri e dell'orbe cattolico, abbiamo proclamata Madre della Chiesa, confirmando solennemente una verità dell'antica tradizione. Infatti la Madre del Salvatore è 'certamente madre delle di Lui membra' come insegnano Sant'Agostino (*De sancta virginitate* 6; PL 40:399), e con lui, omettendo gli altri, Sant'Anselmo, con queste parole: 'Quale più alta dignità si può pensare, che tu sia madre di colui dei quali Cristo si degna di essere padre e fratello?' " (PL 158:945). Text cited as found in *La Civiltà Cattolica* 4 (1976), 7.

245. Cf. Gambero, *Mary and the Fathers*, 219–221, passim: "It was to carry out this function that Mary was chosen by God. Her two prerogatives (to be both mother and virgin) define her personal relationship with the Incarnate Word and with the Church, by expressing the nature of her mission within salvation history. Augustine holds that Mary's role as Mother in the event of the Incarnation must be considered an indispensable condition for safeguarding the true faith. To the heretics who denied Mary's motherhood, supporting their claim with the fact that Jesus called her 'woman' (cf. Jn 2:4), he opposes the words of the same evangelist, who called Mary the Mother of Jesus, not once, but twice in the very same passage (cf. Jn 2:1, 3). . . . According to Augustine, the divine plan, which required Mary to collaborate as a virgin, did not exclude a free choice on her part. . . . Mary had intentionally offered her virginity to God in a kind of vow even before the Annunciation; this vow arose spontaneously from her own will, without any imposition or coercion. This act, then, would have been prompted by her feelings toward the Lord, before He made known His plans to her. By insisting on the free character of virginity consecrated to the God, Augustine accentuates its spiritual component, which gives value to the physical aspect as well. In the West, Augustine appears to be the first Father of the Church to have expressed the conviction that Mary made a vow of virginity. We know that in the East, Gregory of Nyssa thought the same way. According to Augustine, proof of this vow may be deduced from Mary's own words in response to Gabriel. Indeed he is convinced that, if Mary had intended to lead a normal conjugal life, she would not have been amazed by the angel's words."

246. *De Sancta Virginitate* 2, 2 (PL 40:397).

247. Cf. St. Augustine, *Sermo* 178, 4 (PL 38:1005). St. Augustine writes: "Today the Virgin birth is celebrated by the Virgin Church. For to her it was that the Apostle said: 'I have espoused to you one husband that I may present you as a chaste virgin to Christ' (2 Cor 2:2). Why a chaste virgin, unless because of her purity in faith, hope and charity? The Virginity, which Christ desires in the heart of the Church, he assured first in the body of Mary. But the Church could only be a virgin if she has a spouse to whom she should give herself entire; and he is a virgin's son."

248. Cf. St. Augustine, *Tract.* 1, 8; *Sermo* 25, 8; *Enarrationes in Psalmos* 127, 12 (PL 37:1685). In this last work St. Augustine writes: "She is most truly our mother, because the Church every day in Baptism brings new Christians to birth, who simply because they are Christians form the one and the only Christ."

249. Gambero, *Mary and the Fathers*, 222–224, passim: "Even though our doctor recognizes the holy Virgin's sublime dignity and her unique, privileged mission in the divine economy, he doe not hesitate to consider her a part or member of the Church. He states categorically that Mary's place is within the Church, with which she is profoundly and indissolubly linked. In a certain sense the Church is absolutely greater than Mary. . . . Taking St. Paul's theology of the Mystical Body as his point of departure, Augustine is convinced that no Christian can be outside of the body of Christ, the Church of which Christ is the Head. Mary cannot be an exception to this rule. She is the Mother of the Head on the level of the flesh, but in the order of salvation she belongs to the whole Christ, as a member, because she too, has been saved by Christ. Moreover he attributes to the Lord's Mother a certain maternal relationship with regard to all the other members of the Mystical Body. . . . Augustine preferred to conceive of Mary's spiritual motherhood as applying to the faithful as individual members of the Church, rather than toward the unity of the Mystical Body. This spiritual relationship is based on Mary's physical motherhood of Christ, the Head of the Church. Mary's motherhood and the motherhood of the Church toward the faithful are two realities that, in Augustine's thought, are often mixed together or identified outright. . . . Taking up Ambrose's line of thought, Augustine sees Mary as the type or model of the Church. Actually, he applies the term *typus* to the Church only once. . . . But the concept recurs frequently in his writings, and, in general, we can assert that it assumes important dimensions in his reflection and brings the already happy intuitions of St. Ambrose to a significant level of development."

250. Cf. LG 64: "She herself is a virgin, who keeps whole and entire the faith given to her by her spouse. Imitating the mother of her Lord, and by the power of the Holy Spirit, she keeps with virginal purity an entire faith, a firm hope and a sincere charity."

251. Cf. LG 64: "The Church indeed, contemplating her hidden sanctity, imitating her charity and faithfully fulfilling the Father's will, by receiving the Word of God in faith becomes herself a mother. By her preaching she brings forth to a new and immortal life the sons who are born to her in baptism, conceived of the Holy Spirit and born of God."

252. *De Sancta Virginitate* 6, 6 (PL 40:399). Cf. LG 53 and its citation of this text of Augustine.

253. Cf. LG 64–65. Herein the Council Fathers cite Augustine twice as evidence of the Church's belief in Mary as model and spiritual mother of the Church. Cf. St. Augustine, *In Ioannis Tractatum*, 13, 12 (PL 35:1499); *Sermo* 191, 2, 3 (PL 38:1010).

254. Cf. Kelly, *Early Christian Doctrines*, 497: "Like Ambrose, he stressed the special relationship between Mary and the Church, the one a virgin who brought forth Christ and the other a virgin who brings forth Christ's members to birth."

255. Cf. AAS 56, 1018. Pope Paul VI's Discourse at the Closing of the Third General Session of the Second Ecumenical Vatican Council in which he proclaimed Mary "Mater Ecclesiæ," on 21 November 1964. Father Raimondo Spiazzi, O.P., comments: "Come tutti i discorsi di apertura e di chiusura delle

sessioni concliari, anche quello del 21 Novembre 1964 e strettamente connesso agli atti del Concilio e anzi esso ha una particolare importanza perché espressivo della intenzione di Paolo VI di chiarire e integrare col magistero papale quello del Concilio, che in quello stesso giorno aveva votato la Costituzione Dogmatica *Lumen Gentium* su la Chiesa."—*Maria Santissima nel Magistero della Chiesa: I Documenti da Pio IX a Giovanni Paolo II* (Milan: Massimo, 1987), 218. See also AAS 58, 745: Pope Paul VI's apostolic exhortation *Signum Magnum*, written on the occasion of the 50th anniversary of the apparitions at Fatima (13 May 1967); *Insegnamenti di Paolo VI*, 6:302: Pope Paul VI's "The Credo of the People of God," written in celebration of "the Year of Faith" (30 June 1968). Spiazzi writes: "La formula mariana di Paolo VI in questo testo appartiene al magistero ordinario della Chiesa e del Papa, ma svolto in modo particolarmente solenne e impegnativo, tanto che sembra sfiorare quello straordinario. . . " (*Maria Santissima nel Magistero della Chiesa*, 236).

256. "A Great Sign." The title of Pope Paul VI's apostolic exhortation is based on Rev 12.

257. Trapè, *Sant'Agostino—Maria "Dignitas Terræ*," 47f. See also 49–50.

258. Cf. Song of Songs 4:7, "You are all-beautiful, my beloved, and there is no blemish in you." The NAB footnote for this verse reads: "Cf. St. Paul's description of the church in Eph 5, 27. This verse is also applied to Our Lady, especially in the liturgy of the feast of the Immaculate Conception. The liturgical antiphon, based on the Latin Vulgate version of this text, reads: "*Tota pulchra es, Maria; non est macula in te*." This Latin text adorns the façade of the Roman church known as "*Chiesa Nuova*," or "New Church," wherein St. Philip Neri, founder of the Congregation of the Oratory to which Cardinal Newman belonged, is buried. The official title of this Church is "*Santa Maria in Vallicella*," or "Holy Mary in the Little Valley."

259. MD, 6.

260. MD, 31. Cf. CCC 1807—on the cardinal virtue of justice.

261. MD, 32.

262. Ibid.

263. Ibid.

264. MD, 17.

265. Ibid. Admiration for the Virgin is not completely foreign to non-Christians. The Muslims, for example, have a profound respect for Our Lady, especially for her virginity. This is evident in the Koran. Cf. Jaroslav Pelikan, *Mary through the Centuries: Her Place in the History of Culture* (New Haven, Conn.: Yale University Press, 1985), 67–79. See also *Jesus Christ and Mary: In the Noble Qur'an* (Istanbul, Turkey: Call to Unity Publications, 2000), 10–18.

266. MD, 19.

267. MD, 61. Cf. CCC 1808—on the cardinal virtue of fortitude.

268. Cf. Augustine's *Sermo* 196, 1 (PL 38:1019).

269. Cf. Lk 8:20: "You mother and your brethren are standing outside, desiring to see you." Cf. also Pope John Paul II, *Mary, Mother of God*, 106.

270. Trapè, *Sant'Agostino—Maria "Dignitas Terræ*," 48f. Cf. also 49–54. Pope John Paul II, in his apostolic letter commemorating the fifteenth centenary of Augustine's conversion, relying on Augustine's *Sermo* 22, 10 and *De*

Cath. Rud. 15, 23, makes the following observations: "La Chiesa dunque è madre: due infatti ci hanno generato per la morte, Adamo ed Eva, e due per la vita, Cristo e la Chiesa. Madre, ma anche vergine. Come Maria. Madre per l'ardore della carità, poichè la carità "a nessuno è nemica e a tutti è madre," vergine per l'integrità della fede che è appunto la verginità della mente, la più preziosa, la più necessaria" (as cited in Trapè, 39f.).

271. Cf. Pope John Paul II, *Mary, Mother of God*, 179–181. Also, LG 58: "In the course of her Son's preaching she received the words whereby, in extolling a kingdom beyond the calculations and bonds of flesh and blood, he declared blessed (cf. Mk 3:35, par.; Lk 11:27–28) those who heard and kept the Word of God, as she was faithfully doing (cf. Lk 2:19,51)."

272. Father Serra comments: "Maria fu vicinissima a Dio perchè, insegna sant'Agostino, portò Gesù più nel cuore che nel grembo. Grande cosa fu per la Santa Vergine allattare il Figlio dell'Altissimo, ma cosa ancor più grande fu per lei l'essersi nutrita di quel mistico latte che è la parola di Dio" (cf. Serra, *Maria di Nazaret*, 57f.). In note 12 on page 58 of the aforementioned work, Serra cites Augustine's *De sancta virginitate*, 3: "[Maria] se fu beata per aver concepito il corpo di Cristo, lo fu maggiormente per aver accettato la fede nel Cristo. . . . Di nessun valore sarebbe stata per lei la stessa divina maternità, se lei il Cristo non l'avesse portato nel cuore, con una sorte più fortunata di quando lo concepì nella carne." Cf. PL 40:398. Also, Sant'Agostino, *Matrimonio e Verginità*, trans. V. Tarulli (Rome: Città Nuova, 1978), 77.

273. Lk 11:28. Cf. Lk 8:21: "My mother and my brethren are those who hear the Word of God and do it."

274. FP, 86. Cf. Diff II, 36.

275. FP, 86f.

276. FP, 87.

277. Cf. St. Augustine, *Sermo 13 in Nat. Dom.*; *Sermo 293*.

278. FP, 92.

279. Trapè, *Sant'Agostino—Maria "Dignitas Terræ,"* 27f.

280. FP, 86–89, passim.

281. Jean Guitton, *Il Secolo Che Verrà*, trans. Antonietta Francavilla (Milan: Saggi Tascabili Bompiani, 1999), 144. Cf. Gambero, *Mary and the Fathers*, 217 (under the section entitled "A Mariology for the Future"). Father Gambero notes: "The extraordinary genius of the bishop of Hippo is also evident in his relfections on the mystery of the Lord's Mother. He continued the tradition of Marian theology, which had already reached considerable heights in other Fathers before and contemporary with him, while also leaving the impress of his own understanding, influenced by the originality of his great conversion experience. His intuitions and perspectives on Marian doctrine are singularly profound and anticipate the statements of the Second Vatican Council. Suffice it to say that Augustine is the Father of the Church most often cited by the Council and that citations of or references to his works and teaching are to be found in almost all of the conciliar documents. In his Marian doctrine, which anticipates the perspectives of Vatican II by centuries, Augustine examines the Blessed Virgin in relation to the mystery of her Son and to the Church; this allows him to give the proper place to her person and mission within salvation history."

282. Cf. Diff II, 137. Boyce writes: "The only real objection which Newman knows against the doctrine was the fact that some eminent Fathers of the fourth century, such as Origen, Tertullian, St Basil, St Chrysostom and St Cyril of Alexandria, thought that our Lady did become a victim to some of the infirmities of our nature by committing slight imperfections or venial sins (such as initial doubt) at the moment of the Annunciation and under the Cross. Consequently, Newman added a lengthy examination of these texts in the published volume of his *Letter to Pusey*. He shows that these were mere personal opinions of individual Fathers and not indications of a living and widespread tradition in the Church (cf. *Difficulties of Anglicans*, II, Note III, pp. 128–152). On this question one can get a fuller summary in Domenico Bertetto, *Maria la Serva del Signore: Trattato di Mariologia* (Napoli, 1988), pp. 88–108." See *Mary in the Writings of JHN*, 54, note 9. Father Velocci clarifies the nature of Newman's position vis-à-vis the erroneous interpretations of Sts. Basil, Chrysostom, and Cyril concerning some key Marian passages of Scripture. "Newman ribatte vigorosamente a tali affermazioni, dimostrando, con argomentazione serrata e convincente che tale contesto i suddetti Padri parlano solo come teologi privati ed esprimono soltanto un loro pensiero" (*Il Coraggio*, 147).

283. The reader, obviously, should understand Father Toniolo's reference to "the impulses of the flesh and of blood" as referring to the possibility of Mary having been exposed to and to her having overcome temptations, not to her having had to overcome concupiscence, from which she was exempt.

284. Ermanno Toniolo, "Padri della Chiesa," NDM, 1064f.

285. HS, 288f.

286. Newman gives only his own translation of Chrysostom in the *Letter to Pusey*; he does not give the actual Greek text or even a Latin translation. Nevertheless, Newman's English translation of Chrysostom in the *Letter to Pusey* is based on the Greek text and not on a Latin translation since he refers, where he deems necessary, to actual Greek terms used by Chrysostom. The texts which Newman cites as follows: *In Matth. Hom iv*; *In Matth. Hom xliv* (cf. also *In Joann. Hom. xxi*). Cf. PG 57:40–54; 59:127–134; also, *In Joann. Hom. xxii* (PG 59:133–138).

287. *In Matth. Hom. iv*. Cf. Diff II, 130.

288. Diff II, 133f.

289. Diff II, 134.

290. Ibid.

291. *In Matth. Hom. iv*. Cf. Diff II, 130.

292. Diff II, 134.

293. Of course, this preparation is begun from the very moment of her conception and consists in her being "full of grace"—as the Angel addresses her at the Annunciation.

294. *In Matth. Hom. iv*. Cf. Diff II, 131. Cf. also Diff II, 134 ("ministered to the mystery").

295. AP, 239. This quotation is cited by CCC 157. The *Catechism* also cites Newman at numbers 1723, 1778, and 2144. See also the following works of Newman: *Discourses to Mixed Congregations*, 5, on holiness; *Letter to the Duke of Norfolk*, 5; *Parochial and Plain Sermons*, 5, 2, pp. 21–22.

296. Chrysostom makes a distinction between what he considers an imperfection and that which he would consider sinful. Newman does not see how such a distinction can be made.

297. *In Matth. Hom. xliv.* Cf. Diff II, 131 (PG 57:463–466).

298. *In Matth. Hom. xliv.* Cf. Diff II, 132 (PG 57:463–466): "οὐδε γὰρ ἐξαπορῶσαι θέλων, ἀλλ᾽ ἀπαλλάξαι τοῦ τυραννιχωτάτου πάθους, καὶ κατὰ μικρὸν ἐναγγεῖν εἰς τὴν προσήκουαν περὶ αὐτοῦ ἔννοισαν, καὶ πεῖσαι ὅτι οὐχὶ υἱὸς αὐτῆς μόνον ἐστὶν, ἀλλὰ καὶ Δεσπότης."

299. Diff II, 134.

300. Diff II, 135f.

301. St. Thomas Aquinas, who throughout his works, especially in his *Summa Theologica*, heavily relies on the scriptural commentary (among other writings) of Chrysostom, summarily dismisses St. John Chysostom's negative criticism of the Virgin as revealed in his exegesis of certain Marian texts (e.g., those discussed by Newman in the *Letter to Pusey*) with the following terse statement: "In verbis illis Chrysostomus excessit." See *Summa Theologica*, III, q. 27, a. 4 ad 3.

302. Diff II, 136.

303. Ibid. Newman's statement about not having explicit proof of the Marian devotion of Sts. Basil, Cyril and Chrysostom to the Virgin is best understood in conjunction with Newman's distinction, proposed throughout the *Letter to Pusey*, between doctrine and devotion. In his discussion with Pusey about the necessity of direct devotion to or invocation of Mary for salvation, Newman writes: "If it were so, there would be grave reasons for doubting of the salvation of St. Chrysostom or St. Athanasius, of the primitive martyrs; nay, I should like to know whether St. Augustine, in all his voluminous writings, invokes her once" (Diff II, 105) Nevertheless, with all due respect to Newman's distinction between doctrine and devotion (see Chapter One), it would seem, taking in consideration what Newman writes (cf. for example, Diff II, 50, 65, 67, 149f.), that one could also be led to attribute to these Fathers at least an implicit devotion arising from their doctrinal considerations, even if this devotion was not explicitly mentioned in their writings as such and/or found under the form of direct Marian invocation. It seems, at times, that too strict a separation between doctrine and devotion can lead some to make a faulty line of demarcation between the two, thus forcing a separation between the head and the heart in both doctrinal and spiritual matters.

304. Diff II, 136.

305. The role of women in first-century Palestine is a widely debated topic that is beyond the scope of this book.

306. Cf. Diff II, 141: PG 59:127–134.

307. Cf. John Chrysostom, *In Joann. Hom. XXI* (PG 59:129): "Ἄξιον ἐνταῦθα ζητῆναι περὶ τοῦ παιδός. Οὐδὲ γὰρ σημεῖ   ον ἦν τι πεποιηκώς

308. Cf. John Chrysostom, *In Joann. Hom. XXII* (PG 59:134): Εἰ γὰρ ὑπέκειτο, πῶς ἂν τῆς προσηκούσης ὥρας μὴ παραγενομένης ἔπαξεν; Ἔπειτα δε καὶ τιμῶν τὴν μητέρα. . . .

309. Cf. John Chrysostom, *In Joann. Hom. XXI* (PG 59:131).

310. Cf. Friedel, *The Mariology of Cardinal Newman*, 246f.: "Newman views the question first in the light of the Fathers. St. Athanasius, with Chrysostom

and Theophylact, sees here a rebuke to the Blessed Virgin. Chrysostom even seems to consider the Virgin guilty of a slight sin of vain-glory on this occasion. Athanasius holds the words as a proof of Our Lord's humanity, since He appeared to decline a miracle; while other Fathers see there a reminder that He is the Son of God. Irenæus thinks Mary was rebuked because of her eagerness to drink of His cup."

311. Diff II, 141.

312. Cf. Friedel, *The Mariology of Cardinal Newman*, 246f.: "This passage has ever aroused the interest of Scripture students from the days of Augustine and Chrysostom, and various explanations have been offered. Newman derives his from St. Augustine" (cf. *Selected Treatises of Athanasius* 2:277). Cf. also the article "Il Vangelo di Giovanni nell'Esegesi di Agostino," by Gætano Lettieri in *Letture Patristiche: La Bibbia nei Padri della Chiesa: Il Nuovo Testamento*, ed. Mario Naldini (Bologna: Edizioni Dehoniane, 2000), 64: "Significativa in proposito l'interpretazione allegorica delle nozze di Cana: Cristo è la potenza di grazia capace di tramutare l'acqua della natura umana (o delle stesse profezie ancora prive del Senso rivelato che le svela) nel vino della creatura redenta (o di Cristo Redentore e della Trinità, Dio della grazia), che rivela il Nuovo Testamento: cf. *Tr Ioh* 8, 3 e 9, 1–17)."

313. Diff II, 147.

314. Ibid.

315. Ibid.

316. Cf. Diff II, 147f. Newman makes a brief list of examples of "successive outbreaks of heresy" in the Antiochean school, starting from Paul of Samosata to Diodorus, a teacher of Chrysostom at Antioch, and finally, to a classmate of Chrysostom's by the name of Theodore. Newman advises Pusey to consult his *Essay on the Development of Christian Doctrine* (chapter 5, section 2) for more information. What is of most pertinence to our present discussion is Newman's illustration of the continuity of principles in terms of how a certain theological school arrives at certain doctrinal conclusions based on its principles or rules of "scriptural interpretation," and other doctrinal, spiritual or philosophical principles. (Cf. Dev. D., 179f.). See also CCC 465. Also, LD, 14:361–370. Boyce, *Mary in the Writings of JHN*, 321: ". . . denied by the Synod of Antioch in 268 because the term was used in a false sense by Paul of Samosata who took it to mean that the Son was not really a person of His own, distinct from the Father."

317. Diff II, 149.

318. Cf. Gambero, *Mary and the Fathers*, 143–149, passim: "Those of his texts that hold the greatest of interest for Marian doctrine are the *Homily on the Generation of Christ* and *Letter* 260. . . . Mary is called to collaborate with God's almighty power by offering her own body. Basil, with a sense of profound realism, calls Mary's womb a 'workshop': 'But what is the workshop [*ergastrion*] of this economy? The body of a holy Virgin. And what are the (active) principles of this birth? The Holy Spirit and the overshadowing power of the Most High.' . . . The bishop of Cæsarea considers that the consensus of the faithful is more than sufficient argument to establish that the perpetual virginity of the Mother of God is an indispensable requirement of ecclesial faith. . . . In the homily on the generation of Christ, our author shows that he is very interested

in the Virgin's marriage to St. Joseph. he justifies it by referring to well-known arguments, drawn from the writings of Origen. Among others, he offers the witness of St. Ignatius of Antioch. . . . But the motivations that Basil stresses are primarily those of a moral character. He wishes, above all, to affirm the religious character of Christian marriage. . . . The marriage also had the purpose of creating a context that protected and safeguarded the virginity of Jesus' Mother. . . . Basil does not make any explicit statements about the Virgin Mother's holiness. He limits himself to calling her holy, to recalling her purity and perseverance in holy virginity. In a homily, he stresses her poverty. . . . However, he considers himself justified in affirming that the Virgin's holiness was not totally without shadow. He refers to the doubt she suffered at the moment of her Son's Passion, which Simeon had foretold, using the metaphor of the sword. . . . Like the disciples, Mary also doubted at the foot of the Cross. But Jesus strengthened the faith of His disciples and His Mother, so that she subsequently became a shining example of faith. In conclusion, we can perceive how the bishop of Cæsarea preferred to bring Mary's role within the context of the mystery of the Incarnation, instead of praising her attributes or her personal merits. In this perspective, we can see how this Marian thought was essentially shaped by Christology, from which it draws its confidence and vigor."

319. St. John Chrysostom has just been treated.

320. Diff II, 135. Cf. CCC 489.

321. Diff II, 29. For original text, see PG 32:953–968.

322. Cf. Diff II, 129.

323. Mt 26:31.

324. Newman refers to Origen as the first among the early theologians to give a particular interpretation to the mention of the sword in Simeon's prophecy. Cf. Diff II, 144.

325. Diff II, 143.

326. Ibid.

327. Diff II, 143f.

328. Diff II, 144. Newman observes: "St. Cyril, who, though an Alexandrian as well as Origen, represents a very different school of theology, has, as we have seen, the same interpretation for the piercing sword" (Diff II, 144). Cf. PG 72: 505–506.

329. Cf. Diff II, 135.

330. Diff II, 133. The text is cited by Newman as: St. Cyril *in Joann.* lib. xii., 1064 (PG 74:661–665).

331. NDM, 1066.

332. Diff II, 135.

333. Diff II, 144.

334. Diff II, 148.

335. Diff II, 143.

336. Diff II, 144.

337. Friedel synthetically presents Newman's criteria and applications of the principles in Diff II, 137–143 for determining whether or not a particular teaching, especially that of a Father of the Church (e.g., scriptural interpretation), is consonant with or contrary to the Apostolic Tradition. "1. The Fathers not only

represent the people or countries for which they write, but they must witness to an uninterrupted tradition handed down from the Apostles; if they do not, their testimony is of no value. 2. In its *matter* the tradition must be a *positive* belief, whether the proposition itself be affirmative or negative. Thus 'Christ is God,' is an example of an affirmative tradition; 'no one born of woman is in God's favor' represents a negative tradition. 3. Before any tradition has weight, it needs interpretation. 4. Traditions are explicit or implicit. 5. A tradition may be determined as apostolical, *a*. When credible witnesses declare it such. *b*. When independent witnesses enunciate one and the same doctrine. The application of these principles follows most naturally. Newman deduces the tradition of Mary's sinlessness as apostolical from the tradition of the 'second Eve,' which has, as he affirms, one of the two tests prescribed and which is an explicit tradition, whereas that of Mary's sinlessness is implicit, contained in the doctrine that she is the New Eve" (Friedel, *The Mariology of Cardinal Newman*, 283f.). These criteria should also be read with an eye to what has been said in Chapter One concerning Newman's seven principles of authentic doctrinal development as found in his *Essay* and his twelve principles of dogmatic evolution.

338. Diff II, 137.

339. Friedel, *The Mariology of Cardinal Newman*, 284f.

340. Ephrem is nicknamed "the harp of the Spirit." Owen Cummings observes that "in 1920, Pope Benedict XV made Ephrem a Doctor of the Church and said of him: 'The harp of the Holy Spirit never sings sweeter songs than when he has set strings to sing the praises of Mary.' Marist [sic] theologian Bertrand Buby compares Ephrem with Hans Urs von Balthasar in his appreciation of the beautiful and the aesthetic, calling him 'Mary's first poet' " ("The Mariology of St. Ephrem," in *Lay Witness*, December 1998, 38). Patrick J. Hamell makes this assessment: "His poems are doctrinal, moral, polemical, liturgical, poems of Nisibis, etc. and 'his harp resounds to the praises of Mary more frequently than that of any other poet or orator of Christian antiquity. He loves to sing of her stainless virginity, her truly divine maternity, her freedom from sin' (Bardenhewer)": *Handbook of Patrology* (New York: Alba House, 1968), 125. Sebastian Brock, in *The Harp of the Spirit: Eighteen Poems of Saint Ephrem*, makes this evaluation: "Among the Syriac poets . . . one stands out head and shoulders above all others, St. Ephrem, described recently as 'the greatest poet of the patristic age and, perhaps, the only theologian-poet to rank beside Dante.' Ephrem is a poet who combined an astonishing technical artistry with a richness of imagery that is at times quite breath-taking in its application. Living at a time before the Syriac-speaking churches had undergone any extensive hellenization, he is one of the few surviving representatives of a truly Semitic Christianity, and throughout his writing he displays that characteristically Semitic love of parallelism and antithesis, which, in his hands, proves a tool admirably suited to the expression of the various paradoxes of the Christian mystery" (Fellowship of St. Alban and St. Sergius, 1983, 6).

341. Diff II, 39f.

342. In the *Letter to Pusey*, Newman relied on Greek and Latin translations of Ephrem's Syriac texts, found in *Omnia Opera Patrum Syriacorum* (six volumes). However, as concerns the writings of Ephrem which are cited in this work and

that are not found in the *Letter to Pusey*, I have relied on contemporary English translations based on the original Syriac texts.

343. De Margerie makes a helpful contribution when he writes: "Ephrem's exegetical universe is precise and consistent in some instances, but rather lyrical, vague and imprecise in others. It does not seem to have been his principal concern to read and explain what the human author or even what the divine author meant or did not mean, but rather what his inspired text suggests to the believing reader whose concern is to read it within the analogy of the Church's faith. To be sure, Ephrem is not the only one of the Fathers to leave us with this impression. But it is more accentuated in this case, and we cannot deny that the interpretations he offers and especially the comparisons he makes generally give some insight into the sense that the divine author wished to communicate to us" (*A History of Exegesis: The Greek Fathers*, 1:147).

344. Cummings, "The Mariology of St. Ephrem," 38.

345. Cf. St. Ephrem, *Evangelii Concordantis Expositio*, ed. Moesignor, p. 49, as found in Hugo Ranher, *Our Lady and the Church*, ix. Ephrem writes: "Mother Earth it was that bore all flesh, and for the sake of the flesh that is the Church incorruptible, this fleshly earth was blessed from the beginning for Mary was the Mother Earth that brought the Church to birth."

346. Cummings, "The Mariology of St. Ephrem," 39.

347. *St. Ephrem the Syrian, Hymns on Paradise*, trans. Sebastian Brock (New York: St. Vladimir's Seminary Press, 1990), 99, hymn 4, 5.

348. Cummings, "The Mariology of St. Ephrem," 39.

349. De Margerie, *A History of Exegesis: The Greek Fathers*, 1:144f.

350. Brock notes: "The terms 'symbol' (the Syriac word literally means "mystery") and 'type' are recurrent in Ephrem's poetry, and it is they which provide the key to his understanding of the Bible—and indeed of Creation as whole. Perhaps no other writer has ever put typological exegesis to such creative use, employing it to provide an intricate network of links between the two Testaments, between this world and the heavenly world. (Brock, *The Harp of the Spirit*, 11).

351. Cf. Ephrem, *Diatessaron* (Syr. Arm.), SC 121:66: 2:2. Cf. Epiphanius of Salamis, *Panarion* 3, 2, 78 (PG 42:728–729). Epiphanius writes: "Eve looks forward to Mary, and her very name 'Mother of all the living' (Gen 3:20) is a mysterious presage of the future, for life itself was born of Mary, where she became more fully 'the Mother of all the living.' . . . Nor can we see the passage 'I will put enmities between between thee and the woman' (Gen 3:15) as applying to Eve alone: it received its true fulfillment when that holy and unique One came, born of Mary without work of man. . . . And then there is that other text nearby 'Wherefore a man shall leave father and mother, and shall cleave to his wife, and they shall be two in one flesh.' (Gen 2:24), and this also we can understand of Mary, and I would even say, of the Church, for the Apostle says of this passage, 'This is a great mystery—I mean in reference to Christ and to the Church' (Eph 5:32). His own body He fashioned from Mary, and the Church He fashioned from the wound in His own side, when the spear pierced His breast and there flowed out for us the twin redeeming mysteries of the water and the blood."

352. Once again Brock is helpful: "A good example of the way in which St. Ephrem often used typology in the course of his extended meditations on Scripture is provided by his treatment of the verse in St. John's Gospel, 'One of the soldiers pierced the side of Jesus with a lance and from it there immediately came forth blood and water' (19:34). The 'side' and the 'lance' for Ephrem, point back to the opening chapters of Genesis, to Adam's 'side' that miraculously gave birth to Eve, and to the 'sword' that barred the entrance of Paradise to fallen Adam and Eve (Ephrem often use the same word for both weapons); the 'blood and the water,' on the other hand, point forward to the sacraments, to Baptism and the Eucharist (the order of the two words in John 19:34 is often reversed). We are thus provided with the pattern: Adam's side : Eve :: Christ's side : Church. Adam's side gave birth to Eve, at whose listening to the evil counsel of the serpent the primordial pair were stripped of their original 'robe of glory' and banished from Paradise, kept out by the revolving sword of fire. A second weapon undoes this damage, by piercing another side, from which 'flow forth' (Ephrem sometimes deliberately uses the word 'flow,' borrowed from John 7:38) the two sacraments that wash away sin and effect the potential re-entry of the baptized into Paradise, enabling them to feed on Christ the Tree of Life, Baptism having clothed them once again in that 'robe of glory' which Adam and Eve had lost at the Fall. Eve's miraculous 'birth' from Adam's side is in turn linked typologically with Mary's miraculous birth of Christ, thus providing the chiastic pattern: Adam : Eve :: Mary : Christ" (second Adam).—Brock, *The Harp of the Spirit*, 11.

353. Cf. Ephrem, *Hymns of Paradise*, SC 137:xii, 15–16, 161–162.

354. Gambero, *Mary and the Fathers*, 115.

355. *Nuovo Dizionario di Mariologia* offers the following: "Sotto il profilo mariano, egli è insieme antico e nuovo: veste infatti di immagini liriche i contenuti tradizionali di fede. Riprendendo ad esempio, l'antico parallelismo Eva–Maria, paragona le protagoniste della storia umana ai due occhi del corpo: "Guarda il mondo: due occhi ha avuto: Eva, l'occhio sinistro, quello cieco; Maria, occhio luminoso, quello destro. Per colpa dell'occhio sinistro si ottenebrò il mondo e rimase nel buio. . . . Ma mediante Maria, occhio destro, s'illuminò il mondo con la luce celeste che abitò in lei, e gli uomini ritrovarono l'unità" (NDM, 1060). Cf. *Inni sulla chiesa*, 37 (CSCO 199:90).

356. Thus, Gambero: "Mary and Eve are like a kind of eye for the world, yet how different one is from the other! While the one eye is closed to the light, the other radiates splendor on all men, who in this way will retrieve their lost unity" (*Mary and the Fathers*, 116).

357. Cignelli writes: "Efrem interpreta il Protovangelo in senso cristologico-mariologico e sottolinea il carattere libero e meritorio della partecipazione di Maria all'opera redentrice. La azione salvifica della Vergine abbraccia sia il proprio sesso che l'intera umanità: essa ripara l'operato di Eva, ne provoca la guarigione e benefica per tutte le donne. . . . Egli poi, come Origene, mette in luce la dipendenza di Maria dal Cristo, Figlio e Sposo, sia nell'essere che nell' operare. La Vergine deve al Cristo salvatore tutto il suo splendore di santità, e non è sotericamente attiva che in forza del suo legame con lui" (*Maria Nuova Eva nella Patristica Greca*, 49).

358. "Davvero, Gesù, tu e tua madre siete i soli ad essere bellissimi in tutto. In te infatti, O Signore, non esiste difetto alcuno; né vi è macchia nella tua madre" (*Carmi nisibeni* 27, 8; CSCO 219:76). Cf. also Gambero, *Mary and the Fathers*, 109 –111.

359. Jn 1:9.

360. Cited by Newman as *Opp. Syr.* ii. p. 318. Cf. Diff II, 121. "Through Eve, the beautiful and desirable glory of men was extinguished; but it has revived through Mary" (Diff II, 39).

361. Cited by Newman as *Opp. Syr.* iii. p. 607. Cf. Diff II, 121f. Newman's translation: "In the beginning, by the sin of our first parents, death passed upon all men; to-day, through Mary we are translated from death unto life. In the beginning, the serpent filled the ears of Eve, and the poison spread thence over the whole body, to-day, Mary from her ears received the champion of eternal happiness: what, therefore, was an instrument of death, was an instrument of life also" (Diff II, 39f.).

362. Brock, *The Harp of the Spirit*, 66.

363. PPS, II, 128–130, passim.

364. Brock, *Harp of the Spirit*, 62. Cf. NDM, 1060; *Carmina* 'Sogita,' 1, 4: CSCO 187:179. Ephrem's words, "not shrinking from such a home," express the theological truth one finds in the words of the *Te Deum*, "non horruisti Virginis uterum," which, as has already been pointed out, are mentioned by Newman in his praise of Our Lord's Incarnation, as well as Mary's Divine Motherhood and Perpetual Virginity. Cf. Gambero, *Mary and the Fathers*, 113: "It seems that Ephrem thought of virginity as a prerogative of Mary's person. The prophesies and symbols of the Old Testament prefigured her in this light. The virgin earth that gave birth to Adam, the virgin Eve, the bush, burning yet unconsumed, that Moses saw on Mount Sinai, the famous prohecy of Isaiah, and other figures as well are to be applied to Mary's virginity. Finally, in Jesus' Resurrection from the tomb, Ephrem perceives a posthumous confirmation of His virginal birth from Mary."

365. Cf. PPS, II, 297: "Such is the Creator in His Eternal Uncreated Beauty, that, were it given to us to behold it, we should die of very rapture at the sight. Moses, unable to forget the token of it he had once seen in the Bush, asked to see it fully, and on this very account was refused. 'He said, Show me Thy glory; and He said, Thou canst not see My Face; for man shall not see Me and live.'"

366. Cf. MD, 13–14. This meditation is here only mentioned in passing since it is discussed at greater length in Chapter Four: "Newman's Understanding of Mary's Cooperation in the *Œconomia Salutis* as *Theotokos* and New Eve."

367. PPS, II, 36.

368. PPS, II, 36f. See also CCC 465–483, especially 465 and 471.

369. *Liturgia Horarum*, vol. 1 (Editio Typica Altera, Vatican City: Libreria Editrice Vaticana, 1985), 411.

370. Brock, *Harp of the Spirit*, 65. Ephrem's words "which for our sakes leaned down . . ," express the doctrine contained in the Nicene-Constantinoplitan Creed: "Qui propter nos homines et propter nostram salutem descendit de cælis. Et incarnatus est de Spiritu Sancto ex Maria Virgine, et homo factus est." Indeed, the Church instructs to make a profound bow (a genuflection on

the Solemnities of the Annunciation and Christmas) at these words. Thus, the condescension of the Word Incarnate is appropriately acknowledged by a concrete physical action which expresses our profound humility before the humility of our God Who has become in Christ "bone of our bone, flesh of our flesh."

371. The first antiphon of First Vespers for the Solemnity of the Holy Mother of God for the present Liturgy of the Hours in the Roman rite reads: "O admirabile commercium! Creator generis humani, animatum corpus sumens, de Virgine nasci dignatus est; et, procedens homo sine semine, largitus est nobis suam Deitatem" (*Liturgia Horarum*, 1:411).

372. Brock, *Harp of the Spirit*, 67.

373. The Evangelist John carefully worded his Prologue in Greek to express the divine intimacy with which the Second Person of the Blessed Trinity is eternally present in the bosom of the Eternal Father. Thus, the preposition πρoς (πρoς τov Θεov) underscores Christ's eternal presence in the inner life of the Trinity as one of perpetual movement toward the Father. Hence, it is also common among theologians to refer to the *perichoresis* of the Trinitarian Persons in relationship to each Other.

374. PPS, II, 38–40, passim.

375. Cf. St. Ephrem, *Hymns of the Unleavened Bread*, 6, 6–7.

376. St. Ephrem, *Hymns on Faith*, 10, 17.

377. Cummings, "The Mariology of Ephrem," 39.

378. PPS, VI, 151.

379. Ibid. Cf. Jn 20:28.

380. DMC, 376.

381. *St. Ephrem: Hymns on the Nativity*, no. 11 (verses 6–8). *Ephrem the Syrian Hymns*, trans. Kathleen E. McVey (New York: Paulist Press, 1989), 132.

382. Just as the Incarnation is understood by Newman in this sermon as a "pledge of our future birth," unto eternal salvation through spiritual rebirth at Baptism, so too does the Church reflect on the Eucharist as the pledge of our future glory at the eternal wedding feast of the lamb. For example, an ancient prayer of the Church reads: "O Sacrum Convivium, in quo Christus sumitur, recolitur memoria passionis ejus; mens impletur gratia et futuræ gloriæ nobis pignus datur." Cf. CCC 1402.

383. PPS, V, 87–92, passim. In Sermon VII, "The Mystery of Godliness," Newman makes several allusions to or actual citations of Sacred Scripture, for example, Gen 3:15; Is 7:14; Mt 1:23; Lk 1:28–35; Jn 1:5; Gal 4:4; Eph 1:3–14; 1 Tim 6:16; Heb 5:3; 7:26–28; Rev 19:7–8.

384. PPS, V, Sermon VII, 92f., passim. The Collect for Christmas of which Newman speaks is one of the optional collects for Christmas in the present Book of Common Prayer. Its traditional rendering is: "Almighty God, Who hast given us thy only-begotten Son to take our nature upon Him and at this time to be born of a pure virgin: Grant that we, being regenerate and made thy children by adoption and grace, may daily be renewed by thy Holy Spirit; through the same our Lord Jesus Christ, Who liveth and reigneth with thee and the same Spirit ever, one God, world without end. Amen."—*The Book of Common Prayer* (New York: Oxford University Press, 1990), 161. In this text, Newman makes several allusions to or actual quotations of Sacred Scripture, for

example, Rom 5:12, 15; 1 Cor 15:21; Eph 5:25–27; Col 1:3–23; 3:16; 1 Pet 1:15, 19; 2 Pet 1:4.

385. Diff II, 67.

386. Brock, *Harp of the Spirit*, 59f. (stanzas 1, 3, 4). Compare use of poetic metaphor and other images to Hippolytus' text entitled *The Blessing of Moses*. Hippolytus writes: " 'Moses said: 'Through God's blessing His land shall remain His own, and be blessed with the dew of heaven' (cf. Deut 33:13). This was said of Mary, who was the blessed land, and the Word was made flesh, coming down as the dew. But it can also be said of the Church, for she is blest by the Lord as a holy land and a paradise of bliss, and the dew is the Lord, the Redeemer Himself. For this holy land has inherited all the Lord's blessings from the holy House, from the Virgin birth, as these latter ages have shown"—*Texte und Untersuchungen* 266, p. 66.

387. Brock, *Harp of the Spirit*, 60 (stanza 5).

388. MD, 15.

389. MD, 16.

390. Giorgio Zevini, *Commenti Spirituali del Nuovo Testamento: Vangelo secondo Giovanni* (Rome: Città Nuova Editrice, 1992), 1:64. Cf. Ex 25:8; 40:35; Ezra 37:27; Joel 4:17; Jn 1:14.

391. MD, 33.

392. Ibid. John Keble's poem is entitled "The Purification," and is found in *The Christian Year*, 282f.

393. MD, 52.

394. Ibid.

CHAPTER FOUR

1. Cf. F. Friedel, "Mother of God and Second Eve," *Catholic World* 141 (1935), 228–229; Carleton Jones, O.P., *John Henry Newman and Mary: Mother of God, the New Eve*, an address to the annual conference of the New England region of the Mariological Society of America, at Providence College, 19 October 1996.

2. Cf. Peter M. J. Stravinskas, *Our Sunday Visitor's Catholic Dictionary* (Huntington, Ind.: Our Sunday Visitor Publications, 1993), 188; *Lexicon: Dizionario Teologico Enciclopedico* (Casale Monferrato: Piemme, 1993), 336f; Gerald O'Collins and Edward G. Ferrugia, eds., *Dizionario Sintetico di Teologia* (Vatican City: Libreria Editrice Vaticana, 1995), 121; "Oikonomía" in *Theological Dictionary of the New Testament*, one volume, abridged version by Geoffrey W. Bromiley (Grand Rapids, Mich.: Eerdmans & Company, 1985), 689.

3. Cf. Gerard Magil, "Newman's Personal Reasoning: The Inspiration of the Early Church," *Irish Theological Quarterly* 58.1 (1992), 307: "The principle of economy in the early Church fascinated Newman. He was attracted to the Alexandrian Church whose teachings were based upon the 'various Economies or Dispensations of the Eternal' (*Apologia* 36). That is, the theological doctrines of that Church were consciously limited expressions of divine mystery (revelation) in human language (ecclesial doctrine). Hence, the principle of economy expressed the sacramental character of theology" (308).

4. PPS, II, 32.

5. DMC, 368f. Cf. Rom 11:16.

6. PPS, II, 27.

7. DMC, 300.

8. DMC, 302. In the context of Newman's description of Our Lord's Passion, reference is made to the image of the suffering servant of Yahweh in Isaiah 53, especially to verses 2, 3, and 4 from which he quotes as follows: " 'He hath no beauty or comeliness; He is despised and the most abject of men, a Man of sorrows and acquainted with infirmity;' nay, He is a 'leper, and smitten of God, and afflicted.' "

9. DMC, 300.

10. Ibid.

11. MD, 300.

12. DMC, 300.

13. Cf. CCC 465–483, 495. Newman's emphasis on the reality of Christ's Sacred humanity not only reaffirms the natural ties of Our Lord to the Blessed Virgin in terms of physical resemblance but it also should be understood as an affirmation, although not expressly so in this instance, of the Church's teaching on the human will of Christ against the heresy of Monothelitism (DS, 550–552, 553–559). Hence, his reference in the sermon to "the operations of a human soul" in the hypostatic union (cf. DMC, 300).

14. The teaching of the Church concerning the Sacred Humanity of Christ as really and truly being formed of Mary the Virgin by the power of the Holy Spirit was already asserted by the insertion of Mary into the Nicean-Constantinopolitan Creed at the Council of Constantinople I in 381. This insertion is of fundamental Christological and Mariological importance: "Esprime una essenzialità dottrinale circa l'apporto materno dato da Maria all'Incarnazione del Verbo . . . e la sua opera salvifica . . . la persona di Maria risulta grammaticalmente e dottrinalmente congiunta con lo Spirito Santo, come coprincipio umano dell'incarnazione e della umanizzazione del Figlio di Dio per la salvezza dell'uomo. . . . Estremamente significativo è il termine *virgine* legato alla persona di Maria. . . . È la Vergine per autonomasia: la qualifica determinante dell'apporto di Maria sia per l'incarnazione in sé sia per la salvezza che ne consegue, così come la interpreta Matteo alla luce della profezia messianica di Isaia" (NDM, 814–815, passim). Cf. also the entire treatment of this topic under the entry, "Madre di Dio" in NDM, 813–815. Of particular interest, in terms of our present discussion, is the explanation of the actual grammatical formula of the Greek original vis-à-vis the Latin versions of the creedal insertion, which brings to light the significance of Mary's role of cooperation in the *œconomia salutis*. Father Galot's starting point is the mention of the Holy Spirit in the Nicean-Constantinopolitan Creed. Mary's particular cooperation in the economy of salvation at the moment of the Incarnation is a harbinger of our own cooperation with the Holy Spirit so that God the Father might allow Christ to be formed within us. Cf. the article of Jean Galot, S.J., "Vita di Cristo, Vita dello Spirito," *Civiltà Cattolica* 4 (1985), 118–130.

15. PPS, II, 31.

16. MD, 37.

17. MD, 261. Newman's source for this phrase is a homily attributed to St.

Epiphanius of Salamis wherein he compares Mary to the incomparable book in which the Word is read (cf. PG 94:1029).

18. Cf. LG 56: ". . . adorned from the first instance of her conception with the radiance of an entirely unique holiness." Also, LG reads in part that Mary was, "fashioned by the Holy Spirit and formed as a new creature." Furthermore, the following references should likewise be noted: Bishop Theoteknos of Livia, *Panegyric for the Feast of the Assumption*, 5–6; St. Gregory of Nazianzen, *Oratio 38*, 16; St. Andrew of Crete, *Sermon I on the Birth of Mary, Sermon I on the Dormition of Mary*—discussed by Pope John Paul II in *A Catechesis on Mary, Mother of God*, 90–92.

19. MD, 62.

20. See Pope John Paul II, *Mary, Mother of God*, 130–132.

21. Donald Dawe, an Evangelical theologian, establishes the linkage thus: "All those Christians who have never ceased to affirm the mystery of the Incarnation recognize the need to revere the Lord's Mother. Mary stands so close to her Son as to share fully in the graces God bestowed in the Incarnation on Him. Her being reflects the very process by which the Incarnation took place. From the doctrine of the Incarnation . . . the Christian mind has derived a number of secondary dogmas or *theologoumena*. These form the basis of the legitimate Marian doctrines. . . . At the head of the list is the dogma of Mary as *Theotokos*. . . . But the list continues with the Immaculate Conception, Mary's perpetual virginity, and her bodily Assumption . . . correlates of the doctrine of the Incarnation."—"*The Blessed Virgin and Depth Psychology—A Theological Appraisal*" (unpublished manuscript), page 18.

22. Diff II, 62f.

23. A more complete study of Newman's understanding of the New Eve theology is given in the second part of this chapter and in Chapter Three on Newman's use of the Fathers of the Church in support of his understanding of Mary's cooperation in the economy of salvation. Cf. J. McGuire, *Holy Virgin Mary: The Mystery of Grace, a True Mystery of the Incarnation As Presented in the Writings of John Henry Cardinal Newman*, dissertation at the Pontificia Universitas Gregoriana, Rome, 1975.

24. PPS, II, 32. The reader should note that at the time, Newman was still an Anglican and, therefore, he did not yet adhere to the Catholic doctrine of the Immaculate Conception, for which he would become a most ardent herald both before, during, and after its solemn dogmatic definition in 1854. Newman's predilection for this Marian dogma is revealed throughout his Catholic writings, most especially in his *Meditations and Devotions* and in the *Letter to Pusey*. Newman, as he would point out time and again, derives a truly Catholic apologetic for this doctrine from a careful study of the Fathers of the Church and, in particular, from their teachings on Mary as the New Eve. Cf. D. Victory, "The Immaculate Conception in Newman," *Euntes Docete* 7 (1954), 147–156.

25. The Song of Songs 4:12, reads: "You are an enclosed garden, my sister, my bride, an enclosed garden, a fountain sealed." The New American Bible, in its introduction to the Song of Songs, says the following: "In Christian tradition, the Song has been interpreted in terms of the union between Christ and the Church and, particularly, by St. Bernard, of the union between Christ and

the individual soul. Throughout the liturgy, especially in the Little Office, there is a consistent application of the Song of Songs to the Blessed Virgin Mary." An entry in Michael O'Carroll's *Theotokos*, entitled "The Song of Songs," sums up the Marian interpretation of this book of the Bible on the part of several of the Fathers of the Church. As regards the interpretation of 4:12 in reference to the perpetual virginity of Mary, O'Carroll cites Sts. Epiphanius and Isidore of Seville. He also notes that: "St. Jerome interpreted 4:21 of Mary's virginity and 4:13 of the harmony of other virtues with her virginity": "The Song of Songs," *Theotokos: An Encyclopedia of the Blessed Virgin Mary* (Collegeville, Minn.: The Liturgical Press, 1982) 327.

26. DMC, 300f.

27. Yves Congar reflects on the Immaculate Conception as the mystery by which Mary's womb is prepared as the wedding chamber of the *totus Christus*, that is, of the Incarnate Son and His Mystical Bride, the Church: "From the instance of her conception God, preserving her from sin and sin's slavery, forestalled her, as it were, by His grace and 'prepared her so that His only Son might be born of her and with Him the Church in its wholeness.' For it was in her—that is, in her womb—'that the whole Church was betrothed to the Word and united to God by an eternal alliance'; 'Partus Mariæ, fructus Ecclesiæ'" (*Christ, Our Lady and the Church*, 254).

28. "Anagogical Way." Cf. CCC 117.

29. Giacomo Biffi, *Il Canto Nuziale* (Milan: Jaca Book, 2000), 21.

30. Biffi, *Il Canto Nuziale*, 85.

31. Cf. Rev 19:9.

32. PPS, II, 31f.

33. Cf. Mario Naldini, "Il Libro della Creazione," *Letture Patristiche: La Bibbia nei Padri della Chiesa: L'Antico Testamento*, ed. Mario Naldini (Bologna: Edizioni Dehoniane, 1999), 51–66.

34. Cf. Guido Innocenzo Gargano, "I Commenti Patristici al Cantico dei Cantici," in *Letture Patristiche*, 127–150.

35. Cf. Hugo Rahner, *Our Lady and the Church*, 16: "There is another place in Scripture where the Fathers saw a reference to this victory of the Immaculate Mother, first fulfilled in Mary and then in the Church's struggles. It is in the longing cry of the bride in the Canticles (Cant 5:2): 'Open to me, my sister, my love, my dove, my perfect one.' The Latin text, as used by the Latin Fathers for the Hebrew 'my perfect one,' has *immaculata mea*, a title given in the earliest times to Our Lady." Also, Honorius, *Commentary on the Canticle* 5 (PL 172:435); St. Ambrose, *Commentary on Luke* 11:7 (CSEL 32:4, p. 45).

36. Michael J. Perrott, *Newman's Mariology* (England: The St. Austin Press, 1997), 26f., passim.

37. Cf. SN, 14. Newman makes reference to Mary's "vow of virginity," in connection to the fulness of grace she enjoyed from the moment of her Immaculate Conception, that is to say, "grace before Gabriel (i.e., before the Annunciation), before the vow of virginity." Thus, implicitly, Newman makes two significant theological statements about the Virgin Mary. First, he acknowledges that Mary's plenitude of grace was already a well-integrated part of the mystery of Mary's person/mission before it is recognized by the Angel Gabriel

who greets her as "full of grace." Secondly, Newman hints at Mary's question to the Angel Gabriel: "How can this be since I do not know man?" as indicative of a vow of virginity that she made well in advance of his announcement concerning her divine maternity.

38. MD, 44.

39. DMC, 302f. Cf. The Song of Songs 5:10–16. Note that Jews read from the Song of Songs during the celebration of Pesach or Passover.

40. Henri Cardinal de Lubac explains how the mystery of Mary's motherhood of the Divine Word is intimately related to her spiritual maternity of the Church. De Lubac, following the tradition of several of the Fathers and Doctors of the Church, considers the divine and spiritual maternity of Mary in terms of her mystical spousal relationship to the Head and members of the Mystical Body. "When in the mystery of the Incarnation, the heavenly King celebrated the wedding of His Son, giving Him the Holy Church as his companion, Mary's womb was the bridal bed for the royal Spouse. It was a unique and privileged position for Mary, and a number of writers express it aptly by means of an image which has long had classical status, but the usual symbolism of which they have modified. Guided, apparently, by the letter of the Canticle of Canticles, which compares the neck of the Bride with the Tower of David, they see in the neck something more than the image of Christ the Mediator, or the Church, or the Church's preachers and teachers, or even Scripture itself, which brings to us both doctrine and the indication of the divine will; they compare Mary to the neck which connects the Head to the other members of the body. Others, following St. Bernard, depict her crowned with the sun and holding the moon under her feet—that is, as the living link between the two stars, the Church and Christ" (*The Church and Our Lady*, 254f.).

41. PPS, II, 128f.

42. PPS, II, 132, 136f.

43. Cf. CCC 490–494.

44. Cf. LG 58. Cf. also CCC 964f.

45. PPS, VII, 90.

46. Perrott, *Newman's Mariology*, 49.

47. See, for example, the bull *Sollicitudo*, of Pope Alexander VII in 1661 (DS, 2017); the bull *Ineffabilis Deus*, of Blessed Pius IX, defining the dogma of the Immaculate Conception in 1854 (DS, 2803); the encyclical *Fulgens Corona*, of Pope Pius XII in 1953 (AAS 45, 580–81)

48. Roderick Strange, *Newman and the Gospel of Christ* (New York: Oxford University Press, 1981), 49f.

49. Cf. Council of Ephesus: DS, 251; CCC 495.

50. Cf. Boyce, *Mary in the Writings of JHN*, 255: "like Theodoret a friend and supporter of Nestorius." The reader should note that when St. Cyril of Alexandria had the Council of Ephesus convoked before John of Antioch and the other Antiochean supporters of Nestorius arrived that the outraged Nestorius decided not to attend the Council. Nestorius eventually obtained permission from the Emperor to retire in a monastery in Antioch.

51. Cf. Boyce, *Mary in the Writings of JHN*, 259: "John Cassian (360–435) a monk who came from the East and settled in France. He is well-known for his

monastic studies, the *Institutes* and the *Conferences*. Newman, in his *Select Treatises of St. Athanasius*, refers to his 7 vol. theological work *De Incarnatione
Domini*."

52. Cf. Diff II, 63–65, passim. Also, *Select Treatises of St. Athanasius with the
Arians* (London, 1903), 2:210–215, 367–369.

53. Cf. The article of Rino Fisichella, "La Vergine Maria nella Professione
di Fede della Chiesa Antica," in *La Vergine Madre nella Chiesa delle Origini*,
Itinerari Mariani dei Due Millenni, vol. 1.16 of the series Fine d'Anno con
Maria (Rome: Centro di Cultura Mariana "Madre della Chiesa," 1996), 43–54.

54. PPS, II, 28. Cf. Jared Wicks, "I Simboli della Fede," in *Catechismo della
Chiesa Cattolica: Testo Integrale e Commento Teologico*, ed. Rino Fisichella (Casale
Monferrato: Piemme, 1993), 655–666.

55. Cf. 1 Tim 3:16; 2 Cor 5:19; Is 9:6; Rom 9:5; Jn 20:28; Rev 1:8; Heb
1:2–3.

56. PPS, II, 28

57. PPS, II, 29.

58. PPS, II, 37.

59. PPS, II, 29.

60. PPS, II, 31.

61. Diff II, 36.

62. Giovanni Velocci, *Introduzione alla Lettera al Rev. Pusey su Maria e la Vita
Cristiana* (Rome: Città Nuova Editrice, 1975), 70.

63. Diff II, 65f.

64. Diff II, 65. Cf. Diff II, 66: "Thus Jerome inveighs against Helvidus, St
Cyril Nestorius, and St. Ambrose Bonosus." See also Newman's meditation on
the title *Janua Cæli*, MD, 36–38. Jerome did much in his own apologetic in favor
of the perpetual virginity of Mary against Helvidius. Newman, writing in his
Select Treatises of St. Athanasius II, 205f., addresses some of the questions raised
by those who object to the doctrine in the same vein as Helvidius did. Concerning the brothers and sisters of Jesus mentioned in the Gospels, Newman responds that they refer to Our Lord's cousins, close relatives, or, perhaps,
stepbrothers and -sisters. Newman does not prefer the latter position, accepting
a traditional belief that Joseph, like Mary, remained a virgin during his entire
life. However, the Protestant objection to Mary's perpetual virginity based on
Matthew 1:25 is another apologetical challenge that Newman does not hesitate
to face, like St. Jerome centuries earlier. Concerning the Evangelist's words:
"And he knew her not till she brought forth her first-born son," "Newman," as
Friedel tells us, "explains that the word 'till' need not imply a termination at a
certain point of time, but may be given as information up to a certain point, and
often after that there can be no doubt" (cf. Friedel, *The Mariology of Cardinal
Newman*, 229). Furthermore, Newman's explanations clarify how this can be the
case. If someone were to say that a person prayed until the day of his death, this
would not mean he prayed afterwards. On the other hand, if one were to say that
a person prayed up until the day of his conversion, this would not mean that
such a person ceased to pray after his conversion. Likewise, as Newman points
out, the Sacred Scriptures (cf. Gen 28:15; Deut 34:6; 1 Sam 15:35; 2 Sam 6:35;
Mt 28:20—this last Matthean text being of considerable support in the Church's

fight against the heresy of Marcellus of Ancyra, who believed that Christ's Kingdom would end; see J. N. D. Kelly, *Early Christian Doctrines* (London: Black, 1993) 241. Hence also, the significance of Lk 1:33 and of the statement in the Nicene Creed, "And of His Kingdom there will be no end." All of this evidence points to the reason why the word "till" or "until" need not imply a termination at a certain point in time, so that, in the case of Matthew 1:25, the word *till* (*until*) does not, by any means, suggest that the Virgin Mary had sexual relations after she gave birth to Jesus. The teaching of the Church, at the First Lateran Council (649), solidified the Church's teaching on Mary's perpetual virginity (cf. DS, 502–503). In his apologetic of the doctrine of Mary's perpetual virginity in the *Select Treatises of Athanasius* 2:205, Newman also employs the four principles of St. Thomas Aquinas, as he understood them in the work of a contemporary Catholic apologist of his day (Pearson). Here, they are briefly summarized: 1) Mary was forever a virgin because of pre-eminent dignity as the Mother of God. Her vow of perpetual virginity expresses her unreserved love of God; 2) It is a tribute of special honor and reverence to Christ and to her since Our Lord is both the Only-Begotten Son of the Father and her only Son; 3)The perpetual virginity of Mary guarantees that the Holy Spirit is the active divine principle in the Incarnation (no male seed). Therefore, Jesus has only one Father (Who is God the Father—Joseph being Our Lord's putative father and guardian) and "the overshadowing of the Holy Spirit" emphasizes Our Lord's sanctity both as God and Man; 4) The perpetual virginity of the Blessed Mother is also an argument in favor of the piety and purity of Joseph, who is called a "just man" in the Gospels. Joseph, as one tradition holds, was probably a virgin himself, indeed, he too made a vow of virginity. And, even if he had not been a virgin, he would have nonetheless justly respected Mary's own vow of virginity. Mary's perpetual virginity is most commonly expressed in three Latin phrases with which Newman was probably familiar: "*ante partum, in partu, post partum.*" Finally, it should be noted that Newman in his meditations on the Litany of Loreto reflects on Mary's virginity under her titles of *Virgo Purissima, Virgo Prædicanda, Virgo Veneranda, Virgo Prudentissima, Virgo Potens, Virgo Fidelis.* Cf. also CCC 496–511.

65. Diff II, 65–67, passim.

66. DMC, 347.

67. Cf. NDM, 820f.

68. Cf. Friedel, *The Mariology of Cardinal Newman*, 169: "The *Theotokos*, in fact, is the shibboleth of the pure, unadulterated doctrine of Christianity; to deny the title is to fabricate an entire system of false conceptions. There no longer remains any internal union; it is only something external, a mere juxtaposition. Anyone could thus be united with God, since no real unity is required. Christ becomes two hypostases, two persons, two sons, the being to which Mary gave birth then, is not God."

69. Cf. NDM, 815–818.

70. Cf. Hugo Rahner, *Our Lady and the Church*, 34f.: "And when in the fifth century, under the influence of the speculations of the later Greeks, the title came to be denied her, the faithful conscience of the whole Church of the East rose up, and at the General Council of Ephesus in 431 the truth of Mary's

dignity as Mother of God was solemnly proclaimed." See also Pope Pius XII, *Lux Veritatis* (25 December 1931), in AAS 25 (1931), 512.

71. Dev. D., 145.

72. This analogy, however, does not admit of a hypostatic union between Mary and the Godhead (e.g., hypostatic union with the Holy Spirit) as has been put forth as a theological hypothesis by a contemporary theologian such as Leonardo Boff. See Angelo Amato, *Maria e La Trinità* (Milan: Edizioni San Paolo, 2000), 99–101. Mary is a creature; her custody of the Incarnation, that is, her cooperation in the mystery of the Incarnation, cannot be equated with the work of the Holy Spirit in the same event.

73. DMC, 348f.

74. Diff II, 62.

75. PPS, II, 135–136, passim.

76. See Pope John Paul II, *Mary, Mother of God*, 149–151. Also, St. Augustine writes: "if the Mother were fictitious, the flesh would also be fictitious . . . and the scars of the resurrection" (*Tract. In Ev. Ioannis*, 8, 6–7).

77. The interrelationship among these doctrines is underscored throughout the Tradition of the Church. Please note the following: St. Epiphanius, *Ancoratus*, 119, 5 (DS, 44); Second Council of Constantinople (553) in DS, 422; Fourth Lateran Council (1215) in DS, 801; Second Council of Lyons (1274) in DS, 852; the definition of the dogma of the Assumption (1950) in DS, 3903; Second Vatican Council, LG 57: "did not diminish his Mother's virginal integrity but sanctified it."

78. Cf. the article "Icone" in NDM, 670–679. Mary is the *Hodigítria par excellence*. She indicates (points to) Him Who is the Way, the Truth and the Life; she contemplates the Christ child seated on her lap and beckons us to enter into that same contemplation, so that, having received the blessing of the Savior to Whom she gave birth and from Whom she is never separated, we too might never be separated from Him. Along similar lines, one could say that the image of Our Lady in the *orans* position, with the Child Jesus resting on her lap, as found in the paintings of the catacombs of Rome, was, for Newman, a western version of the *Hodigítria* (and its derivations in Eastern iconography); cf. Diff II, 55f.

79. MD, 38–41, passim.

80. Cf. Jn 1:11–14, 1 Jn 3:1–10. We are *"filii in Filio."* It should be noticed, for example, how Jn 1:11–14 makes an implicit but nonetheless theologically significant mention of our divine filial adoption in connection with Our Lord's virgin birth. This theology of our divine, adoptive filiation in Christ and the accompanying, implicit reference to the Virgin Mary's divine maternity in John's Gospel is most akin to the one we find in Galatians 4:4–7. Cf. CCC 502–507, most especially no. 505. Because we are sons of the Father in Christ and Christ is our Brother through His Incarnation, "conceived of the Holy Spirit and born of the Virgin Mary," this divine logic leads us to understand how Mary's divine maternity likewise includes her spiritual maternity of us, brothers and sisters of Jesus through grace, Baptism and faithful discipleship in His Church. The Evangelist John, in fact, makes constant use of an ecclesial "we," "us," and "our" in his writings.

81. These words are taken from the concluding part of the embolism prayer, which the priest recites immediately after the Our Father, based on St. Paul's Epistle to Titus 2:13.

82. Cf. Friedel, *The Mariology of Cardinal Newman*, 188f.: "His treatment of Mary's position as Second Eve really merits the designation of *'magisteriale'* [italics added] as given by Terrien. His method is not merely historical; the foundation for the belief is indirectly placed in Scripture. He explains it and then strengthens it by the testimony of the Fathers."

83. Newman clearly sees the theology of the New Eve as scripturally based on the *Protoevangelium* and Chapter 12 of the Apocalypse. These texts, for Newman, interpret each other and such an interpretation is confirmed by the constant witness of Tradition. In his *Letter to Pusey*, Newman offers a herme-neutic for interpreting these biblical texts (cf. Diff II, 58–61, passim). One finds here a significant example of his method of interpretation, already cited in Chapter Two. Cf. CCC 410–412, 494, 726, 2618, 2853.

84. Diff II, 63.

85. Father Jones uses here a transliteration of the Greek word rather than its Latin counterpart, namely, *Protevangelium.*

86. Carleton Jones, O.P., "John Henry Newman and Mary: Mother of God, the New Eve," An Address to the Annual Conference: The New England Region of the Mariological Society of America, *Newsletters of the Dominican Fathers and Brothers of the Province of St. Joseph* (Providence, R.I.: Providence College, 19 October 1996), 6.

87. Agnes Cunnigham, "Mary's Faith: The Supreme, Abiding Gift of the Holy Spirit," *Communio* (Summer 1998), 283.

88. MD, 82.

89. Dev. D., 384.

90. The patristic texts to which he refers are: St. Justin Martyr, *Dialogus cum Trypho*, 100 (PG 6:709); St. Irenæus, *Adversus Hæreses*, 3, 22, 34 (PG 7:958ff.); *Adv. Hær.* 5, 19 (PG 7:1175); Tertullian, *De Carne Christi*, 17 (PL 2:782).

91. Cf. 1 Cor 15:21–22; 45–47.

92. Nicolas writes: "La force de parallelisme Ève–Marie vient du parallel-isme Adam–Jésus. St. Paul nous apprend que le Christ est le nouvel Adam, le nouveau homme, en qui l'humanité prend, par le baptême, une vie nouvelle, une origine nouvelle. L'obéissance du Christ nous sauve et se transmet à nous, comme la désobéissance d'Adam nous avait perdus en se transmettant à nous. Si vraiment, dans cette repris du plan créateur, dans cette régénération de l'espèce humaine, Marie est la nouvelle Ève, la nouvelle première femme, n'est-elle pas en conséquence la mère des nouveaux vivants par intime association à celui qui en est le Chef?"—M. J. Nicolas, *Essai de Synthèse Mariale*, vol. 1 (Paris: Beauchesne, 1949), 732.

93. Carleton Jones, O.P., "John Henry Cardinal Newman and Mary: Mother of God, the New Eve," 7. Francis Friedel comments: "Consequently it is most natural to find the early Christians all impregnated with the idea of Christ's role; the parallelism between the fall and the restoration could not long remain incomplete. Instinctively the Christians would seek the woman who was instrumental in man's redemption, as the first Eve was the occasion of man's

NOTES: *Chapter Four*

ruin. Where would they look if not to Jesus, the second Adam, to find associated with Him, the second Eve" (*The Mariology of Cardinal Newman*, 188).

94. Diff II, 32.

95. Diff II, 45.

96. Cf. Jean Galot, S.J., *Maria la Donna nell'Opera della Salvezza* (Rome: Università Gregoriana Editrice, 1984), 272. Cf. also Velocci, *Il Coraggio*, 138.

97. MD, 37.

98. Diff II, 45–49, passim.

99. Cf. Gerhard Luwig Müller. *Dogmatica Cattolica: Per lo Studio e la Prassi della Teologia* (Milan: Edizioni San Paolo, 1999), 620: "Una dottrina su Maria deve comunque sempre partire dall'amore e dalla promessa . . . da Dio di concederle la pienezza della grazia nella presenza del Signore, amore e promessa che determinano in modo unitario la sua persona e la sua missione. In virtù di questa promessa e di questa presenza Maria è abilitata a pronunciare il suo sì." Müller also reflects on Mary's *fiat* as the principal means by which she cooperated not only in the redemptive act of the Incarnation but in the entire redemptive activity of Christ "in quanto il sì da lei pronunciato è l'accettazione umana, sorretta dall grazia, di tale autocomunicazione" (621f.). Müller clearly distinguishes this self-communication/revelation of God in Christ (i.e., hypostatic union) from Mary's cooperation/participation since the cooperation of the God-Man is ontologically different than the cooperation of the Virgin. Nevertheless, in both Christ the God-Man and Mary the creature, Müller identifies that a "compendio di salvezza" exists because of their distinct but related cooperation in response to the Father's plan of salvation or, as Müller writes: "il compendio della salvezza non è semplicemente l'autocomunicazione di Dio, ma l'autocomunicazione di Dio *accolta* dalla nostra libertà nella grazia" (622).

100. Friedel, 191.

101. Diff II, 44.

102. Diff II, 36. Cf. *Histoire des Dogmes: Les Signes du Salut*, vol. 3, *Les Sacrements, l'Église, la Vierge Marie*, ed. Bernard Sesboüé et al. (Paris: Desclée, 1995), 581: "Ce thème sotériologique trés ancien intègre donc Marie à la totalité de l'histoire du salut et met aussi en opposition la credulité mauvaise d'Ève et la foi de la Vierge, le caractère libérateur d'une coopération ordonnée au salut."

103. PPS, 1, 8–14, passim.

104. LDJ, 2.

105. Diff II, 123: "Benedicta tu in mulieribus. Quia in quibus Eva maledicta puniebat viscera; tunc in illis gaudet, honoratur, suspicitur Maria benedicta. Et facta est vere nunc mater viventium per gratiam quæ mater existit morientium per naturam. . . . Quantus sit Deus satis ignorat ille, qui hujus Virginis mentem non stupet, animum non miratur: pavet cælum, tremunt Angeli, creatura non sustinet, natura non sufficit, et una puella sic Deum in sui pectoris capit, recipit, oblectat hospitio, ut pacem terris, cælis gloriam, salutem perditis, vitam mortuis, terrenis cum cælestibus parentelam, ipsius Dei cum carne commercium. . . " (cf. Diff II, 43 for Newman's English translation).

106. Diff II, 43.

107. Aidan Nichols, *Epiphany: A Theological Introduction to Catholicism*, 185: "Grace is operative in our lives, but it is also *co-operative* with us. This is the basis

of the distinction between justifying *grace* and *merit*. . . . In the New Testament there is, in this sense, a concept of *reward*. Our deeds 'earn' a place in the Kingdom, making us into the kind of person who is able to live under the rule of God. . . . Though we cannot merit the grace that moves us, once moved we can merit the end."

108. LDJ, 35.

109. Cf. DS, 1520–83.

110. Diff II, 35.

111. Blehl, *The White Stone*, 113: "God could have redeemed man from his fallen state and reconciled him to Himself without becoming Man, but once the Incarnation was decreed, . . . she was destined to be associated with Him, not just by giving birth to Him, but in the total economy of the Incarnation. Just as Christ's redemptive action was a *free* fulfillment of His Father's will, so Mary's conception of the Word was an act of complete obedience and surrender to the divine will."

112. The Greek past perfect participle κεχαριτωμένη (Lk 1:28) implies that Mary already received the fullness of grace and continued to live in the state of that fullness before and after her consent to the Archangel Gabriel.

113. Blehl, *The White Stone*, 115: "Although Mary could not *merit* the first grace of the Immaculate Conception, she could *merit* by her faith and obedience the gift of being the Mother of our Redeemer."

114. Diff II, 51f.

115. Diff II, 52.

116. Cf. SC 103: "admires and exults in Mary, the most excellent fruit of the Redemption."

117. PPS, V, 166. Sermon 12, "The New Works of the Gospel": "Now there can be no doubt at all that salvation is by faith, and that its being by faith is one of those special circumstances which make the Gospel a new covenant; but still it may be by works also; for, to use a familiar illustration, obedience is the *road* to heaven and faith the *gate*."

118. Diff II, 52.

119. Diff II, 63.

120. Diff II, 48.

121. Cf. Diff II, 48. Newman is not using the word "positive," in reference to sin, to mean that Protestants consider it to be something good. This would be an absurd and contradictory statement on Newman's part or on the part of any Christian. Rather, Newman intends to use the word "positive" as a figurative manner of speaking, to highlight the fact that, knowingly or unknowingly, much Protestant doctrine, as Newman understood it, tends to attribute to sin a power inherent in man's nature that only grace is meant (has a right) to exercise according to God's original plan for our salvation. This original plan of salvation is fully realized in the Blessed Virgin Mary, the New Eve. Man, therefore, to paraphrase a key expression of *Gaudium et Spes* 22, cannot be fully understood but in light of his Redemption in and through the mystery of the Incarnate Word, Who is Christ the New Adam. And so too, Mary. This is the true "positive," upon which man must focus, not upon his sinfulness as such. Thus, simply speaking, holiness, for Newman, is a positive to be achieved in coopera-

tion with God's grace; while, sin, on the contrary, is a negative to be avoided. If this very important distinction is lost, then one could easily be led to believe that since all men (save Our Lord and Our Lady) have inherited the sin of Adam through conception, man's only real inheritance is sin. For Newman, nothing could be further from the truth. Consequently, the Catholic understanding of man's cooperation in the work of his own salvation and the salvation of others, while inseparable from the reality of sin and its consequences, nevertheless considers the salvific efficacy of the Redemption as being most evident not in a mere extrinsic justification, but in both an intrinsic and extrinsic justification, which comports an interior renewal of man's whole being that manifests itself in both faith and good works in cooperation with Divine Grace. The whole question of the relationship of justification to the process of man's cooperation in the work of salvation is a thorny issue which continues to be the source of fruitful ecumenical dialogue. Though very much pertinent to our present discussion, it remains, nonetheless, beyond the scope of this discussion. Cf. LD, 19:361–370: letter dated 15–17 June 1860. See also LD, 19:437–438: letter to William Wilberforce, written 9 December 1860.

122. Diff II, 48.

123. Diff II, 48.

124. The Fathers of the Second Vatican Council cite several important texts of the Fathers of the Church in Chapter Eight of *Lumen Gentium* concerning the New Eve Theology. Newman relied upon some of these authors in his Summa Mariologica, *A Letter to Pusey*. Cf. Irenæus, *Adv. Hæreses*, 3, 22, 4 (PG 7:959A); Epiphanius, *Hær*, 78, 18 (PG 42:728CD–729AB); Hieronymus, *Epist.* 22, 21 (PL 22:408). See, for example, Diff II, 34f.

125. Diff II, 140.

126. Diff II, 45f.

127. Cf. Diff II, 36.

128. Diff II, 52.

129. Cf. Velocci, *Il Coraggio*, 139.

130. MD, 36f.

131. The insights of Robert Auman are worth citing. He believes that the subordinate role of Mary to Christ in the work of salvation does not prevent one from using the title "Co-Redemptrix" as expressive of this role. His concluding argument is interesting since he parallels Mary's cooperation with Christ the Redeemer to the indissoluble union that exists between a husband and his wife in the sacrament of marriage (cf. Mt 19:6; Gen 2:24). Auman writes: "We know that the Redemption was accomplished by Christ alone, by His merits alone, for we have salvation in no other name. Similarly, we know that the Fall of mankind was due to Adam, was a direct result of his sin alone. Eve's sin did not cause the Fall of mankind, but it surely had a part in the Fall. Her sin united itself to that of Adam's through her cooperation in his sin by giving him the forbidden fruit. Morally speaking, theirs was one sin, a combined sin, although the Fall was a direct result of Adam's disobedience only, not upon Eve. But the matter is purely hypothetical, to say that had only Eve disobeyed, the Fall of mankind would never had occurred, because the Fall of mankind was dependent upon Adam only, not upon Eve. But the matter is purely hypothetical; and it would

have been incongruous on God's part to transmit to mankind the supernatural, preternatural gifts through an innocent father and a guilty mother. Therefore, considering the entire matter as it actually happened, we must consider the scene in the Garden as one moral evil consisting in Eve's personal sin, her subsequent inducement of Adam, and Adam's sin to which was specifically attached the evils of the Fall. Eve's cooperation in Adam's sin made her a principle combined with that of Adam's. In much the same way, but far more intimately, Mary's cooperation in the Redemption made her a principle, but only a cooperative, subordinate principle combined with Christ, the constitutive, effectual principle, from which our salvation flows. We have, therefore, one and only one Redeemer, Who for the greater honor of the human race, especially of women and particularly of Mary, chose to join to Himself a Co-redemptrix in bringing about the salvation of the world. May we not apply here the words the Redeemer spoke in a different context, 'What God has joined together let no man put asunder.'" See his "Divine Vengeance and Mary's Consent," *Homiletic and Pastoral Review* (November 1998), 49f.

132. Gianni Colzani explains the nature of Mary's cooperation as the New Eve in these terms: "Se, in sintonia con un antichissima tradizione, dobbiamo parlare di un'adesione di Maria all'unica azione redentrice di Cristo, di una comunione della novella Eva con la logica spirituale che muove il nuovo Adamo, allora possiamo parlare solo di una cooperazione ministeriale, solo di un servizio voluto da Dio per i suoi disegni e prestato da Maria nella libertà della sua fede. Come Eva non ebbe un influsso diretto sul peccato di Adamo, ma fu lo strumento attraverso cui fu realizzata la colpa originaria, così la nuova Eva non diminuisce il carattere independente e autosufficiente dell'opera di Cristo; anzi la redenzione di Cristo comprende pure il modo particolare di conformazione a Cristo con cui Maria, salvata da lui, aderisce totalmente ai suoi disegni. La cooperazione ministeriale insomma, 'disegna al tempo stesso con la totale subordinazione anche la più intima unione di Maria con il Redentore.'"— *Maria: Mistero di Grazia e di Fede* (Milan: Edizioni San Paolo, 1996), 276.

133. LG, 53; 56.

134. St. Anselm writes: "You are the mother of reconciliation and the reconciled, the mother of salvation and the saved." *Oratio 52*, 8 (PL 158:957A).

135. Diff II, 82f.

CHAPTER FIVE

1. Newman gives a short-hand definition of martyrdom, highlighting it as a privileged means of co-suffering (*compassio*) for the sake of the Body of Christ the Church in his *Sermon IV* on the feast of St. Stephen's Martyrdom: "A martyrdom is a season of God's especial power in the eye of faith, as great as if a miracle were visibly wrought. It is a fellowship of Christ's sufferings, a commemoration of His Death, a representation filling up in figure, 'that which is behind of His afflictions, for his Body's sake which is the Church'" (PPS, II, 47f.).

2. PPS, II, 402.

3. PPS, III, 139.

4. PPS, III, 140.

5. Ibid.

6. SN, 123. "The Seven Dolors," or "The Seven Sorrows."

7. In his Sermon Note for February 16 (Septuagesima) entitled "On Labor—Our Work Here," Newman writes, in reflecting on the discipline of Lenten penance: "Suffering is a work. On satisfaction and *satispassio*; on bearing pain with sweetness or patience, with sweet faces, ways, voice, etc., etc. On the discipline when associated with the thought of Christ's suffering, more meritorious; for the mind goes with it and is not otiose. Thus let us begin this sacred time" (SN, 62). Newman explains the meaning of the word *satispassio* as "paying the full penalty—the last farthing."

8. PPS, III, 140.

9. PPS, III, 140f.

10. Cf. Lk 14:27.

11. Newman refers the reader to 2 Cor 4:10. Cf. also 2 Cor 12:9–10; CCC 1508.

12. PPS, III, 142–148, passim.

13. SD 18–19.

14. *A Catechesis on the Creed: Jesus—Son and Savior* (Boston: Pauline Books and Media, 1996), 2:447–449, passim.

15. Vincent Blehl, S.J., *The White Stone: The Spiritual Theology of John Henry Newman* (Petersham, Mass.: St. Bede's Publications, 1993), 119.

16. CCC 618.

17. MD, 51.

18. MD, 53. Cf. SN, 104–105.

19. SN, 104–105.

20. Here, Mary is seen as benefitting from the fulness of redemption, insofar as she was immaculately conceived and assumed body and soul into heaven.

21. MD, 56. Cf. Hugo Rahner, *Our Lady and the Church*, 53: "It is necessary in order to understand the depths of such mysteries to have, as Jerome once said a 'godly' heart. And Origen similarly, in his introduction to St. John's Gospel, says that none can penetrate this mystery save one who 'himself has rested on the breast of Jesus and from Jesus has taken Mary as his mother to his own."

22. Literally, "inclusion." This device is sometimes used in a literary context, such as in the Gospel of John, for indicating that the beginning and end of something encompass the same reality.

23. MD, 57.

24. Ibid.

25. PPS, IV, 323f.

26. Cf. Rom 7:17–23; 1 Cor 1:7; 2 Cor 4:10; Phil 3:10; Col 1:24; Col 3:4.

27. Cf. CCC 1809—on the cardinal virtue of temperance, which is not unrelated to the virtues of patient vigilance (i.e., waiting) and forbearance in suffering—essential virtues of Christian discipleship.

28. MD, 58.

29. Ibid.

30. Giacomo Biffi, *La Merviglia dell'Evento Cristiano*, 241: "Questa pena propria delle madri è stata interamente assaporata anche da lei, dalla Vergine Madre di Dio; ma in lei era una pena trasfigurata dall'intima consapevolezza di

contribuire così alla salvezza del mondo, e intimamente sublimata dalla stessa potenza d'amore che faceva del Crocefisso del Golgota il Redentore dell' universo.... A questo amore del Padre Maria ha unito il suo, di creatura obbediente, elevata a un compito altissimo e singolare. Anche lei ci ha tanto amato da regolarci il suo Gesù, il suo solo amore, nel travaglio maternamente condiviso della passione redentrice."

31. John Saward, *The Beauty of Holiness and the Holiness of Beauty* (San Francisco: Ignatius Press, 1997), 137f.: "The Blessed Virgin was not passively deployed by God. No, she freely cooperated with the work of our salvation through her faith and loving obedience. This cooperation began at the Annunciation when she said Yes to God the Son's becoming incarnate from her by the Holy Spirit, and it continued all the way to the Cross and the Empty tomb. The cooperative Yes of Our Lady is beautiful, first of all, because it reveals the infinite courtesy of God the Father. He does not impose His Son on mankind.... Our Lady's cooperation with our Redemption is also beautiful because it is an act of pristine Christian faith.... Finally, Our Lady's cooperative Yes is beautiful, because it is a cooperation with the incarnate Son's restoration of mankind to the beauty of deifying grace."

32. SN, 74.

33. SN, 74f.

34. SN, 114. For the entire text of the Sermon Note, see pages 112–114.

35. The ancient Greeks spoke of virtue in the terms of excellence (*arete*). Etymologically speaking, this word *arete* seems to be related to Ares or Mars, the pagan god of war. This Greek virtue of *arete* expresses "manliness," in the sense of strength of mind, body and will engaged in the noble pursuit of self-actualization and happiness. The root of the Latin word "*virtus*," from which we derive the English word virtue, is the word "*vir*" meaning "man." The ancient Romans like Virgil praised the virtue of *pietas* (e.g., *pius Aeneas*)—fidelity to one's duty in life regardless of the suffering which had to be endured in order to maintain that fidelity. In a Christian scheme of things, these pagan concepts of manly virtue received their proper "baptism," in the Gospel of Christ and are attributed in the most feminine and exemplary way possible to the Virgin. Prudence is considered the first of the four cardinal virtues and was deemed the *auriga omnium virtutum*, "the charioteer of all the virtues," in the writings of the Greek philosopher Aristotle.

36. Pope John Paul II, *Mary, Mother of God*, 158–160. On p. 160, we read: "Beginning with Simeon's prophecy, Mary intensely and mysteriously united her life with Christ's sorrowful mission. She was to become her Son's faithful co-worker for the salvation of the human race."

37. This ties into the theme of Newman's sermon "Watching" (PPS, ?, ??), which reiterates the idea of the Christian virtue of prudence and forbearance in suffering, as exemplified in the life of the Virgin.

38. MD, 59.

39. Father von Balthasar writes: "This physical union provides the assurance of being present with the Son, when on the Cross, He takes way the sins of the world in initive sufferings: in the impenetrable mystery in which the new Adam *alone* carries all things through the end (including the Church and also Mary,

who was pre-redeemed by virtue of the Cross), and yet he nevertheless takes the woman eucharistically and bodily with Him under the Cross, so that *Mater Dolorosa* may indeed become *co-redeemer*": "Faith and the Expectation of an Imminent End," *Communio* 26 (Winter 1999), 694. Balthasar continues by presenting the grounds upon which he builds the rationale for an acceptance of a theology of co-redemption in subordination to the unique work of the Redeemer on Calvary: "That this is possible is rooted in the radical and original being-in *communion* of Christ, as Christ-Man and Christ-Child (*Christus-Mensch und -Kind*), with every human being (*Menschenkind*); it is even more deeply rooted in the fact that the servant of Yahweh, from the beginning, is an individual as well as a people; but it is most deeply rooted in the fact that Jesus, Who has invited and taken others along this path of faith, does not afterward allow these others to stand just anywhere. . . . To be sure, the final step into darkness can be undertaken only by the Son of absolute light: a step more for us than with us" (694).

40. Again, Von Balthasar is helpful: "In Christians' co-bearing of the mortal suffering of Christ there is undoubtedly a graduated scale in operation. The promise to Peter that he will be (co-)crucified (John 21:9), the grace given to John and to Mary that they may stand at the foot of the Cross, the sufferings of Paul—these occupy a place of their own vis-à-vis community and Church. In Mary and the women saints at the foot of the Cross, we find a representation of the nuptial character of the new covenant" (*Mysterium Paschale*, 136).

41. Von Balthasar, *Mysterium Paschale*, 136.

42. Von Balthasar, *Mysterium Paschale*, 132–136.

43. There are two separate Sermon Notes for September 28 (Tenth Pentecost). Cf. SN, 135–136. The one currently being considered is simply entitled "Seven Dolours."

44. SN, 91f.

45. MD, 37.

46. MD, 49.

47. Cf. AAS 46 (1954), 634. Also Pope John Paul II, *Mary, Mother of God*, 210: "In his encyclical *Ad Cæli Reginam* to which the text *Lumen Gentium* refers, . . . Pius XII . . . recalls the liturgical text: 'There was St. Mary, Queen of heaven and Sovereign of the world, sorrowing near the cross of our Lord Jesus Christ.' "

48. MD, 60f.

49. MD, 51.

50. RM 16, 2.

51. RM 18, 3.

52. See the traditional Lenten Hymn "Stabat Mater" ("At the Cross, Her Station Keeping").

53. Cf. Hugo Rahner, *Our Lady and the Church*, 81–83, passim. "The classical passage in praise of this strength in Mary and in the Church, cited by the Fathers and mystics, is the poem of the *Mulier Fortis* at the end of the Book of Proverbs (Prov 31:10–31). . . . The history of the interpretation of the valiant woman by the Fathers of the early Church and the mystics of the early Middle Ages is one of the special treasures of the theology of Mary and the Church. The Fathers saw in the song of the valiant woman above all an application to the

Church our mother; so much so, in fact, that their interpretation gave rise in Medieval times to the tenderest expressions of love of Our Lady, the woman who in herself includes all the mysteries of the Church. And at the same time they saw the symbolism of our own sanctification: for the figure of the valiant woman is fulfilled not only in Our Lady and in the Church, but also in ourselves, since (to use the phrase of Ambrose) by our Baptism we become not only 'Mary' but are identified with the Church. Thus a mystic of the school of Bernard of Clairvaux sees Mary, the Church, and the soul all in one: 'under the figure of the valiant woman we can see Mary, the mother of divine wisdom, or the Church, the mother of the wise, of the soul, which is where wisdom resides.' . . . It is this mystery of her life, and her life already at Nazareth where 'love is strong as death' (Cant 8:6), that the Cistercian mystic refers, when he sees in the moment of the Incarnation the fulfillment of the valiant woman: 'A Lady full of bravery: she traveled through her mortal life upon this evil world, yet through the majesty of her spirit she surpassed all creation. For it was to her, the valiant woman, that Gabriel was sent—his very name means 'God's valiant man.' Was she not indeed valiant this woman, Mary, whose love was stronger than death?" For her acceptance of the Incarnation was the acceptance of death. Her blood she gave Him, only for Him to shed it. And this also is fulfilled in the Church: the Church, like Mary, is the woman who brings Christ into the world, only to be sacrificed on the altar."

54. Nichols, *Epiphany: A Theological Introduction to Catholicism*, 353.

55. Saward, *The Beauty of Holiness*, 140.

56. MD, 53.

57. Nichols, *Epiphany, A Theological Introduction to Catholicism*, 353.

58. The Christian virtue of piety, which is one of the gifts of the Holy Spirit, should not be identified with the pagan notion of *pietas*, which was often based on the principles of Stoic philosophy. Cf. CCC 186, 385, 575, 901, 971, 1303, 1437, 1478, 1674, 1686, 1809, 1831, 1966, 2186, 2215, 2606, 2688.

59. Saward, *The Beauty of Holiness*, 140.

60. It should be noted that Newman composed two editions of the Stations of the Cross, one longer and one shorter; we are concerned with his shorter meditations here (used by Pope John Paul II for Good Friday 2001).

61. MD, 158.

62. Cf. Pope John Paul II, *Mary, Mother of God*, 155–164.

63. Ibid, 165–168.

64. Ibid, 169–172.

65. MD, 133.

66. Ibid.

67. MD, 133f.

68. MD, 159. St. Paul uses the Greek noun (always in its plural form) *synergoí*, meaning "co-workers," to refer to those who are collaborators of his in the work of salvation. This fellowship is not limited to their preaching of the Gospel; it also includes all the different forms of suffering they had to endure on account of their witness to Christ and the Gospel.

69. MD, 159.

70. Ibid.

71. Ibid.
72. St. Augustine, *Sermo* 169, 1113.
73. MD, 159.
74. MD, 136f.
75. Cf. SN, 135–136.
76. MD, 234f.
77. MD, 241–243, passim.
78. MD, 245.
79. MD, 258.
80. Cf. Pope John Paul II, *Mary, Mother of God*, 145–147. Also, LG 57: "The Mother of God joyfully showed her first-born Son."
81. SN, 135.
82. Ibid.
83. SN, 136.
84. Ibid.

CHAPTER SIX

1. The Reverend Francis Friedel, writing in reference to the *Letter to Pusey*, gives the following appraisal: "Newman gives one of the finest psychological analyses of devotion to Mary ever penned by a Catholic writer."—*The Mariology of Cardinal Newman* (New York: Benzinger Brothers, 1928), 135. Cf. Philip Boyce, *Mary: The Virgin Mary in the Writings of John Henry Newman* (Grand Rapids, Mich.: Eerdmans, 2001), 37–39, passim. Bishop Boyce writes: "The context that prompted this Mariological work was the following: the Definition of the dogma of the Immaculate Conception by Pope Pius IX in 1854 raised many fears and criticisms of the Rome outside the Church. Some of them stemmed from ignorance or misconceptions of what the doctrine exactly meant. Others came from prejudice against the See of Rome and against any solemn declaration made by the Pope. Although Papal Infallibility had not yet been defined, there was a clear reference to it in the Papal pronouncement of 1854. The dogma was not proclaimed by an Ecumenical Council but by the Pope alone, ("by the virtue of the authority of the holy Apostles Peter and Paul and of Our own authority,") using the full weight of his apostolic authority to bind the consciences of all the faithful on a particular point of doctrine. . . . Pusey had the merit of formulating in his *Eirenicon* the fears and objections of sincere Anglicans in a learned and exhaustive fashion, and thus evoking a singularly well-established, documented and ecumenical response from Newman. Although Newman considered that his friend discharged his olive branch of peace (*Eirenicon*) 'as from a catapult,' Pusey's aim was not polemical as his text would at times suggest." See also *John Henry Newman: The Mother of God*, ed. Stanley L. Jaki (Pinckney, Mich.: Real View Books, 2003), vii–lxxxi.
2. Boyce, *Mary in the Life and Writings of JHN*, 95.
3. Dev. D., 93f.
4. Roger Jupp, "'Awfully gifted of the children of men': Some Aspects of Newman's Devotion to the Blessed Virgin Mary As an Anglican," in *Newman on Mary: Two Papers in Development* (Oxford: The Ecumenical Society of the Blessed Virgin Mary, 1996), 10. (Hereafter cited as "Some Aspects.")

5. Cf. H. Francis Davis, "Newman and Our Lady," in *The Clergy Review* 34 (1949), 377: "We might mention Newman's basing the honouring of saints on the Athanasian principle that Christians are made one with the flesh of Christ, and live by His life. Christians, insofar as they are Christians, are said by Athanasius and many others of the Fathers to be deified or divinized. This dignity is greater in Mary than in us, because she is so much more closely joined to Christ; she is much more closely one with His life-giving flesh, and with His very God-head. Because of this, her life had to be a life more Christlike than that of other creatures."

6. Giovanni Velocci, "Maria nella Vita di John Henry Newman," in *Theotokos* 6 (1998), 280f.

7. PPS, IV, 172f. Cf. Heb 12:22–24.

8. Newman furnishes us with an excellent scripturally based understanding of the communion of the saints: "Christ went to intercede with the Father, we do not know, we may not boldly speculate, yet it may be that saints departed intercede, unknown to us, for the victory of the Truth upon earth; and their prayers above may be as really indispensable conditions of that victory as the labors of those who remain among us. They are taken away for some good purpose surely; their gifts are not lost to us; their soaring minds, the fire of their contemplation, the sanctity of their desires, the vigor of their faith, the sweetness and gentleness of their affections, were not given without an object. Yea, doubtless they are keeping up the perpetual chant in the shrine above, praying and praising God day and night in His temple like Moses upon the Mount, while Joshua and his host fight with Amalek. Can they be allotted greater blessedness than to have a station after the pattern of that Savior who has departed hence? Has He no power in the world's movements because he is away? And though He is the living and exalted Lord of all, and the government is on His shoulders, and they are but His servants without strength of themselves, laid up, moreover apart from the conflict of good and evil in the paradise of God, yet so much light as this is given us by the inspired pages of the Apocalypse, that they are interested in the fortunes of the Church" (PPS, II, 214). In a personal communication, Mr. Gerard Tracey, late Archivist of the Birmingham Oratory, wrote the following to this author: "It is interesting to note that (this sermon) is one of the five sermons that were written for publication rather than preaching (and the only ones that were ever composed as such throughout his whole corpus). The subjects treated suggest that they were intended as an implicit response to the theological position adopted by R. D. Hampden in the pamphlet, *Observations on Religious Dissent* (a work that Newman thought made a 'shipwreck' of Christianity) that had appeared in the previous month" (16 April 1999).

9. Newman, in referring to "the citizens of the City of God," may have been inspired by the title of St. Augustine's magnum opus, *Civitas Dei*. Cf. Ps 86:3.

10. PPS, IV, 176–178, passim.

11. Cf. Heb 4:14–16.

12. Cf. Velocci, "Maria nella Vita di John Henry Newman," 282: "Ma durante gli anni '30 Newman, forse per un esagerato letteralismo biblico, dovette affrontare un'altra difficoltà: quella di conciliare la presenza attiva dei santi nella

Chiesa e l'insegnamento della Scrittura, secondo il quale essi sono nella pace e nel riposo. La superò facilmente convincendosi che la loro attività non comporta nessuna fatica."

13. PPS, III, 350–363, passim. Cf. CCC 2616. The reference to St. Augustine's work is *Enarratio in Psalmos*, 85, 1. Cf. also *Principles and Norms for the Liturgy of the Hours*, 7.

14. Cf. CCC 328–336.

15. Jupp, "Some Aspects," 11.

16. AP, 113.

17. Meriol Trevor, *Newman: The Pillar of the Cloud*, vol. 1 (London, 1962), 91f. Cf. Jupp, "Some Aspects," 5.

18. AP, 114.

19. Jupp, "Some Aspects," 3.

20. AP, 112. Cf. Dermot Fenelon, "The Mystery of Newman," *Louvain Studies* 15 (1990), 121: "Celibacy in the priestly state was accompanied, in Newman, with a great love of the Virgin Mary. He saw in her the pattern of humility and of obedience to the Revealed Word."

21. Velocci, "Maria nella Vita di John Henry Newman," 283: "In questo periodo (1833–1839) Newman fu animato da un forte spirito polemico, specialmente nei confronti della Chiesa di Roma, e andò alla ricerca di tutti i suoi punti deboli per denunciarli e condannarli. Così tra altro, criticò severamente la dottrina di alcuni teologi, come quella di P. Crasset, il quale sembra affermare che la forza della preghiera di Maria è così grande che può salvare gli uomini, anche se questi non conducono una vita cristiana. Criticò pure l'opinione di altri scrittori, secondo i quali le preghiere di Maria sono un comando per il Figlio. Quando Newman si esprimeva in questi termini, sentiva sicura la sua posizione; solo cercava una base teologica per il suo anglicanesimo che credette trovare nella *via media* tra il cattolicesimo e il protestantesimo."

22. AP, 101. Cf. Diff II, 24.

23. Jupp, "Some Aspects," 5.

24. AP, 135.

25. Cf. Jupp, "Some Aspects," 5f. Also, AP, 101, 136, 222, 244f., 246.

26. Jupp, *Some Aspects of Newman's Devotion to the Blessed Virgin Mary As an Anglican*, 8: "It is Michael O'Carroll's view that 'between 1832–1845, (Newman) the Anglican . . . developed a theology of Mary, not only unexampled in his own communion, but superior to most contemporary thinking on the subject in the Catholic or Orthodox churches.'"

27. Jupp, "Some Aspects," 8.

28. Ibid.

29. Jupp, "Some Aspects," 10.

30. Ibid.

31. Ibid.

32. Jupp, "Some Aspects," 11.

33. Newman wrote Tract 75 on the Roman Breviary.

34. Jupp, "Some Aspects," 12. Cf. AP, 152.

35. Trevor, *The Pillar of the Cloud*, 195f. Cf. Jupp, "Some Aspects," 12.

36. Jupp, "Some Aspects," 12.

37. The Articles of Religion (Article 22, "Of Purgatory") found in *The Book of Common Prayer* (New York: Oxford University Press, 1990), 874. Cf.: CCC 1030–1032, 1472 (Purgatory); CCC 336, 956, 958, 1434, 2156, 2683 (intercession of the angels and saints); CCC 969, 2673–2679, 2827 (intercession of the Virgin Mary); CCC 476f. (sacred images); CCC 1075, 1667ff, 1688ff (sacramentals). Most noteworthy are the following scriptural quotations that are foundational for these doctrines: 1 Cor 3:15, 1 Pet 1:7, Mt 12:31, 2 Mac 12:45–46, Job 1:5 (Purgatory); Heb 12:1f., Mt 25:21 (intercession of the saints); Job 33:23f., Zacc 1:12, Tob 12:12, Mt 18:10, Rev 8:3f. (intercession of the angels); Lk 1:48, Jn 2:1–11, Rev 12:1f. (intercession of the Virgin Mary); Ex 25:18–22, Num 21:4–9, Gal 3:1, 1 Jn 1:1–4 (sacred images); Lk 8:43–48, Jn 9:5–7, Acts 5:12–16 (sacramentals/relics).

38. Jupp, "Some Aspects," 13.

39. Cf. Friedel, *The Mariology of Cardinal Newman*, 52.

40. Cf. VM, II, 304.

41. Cf. AP, 197.

42. Jupp, "Some Aspects," 19.

43. Newman was Faber's spiritual advisor.

44. Cf. Friedel, *The Mariology of Cardinal Newman*, 70.

45. Velocci, "Maria nella Vita di John Henry Newman," 284–285.

46. Cf. AP, 24f.

47. Cf. Stephen Dessain, *Cardinal's Newman's Teaching about the Blessed Virgin Mary* (The Oratory at Birmingham, England: The Friends of Cardinal Newman, n.d.), 4f. The quotations of Newman are taken from EHC, 36, 438.

48. EHC, 452f. Newman placed a picture of the Madonna in the room of his young brother, Frank, when Frank arrived at Oxford.

49. EHC, 453.

50. Velocci, *John H. Newman: Lettera al Rev. Pusey su Maria e la Vita Cristiana* (Rome: Città Nuova Editrice, 1975), 20f. Cf. Velocci, "Maria nella Vita di John Henry Newman," 285: "Grazie ai ripetuti incontri con Keble, Newman giunse ad assimilare le idee lentamente su Maria: sulla sua grandezza e santità, nella sua missione nella storia della salvezza e nella comunione dei santi si avvicinò senza pregiudizi alla Chiesa di Roma, sentì per essa rispetto e venerazione, la guardò con delicatezza e simpatia."

51. Velocci, *John H. Newman: Lettera*, 67f.

52. Cf. Friedel, *The Mariology of Cardinal Newman*, 108: "The *Letter to Pusey* purports to be an answer to this renowned Anglican's *Eirenicon*—a letter addressed to John Keble. This in turn had been an answer to a letter of Manning. . . . In his volume Pusey at first merely defended the English Church against the implications of Manning, following somewhat on the lines of Newman's Tract 90, by showing that the divergences between the Articles and the Tridentine Decrees were merely differences of words. But as he reached the great point of contest, namely, Article 22, which treats of the 'Romish practices such as invocations, pardons, etc.', he changed his tactics and made his answer a plea for reunion."

53. Friedel, *The Mariology of Cardinal Newman*, 120.

54. Diff II, 51f.

55. Karl Adam offers many insights into the nature of the communion of saints (with particular reference to their intercessory role, their cooperation in the redemptive work of Christ, and their share in Christ's mediation—all themes of Newman decades earlier): "They do not help us through any strength of their own, but through the strength of God, and they help us only so far as creatures may. They cannot themselves sanctify us. For sanctification, the new life in God, is to be obtained only from Him Who is Himself the divine life, that is from our divine Redeemer. St. Augustine tells us that the power of awakening souls to this life belongs to God alone. So the Catholic knows that he belongs to God alone, is related only to Him and lives only in Him, and that not only in the substance of his natural being, but also in his supernatural life. In comparison with our intimate and vital conjunction with God, and with that marvelous contact with the Infinite Being, where difference is annulled and where the Divine Life penetrates our souls and continually pervades them anew, the activity of even angels and saints pales into insignificance. For it is God and God only Who redeems us and gives us life. Yet angels and saints have the power to accompany the great work of our redemption with their fostering love and by their 'intercession' (*intercessione*) to elevate our prayers for help into the great solitary prayer of the whole Body of Christ. It is true that God knows our necessities, and needs no saints to tell Him. And it is true also that His Only-begotten Son by His Sacrifice on the Cross merited His grace and mercy for us once and for all, so that they are ever near us. Yet, for the very reason that Jesus Christ, the God-Man, is the Mediator of our Redemption, the saints also have a share in it. For they are members of our Redeemer. He is not without them, and they are not without Him. No help comes to us, but that the members of Christ in their manner cooperate with their Head. We say 'in their manner,' that is, otherwise than the Head. This is the fulfilment of the law of love, the great structural law of the Kingdom of God. God redeems men in such a way that every love-force in the Body of Christ has its proper share in the work. The Body of Christ of its very nature implies communion and cooperation, and so the divine blessing never works without its members, but only in and through their unity. God can help us without the saints; but He will not help us without their cooperation, for it is His nature and will to be communicative love."—*The Spirit of Catholicism* (Garden City, N.Y.: Image Books, 1954), 123f.

56. Diff II, 52.

57. Diff II, 52.

58. LD, 22:68, 90.

59. LD, 22:68.

60. Father Friedel comments: "Seated at the right hand of her Son in glory, raised to the dignity of Queen of Angels and Sts., Mary cannot forget the Church militant, for the salvation of which she had consented to become the Mother of the Redeemer, had cooperated in the Redemption, and had suffered courageously the greatest spiritual anguish that could ever have been endured by a mere creature" (*The Mariology of Cardinal Newman*, 327).

61. The Holy Father, Pope John Paul II writes: "The first known Marian invocation goes back to the third century and begins with the words: 'We fly to thy protection ("*sub tuum præsidium*"), O holy Mother of God. . . .' However,

since the 14th century the most common prayer among Christians has been the Hail Mary.... The Eastern hymn *Akáthistos* repeatedly stresses this 'rejoice' " (*Mary, Mother of God*, 255).

62. Diff II, 37. Newman does not give any indication as to what other possible words the evangelists might have used instead of the Greek word παράκλητος.

63. See LG 62. Also, Pope John Paul II writes: "Mary exercises her role as 'Advocate' by cooperating both with the Spirit (the Paraclete) and with the one who interceded on the cross for his persecutors (cf. Lk 23:34), whom John calls our 'advocate with the Father' (1 Jn 2:1)."

64. Cf. Friedel, *The Mariology of Cardinal Newman*, 104.

65. Although the concept of intercessory prayer is not necessarily excluded by Irenæus' use of the term "advocate," it does not seem to be his intention to emphasize this particular doctrine with regard to Mary when he refers to her as "Advocate" of Eve in the *Adversus Hæreses*.

66. SN, 92f.

67. SN, 105.

68. SN, 114.

69. Cf. LG 54: " ... the duties of the redeemed toward the Mother of God, who is the Mother of Christ and Mother of men, particularly of the faithful."

70. SN, 134.

71. Cf. DS, 1821: "bonum atque utile esse, suppliciter eos invocare et ob beneficia impetranda ... "

72. Diff II, 68.

73. Ibid.

74. In DS, 1821, the appropriateness of invoking the saints is immediately followed by an important series of modifying clauses, namely that the benefits we receive through their intercession come to us, "a Deo per Filium eius Iesum Christum Dominum nostrum, qui solus noster Redemptor et Salvator est, ad eorum orationes, opem auxilumque confugere; illos vero, qui negant, Sanctos, æterna felicitate in cælo fruentes, invocandos esse; aut qui asserunt, vel illos orare, vel eorum, ut pro nobis etiam singulis orent, invocationem esse ido(lo)latriam, vel pugnare cum verbo Dei, adversarique honori 'unius mediatoris Dei et hominum Iesu Christi' (cf. 1 Tim 2:5); vel stultum esse, in cælo regnantibus voce mente supplicare: impie sentire."

75. LG 60–62.

76. Diff II, 68.

77. Cf. LG 59. Also, Hugo Rahner, *Our Lady and the Church*, 93: "Here indeed is fulfilled in all mankind what was begun in the heart of the Virgin at the instant of the Incarnation: in the sanctuary of the immaculate heart, in her innermost being, in her trusting and obedient spirit, in her spotless womb, when the overshadowing grace of the Holy Spirit came in. The heart of Mary is the beginning of the story: in her heart was prepared in secret, what now at Pentecost is open to the gaze of all mankind. The heart of Mary is the original upper room, where redeemed mankind is gathered."

78. Pope John Paul II, *Theotokos: Woman, Mother, Disciple*, vol. 5 (Boston: Pauline Books and Media, 2000), 17–20, 197–199. Also RM 26: "The Holy

Spirit had already come down upon her, and she became his faithful spouse at the Annunciation, welcoming the Word of the true God. . . ."

79. Diff II, 69. Cf. Acts 1:14. Also, CCC 2617.

80. Cf. Diff II, 69: "St. Paul enjoins his brethren to 'pray with all prayer and supplication at all times in the Spirit, with all instance and supplication for all the saints,' to 'pray in every place,' 'to make supplications, prayers, intercessions, giving thanks, for all men.' And in his own person he 'ceases not to give thanks for them, commemorating them in his prayers,' and 'always in all his prayers making supplication for them all with joy.'" Cf. 1 Tm 2:1–7.

81. Diff II, 71.

82. Diff II, 69f.

83. Diff II, 70. Here Newman accepts both the intercession of the saints and the direct invocation of the saints on the part of believers—the latter which, as we have already noted, was a major difficulty during his Anglican period.

84. Diff II, 70. The following versicles of the Roman Liturgy of the Hours, taken from the *Antiphonale Monasticum*, express well the theme of intercessory prayer contained in the Book of Revelation: 1) *V.* Dirigatur, Domine, oratio mea. *R.* Sicut incensum in conspectu tuo. 2) *V.* Vespertina oratio ascendat ad te, Domine. *R.* Et descendat super nos misericordia tua. Cf. Ps 140.

85. Diff II, 70.

86. Diff II, 71.

87. Cf. Heb 12:1–2.

88. Diff II, 71. Cf. Rom 8:26–27

89. Diff II, 71.

90. Diff II, 71f. Cf. Jn 9:31; Jas 5:16 (cf. also 5:15); 1 Jn 3:2–23 (cf. also 5:13–21). Also, Jn 4:23f.

91. Diff II, 72. See, for example, Gen 19:16–33; Ex 32:1–14.

92. Diff II, 72.

93. Newman writes: "To the friends of Job it was said, 'My servant Job shall pray for you; his face I will accept.'" Cf. Diff II, 72; Job 33:26.

94. Cf. Diff II, 72. Newman writes: "Elias by his prayer shut and opened the heavens." Some references to the power of Elijah's intercessory prayer: 1 Kings 18:36–39; 2 Kings 1:9–12; Jas 5:17–18.

95. Cf. Jer 11:23–25.

96. Cf. 1 Sam 8:1–10.

97. Cf. Gen 8:20–22.

98. Cf. Dan 6:11; 9:1–27.

99. Cf. Lk 16:19–31.

100. Diff II, 72.

101. SN, 92.

102. The number six, in biblical terms, is generally considered to be a number of imperfection. Christ's sign at Cana takes place on the seventh day of His public ministry according to the chronology laid out by John. Thus, the first sign of Christ's inaugurates the work of a new creation reminiscent of the six days of creation in the Book of Genesis. In fact, the sign manifesting Our Lord's glory at Cana is the first of seven major signs in John's Gospel culminating in the Resurrection of Our Lord "on the third day." The third day, according to

the Gospels, is the first day of the week (i.e., Sunday). The "eighth day" is a theological expression of eschatological import. It is used to refer to the life of heaven, that is, to the day of the Lord that will never end. See CCC 314, 349, 639, 2174–2176.

103. The Reverend Francis M. William, O.P., reflects on Newman's understanding of Mary's intercessory power as revealed in the latter's *Sermons on the Subjects of the Day*, particularly one entitled "Our Lord's Last Supper and Its First," which he delivered on 23 February 1843. Father William writes: "Sub 'primo convivio' intelligit nuptias apud Canam, in quibus Jesus, matre precante, primum miraculum patravit. Sub 'ultimo convivio' intelligit cænam Domini, in qua Sacrificium Missæ instituit et apostolos eorumque successores ordinavit eisque mandavit, ut hoc sacrificium incruentum tamquam suas vices gerentes semper offerent atque ita de inexhausta benedictione motis suæ in crucis fidelibus communicarent. Inde a nuptiis Canæ Iesus a Matre sua per tempus determinatum, nempe per dies vitæ suæ publicæ, discessit. Postea, cum venit hora eius, in opere redemptionis exsequendo iterum ad latus eius accessura erat. Huic interruptioni commorationis externæ Iesu cum discipulis tempore passionis et mortis suæ apponit. Cognitioni hic sibi illucescenti hance tribuit formam: Si Iesus hic apostolis pro tempore, quo iterum sibi coniuncti erunt, tantam intercessionis potentiam pollicetur, quantam intercessionis Mariæ, matri virginis suæ, in cælis concedere debet, quæ in exsecutionem historicam operis redemptionis condicionato modo est inducta! Suscipiens— angelo ei condicionem quoad eum sine condicione, via facti relationem ingressa est non solum ad Iesum, sed etiam ad omnes homines, ad quos redimendos Filius Dei incarnari voluit. Postquam de significatione symbolica convivii festivi universe locutus est. . . . Transit deinde Newman ad comparationem separationis transitoriæ Iesu a Maria post nuptias Canæ cum separatione ab apostolis in ipsa cæna dominica sub respectu momenti interni. Ita valedixit matri in convivio festivo, sicut postea valedixit in alio convivio."— "Doctrina Mariana Cardinal Newman et Motus Œcumenicus," *De Mariologia et Œcumenismo* (Rome: Pontificia Academia Mariana Internationalis, 1962), 265–268, passim. Cf. SD 27–39.

104. Diff II, 72f.

105. MD, 312. Cf. H. Francis Davis, "La Sainte Vierge dans la Jeunesse de Newman," 546: "Ces paroles mystérieuses, les autres réprimandes—ou qui nous semblent telles—que Notre Seigneur adressa à Marie au début de son ministère, sont interprétées par Newman comme une indication donnée à Sa Mère: jusqu'à la fin de Sa vie publique, jusqu'à Sa mort et Sa résurrection, il ne lui serait plus possible de participer directement à son œuvre. Elle ne pourrait que souffrir, et prier, et offrir ces souffrances et ces prières pour Ses membres, pour qu'ils ne refusent pas grâces gagnées par Lui et qu'ils écoutent son enseignement. C'est après la résurrection de son Fils que commencerait son rôle publique et officiel dans l'Église."

106. It is interesting that the Evangelist does not say that Mary came to believe in Jesus as a result of the sign worked at Cana. Perhaps, this is to indicate that her faith was already well-established and indeed what prompted her to ask Jesus to perform the sign at Cana. Likewise, her words to the servants: "Do

whatever He tells you," are most indicative of her singular obedience of faith, which she, in turn, engenders in others. Jn 2:12 tells us that after having completed His sign manifesting His glory, Jesus goes down from Cana in Galilee to Capernaum in the company of Mary, His brothers and His disciples. Here, the Evangelist seems to have envisioned the formation of the new messianic family which will be further delineated at Calvary in the persons of Mary and the Beloved Disciple. Cf. The article "Bibbia," by Aristide Serra in NDM, 283: "'al'termine dell'episodio, la Vergine, i fratelli e i discepoli di Gesù appaiono come un sol gruppo, stretto attorno a Lui. Con molta probabilità, l'evangelista vuol dire che il motivo di tale fusione è *la fede in Gesù*, dimostrata sia dalla Vergine (v. 5), sia dai discepoli (v. 11). Anzi, sul piano della fede non v'è differenza tra i parenti (madre, fratelli) e i discepoli. Commenta M. Thurian: 'Alla fine del racconto, Maria e i discepoli formano una comunità messianica, unita nella fede al Figlio di Dio che ha appunto manifestato la sua gloria; lì sta il nucleo della Chiesa attorno al suo Signore . . .'" (*Maria, Madre del Signore*, 158). Moses gave the Law (Torah) to the Israelites "on the morning of the third day," after having entered into the desert of Sinai (cf. Ex 19:16ff.). Jesus performs the miracle at Cana "on the third day" and thus fulfills and surpasses the Law of Moses—by changing the water of the Old Covenant into the new and more choice wine of His gospel (cf. Jn 2:1–11).

107. Cf. Hugo Rahner, *Our Lady and the Church*, 50f.: "When we read in the story of the marriage at Cana the simple words 'and the mother of Jesus was there' (Jn 2:2) we are already deep in symbolism. It was a marriage, and the God-Man changed the water of human nature into the wine of the divine; at the feast of Jesus through all time, that is in the Church, the Mother of Jesus is there. The history of the Incarnation begins in her; at her motherly request the guests at the table became His guests, receiving what He had to give them. The Syrian Ephrem in one of his hymns on the mysteries of the Lord exclaims: 'Cana is the praise of thee, for through thee came the joy of this feast. The bride is thy holy Church, the guests of the table are thy guests, and the triumph of the miracle looks forward to thy coming in majesty (*Hymn on the Lord's Mysteries* 34, I; ed. Lamy, II, p. 822).' This deep significance of the marriage at Cana therefore includes the whole history of salvation from the first coming at the Incarnation to Our Lord's return at the end of days. Throughout this history, extending through the centuries humanity is being changed into the wine of the life of grace, while Mary is there, the mother who cares and who intercedes, standing at the very centre of the mystery in which God takes human nature from the child of Eve: Mary is the mother of all who are sanctified by their faith in this coming of God."

108. St. Thomas Aquinas, *In Johannem Evangelistam expositio*, 330–332.

109. Diff II, 73.

110. Diff II, 21.

111. Diff II, 100.

112. Diff II, 104f. See, also LD, 22:68: "But there is all the difference in the world between saying that 'without her intercession no one is saved—' and 'without her invocation no one is saved—' whereas Pusey at page 102 passes from the one idea to the other, as if authors who said the one must necessarily

say, may be taken and understood to say, the other. He quotes Suarez for the power of her intercession—he quotes St. Bernardine (or Eadmer) for the necessity of her invocation, or of devotion to her—but Suarez is an authority quite in a different line of importance from St. Bernardine—(or rather Eadmer—). The former is a theologian, laying down doctrine—the latter is a devotional author,—and moreover writes for Italians, for those who already knew and held the doctrine of her intercession, and were in a country where to neglect devotion to her would have been a rejection of a privilege which they *possessed*. I never can deny my belief that the Blessed Virgin prays efficaciously for the Church, and for individual souls in and out of it. Nor can I deny that to be devout to her is a duty *following* on this doctrine—but I will never say, even though St. Bernardine said it, that no one is saved who is not devout to her, and (tho' I don't know St. Bernardine's writings) I do not think *he* would have said it had he not been in his own Christendom, or had he known the history of the first centuries, or had he seen the religious state of things we see ourselves." The St. Bernardine to whom Newman is referring is most likely St. Bernardine of Siena. Newman, writing in *A Letter to Pusey* (cf. Diff II, 98) makes reference to the fact that he was unaware of the existence of another writer by the name of Bernardine de Bustis about whom Pusey makes reference in his *Eirenicon* along with St. Bernardine of Siena. It is interesting to note that the mention of both of these men in *A Letter to Pusey* occurs in the context of a discussion of Catholic Marian devotions, Anglican misconceptions, and Catholic excesses of the same. Newman highlights how both of these men, but especially St. Bernardine of Sienna (Newman misspells this city's name or is relying on an earlier spelling), exhibited a great devotion to Mary but always in a way that was subordinate to their "burning love for our Lord" and their "conspicuous" "zeal" "for the Holy Name" "of Jesus." With this background provided by Newman, perhaps his criticism of St. Bernardine of Siena (or Eadmer) in a letter to John Keble is mitigated. Nevertheless, if Newman had given precise references to St. Bernardine's words (or Eadmer's), then perhaps his criticism of him (them) could be better evaluated. Cf. also LD, 22:89–91.

113. Diff II, 118.

114. Diff II, 170.

115. Newman took "Mary" as his Confirmation name.

116. Dermot Fenelon, "The Mystery of Newman," *Louvain Studies* 15 (1990), 222.

117. Diff II, 76.

118. Cf. LG 60: "The salvific influence of the Blessed Virgin on men originates, not from some inner necessity, but from the divine pleasure. It flows forth from the superabundance of the merits of Christ, rests on his mediation, depends entirely on it and draws all its power from it." Again, at LG 60: "The maternal duty of Mary toward men in no way obscures or diminishes this unique mediation of Christ, but rather shows his power." Finally, in the same paragraph, the Council Fathers explain that Mary's maternal mediation does not, "impede, but rather does it foster the immediate union of the faithful with Christ."

119. Cf. SN, 118.

120. See also MC 16: "That the Blessed Virgin is an exemplar in this field derives from the fact that she is recognized as a most excellent exemplar of the Church in the order of faith, charity and perfect union with Christ, that is, of that interior disposition with which the Church, the beloved spouse, closely associated with her Lord, invokes Christ and through him worships the Eternal Father."

121. SN, 42f.

122. Cf. SN, 129–131.

123. SN, 130.

124. Ibid.

125. Ibid. This theological distinction between the once-for-all act of redemption—which Jesus alone could accomplish as the God-Man according to the Father's will (divine economy)—and the on-going work of our salvation is a distinction that can well serve our present discussion concerning creaturely (e.g., human, ecclesial, Marian) cooperation in the *œconomia salutis* as it preserves the historical uniqueness of the Paschal Mystery in contradistinction to but not in contradiction to the manner in which the infinite merits of those redemptive acts are then subjectively applied to the individual believer.

126. SN, 130.

127. Cf. St. Thomas Aquinas, *Summa Theologica* III, q. 68, a. 2: "Deus non alligatur sacramentis"; Pope Pius XII's encyclical letter *Mystici Corporis*, 101.

128. SN, 130.

129. SN, 130. Cf. LG 1, 9; GS 45.

130. SN, 130f.

131. SN, 131.

132. Diff II, 84.

133. Cf. LG 63: "By reason of the gift and role of divine maternity, by which she is united with her Son, the Redeemer, and with his singular graces and functions, the Blessed Virgin is also intimately united with the Church."

134. Cf. Pope John Paul II, *Theotokos: Woman, Mother, Disciple*, 52. Also, LG 61, 62.

135. Diff II, 85. Newman is referring to the poet William Wordsworth.

136. Diff II, 85.

137. Diff II, 426f.

138. Dev. D., 354f. Cf. Jn 12:20–26. See also for example, Jn 1:40–42 and Jn 1:43–51, in which Andrew evangelizes his brother Peter and Philip evangelizes the apostle Nathanael (also known as Bartholomew). See also Acts 8:26–40. St. Philip evangelizes the Ethiopian eunuch and subsequently baptizes him. All of the aforementioned passages relate evangelization to discipleship and vice versa. Furthermore, the preaching of God's Word and the administration of the sacraments to the neophytes by the apostles and disciples of the Lord clearly express the Lord's will that the offer of salvation be made through human mediation, most especially through the mediation of the Church and her Sacred Ministers. Hence, the significance of the Apostolic Tradition and the Apostolic Succession of Bishops as integral doctrines that express the importance of ecclesial mediation and human cooperation in the *œconomia salutis*.

139. MD, 71.

140. Cf. LG 54: "... occupies a place in the Church which is the highest after Christ and yet very close to us."

141. Cf. Arnold of Chartres, *De Septem Verbis Domini in Cruce*, 3 (PL 189:1694). He writes: "What the Mother asks, the Son approves and the Father grants."

142. Cf. AP, 165. Also, Velocci, "Maria nella Vita di John Henry Newman," 277.

143. Velocci, "Newman e *l'Ecclesia Mater*," *Mater Ecclesiæ* 3 (1965), 162.

144. Charles Reding, the principal character of Newman's novel *Loss and Gain*, having returned from a meeting with a friend who had converted to Catholicism and overwhelmed with joy, begins, in almost litanic form, to invoke the Church as his great and powerful mother, begging of her the grace of final conversion.

145. Diff II, 104.

146. Diff II, 91. However, Newman's recourse to the Greek Church (Liturgy) need not have been, in the opinion of this author, so harshly critical and ecumenically insensitive, especially when he writes, by way of comparison, that "the Latins have more mental activity, more strength of intellect, less of routine, less mechanical worship among them, than the Greeks. We [i.e., Latins] are able, better than they, to give an account of what we do; and we seem to be more extreme, merely because we are more definite." Newman's criticism falls short of acknowledging a whole set of factors (historical, theological, etc.) which, taken as whole, would help to explain the differences between the Western and Eastern Rites. Unfortunately, Newman does not allude to these factors, and a discussion of them is far beyond the scope of this present discussion.

147. Diff II, 91.

148. Diff II, 101.

149. Ibid.

150. Ibid.

151. Diff II, 105.

152. Ibid.

153. Diff II, 104.

154. Diff II, 105f.

155. Diff II, 104. Newman writes: "To say, for instance, dogmatically, that no one can be saved without personal devotion to the Blessed Virgin, would be an untenable proposition; yet it might be true of this man or that, or of this country at this or that date; and, if that very statement has ever been made by any writer of consideration (and this has to be ascertained), then perhaps it was made precisely under these exceptional circumstances."

156. Cf. Diff II, 106. Newman writes: "... and I certainly think it would be a very grave act, if in a Catholic country (and of such the writers were speaking, for they knew of no other), with Ave-Marias sounding in the air, and images of the Madonna in every street and road, a Catholic broke off or gave up a practice that was universal, and in which he was brought up, and deliberately put her name out of his thoughts."

157. Diff II, 105.

158. Newman's novel *Loss and Gain* is autobiographical in inspiration. Its

main theme is the conversion story of a character by the name of Charles Reding who, as a student at Oxford, discovers and accepts the truths of Roman Catholicism through his discussions/relationships with his fellow students and family members. One of the many difficulties that Charles Reding had to overcome along the path to his conversion was the question of Roman Catholic Marian doctrine and devotion. In fact, Charles, while at the University, engages in on-going debates of a theological and spiritual nature about the distinction between intercession and invocation of Our Lady and the saints. He expresses frustration and dismay when he learns of the accusations of idolatry or Mariolatry on the part of the Roman Church which are, for example, either raised by some of his fellow students (e.g., a character by the name of Bateman) or not properly addressed by converts to Catholicism (e.g., a character named Willis). Eventually, Charles becomes a most adamant apologist of Roman Catholic teachings, expressing a special love and devotion to Our Lord's Real Presence in the Eucharist and Our Blessed Mother—two essential catalysts of his conversion. At the end of the story, Charles is received into full communion with the Catholic Church at a Passionist monastery and decides to pursue studies for the priesthood.

159. Cf. Edward B. Pusey, *Letter to the Lord Bishop of Oxford* (New York: J. S. Redfield Publishers, 1843), 138. Cf. also Karl Rahner, "Why and How Can We Venerate the Saints?" in *Theological Investigations*, vol. 8 (New York: Herder and Herder, 1971), 3–29.

160. See the Conclusion of the work for a more detailed analysis of Newman's treatment of the title of Mary Co-Redemptrix.

161. DMC, 143–144, passim.

162. Basil of Seleucia actually uses the word "mediatress" (*mesiteuosa*) in reference to Mary (PG 77:992).

163. De Margerie, "Mary, Co-Redemptrix in the Light of Patristics," in *Mary, Co-Redemptrix, Mediatrix, Advocate* (Santa Barbara, Calif.: Queenship Publishing, 1995), 20. The citation is from Basil's Homily 39 (PG 85:448–449).

164. De Margerie, "Mary, Co-Redemptrix in the Light of Patristics," 20. Newman most certainly relies upon Basil of Seleucia as a testimony of the Church's belief in Mary as Mediatrix. However, the other conclusions that De Margerie draws from Basil do not appear explicitly in the writings of Newman.

165. De Margerie, "Mary, Co-Redemptrix in the Light of Patristics," 20.

166. SN, 138.

167. SN, 46f.

168. SN, 151.

169. SN, 193.

170. Dev. D., 144.

171. Dev. D., 145.

172. Ibid.

173. Velocci, "Maria nella Vita di John Henry Newman," 294.

174. Cf. CCC 332. The following scriptural texts are most noteworthy in this connection: cf. Job 38:7, Gen 3:24, Gen 19, Gen 21:17, Gen 22:11, Ex 23:20–23, Judg 13, Judg 6:11–24, 1 Kings 19:5, Is 6:6, Mt 1:20, Mt 2:13.19, Acts 7:53.

175. Cf. Dev. D., 140: "The more plausible was the heretical argument against His Divinity from these texts, the more emphatic is St. Athanasius' exaltation of our regenerate nature by way of explaining them. . . . The sanctification, or rather the deification of the nature of man, is one main subject of St. Athansius' theology."

176. Velocci, "Maria nella Vita di John Henry Newman," 294.

177. Dev. D., 140.

178. The quotations from Proclus of Constantinople are on pages 146 and 147 of *An Essay on the Development of Christian Doctrine*.

179. Cf. St. Bernard of Clairvaux, Serm. 3 *in Purif.*, 2 (PL 183:370).

180. Dev. D., 146f.

181. MD, 391–393, 393–395.

182. MD, 391. Cf. CCC 659–667. See also for example, the following key scriptural texts having to do with Our Lord's Ascension and His priestly intercession on behalf of our salvation: Jn 12:32; Heb 7:25, 9:11, 9:24; Rev 4:6–11.

183. MD, 392.

184. If Newman intends, in this instance, that prayer after the grave (death) becomes "obsolete," then one would obviously have to admit that he did not yet fully understand the Catholic doctrines of purgatory and the communion of saints.

185. MD, 395.

186. MD, 83f.

187. Cf. Jn 1:9

188. Cf. Pope Pius XII, *Mystici Corporis*, in AAS 35 (1943), 248: "We have without hesitation consecrated all mankind to the immaculate heart of Mary. May she, the most holy Mother of all the members of Christ, radiant now, body and soul in heaven, and gloriously reigning with her Son, earnestly implore of Him, that mighty streams of grace may ceaseless flow from the majestic head upon all members of the Mystical Body."

189. MD, 246.

190. MD, 236f.

191. Hence, also, the title of Mary: "Our Lady of Victory."

192. Vincent Blehl, S.J., *The White Stone: The Spiritual Theology of John Henry Newman* (Petersham, Mass.: St. Bede's Publications, 1993), 119.

193. Cf. Dermot Fenelon, "The Mystery of Newman," 221.

194. Cf. Friedel, *The Mariology of Cardinal Newman*, 95f.

195. Blehl, *The White Stone*, 119f.

196. Diff II, 103.

197. SN, 39.

198. René Laurentin, *Maria Chiave del Mistero Cristiano* (Milan: Edizioni San Paolo, 1996), 23f.

199. Friedel, *The Mariology of Cardinal Newman*, 142.

CHAPTER SEVEN

1. Blehl, *The White Stone*, 113.

2. MD, 158. See also the Fourth Station in Newman's longer version of the Stations of the Cross.

3. MD, 167.

4. LG 61.

5. AP, 195.

6. The "solus cum solo" principle also stems from Newman's quest for the interiorization of the simplicity of Gospel truths. The Catholic Newman, Newman the Oratorian and Prince of the Church does not adhere to the notion of a rugged, individualistic, private, isolationist approach to religious matters, whether doctrinal or devotional, as was taught him in his Evangelical up-bringing. However, while never divorcing the individual's life of faith from the life of faith of the whole Church, Newman's keen sense of personhood, the individual soul, and the individual conscience does not permit him to accept the notion that the one is subsumed into the other, but is to be integrated into it.

7. Newman actually uses another form of the same title: "Co-redemptress."

8. Diff II, 78. Let us leave aside the appropriateness of the title "priestess" because it does not enter into our purpose.

9. Cf. For a treatment of this section of the *Letter to Pusey*, see Chapter One, "Newman's Critique of the Protestant (Anglican) Problem with Marian Doctrine and Devotion."

10. Diff II, 78.

11. Diff II, 79.

12. Cf. Diff II, 43.

13. Diff II, 84f.

14. Cf. Friedel, *The Mariology of Cardinal Newman*, 209f. Friedel comments on Diff II, 78, in light of what Newman writes in Diff II, 84: "She does not usurp the place of her Divine Son in the work of Redemption. . . . This is elementary dogma known by the simplest Catholic. No matter how we elevate Mary—and we may raise her to a height short of the infinite—She remains ever a creature as one of us, though a very privileged one. Her function of Mediatrix or Co-Redemptress was not absolutely necessary *necessitate medii*, as the Schoolman would say; yet it was necessary according to the designs of Divine Providence. He willed that she should have a real share in the work of the Redemption. The Fathers manifest this clearly when they speak of her as the cause of salvation to the human race. From the doctrine of the Second Eve springs that of the spiritual maternity. She is truly the Mother of men; like Eve, she has become the Mother of all the living. By becoming the Mother of God and therefore the instrument of the Incarnation, she has entered into an intimate relationship with us in what concerns the spiritual life, for through the Incarnation we become brethren of Christ and heirs of heaven. Grace was restored by the coming of Christ, human nature is sanctified. Christ dwells in His elect personally; He is the immediate source or principle of the spiritual life in them. This Physician, as St. Ignatius calls Him, is from Mary; He gave Himself first through Mary; she was associated with Him in the first act that led to our Redemption; she became thus the cause of our salvation; should she not, then, participate also in the fruits of the Redemption by becoming Mother of all the living, the Mother of 'fair love and fear and knowledge and holy hope,' the health of the weak, the Refuge of sinners, the Comforter of the Afflicted?" (Cf. DMC, 363.)

15. Newman, in speaking of St. Athanasius as the "first and the great teacher" (i.e., post-biblical theologian) of the Incarnation, claims as a consequence of this fact his having "engraved indelibly upon the imaginations of the faithful, as had never been before, that man is God and God is man, that in Mary they meet, and that in this sense Mary is the centre of all things" (Diff II, 87). Furthermore, in the *Letter to Pusey*, Newman, in discussing the qualification of Mary's intercessory prayer as "omnipotent," highlights how this qualification is made in strict relationship to the doctrine of the Incarnation. Newman writes: "Again, to say that Mary is the centre of all being, sounds inflated and profane; yet after all it is only one way, and a natural way, of saying that the Creator and the creature met together, and became one in her womb. . . " (Diff II, 104).

16. DMC, 355. Cf. Diff II, 101: ". . . she is nothing more than an Advocate and not a source of mercy." A more thorough examination of the meaning of this text in Newman's overall thought on Mary's maternal mediation is presented in Chapter Six.

17. Cf. Dev. D., 435.

18. Friedel, *The Mariology of Cardinal Newman*, 340. Cf. MD, 70–71. This meditation of Newman's on the title "Virgo Potens" is discussed in Chapter Six.

19. Diff II, 97.

20. Diff II, 92.

21. Diff II, 93.

22. Ibid.

23. Ibid.

24. Diff II, 94.

25. Ibid.

26. Diff II, 94–95, passim. The statement about the little mention of Mary in the proper of the Mass of the Roman Rite should not be construed as a deprecation of Our Lady's rightful place in the Liturgy or of her intimate association with the redemptive work of Christ at Calvary; it is meant as a mere statement of fact. Furthermore, the Catholic Newman understands clearly that one of the important consequences of the Virgin Mary's intimate association with the mystery of the Incarnation is her love and devotion to her Eucharistic Son, which she learned from the apostles (especially John the Beloved) and transmits by example to the Church. (cf. his sermon "The Glories of Mary for the Sake of Her Son," in DMC, 376). The reader of the *Letter to Pusey* should also appreciate the realism of Newman's pastoral sensibility insofar as he plainly acknowledges theat Pusey and others could be led to the facile and wrong conclusion that the behavior of many Catholics during the celebration of the Mass—whereby they attend informally to Marian devotions (e.g., the veneration of an image of Our Lady)—is synonymous with doctrinal error. Newman writes: "They may be tempted . . . to call such a temple, not a 'Jesus church,' but a 'Mary church'" (cf. Diff II, 95). To this Newman adds an explanation which, although historically conditioned (e.g., the mention of the distinction between High Mass and Low Mass and the time of Mass being limited to morning celebrations), is nonetheless instructive. He writes: "But, if they [Newman is referring to some Protestant observers of the Mass, especially

to those who have communicated their observations to Pusey] understood our ways, they would know that we begin the day with Our Lord and then go on to His Mother" (cf. Diff II, 95). Likewise, Newman responds to yet another possible objection on the part of non-Catholic Christians when he writes that: "Nor is there any reason why those who have been at Low Mass already, should not at that hour proceed to ask the intercession of the Blessed Virgin for themselves and for all that is dear to them" (cf. Diff II, 95). In the *Letter to Pusey*, Newman "recollects" hearing that in the time of Pope Gregory XVI some Catholic devotional books were in circulation that put forth what he terms "the shocking notion that the Blessed Mary is present in the Holy Eucharist, in the sense in which Our Lord is present." However, Newman immediately adds this qualification: "but I have no means of verifying the information I then received" (Diff II, 107).

27. Cf. Diff II, 97f.

28. Diff II, 98.

29. Ibid.

30. Cf. Diff II, 98. Newman writes: " . . . the bulk of our laity, not to say of our clergy."

31. Cf. Diff II, 97: "Such men are on a level very different from our own, and we cannot understand them."

32. Diff II, 99

33. Diff II, 101f.

34. Diff II, 103.

35. Ibid.

36. Blehl, *The White Stone*, 113: "God could have redeemed man from his fallen state and reconciled him to Himself without becoming man, but once the Incarnation was decreed, its economy included . . . she was destined to be associated with Him, not just by giving birth to Him, but in the total economy of the Incarnation. Just as Christ's redemptive action was a free fulfillment of His Father's will, so Mary's conception of the Word was an act of complete obedience and surrender to the divine will."

37. Diff II, 103.

38. It seems as though Newman's objection to this statement is primarily based on his zealous desire to preserve the unity of Our Lord's person. In other words, our Lord, in every case, even once the Incarnation took place, remained a divine Person (of one substance with the Father). He did not become a human person, even though He most definitely assumed from the Most Blessed Virgin a human nature which was then consubstantially united to His divine Person at the moment of His Incarnation. In the Letter to the Hebrews, we read that the Incarnate Word "reflects the glory of God and bears the very *stamp* of His nature" (Heb 1:3). In St. Paul's Letter to the Philippians, we read that "Christ Jesus, who though He was in the *form* of God, did not count equality with God, a thing to be grasped, but emptied Himself, taking the *form* of a servant, being born in the likeness of men. And being found in *human form*, He humbled Himself and became obedient unto death, even death on a cross" (Phil 2:5–8). Both of these passages preserve a perfect balance in explaining the unity of the two natures (human and divine) in the one, divine Person of Our Lord. It is just

such a balanced theology that Newman himself expresses when he writes: "Her (Mary's) very *image* is as a book in which we may read at a glance the mystery of the Incarnation, the mystery of the Redemption" (MD, 261).

39. Diff II, 113f.

40. Diff II, 114.

41. Ibid. The mention of *The Imitation of Christ* is not as formidable an argument since, unlike the other books, it is a devotional and not a dogmatic source, albeit one of the most widely read and appreciated of Christian devotional literature.

42. Diff II, 114.

43. Diff II, 115.

44. Newman distinguishes between the *scandalum parvulorum* and the *scandalum pharisæorum*. This distinction is not merely a distinction between learned and unlearned but even more so a distinction between those who are pure of heart and those who have pride of heart. Newman leaves this judgment in his regard up to his readers. In any case, Newman, without fear of human respect, speaks his mind and judges these statements according to how they strike him at both an intellectual and visceral level.

45. Diff II, 115.

46. Ibid.

47. Friedel, *The Mariology of Cardinal Newman*, 376.

48. Newman writes: "I do not, however, speak of these statements, as they are found in their authors, for I know nothing of the originals, and cannot believe that they have meant what you say; but I take them as they lie in your pages" (cf. Diff II, 115).

49. There seems to be no necessity to apply Newman's principles to the Marian titles of Mediatrix and Advocate since there is ample evidence of their use and acceptability in both doctrine and devotion; indeed, *Lumen Gentium* notes them in passing as thoroughly legitimate, while exhibiting total silence with reference to that of Co-Redemptrix. As Perrella observes: "Il Concilio Ecumenico si mostrò riluttante a fare proprio il lessico della corredenzione, che era in voga nei trattati mariologici degli anni immediatamente precedenti il Vaticano II. Ma il rifiuto del lessico teologico non significava disinteresse per il tema: la questione infatti della partecipazione attiva di Maria all'opera della salvezza di Cristo redentore verrà, seguendo una linea biblico-patristica, ripresa e approfondita in termini soprattutto di cooperazione subordinata e di maternità spirituale. La dottrina conciliare sul ruolo salvifico della Madre e Serva del Signore, imboccava la strada del recupero, della integrazione e degli approfondimenti teologici, suscitata dall'interessante dibattito preconciliare, avendo particolare cura di presentare un insegnamento mariano sobrio, esauriente, e universalmente accettabile anche dalle altre confessioni cristiane."—Salvatore Perrella, *I Vota e I Consilia dei Vescovi Italiani sulla Mariologia e sulla Corredenzione nella Frase Antepreparatoria del Concilio Vaticano II* (Rome: Scripta Pontificæ Facultatis Theologicæ Marianum, 1994), 223.

50. Perrella, *I Vota e I Consilia*, 171.

51. Antonio Maria Calero, *La Vergine Maria nel Mistero di Cristo e della Chiesa* (Turin: Editrice Elle di Ci, 1995), 287.

52. Carlos Ignacio González, *Mariologia: Maria, Madre e Discepola* (Casale Monferrato: Piemme, 1989), 247.

53. Cf. G. M. Roschini, *Mariologia*, 4 vol. (Rome, 1947–1948); J. B. Carol, *De Corredemptione* (Città del Vaticano: Libreria Editrice Vaticana, 1950); Domenico Bertetto, *Maria: Corredentrice: La Cooperazione Prossima e Immediata di Maria alla Redenzione Cristiana* (Alba: Edizioni Paoline, 1951); R. Laurentin, *Le Titre de Corédemptrice: Étude Historique* (Paris: Lethiellieux, 1951); Jean Galot, "La Plus Ancienne Affirmation de la Corédemption Mariale: La Témoignage de Jean le Géomètre," *Recherches de Science Religieuse* 45 (1957), 187–208; C. Dillenschneider, *Maria Corredentrice: Il Merito Mediatore della Nuova Eva nell'Economia della Redenzione* (Rome: Edizioni Paoline, 1955); Bertetto, *Maria: La Serva del Signore* (Napoli: Edizioni Dehoniane, 1988); Brunero Gherardini, *La Corredentrice nel Mistero di Cristo e della Chiesa* (Rome: Edizioni Vivere In, 1998); Dillens, *Le Mystère de la Corédemption Mariale* (Paris: VRIN, 1951); W. Goosens, "Estne Mater Redemptoris Immediate Cooperata ad Redemptionem Obiectivam seu ad Acquisitionem Gratiarum?" *Collationes Gandavenses* 24 (1937) and 25 (1938); Y. Congar, "Bulletin de Théologie," *Revue des Sciences Philosophique et Théologique* 27 (1938), 332–341; J. Rivière, "Marie: Corémptrice," *Revue des Sciences Religieuses* 19 (1939), 332–341; H. Lennerz, "Considerationes de Doctrina Beatæ Mariæ Virginis Mediatricis, *Gregorianum* 28 (1947), 420–444; and his "De Cooperatione Beatæ Virginis in Ipso Opere Redemptionis," *Gregorianum* 28 (1947), 574–597, and 29 (1948), 118–141; Gianni Colzani, *Maria: Mistero di Grazia e di Fede* (Milan: Edizioni San Paolo, 1996), 197–199, 275–283.

54. *Mary: Co-Redemptrix, Mediatrix, Advocate* (Santa Barbara, Calif.: Queenship Publishing Co., 1996), 4f., passim.

55. Ibid., 8.

56. Bertrand de Margerie, "Mary, Mother of God, Cooperated with Our Redemption and Is Our Advocate," a homily delivered at Oxford on 10 August 1998. In a personal communication, the Reverend Bertrand de Margerie, S.J., admitted that his subsequent research led him to note that Newman does not, in fact, use the title "Co-Redemptress," in his *Sermon Notes*, or express disapproval of its use. My own research has also led me to this same conclusion. Nevertheless, any future research in this area, that either confirms the present research or modifies it in any way, would be most helpful.

CONCLUSION

1. Discussing Newman and the Church after Vatican II, specifically the Marian dimension, Ker makes the following observation: "Before leaving *Lumen Gentium*, a word should be said about Marian devotions. Although, as has been said, Newman would have welcomed the constitution's balanced Mariology and although, in view of past distortions and exaggerations that he himself deplored, he would have appreciated the difficult decision the Council Fathers took not to treat Our Lady in a separate document but to view her in the context of the whole mystery of the Church—there is no doubt that the recent tendency to deprecate and depreciate devotion to Mary would not have struck any responsive chord in Newman. An unease at certain manifestations of emotional

devotionalism by no means meant that Newman himself did not have a deep Marian piety."—Ian Ker, "Newman and the Post-Conciliar Church," in *Newman Today*, Proceedings of the Wethersfield Institute, vol. 1 (San Francisco: Ignatius Press, 1989), 130.

2. A possible explanation of why the Second Vatican Council did not include the title of Mary as Co-Redemptrix is offered by G. Iammarrone when he writes: "I motivi di questo abbandono sono stati di carattere ecumenicao (i protestanti non accettano in nessun modo che si parli di 'corredenzione' di Maria o di altri accanto alla redenzione dell'unico Mediatore Gesù Cristo) e pastorale i Padri conciliari hanno voluto evitare termini che potrebbero essere equivocati dato che hanno bisogno di complessi chiarimenti teologici per essere intesi nel loro senso esatto e accettabile."—"Socia del Redentore/Cooperatrice alla Redenzione," in *Lexicon Dizionario Teologico Enciclopedico* (Casale Monferrato: Edizioni Piemme, 1993), 969.

3. The Reverend Juniper B. Carol, O.F.M., stakes out the theological terrain in this regard—although it must be stressed that we have little way of knowing how much of his approach or understanding would have been shared by Newman. However, Carol's analysis is helpful because it summarizes well the terminology used up to and including the conciliar era. "What does the word 'Co-Redemptrix' mean? For some theologians, it refers to Mary's cooperation in the Redemption in the sense that she knowingly and willingly gave birth to the Redeemer (indirect, remote cooperation), and that she dispenses to us the fruits (graces) of the Redemption already accomplished by Christ alone (technically: cooperation in the *subjective* Redemption). The majority, however, believe that, besides the two types of cooperation just mentioned, Mary also contributed to the Redemption itself, i.e., to the redemptive action of Christ which was consummated on Calvary (called *objective* Redemption)."—"Co-Redemptrix," *Dictionary of Mary* (New York: Catholic Book Publishing, 1985), 57. Mark Miravalle makes the following definition of terms: "'Objective' Redemption is the price Jesus paid for our forgiveness and grace. 'Subjective' Redemption is God's distribution of grace to us. Mary's cooperation in our objective Redemption is either 'immediate' (she shared in some way in His payment of the price for our forgiveness and grace), or it is 'remote' (she merely gave us Jesus, Who paid the price for our Redemption). Mary's cooperation in our subjective Redemption is either 'immediate' (as an instrument, like the sacraments) or 'remote' (she merely intercedes for grace). There is a primary need for theologians to clarify the interdependence of Mary's titles: Co-Redemptrix and Mediatrix."—*Mary: Co-Redemptrix, Mediatrix, Advocate*, 216.

4. Michæl Schmaus writes: "In the development of the faith after the patristic age, the thought of the divine motherhood of Mary was completed by that of her participation in the cross of Jesus. Her salvific function is considered here. As Mother of the Redeemer, Mary herself is called Redemptrix, from the ninth century on. This term was changed into Co-redemptrix in the fifteenth century. In the seventeenth and eighteenth centures, Mariology was strongly determined by feelings and polemics—'no praises too great.' A Mariology founded on the patristic data was introduced by J. H. Newman and M. J. Scheeben. The main questions centered on Mary's share in the redemption.

The problem crystallized in the question of Mary's relationship to the Church and vice versa. In 1950, Pius XII defined the doctrine of Mary's bodily assumption into Heaven."—"Mariology," *Sacramentum Mundi* (New York: Seabury Press, 1975), 897.

5. Cf. the Reverend S. Perrella, O.S.M., *I Vota I Consilia dei Vescovi Italiani sulla Mariologia e sulla Corredenzione nella Fase Antipreparatoria del Concilio Vaticano II* (Rome: Scripta Pontificiæ Facultatis Theologicæ Marianum, 1994).

APPENDIX I
GLOSSARY

1. Giovanni Velocci, *Newman: Il Coraggio della Verità* (Vatican City: Libreria Editrice Vaticana, 2000), 59f.

2. Samuel D. Femiano, *Infallibility of the Laity* (New York: Herder & Herder, 1967), Glossary.

3. Femiano, Glossary.

4. Velocci, 44–46, passim.

5. Owen Chadwick, *Newman* (New York: Oxford University Press, 1983), 42f.

6. Femiano, 47.

7. Dev D, 325.

8. Walter P. Burke, "The Beauty Ever Ancient, Ever New," in John K. Ryan and Edmond Darvil Benard, eds., *American Essays for the Newman Centennial* (Washington, D.C.: The Catholic University of America, 1947), 195f.

9. Chadwick, 32.

10. Francesco Turvasi, "The Development of Doctrine in John Cardinal Newman and Alfred Loisy," in Michael E. Allsopp and Ronald R. Burke, eds., *John Henry Newman: Theology and Reform* (New York: Garland Publishing, 1992), 171.

11. Diff II, 26.

12. Femiano, Glossary.

13. Chadwick, *Newman*, 36.

14. *On Consulting the Faithful in Matters of Doctrine*, ed. John Coulson (New York: Sheed & Ward, 1961), 44.

15. DMC, 324–344.

16. *John Henry Newman: Roman Catholic Writings on Doctrinal Development*, trans. J. Gaffney (Kansas City: Sheed & Ward, 1997), 5.

17. Newman, *The Arians of the Fourth Century*, ed. Rowan Williams (University of Notre Dame Press, 2001), 74.

18. Yves Congar, *Thomas d'Aquin: Sa Vision de Théologie et de l'Église* (London: Variorum RePrints, 1984), 79f.

19. Femiano, 123f.

20. AP, 110f.

21. Ian Ker, *Newman and the Fullness of Christianity* (Edinburgh: Clark, 1993), 104f.

22. Chadwick, *Newman*, 43.

23. Christopher Hollis, *Newman and the Modern World* (Garden City, N.Y.: Doubleday, 1968), 57.

24. Webster T. Patterson, *Newman: Pioneer for the Layman* (Washington, D.C.: Corpus Books, 1968), 66.

25. Patterson, *Newman*, 70, note 18.

26. *John Henry Newman: Roman Catholic Writings*, 6.

27. VM, I, 32.

28. ES, 287.

29. Geoffrey Rowell, *The Vision Glorious: Themes and Personalities of the Catholic Revival in Anglicanism* (New York: Oxford University Press, 1983), 60.

Bibliography

PRIMARY SOURCES

Anglican Difficulties. With an Introduction and Notes by Stanley L. Jaki, O.S.B. Fraser, Mich.: Real-View-Books, n.d.

Apologia pro Vita Sua: Being a History of His Religious Opinions. New York: Longmans, Green & Co., 1908.

The Arians of the Fourth Century. New York: Longmans, Green & Co., 1908.

The Arians of the Fourth Century. With an Introduction and Notes by Rowan Williams. South Bend, Ind.: University of Notre Dame Press, 2001.

Certain Difficulties Felt by Anglicans in Catholic Teaching. 2 volumes. New York: Longmans, Green & Co., 1907–1908.

The Church of the Fathers. New York: John Lane, 1928.

The Church of the Fathers. With an Introduction and Notes by Francis McGrath, F.M.S. South Bend, Ind.: University of Notre Dame Press, 2002.

Discourses Addressed to Mixed Congregations. New York: Longmans, Green & Co., 1909.

Discourses Addressed to Mixed Congregations. With an Introduction and Notes by James Tolhurst. South Bend, Ind.: University of Notre Dame Press, 2002.

An Essay in Aid of a Grammar of Assent. New York: Longmans, Green & Co., 1909.

An Essay on the Development of Christian Doctrine. New York: Longmans, Green & Co., 1909.

An Essay on the Development of Christian Doctrine. Westminster, Md.: Christian Classics, 1968.

An Essay on the Development of Christian Doctrine. With Foreword by Ian Ker. South Bend, Ind.: University of Notre Dame Press, 1989.

Essays Critical and Historical. Volume 2. New York: Longmans, Green & Co., 1895.

Faith and Prejudice and Other Unpublished Sermons of Cardinal Newman. New York: Sheed & Ward, 1956.

Fifteen Sermons Preached before the University of Oxford [between 1826 and 1843]. New York: Longmans, Green & Co., 1909.

Historical Sketches. Volume 2. New York: Longmans, Green & Co., 1906.

Lectures on the Present Position of Catholics in England. New York: Longmans, Green & Co., 1908.

Bibliography

Letters and Diaries of John Henry Newman. Edited by Charles Stephen Dessain, C.O. London: Thomas Nelson and Sons, 1961.

Meditations and Devotions. New York: Longmans, Green & Co., 1907.

On Consulting the Faithful in Matters of Doctrine. Edited and with an Introduction by John Coulson. New York: Sheed & Ward, 1961.

Parochial and Plain Sermons. 8 volumes. New York: Longmans, Green & Co., 1907–1909.

———. San Francisco: Ignatius Press, 1987.

Prayers, Verses, and Devotions. San Francisco: Ignatius Press, 1989.

Roman Catholic Writings on Doctrinal Development. Translated, with commentary, by James Gaffney. Kansas City: Sheed & Ward, 1997.

Select Treatises of Saint Athanasius in Controversy with the Arians. 2 volumes. New York: Longmans, Green & Co., 1903.

Sermon Notes. New York: Longmans, Green & Co., 1914.

Sermon Notes of John Henry Cardinal Newman, 1849–1878. With an Introduction and Notes by James Tolhurst. South Bend, Ind.: University of Notre Dame Press, 2000.

Sermons, 1824–1843. Volume 1: *Sermons on the Liturgy and Sacraments and on Christ the Mediator.* Edited by Placid Murray, O.S.B. Oxford: Clarendon Press, 1991.

———. Volume 2: *Sermons on Biblical History, Sin and Justification, the Christian Way of Life, and Biblical Theology.* Edited by Vincent Ferrer Blehl, S.J. Oxford: Clarendon Press, 1993.

The Theological Papers of John Henry Newman on Biblical Inspiration and on Infallibility. Edited by J. Derek Holmes. Oxford: Clarendon Press, 1979.

Tracts Theological and Ecclesiastical. Westminster, Md.: Christian Classics, 1974.

The Via Media of the Anglican Church. 2 volumes. New York: Longmans, Green & Co., 1901/1908.

SECONDARY SOURCES

Adam, Karl. *The Spirit of Catholicism.* Garden City, New York: Image Books, 1954.

Agostino, S. *Maria: Dignitas Terrae.* Rome: Città Nuova Editrice, 1995.

Aleizalde Bastero, S.-L. "Paralelismo Eva–María en S. Ambrosio de Milan," *Estudios Marianos* 50 (1985), 71–88.

Alfaro, J. *Cristologia e Antropologia.* Assisi: Cittadella, 1973.

Alighieri, Dante. *La Divina Commedia: Il Paradiso.* Milan: Edizioni San Paolo, 1987.

Alonso, J. "La Mariologia del Cardenal Newman y Evolución de Su Pensamiento," *Epherimedes Mariologicæ* 27 (1977), 81–84.

———. "La Maternidad Divina de Maria desde Efeso hasta Nuestros Días," *Epherimedes Mariologicæ* 31 (1981), 365–381.

Alsopp, Michael E., and Ronald R. Burke. *John Henry Newman: Theology and Reform*. New York: Garland Publishing Inc., 1992.

Amata, Biaggio. "Intuizioni Ambrosiane sulla Centralità Mediatrice di Maria nel *Mysterium Salutis*," *Marianum* 59 (1997), 139–157.

Amato, Angelo, S.D.B. *Maria e la Trinità*. Milan: Edizioni San Paolo, 2000.

———. "Verso un Altro Dogma Mariano?" *Marianum* 58 (1996), 229–232.

Anderson, H. George, et al., eds. *The One Mediator, the Saints, and Mary: Lutherans and Catholics in Dialogue, VIII*. Minneapolis: Augsburg Publishing House, 1992.

Aquinas, Saint Thomas. *Commentum in Matthæum et Johannem*. Parma: Typis Petri Fiaccadori, 1861.

———. *Summa Theologica*. Rome: Ex Typographia Forzani et S. Ioannis Bardi, 1923.

Artz, J. "Newman: Une Psychologie Concrète de la Foi et une Apologétique Existentielle," *Cahiers de Lumen Vitae* 4 (1950), 69–76.

Auer, Johann, and Joseph Ratzinger. *Gesù il Salvatore: Soteriologia-Mariologia: Piccola Dogmatica Teologica*. Volume 21, edited by Carlo Molari. Assisi: Editrice Cittadella, 1993.

Balio, C. "De Titulo 'Mediatrix' BVM Adscripto," *Acta Congressi Mariologici-Mariani Internationalis* 4 (1971), 282–283.

Barberi, Domenico della Madre di Dio. *Lettera ai Professori di Oxford—Relazioni con Newman e i suoi Amici*. Edited by Fabiano Giorgini, C.P. Rome: Editrice C.J.P.I., 1990.

Bastero de Eleizade, Juan Luis. *Maria: Madre del Redentor*. Pamplona: Edición Universidad de Navarra, 1995.

Baumer, I. "Pascal—Newman—Chardin," *Orientierung* 26 (1962), 204–208.

Bea, Agostino Cardinal. "La Sacra Scrittura 'Ultimo Fondamento' del Domma dell' Assunzione," *La Civiltà Cattolica* 4 (1950), 556f.

Bearsley, Patrick J. "Mary the Perfect Disciple: A Paradigm for Mariology," *Theological Studies* (September 1980), 461–504.

Beggiani, Seely J. *Early Syriac Theology*. New York: University Press of America, 1983.

Benard, Edmond Darvil. *A Preface to Newman's Theology*. St. Louis, Mo.: B. Herder Book Co., 1945.

Bennett, Sr. Catherine M. "Mary, the Fathers and the Bible," *The Bible Today* (October 1966),1900–1905.

Bertagna, M. "Elementa Cultus Mariani apud Sanctum Ambrosium Mediolanensem," *De Primordiis Cultus Mariani* 3 (Rome, 1970), 1–15.

Bertetto, Domenico. *Maria Corredentrice: La Cooperazione Prossima e Immediata di Maria alla Redenzione Cristiana*. Alba: Edizioni Paoline, 1951.

———. *Maria: La Serva del Signore*. Naples: Edizioni Dehoniane Napoli, 1988.

Biemer, Gunter. *Newman on Tradition*. Translated by K. Smyth. New York: Herder & Herder, 1967.

Biffet, Esquerda J. *La Virgen del Vaticano II*. Bilbao: Desclée de Brouwer, 1966.

Biffi, Giacomo Cardinal. *Il Canto Nunziale*. Milan: Jaca Book, 2000.

———. *Esplorando il Disegno*. Turin: Editrice Elle Di Ci, 1994.

Blehl, Vincent Ferrer, S.J. "The Holiness of John Henry Newman," *Month* 19 (1958), 325–334.

———. "L'Humanisme Patristique de John Henry Newman." Manuscript. Address to Cardinal Newman Symposium, Rome, 3–8 April 1975.

———. "The Importance of the 'Real' for the Interpretation of Newman's Spirituality and Holiness," *Louvain Studies* 15 (1990), 226–232.

———. "Newman: The Bishops and *The Rambler*," *Downside Review* 90 (1972), 20–40.

——— [postulator]. *Positio super Virtutibus for the Cause of Canonization of the Servant of God John Henry Cardinal Newman Presented by the Fathers of the Oratory at Birmingham in England to the Congregation for the Causes of the Saints*. Rome, 1989.

———. *The White Stone: The Spiritual Theology of John Henry Newman*. Petersham, Mass.: St. Bede's Publications, 1993.

Boekraad, A. J. "A Meditation on Cardinal Newman," in *Cardinal John Henry Newman: A Study in Holiness*. London: The Guild of Our Lady of Ransom, 1980. Pages 1–3.

———. "Newman en Heilege Schrift," *Schrift und Tradition* 7 (1954), 385–388.

———. "Newman, the Cardinal, the Saint," in *Cardinal John Henry Newman: A Study in Holiness*. London: The Guild of Our Lady of Ransom, 1980. Pages 27–34.

The Book of Common Prayer. New York: Oxford University Press, 1990.

Comunità di Bose, ed. *Maria: Testi Teologici e Spirituali dal I al XX Secolo*. Milan: Arnoldo Mondadori Editore, 2000.

Bouyer, Louis, C.O. *Histoire de la Spiritualité Chrétienne*. Volume 1. Paris: Éditions Montaigne, 1960.

———. *The Meaning of Sacred Scripture*. London: Darton, Longman & Todd, 1958.

———. *Newman: His Life and Spirituality*. Translated by J. Lewis May. New York: P. J. Kenedy & Sons, 1958.

————. *Newman's Vision of Faith*. San Francisco: Ignatius Press, 1986.

————. *Orthodox Spirituality and Protestant and Anglican Spirituality*. London: Burns and Oates, 1965.

————. *La Trône de la Sagesse*. Paris: Éditions du Cerf, 1957.

Bover, J. M. "Suarez Mariologo," *Estudios Eclesiasticos* 22 (1948), 311–337.

Bower, J. M. "La Mediación Universal de María segun San Ambrosio," *Gregorianum* 5 (1924), 24–45.

Boyce, Philip, O.C.D. "The Birth and the Pursuit of an Ideal of Holiness," in *Cardinal John Henry Newman: A Study in Holiness*. London: The Guild of Our Lady of Ransom, 1980. Pages 11–26.

————. "Euntes Docete: Newman As Preacher," *Ensign* (1972), 1–12.

————. *John Henry Newman: Maria, Pagine Scelte*. Milan: Edizioni Paoline, 1999.

————. *Mary: The Virgin Mary in the Life and Writings of John Henry Newman*. Grand Rapids, Mich.: Eerdmans Publishing Co., 2001.

————. Personal communication, 4 May 2001.

————. Telephone interview, 26 July 2000.

Brandreth, Henry R. T. *The Ecumenical Ideals of the Oxford Movement*. London: Society for Promoting Christian Knowledge, 1947,

Brechtken, J. *Kierkegaard–Newman: Wahrheit und Existenzmiteilung*. Munich: A. Harm, 1970.

Breck, John. "Mary in the New Testament," in *Hopes and Visions: Papers of the Ecumenical Society of the Blessed Virgin Mary in the United States of America*. Washington, D.C.: The Ecumenical Society of the Blessed Virgin Mary, May 1988. Pages 1–22.

Brent, A. "Newman and Perrone: Irreconcilable Theses on Development," *Downside Review* 102/349 (1984), 276f.

Brit, John, "Newman's Use of Sacred Scripture in Texts on the Incarnation and Mary," *Marian Studies* 24 (1995), 198–264.

————. "A Status Quæstionis and Analytic Study of the Use of the Apocalypse 12 by Newman in *A Letter to Dr. Pusey*." Dissertation. University of Dayton: Marian Library Institute, 1978.

————. "The Use of My Rhetorical Approach to Poetry on Newman and Mary," address to the National Danforth Conference, Ohio University, 1994.

Brock, Sebastian P. *The Harp of the Spirit: Eighteen Poems of Saint Ephrem*. Fellowship of St. Alban and St. Sergius, 1983.

————. *The Luminous Eye: The Spiritual World Vision of Saint Ephrem*. Rome, 1985.

————, translator. *Saint Ephrem the Syrian: Hymns on Paradise*. New York: St. Vladimir's Seminary Press, 1990.

Bromiley, Geoffrey, ed. *Theological Dictionary of the New Testament.* Grand Rapids, Mich.: William B. Eerdmans, 1985.

Brown, David, ed. *Centenary Essays: Newman—A Man for Our Time.* Harrisburg, Penn.: Morehouse Publishing, 1990.

Brown, Peter. *Augustine of Hippo: A Biography.* Berkeley: University of California Press, 1969.

Brown, Raymond E., S.S. *Biblical Exegesis and Church Doctrine.* New York: Paulist Press, 1985.

———. *The Birth of the Messiah.* New York: Doubleday, 1977.

———. *The Gospel According to John.* 2 volumes. New York: Doubleday, 1979.

———. *An Introduction to the New Testament.* New York: Doubleday, 1997.

——— et al., eds. *Mary in the New Testament.* New York: Paulist Press, 1978.

——— et al., eds. *The New Jerome Biblical Commentary.* Englewood Cliffs, N.J.: Prentice Hall, 1990.

Buby, Bertrand, S.M. *Mary of Galilee.* 3 volumes. New York: Alba House, 1994, 1995, 1997.

Bur, J. "La Vierge Marie dans l'Économie du Salut," *Divinitas* 12 (1968), 229–251.

Burke, Cormac. "Development of Doctrine," *Encyclopedia of Catholic Doctrine.* Edited by Russell Shaw. Huntington, Ind.: Our Sunday Visitor Press, 1997. Pages 168–170.

Burke, Eugene M. "The Use of Sacred Scripture As a *Locus Theologicus*," The Catholic Theological Society of America: *Proceedings* of the Fourteenth Annual Convention. New York: St. Joseph's Seminary, 1959. Pages 54–96.

Butler, Perry, ed.. *Pusey Rediscovered.* London: Society for Promoting Christian Knowledge, 1983.

Caffey, D. "The Sources of Newman's Scriptural Quotations in His Sermons." Dissertation. Fordham University, 1949.

Calero, Antonio Maria. *La Vergine Maria nel Mistero di Cristo e della Chiesa: Saggio di Mariologia.* Turin: Editrice Elle di Ci, 1995.

Calkins, Arthur B. "The Heart of Mary As Co-Redemptrix in the Magisterium of Pope John Paul II," in *Studi Tomistici*, volume 59 (Autori Vari San Tommaso Teologo Richerche in Occasione dei Due Centenari Accademici, ed. Antonio Piolanti). Rome: Libreria Editrice Vaticana, 1995. Pages 320–335.

———. "Mary's Presence in the Mass," *Homiletic and Pastoral Review* (July 1997), 8–15.

———. "The Proposed Marian Dogma: The 'What' and the 'Why'." Privately published manuscript, n.d.

————. "Towards Another Marian Dogma? A Response to Father Angelo Amato, S.D.B.," *Marianum* 59 (1997), 159–167.

Callegari, Lina. *Newman: La Fede e le Sue Ragioni.* Milan: Edizioni Paoline, 2001.

Cantalamessa, Raniero, O.F.M. Cap. *Maria—Uno Specchio per la Chiesa.* Milan: Ancora Editrice, 1989.

Carol, Juniper B., O.F.M. *De Corredemptione.* Vatican City: Libreria Editrice Vaticana, 1950.

————. *Dictionary of Mary.* New York: Catholic Book Publishing Co., 1985.

————. "Mary and the Church," *New Catholic Encyclopedia.* New York: McGraw-Hill Book Co., 1967.

Carroll, Eamon, et al., eds. *Mary in Ecumenical Perspective: Three Papers.* Washington, D.C.: The Ecumenical Society of the Blessed Virgin Mary, 1996.

Catechism of the Catholic Church. Vatican City: Libreria Editrice Vaticana, 1997.

Cere, Daniel. "Newman, God, and the Academy," *Theological Studies* 55 (March 1994), 3–23.

Ceuppens, F. *De Mariologia Biblica*, volume 4 of *Theologia Biblica* (Rome, 1948).

Chadwick, Henry. *The Early Church.* New York: Dorset Press, 1967.

————. "Newman's Significance for the Anglican Church," in *Centenary Essays: Newman—A Man for Our Time.* Harrisburg, Penn.: Morehouse Publishing, 1990. Pages 52–74.

Chadwick, Owen. "A Consideration of Newman's *Apologia Pro Vita Sua*," in *Newman from Oxford to the People.* Edited by Paul Weiss. Trowbridge, Eng.: Witshire, 1996. Pages 163–185.

————. *From Bossuet to Newman: The Idea of Doctrinal Development.* Cambridge: The University Press, 1957.

————. *The Mind of the Oxford Movement.* Stanford, Calif.: Stanford University Press, 1960.

————. *Newman.* New York: Oxford University Press, 1983.

————. *The Spirit of the Oxford Movement: Tractarian Essays.* New York: Cambridge University Press, 1990.

Chapman, J. "Newman and the Fathers," *Blackfriars* 14 (1933), 578–590.

Charley, Julian. "Mary in Recent Catholic Theology," in *Chosen by God: Mary in Evangelical Perspective.* Edited by David F. Wright. London: Marshall Pickering, 1989. Pages 200–215.

Chavannes, H. "La Mediación de Maria y la Doctrina de la Participación," *Epherimedes Mariologiæ* 24 (1974), 39–47.

————. "Remarques sur la médiation de Marie en relation avec la doctrine de la Participation," *Epherimedes Mariologæ* 26 (1976), 135–141.

Chiminelli, Piero. *J. H. Newman: L'Annunciatore della 'Seconda Primavera' della Cattolicità in Inghilterra: 1801–1890*. Modena: Paoline, 1964.

———. "Maria nella Vita e nel Pensiero di J. H. Newman," *Studium* 35 (1939), 285–98.

Cignelli, Lino. *Maria—Nuova Eva nella Patristica Greca*. Assisi: Studio Teologico "Porziuncola," 1966.

Colzani, Gianni. *Maria: Mistero di Grazia e di Fede*. Milan: Edizioni San Paolo, 1996.

———. "Comment on Marian Academy's Declaration: A New Marian Dogma?" *L'Osservatore Romano* (25 June 1997), 10.

Congar, Yves, O.P. "Bulletin de Théologie," *Revue des Sciences Philosophique et Théologique* 27 (1938), 647–648.

———. *Christ, Our Lady and the Church*. Westminster, Md.: Newman Press, 1957.

———. "Écriture et Tradition comme formes de communication," *Istina* 8 (1962), 411–436.

———. *Jalons pour une théologie Mariale*. Paris: Lethielleux, 1953.

———. "Marie l'Église dans la pensée patristique," *Revue des Sciences Philosophique et Théologique* 38 (1954), 3–38.

———. *Thomas d'Aquin: Sa Vision de théologie et de l'Église*. London: Variorum Prints, 1984.

———. *Vraie et fausse réforme dans l'Église*. Paris: Cerf, 1950.

Congregation of the Doctrine of the Faith. *Dominus Jesus—On the Unicity and Salvific Universality of Jesus Christ and the Church*. Vatican City: Libreria Editrice Vaticana, 2000.

Congregazione per l'Educazione Cattolica. *La Vergine Maria nella Formazione Intellettuale e Spirituale*. Bologna: EDB, 1988.

"Co-Redemptrix," in *Annali Mariani*. 2 volumes. Castelpetroso (Isernia): Santuario dell'Addolorata, 1995–1996.

Cornelis, E., et al. "Le Déploiement de l'évènement Jésus-Christ," *Mysterium Salutis*. Volume 13. Paris: Les Éditions du Cerf, 1972. Pages 13–176.

Cossiga, Francesco. "Newman the Man, Newman and Italy," in *Centenary Essays: Newman, a Man for Our Time*. Edited by David Brown. Harrisburg, Penn.: Morehouse Publishing, 1990. Pages 19–23.

Coulson, John. *Newman and the Common Tradition: A Study in the Language of Church and Society*. Oxford: Clarendon Press, 1970.

Coupet, Jacques, O.P. "Le Rôle de Marie dans le cheminement de Newman," *Nouveaux Cahiers Marials* (February 1990), 6–12.

Courth, Franz, and Ulrich Wickert. "Mariology," *The Oxford Encyclope-*

dia of the Reformation. Volume 3, edited by Hans J. Hillerbrand. New York: Oxford University Press, 1996. Pages 10–14.

Cross, F. L., and E. A. Livingston, eds. *The Oxford Dictionary of the Christian Church.* New York: Oxford University Press, 1983.

Cummings, Owen. "The Mariology of Saint Ephrem," *Lay Witness* (December 1998), 38f.

D'Arcy, Eric. "Newman's Significance for the Roman Catholic Church," in *Centenary Essays: Newman, a Man for Our Time.* Harrisburg, Penn.: Morehouse Publishing, 1990. Pages 75–97.

Da Spinetoli, Ortensio. *Maria nella Bibbia.* Bologna: Edizioni Dehoniane Bologna, 1988.

Davies, Michael. *Lead Kindly Light: The Life of John Henry Newman.* Long Prairie, Minn.: Neumann Press, 2001.

Davis, H. Francis. "Doctrina Mariana Cardinalis," *Alma Socia Christi* 11 (1953), 233–243 (Acta Congressus Mariologici-Mariani Romæ).

———. "La Mariologie de Newman," in volume 22 of *Maria: Études sur la Sainte Vierge.* Edited by D'Hubert du Manoir, S.J. Paris: Beauchesne and Ses Fils, 1954. Pages 532–552.

———. "Newman and Our Lady," *The Clergy Review* 34 (1950), 369–378.

———. "Newman and Thomism," *Newman Studien* 3 (1957), 157–169.

———. "Newman: The Bible and the Obiter Dicta." *Louvain Studies* (1954), 398–407.

———. "Newman: Theologian of the Word in Christian Life," *Blackfriars* 42 (April 1961), 150–156.

———. "La Sainte Vierge dans la jeunesse de Newman," *Doctrine Mariale*, 535–552.

Dawe, Donald G. "The Blessed Virgin and Depth Psychology: A Theological Appraisal." Unpublished manuscript.

Dawson, Christopher. "Newman and the Modern World," *Tablet* 226 (1972), 733–734.

De Aldama, J. A. *Maria en la Patristica de los Siglos I-II.* Madrid, 1970.

De Fiores, Stefano. *Corso di Teologia Sistematica: Maria Madre di Gesù—Sintesi Storico-Salvifica.* Bologna: Edizione Dehoniane, 1992.

———. *Maria nel Mistero di Cristo e della Chiesa.* Rome: Edizioni Montfortane, 1995.

———. "Maria nella Teologia Postconciliare," *Vaticano II: Bilancio e Prospettive Venticinque Anni Dopo (1962–1987).* Edited by René Latourelle. Assisi: Cittadella Editrice, 1987. Pages 417–470.

De Fiores, Stefano, and Salvatore Meo, S.M.M. *Nuovo Dizionario di Mariologia.* Milan: Edizioni Paoline, 1986.

De la Haye, Karl. *Ecclesia Mater chez les Pères des trois premiers siècles.* Paris: Les Éditions du Cerf, 1964.

De la Potterie, Ignace, S.J. "La Figlia di Sion: Lo Sfondo Biblico dalla Mariologia dopo il Concilio Vaticano 11," *Marianum* 49 (1987), 356–376.

———. "La Madre di Gesù e il Mistero di Cana," *La Civiltà Cattolica* 130 (1979), 425–440.

———. *Mary in the Mystery of the Covenant.* New York: Alba House, 1992.

de Lubac, Henri, S.J. *Exégèse Médiévale: Les Quatre Sens de l'Écriture.* 4 volumes. Paris, 1959.

———. *The Medieval Exegesis: The Four Senses of Scripture.* 4 volumes. Grand Rapids, Mich.: William B. Eerdmans, 1998.

———. *The Splendour of the Church.* New York; Sheed & Ward, 1956.

De Margerie, Bertrand, S.J. "Dogmatic Development by Abridgement or by Concentration?" *Marian Studies* 27 (1976), 64–98.

———. *An Introduction to the History of Exegesis.* Volume 1. *The Greek Fathers.* Petersham, Mass.: St. Bede's Publications, 1993.

———. *An Introduction to the History of Exegesis.* Volume 2. *The Latin Fathers.* Petersham, Mass.: St. Bede's Publications, 1991.

———. *An Introduction to the History of Exegesis.* Volume 3. *Saint Augustine.* Petersham, Mass.: St. Bede's Publications, 1991.

———. "Mary, Mother of God, Cooperated with Our Redemption and Is Our Advocate," homily delivered at Oxford, 10 August 1998.

———. "Newman and Mary, Mother of God," *The Month* (May 1999), 189–191.

———. Personal communication, 4 May 2001.

De Sanctis, E. "Newman's Concept of the Church in the World in his Parochial and Plain Sermons," *American Benedictine Review* 21 (1970), 268–282.

Dessain, Charles Stephen, C.O. "Cardinal Newman and the Eastern Tradition," *The Downside Review* 94 (April 1976), 83–98.

———. "Cardinal Newman and Ecumenism," *Clergy Review* 2/3 (1965), 119–137.

———. "Cardinal Newman and Our Lady," *Our Lady's Digest* 27 (January-February 1973), 172.

———. *Newman's Spiritual Themes.* Dublin: Veritas Publications, 1977.

———. *Cardinal Newman's Teaching about the Blessed Virgin Mary.* Birmingham, Eng.: Friends of Cardinal Newman, 1971.

Di Berardino, Angelo, and Basil Studer, eds. *History of Theology: The Patristic Period.* Volume 1, translated by Michael J. O'Connell. Collegeville, Minn.: The Liturgical Press, 1996.

Dickson, Charles. *A Protestant Pastor Looks at Mary*. Huntington, Ind.: Our Sunday Visitor Press, 1996.

Dillenscheider, C. *Maria Corredentrice: Il Merito Mediatore della Nuova Eva nell'Economia della Redenzione*. Rome: Edizioni Paoline, 1955.

———. *Le Mystère de la Corédemption Mariale*. Paris: Vrin, 1951.

Dillon, John J. *Mary As the Second Eve: A Patristic Viewpoint*. Washington, D.C.: The Ecumenical Society of the Blessed Virgin Mary, 1998.

Di Napoli, Emmanuele. "Attualità di uno Studio sul Vaticano II tra Mariologia e Correndenzione," *Marianum* 59 (1997), 169–181.

Di Nola, Gerardo, ed. *Ambrogio—Cristo, Eucaristia, La Vergine Madre del Signore: In Occasione del XVI Centenario della Morte di Sant' Ambrogio Vescovo e Dottore della Chiesa e in Preparazione al Giubileo 2000*. Latin-Italian edition. Vatican City: Libreria Editrice Vaticana, 1997.

Dombes, Gruppo di. *Maria nel Disegno di Dio e nella Comunione dei Santi*. Magnano: Edizioni Qiquajon, 1998.

Donald, Gertrude, *Men Who Left the Movement: John Henry Newman, Thomas W. Allies, Henry Edward Manning, Basil William Maturin*. London: Burns, Oates & Washbourne, 1933.

Ducci, M. S. "Senso della Tipologia Mariana in S. Ambrogio e suo Rapporto con lo Sviluppo Storico e Dottrinale," *Ecclesiastica Xaveriana* 21 (1971), 137–192.

————. "Sviluppo Storico e Dottrinale del Tema Maria-Chiesa e suo Rapporto con il Pensiero Teologico Mariano di S. Ambrogio," *Ephemerides Mariologicæ* 23 (1973), 363–404.

Dufour, Leon-Xavier, S.J. *Dictionary of Biblical Theology*. Boston: St. Paul Books and Media, 1995.

Du Manoir, H. "Marie, Nouvelle Ève, dans l'œuvre de Newman," *BSFEM* 14 (1956), 67–90.

Duggan, Paul E. *The Assumption Dogma: Some Reactions and Ecumenical Implications in the Thought of English-Speaking Theologians*. Dayton, Oh.: International Marian Research Institute, 1989.

Dulles, Avery Cardinal, S.J. "From Images to Truth: Newman on Revelation and Faith," *Theological Studies* 51 (June 1990), 252–267.

———. *John Henry Newman*. New York: Continuum, 2002.

———. "Justification in Contemporary Catholic Theology," in *Justification by Faith: Lutherans and Catholics in Dialogue*. Volume 7. Minneapolis: Augsburg Publishing House, 1985. Pages 256–277.

———. "Newman, Conversion and Ecumenism," *Theological Studies* 51 (December 1990), 717–731.

———. "Newman on Infallibility," *Theological Studies* 51 (September 1990), 434–449.

————. *The Splendor of Faith: The Theological Vision of Pope John Paul II.* New York: Crossroad Publishing Company, 1999.

————. *The Survival of Dogma: Faith, Authority, and Dogma in a Changing World.* Garden City, New York: Image Books, 1973.

Elwood, J. Murray. *Kindly Light: The Spiritual Journey of John Henry Newman.* Notre Dame, Ind.: Ave Maria Press, 1979.

Fagiolo, Vincenzo Cardinal. *Catechesi Mariane.* Casale Monferrato: Piemme, 1998.

Felici, Sergio. *La Mariologia nella Catechesi dei Padri (Età Prenicena).* Rome: Libreria Ateneo Salesiano, 1989.

Femiano, Samuel D. *Infallibility of the Laity: The Legacy of Newman.* New York: Herder & Herder, 1967.

Fenelon, Dermot. "'The Aristocracy of Talent' and the Mystery of Newman," *Louvain Studies* 15 (1990), 220–226.

Fernandez, D. "El Concilio de Efeso y la Maternidad Divina de Maria," *Epherimedes Mariologicæ* 31 (1981), 365–381.

Feuillet, A. *The Apocalypse.* Translated by T. E. Crane. New York: Alba House, 1965.

————. "L'Heure de la Femme (Jn 16:21) et l'heure de la Mère de Jésus (Jn 19:25–27)," *Biblica* 47 (1966), 565–569.

Ffinch, Michael. *Newman: Towards the Second Spring.* San Francisco: Ignatius Press, 1992.

Finan, Thomas, and Vincent Twomey, eds. *Scriptural Interpretation in the Fathers: Letter and Spirit.* Dublin: Four Courts Press, 1995.

Fine d'Anno con Maria. Volume 1, *La Vergine Madre nella Chiesa delle Origini.* Volume 2, *La Vergine Madre dal Secolo VI al Secondo Millennio.* Rome: Centro di Cultura Mariana "Madre della Chiesa," 1996.

Fine d'Anno con Maria. Volume 4, *La Vergine Maria dal Rinascimento a Oggi.* Rome: Centro di Cultura Mariana "Madre della Chiesa," 1999.

Flanagan, Donal. "The Blessed Virgin Mary, Mother of God, in the Mystery of Christ and the Church," in *The Church: A Theological and Pastoral Commentary on the Constitution on the Church.* Edited by Kevin McNamara. Dublin: Veritas Publications, 1993. Pages 317–356.

Flannery, Austin, O.P., ed.. "Dogmatic Constitution on the Church" and "Dogmatic Constitution on Divine Revelation," in *Vatican Council II: The Conciliar and Post-Conciliar Documents.* New York: Costello Publishing Co., 1981.

Flores Folgado, S. "María Modelo de la Iglesia en San Ambrosio," *Estudios Marianos* 39 (1974), 57–77.

————. "Contorno Teológico de la Virginidad de María en S. Ambrosio," *Marianum* 44 (1982), 286–315.

Folghera, J. D. *Newman's Apologetic.* St. Louis: B. Herder Book Co., 1928.

Ford, John T. "Newman on 'Sensus Fidelium' and Mariology," *Marian Studies* 28 (1977), 120–145.

Forte, Bruno. *Maria: La Donna Icona del Mistero—Saggio di Mariologia Simbolico-Narrativa.* Milan: Edizioni Paoline, 1989.

Friedel, Francis J. *The Mariology of Cardinal Newman.* New York: Benziger Brothers, 1928.

———. "Mother of God and Second Eve," *Catholic World* 141 (1935), 228–229.

———. "Our Lady and the Devotion of the Anglican Newman," *Ampleforth Journal* (1979), 20–30.

Frosini, Giordano. *Teologia Oggi.* Bologna: Edizioni Dehoniane Bologna, 1996.

Frost, F. "Le Personalisme dans l'itineraire théologique et spirituel de John Henry Newman," *Mélange de Science Religieuse* 35 (1976), 57–70.

Gaffney, James, translator and commentator. *John Henry Newman: Roman Catholic Writings on Doctrinal Development.* Kansas City: Sheed & Ward, 1997.

Galot, Jean, S.J. *La Fede di Maria e la Nostra.* Assisi: Cittadella, 1973.

———. *Maria, la Donna nell'Opera di Salvezza.* Rome: Univ. Greg. Ed., 1984.

———. "Maria, Immagine della Donna," *Civiltà Cattolica* 2 (1974), 217–229.

———. "Maria, Madre della Chiesa: Resistenze e Progressi a Vent' Anni dal Vaticano II," *Civiltà Cattolica* 4 (1985), 118–130.

———. *Marie dans l'Évangile.* Paris: Desclée de Brouwer, 1965.

———. "La Plus Ancienne Affirmation de la Corédemption Mariale: Le Témoignage de Jean le Géometre," *Recherches de Science Religieuse* 45 (1957), 187–208.

———. "Vita di Cristo, Vita dello Spirito," *Civiltà Cattolica* 2 (1996), 233–245.

Gambero, Luigi, S.M. *Maria nel Pensiero dei Padri della Chiesa.* Milan: Edizioni Paoline, 1991.

———. *Maria nel Pensiero dei Teologi Latini Medievali.* Milan: Edizioni San Paolo, 2000.

———. *Mary and the Fathers of the Church.* Translated by Thomas Buffer. San Francisco: Ignatius Press, 1999.

Garcia, Pablo. *Domingo Barberi, Precursor y Profeta.* Salamanca: Ediciones Sigueme, 1997.

Garcia-Paredes, José, C.R. *Mariologia.* Madrid: Biblioteca de Auctores Cristianos, 1995.

Gargano, Guido Innocenzo. "I Commenti Patristici al Cantico dei Cantici," *Letture Patristiche—La Bibbia nei Padri della Chiesa: l'Antico Testamento*. Edited by Mario Naldini. Bologna: Edizioni Dehoniane Bologna, 1999.

Gauthier, Pierre. "R. H. Froude's Influence on Newman and the Oxford Movement," in *Newman from Oxford to the People*. Edited by Paul Weiss. Wiltshire, Eng.: Trowbridge, 1996. Pages 255–286.

Gaventa, Beverly Roberts. *Mary: Glimpses of the Mother of Jesus*. Columbia, S.C.: University of South Carolina Press, 1995.

Geisler, Michael. "Co-Redemption," *The Catholic Answer* (March/April 1995), 44–50.

Geissler, Hermann, and Roger Jupp. *Newman on Mary: Two Studies in Development*. Chichester, Eng.: The Ecumenical Society of the Blessed Virgin Mary, 1995.

Gherardini, Brunero. *La Corredentrice nel Mistero di Cristo e della Chiesa*. Rome: Edizioni Vivere In, 1998.

Gilley, Sherindon. "The Ecclesiology of the Oxford Movement: A Reconsideration," in *Newman from Oxford to the People*. Edited by Paul Weiss. Wiltshire, Eng.: Trowbridge, 1996. Pages 60–75.

———. *Newman and His Age*. London: Darton, Longman & Todd, 1990.

Gillieron, Bernard. "Adorare," *Lessico dei Termini Biblici*. Turin: Elle di Ci Editrice, 1992. Pages 15f.

Giovannini, Luigi, ed. *Storia della Chiesa Cattolica*. Milan: Edizioni San Paolo, 1989.

Gonzalez, Carlos Ignacio. *Maria: Madre e Discepola*. Casale Monferrato: Edizioni Piemme, 1988.

Goosens, W. "Estne Mater Redemptionis Immediate Cooperata ad Redemptionem Obiectivum seu ad Acquisitionem Gratiarum?" *Collaudationes Gadavenses* 24 (1937), 187–202, 270–285.

Gorce, Denys. *Introduction à Newman*. Paris: Les Éditions du Cèdre, 1952.

———. *Newman et les Pères*. Bruges: Bayaert, 1947.

Govaert, Lutgart. " 'From Henceforth All Generations Shall Call Me Blessed' (Lk 1:48): J. H. Newman on Our Lady," *Marianum* 53 (1991), 17–41.

———. *Kardinal Newmans Mariologie und sein personischer Wedergang*. Salzburg und Munchen, 1975.

———. "Newman's Mariology: Its Development," in *De Cultu Mariano Sæculis XIX-XX*. Actus Congressus Mariologici-Mariani Internationalis, anno 1987 celebrati. Rome: Pontificia Academia Mariana Internationalis, 1991. Pages 545–555.

Graef, Hilda. *Mary: A History of Doctrine and Devotion*. Westminister, Md.: Christian Classics, 1985.

Gray, Robert. *Cardinal Manning: A Biography*. New York: St. Martin's Press, 1985.

Griese, Vincent. *John Henry Newman: Heart to Heart*. New York: New City Press, 1993.

Griffin, John R. *A Historical Commentary on the Major Catholic Works of Cardinal Newman*. New York: Peter Lang Publishing, 1993.

————. "Newman and Ecumenism," *Faith and Reason* 8 (Winter 1982), 288–301.

————. "Newman and the Mother of God," *Faith and Reason* 15 (Winter 1989), 91–109.

Guitton, Jean. "Newman As a Modern Father of the Church," *Tablet* 218 (1964), 814ff.

————. "Parallel de Saint Augustin et de Newman," *Augustinus Magister* 11 (1954), 105–109.

————. *La Philosophie de Newman: Essai sur le rôle du dévelopement*. Paris: Éditions Montaigne, 1933.

————. *Il Secolo che Verrà: Conversazioni con Phillipe Guyard*. Translated by Antonietta Francavilla. Milan: Bompiani, 1999.

Gwynn, Denis. *Father Dominic Barberi*. Buffalo, N.Y.: Desmond & Stapleton, 1948.

Hamell, Patrick J. *Handbook of Patrology*. New York: Alba House, 1968.

Hammerschmidt, E. "John Henry Newmans Patristichen Studien," *Internationale Kirchliche Seitschrift* 53 (1963), 105–115.

Hardon, John, S.J. "Cardinal Newman, Apologist of Our Lady," *Review for Religious* 11 (May 1952), 113–124.

Harrison, Ignatius, C.O. "Timeless Truth in an Ever-Changing World," *Friends of Cardinal Newman Newsletter* (Christmas 1998), 7f.

Harrold, Charles F. *John Henry Newman: An Expository and Critical Study of His Mind, Thought, and Art*. New York: Longmans, Green & Co., 1945.

Healy, J. "Cardinal Newman on the Inspiration of Scripture," *Irish Ecclesiastical Review* (1884).

Hefting, Charles C. *Why Doctrines?* Boston: Cowley Publications, 1984.

Hertling, Ludwig. *Storia della Chiesa*. Rome: Città Nuova Editrice, 2001.

Hollis, Christopher. *Newman and the Modern World*. Garden City, N.Y.: Doubleday & Co., 1968.

Holmes, J. Derek. "Newman's Attitude towards Historical Criticism and Biblical Inspiration," *Downside Review* 89 (1971), 22–37.

Honoré, Jean Cardinal. *Itinéraire Spirituel de Newman*. Paris: Édition du Seuil, 1964.

———. *Présence au Monde et Parole de Dieu: La Catéchèse de Newman*. Paris: Fayard-Mame, 1969.

———. *The Spiritual Journey of Newman*. Translated by Sr. Mary Christopher Ludden, S.C. New York: Alba House, 1992.

Hovers, Harrie J. F. "John Henry Newman's Use of Scripture in His Discourse on the Mental Sufferings of Our Lord in His Passion" [manuscript]. Rome: Pontificia Università Urbaniana, n.d.

Huhn, J. *"Das Mariengeheimnis beim Kirchenvater Ambrosius," Münchener Theologische Zeitschrift* 2 (1951), 130–146.

———. *Das Geheimnis der Jungfrau-Mutter Maria nach dem Kirchvater Ambrosius*. Würtzburg, 1954.

Hume, Basil Cardinal, O.S.B. "Cardinal John Henry Newman: A Saint for Our Time," *The Guild of Our Lady of Ransom*, 2–7.

Hutton, Richard H. *Cardinal Newman*. New York: Houghton, Mifflin & Co., 1891.

"International Theological Commission: Select Questions on the Theology of God the Redeemer," *Communio* 19 (Spring 1997) 160–214.

Jaki, Stanley, O.S.B., ed. *Newman's Challenge*. Grand Rapids, Mich.: Eerdmans Publishing Co., 2000.

———. *Newman Today: Papers Presented at a Conference on John Henry Cardinal Newman*. San Francisco: Ignatius Press, 1989.

———. *The One True Fold: Newman and His Converts*. Royal Oaks, Mich.: Real View Books, 1998.

Jazwisuka, M. "Cardinal Newman and Devotion to Our Lady," *Unitas* 10 (1958), 162–173.

Jelly, Frederick, O.P. "Mary's Intercession: A Contemporary Reappraisal," *Marian Studies* 32 (1981), 76–95.

———. "Roman Catholic Ecumenical Response to the Theme ("Ut Unum Sint" PT 3)," *Marian Studies* 48 (1997), 129–137.

Jesus Christ and Mary: In the Noble Qur'an. Istanbul, Turkey: Call to Unity Publications, 2000.

John Paul II, Pope. *Catechesi Tradendæ: On Catechesis in Our Time*. Boston: St. Paul Editions, 1979.

———. *A Catechesis on the Creed: Jesus—Son and Savior*. Volume 11. Boston: Pauline Books and Media, 1996.

———. *Lettera Apostolica, "Agostino d'Ippona,"* commentary by Agostino Trapè. Rome: Città Nuova Editrice, 1988.

———. "Letter to Archbishop Vincent Nichols of Birmingham, England, marking the 200th Anniversary of the Venerable John Henry Cardinal Newman's Birth," *Origins* (15 March 2001), 631f.

———. "Message of His Holiness to the Most Reverend G. P. Dwyer," *L'Osservatore Romano* (14 May 1980), 1.

———. "On the Centenary of Cardinal Newman's Elevation to the Sacred College," in *Cardinal John Henry Newman: A Study in Holiness.* London: The Guild of Our Lady of Ransom, 1980. Pages ix-x.

———. *Redemptoris Mater,* in *The Encyclicals of John Paul II.* Edited by J. Michael Miller, C.S.B. Huntington, Ind.: Our Sunday Visitor Press, 1996. Pages 353–410.

———. *Theotokos: Woman, Mother, Disciple—A Catechesis on Mary, Mother of God.* Boston: Pauline Books and Media, 2000.

Johnson, H. "Leo XIII, Cardinal Newman and the Inerrancy of Scripture," *Downside Review* 69 (1951), 411–427.

Jones, Carleton, O.P. "John Henry Cardinal Newman and Mary: Mother of God, the New Eve," address to the Mariological Society of America, at Providence College, 19 October 1996.

Jones, Hubert Cunliffe. *A History of Christian Doctrine.* Philadelphia: Fortress Press, 1980.

Jouassard, G. "Deux Chefs de file théologie Mariale dans la seconde moitié du IV siècle: St. Epiphanie et St. Ambroise," *Gregorianum* 42 (1961), 5–36.

———. "Une Portrait de Ste. Vierge par St. Ambroise," *Vie Spirituelle* 90 (1954), 477–489.

Joumet, Charles. *L'Église du Verbe Incarné.* 3 volumes. Paris: Desclée de Brouwer, 1951.

Jurgens, William A. *The Faith of the Early Fathers* 3 volumes. Collegeville, Minn.: The Liturgical Press, 1970–1979.

Kelly, J. N. D. *Early Christian Doctrines.* London: A & C Black, 1977.

Ker, Ian. *The Achievement of John Henry Newman.* London: Harper Collins Publishers, 1991.

———. "The Greatness of Newman," *The University of Leeds Review* 33 (1990–1991), 101–117.

———. *John Henry Newman: A Biography.* New York: Oxford University Press, 1988.

———. "The Mind of Newman," *Tablet* (26 May 1986), 665–666.

———. *Newman and Conversion.* Edinburgh: T & T Clark, 1997.

———. *Newman and the Fullness of Christianity.* Edinburgh: T & T Clark, 1993.

———. "Newman and the 'Orphans' of Vatican II," *Louvain Studies* 15 (1990), 119–135.

———. "Newman and the Post-Conciliar Church," *Newman Today: Proceedings of the Wethersfield Institute.* Volume 1. San Francisco: Ignatius Press, 1989. Pages 130f.

————. *Newman on Being a Christian*. London: Harper Collins Publishers, 1991.

————. "Newman's View of the Relationship between Magisterium and Theologians," *Scripta* [manuscript]. Rome: Pontificia Università Urbaniana (1979).

————. Personal interview, 14 February 1999.

————. "Were Newman Here...," *Catholic World Report* (January 1993), 30–31.

————. "What Kind of Book Is the *Apologia?*" in *Newman from Oxford to the People*. Edited by Paul Weiss. Witshire, Eng.: Trowbridge, 1996. Pages 186–197.

Kirsch, J. *The Doctrine of the Communion of Saints in the Anglican Church*. Translated by J. R. McKee of the Oratory. St. Louis: Herder, 1911.

Kisner, Madaline, A.S.C. "From Shadows and Images into Truth: Development As a Personal Journey." Manuscript. Rensselaer, Ind.: The National Newman Conferences, 3–5 August 1995.

Knox, Wilfrid L. *The Catholic Movement in the Church of England*. London: Philip Allan & Co., 1923.

Kroger, James. "Gleanings: Newman on the Consensus of the Faithful and the Magisterium," *East Asian Pastoral Review* 4 (April 1987), 360–378.

Lamm, William R. *The Spiritual Legacy of Newman*. Milwaukee: Bruce Publishing Co., 1934.

Laurentin, René. *Court Traité de Théologie Mariale*. Paris: Lethielleux, 1953.

————. *La Madonna, Questioni di Teologia*. Brescia: Morcelliana, 1964.

————. *Maria: Chiave del Mistero Cristiano*. Milan: Edizioni San Paolo, 1996.

————. *Maria nella Storia della Salvezza*. Turin: Marietti, 1972.

————. *Marie, l'Église et le Sacerdoce*. 2 volumes. Paris: Lethillieux, 1952–1953.

————. *Mary in the Communion of Saints*. Wallington, Eng.: Ecumenical Society of the Blessed Virgin Mary, 1973.

————. *Le Titre de Corédemptrice: Étude Historique*. Paris: Lethiellieux, 1951.

Lennerz, H. "Considerationes de Doctrina Beatæ Virginis Mediatricis," *Gregorianum* 19 (1938), 420–444.

————. "De Cooperatione Beatæ Virginis in Ipso Opere Redemptionis," *Gregorianum* 28 (1947), 574–597.

————. "De Cooperatione Beatæ Virginis in Ipso Opere Redemptionis," *Gregorianum* 29 (1948), 118–141.

Lexicon: Dizionario Teologico Enciclopedico. Casale Monferrato: Edizioni Piemme, 1993.

Lietzmann, Hans. *A History of the Early Church*. 2 volumes. Cambridge: James Clark, 1993.

Lilly, William Samuel. *Characteristics from the Writings of John Henry Newman*. London: Henry S. King & Co., 1874.

———. "Newman: The Perfect Ecumenist," *Homiletic and Pastoral Review* (July 1984), 28–32.

Linera, A. "La Vida y la Mentalidad del Cardinal Newman," *Las Ciencias* 13 (1948), 385–405.

Liturgia Horarum. Editio Typica Altera. Vatican City: Libreria Editrice Vaticana, 1985.

Lortz, Joseph. *Storia della Chiesa: Considerata in Prospettiva di Storia delle Idee*. 2 volumes. Milan: Edizioni Paoline, 1987.

Ludden, Sr. Mary Christopher, S.C. "John Henry Newman," *Process: Journal of the Catholic Campus Ministry Association* 5 (1979), 16.

———. "Venerable John Henry Newman: Prophet and Teacher," *The Catholic Answer* (March/April 1998).

McGuire, James E. "Holy Virgin Mary: The Mystery of Grace in the Mystery of the Incarnation As Presented in the Writings of John Henry Cardinal Newman." Dissertation extract. Rome: Pontificia Studiorum Universitas a S. Thoma Aq. in Urbe, 1975.

McHugh, John. "The Second Eve: Newman and Irenæus," *The Way Supplement* 45 (June 1982), 3–21.

MacKenna, B. "Our Lady As Seen by Cardinal Newman," *Ecclesiastical Review* (1929), 480ff.

McManus, Jim, C.Ss.R. *All Generations Will Call Me Blessed*. New York: Crossroad Publishing Company, 1999. Page 41.

McPartlan, Paul. *Mary for Teilhard and de Lubac*. Wallington, Eng.: Ecumenical Society of the Blessed Virgin Mary, 1987.

Macquarrie, John. *Mary for All Christians*. Grand Rapids, Mich.: Eerdmans; Publishing Co., 1990.

McVey, Kathleen, translator and editor. *Ephrem—the Syrian Hymns*. New York: Paulist Press, 1989.

Magill, Gerard. "Moral Imagination in Theological Method and Church Tradition: John Henry Newman," *Theological Studies* 53 (September 1992), 451–475.

———. "Newman's Personal Reasoning: The Inspiration of the Early Church," *Irish Theological Quarterly* 58 (1992), 305–313.

Manoir, H. "Marie, Nouvelle Ève, dans l'œuvre de Newman," *Études Mariales* 13 (1955), 67–90.

Maria Corredentrice: Storia e Teologia. Frigento: Casa Mariana Editrice, 1998.

Martlett, Jeffrey D. "Conversion Methodology and the Case of Cardinal Newman," *Theological Studies* 58/4 (December 1997), 669–685.

Medina-Estevez, Jorge Cardinal. "The Blessed Virgin." *Vatican II—An Interfaith Appraisal*. International Theological Conference. Edited by John H. Miller, C.S.C. Notre Dame, Ind.: University of Notre Dame Press, 1966. Pages 301–315f.

Melotti, Luigi. *Maria la Madre dei Viventi: Compendio di Mariologia*. Turin: Editrice Elle DiLeumann, 1989.

Merrigan, Terrence. "Newman the Theologian," *Louvain Studies* 15 (1990), 103–118.

Meyer, Harding. "The Ecumenical Unburdening of the Mariological Problem: A Lutheran Perspective," *Journal of Ecumenical Studies* 26 (1989), 681–696.

Meyer, N. *Motives for a Christian Life in the Sermons of Cardinal Newman*. Teutopolis: Worman Co., 1960.

Middleton, R. D. *Newman at Oxford: His Religious Development*. New York: Oxford University Press, 1950.

Miller, Frederick. "The Marian Orientation of Spirituality in the Thought of John Paul II," *Communio* 17 (Winter 1990), 566–579.

Miravalle, Mark I., ed. *Mary: Co-Redemptrix, Mediatrix, Advocate—Theological Foundations towards a Papal Definition?* Santa Barbara, Calif.: Queenship Publishing, 1995.

———. *Mary: Co-Redemptrix, Mediatrix, Advocate*. Santa Barbara, Calif.: Queenship Publishing, 1996.

Misner, P. "Newman's Concept of Revelation and the Development of Doctrine," *Heythrop Journal* 11 (1970), 32–47.

Montague, George, S.M. *The Vision of the Beloved Disciple: Meeting Jesus in the Gospel of John*. New York: Alba House, 2000.

Morales, José. "La Mariología de John H. Newman," *Scripta de María* 3 (1980), 493–524.

———. *Religión, Hombre, Historia*. Estudios Newmanianos. Navarre: Ediciones Universidad de Navarra, 1989.

Most, William. "The Knowledge of Our Lady," *Faith and Reason* 11 (1985), 51–76.

Moyer, Matthew F., O.P. "Mary, The Maternal Instrument in God's Saving Act," *Marian Studies* 44 (1993), 9–18.

Muller, Alois. *Ecclesia-Maria: Die Einheit und der Kirche*. 2 volumes. Fribourg, 1955.

———. "La Posizione e la Cooperazione di Maria nell'Evento di Cristo," *Mysterium Salutis* 3.2 (Paris: Les Éditions du Cerf, 1972), 495–641.

———. "Place et cooperation de Marie dans l'évènement Jésus Christ," *Mysterium Salutis* 12.40 (Paris: Les Éditions du Cerf, 1972), 24.

Muller, Ludwig Gerhard. *Dogmatica Cattolica per lo Studio e la Prassi della Teologia*. Milan: Edizioni San Paolo, 1999.

Murphy, R. "Mary in the Apocalypse," *Theological Studies* (1949), 565–573.

Murphy, T. "Newman and Devotion to Our Lady," *Irish Historical Record* 72 (1949), 385–396.

Murray, Placid, O.S.B. *Newman the Oratorian*. London: Fowler Wright Books, 1968.

———. "Tower of David: Cardinal Newman's Mariology," *Furrow* 27 (1976), 26–34.

Naldini, Mario, ed. *Letture Patristiche*. Volume 7, *La Bibbia nei Padri della Chiesa: L 'Antico Testamento*. Volume 8, *La Bibbia nei Padri della Chiesa: Il Nuovo Testamento*. Bologna: Edizioni Dehoniane, 1999.

National Conference of Catholic Bishops. *Behold Your Mother: Woman of Faith*. Washington, D.C.: United States Catholic Conference, 1973.

Neill, Stephen. *The Interpretation of the New Testament, 1861–1961*. New York: Oxford University Press, 1966.

Nesbitt, Roger. *Mary, Model of the Church*. Wallington, Eng.: Ecumenical Society of the Blessed Virgin Mary, 1994.

Neumann, Charles William, S.M. "The Virgin Mary in the Works of Saint Ambrose," *Paradosis: Contributions to the History of Early Christian Literature and Theology*. Volume 17. Fribourg, Switzerland: The University Press, 1962.

The New American Bible. New York: Oxford University Press, 1990.

The New Oxford Annotated Bible: Revised Standard Version. New York: Oxford University Press, 1973.

Nichols, Aidan, O.P. *Epiphany: A Theological Introduction to Catholicism*. Collegeville, Minn.: Liturgical Press, 1996.

———. *From Newman to Congar: The Idea of Development from the Victorians to the Second Vatican Council*. Edinburgh: T & T Clark, 1990.

Nicolas, M. J. "Essai de synthèse Mariale," *Maria*. Volume 1. Paris: Beauchesne, 1949.

Norris, T. J. *Newman and His Theological Method: A Guide for the Theologian Today*. Leiden, 1977.

O'Brien, Felicity. *Not Peace but a Sword*. England: St. Paul Publications, 1990.

O'Carroll, Michael. "Our Lady in Newman and Vatican II," *Downside Review* 89 (1971), 38–63.

———. *Theotokos: A Theological Encyclopedia of the Blessed Virgin Mary*. Collegeville, Minn.: Liturgical Press, 1982.

O'Collins, Gerald, S.J., and Edward G. Ferrugia, eds. *Dizionario Sintetico di Teologia*. Vatican City: Libreria Editrice Vaticana, 1995.

O'Connell, J. *The Mariology of Cardinal Newman in Light of His Contro-versy with the "Eirenicon" of E. B. Pusey.* Dissertation. Pontificia Universitas Gregoriana, 1959.

O'Connell, Marvin R. "Newman: The Victorian Intellectual As Pastor," *Theological Studies* 46 (June 1985), 329–344.

———. *The Oxford Conspirators: A History of the Oxford Movement, 1833–1845.* London: Macmillan, 1969.

Olive, Martin M, O.P. "Un Petit Traité de Mariologie selon les Pères des premiers siècles: La 'Lettre à Pusey' de Newman (1865)," *De Primordiis Cultus Mariani.* Acta Congressus Mariologici-Mariani in Lusitania anno 1967 celebrati. Volume 3. *De Fundamento Cultus B.V. Mariæ in Operibus Sanctorum Patrum et Scriptorum Ecclesiasti-corum (post sæc. II).* Rome: Pontificia Academia Mariana Inter-nationalis, 1970. Pages 303–332.

The Oratory Magazine (August 2000), 13.

Orbe, Antonio. "La 'Recirculación' de la Virgen María en San Ireneo," *La Mariologia nella Catechesi dei Padri (Età Prenicena).* Rome: Libreria Ateneo Salesiano, 1989.

Padovese, Luigi. *Introduzione alla Teologia Patristica.* Casale Monferrato: Edizioni Piemme, 1992.

Pagnamenta, A. *La Mariologia di S. Ambrogi.* Milan, 1932.

Palmer, Paul F. *Mary in the Documents of the Church.* Westminster, Md.: Newman Press, 952.

Panido, M. "Newman e Evoluçao do Dogma Catholico," *Revista Ecclesia Brasilera* 5 (1946), 233–263.

Parspartis, Minima. *Some Side-lights on the Oxford Movement.* London: Art & Book Co., 1895.

Pasquier, C. "Newman Prédicateur," *Nouvelle Revue Théologique* 69 (1947), 839–851.

Patterson, Webster T. *Newman: Pioneer for the Layman.* Washington, D.C.: Corpus Books, 1968.

Paul VI, Pope. "D'Actualité de Newman," *Monitor Ecclesiasticus* 95 (1970), 494–496.

———. "Epistola Enciclica *Christi Mater*," in *Civiltà Cattolica* 4 (1966), 5–9.

———. *Marialis Cultus.* Washington, D.C.: United States Catholic Conference, 1974.

Payne, Robert. *The Fathers of the Eastern Church.* New York: Dorset Press, 1989.

———. *The Fathers of the Western Church.* New York: Dorset Press, 1989.

Pelikan, Jaroslav. *Jesus through the Centuries: His Place in the History of Culture.* New Haven: Yale University Press, 1985.

————. *Mary through the Centuries: Her Place in the History of Culture.* New Haven: Yale University Press, 1996.

Perrella, Salvatore M, O.S.M. "L'Immagine Teologica di Maria, Oggi: Il Contributo del Magistero e della Teologia," *Fine d'Anno con Maria*. Volume 4, *La Vergine Maria dal Rinascimento a Oggi, Itinerari Mariani dei Due Millenni*. Rome: Centro di Cultura Mariana "Madre della Chiesa," 1999. Pages 103–165.

————. "Maria di Nazareth nel Mistero di Cristo e della Chiesa tra il Vaticano II e la *Tertio Millennio Adveniente* (1959–1998)," *Ephemerides Mariologicæ* 60:385–530.

————. "Present State of the Question: Mary's Cooperation in the Work of Redemption," *L'Osservatore Romano* (2 July 1997), 9f.

————. *I Vota e i Consilia dei Vescovi Italiani sullo Mariologia e sulla Corredenzione nella Frase Antipreparatorio del Concilio Vaticano II.* Rome: Scripta Pontificiæ Facultatis Theologicæ Marianum, 1994.

Perrott, Michael J. L. *Newman's Mariology*. South Hampton, Eng.: St. Austin Press, 1997.

Philips, Gerard. *La Chiesa e il Suo Mistero: Storia, Testo e Commento della Costituzione "Lumen Gentium."* Milan: Jaca Books, 1975.

Poffet, Jean-Michel. *I Cristiani e la Bibbia: Per una Storia d'Occidente Chiesa e Stato*. Translated by Matina Rosignotti. Milan: Jaca Books, 2001.

Pontifical Biblical Commission. *The Interpretation of the Bible in the Church.* Vatican City: Libreria Editrice Vaticana, 1993.

Potter, G. *The Idea of Preaching According to John Henry Newman*. Dissertation. Pontificia Universitas Gregoriana, 1963.

Pozo, Candido. "Development of Dogma," in *Encyclopedia of Theology: The Concise Sacramentum Mundi.* Edited by Karl Rahner, S.J. New York: Seabury Press, 1975. Pages 356–360.

Przywara, Erich, S.J. *The Heart of Newman.* San Francisco: Ignatius Press, 1997.

Pusey, Edward B. *Letter to the Lord Bishop of Oxford* [*Eirenicon*]. New York: J. S. Redfield Publishers, 1843.

Pusinieri, G. "Spiriti Rosminiani nella Conversione di Enrico Newman," *Rivista Rosminiano di Filosofia e di Cultura* 39 (1945), 69f.

Quasten, Johannes. *Patrology*. 4 volumes. Westminister, Md.: Christian Classics, 1986, 1988.

Quinn, J. Richard. *The Recognition of the True Church According to John Henry Newman.* Washington, D.C.: The Catholic University of America Press, 1954.

Rahner, Hugo. *Maria e la Chiesa.* Milan: Jaca Books, 1991.

Rahner, Karl, S.J. "Dogma," in *Encyclopedia of Theology: The Concise Sacramentum Mundi*. Edited by Karl Rahner, S.J. New York: Seabury Press, 1975. Pages 352–356.

————. *Nature and Grace: Dilemmas in the Modern Church*. New York: Sheed & Ward, 1964.

————. "One Mediator and Many Mediations," *Theological Investigations*. Volume 9. London: Darton, Longman & Todd, 1972. Pages 169–184.

————. "Why and How Can We Venerate the Saints," *Theological Investigations*. Volume 8. New York: Herder & Herder, 1971. Pages 3–23.

Ratzinger, Joseph Cardinal. *La Figlia di Sion*. Milan: Jaca Book, 1995.

————. *Introduction to Christianity*. San Francisco: Ignatius Press, 1990.

Ravasi, Gianfranco. *L'Albero di Maria: Trentun Icone Bibliche Mariane*. Milan: Edizioni San Paolo, 1993.

————. *La Buona Novella: Le Storie, le Idee, i Personaggi del Nuovo Testamento*. Milan: Arnoldo Mondadori Editore, 1996.

————. *Il Racconto del Cielo: Le Storie, le Idee, i Personaggi dell'Antico Testamento*. Milan: Arnoldo Mondadori Editore, 1995.

Reilly, Joseph J. *The Fine Gold of Newman*. New York: Macmillan, 1932.

Reynolds, E. E. *Three Cardinals: Newman, Wiseman, Manning*. New York: P. J. Kenedy & Sons, 1958.

Rickaby, Joseph. *Index to the Works of John Henry Cardinal Newman*. Westminister, Md.: Christian Classics, 1977.

Rigamonti, G. *Maria Ideale di Vita Cristiana nella Dottrina di S. Ambrogio*. Milan, 1960.

Riviere, J. "Marie: 'Corédemptrice,'" *Revue des Sciences Religieuses* 19 (1939), 332–341.

Roschini, G. M. *Mariologia*. 4 volumes. Rome, 1947–1948.

Roten, Johann, S.M. "Mary and the Way of Beauty," *Marian Studies* 49 (1998), 109–127.

Rouet, A. "Marie et la vie Chrétienne: Marie Témoin de la Foi de l'Église. Voir ce que Dieu accomplit dans le croyant. Une Femme Fidèle et Engagée," in *Croire Aujourd'hui*. Paris: Desclée de Brouwer, 1978. Pages 138f.

Rowell, Geoffrey. "Newman, John Henry," *The Blackwell Encyclopedia of Modern Christian Thought*. Edited by Alister E. McGrath. Cambridge, Mass.: Blackwell Publishers, 1993.

————. *The Vision Glorious: Themes and Personalities of the Catholic Revival in Anglicanism*. Oxford: Oxford University Press, 1983.

Ryan, John K., and Edmond Darvil Benard, eds. *American Essays for the Newman Centennial*. Washington, D.C.: The Catholic University of America Press, 1947.

Salgado, Jean-Marie, O.M.I. "La Maternité spirituelle de la Très Sainte Vierge Marie," *Studi Tomistici*. Volume 36. Rome: Libreria Editrice Vaticana, 1990.

Sandeen, Ernest K. *The Roots of Fundamentalism: British and American Millenarianism, 1830–1930*. University of Chicago Press, 1970.

Saward, John. *The Beauty of Holiness and the Holiness of Beauty*. San Francisco: Ignatius Press, 1997.

―――. *Christ Is the Answer: The Christ-Centered Teaching of Pope John Paul II*. New York: Alba House, 1995.

―――. "The Christocentricity of Pope John Paul II," *Communio* 18 (Fall 1991), 332–355.

―――. *Redeemer in the Womb*. San Francisco: Ignatius Press, 1993.

Schillebeeckx, Edward, O.P. *Mary, Mother of the Redemption*. New York: Sheed & Ward, 1964.

Schmaus, Michael. "Mariology," *Encyclopedia of Theology: The Concise Sacramentum Mundi*. Edited by Karl Rahner, S.J. New York: Seabury Press, 1975. Page 897.

Schnackenburg, Rudolf. *La Persona di Gesù Cristo nei Quattro Vangeli*. Brescia: Paideia Editrice, 1995.

Schneider, Paul Peter, O.S.B. "Das Marienbild des anglikanischen Newman," *Newman-Studien*. Volume 2. Nürenberg: Glock und Lutz, 1954. Pages 103–109.

Schneider, Theodore, ed. *Nuovo Corso di Dogmatica*. 2 volumes. Brescia: Editrice Queriniana, 1995.

Schokel, Alonso Luis. *Il Dinamismo della Tradizione*. Brescia: Paideia, 1970.

Schriffers, N. "Schrift und Tradition bei John Henry Newman," *Schrift und Tradition* (Essen, 1962), 250–266.

Scola, Angelo. *Questioni di Antropologia Teologica*. Milan: Edizioni Ares, 1996.

Semmelroth, Otto. "Chapter VIII, The Role of the Blessed Virgin Mary, Mother of God, in the Mystery of Christ and the Church," *Commentary on the Documents of Vatican II*. Volume 1. New York: Herder & Herder, 1967. Pages 285–296.

―――. *Mary: Archetype of the Church*. New York: Sheed and Ward, 1963.

Serra, Aristide. *Dimensioni Mariane del Mistero Pasquale*. Milan: Edizioni Paoline, 1995.

―――. *Maria a Cana e Presso la Croce: Saggio di Mariologia Giovannea (Gv 2, 1–12 e Gv 19, 25–27)*. Rome: Centro di Cultura Mariana "Madre della Chiesa," 1991.

―――. *Maria di Nazareth: Una Fede in Cammino*. Milan: Edizioni Paoline, 1993.

Servotte, Herman. "'Loss and Gain': A Grammar of Conversion," *Louvain Studies* 15 (1990), 256–266.

Sesboüé, Bernard, et al., eds. *Histoire des Dogmes—Les Signes du Salut.* Volume iii. *Les Sacrements, l'Église, La Vierge Marie.* Paris: Desclée, 1995.

Seynaeve, Jaak. "Doctrine scriptuaire de Cardinal Newman," *Dictionnaire de la Bible.* Paris, 1928. Pages 427–474.

―――. "La Doctrine Scriptuaire du Cardinal Newman sur l'Inspiration d'après les Articles de 1884," *Epherimedes Theologicæ Louvanenses* 18 (1950), 356–382.

―――. "Newman's Biblical Hermeneutics," *Louvain Studies* 15 (1990), 282–300.

Sheen, Fulton J. *The World's First Love.* New York: McGraw-Hill Book Co., 1952.

Sheenan, B. *Worship and Christian Life in the Anglican Sermons of John Henry Newman.* Dissertation. Louvain, 1974.

Sheran, W. "Newman's Devotion to Our Lady," *Catholic World* 93 (1911), 174–183.

Sicari, Antonio. "Mary, Peter and John: Figures of the Church" *Communio* (Summer 1992), 198f.

Sierra, Martinez A. "Significado e Importancia del Concilio Vaticano para la Mariología," *Epherimedes Mariologicæ* 36 (1986), 205–219.

Simonetti, Manilio. *Lettera ed Allegoria: Un Contributo alla Storia dell'Esegesi Patristica.* Rome: Studia Ephemeridi Augustinianum, 1985.

Söll, Georg. *Storia dei Dogmi Mariani.* Rome: Accademia Mariana Salesiana, 1981.

Spedalieri, Francesco, S.J. *Maria nella Scrittura e nella Traditione della Chiesa Primitiva.* Studio Diretto sulle Fonti. Volume 1. Rome: Herder Editrice e Libreria, 1968.

―――, ed. *Maria nella Scrittura e nella Tradizione della Chiesa Primitiva: Studi e Problemi.* Volume 2, *I Privilegi.* Rome: Herder Editrice e Libreria, 1975.

Spiazzi, Raimondo, O.P. *Maria Santissima nel Magistero della Chiesa: I Documenti da Pio IX a Giovanni Paolo II.* Milan: Massimo, 1987.

Stacpoole, Alberic, O.S.B. *Mary in Doctrine and Devotion.* Collegeville, Minn.: The Liturgical Press, 1990.

Stark, Anthony. "John Henry Newman: A Biographical Sketch," *Cardinal John Henry Newman: A Study in Holiness.* London: The Guild of Our Lady of Ransom, 1980. Pages 4–10.

Stern, Jean, M.S. *La Bible et Tradition chez Newman.* Paris. 1948.

―――. *Bible et Tradition chez Newman aux origines de la théorie du développement.* Paris: Auber-Montaigne, 1967.

————. "Le Culte de la Vierge et des Saints et la Conversion de Newman au Catholicisme," *La Vie Spirituelle* 117 (1967), 159–168.

————. "Le Développement du dogme selon Newman et la Constitution Dogmatique sur la Révelation Divine du Vatican II," *Euntes Docete* 33 (1980), 47–61.

————. "Le Dogme chez John Henry Newman," *AXES* 8 (1976), 53–62.

————. "L'Infallibilité de l'Église dans la pensée de John Henry Newman," *Recherches de Science Religieuse* 61 (1973), 161–185.

————. Personal interview, 1998.

————. "Le Saint Esprit dans le Mystère du Christ et de sa Mère selon John Henry Newman," *Cahiers Marials* 73 (1970), 183–190.

————. "Les Théologiens et le Magistère selon John Henry Newman." Manuscript.

————. "Tradition et Intégrisme: Les Modèles Théologiques du cinquième siècle selon John Henry Newman," *Studia Ephemerides Augustinianum* 31 (1990), 443–454.

————. "La Vierge Marie dans le chemin de Foi parcouru par John Henry Newman," *Marianum* 53 (1991), 42–68.

Strange, Roderick. "The Development of Newman's Marian Thought and Devotion," *One in Christ* 16 (1980), 114–126.

————. *Newman and the Gospel of Christ*. Oxford: Oxford University Press, 1981.

————. "Newman at Oxford: Preaching a Living Faith," in *Newman from Oxford to the People*. Edited by Paul Weiss. Trowbridge, Eng.: Witshire, 1996. Pages 223–238.

————. "Newman on Infallibility," *American Journal* 80 (1975), 61–70.

Stravinskas, Peter M. J. *Mary and the Fundamentalist Challenge*. Huntington, Ind.: Our Sunday Visitor Press, 1998.

————. *Our Sunday Visitor's Catholic Dictionary*. Huntington, Ind.: Our Sunday Visitor Press, 1993.

Strolz, W. "Newman, Kirchvater der Neuzeit," *Word und Wahrheit* 10 (1955), 396–399.

Strolz, W., and Margarete Binder, eds. *John Henry Newman—Lover of Truth*. The Papers of the Academic Symposium and Celebration of the First Centenary of the Death of John Henry Newman, Rome, 26–28 April 1990. Rome: Urbaniana University Press, 1991.

Studer, Basil. *Trinity and Incarnation: The Faith of the Early Church*. Edited by Andrew Louth. Edinburgh: T & T Clark, 1993.

Tavard, George H. *The Thousand Faces of the Virgin Mary*. Collegeville, Minn.: The Liturgical Press, 1996.

Theis, N. "Newman und die Bibel," *Beilagen zum Kirchlichen Anzeiger* (1955), 27–30.

Thomas, F. *The Spiritual Doctrine of Cardinal Newman in His Sermons and Other Writings.* Dissertation. Pontificia Universitas Gregoriana, 1959.

Thomas, Stephen. *Newman and Heresy: The Anglican Years.* New York: Cambridge University Press, 1991.

Thornhill, John. "The Mystery of Mary and the Church," *Homiletic and Pastoral Review* (October 1966), 31–40.

Tillman, Mary Katherine. "The Two-fold Logos of Newman and Pascal: l'Esprit Géométrique," *Louvain Studies* 15 (1990), 233–256.

Todd, J. "On Mary: The New Eve," *Orate Fratres* 27 (1953), 273–278.

Tracey, Gerard (archivist of Birmingham Oratory). Personal interview, 17 February 1999.

———. Personal communication, 16 April 1999.

———. Personal communication, 1 May 2001.

Trapè, Agostino. *Sant'Agostino—Maria "Dignitas Terræ."* Rome: Città Nuova Editrice, 1988.

Trevor, Meriol. *Newman: Light in Winter.* Garden City, New York: Doubleday & Co., 1963.

———. *Newman: The Pillar of the Cloud.* Garden City, New York: Doubleday & Co., 1962.

———. *Newman's Journey.* London: Harper & Collins, 1996.

Tristram, Henry, C.O. "Dr. Russell and Newman's Conversion," *Irish Ecclesiastical Record* 66 (1945), 189–200.

———. *Newman and His Friends.* London: John Lane, 1933.

Unger, Dominic J. "Cardinal Newman and Apocalypse XII," *Theological Studies* 11 (1950), 356–367.

Vacant, A., et al., eds. *Dictionnaire de Théologie Catholique.* Paris: Librairie Letouzey et Ane, 1925.

Valentini, Alberto. "L'Immagine Biblica di Maria," in *Fine d'Anno con Maria.* Volume 4, *Vergine Maria dal Rinascimento a Oggi: Itinerari Mariani di Due Millenni.* Rome: Centro di Cultura Mariana "Madre della Chiesa," 1999. Pages 169–191.

———. *Il Magnificat: Genere Letterario: Struttura Esegesi.* Bologna: Edizioni Bologna Dehoniane, 1987.

Vanhoye, A., S.J. "Intérrogation Johannique et exégèse de Cana [Jn 2, 4]," *Biblica* 55 (1971), 157–167.

Velocci, Giovanni, C.Ss.R. "John Henry Newman, l'Ultimo dei Padri," *L'Osservatore Romano* (17 July 1974).

———, translator. *Lettera al Rev. Pusey su Maria e la Vita Cristiana.* Rome: Città Nuova Editrice, 1975.

———. "La Madonna in Newman," *Ecclesia Mater* 6 (1968), 139–161.

————. "Maria nella Vita di John Henry Newman," *Theotokos* 6 (1998), 277–300.

————. "Maria nella Vita e nel Pensiero di Newman," *Sacra Doctrina* (1973), 301–308.

————. "La Mariologia di Cardinal Newman," *Divinitas* 11 (1967), 1021–1046.

————. "Newman e *l'Ecclesia Mater*," *Mater Ecclesiæ* 3 (1965/1), 159–163.

————. *Newman: Il Coraggio della Verità*. Vatican City: Libreria Editrice Vaticana, 2000.

————. *Newman Mistico*. Rome, 1964.

————. "Newman, Uomo Ecumenico," *Humanitas* 21 (1966), 488–497.

————. Personal interview, March 2001.

————. "Sant'Alfonso Visto da Newman," *Rivista di Vita Spirituale* 40 (1986), 167–180.

————. "San Tommaso d'Aquino 'Visto' dal Cardinale John Henry Newman," *L'Osservatore Romano* (1 February 1996), 7.

————. "Senso e Teologia della Provvidenza in Newman." Manuscript. Rome: Cardinal Newman Academic Symposium, 3–8 April 1975.

Victory, D. "The Immaculate Conception in Newman," *Euntes Docete* 7 (1954), 147–156.

Vismara, E. "Il Testamento del Signore nel Pensiero di S. Ambrogio e la Maternità di Maria SS. verso gli Uomini," *Salesianum* 7 (1945), 7–38, 97–143.

von Balthasar, Hans Urs. "Marie et l'Église dans l'Œuvre de la Rédemption," address to the Association Sacerdotale "Lumen Gentium." No. 43. Paris: Rue des Petites Écuries, 1978.

————. "Mary—Church—Office," *Communio* 23 (Spring 1996), 193–198.

————. *"Mysterium Paschale: Revival and Renewal—Ressourcement in Catholic Thought*. Grand Rapids, Mich.: William B. Eerdmans Publishing Company, 1990.

————. *The Office of Peter and the Structure of the Church*. San Francisco: Ignatius Press, 1986.

von Esbroeck, M. "Apocryphes Géorgiens de la Dormition," *Analecta Bollandiana* 91 (1973), 55–75.

————. "L'Assomption de la Vierge dans un Transitus Pseudo-Basilien," *Analecta Bollandiana* 92 (1974), 125–163.

Walgrave, J. H. *Newman the Theologian: The Nature of Belief and Doctrine As Exemplified in His Life and Works*. New York: Sheed & Ward, 1960.

————. "Le Sens Ecclésial de Newman," *Dictionnaire de Spiritualité Ascetique et Mystique*. Paris, 1958.

Ward, Wilfrid. *The Life of John Henry Cardinal Newman*. 2 volumes. New York: Longmans, Green & Co., 1912.

———. *William George Ward and the Catholic Revival*. Reprint: New York: Macmillan & Co., 1969.

Warren, Ira. *The Causes and the Cure of Puseyism*. New York: M. W. Dodd, 1847.

Weatherby, Harold L. *Cardinal Newman in His Age: His Place in English Theology and Literature*. Nashville: Vanderbilt University Press, 1973.

White, W. D. *The Preaching of John Henry Newman*. Philadelphia, 1969.

Whyte, Alexander. *Newman: An Appreciation in Two Lectures: With the Choicest Passages of His Writings Selected and Arranged*. London: Oliphant, Anderson and Ferrier, 1901.

William, Franciscus, O.P. "Cardinalis Newman Theses de Doctrina et Devotione Mariana et Motus Œcumenicus," in *De Mariologia et Œcumenismo*. Rome: Pontificia Academia Mariana Internationalis, 1962. Pages 257–274.

———. "Kardinal John Henry Newman und die Kirchlichen Lehrtradition," *Orientierung* 22 (1958), 61–66.

Withey, Donald A. *John Henry Newman: The Liturgy and the Breviary, Their Influence on His Life As an Anglican*. London: Sheed & Ward, 1992.

Wood, Susan K. *Spiritual Exegesis and the Church in the Theology of Henri de Lubac*. Grand Rapids, Mich.: William Eerdmans Publishing Co., 1998.

Wright, David F, ed. *Chosen by God: Mary in Evangelical Perspective*. London: Marshall Pickering, 1989.

Young, Urban. *Dominic Barberi in England: A New Series of Letters*. London: Bums, Oates & Washbourne, 1935.

Zanini, Giorgio. *Commenti Spirituali del Nuovo Testamento: Vangelo secondo Giovanni*. Volume 1. Rome: Città Nuova Editrice, 1992.

Zoffoli, Enrico, C.P. *Cristianesimo: Corso di Teologia Cattolica*. Udine: Edizioni Segno, 1993.

GENERAL INDEX

Abimelech, 146

Abraham, 103, 106, 107, 131, 146,
163, 240, 279, 379–381, 388

Achilles, 433

Advocata Evæ (Marian title), 211–213

Alexander of Egypt, 307

Alphonsus Liguori, Saint, 134, 366,
370, 395–396, 412, 425–428, 445

Ambrose, Saint, 159, 185, 220–233,
238–241, 268, 292, 307, 310, 325,
332, 372, 444

Ammonius of Thrace, 307

Amphilochus, 307

"An Essay on the Miracles of
Scripture" (Newman), 77, 79

Andrewes, Lancelot, 364

"Anglican Claims of Apostolic
Succession, The" (Wiseman),
188

Antiochus of Syria, 307

Apollonarianism, 279

Apologia pro Vita Sua (Newman), 24,
27, 29, 33, 38, 75, 132, 188–190,
363, 367, 415

Aquinas, Saint Thomas, 27–28, 55,
59, 164, 382, 383

Arian controversy, 34, 107

Arianism, 137, 267, 297, 311, 400

Arians of the Fourth Century, The
(Newman), 34, 46, 74

Arius, 34, 41, 68, 190

Articles of Religion (Anglican), 193,
362

Assumption of Mary (dogma), 46,
53, 153, 154, 156, 158, 160, 164–
173, 182, 191, 218, 235, 298,
328, 339, 342, 444, 446, 449

Athanasian Creed, 279, 280, 308,
309

Athanasius of Alexandria, Saint, 107,
159, 181, 189, 190, 222, 307,
309, 331, 395, 401

Augustine of Hippo, Saint, 31, 43,
55, 72, 84, 85, 88, 93, 142, 144,

159, 185, 186, 187, 188, 191,
210, 241–257, 267, 272, 292, 307,
351, 395, 331, 444

Auxilium Christianorum (Marian
title), 406

"Ave Maris Stella" (Newman), 405

Balaam, 158–159

Barberi, Blessed Dominic
(Domenico), 28, 31–33, 425

Baronius, Cesare Cardinal, 76

Basil of Cæsarea, Saint, 189, 257,
267–273, 292

Basil of Seleucia, 310, 398–399, 412

Bernard of Clairvaux, Saint, 55, 93,
164, 235

Bernardine of Siena, Saint, 370

Blehl, Vincent, 76, 338, 406, 407,
414

Blondel, Enrichetta, 29

Book of Common Prayer, The, 364

Brit, John, 82, 83, 112, 174

Capriolus, 307

celibacy of Jesus, 95, 97, 106

Chalcedon, Council of, 41–42, 63–
64, 110, 311

Chrysologus, Saint Peter, 55, 145,
323, 332, 412, 419

Chrysostom, Saint John, 84, 85, 142,
144, 181, 191, 253, 257–268, 273,
292, 307, 395

Cignelli, Lino, 213–215

Constantinople, Second Council of,
41

Cooperatrix (Marian title), 413-441

Co-Redemptress (Marian title), 413,
416, 418–419, 448, 450

Co-Redemptrix (Marian title), 19,
23, 24, 42, 168, 318, 348, 349,
397, 407, 408, 413, 416, 422,
434–440, 442, 445, 448, 450–453

Commentary on the Diatesseron
(Ephrem), 274

SCRIPTURE INDEX